Psychotherapy in the Third Reich

Psychotherapy in the Third Reich

THE GÖRING INSTITUTE

Second Edition, Revised and Expanded

Geoffrey Cocks

Routledge
Taylor & Francis Group
LONDON AND NEW YORK

First published 1997 by Transaction Publishers

2 Park Square, Milton Park, Abingdon, Oxfordshire OX14 4RN
711 Third Avenue, New York, NY 10017

Routledge is an imprint of the Taylor & Francis Group, an informa business

First issued in hardback 2018

Library of Congress Catalog Number: 96–34060

Library of Congress Cataloging-in-Publication Data

Cocks, Geoffrey, 1948–
Psychotherapy in the Third Reich : the Göring Institute / Geoffrey Cocks. — 2nd ed., rev. and expanded.
p. cm.
Includes bibliographical references and index.
ISBN 1–56000–904–7 (paper : alk. paper)
1. Psychotherapy—Political aspects—Germany—History—20th century. 2. National socialism. 3. Germany—History—1933–1945. I. Title.
RC450.G3C63 1997
616.89'14'09430904—DC20 96–34060
CIP

ISBN 13: 978-1-56000-904-7 (pbk)
ISBN 13: 978-1-138-53115-4 (hbk)

Contents

Illustrations

Abbreviations

BA	Bundesarchiv
BA-MA	Bundesarchiv-Militärarchiv
BDC	Berlin Document Center
DAF	Deutsche Arbeitsfront
DFG	Deutsche Forschungsgemeinschaft
DGPT	Deutsche Gesellschaft für Psychotherapie und Tiefenpsychologie
DPG	Deutsche Psychoanalytische Gesellschaft
DPV	Deutsche Psychoanalytische Vereinigung
IPA	International Psycho-Analytic Association
NSDAP	Nationalsozialistische Deutsche Arbeiterpartei
NSV	Nationalsozialistische Volkswohlfahrt
NWH	Nordrhein-Westfälisches Hauptstaatasarchiv
OKW	Oberkommando der Wehrmacht
RFR	Reichsforschungsrat
SA	Sturmabteilung
SD	Sicherheitsdienst
SS	Schutzstaffel
ZfP	*Zentralblatt für Psychotherapie und ihre Grenzgebiete einchliesslich der medizinischen Psychologie und psychischen Hygiene*

Preface

It has been twenty years since I completed my dissertation on the history of the so-called Göring Institute and ten years since the first edition of this book was published. A second edition is justified by the great amount of research that has been done since that time, not only on the history of psychotherapy and psychoanalysis in Nazi Germany, but also on the Third Reich itself, especially its social history, as well as on the history of the professions, particularly medicine. Much of my subsequent work on this topic has been informed and enriched by the critical viewpoints and additional documentation brought to the subject by young German psychoanalysts and historians; chief among these is Regine Lockot. I have also taken the opportunity to reorganize the volume along chronological and narrative lines for greater ease of reading for a general educated audience. The first edition was based a topical approach more conducive to scholarly use through reference to the index and to chapter subdivisions listed in the table of contents. Those readers of this second edition who wish to read more for scholarly purposes might want to read chapter 16 on the large historiographical issues first. I have placed these thoughts at the end of the book in order to allow for the greater flow of narrative and chronology in the text for the benefit of the more general reader.

There are other individuals whose assistance I gladly acknowledge: Hildegard Achelis, Mitchell G. Ash, Barbara Bauer of the Barbara Bauer Literary Agency, Inc., Dan Burdett, Georg Cimbal, Greg Eghigian, Richard Evans, John Fout, Volker Friedrich, Michael Geyer, Ludger Hermanns, Konrad Jarausch, Wolfgang Kretschmer, Robert Jay Lifton, Charles McClelland, Alain de Mijolla, Alice Wiley Moore, Timothy Pytell, Eva Rittmeister-Hildebrand, Claudia Schoppmann, Ulrich Schultz-Venrath, Michael Van Houten, and Uwe Zeller.

Institutions to which I am newly indebted are: the Library of Congress in Washington, D.C., the Zentrales Staatsarchiv and Staatsarchiv

Potsdam, the Nordrhein-Westfälisches Hauptstaatsarchiv in Düsseldorf, the Archiv zur Geschichte der Psychoanalyse in Berlin and the Bundesarchiv in Coblenz, the Staatsarchiv Hamburg, and publishers Georg Thieme and S. Hirzel. I am especially grateful to Albion College and its donors for support through the Royal G. Hall Professorship in History. The following agencies provided generous grants for various aspects of my research since 1985: the National Endowment for the Humanities, the German Academic Exchange Service, the International Research and Exchanges Board, the American Historical Association, the National Institutes of Health, and the Faculty Development Committee of Albion College.

Portions of a number of chapters in this edition of *Psychotherapy in the Third Reich* originally appeared in other publications. I gratefully acknowledge the following publishers for permission to reprint this material:

Chs. 1, 7, 10, 11, 16: Excerpted from "The Professionalization of Psychotherapy in Germany, 1928–1949," *German Professions, 1800–1950,* edited by Geoffrey Cocks and Konrad H. Jarausch. Copyright © 1990 by Oxford University Press, Inc. Reprinted by permission.

Chs. 3, 16: Excerpted from "The Old as New: The Nuremberg Doctors' Trial and Medicine in Modern Germany," *Medicine and Modernity: Public Health and Medical Care in Nineteenth- and Twentieth-Century Germany,* edited by Manfred Berg and Geoffrey Cocks. Copyright © 1996 by Cambridge University Press.

Ch. 6: Excerpted from "The Nazis and C.G. Jung," *Lingering Shadows: Jungians, Freudians, and Anti-Semitism,* edited by Aryeh Maidenbaum and Stephen A. Martin; © 1991. Reprinted by arrangement with Shambhala Publications, Inc., 300 Massachusetts Avenue, Boston, MA 02115.

Ch. 12: Excerpted from "Partners and Pariahs: Jews and Medicine in Modern German Society," *LBI Yearbook* 36 (1991): 191–205. Copyright © 1991 by the Leo Baeck Institute.

Ch. 14: Excerpted from "Repressing, Remembering, Working Through: German Psychiatry, Psychotherapy, and Psychoanalysis and the 'Missed Resistance' in the Third Reich," *Journal of Modern History* 64 (1992): 5204–26. Copyright © 1992 by The University of Chicago. All rights reserved.

Ch. 15: Excerpted from "German Psychiatry, Psychotherapy, and Psychoanalysis During the Nazi Period: Historiographical Reflections,"

Preface to the First Edition

The idea for this book sprang, quite simply, from curiosity. As a student of German history and of psychoanalysis, I came to wonder what had happened in the new, dynamic field of medical psychology in Germany with the advent of Hitler. The very use of the preposition "in" marked a departure from previous thought on the subject since the traditional—and limited—historical view employed the preposition "to" in a declarative sentence: The Nazis did to the field of medical psychology what they did to science and knowledge in general in Germany; that is, they polluted and destroyed it. This traditional judgment was based primarily on the spectacle and testimony of those in the field who had emigrated from Germany to escape Nazi persecution.

Such a judgment had, and still has, considerable merit. The psychoanalytic movement that had revolutionized the treatment of mental disorders was forced to move the loci of its activities from Vienna and Berlin to London and New York. Jewish psychoanalysts who did not flee were tortured and murdered in Nazi concentration camps. The fist of Nazi totalitarianism closed around the Freudian movement so tightly as to squeeze out light and life.

But there were several interesting shards of evidence that pointed to the possibility that one could reconstruct a history of developments in German medical psychology, as well as the damage done to it, beginning in 1933: the existence of a journal for psychotherapy published continuously from 1928 to 1944; accounts of a psychotherapist who assumed leadership of his colleagues and who was a relative of the powerful Nazi leader Hermann Göring; the fact of a strong psychotherapeutic lobby in German medicine that was impoverished but apparently not destroyed by the expulsion of the prominent and predominantly Jewish psychoanalytic movement; and research into the domestic history of the Third Reich revealing the seams, cracks, and niches that marked the facets of an order that its Nazi masters had proclaimed as smooth as the rally of stones at Nuremberg.

Fortunately, the leads for the pursuit of this history were not as cold as Albert Speer's blocks piled up in Dutzendteich. From psychoanalysts who had emigrated to the United States in the 1930s, I learned of colleagues who had remained in Germany and who, together with non-Freudian psychotherapists, had pursued their profession under the aegis of the so-called Göring Institute. My research in Germany thus began with interviews and hours of research in libraries and archives. The institute building itself had been destroyed in 1945, so from the beginning this research took me to a wide variety of sources and locales. With time, of course, resources and recourses multiplied. As a result, the list of those to whom I must express my gratitude is long, but such gratitude is anything but a burden and, moreover, it is a special pleasure for a historian to look back over the history of a project in order to thank the many organizations, institutions, and individuals whose assistance was so generously given.

A fellowship from the Deutscher Akademischer Austauschdienst provided for the first year of indispensable and timely research in Europe. An additional grant from the National Endowment for the Humanities enabled me to see this project through to its completion. A major grant from the Faculty Development Committee, out of funds awarded Albion College by the Andrew W. Mellon Foundation, assisted in the final revision of the manuscript. In addition, two smaller grants from the same source were forthcoming—one making possible a quick trip to Germany in 1979 to tape a crucial interview and the other helping cover the cost of preparing the index. I am also indebted to Julian Rammelkamp, former chair of the Department of History at Albion College; to Neil Thorburn, former dean of the faculty at Albion; and to the latter's successor, Russell Aiuto, for their support of my work. I also wish to thank the Department of History at UCLA and its chair, Hans Rogger, for a term of university teaching that made possible, and complemented, some of the final stages of research. The department at UCLA was also generous in the provision of funds for some technical costs in the reproduction of illustrations.

I also extend my appreciation to the following institutions whose resources and staffs were instrumental in the completion of the research. The Berlin Document Center in Berlin-Zehlendorf, under its late director, Richard Bauer, present chief Daniel Simon, and with the assistance of Werner Pix, served as a consistently exciting source of documentation. I am also grateful to the Bundesarchiv and the Bundesarchiv-Bildarchiv in Coblenz; the Bundesarchiv-Militärarchiv in Freiburg im Breisgau; the Institut für Zeitgeschichte in Munich; the Institute for Contemporary History and Wiener Library in London; the National Archives in Washington, D.C.; the Geheimes Staatsarchiv in Berlin-Dahlem; the Hoover Institution on War, Revolution and Peace at Stanford University; Hadassah Modlinger of the Central Archives for the Disaster and the Heroism at Yad Vashem in Jerusalem; the Sigmund Freud-Gesellschaft in Vienna; the Bundesärztekammer and Kassenärztliche Bundesvereinigung in Cologne; the Bundesminister der Verteidigung and Sanitätsamt der Bundeswehr in Bonn; the Niedersächisches Hauptstaatsarchiv in Hanover; the Institut für Geschichte der Medizin der Freien Universität Berlin; the Staatsbibliothek Berlin; the Landesarchiv Berlin; the Bildarchiv Preussischer Kulturbesitz in Berlin; the Institut für Medizinische Psychologie und Psychotherapie der Technischen Universität München; and, to a lesser extent, the Zentrales Staatsarchiv in Potsdam. The research and medical libraries of the Free University of Berlin, the Friedrich-Alexander University in Erlangen, the University of California at Los Angeles, and the University of Michigan provided efficient access to a wide range of primary and secondary sources. The libraries of Occidental College, Albion College (with special thanks to Judy Johnson), Portland State University, Stanford University, and the Monterey Institute of International Studies, along with the Carmel (California) Public Library, also served as valuable sources of material. Finally, I am grateful to the National Library of Medicine for an off-line bibliographic citation list generated by Medlars II.

Apart from those men and women who consented to be interviewed about their roles in, and perspectives on, the history of psychotherapy in the Third Reich and whose contributions are credited in the bibliography, I must thank Gerhard Adler, M.D.; Thomas Aichhorn; Ellen Bartens; Bruno Bettelheim; Dr. med. Adolf-Martin Däumling; Lloyd deMause; Dr. med. Annemarie Dührssen; Judith Elkin; Ernst Federn; Dietmar Frenzel of the Embassy of the Federal Republic of Germany in Washington, D.C.; Daniel Goleman of the *New York Times;* Martin

Grotjahn, M.D.; David Heron of the Hoover Institution; Dr. med. Johanna Herzog-Dürck; Zoe Heyer; James Hillman; Dr. med. Wolfgang Hochheimer; Dr. sc. med. Kurt Höck of the Haus der Gesundheit in East Berlin; Klaus Hoppe, M.D.; Wolfgang Huber; Aniela Jaffé; Dr. med. Heinz Knoche, director of the Arbeitsgruppe "Geschichte der Deutschen Luft- und Raumfahrtmedizin" of the Deutschen Gesellschaft für Luft- und Raumfahrtmedizin in Bonn; Dr. med. Gisela Krichhauf; Bernhard Kroner; Peter Loewenberg; Hans-Martin Lohmann; William McGuire; Dr. med. C. A. Meier; Dr. med. Adolf-Ernst Meyer; William Miller; Paul Moor; Dr. med. Hans Müller-Braunschweig; Hermann O. Pineas, M.D.; Monika Richarz; George Rosenwald; Diane Snell and Stella Restropo of CEUCA in Bogotá, Colombia; Albert Speer; Rose Spiegel, M.D.; James Steakley; Sanford Thatcher; John Toland; and Robert Wolfe of the National Archives. I am also grateful to the editor of *Psyche* and *Zeitschrift für klinische Psychologie und Psychotherapie;* to the staffs of the Consulate General of the Federal Republic of Germany in Detroit, the Leo Baeck Institute in New York, the Landgericht Lüneburg, and the Amt für Einwohnerwesen in Düsseldorf; and to Charles Scribner's Sons of New York. Special appreciation goes to two colleagues formerly at the Free University of Berlin, Ulfried Geuter (Psychological Institute) and Regine Lockot (Institute for Medical Psychology).

The original thesis on which this book is based was ably directed by Peter Loewenberg and read by Albert Hutter and Hans Rogger. More than anyone else, Peter Loewenberg taught me by word and by deed the skills, the responsibilities, and the joys of the historian, a process so capably begun by John Rodes and Andrew Rolle.

In Germany, Michael and Gwen Wolff of Fürth were more than generous with their hospitality. In the task of revising the thesis into a book, I am grateful to good friends in Los Angeles for joyful and scholarly sanctuary at St. Albans. The production of the final manuscript owes a great deal to the kind and patient expertise of Sara Blackburn of New York City. Grace Waterbury, Carole Steinaway, and Gwen Fellenberger of Ann Arbor typed the final copy. At Oxford University Press, Nancy Lane proved to be an able and generous editor and was efficiently aided by a number of associates, in particular, Joan Knizeski. The index was prepared by Dorothy Hoffmann. I am grateful to all these fine professionals. Finally, I thank my wife Sarah for her assistance, her support, and, all too often, her tolerance.

All translations are my own unless otherwise noted. And, of course, in spite of the help I have received, the responsibility for any errors of fact or interpretation is mine alone.

G.C.
Albion, Michigan

June 1984

1

Medicine and the Mind in Modern Germany

On April 27, 1945, Soviet troops of Vassili Chuikov's Eighth Guards Army were fighting toward the Landwehr Canal at the western edge of the Berlin city center. The canal would be the jumping-off point for an assault on the Reichstag, the chief Russian objective in the conquest of the Nazi capital. The Russians were encountering heavy resistance from German positions in the Eden Hotel on the Budapesterstrasse at the southern end of the Tiergarten, Berlin's central park. But Russian tanks soon broke into the grounds of the Zoological Gardens and were firing on the huge flak tower there. By the end of the day, the Soviets had established positions along the Landwehr Canal all the way from the Tiergarten southeast to the Halle Gate.[1] In the course of these operations, the Russians occupied the Keithstrasse just east of the Budapesterstrasse. On the west side of the Keithstrasse at number 41 stood a building designated as a military hospital by the Red Cross flag hanging from it. As the Russians began to inspect the grounds, however, the officer in charge was shot by one of a group of SS soldiers hiding on one of the upper floors. The inhabitants of the building were herded into the cellar and the building was set on fire. Those in the cellar escaped though a hole in the wall as the building burned to the ground. The German in charge, dressed in the uniform of a Luftwaffe officer, was taken prisoner.[2] Though the Soviets were surely unaware of it, this action marked the end of one of the more remarkable stories in the brief history of the Third Reich. The man they had taken prisoner at Keithstrasse 41 on April 27 was Matthias Heinrich Göring.[3] During the previous twelve years Göring had emerged from personal and professional obscurity to become a significant public figure in Nazi Germany.

Three years before, on October 23, 1942, a letter from the office for science in Alfred Rosenberg's Nazi party organization for the oversight of doctrine had been sent to the party chancellery in Munich. This letter concerned psychotherapist Johannes Heinrich Schultz, deputy director of the German Institute for Psychological Research and Psychotherapy at Keithstrasse 41 in Berlin. Rosenberg's office had no objection to Schultz giving public lectures on psychotherapy since he was a noted psychotherapist and displayed no political, philosophical, or personal blemishes. Moreover, the letter went on, the institute with which Schultz was associated was directed by Matthias Heinrich Göring, "a close relative of the Reich Marshal."[4] In Nazi Germany, to be a relative of a powerful figure like Hermann Göring was a political imprimatur or, for a rival, most often a sign that nothing was to be done. In this case, Schultz, whatever his own merits or demerits as far as the Nazis were concerned, was safe and even favored because of his association with the Göring name.

The role played by Matthias Heinrich Göring, who was a neurologist and psychotherapist from Wuppertal-Elberfeld in the Ruhr, in the history of psychotherapy in Germany is a prime example of the importance not only of the individual but also of historical accident. Göring provided the protection and prestige necessary for the institutionalization of a marginal medical discipline between 1936 and 1945. The accident of a Göring connection, however, brought to partial professional fruition a number of dynamic intellectual and institutional trends in the realms of medicine, psychology, and social policy in Germany during the first half of the twentieth century. Finally, as we shall see, the story of the so-called "Göring Institute" also contributes to recent scholarship on the surprising complexities—and disturbing continuities—in the history of German society under Nazism.

The Third Reich accelerated a process of professionalization among German psychotherapists that had begun in 1928 with the official founding of the General Medical Society for Psychotherapy. This society, which by 1930 counted almost 500 members, was the chief organizational expression of a strong new trend among physicians, especially neurologists (*Nervenärzte*), toward psychological explanations of illness. This trend, which was embodied most significantly in the psychoanalytic movement under Sigmund Freud emerging from

Vienna at the turn of the century,[5] had been strengthened during the First World War when cases of "shell shock" were successfully treated by psychotherapeutic methods. This was a direct challenge to the reigning psychiatric establishment in Germany, which had traditionally regarded mental illness as physical in origin and rejected "psychodynamic" interpretations as unscientific and indulgent of supposed conflict in the patient's mind. But the psychogenic point of view gained significant ground even among psychiatrists during the war. In any case, although the German wartime government displayed some interest in this new approach, after the war the government and the psychiatric establishment took a hard line against compensation for those suffering from war neuroses.[6]

The General Medical Society for Psychotherapy had embraced a diversity of views on the status and role of psychotherapy in medicine, but it was led after 1933 by those who since its founding had sought professional autonomy for the discipline. The Nazis in their campaign against "the Jew" were to destroy the autonomous Freudian movement and favor traditional psychiatry in a ruthless "biological" program of sterilization and "euthanasia" against a broad grouping of the "incurably insane,"[7] but conditions in Hitler's Germany also benefited the professional ambitions of the psychotherapists who had reorganized themselves under Göring's leadership. Aside from Göring, opportunistic psychotherapists exploited the organizational disorder of the Third Reich as well as the Nazis' interest in an Aryanized field of psychology to ensure the "care and control" (*Betreuung*) of a loyal and productive *Volk*. The resultant professional gains provided for a continuity of institutional development along the disciplinary boundaries between medicine and psychology after 1945. This has created a tie between past and present, which had been earlier obscured by professionally protective claims for either the complete suppression of psychology in medicine under the Nazis or its clandestine preservation.[8] So even though psychotherapists in the Third Reich exploited the unique advantage of the Göring name, their experience between 1933 and 1945 also shows that basic characteristics of professional life in Germany were compatible with the Nazi dictatorship.

The professionalization of psychotherapy in the Third Reich was the culmination of a number of important developments in medicine and psychiatry during the nineteenth and early twentieth centuries in Germany. Psychotherapy itself had a long intellectual history there. Its modern origins lay in Romantic natural philosophy (*Naturphilosophie*) and specifically derived from Friedrich W. J. Schelling's mysticism, pantheism, and monism that stressed the basic unity of all life. This philosophy reflected a holistic tradition that was particularly pervasive in German thought. While the Englishman Thomas Hobbes believed that any unity of body and soul could be deduced through the application of mathematics and mechanics, Goethe emphasized the sovereign and all-encompassing realm of nature, of which humanity was the *sensorium commune*. The Romantics resurrected the vitalist tradition of the philosopher Georg Ernst Stahl, which declared that within every living system there exists a substantial entity that imparts to the system powers and qualities not possessed by inanimate bodies. This vital force could not be understood in mechanical terms; it was basic and irreducible and not accessible to scientific verification. As a result of these traditions and in the absence of later physiological investigation of the brain and the nervous system, early nineteenth-century physicians concerned themselves with the subjective realms of the emotional and the irrational:

> They held beliefs now considered quite sophisticated: the notion of inner conflict; the idea of the human being as psychobiological entity; that if intense and ungratified "passions" could not find an outlet, the result might be a breakdown of personality function; that ideas can become symbolized and expressed in physical reactions; the belief in an unconscious.[9]

It was this "mentalist" and philosophical preoccupation with the mind that university psychiatrists in Germany would reject during the latter half of the nineteenth century.

The concepts of the unity of body and mind and of the unconscious can be traced as far back in medical history as Heraclitus in the sixth century before Christ. Carl Haeberlin, a charter member of the General Medical Society for Psychotherapy, for one, identified Heraclitus as the first in a series of thinkers diverging from a "logocentric science" toward a "biocentric characterology."[10] Heraclitus, like Rousseau centuries later, believed that though reason was common to persons, it alone could not define the uniqueness of any given individual. During ancient times this conception of the individual as a unitary, biological system rather than a mechanical object of autonomous parts gained strength, particularly with Galen's notion of the bodily consensus. Yet it was not until the sixteenth century that the two chief orientations in psychology, between which the nineteenth century was to draw distinct battle lines, became manifest. The physiological and empirical approach was advocated by Francis Bacon, while the perspective that attempted to deal with human motivation apart from corporeal determinants was expressed by the Spanish religious humanist Juan Luis Vives and the Basel physician Theophrastus Bombastus von Hohenheim.

The latter Latinized his name to Paracelsus. He became a major critic of witch-hunts and, in a wildly unsystematic way, "envisioned the human personality as a whole, as made up of spiritual and corporeal parts intimately connected with the soul."[11] Among other things, Paracelsus became somewhat of a legendary figure in Nazi medical circles. Some Nazis heralded his advocacy of natural health and his professional use of written German in place of Latin. In 1943 the prominent film director G. W. Pabst produced a lavish film version of his life.[12] Paracelsus's notion of each individual as a microcosm mirroring the macrocosm was also implicit in the monadology of Leibniz, who conceived of an irreducible entity of life force. Leibniz's view of the human being as a biological unit contradicted Descartes's conception of the human organism as a soulless machine.

The figure of Leibniz in fact was one means by which psychotherapists in Germany after 1933 attempted to fabricate an exclusive German tradition of discovering, exploring, and analyzing the human unconscious. According to this opportunistic but also proprietary view, it was not (the Jewish) Freud but rather (the German) Leibniz who had recognized repression and sublimation as mental phenomena and free association as a valuable method of healing. Matthias Heinrich Göring noted that

> had not his work remained completely unknown until 1765 and the later, resulting, work or a better translation of Christian Wolff gone unrecognized, the path toward the research and management of unconscious mental functions would never have been that of Freud and his school.[13]

Wolff objected to the Cartesian idea that nothing could be in the mind of which it was not aware. It is true that Wolff, in advancing from the medieval theurgy of Leibniz's thought, "served as a stimulus to the development of neurology and also of the theory of instincts which Freud introduced early in the twentieth century."[14] But Göring, in his rush to affirm the German pedigree of psychotherapy to the Nazi regime, ignored the fact that it was precisely Freud's great contribution to combine Romantic preoccupation with "hidden forces" in the psyche with the materialism of the late nineteenth-century scientific tradition to produce a method by which the unconscious could be revealed and treated.[15]

Physician and painter Carl Gustav Carus was another early advocate of the unity of body and mind. Drawing from Schelling's seminal *Philosophy of Nature* (1797), Carus defined psychology as the science of the soul's evolution from the unconscious to the conscious: "The unconscious itself is the subjective expression of that which we must objectively recognize as nature."[16] It followed that the emphasis in curing mental illness had to rest on curing the whole individual, not a particular part or organ, and on an appreciation of human aims and desires. This position, as we shall see, was what caused many German psychotherapists to prefer Alfred Adler's individual psychology to the sexual emphasis of Freud's psychoanalysis. Also implicit in this approach, and in its later glorification in the German national and cultural milieu, was the philosophical and religious grandeur it imparted to the human psyche, a quality that was to make Carl Jung's spiritual outlook as well preferable to Freud's instinctual one in the minds of many German psychotherapists. As one such Jungian put it, "[t]he unconscious according to Carus is at a deeper level and at its core not influenced by instinctual drives."[17]

Carus and his most influential work, *Psyche, zur Entwicklungsgeschichte der Seele* (1846), became a chief source of inspiration for Göring and some of the other German psychotherapists in the Third Reich. Other important influences were the works of two Romantic thinkers of the early nineteenth century who were struck from the same mold as Carus: Carl Wilhelm Ideler and Ernst von Feuchtersleben. Feuchtersleben in particular, with his *Diätetik der Seele* (1838), urged the view that mental diseases were diseases of the personality and stressed the need for an "educational" psychotherapy. For Göring, Feuchtersleben, like Leibniz, Carus, and others, was still another historical witness to the richness of a specifically German psychotherapeutic tradition and further proof of the consequent relative insignificance of Freud's mechanistic misinterpretation of the human unconscious.[18] The nineteenth-century Romantic tradition in medicine and psychology reached its peak in Eduard von Hartmann's *Philosophie des Unbewussten* (1869). Hartmann was one of the last in a line of

German philosophers who emphasized the will over reason, the unconscious over the conscious, and nature over ego. The Romantic tradition then went underground in Germany, mining inspiration from the literature of Goethe and Dostoyevsky and the philosophy of Nietzsche, while overhead reigned the self-assured age of medical positivism and psychiatric nosology. In this way, too, Nietzsche as well became an important forerunner of modern psychotherapy in Germany.[19]

From the middle of the nineteenth century in Germany in particular the new medical sciences of the mind were dominated by a strictly somatological psychiatry.[20] At mid-century the rational confidence of the Enlightenment had begun to take hold in German scientific thought, producing in Germany and Austria physiologists like Johannes Müller, Emil Du Bois-Reymond, and Ernst Brücke, pathologist Rudolf Virchow, psychologist Wilhelm Wundt, and the three great psychiatrists of the age, Wilhelm Griesinger, Theodor Meynert, and Emil Kraepelin. The work of Du Bois-Reymond and Brücke, as well as that of others, was subsumed under what has been called the "school of Helmholtz": Physiologist Hermann von Helmholtz espoused a belief in materialism and the primacy of experimentation and observation, to wit, the classic scientific method. It was Griesinger who drew psychiatry away from an exclusive relationship with the asylum and toward the university with the dictum that mental disease was brain disease. Meynert concentrated on disorders of the frontal lobe of the brain, mocked his student Freud, but died confessing himself a hysteric to the father of psychoanalysis. Kraepelin's personal impact was especially great as well as revealing of a common scientific, professional, and cultural authoritarianism among psychiatrists and doctors in general:

> After he assumed the directorship of a hospital and clinic there was never a question of who was the man in charge. "Imperial German Psychiatry" was said to have gained prominence under the "chancellorship" of Kraepelin, one of Bismarck's admirers.[21]

Kraepelin's manner reflected a psychiatric doctrine that had imbibed the strutting rigor of the Prussian unification of Germany. Like Bismarck in his critique of the failure of the idealistic German liberals in 1848, the *Realpolitik* of the university psychiatric clinic was decreed to be no place for fuzzy-headed and indulgent notions of psychotherapy. The laboratory, classroom, clinic, and asylum were places where strict scientific observation could take place. Since the precise physical sources for mental disorders remained elusive, however, somatic psychiatrists increasingly evinced a pessimism about the possibilities for treatment and cure. Therapy remained marginal and crude. It was this unbending environment that nurtured the work of those, like neurologist Wilhelm Erb, who pioneered the medical use in Germany of electric therapy, a method which Freud was later to find of absolutely no use in a majority of neurotic cases.

Yet within the psychiatric ranks themselves, the "psychological" orientation was beginning to assert itself. For not only were the categories of mental disease that were worked out by Kraepelin silent on treatment, they also did not address a wide variety of psychological complaints among patients. Psychiatrists in the new century, such as Ernst Kretschmer and Robert Gaupp, turned increasingly toward viewing the human being as a psychophysical totality. This provided some of the impetus for the study of the human psyche that was to bring psychiatry, or at least a number of its practitioners, closer to a psychotherapeutic point of view.[22] Kretschmer, with his theory of the relationship between body type and character, would appeal to many psychiatrists frustrated at the seeming random incurability of psychiatric disorders. He would also, as we shall see, play a significant role in the development of a psychotherapeutic movement after the First World War. Still, German psychiatry remained overwhelmingly somatic and positivistic in its outlook. A revealing contrast in this respect was the leading role in the development of psychoanalysis and psychotherapy assumed by the Swiss psychiatrists Adolf Meyer, Auguste Forel, Eugen Bleuler, and Carl Jung. Another contrast was the inspiration and instruction Freud acquired from the French clinician Jean-Martin Charcot, who, unlike the German psychiatrists, took hysteria seriously.[23]

The continuing psychiatric attacks against psychoanalysis, which was emerging from Vienna at the turn of the nineteenth century, were the products of a marked degree of professional anxiety. As Gregory Zilboorg observes:

> No adequate and equitable appraisal of Freud's contribution is possible unless one takes cognizance of the fact that formal descriptive psychiatry, having reached its peak in the closing years of the past century, stood rather puzzled at the end of the blind alley it had reached.[24]

The threat was deeply personal as well as professional, however. The dismantling of the scientific scaffolding that surrounded the mental patient, from the heights of which psychiatrists and academic psychologists could study, classify, and prescribe, represented a considerable personal threat to the comfortable brahmin assessments of severe psychic disarray in the "other." This was particularly the case with male psychiatric judgments about women and the feminine biological and genetic "weakness" allegedly revealed most commonly by hysteria. Now, however, mental disorders could no longer be written off simply as matters of mechanics and heredity or divorced from the pliable emotions and environments common to all human beings. The horrors of many segments of the psychiatric community at the sexual content of Freudian theory revealed its members' own discomfort with the universality of such human characteristics. The division between subject and object betrayed psychiatry's heavy and longstanding intellectual debt to Cartesian dualism. The psychiatrist was a scientist, wedded to matter through the ceremony of experimentation. The empirical ethos was in the best tradition of eighteenth-century rationalism and nineteenth-century positivism. It also reflected a confidence, brimming over from the Enlightenment, that science was the sure way to the betterment of the human condition. There was no room in this model of the mind for such an "unscientific" notion as the unconscious. Psychiatrists drew from Descartes the dualism of mind and body, and they used the descendant doctrine of psychophysical parallelism to affirm the primacy of organic processes. Thus, any attempt to analyze the mind was simply unscientific. Du Bois-Reymond had summed up the mechanistic opposition to any attempt to smuggle "philosophical" or "metaphysical" elements into the study of the brain's operations with the words "*ignoramus et ignoramibus*—we do not know and we shall never know."[25]

This strict mechanistic empiricism of German psychiatry was also actually a reaffirmation of the German tradition of idealism. By rigorously excluding all Romantic-rooted medical interest in final cause, teleology, and human attitudes, the psychiatric profession left the realm of the "soul" to the philosophers and theologians, and proclaimed the impossibility of any attempt to go beyond what could be achieved by physiology. With this approach, medical psychology in the late nineteenth century followed Kant in his delineation of what was knowable and what was not. The psychiatrists ventured beyond Kant, however, by seeking to bar any medical iconoclasm that might be so daring as to question the conception of the soul.[26] Freud, whatever materialism was inherent in his theory of psychodynamics, turned the study of human behavior away from the notion of the individual as the sum of his or her physical parts and toward an understanding of the interactions among mind, body, and environment. As was the case with psychotherapy in general, even among German psychiatrists there was some interest in Freud's psychoanalysis. This was due not only to scientific curiosity but also to some sense of frustration at the inability of formal descriptive psychiatry to make significant headway in the search for the causes and cures of mental illnesses.

Freud's work, beginning with his classic statement of 1900, *The Interpretation of Dreams,* had signaled the onset of a revolution in scientific and medical thought in the field. Freud secularized the old "mentalist" point of view by removing behavior and its causes from the realm of morality and theology and placing them in the realms of wishes, desires, and drives.[27] Operating in the tradition of Charcot and Hippolyte-Marie Bernheim, the great French medical hypnotists, Freud and Viennese colleague Josef Breuer discovered the "talking cure" in the course of the treatment by hypnosis of a case of hysteria (conversion of affect into somatic symptoms). Freud was subsequently to discard hypnosis altogether, replacing it with analysis of the free associations made by the conscious patient. Freud's influence grew rapidly—the German Psychoanalytic Society was founded in 1910—but his theories also aroused tremendous controversy, principally because of their frank treatment of adult and childhood sexuality.[28]

Psychoanalysis itself was not a monolith, a fact of some importance for the further development of psychotherapy in Germany. Freud would revise his thought considerably over his lifetime. While Melanie Klein and her school reaffirmed the biological determinants of early infantile experience, subsequent object relations theorists have turned the analytic emphasis away from Freud's Oedipus complex to the early relationships with the mother. Freud himself devoted greater energy to the study of ego functions, a direction anticipated and followed by a number of other psychoanalysts who became known collectively as neo-Freudians:

> The inevitability of anatomy in determining the psychological differences between the sexes, the inevitability of the stages of libido [drive] development and the Oedipus complex, were rejected and the importance of interpersonal relations and the cultural background emphasized, and in psychotherapy an attempt was often made to substitute short and active methods for prolonged and passive ones.[29]

Freud and his orthodox followers rejected short-term suggestive methods of therapy in advocating the "pure gold" of long-term analysis. For Freud, the quest was for self-knowledge as a means of mitigation of mental conflict, not the mere alleviation or elimination of symptoms. The patient, according to psychoanalytic practice, was to "work though" his or her own conflicts with only occasional interpretations and no gratification from the "passive" analyst. This would allow the "transference" of unconscious feelings from the patient's past onto the neutral analyst so that they could be recognized and analyzed. In fact, Freud himself did not exercise strict psychoanalytic neutrality, but it was Sandor Ferenczi, one of his early followers, who first began systematically advocating and practicing personal involvement between analyst and analysand.[30] This would become part of a broader departure from strict psychoanalytic method manifested not only among neo-Freudians but also among psychotherapists and physicians in general who called for the "active" engagement—even leadership—of the therapist in the healing process. In place of the isolated psychoanalytic dyad there would be an opening up to a variety of interpersonal, social, and cultural approaches and dynamics in psychotherapy.

Alfred Adler emerged before the First World War as the first major prophet of this cultural/interpersonal orientation. Adler had developed a profound social consciousness in his work with laborers in Vienna. This experience revealed to him the high incidence of somatic defect among his patients. Drawing from his own childhood—which was marred by rickets, pneumonia, and a number of accidents—as well as from Freud's drive theory, Adler evolved his theory that the aggressive drive is a means by which an individual adapts to arduous life tasks. For Adler, the crucial element in the human psyche was the individual's reaction to feelings of inferiority, which originated in the child's early relationship to the adult. Sexuality became symbolic of this basic struggle, posing the "masculine protest" against feminine "weakness." This approach emphasized the reality and importance of the social environment and the social "instinct" in every human being. Freud was a pessimist, at best a meliorist, while Adler and other neo-Freudians adopted a more optimistic stance in balancing human pathology with human potential. Adler abandoned causality in favor of teleology, embarking on a campaign to involve the individual psychologist in the process of bringing human beings and the social environment into mutual harmony.

Aside from Adler, the three principal representatives of the neo-Freudian, or social Freudian, school were Karen Horney, Erich Fromm, and the American Harry Stack Sullivan. Although each evolved a unique theory, they argued in unison that Freud's biological determinism was inadequate to comprehend the dynamics of humanity's existence as an aggregate of social beings, and that instead of the search for pleasure and the avoidance of pain, the basic human drive was for self-expression and social recognition. Theodor Reik called this "wholeness," and Erik Erikson labeled it "totality." While Horney and the others subscribed to the three basic Freudian precepts of psychic determinism, repression, and the personality as dynamic and not static, they challenged other parts of Freud's theory. These included: Freud's biological orientation; his indifference to contemporary anthropology and sociology with their emphasis on the relative quality of "human nature"; the dualism of the life and death instincts; Freud's abstention from moral judgment; and his "mechanistic-evolutionistic" thinking, which, according to many critics, cast human behavior as nothing but (*nichts als*) a repetition of childhood patterns.[31] By contrast, Adler and the social Freudians believed that the individual and, eventually, society could be improved through the active and empathic intervention of the therapist. Though this was a politically progressive or even socialist orientation, the desire they shared for short-term, inexpensive modes of psychotherapy and their faith in the prospects of psychosocial engineering were also tacks that conservative and fascist psychotherapists in Germany were to use to advantage in the Third Reich.

Psychoanalysis also faced a strong challenge from Carl Gustav Jung. In 1900 Jung, who came from a Swiss Reformed religious background, went to the Zurich mental hospital and university psychiatric clinic, the Burghölzli, to study under Bleuler. There he became convinced that dementia praecox (schizophrenia), a common psychotic condition, was treatable by psychotherapeutic means. Jung became an enthusiastic proponent of Freudian theory, but broke with Freud over the nature of the drives, positing a vast area beyond Freud's conception of the unconscious as a "collective unconscious." He rejected Freud's emphasis on neurotic causation in favor of a teleological point of view. As Philip Rieff has put it: "While for Jung the unconscious is all that consciousness can become, for Freud it is, more simply, all that consciousness is not."[32] Jung scoured the realm of mythology for inspiration from the past to guide the patient's future, while Freud used the patient's unconscious as a guide to myth, as proof of individual and collective enslavement to the past. Here, too, the wind that filled Jung's sails was to blow strongly among German psychotherapists.

But before then all three disciplines in Germany—psychotherapy, psychiatry, and psychoanalysis—were thrown together in the maelstrom of the First World War. The first year of this first "industrial war" confronted army psychiatrists with a phenomenon known as "mass psychosis," a collection of symptoms without any detectable organic basis. The mental casualty rate was increased as a result of the relatively poor monitoring and screening procedures inherent in the massive, rapid, and enthusiastic mobilization as well as by the questionable health of a good part of the German population. What was typical of these "mass psychoses" was the inverse proportion of their frequency to proximity to the front. The common symptoms—sleeplessness, shaking, and disorders of speech, sight, gait, or hearing—turned out to be caused by the effects of rumor, anxious expectations, and fantasies that were the outcome of long periods of waiting behind the lines. Once susceptible personalities had been weeded out, however, and the war had settled into a more individualized mode of trench warfare and small-group operations, these particular psychological manifestations declined to almost zero. But by the winter of 1917, war neuroses in general had risen to the point of parity with organic disorders. The effect of incessant artillery bombardment, for example, had led to an increase in traumatic neuroses from 14 percent in 1914 to 45 percent in 1917.[33]

The medical troops of "Imperial German psychiatry" who were mobilized for battle in 1914 still went to war against organic disease, the external invader of a healthy system or the resident source of an unhealthy one, not neurosis, the internal imbalance of psychodynamics, environment, and history. But the reality of war neurosis in the First World War challenged psychiatry's initial wartime protests of an organic basis for mental illness. The fact that most of those affected during 1914–15 came from the rear areas or were afflicted during long pauses in activity at the front cast grave doubt over the early sanguine diagnosis of alterations in the brain's cortex stemming from the physical shocks of battle. At the famous war session of the German Association for Psychiatry in Munich in September 1916, Robert Gaupp, Max Nonne, Karl Bonhoeffer, and Oswald Bumke, among others, attempted to come to psychiatric terms with the concept of neurosis as symptomatic of psychological disorder. Nonne, for one, had success with hypnosis. In fact, the first studies of war neurosis performed during the Russo-Japanese War had been published in a German psychiatric journal almost a decade before.[34] The German psychiatrists at Munich rejected the mostly organic thesis advanced by Hermann Oppenheim, deciding instead on a formula that recognized the psychogenic factor in the cause, or etiology, of war neuroses. Still, they maintained, it was the body that was the chief source for wish fantasies, and that this joined with the psychological disposition to produce a trauma with a subsequent psychogenic recreation.[35]

The psychiatrists also continued to challenge their most autonomous and unified competitors, the psychoanalysts. Among other things, many of them argued that the cases of war neuroses which were flooding the military clinics actually disproved Freudian theory: Where, they asked, was the sexual etiology?[36] In spite of such ongoing opposition, psychoanalysis in particular was winning unprecedented attention from official sources. At the Fifth International Psycho-Analytical Congress held in Budapest in September 1918, representatives of the German and Austrian governments were in attendance for the first time. Such prominent psychoanalysts as Karl Abraham, Max Eitingon, Ernst Simmel, and Sandor Ferenczi had all contributed valuable clinical experience to the problem of war neurosis, and there were plans for establishing psychoanalytic clinics throughout Germany and Austria-Hungary.[37] The November armistice precluded the implementation of any such program, but the concept of the unconscious life of the individual and its medical treatment had achieved significant public validation and notoriety.

The state of German psychiatry during the First World War thus represented a final crisis of sorts, though also an opportunity for a recently troubled medical newcomer to prove its technical and national credentials. Both within and without the discipline, there was serious questioning of the theory and practice of psychiatry. In the words of Thomas Kuhn on the shifting of scientific paradigms: "Failure of existing rules is the prelude to a search for new ones."[38] While according to Kuhn's definition, psychiatry may not be a science, the dramatic wartime failure of German psychiatry's principles marked the end of the exclusive dominance of an entire late nineteenth-century tradition in science and medicine. One contemporaneous observer saw it this way:

> Medicine is so deeply imbued with materialism that the majority of its members earnestly proceed with the search for some mythical toxins as the one and only causative factor of mental abnormality, with the result that the human factor, the individual conflict with the environment and the social and biological standpoints are quite lost sight of.[39]

The psychogenic challenge to somatic psychiatry also embodied an important trend in the treatment of mental illness that would play a major role in the subsequent history of psychotherapy in Germany and the West. The traditional view of this challenge has often been put in terms of ethics. This view holds that psychotherapists and psychoanalysts humanized an otherwise brutal psychiatric approach to those soldiers suffering from war neuroses. It is true that the majority of German psychiatrists saw war neurosis as a manifestation of either congenital defect or a lack of will. And it is also true that psychiatric treatment of these disorders most often fell under the cloak of harsh "disciplinary therapy" designed to force the soldier back into service.[40] But psychotherapists and psychoanalysts were also committed to returning the soldier to combat, even if their attitudes and methods were more compassionate. As Paul Lerner has argued, this commitment was part of an ongoing trend in the West toward the medicalization and rationalization of society.[41] Medicalization involved a combination of healing, professional interest, and social control. Rationalization, which would be a powerful force in the Weimar Republic after the First World War, emphasized economic productivity and efficiency in the context of a new industrial order. And an emphasis on will and the responsibility to get well and be productive, an ethos that would become the hallmark of psychotherapists seeking professional validation, would also meld dangerously with National Socialism in peace and at war.

However, the practical success and official recognition that psychotherapy and psychoanalysis experienced during the First World War did not lead, as its proponents had hoped, to uninterrupted growth in influence and application after 1918. Psychoanalysts in Germany and Austria, trading on Freud's brilliance and fame, established their own institutes for training and treatment in Berlin in 1920 and in Vienna in 1922. But Germany's defeat and the resultant political chaos of the immediate postwar years prevented the realization of a plan for the systematic study and treatment of war neurotics. Such a plan, involving the widespread use of psychotherapy, had been announced by psychiatrist Max Nonne and the army medical service in 1916.[42] The period of catastrophic postwar inflation which racked Germany from the end of the war added further difficulties. Doctors, like almost everyone else, had to scramble to make ends meet and did not have the luxury of expanding their practices by investment in training or practicing psychotherapy. Moreover, the burgeoning demand for disability pensions, particularly as a result of the huge numbers of soldiers suffering the effects of wartime neuroses, put such pressure on the insurance funds that in 1926 the Reich Insurance Office withdrew recognition of traumatic neurosis as an indemnifiable illness altogether.[43] Finally, many psychiatrists remained skeptical of psychotherapy and in general suspicious of claims from patients, whether civilian or military, for mental suffering. Psychotherapist Walter Cimbal saw this last phenomenon as the intensification of a trend when he concluded: "German medical science turned ever more sharply toward a mechanistic-materialistic way of thinking."[44]

But trends in favor of the professional development of psychotherapy were also present during the Weimar Republic. First, of course, was the very fact of ongoing interest in the field on the part of psychiatrists, physicians, representatives of other disciplines concerned with human welfare, and not least of all the public—potential and actual patients—in general. Second, the successive crises of war, defeat, and economic disorder increased the need and demand for medical services, including psychotherapy: "German society found itself overwhelmed by the conditions of impoverishment, unemployment, and illness."[45] The war had spawned unprecedented mental as well as physical casualties, while the defeat deprived Germany of the opportunity to pay for its human and material damage through victory, conquest, booty, and reparation. Pensions could not keep up with the disastrous inflation of the early postwar years, while the subsequent stabilization measures beginning in 1924 also hurt pensioners and others on fixed incomes. Demand for pensions had been up sharply since the war. The government's commitment to compensate victims of the war led a wide range of other pensioners to agitate for like compensation.

While relatively few of these people were economically or emotionally disposed to take on the cost of psychotherapeutic treatment, even had it been more widely available during these years, the ethos within government, business, and professional circles was turning toward the substitution of treatment and rehabilitation for the monetary compensation of pensions and allowances.[46] Psychotherapy and psychoanalysis were even included—marginally (see chapter 9)—in the revised fee schedules worked out by doctors and the sickness funds in 1924.[47] The same point of view was growing among psychiatrists who wished to turn the asylums into places of active treatment rather than passive confinement. Such reformers were seeking to adapt psychiatry to the changed political, social, and economic conditions in Germany. Treating patients instead of warehousing them was seen to be more economical, consistent with the contemporary standard of social integration, and a contribution to the demand for individual productivity under the stabilization policies of the latter half of the 1920s.[48] Such an emphasis on social productivity was in keeping both with the demands of a resurgent and highly cartelized capitalism and with the paternalistic state tradition embedded in Bismarck's original conception for the social welfare system that had been established in the 1880s. It was also an extension of the type of therapeutic rationalization Lerner describes as occurring among psychiatrists during the First World War. And, as we shall see, it became an important element in the mutual attraction between psychotherapists and the Nazi regime. Even more fateful among psychiatrists in this regard was the turn during the onset of Great Depression in 1929 toward eugenics. With the resultant diminished prospects for the integration of the mentally ill into the economy, there was greater emphasis on distinguishing the curable from the incurable. For the latter, sterilization was increasingly regarded as the best solution.[49]

In spite of many difficulties, therefore, the psychotherapeutic point of view in medicine and psychiatry stood to gain ground in Germany in the years after the First World War. Psychoanalysis even became culturally fashionable on both sides of the Atlantic and extended its influence outside of medicine into the arts and literature. As early as 1918 Berlin psychoanalyst Karl Abraham even expressed misgivings to Freud about the scientific and professional dangers of too great a "popularization" of psychoanalysis.[50] Such concerns did not, however, prevent Abraham in 1925 from serving as an expert consultant on a feature film about psychoanalysis. Freud was not enthusiastic about the project, having earlier turned down an offer out of Hollywood from Samuel Goldwyn for a psychoanalytic film about the great love affairs in history. Abraham, president of the German Psychoanalytic

Society, and fellow analyst Hanns Sachs both consulted on *Geheimnisse einer Seele* (*Secrets of a Soul*), produced by the giant German film studio Ufa, directed by G. W. Pabst, and starring Werner Kraus. The hyperbole that surrounded the film's release in 1926 only confirmed Freud in his reservations. The film in fact was a pale, indeed misleading, exercise in psychoanalysis, although its simplifications helped generate greater popular interest in the film and thus, perhaps, also in psychoanalysis. One of Abraham's arguments to Freud in favor of psychoanalytic collaboration on the film, however, also demonstrates the liveliness and contentiousness in the field of psychotherapy in Berlin at the time. Abraham argued that if the psychoanalysts did not accept Ufa's offer to cooperate in the production of the film, then the offer might go to the "'wild' analysts in Berlin—if only to mention Kronfeld, Schultz, and Hattingberg who would be only too keen to grasp at an offer should we decline."[51]

Freud himself wrote on what he labelled "wild psychoanalysis," observing that it generally sacrificed depth analysis for initial transference improvements based shakily on the early establishment of a positive relationship between therapist and patient, offered rational help and unspecific guidance under a veil of personal and emotional involvement, and only occasionally provided limited depth interpretations. These methods, Freud believed, rested more on intuitive inquiry than on proper scientific investigation.[52] Freud's colleague Otto Fenichel dismissed these practices in observing that such

> methods of psychotherapy . . . have remained the same since the times of the earliest witch doctors; the results were perhaps not bad, but they were not understood and thus were unreliable. You could never tell whether or not they would be achieved at all.[53]

The psychoanalytic movement would remain committed to the neutral and relatively passive role of the analyst for the sake of the analysand's own long-term "working through." The patient should receive no gratification from the analyst. Psychotherapists—or "wild psychoanalysts"—were more interested in practical short-term therapies based on the active involvement of the therapist as a guide, a friend, an educator, a doctor.

It was true, as Jung had pointed out in his presidential address to the International Psycho-Analytical Congress in 1911, that there were any number of dubious practitioners in this particular field, especially in

Germany, with its lack of legal restrictions on quackery and its turn-of-the-century bourgeois passion for sexology.[54] But the ferment about the varieties of technique also indicated the widespread interest in psychoanalysis and psychotherapy that prevailed in Germany among members both of the general public and among doctors and other professionals. The medical profession's interest in psychoanalysis in particular ranged from enthusiasm through various degrees of reservation to outright rejection. Hans von Hattingberg, one of those cited anxiously by Abraham in 1925, had been secretary of the International Psycho-Analytical Association in 1911.[55] Abraham's dubbing of Hattingberg as a "wild" psychoanalyst stemmed from Hattingberg's idiosyncratic fusion of various psychodynamic models, a melding that was squarely in the German Romantic tradition. Hattingberg's practice typified the large number of German physicians who were evolving their own versions of psychoanalysis and psychotherapy from a rich nineteenth-century heritage that had been brought to startlingly new and fruitful life by Freud and his followers. In 1926, as we shall see in the next chapter, many of these physicians began to organize themselves in a way that would seven years later lead them into a fateful collaboration with the Nazi regime.

Notes

1. Anthony Read and David Fisher, *The Fall of Berlin* (New York, 1993), pp. 424–5.
2. Harald Schultz-Hencke, Zweiter protokollarsicher Bericht May 24, 1945, p. 2, Kl. Erw. 762/7. BA. Werner Kemper, director of the Göring Institute's outpatient clinic from 1942 to 1945, claims that the institute must have been destroyed in one of the last air raids on Berlin: see Ludwig J. Pongratz, ed., *Psychotherapie in Selbstdarstellungen,* p. 293. Schultz-Hencke's version, however, is more specific as well as definite, accords with the course of the battle for Berlin, and also accounts for Göring being taken prisoner. It is based on an apparently firsthand report from Cäcilie Otten, who was also taken prisoner by the Russians and after the war became a member of the Institute for Psychotherapy in Berlin: see Regine Lockot, *Die Reinigung der Psychoanalyse,* p. 58, n. 62.
3. Pongratz, *Psychotherapie,* p. 277.
4. MA 116/15. Institut für Zeitgeschichte, Munich.
5. Hannah S. Decker, *Freud in Germany.*
6. Robert Weldon Whalen, *Bitter Wounds: German Victims of the Great War, 1914–1939* (Ithaca, 1984), p. 63.
7. Hans-Walter Schmuhl, *Rassenhygiene, Nationalsozialismus, Euthanasie. Von der Verhütung zur Vernichtung "lebensunwerten Lebens," 1890–1945* (Göttingen, 1987).
8. Regine Lockot, *Erinnern und Durcharbeiten*; Karen Brecht et al., *"Hier geht das Leben auf eine sehr merkwürdige Weise weiter…".*

9. Decker, *Freud in Germany,* p. 28.
10. Carl Haeberlin, "Die Bedetung von Ludwig Klages und Hans Prinzhorn," p. 39. See also idem, "Über das vital Unbewusste, Bewusstsein und Charakter"; and Gregory Zilboorg, *A History of Medical Psychology,* p. 39.
11. Franz G. Alexander and Sheldon T. Selesnick, *The History of Psychiatry: An Evaluation of Psychiatric Thought and Practice from Prehistoric Times to the Present* (New York, 1966), pp. 85–6. On this debate, see Zilboorg, *Medical Psychology,* pp. 180–200.
12. David Stewart Hull, *Film in the Third Reich: A Study of the German Cinema, 1933–1945* (Berkeley, 1969), pp. 246–8; Erich Otto, "Der Paracelsus Film: Zur Salzburger Uraufführung," *Deutsches Ärzteblatt* 73 (1943): 131.
13. Quoted in Ilse Döhl, "Gottfried Wilhelm Leibniz als Entdecker des Unbewussten," in idem et al., *Leibniz, Carus und Nietzsche als Vorläufer unserer Tiefenpsychologie,* p. 8. See also the review by Josef Meinertz in *ZFP* 14 (1942): 175–7; and Döhl, *Bewusstseinsschichtung: Ein Beitrag zur Entwicklung ihrer Theorie, insbesondere durch Nachweis von Ursprüngen bei Leibniz* (Berlin, 1935).
14. Zilboorg, *Medical Psychology,* p. 253; see also Lancelot L. White, *The Unconscious Before Freud* (Garden City, N.Y., 1962).
15. See Siegfried Bernfeld, "Freud's Earliest Theories and the School of Helmholtz," *Psychoanalytic Quarterly* 13 (1944): 341–62, which places Freud in the tradition of the nineteenth-century German materialistic reaction to natural philosophy. Such a view of Freud is consistent—if not an inevitable outcome—of Bernfeld's Marxism. See also Frank J. Sulloway, *Freud, Biologist of the Mind: Beyond the Psychoanalytic Legend* (New York, 1979).
16. C. G. Carus quoted in Haeberlin, "Unbewusste, Bewusstsein und Charakter," p. 285.
17. Gustav Graber, "Carl Gustav Carus als Erforscher des Unbewussten und Vorläufer unserer Seelenheilkunde," in Döhl et al., *Leibniz, Carus und Nietzsche,* p. 37. On Carus, see Henri Ellenberger, *The Discovery of the Unconscious,* pp. 207–8; Alexander and Selesnick, *Psychiatry,* 169–70; and Decker, *Freud in Germany,* p. 259.
18. Matthias Heinrich Göring, "Grundlagen der Psychotherapie"; see also Ellenberger, *Discovery,* pp. 210–15; and Zilboorg, *Medical Psychology,* pp. 475–8.
19. Fritz Mohr, "Friedrich Nietzsche als Tiefenpsychologe und Küster eines neuen Arzttums," in Döhl et al., *Leibniz, Carus und Nietzsche,* p. 55. On Hartmann, see Kurt Gauger, "Die Lehre vom makrokosmischen Zweckprozess bei Eduard von Hartmann" (Inaugural dissertation, Rostock, 1922). For a critical view of the Romantics and science, see Charles Coulston Gillispie, *The Edge of Objectivity: An Essay in the History of Scientific Ideas* (Princeton, 1960), pp. 178–201.
20. Zilboorg, *Medical Psychology,* pp. 287–91, 319–41; Ellenberger, *Discovery,* pp. 210–12.
21. Alexander and Selesnick, *The History of Psychiatry,* p. 163; see also Decker, *Freud in Germany,* pp. 47–54.
22. Decker, *Freud in Germany,* pp. 36–72; see also Robert Gaupp, "Psychiatrische Probleme der Gegenwart," *Zeitschrift für ärztliche Fortbildung* 38 (1941): 257–9.
23. Decker, *Freud in Germany,* pp. 77–81; see also Jan Goldstein, "The Hysteria Diagnosis and the Politics of Anticlericalism in Late Nineteenth-Century France," *Journal of Modern History* 54 (1982): 209–39.
24. Zilboorg, *Medical Psychology,* pp. 494–5.
25. Decker, *Freud in Germany,* pp. 46, 202, 324–8.
26. Robert Gaupp, "Some Reflections on the Development of Psychiatry in Germany," *American Journal of Psychiatry* 108 (1952): 721–3.

27. Annemarie Dührssen, *Ein Jahrhundert Psychoanalytische Bewegung in Deutschland,* pp. 14–15.
28. See Decker, *Freud in Germany*; Johannes Heinrich Schultz, *S. Freud's Sexualpsychologie: Kritische Einführung für Gerichtsärzte, Ärzte und Laien* (Berlin, 1917); and Carl Haeberlin, *Grundlinien der Psychoanalyse* (Munich, 1927). The same was true across the Atlantic Ocean: see Nathan G. Hale, *Freud and the Americans: The Beginnings of Psychoanalysis in the United States, 1876–1917* (New York, 1971).
29. J. A. C. Brown, *Freud and the Post-Freudians* (London, 1972), p. 129.
30. Janet Malcolm, *Psychoanalysis: The Impossible Profession* (New York, 1981), pp. 36–47.
31. Ibid., pp. 129–73.
32. Philip Rieff, *Freud: The Mind of the Moralist,* 3rd ed. (Chicago, 1979), p. 35. See also Alexander and Selesnick, *Psychiatry,* pp. 234–48. On the crucial period from 1906 to 1914, see Sigmund Freud, *The Freud/Jung Letters: The Correspondence Between Sigmund Freud and C. G. Jung,* ed. William McGuire and trans. Ralph Manheim and R. F. C. Hull, Bollingen Series XCIV (Princeton, 1974).
33. Heinz Hartmann, "Die k.u.k. Nervenklinik Graz im Dienste des Krieges," *Archiv für Psychiatrie* 59 (1918): 1162; neurasthenia, a physiological nervous disorder, showed a marked stability after 1914 as the soldiers became more accustomed to the war environment.
34. P. M. Awtokratowo, "Die Geistekrankheiten im russischen Heere während des japanischen Krieges," *Allgemeine Zeitschrift für Psychiatrie* 64 (1907): 286–319.
35. Konrad Hummel, "Vergleichende Untersuchungen," pp. 26–7. For discussion of this among German psychiatrists and psychoanalysts between 1918 and 1945, see Gustav Störring, "Die Verschiedenheiten der psycho-pathologischen Erfahrungen im Weltkriege und im jetzigen Krieg und ihre Ursachen"; Robert Sommer, *Krieg und Seelenleben* (Giessen, 1918); and Hilda Abraham and Ernst Freud, eds., *A Psychoanalytic Dialogue: The Letters of Sigmund Freud and Karl Abraham, 1907–1926,* trans. B. Marsh and H. C. Abraham (New York, 1965), p. 265.
36. Ernest Jones, *Papers on Psychoanalysis,* 5th ed. (London, 1948), pp. 300–1.
37. Ernest Jones, *The Life and Work of Sigmund Freud,* 2:197–8, 251–4; see also idem, ed., *Psychoanalysis and the War Neuroses* (Vienna, 1921); and Ernst Simmel, *Kriegs-Neurosen und psychische Trauma* (Berlin, 1918).
38. Thomas S. Kuhn, *The Structure of Scientific Revolutions* (Chicago, 1962), p. 68.
39. C. Stanford Read, "A Survey of War Neuropsychiatry," *Mental Hygiene* 2 (1918): 360.
40. Eric J. Leed, *No Man's Land: Combat and Identity in World War I* (London, 1979), pp. 63–92.
41. Paul Lerner, "Rationalizing the Therapeutic Arsenal: German Neuropsychiatry in the First World War," in Manfred Berg and Geoffrey Cocks, eds., *Medicine and Modernity,* pp. 121–48.
42. Walter Cimbal, "Erinnerungen eines alten Arztes an die Frühzeit der Psychotherapie in Deutschland," p. 39: Paul Frederick Lerner, "Hysterical Men: War, Neurosis, and German Mental Medicine, 1914–1921" (Ph.D. dissertation, Columbia University, 1996).
43. Greg Eghigian, "Die Bürokratie und das Entstehen von Krankheit."
44. Cimbal, "Erinnerungen," p. 40.
45. Greg A. Eghigian, "The Politics of Victimization: Social Pensioners and the German Social State in the Inflation of 1914–1924," *Central European History* 26 (1993): 381.

46. Ibid., p. 399.
47. Dührssen, *Ein Jahrhundert Psychoanalytische Bewegung*, pp. 157–8.
48. Hans-Ludwig Siemen, "Die Reformpsychiatrie der Weimarer Republik: Subjektive Ansprüche und die Macht des Faktischen," in Franz Werner Kersting et al., eds., *Nach Hadamar: Zum Verhältnis von Psychiatrie und Gesellschaft im 20. Jahrhundert* (Paderborn, 1993), p. 103.
49. Ibid., p. 106; see also Hans-Walter Schmuhl, "Kontinuität oder Diskontinuität? Zum epochalen Charakter der Psychiatrie im Nationalsozialismus," in Kersting, *Nach Hadamar*, pp. 126–7. On the concept of an overarching ethos of a peculiarly German "therapeutic intervention to heal society," see Michael Geyer, "The Stigma of Violence, Nationalism, and War in Twentieth-Century Germany," *German Studies Review* (Special Issue, Winter 1992): 75–110.
50. Abraham to Freud, October 27, 1918, in Abraham and Freud, eds., *Psychoanalytic Dialogue*, pp. 279–80.
51. Ibid., p. 382; see also Jones, *Freud*, vol. 2, pp. 114–15.
52. Sigmund Freud, "Some Observations on 'Wild' Psychoanalysis," in idem, *Collected Papers*, vol. 2, trans. Joan Riviere (London, 1949), 297–304; see also Ellenberger, *Discovery*, p. 805.
53. Otto Fenichel, *The Psychoanalytic Theory of Neurosis* (New York, 1945), p. 565.
54. Decker, *Freud in Germany*, p. 187.
55. "Aktuelles," ZfP 16 (1944): 1. In 1910 Leonhard Seif, another prominent German psychotherapist of the period, had emerged at the first congress of Oskar Vogt's and Auguste Forel's International Society for Medical Psychology and Psychotherapy in Brussels as a vigorous young defender of Freud's ideas: see Ellenberger, *Discovery*, pp. 805–6.

2

The General Medical Society for Psychotherapy, 1926–1933

Due to the economic and political chaos in Germany, doctors interested in psychotherapy would first begin to organize only several years after the First World War. In 1925 the annual meeting of German psychiatrists and neurologists convened in Kassel and the usual arguments for and against psychotherapy were aired. Walter Cimbal presented a paper on the psychodynamics of war neurotics and was sharply criticized for being sentimental and unscientific.[1] Shortly thereafter, however, in April of the following year, Wladimir Eliasberg of Munich and Robert Sommer of Giessen presided over the first General Medical Congress for Psychotherapy in Baden-Baden. The founding of an international General Medical Society for Psychotherapy followed in 1928, along with the appearance of the *Allgemeine Ärztliche Zeitschrift für Psychotherapie und psychische Hygiene,* edited by Eliasberg and Sommer. This journal was renamed in 1930 as the *Zentralblatt für Psychotherapie und ihre Grenzgebiete einschliesslich der medizinischen Psychologie und psychischen Hygiene*. Among the co-founders of the society were Cimbal, Haeberlin, Arthur Kronfeld, Schultz, Hattingberg, Gustav Richard Heyer, Harald Schultz-Hencke, and Fritz Künkel. By 1928, when regional branches (*Ortsgruppen*) were established in Berlin and Munich, Schultz and Künkel were major figures in Prussia, while Leonhard Seif joined Hattingberg and Heyer as a leader of the movement in Bavaria. Most of these men were around thirty years of age in 1918 and they thus by and large constituted a young avant-garde in medicine whose humanistic, national, and cultural ideals had been sharpened by the war and by Germany's predicament in the 1920s.[2]

A large majority of the members of the General Medical Society came from the ranks of internists and neurologists. Internists came by way of their confrontation with psychosomatic disorders. Neurology, or the study of the human nervous system, had first made its appearance in seventeenth-century England and France and incorporated the Hippocratic dictum that the seat of madness was in the brain. In the nineteenth century, neurologic research brought scientific discipline to the study of mental illness and helped revolutionize asylum care by instigating reasoned investigation of each patient's mental life. This innovation provided an understanding that was not available from the rigid system of strict psychiatric classification and genetic inquiry. Late in the century psychiatry in Germany also benefited in this way from the therapeutic zeal of such pioneering pathologists as Adolf Meyer. And although neurology in Germany remained subordinate to psychiatry, increasing numbers of physicians chose to specialize in neurology as a way to concentrate on the practical treatment of psychological disorders. Of twenty-four representative psychotherapists prominent before and after 1933, thirteen had become neurologists (*Nervenärzte*), four were specialists in internal medicine, four were psychologists, four were general practitioners, and only two had specialized in psychiatry.[3]

The first congress concerned itself primarily with the antagonistic stance of the bulk of psychiatrists and the incumbent dangers to psychotherapy. This concern stemmed from the desire of these psychotherapeutically inclined physicians to oppose a powerful tradition in German medicine that they believed obstructed physicians' control and development of a scientific and humanistic array of psychotherapeutic techniques. From this standpoint, psychotherapy could not be left in the hands of the German psychiatric establishment. Eliasberg later noted how the psychotherapists conceived of the case histories they presented at the congresses of the General Medical Society as an important challenge to the medical establishment as a whole: "We wanted to confront the 'systems' with the reality of life as it is seen in the offices of the practitioners, the specialists, and in the hospitals."[4] The primary purpose of the society and its annual congresses from 1926 to 1931 was to minimize the dissension among the various theories of psychotherapy and to encourage its practice in all branches of medicine, and to encourage research in the young field.

The first announcement from the society, circulated in 1925, contained an agenda for the 1926 congress that concerned itself not only with the development of psychotherapy as a profession but also with its place in the so-called "crisis in medicine" movement. This movement was generally comprised of younger and politically right-wing doctors who complained of an oversupply of doctors and consequent falling incomes, and who joined in the traditional animus of many older and politically conservative doctors against a state health insurance system heavily populated with socialists and allegedly inimical to the interests of doctor and patient.[5] Such complaints also engaged a holistic critique of "materialistic" and "mechanistic" medicine associated with the "fragmentation" of culture embodied in modern industrial society and the Weimar Republic. This *völkisch* orientation would help lead many doctors into the ranks of the Nazis, while there were also liberal and socialist variants of what has been called the "fevered holism" of the 1920s in Germany.[6] It was also generally in accord with many psychotherapists' rejection of a similarly mechanistic German psychiatry. What the announcement termed the "domestic policies" for psychotherapy concentrated on the achievement of the status of a distinct profession: definition of a body of knowledge; standards for, and control of, training; professional ethics; and differentiation from neighboring disciplines. The "foreign policies" addressed themselves to psychotherapy's various interfaces with the medical profession and with the social problems and issues which surrounded doctors. The notion of unity, therefore, was intended not only to further the professional aims of psychotherapy but also to solve the broader problems confronting medicine as a whole.[7]

Critics of the medical establishment, including many psychotherapeutically oriented physicians, saw the reigning "systems" as hopelessly beholden to science, research, classification, and political influence: out of touch with "the reality of life," as Eliasberg had put it. The demand for increased attention to what was called "social hygiene" was another front in the challenge to the establishment. Mental hygiene, as part of the social hygiene movement in Germany, had first been professionalized in America by Clifford Beers. In 1909 Beers, Adolf Meyer, and William James were responsible for the foundation of the National Committee for Mental Hygiene. This phenomenon reflected not only the growing international scientific interest in the complexities of human psychology, it also represented a "shift in emphasis of philosophy from the salvation of the individual to the reconstruction of society."[8] In Germany, Max von Pettenkofer and Robert Koch had pioneered the practice of social hygiene during the late nineteenth century. In Austria, two members of the General Medical Society before and after 1933, Erwin Stransky and Heinrich von Kogerer, were leaders of the movement.[9] Subsequently, Robert Sommer, who turned from an early traditional opposition to such activism, became the moving spirit behind the movement in Germany. From his particular point of view, of course, psychotherapy was to play a vital role in this enterprise. The General Medical Society for Psychotherapy, in its desire to mobilize all the sciences of the mind into a united front against mental illness, as well as against the skeptics within the medical establishment, claimed a variety of provinces for its potential practice: child care, industrial psychology, clinical practice, and pedagogy were specifically mentioned.

Adolf Friedländer, in an address in 1928 to the third congress of the General Medical Society, claimed that the medical profession as a whole was disunited, that it had failed as both a scientific and as a social entity. He complained about communistic doctors, overbureaucratization, the warring factions in psychotherapy, the clashes between homeopathy and "school medicine," the overprescription of drugs, and so on. Friedländer demanded a broader kind of academic medicine, a decrease in the prescription of drugs, a concern for social health programs, and, most importantly, physicians who would exhibit more concern for *Volksgesundheit* than for political power.[10] The General Medical Society was particularly enthusiastic about modes of simple, or *kleine*, psychotherapy that could be used medically and humanistically by all physicians. Such an emphasis, they believed, was a necessary to complement to the development of large (*grosse*) theory in the field. Its mission, the society announced, was

> to contribute to an inductive, rational, clinical psychotherapy, which stands in exactly the same relationship to special psychotherapeutic methods like psychoanalysis and individual psychology, among others, as the clinic for internal medicine does to physiological chemistry.[11]

Somewhat hyperbolically, but also with an eye for professional opportunity, the General Medical Society declared this mission as urgent, since psychotherapy was a crucial element in the "battle against the national epidemic [*Volksseuche*] of neurosis."[12]

Despite this criticism of the medical establishment—and because of it—the General Medical Society was also careful to underline its loyalty to the discipline of medicine on the first page of the first issue of its journal in 1928:

> The most basic orientation of psychotherapy is not that spiritualism should take the place of that materialism under whose flag experimental medicine of the nineteenth century became a rational science. . . . Psychotherapy is a matter for doctors. We are doctors and not laymen.[13]

Only doctors were allowed to participate in the society's first congress and all press reports on the meeting had to be vetted by physicians.[14] These measures were taken to defend the new organization from association with the many so-called "quacks" who practiced various types of healing under the "freedom to practice" (*Kurierfreheit*) allowed by German law. Psychotherapy was particularly vulnerable to attack on these grounds from skeptical or hostile doctors and psychiatrists since the nature of the discipline was so closely tied to the realm of the spirit. The society's special concern about the press reflected both the popularization of psychological healing through reports in the press as well as the frequent advertisements appearing in papers and magazines for such cures.[15]

But while the official position of the society continued to be that psychotherapy should be practiced only by doctors, there was an inherent tension over this matter among members of the General Medical Society. Many argued for a formal medical specialization in psychotherapy (*Facharzttitel*) for doctors in order to establish the practice of psychotherapy as a medical specialty, to distinguish psychotherapy from quackery, and prevent the unsystematic use of it by doctors themselves.[16] Psychiatrist Ernst Kretschmer, who became president of the society in 1930, was in a distinct minority of those who wished to render psychotherapy a tool to be used only by psychiatrists. At the other end of the spectrum, there was a larger and growing minority who felt that the practice of psychotherapy should not be confined to physicians. Both the perceived and actual need for widespread treatment of neurosis as well as the desire to achieve professional status would after 1933 impel the psychotherapists in the direction of the training and medical supervision of nonmedical psychotherapists and psychologists. At the third congress in 1928 nondoctors (philosopher Ludwig Klages and psychologist Kurt Lewin) were on the program for the first time.[17] This position of favoring the extension of psychotherapy's practical domain was strengthened by the rise in general suffering occasioned by the Great Depression of 1929.[18] Moreover, private interests and public agencies, including most significantly the Nazi regime, became increasingly interested in cultivation and control of mental health in as many ways as possible.

Arguments in favor of expanding the practice of psychotherapy to disciplines outside medicine were also given added force by the commitment of the General Medical Society to control quackery (*Kurpfuschertum*), a commitment of particular concern for two specific groups: physicians who wished to expand the control of scientific medicine, and psychotherapists and psychologists who were eager to avoid the label of quack. Moreover, the very nineteenth-century Romantic tradition in psychiatry and medicine that had helped create the modern psychotherapeutic movement was a strong force among members of the society, as we shall see below, and its origins in philosophy and religion as well as medicine oriented psychotherapy toward disciplinary inclusiveness rather than compartmentalization. For example, a report on the first five congresses of the General Medical Society spoke strongly against psychotherapeutic training of laypersons while at the same time it spoke of the need for doctors to work closely with practitioners in "medical psychology," law, education, marriage counseling, and religion.[19] The disagreements among the members of the General Medical Society on this fundamental question of disciplinary orientation remained unresolved, however. In 1927 the society failed to reach agreement on a resolution for a medical specialty in psychotherapy, agreeing only on the necessity for the inclusion of psychoanalysis and psychotherapy in the university medical curriculum.[20]

One of the most immediate important tasks for the psychotherapists, in any case, was proselytization among physicians. Chief among such proselytizers was Johannes Heinrich Schultz. Schultz later noted that it was during the 1920s that psychotherapy became socially and professionally acceptable (*salonfähig*).[21] That it did so was in no small measure due to his own skillful and tireless efforts. Schultz placed articles on psychotherapy in the *Deutsche medizinische Wochenschrift* every year from 1927 through 1930. Before 1926 this Berlin journal, which along with the *Münchener medizinische Wochenschrift* was one of the two major medical journals in Germany, had published only reports on meetings and reviews—by Schultz, Kronfeld, Gaupp, and

Kretschmer, among others; the single article on psychotherapy in the journal before 1926 appeared in 1916 and concerned psychotherapy and traumatic neurosis. The same general pattern held for the *Münchener medizinische Wochenschrift;* in 1930 that journal inaugurated a section heading for psychotherapy with an article by, appropriately, Schultz.[22] Beginning in 1928, of course, the psychotherapists had their own journal, and in the same year *Hippokrates,* a journal dedicated to "practical medicine" and "the unity of medicine," made its appearance, providing another forum for a sympathetic discussion of psychotherapy and various related social issues facing medical practice.

The congresses, which regularly attracted over 500 participants, were to provide not only a forum but a medical and scientific foundation for psychotherapy. The 1927 congress at Bad Nauheim was devoted to four themes: psychoanalysis, health pedagogy, training, and the fight against quackery.[23] Back at Baden-Baden in 1928, the third congress of the now formally licensed society included presentations on individual psychology by Künkel, Schultz-Hencke, and Leonhard Seif; on character research by Sommer, Cimbal, Klages, Rudolf Allers, and Georg Groddeck; and on experimental psychology by Schultz and Lewin. There was also a session on religion and psychotherapy, including remarks by one M. H. Göring.[24]

The society continued to grow and to operate as a forum for a wide range of views, both medical and lay, on psychotherapy and neurosis. In 1928 Sommer was still president, with Cimbal as managing director; the executive committee included Seif, Schultz, Eliasberg, Kronfeld, Kretschmer, and Kurt Goldstein. Carl Jung participated in the congress that year for the first time and references to his work multiplied in the 1928 annual report. New members in 1928 included Alfred Adler, Hans Prinzhorn, and psychoanalyst Kurt Birnbaum. Total membership rose to 399 (Germany 334, Switzerland 18, Austria 16, Holland 15, Czechoslovakia 5, Hungary 4, Sweden 3, France 2; Poland and Spain each claimed a single member). The following year saw the attendance of psychoanalyst Franz Alexander, the presentation of a paper by Jung, and, in line with the group's efforts to build bridges to neighboring disciplines, particularly psychiatry, a paper by Ernst Kretschmer. In 1930 Kretschmer was elected president and Jung vice president.[25]

Sommer had stepped down as president because of ill health and was named honorary president, although he remained co-editor of the society's journal with Kretschmer. The theme of the 1930 congress was compulsion neurosis with papers by Wilhelm Stekel and Karen Horney. Jacob Wilhelm Hauer, who later as founder of the German Faith Movement was to become a somewhat celebrated cultural adjunct to National Socialism, spoke on yoga and psychotherapy—a subject that was later pursued within the Göring Institute by Schultz and Gustav Schmaltz. The psychiatrist who was to be closest to the psychotherapists in the Third Reich, Hans Luxenburger, also presented a paper, the subject of which was the heredity and family typology of compulsion. The 1930 congress counted 575 participants and the society gained 80 new members.[26] The 1931 congress, in Dresden, considered two major issues: somatology (Heyer) and psychology (Wolfgang Kranefeldt representing Jung). As president, Kretschmer read an address in honor of Freud's seventy-fifth birthday and it was proposed that the next congress be held in Vienna April 7–10, 1932, with papers to be given on the relationship of neurology to psychology, on child and youth psychotherapy, and on hysteria.[27] This seventh congress never took place; the economic crisis had become too severe.

Although it was the aim of the General Medical Society to unify the various schools of thought among psychotherapists, there were inevitably factions: Adlerians (including Adler), Jungians (including Jung), Stekelians (including Stekel), and Freudians such as Groddeck, Horney, Wilhelm Reich, and Sandor Radó (though not including Freud). The great majority of psychoanalysts who were members of the General Medical Society were revisionists like the neo-Freudian Horney, the almost indefinable Groddeck, the free-love communist Reich, and the intensely intellectual rebel Schultz-Hencke. For its part, the German Psychoanalytic Society did not recognize the General Medical Society and increasingly the two organizations found themselves moving further apart rather than closer together.[28] This began as early as 1928 when at the third congress Ludwig Klages argued that Freud had based his book *The Ego and the Id* (1923) on Klages's work and Kurt Lewin presented the results of his laboratory experiments on unconscious thought processes.[29] The psychiatrists in the society, led by Sommer, Kretschmer, Schultz, and Ernst Speer, were divided among themselves on matters of theory and practice. Sommer, for all his commitment to a psychotherapeutic campaign against neurosis, had been an early and vociferous critic of Freud's psychogenic explanation for hysteria.[30] Schultz, a psychiatrist who had turned to neurology in 1926, did emerge, along with Speer, as a vigorous proponent of an eclectic psychotherapy across disciplines, albeit always under strict medical control.[31] Kretschmer, as we have already noted, maintained the position that psychotherapy should be under the control of psychiatry.

As far as politics went, there is evidence that the General Medical Society comprised a more or less conservative, nationalist—and largely Protestant[32]—membership at odds in this way as well with the generally more liberal, cosmopolitan—and largely Jewish—membership of the German Psychoanalytic Society. Although Eliasberg and Rudolf Allers represented a leftist position that Cimbal later described as "eastern-Soviet," by 1928 at the latest such views seemed to be in a distinct minority in the General Medical Society.[33] Many of the psychotherapists prominent in the affairs of the General Medical Society—and subsequently of the Göring Institute—did display a conservative, nationalist, and "unpolitical" attitude that, in combination with both the professional threats and opportunities presented to psychotherapy by the Nazi regime, was easily transformed into varying degrees of enthusiasm and support for National Socialism from 1933 onward. As we have already noted, doctors in general in Germany at the time tended toward the political right: many identified with the conservative and nationalist German National People's Party (DNVP)—or, as in the case with Matthias Heinrich Göring, with the right wing of the German People's Party (DVP)—in the Weimar Republic.[34] In fact, of all professional groups in Germany doctors ended up with the highest percentage (43.4 percent) of Nazi party members.[35] Such a political orientation was also consistent with the holistic Romantic medical tradition out of which psychotherapy came in Germany. An examination of the particular intellectual and philosophical backgrounds of the chief representatives of psychotherapy in Germany before and after 1933 will help us to understand some of the dynamics of the professional development of psychotherapy in Nazi Germany and after 1945. These men fall into four broad groups: Adlerians, Jungians, Freudians, and independents. Each had its own intellectual underpinnings but all united by professional aim, a general cultural background, and shared historical experience.

Adlerians Fritz Künkel, Leonhard Seif, and Matthias Heinrich Göring were the chief proponents within the General Medical Society of what they saw as the therapeutic need for a sense of community. What unified the three was their common belief in what Adler himself after the First World War had described as "community feeling" (*Gemeinschaftsgefühl*). This belief testified not only to the special debt they owed to Adler's psychology but to a peculiarly strong German cultural bias as well. In this respect in particular, the war itself had been a vital experience for these men and for many of their colleagues. All of the leading psychotherapists before and after 1933 were veterans of the First World War. To one degree or another, each was intellectually and emotionally preoccupied with the clash between culture and civilization that the war represented, a phenomenon widespread among German academics in general.[36] This German fixation involved the struggle between *Geist* ("mind") and *Seele* ("soul"). *Geist* stood for the materialistic Western spirit of the Renaissance, triumphant over the fullness and spirituality of the medieval.[37]

Fritz Künkel emerged in Germany during the 1920s as a major teacher of the practical system that Adler had labeled individual psychology. Born the son of a Prussian landowner in Stolzenberg, Brandenburg, in 1889, Künkel studied medicine in Munich. He enlisted in August 1914 and gave his left arm at Verdun for the Iron Cross, first and second class, while serving as a medical assistant with the 48th Infantry Regiment. He was licensed as a physician in 1917. By 1924 he had set up a practice in Berlin-Wilmersdorf as a specialist in nervous disorders and began to gather about him a circle of students who were attracted by his articulation and later modification of Adler's psychology.[38]

Although he came from a conservative East Elbian family, Künkel, according to his son John, had reacted strongly against the acquisitiveness so common to Junker landowners at the turn of the century.[39] This rejection of his familial and social milieu helped turn Künkel away from a career in business or government. He emerged from the First World War without an arm and also without a good deal of the youthful patriotism that had swept him, like so many others, into uniform in 1914. He turned to psychotherapy when he decided that he could not be a good doctor with only one arm. (His younger brother Hans, who had lost his right arm in the war, was not so hindered as a novelist and philosopher.)

The war, however, had also made a deep psychological impression on Künkel. In 1934 he wrote:

> The experience at the front had brought us something new. Through reflection and a turning inward, we no longer found that it was the self at the base of our existence, no longer the private, individual personality, but the group, fellowship, and nationality [*Volkstum*].[40]

As a result of this widely shared experience and of the growing interest in psychology after the war, "we-psychology was in the air," as Künkel's son has put it. Adler's individual psychology was built on the conviction that human beings from their earliest years and relationships have an inborn need and desire for social contact, this in contrast to Freud's opposing of drive and society. Künkel, diverging from Adler's secular, socialist outlook and from the Marxist orientation of the Berlin Adlerians, added a Hegelian and a Christian perspective to individual psychology. Although his chief concern remained the "dialectic" between subject and object, the "I" and the "We," he drew from Klages and Haeberlin a biocentric emphasis on healthy natural rhythms and from Jung a reverence for the depths of the soul. His psychology stressed the importance of the life of action and social commitment in the spirit of Carus's Romantic ideal of the art of living (*Lebenskunst*).[41]

From this point of view, the psychotherapist was as much a clergyman as a physician. In this, Künkel drew appreciable inspiration from Hans Prinzhorn (1883–1933), a neurologist and psychologist from Dresden. Prinzhorn used the word *Priesterdilettant* ("amateur priest") to describe a psychotherapist. For Prinzhorn and Künkel, it was the role of the psychotherapist to engage the patient as a totality in leading him or her to larger wholes of community and faith. In 1926 Künkel criticized the traditional psychiatric establishment in just this vein: "Seventy years ago the asylums were mostly under administration of the church, and that was much less a failing than materialistic medicine would now have us believe."[42] Prinzhorn himself was the leading proponent in Germany at the time of this "totality approach" (*Ganzheitsbetrachtung*).[43] The view of an individual as a whole demanded that a person be regarded as a biological and social entity rather than as a disparate and semi-sovereign bundle of drives. Like Adler and Künkel, Prinzhorn saw the individual as essentially indivisible, a belief that clearly contradicted Freud's conception of fundamental human ambivalence and internal conflict.[44] For Prinzhorn there was no external norm toward which one should aspire in order to achieve health and happiness. Instead, each person laid claim to a private and unique fate (*Schicksal*) that, in the Romantic spirit, had to be fulfilled. But fate was conditioned by social and biological heritage. The psychotherapist, therefore, was not to be a passive analyst but an active partner in the healing process, in leading the neurotic sufferer back into a life-affirming communion with himself and, most important, with a suprapersonal entity such as nature, culture, community, or God.[45] It was on this basis, therefore, that Künkel could criticize Freud for not dealing therapeutically or theoretically with the "whole individual" as did Adler.[46]

This Romantic concern with totality was linked to another strong German intellectual tradition in the field of psychology and medicine that also found particularly strong expression in Künkel's work. This was the study of character, a concept that was to be understood as an integral whole comprised of an organic disposition and specific psychological characteristics within a given cultural environment. The study of character in this sense was much more appealing to many German psychotherapists than Freud's conception of the personality as an expression of the ego and its compromises with the forces of the id and the superego. In many respects this view paralleled some aspects of the neo-Freudian emphasis on culture in the shaping of personality. It also had a wide audience among philosophers, most significantly in the realm of psychology in the person of Eduard Spranger, a student of the philosopher of history Wilhelm Dilthey. Rather than seeing the relationship between individual and environment in causal terms, these philosophers offered a holistic-organic point of view that led to the construction of character typologies.[47] The importance of characterology lay in its attempt to come to grips with the human organism in all its biological, environmental, and historical complexity. In Germany the Romantic emphasis on the unique and the dynamic—as opposed to the "vulgar democracy" of reason—resulted in a peculiarly strong German run of thought, culminating in psychologist Erich Jaensch's fully Nazified character typology. Künkel's character typology based itself on a synthesis of what he called Jung's "continuation" (*Fortsetzung*) of Freudian psychoanalysis with Adler's individual psychology. The fusion of what Künkel called "internal psychology" (*Innenpsychologie*) or "depth psychology" (*Tiefenpsychologie*), and "external psychology" (*Aussenpsychologie*) or "relations psychology" (*Beziehungspsychologie*) produced a "dialectical science of character" that saw individual human development in terms of an active complementarity between internal character and external environment.[48]

Another Adlerian who continued in the mainstream of German psychotherapy and who exerted significant influence between 1933 and 1945 was Leonhard Seif. He was born in Munich in 1866, the son of a railroad official. After studying philosophy for a year in the wake of passing his university qualifying examinations, the *Abitur,* in Freising, he began the study of medicine at the University of Munich. In May of 1895 Seif established a practice in neurology in the Bavarian capital. He was a co-founder of the International Psycho-Analytical Association in 1910 and became president of its Munich branch the following year.[49] In 1922, under the leitmotif of prevention before cure and a typical Adlerian emphasis on concrete, practical, psychotherapeutic assistance, Seif founded an educational counseling center (*Erziehungsberatungsstelle*) in Munich. He became internationally known: in 1927 and again in 1929 he accepted invitations to lecture and teach at Harvard and at Boston University; between 1928 and 1937 he gave a series of lectures at the universities of London, Birmingham, and York. His last summer course ended a few days before the outbreak of war in 1939.[50] Seif, like Künkel, placed a heavy emphasis on Adler's notion of community feeling and, also like Künkel, insisted on the necessity of a spiritual dimension to life. Seif was not the writer and theoretician that Künkel was, but his Munich facility remained the center of psychotherapeutic work with children and families in Germany from the early Weimar years through the Second World War. And so unlike Künkel, who would leave Germany just before the war, Seif would play a major practical role in the affairs of psychotherapy until almost the very end of the Third Reich.

Matthias Heinrich Göring, due to his family name, would achieve notoriety in the field of psychotherapy beyond anything he would likely have imagined—or deserved—on the basis of his work. He was born April 5, 1879, in Düsseldorf into the oldest branch of the Westphalian Görings, from whom his cousin Hermann Göring was also descended. He earned a doctorate in law at Freiburg in Breisgau in 1900. Following travels through Palestine, Ceylon, and India, he took a doctorate in medicine at Bonn in 1907. During 1909 and 1910 he was a medical assistant at Kraepelin's psychiatric clinic in Munich, where he continued his work in forensic medicine. By 1913 he was a member of the clinical psychiatric staff at Giessen under Robert

Sommer, a position to which he returned after the war. It was during this time that Göring became interested in psychotherapy and hypnosis, and in 1923 he set up neurological practice in Wuppertal-Elberfeld in the Ruhr. Göring participated in the 1927 congress of the General Medical Society and joined the society the next year. In 1928, after undergoing a training analysis with Seif in Munich and attending a course of lectures by Künkel, he founded his own educational counseling center in Elberfeld. The following year he formed a study group for psychotherapy in Wuppertal.[51]

By all accounts, Matthias Heinrich Göring was a shy, gentle man with a stammer. He was a patriot of the old school, a member of the nationalistic ex-serviceman's organization, the Stahlhelm, and a dedicated Lutheran Pietist whose domicile, Wuppertal-Elberfeld, was a stronghold of Pietism. According to Lucy Heyer-Grote and others among the psychotherapists active during the period, Göring always carried a Bible with him. The concern for the individual, the attention to the needs of the common man, the emphasis on popular education, as well as the enthusiasm and irrationalism also characteristic of the Pietist outlook decisively influenced his notion of psychotherapy. He once told Werner Kemper, the Freudian director of the outpatient clinic of the Göring Institute, that one of his major objections to psychoanalysis was the physical positioning of the analyst behind the analysand. Eye contact was vital, Göring believed, in order to allow the pair to face mental problems honestly and manfully in the spirit of Christ. As he put it in a 1933 book on the relationship between Adler's individual psychology and religion: "To love means to be able to merge into another, to understand one's fellow man, and to desire to help him in an effective manner."[52]

The Adlerians Göring and Seif would exercise much greater influence over the development of psychotherapy in Germany than did any of their Jungian colleagues. But one Jungian among them, Gustav Richard Heyer, would nevertheless cut a major figure in the field during the Third Reich. Heyer was born in 1890 in Bad Kreuznach on the Rhine River. His father's family had been foresters from the area surrounding nearby Darmstadt. His maternal grandfather was a member of the German Reichstag. Heyer grew up in Bad Kreuznach, Cologne, and Neuwied am Rhein until his father, a district judge, became a ministerial director in the Reich Financial Office in Potsdam. The younger Heyer elected to go into forestry and went to Munich to study. There he became interested in medicine and philosophy and went to Heidelberg after passing his preliminary exam (the *physikum*).[53] During the war he won the Iron Cross, first and second class, and finished his medical education on leaves occasioned by a number of battle injuries. He completed his internship as commander of a field hospital and received a doctorate in medicine in 1918 with a dissertation on paratyphus. Returning to Munich after the war, he worked as an assistant to internist Friedrich von Müller. But Heyer, by his own account, became increasingly estranged from the physical and chemical orientation of his mentor. It was for this reason, he later claimed, that even after five years as his assistant, Müller refused to recommend him for faculty membership.[54]

Heyer quit his post and, abandoning his experiments on the psychological aspects of stomach and intestinal secretions, established a Munich practice in internal medicine and neurology in 1923. Impoverished by the inflation, Heyer remained in private practice but also found the time to give lectures on psychotherapy to interested medical students and physicians. These began in his home and later moved to the University of Munich. In 1918 he had married Lucy Grote, the daughter of a noted chemist. She was a gymnastics teacher, and through her Heyer became convinced of the value of using physical therapy in psychotherapeutic practice. Heyer had also become involved in the growing international psychoanalytic movement, but he quickly discovered differences with the Freudian school and embraced Jungian psychology. In 1928 he founded an informal Jungian discussion group in Munich. But Heyer found Jung too ethereal, a reaction common among German doctors interested in psychotherapy who were concerned with the tasks of the practicing physician rather than the preoccupations of the researcher or philosopher. At the same time, something in Jung's thought continued to tug at Heyer. For all the inheritors of the German Romantic ethos in the field of medicine, the fate of humanity and civilization rested in the diagnosis and treatment of modern ills to free latent creative and assertive energies. This Jungian perspective was very different from Freud's Stoic resignation in the face of what he saw, very unromantically, as inherent conflict within and between the individual and civilization.

There were, however, Freudians among the German psychotherapists, although they too set their own individual and cultural stamp on their interpretations of Freud. Chief among these were Harald

Schultz-Hencke and John Rittmeister. Like the Adlerians Göring and Seif, who would in their own way make a significant mark on psychotherapy in the Third Reich, Schultz-Hencke and Rittmeister would emerge in the 1930s and 1940s as important voices in the discipline, albeit in starkly different—and, in Rittmeister's case, tragic—ways.

Harald Schultz-Hencke was a Berliner by birth. He was born in 1892; his father, a physicist and chemist, had founded a photographic institute in the German capital the year before. The double name came from his grandfather Karl, whose stepfather, Karl-Ludwig Hencke, because of his scientific accomplishments—as an amateur astronomer he had discovered two planetoids—won permission for his stepsons to carry the name Schultz-Hencke. Harald's mother was a graphologist and it was because of her, he later recalled, that he became interested in the "psychological and human sciences."[55] He also early on cultivated a lively interest in biology. Schultz-Hencke began his medical studies at Freiburg in Breisgau, concentrating on anatomy and pathology, but he also pursued his interest in philosophy by attending seminars give by the neo-Kantian Heinrich Rickert and the phenomenologists Edmund Husserl and Martin Heidegger. His experience in the First World War, particularly in the winter battles of 1915–16 on the Hartmannweilerskopf, left him sickly and, he claimed, even stunted his growth. He was forced by this to turn from an active life to one of scholarship. Before the war he had been a member of the Wandervogel Youth Movement; there, he later wrote, he had found "like-minded comrades."[56] After the war, in his new métier of scholar, he edited a series of impassioned little books on the necessity of a revolution by the young against the stagnation bred by political parties.[57]

Schultz-Hencke had learned psychiatry for the first time from Alfred Hoche at Freiburg. Hoche's sharp skepticism toward psychology only encouraged Schultz-Hencke to devote himself to the medical study of the mind. He was further inspired by Freud's work. In 1921 he joined the psychiatric clinic at Würzburg as a volunteer assistant and there he witnessed dramatic confirmation of a number of the central theses of psychoanalytic theory. The following year found Schultz-Hencke at the neurological clinic of the Charité Hospital at the Friedrich Wilhelm University in Berlin. In 1922 he also began his own personal psychoanalysis; Sandor Radó was his training analyst.

After three years of studying and practicing psychoanalysis, however, Schultz-Hencke had become critical of a number of its assumptions. He welcomed what he considered as the necessary expansion upon psychoanalytic theory by the work of Jung and Adler. As his own interest turned every more away from orthodox Freudian doctrine, his views produced friction with his colleagues at the Berlin Psychoanalytic Institute, where by 1927 he was giving lectures and holding seminars. His growing preference for active therapy, as opposed to passive analysis, was regarded with suspicion, and his criticisms of Freudian sexual theory finally resulted in the loss of his teaching position at the institute. Schultz-Hencke's urge for synthesis in psychotherapy, shared by many of his medical colleagues, had been evident as early as 1928, when he had posed the question of how to unite the psychological (psychoanalysis), the organic (internal medicine), and the technical (suggestive [active] therapy).[58] The same year he criticized Künkel for not recognizing the indispensability of Freudian theory.[59]

What Schultz-Hencke saw as fundamentally wrong with psychoanalysis was its claim to universality, a criticism he shared with other neo-Freudians. Acknowledged as part of the neo-Freudian movement within psychoanalysis, Schultz-Hencke subsequently went on to found his own school of thought, which he called "neo-analysis" and which still claimed adherents in Berlin long after the Second World War.[60] He was vigorous in his criticism of traditional psychoanalysis and his eclectic intelligence drew him into regular and rewarding contact with members of other schools of psychotherapeutic thought. His theories were a mixture of Freudian and Adlerian concepts: He described the root of all neuroses and psychoses as "inhibition" (*Hemmung*), discounting the role of the unconscious.[61]

While Harald Schultz-Hencke's professional position and philosophical views resulted in a long and important association with the Göring Institute in Nazi Germany, Freudian John Rittmeister's professional and philosophical background led him to play only a relatively short and ultimately tragic role in the affairs of psychotherapy in the Third Reich. Rittmeister was born in Hamburg in 1898, the eldest son of a businessman of Dutch-English-Huguenot extraction. He had served on the Italian and French fronts during the last two years of the First World War and survived to study medicine at the universities of Marburg, Göttingen, Kiel, Munich, and Hamburg. It was in Munich that he came into contact with psychotherapy for the first time through the work of Hattingberg. Rittmeister continued his medical education in Paris, London, and at the Burghölzli in Zurich. In 1936, after some clinical work in Holland, he settled in Münsingen, Switzerland, at the cantonal sanitarium there.[62]

Rittmeister was much closer than the great majority of the more provincial members of the General Medical Society, including Schultz-Hencke, to the traditional iconoclastic bent within psychoanalysis that had originated with Freud himself. He also shared the tendency among many European psychoanalysts, especially neo-Freudians, to adhere to the social and political left.[63] In contrast to most of his psychotherapeutic colleagues, Rittmeister saw in Jung's "ahistorical image-collectivism" the symptoms of the frightened and confused bourgeois response to the great social changes of the twentieth century. In this critique of Jung, Rittmeister echoed Ernst Bloch's designation of German psychologists Prinzhorn and Klages as well as Jung as "crypto-fascists."[64] Rittmeister did share some of the same Romantic sources of inspiration as his colleagues. Instead of turning, as many of them had, to a fuzzy and ultimately chauvinistic Romanticism, however, Rittmeister had begun to construct a critique of modern civilization in the Freudian spirit that retained a critical rationalism. He thus avoided sliding off into the emotionalism, mysticism, and relativism that he found so troubling in the thought of Jung. Inspired by the work of Eduard von Hartmann and Hartmann's inspirator Schopenhauer, Rittmeister saw the opposing poles in human relations as subjectivism/egocentrism on the one hand and the sovereign independence of the individual self on the other. By subjectivism and egocentrism—what Schopenhauer and Hartmann called egoism—Rittmeister meant the tendency toward enlargement of one's ego at the expense of others, a sort of psychological imperialism. This subjective tendency, Rittmeister believed, deprived others of their own essential individuality, what Schopenhauer and Hartmann labeled the experience of the generous and respectful unity between the self and others. Rittmeister saw this dangerous, grasping subjectivity as "a consequence or at least a danger of the Jungian world view."[65] For Rittmeister, Jung taught the virtues of introversion, a subjective immersion in the self to the exclusion of others, while Freud instructed humanity in the ecumenical virtues of love. Furthermore, against the "refined egoism" of Jung's archetypal mysticism, Rittmeister praised the systematic doubt of Descartes, seeing in such doubt a humble and necessary acknowledgment of human imperfection.[66]

In addition to the Adlerians, Jungians, and Freudians gathered within the General Medical Society for Psychotherapy, there were a large number of even more eclectic thinkers and practitioners. These independents fell into two large groupings. The first, represented by Hans von Hattingberg and Johannes Heinrich Schultz, achieved significant practical and theoretical prominence both before and after 1933. The second, comprised of Werner Achelis, Rudolf Bilz, Walter Cimbal, and Carl Haeberlin, demonstrated greater philosophical harmony with National Socialism but was also much less prominent after 1933, particularly in the organization and praxis of the suddenly rapidly professionalizing discipline of psychotherapy. As with the professional predominance of Adlerians and Freudians over the Jungians (whose psychological ideals were perceived by both psychotherapists and Nazi bureaucrats to be most in line with Nazi ideology), in the case of the independents as well the professional and practical impetus of organizing psychotherapists in Germany during the interwar period would prove more important than ideological consanguinity with "revolutionary"—or "reactionary"—Nazi ideals.

Such a disparity is also historically important, since it demonstrates, as we shall see in succeeding chapters, certain continuities in social and professional developments in Germany (and the West) before, during, and after the Third Reich. Although racism remained the single most powerful and significant element of Nazi rule in Germany and Europe, early on in the Third Reich Nazi "radicals" and their fellow travellers in many spheres lost out to more mainstream and technically useful agencies and practices. It also shows that even the "unpolitical German" portrayed—or caricatured by Western historians—could be and was engaged "politically" in defense of such things as professional interests. Hattingberg, for example, shared the "unpolitical" orientation so common at the time among German academics and professionals. In a lecture at the Academy for Politics in Berlin on February 13, 1931, he had confessed with a touch of Romantic pride that he knew little of politics save that it was the duty of psychotherapists to make people the "objects" of politics.[67] But whatever the degree of this ignorance of—and even disdain for—politics writ large, psychotherapists, like other professionals and interest groups, as we shall see, were only too interested in politics with a small "p" when it came to their own individual and collective aims and ambitions.

Hans von Hattingberg was born in Vienna in 1879, the son of a jurist who had become the director of the lower Austrian State Mortgage Association. Hattingberg at first studied jurisprudence, but an interest in psychology sparked by August Forel at the University of Berne in Switzerland led him to a degree in that subject there in 1906. In addition to studying under Forel, Hattingberg studied zoology in Naples and brain anatomy with Oskar Vogt. He began his medical studies in 1908, passing the *physikum* at Heidelberg and the state licensing examinations in Munich in 1912. He became a Bavarian citizen in 1913 and the same year received his doctorate in medicine with a dissertation on multiple sclerosis and muscle atrophy.

From November 1913 until Easter 1914 Hattingberg worked with Bleuler at the university psychiatric clinic in Zurich. By the fall of 1914 Hattingberg had established himself in practice in Munich as a specialist in psychotherapy. He later recalled how he had wished to join the philosophical faculty at the university there because the presence of Kraepelin on the medical faculty barred work in psychotherapy. During the war he operated a neurological aid station on the Russian front, later claiming to have studied 1000 cases of war neurosis there. His treatment of these cases was based on active therapy, both of the hypnotic-suggestive and psycho-cathartic (acting out) varieties. His impoverishment after the war forced him, however, to abandon his plans for obtaining a university position; he, like Heyer, devoted himself to earning a living for himself and his family as a doctor.

Even before the war Hattingberg had been enthusiastically involved in the affairs of the International Psycho-Analytical Association as well as in those of Forel's International Association for Medical Psychology and Psychotherapy. From the beginning he was critical of much of the Freudian system. Like Schultz-Hencke, though without such great orchestration and effect, Hattingberg eventually found it necessary to divorce himself from the psychoanalytic movement. In searching for a comprehensive solution to the debates among the various psychoanalytic schools, he worked successively on the subjects of ethology, suggestion, and, finally, graphology and physiognomy. This last turn brought him to Berlin in 1924 with the intention of founding an institute for applied anthropology. Although he found graphology (handwriting analysis) erratic in its findings, he helped the publisher, graphologist, and physiognomist Niels Kampmann to found the *Zeitschrift für Menschenkunde* in 1925.

The institute did not work out, partly because Hattingberg's temperament was not that of an administrator, and he returned to Munich to turn his full attention to psychotherapy. There he wrote a biological critique of psychoanalysis and a study of the importance of religion in psychotherapy. In 1932 he resettled in Berlin in order to pursue the possibility of providing psychological training to candidates for the German diplomatic corps. This hope, ultimately disappointed, was based on the fact that in 1924 the Foreign Office had employed Hattingberg to instruct its trainees in anthropology. In November 1932, however, he did establish a psychotherapeutic clinic at St. Gertrude's Hospital in Berlin and, he later wrote, dedicated himself not only to the practice of psychotherapy but to a resolution of the divisions which, in his view, inhibited its acceptance among members of the medical profession. This motive lay behind his desire to gain a teaching position on the medical faculty of the University of Berlin, a post he got in 1933.[68] Hattingberg was particularly concerned about the "private religions" he saw manifested in the psychoanalytic movement.[69] It was this preoccupation that provided a significant degree of continuity to Hattingberg's thoughts and actions before, during, and after 1933. In proselytizing for psychotherapy in front of medical audiences that were often skeptical, if not openly hostile, he always articulated his belief that unity would be necessary among the often warring psychotherapeutic schools if the widespread use of therapy among doctors was to be effected. For Hattingberg, unity did not mean the triumph of one particular psychotherapeutic or psychoanalytic mode over the others, for that was a prospect that his own failed attempts at theoretical synthesis had already told him was unrealizable. Rather, what he aspired to, and what he believed would be most appealing to doctors in general, was a practice based on an eclectic appreciation and exercise of various therapeutic methods. It was precisely this theme that had run through Hattingberg's early writings on behalf of psychoanalysis, namely, that it deserved the attention of the medical profession as one valuable approach among others.[70]

On January 11, 1933, nineteen days before Hitler became chancellor of Germany, Hattingberg addressed the Berlin Medical Society on Freud, Adler, and Jung. He began by praising the psychoanalytic movement's brave and fruitful *analysis* of the unconscious human dynamics that had been ignored by rationalistic "school medicine." This was Freud's fundamental contribution, said Hattingberg. Adler, for his part, had contributed a laudatory emphasis on "therapeutic activity." But it was Jung, Hattingberg declared, who had performed the great breakthrough by moving away from seeing mental conflict purely in medical terms, thus gaining an appreciation of the basic religious nature of humanity and its strivings. Jung's failings, according to Hattingberg, included a tendency to ignore therapy in favor of constructing typologies, as well as a tendency toward sectarianism that was aggravated by his religious musings. Indeed, it was Hattingberg's opinion in January 1933 that the analytic movement had come to a standstill precisely because of an emphasis on the theoretical and because of the resultant academic battles over abstract concepts and narrow scientific dogmas.[71]

The other major independent among the German psychotherapists before and during the Third Reich was Johannes Heinrich Schultz. He has rightly been called "the Nestor of German psychotherapy."[72] His interests and capabilities ranged widely, and he was unsurpassed in his energy and ability to present psychotherapy's case and to represent its interests. While Hattingberg remained an enthusiastic and capable eclectic, Schultz used his position, often with a hard and critical eye, to argue for unity among the various schools of psychotherapeutic thought.[73] He would also, as we will see, use his talents and ambitions to become arguably the single most influential psychotherapist within the Göring Institute.

Schultz was born in Göttingen in 1884 and received his medical license in 1908. He subsequently studied with psychiatrist Otto Binswanger at Jena in 1913. Binswanger was one of the few German psychiatrists to have taken the study of hysteria seriously.[74] By 1914 Schultz had become a specialist in psychology, an indication of his early commitment to the medical treatment of the mind. After serving as a medical officer in the First World War, he became a professor of neurology at Jena in 1919. He also worked with Hans Prinzhorn at Heinrich Lahmann's natural health sanitarium in Dresden. In 1924 he moved to Berlin and established a neurological practice. Most significantly, as we have already seen, after the war Schultz had emerged as an energetic propagandist for all modes of psychotherapy, and especially those based on hypnosis and suggestion.[75] Beginning in 1924, he also became involved in the continuing education program of the Berlin Medical Society, apparently regarding it as an effective means of introducing doctors to the use of psychotherapy in medical practice.[76]

Like Hattingberg and other German psychotherapists, Schultz displayed a weakness for Jung that was also characteristically prudent under Nazism. Jung's emphasis on religion seemed to Schultz to offer a new and comprehensive view of the workings of the human soul.[77] Schultz, too, placed some importance on spiritual guidance (*Seelenführung*) and human religiosity, but he did so without abandoning a strong faith in scientific method. He condemned those Romantically inclined psychotherapists and philosophers who sometimes discarded scientific method as narrow-minded materialism.[78] Schultz himself only rarely slipped into the relatively empty philosophizing that characterized some of his colleagues, especially among the more philosophical of the second group of independents to which we now turn .

The psychotherapists in this second group of independents turned out to be the most enthusiastic about National Socialism, especially early on. Their greater philosophical receptiveness to the Third Reich was by and large accompanied by an intellectual aloofness from any of the major schools of psychotherapeutic thought. What they mostly contributed to the field before and during the Third Reich was rhetorical observation rather than professional substance. This does not mean that their theoretical standpoint in general was necessarily at a variance with their colleagues aligned with the major schools of thought. They shared a common philosophical heritage that in their cases in particular provided the basis for a significant degree of intellectual fraternization with the Nazis.

Werner Achelis is perhaps the best example of this particular breed of German psychotherapist. Born in Berlin in 1897 as the son of a university professor, he studied philosophy and psychology at Berlin and Marburg, taking his degree in philosophy. He served as a reserve officer in the war and during the 1920s concerned himself increasingly with psychotherapy, founding a Jungian discussion group in Berlin.[79] He undertook medical studies, was licensed as a general practitioner in 1939, and completed his dissertation at Berlin in 1940.

Achelis saw the ravages of civilization everywhere. He had no use, however, for what he regarded as the panacea of a "back-to-the-land" campaign, echoing Hattingberg in his rejection of Rousseau as a philosopher of pessimism and resignation. Achelis blamed the fall of Western Civilization on the blurring of sex roles. He argued that the materialistic bourgeois industrial society of the West had been built upon the male attributes of initiative and rationality. But the complexity of the modern world, Achelis believed, was destroying the patriarchy upon which it had been built. Detached from the feminine-irrational ground of earthly being, men found themselves isolated and dispossessed. Women, most systematically under Marxism, had begun to usurp traditional male roles. Women were turning into men (*Vermännlichung der Frau*) and in so doing were destroying the family. This process had begun, Achelis charged, with the declining authority of the husband and was being completed by the increasing independence of the woman as an economic entity under both communism and capitalism and through the pernicious rise of feminism and liberal-socialist doctrine. To return to the old patriarchal order, however, was as undesirable as it was impossible. A new family-centered ethic had to be adopted that would strike a balance between the male-rational and the female-irrational polarities within the species.[80]

Rudolf and Josephine Bilz were the only prominent psychotherapists to join the Nazi Party before 1933. Born a Lutheran in 1898 in Thalheim, a village south of Chemnitz in southeastern Germany, Bilz became a member of the NSDAP in 1930, the year after he was licensed as a physician.[81] In 1934 he had a practice specializing in neurology in Hamburg. His Catholic wife had been licensed as a general practitioner in Hamburg in 1930 and had joined the NSDAP in 1932.[82] She would become an important part of the Göring Institute's educational counseling work, while her husband produced soupy critiques of Western materialism à la Achelis. Bilz blamed the liberal ethos of the French Revolution for spawning the cold and brutal rationality of an urban civilization. He vigorously defended the value of "feeling states" connected to the biological rhythms of birth and orgasm, and the human qualities of love, tenderness, and reverence united in an organic and emotional tie to the *Volk* and the fatherland.[83] Psychoanalysis, he lectured, was only one example of an intellectual tradition that reduced the rich biological, cultural, and religious aspects of humanity to a single explanation. A proper psychotherapy understood the "wholeness" of human experience from the biological to the metaphysical.[84]

Walter Cimbal and Carl Haeberlin were both early activists for psychotherapy before and just after 1933. A generation older than Achelis and Bilz, both faded from professional prominence before the founding of the Göring Institute in 1936. Cimbal had been born in Neisse, a small town south of Breslau, in 1877. He studied medicine in

Breslau, Freiburg, Kiel, and Munich. From 1901 to 1904 he served as an assistant in the mental health clinic at Heidelberg. In 1904 he joined the staff of the psychiatric section of the municipal hospital in Altona, a suburb of Hamburg, and became the section's director in 1911. In 1928 he became managing director of the General Medical Society; in 1930 he was the organization's secretary. While in his writings Cimbal concentrated on the organizational and practical aspects of clinical work, especially with children and adolescents, his emphasis on the active engagement of the psychotherapist in the life of the patient and the active life for the patient that was to come from such engagement was typical of German psychotherapeutic literature of the period. The titles of some of his works reflect this: for example, *Erziehung zur Tüchtigkeit in Schule und Beruf* (1919) and *Neurosen des Lebenskampfes* (1931). Terms like *Tüchtigkeit* ("fitness") and *Kampf* ("struggle") would prove to be, as we will see in chapter 4, Nazi buzzwords.

Haeberlin was born in 1878 in Frankfurt am Main, received his medical license in 1903 with a degree from the University of Munich, and established himself as a general practitioner in 1906. After serving in the First World War, Haeberlin worked at a sanitarium in Bad Nauheim. He apparently had strong nationalistic feelings early on, speaking publicly in the early 1920s on the need for the unity of the German nation and people.[85] He later argued that the battle cry of freedom, equality, and brotherhood from the French Revolution were only the deceptive phrases of charlatans behind which loomed the guillotine.[86] In this, Haeberlin was echoing Prinzhorn, who in 1929 condemned the "revolutionizing" of Western civilization by what he charged were the great utopian deceptions of the modern age: the social and political utopia of "freedom-equality-brotherhood"; the scientific utopia of positivism; and the utopia that was promised by the "doctrine of class conflict."[87] Closer to home, Prinzhorn saw particular perils for Germany lurking in the "democratic and socialistic" features of Freud's thought.[88] Haeberlin gave Freud credit for recognizing the power of the unconscious, but preferred Carus to Freud's materialist view: As Haeberlin put it, Carus approached the unconscious from the unconscious, not from the conscious. In the same vein, Haeberlin praised Nietzsche and Jung for regarding the unconscious not simply as a repository of repressed wishes but as a source of unrepressed powers.[89]

Driven by such ideas, represented by such men, and favored by some circumstance, the General Medical Society for Psychotherapy had by 1933 become the major forum in Central Europe for consensus and dissent in the field of psychotherapy. A fundamental challenge to the organic bias of German university psychiatry arising from the nineteenth-century German philosophy of nature and the *fin de siècle* psychodynamic revival led by Freud had achieved solid organizational status within the German medical profession. It is impossible to say with any certainty which direction the development of psychotherapy as a discipline and as a potential profession would have taken had not Hitler come to power. The manpower and medical demands placed on governments and industries by the Second World War, which resulted chiefly from the rise of Nazism to power in Germany, accelerated greatly the growth of psychology, psychoanalysis, and psychotherapy throughout the West. The flight of many psychoanalysts from fascism spurred the rapid development of that discipline in the United States. So the disastrous political events of 1933 and the disastrous military events of 1939 played a crucial role in the history of this entire field not only in Germany but in the entire Western world. On the other hand, without the eruption of the Nazis it is likely that psychotherapy as a discipline would have continued to grow in medicine and in other fields. The destruction by fascism of the autonomous psychoanalytic movement in Europe actually deprived psychotherapy of the single most dynamic and internationally influential segment of their discipline. Even within the somatic and positivist citadel of German psychiatry, as we have seen, the psychodynamic point of view was gaining currency before the First World War.

It seems likely, however, that in Germany at least both sympathetic psychiatrists like Ernst Kretschmer and the many less sympathetic of his psychiatric colleagues would have been able to exercise far more control over the evolution of psychotherapy than turned out to be the case after 1933. As it was, those seeking to establish psychotherapy as an autonomous, eclectic, broadly concerned profession in itself won the opportunity to determine the direction of their discipline's development. Aside from the founding of the Göring Institute itself, the most striking indication of this, as we will see, was the cultivation of lay therapy. Organized German psychotherapy under the Nazis would move from careful cooperation with lay professionals to their training and supervision in the practice of psychotherapy. Moreover, academic psychologists would organize on their own both in cooperation and competition with psychotherapists.[90] The change in policy on the part of medical psychotherapy was in part an answer to increasing isolation and danger from a psychiatric establishment strongly influenced by Nazi racial biology. But it also reflected not only old issues but new opportunities for psychotherapists. Building upon established influence and organization, the psychotherapists under the protection of the Göring name could respond most opportunistically and effectively to many Nazi demands for the mobilization of all of German society for health, productivity, and war.

Seen in historical context, therefore, the creation of the German General Medical Society for Psychotherapy in 1933 and the German Institute for Psychological Research and Psychotherapy in 1936 represent more than an uncomplicated collaboration with, and moral capitulation to, the Nazi regime. Collaboration—and moral capitulation—were shaped not just by the conditions of Nazi rule and the failings of individuals but also by the psychotherapists' proximate and immediate past. The experience of psychotherapists in the Third Reich, as we shall see, reveals much about the modern history of Germany as a whole in four vital respects: the history of professions in Germany and in the West; the domestic history of Nazi Germany; the social and institutional continuities and discontinuities in German history to, through, and beyond the Third Reich; and the place of Nazi Germany in the history of Germany and the West.

Notes

1. Cimbal, "Erinnerungen," p. 40
2. Dührssen, *Ein Jahrhundert Psychoanalytische Bewegung,* pp. 145–63.
3. BDC: Reichsärztekammer. In German, *Nervenarzt* is synonymous with *Neurologe,* a neurologist, or general nerve specialist. The British translation of the German terms is "neuropathist," an obsolete term replaced in American usage by "neurologist." In this study use of the term neurologist in the context of speaking of psychotherapists means *Nervenarzt,* while the same term in the context of psychiatrists and neurologists means *Neurologe.* Since the early 1930s, *Neurologe* has come to supplant *Nervenarzt* as the official term: in a 1932 German medical dictionary *Nervenarzt* is the only entry for "a specialist in nerve diseases"; in a 1953 English-German dictionary under "neurologist" *Neurologe* is listed first, followed by *Facharzt für Nervenkrankheiten,* and then *Nervenarzt.* By 1987 *Neurologe/Neurologin* replaced *Nervenarzt.*
4. Wladimir Eliasberg, "Allgemeine Ärztliche Gesellschaft für Psychotherapie," pp. 738–9.
5. Michael H. Kater, "Physicians in Crisis at the End of the Weimar Republic," in Peter D. Stachura, ed., *Unemployment and the Great Depression in Weimar Germany* (London, 1986), pp. 49–77.

6. Mitchell G. Ash, *Gestalt Psychology in German Culture, 1890–1967*, pp. 284–306, 311–12, 321; Michael H. Kater, *Doctors Under Hitler*, pp. 120–1.
7. Eliasberg, "Allgemeine Ärztliche Gesellschaft," p. 738. See also *Psychotherapie: Bericht über den 1. Allgemeinen ärztlichen Kongress für Psychotherapie in Baden-Baden 17. bis 19. April 1926*; and Johannes Heinrich Schultz, "1. Allgemeiner ärztlicher Kongress für Psychotherapie, Baden-Baden, 17.-19. IV. 1926," *Deutsche medizinische Wochenschrift* 52 (1926): 937.
8. Henry Steele Commager, *The American Mind* (New Haven, 1950), p. 100.
9. Lockot, *Erinnern und Durcharbeiten*, p. 53.
10. Adolf Friedländer, "Sozialmedizin und Politik," in Eliasberg and Cimbal, eds., *Bericht über den III. Allgemeinen ärztlichen Kongress für Psychotherapie in Baden-Baden 20. bis 22. April 1928*, p. 212.
11. "Zum Geleit," *Allgemeine Ärztliche Zeitschrift für Psychotherapie* 1 (1928): 2.
12. Ibid., p. 4.
13. Ibid., p. 2.
14. Johannes Heinrich Schultz, "Allgemeiner ärztlicher Gesellschaft für Psychotherapie, Baden-Baden, 17.-19. IV. 1926," *Deutsche medizinische Wochenschrift* 52 (1926): 937.
15. Adolf Friedländer, "Das erste Jahrfünft des Allgemeinen Aerztlichen Kongresses für Psychotherapie," p. 992.
16. Dührssen, *Ein Jahrhundert Psychoanalytische Bewegung*, pp. 149–52, 154; see also below, chapters 5 and 14.
17. Lockot, *Erinnern und Durcharbeiten*, p. 57; on Lewin, see Ash, *Gestalt Psychology*, pp. 11–12, 263–75, 327–8, 406.
18. See Fritz Künkel, *Krisenbriefe: Die Beziehungen zwischen Wirtschaftskrise und Charakterkrise* (Schwerin in Mecklenburg, 1932).
19. Friedländer, "Jahrfünft."
20. Dührssen, *Ein Jahrhundert Psychoanalytische Bewegung*, p. 154.
21. Johannes Heinrich Schultz, *Lebensbilderbuch eines Nervenarztes*, p. 150.
22. Johannes Heinrich Schultz, "Psychotherapie und Medizin," *Münchener medizinische Wochenschrift* 77 (1930): 903–5; see also idem, *Taschenbuch der psychotherapeutischen Technik*, Fischer's Therapeutische Taschenbücher, vol. 12 (Berlin, 1924); and idem, *Die seelische Krankenbehandlung, Psychotherapie: ein Grundriss für Fach und Allgemein Praxis*, 4th ed. (Jena, 1930).
23. Wladimir Eliasberg, ed., *Bericht über den II. Allgemeinen ärztlichen Kongress für Psychotherapie in Bad Nauheim 27. bis 30. April 1927*.
24. Eliasberg and Cimbal, eds., *Bericht*.
25. Cimbal, ed., *Bericht über den IV. Allgemeinen ärztlichen Kongress für Psychotherapie in Bad Nauheim 11. bis 14. April 1929*; and Ernst Kretschmer, *Gestalten und Gedanken*, pp. 133–7; on Goldstein, see Ash, *Gestalt Psychology*, pp. 276–83.
26. Ernst Kretschmer and Walter Cimbal, eds., *Bericht über den V. Allgemeinen ärztlichen Kongress für Psychotherapie in Baden-Baden 26. bis 29. April 1930*.
27. Ernst Kretschmer and Walter Cimbal, eds., *Bericht über den VI. Allgemeinen ärztlichen Kongress für Psychotherapie in Dresden 14. bis 17. Mai 1931*. On psychotherapy and Oriental practices, see Heinrich Zimmer, "Indische Anschauungen über Psychotherapie," *ZfP* 8 (1935): 147–62.
28. Jack L. Rubins, *Karen Horney: Gentle Rebel of Psychoanalysis* (New York, 1978), pp. 113–41; Lockot, *Erinnern und Durcharbeiten*, pp. 55–9.
29. Dührssen, *Ein Jahrhundert Psychoanalytische Bewegung*, pp. 162, 169–72.

30. Decker, *Freud in Germany,* p. 84.
31. Schultz, *Lebensbilderbuch,* p. 164.
32. As far as can be determined, of the twenty-two members of the "core group" within the General Medical Society who comprised the leadership of the organization both before and after 1933, at least eleven were Lutheran, only two were Catholic, and two others (psychoanalysts Schultz-Hencke and Felix Boehm) were without religious affiliation (*konfessionslos*). Cimbal was born Catholic, converted to Lutheranism in 1913, and reconverted to Catholicism in 1932. After the Nazi seizure of power, Heyer, Werner Achelis, and Kurt Gauger changed their declared religious affiliation from Protestant (*evangelisch*) to the Nazi-approved "believer in God" (*gottgläubig*). See BDC: Reichsärztekammer; Personalakte Walter Cimbal, Staatsarchiv Hamburg. German Protestants at this time were by and large socially and politically conservative and were proportionally overrepresented among Nazi voters and activists.
33. Walter Cimbal, "Familienchronik," pp. 105, 106–8; idem, "Gründungsgeschichte," p. 1; on psychologist Lewin's Marxist humanism, see Ash, *Gestalt Psychology,* pp. 265, 293, 305.
34. Robert N. Proctor, *Racial Hygiene,* p. 69.
35. Kater, *Doctors Under Hitler,* pp. 54–5. Psychoanalyst Gerhard Scheunert near the end of his life made a distinction between his interest after the First World War in a "national socialism" and the racist anti-Semitism he says distanced him from the Nazi party he joined in 1933: see Scheunert to Carl Nedelmann, March 14, 1993, pp. 2–3; and Mitgliederkartei des Reichsinstituts für Psychologische Forschung und Psychotherapie, BA.
36. Fritz K. Ringer, *The Decline of the German Mandarins,* pp. 180–99.
37. Haeberlin, "Bedeutung von Klages und Prinzhorn," p. 42.
38. Fritz Künkel, Fragebogen für Mitglieder, Reichsverband Deutscher Schriftsteller, e.V., December 20, 1933, p. 1; idem, Fragebogen zur Bearbeitung des Aufnahmeantrages für die Reichsschriftumskammer, May 25, 1938, p. 2, BDC: Kulturkammer; and BDC: Reichsärztekammer.
39. See Kenneth D. Barkin, *The Controversy over German Industrialization, 1890–1902* (Chicago, 1970), p. 278.
40. Fritz Künkel, "Die dialektische Charakterkunde als Ergebnis der kulturellen Krise," p. 73.
41. Helmut Fabricius, "Gemeinschaftspsychologie," pp. 11–12; and Wolfgang Kloppe, "Die Lebenskunst bei Carl Gustav Carus," *Medizinsiche Monatsschrift* 30 (1976): 499–506. See also Fritz Künkel, "Psychotherapie: Eine Übersicht."
42. Fritz Künkel, *Psychotherapie und Seelsorge,* Arzt und Seelsorger, ed. Carl Schweitzer, no. 1 (Schwerin in Mecklenburg, 1926), p. 25.
43. Hans Prinzhorn, *Psychotherapie,* p. 15. On Prinzhorn, psychotherapy, and National Socialism, see Albert Moll, *Ein Leben als Arzt der Seele: Erinnerungen* (Dresden, 1936), pp. 64–6.
44. Ellenberger, *Discovery,* p. 627.
45. Prinzhorn, *Psychotherapie,* p. 16.
46. Fritz Künkel, "Individualpsychologie und Psychoanalyse," in Eliasberg, *Bericht,* pp. 61–71; see also Johannes Heinrich Schultz, *Psychotherapie,* p. 180.
47. Charles Spearman, "German Science of Character II," *Character and Personality* 6 (1937): 48.
48. Fritz Künkel, *Charakter, Einzelmensch und Gruppe,* p. iii.
49. Sigmund Freud, *Freud/Jung Letters: The Correspondence Between Sigmund Freud*

and C. G. Jung, ed. William McGuire and trans. Ralph Manheim and R. F. C. Hull, Bollingen Series XCIV (Princeton, 1974), pp. 214, 224, 226, 233, 257, 267, 280, 329, 410, 417, 420, 444, 513, 520, 521.

50. "Dr. Leonhard Seif, geboren 15.1.1866," *ZfP* 12 (1941); 321–2.
51. C. G. Jung, et al., "Prof. Dr. M. H. Göring zum 60. Geburtstag"; Peter Göring, *Vorarbeit zu einer Geschichte der Sippe* (Munich, 1911), pp. 320–1.
52. Matthias Heinrich Göring, *Die Individualpsychologie als Werkzeug der Bibelbetrachtung,* p. 16; see also idem, "Anregungen zur Bibelbetrachtung," *Evangelischer Religionsunterricht* 50 (1939): 144–56; and Cimbal, *Bericht,* p. 161. On Pietism, conservatism, and nationalism, see Koppel Pinson, *Pietism as a Factor in the Rise of German Nationalism* (New York, 1963). See also Matthias Göring, *Über die Behandlung verwundeter und kranker deutscher Gefangener im Frankreich* (Augsburg, 1919).
53. The *physikum* was taken after five semesters of university study. The state examination (*Staatsexamen*) was taken upon completion of five additional semesters of clinical instruction. Passing these conferred the status of an *approbierter Arzt* eligible for a year's internship at a hospital. After that came licensure to practice by the state (*Bestallung bei der Ärztekammer*) as a *praktischer Arzt.* The academic degree of Dr. med. required another university examination and a publication of a thesis, whereupon the doctor was *promoviert.* Specialization (*Anerkennung zum Facharzt*) was more or less a formality once a doctor had established a practice (*niederlassen*) for a time.
54. Gustav Richard Heyer, Lebenslauf, Berlin, February 29, 1944, pp. 2–4, BDC: Parteikorrespondenz.
55. Harald Schultz-Hencke, Lebenslauf, Berlin-Wilmersdorf, July 3, 1944, p. 1, BDC: Parteikorrespondenz; see also BDC: Reichsärztekammer.
56. Schultz-Hencke, Lebenslauf, p. 1; see also idem, "Das Unbewusste in seiner mehrfachen Bedeutung," *ZfP* 12 (1941): 336–49.
57. Harald Schultz-Hencke, *Die Überwindung der Parteien durch die Jugend,* Das Wollen der neuen Jugend: Eine Auseinandersetzung mit den Grundfragen der Zeit, ed. Harald Schultz-Hencke, vol. 1 (Gotha, 1921).
58. Harald Schultz-Hencke, "Die heutigen Aufgabe der Psychotherapie als Wissenschaft," *Allgemeine Ärztliche Zeitschrift für Psychotherapie* 1 (1928): 238–52.
59. Harald Schultz-Hencke, "Psychoanalyse und Individualpsychologie," in idem, *Psychoanalyse und Psychotherapie: Gesammelte Aufsätze,* pp. 11–14; see also Eliasberg, *Bericht,* p. 207.
60. See Heinz Kohut, *The Curve of Life: Correspondence of Heinz Kohut, 1923–1981,* ed. Geoffrey Cocks (Chicago, 1994), pp. 248–9.
61. See Ellenberger, *Discovery,* pp. 640–1; and Hans Kunz, "Der gehemmte Mensch: Bemerkungen zu den gleichnamigen Buche von H. Schultz-Hencke," *Der Nervenarzt* 14 (1941): 201–14, 241–60.
62. Werner Kemper, "John F. Rittmeister zum Gedächtnis," *Zeitschrift für psychosomatische Medizin und Psychoanalyse* 14 (1968): 147–49; Pongratz, *Psychotherapie,* pp. 276, 281; see also below, chapter 12.
63. See Elisabeth Brainin and Isidor J. Kaminer, "Psychoanalyse und Nationalsozialismus," p. 87, n. 3, p. 92, n. 7.
64. Ernst Bloch, *Erbschaft dieser Zeit* [1935] (Frankfurt a. M., 1973), p. 344, and pp. 84, 345–51.
65. John F. Rittmeister, "Tagebuchblätter," p. 18.
66. Ibid., pp. 25, 18, 17; see also John F. Rittmeister, "Die mystische Krise des

jungen Descartes," the text of an address given at the Göring Institute early in 1942.

67. Hans von Hattingberg, "Zur Problematik des Führertums," p. 142.
68. Hans von Hattingberg, Lebenslauf, Berlin, c. 1940, pp. 1–3, BDC: Reichsschriftumskammer; "Aktuelles," *ZfP* 16 (1944): 1–2.
69. Hans von Hattingberg, "Neue Richtung, Neue Bindung," p. 102.
70. Hans von Hattingberg, "Der neue Weg der Psychoanalyse," *Medizinische Klinik* 21 (1925): 849–51; idem, "Zur Analyse der analytischen Situation," *Internationale Zeitschrift für ärztliche Psychoanalyse* 10 (1924): 34–56.
71. Hans von Hattingberg, "Zur Entwicklung der analytischen Bewegung."
72. Pongratz, *Psychotherapie,* p. 287.
73. Johannes Heinrich Schultz, *Die Schicksalsstunde der Psychotherapie,* Abhandlungen aus dem Gebiete der Psychotherapie und medizinische Psychologie, ed. Albert Moll, vol. 1 (Stuttgart, 1925). Ernest Jones notes that Schultz had made a "serious attempt" in 1909 to come to an understanding of psychoanalysis, but that his attitude remained "negative." Jones, *Sigmund Freud,* vol. 2, pp. 119–20. See Johannes Heinrich Schultz, "Psychoanalyse, die Breuer-Freud'sche Lehre, ihre Entstehung und Aufnahme," *Zeitschrift für angewandte Psychologie* 2 (1909): 440–97; reprinted as "Psychoanalyse und ihre Kritik," in Curt Adam, ed., *Die Psychologie und ihre Bedeutung für die ärztliche Praxis: Acht Vorträge* (Jena, 1921), pp. 73–103. See also Freud, *Freud/Jung Letters,* p. 209; and Schultz, *Lebensbilderbuch,* p. 58.
74. Decker, *Freud in Germany,* p. 78.
75. See Johannes Heinrich Schultz, *Hypnose-Technik; praktische Anleitung zum Hypnotisieren für Ärzte* (Jena, 1935).
76. Schultz, *Lebensbilderbuch,* p. 106; BDC: Reichsärztekammer.
77. Johannes Heinrich Schultz, "Der Yoga und die deutsche Seele," pp. 67–9.
78. Johannes Heinrich Schultz, *Psychiatrie, Psychotherapie und Seelsorge,* Arzt und Seelsorger, ed. Carl Schweitzer, no. 2 (Schwerin in Mecklenburg, 1926), p. 14. See also Eugen von Grosschopf, *Die seelische Behandlung kranker Menschen: Grundlagen und Grundfragen schöpferischer Psychotherapie* (Leipzig, 1940).
79. See Werner Achelis, *Das Problem des Traumes, eine philosophische Abhandlung,* Schriften zur Seelenforschung, ed Carl Schneider, vol. 20 (Stuttgart, 1928).
80. Werner Achelis, "Psychologische Hygiene," pp. 263–4.
81. BDC: Reichsärztekammer and NSDAP-Zentralkartei.
82. BDC: Reichsärztekammer and NSDAP-Zentralkartei.
83. Rudolf Bilz, *Lebensgesetze der Liebe,* pp. 54, 74.
84. Ibid., p. 80.
85. Carl Haeberlin, *Deutsche Einheit: Rede bei der von der Stadt Bad Nauheim veranstalteten Reichsgründungsfeier am 18. January 1921 gehalten von Dr. med. Carl Haeberlin* (Bad Nauheim, 1921).
86. Carl Haeberlin, "Die Bedeutung von Ludwig Klages und Hans Prinzhorn," p. 44.
87. Prinzhorn, *Psychotherapie,* p. 294.
88. Ibid., p. 25.
89. Carl Haeberlin, *Grundlinien der Psychoanalyse* (Munich, 1927), pp. 12–13, 59, 92.
90. Ulfried Geuter, *Die Professionalisierung der deutschen Psychologie im Nationalsozialismus*; a second, slightly revised edition of this book appeared in 1988 and subsequently a somewhat abridged English translation: idem, *The Professionalization of Psychology in Nazi Germany,* trans. Richard J. Holmes (Cambridge, 1992); all references here are to the first edition.

3

Nazi Medicine and the "Jewish Science"

In 1934 Bavarian Minister of Culture Hans Schemm defined National Socialism as "applied biology."[1] For the Nazis, race was the determining factor of human existence. Biology, not politics, was the solution to the problems facing humanity. Life was not a matter of equality or justice, but of the "survival of the fittest." It was the responsibility of the state to ensure that the racially and biologically desirable members of society thrive and that the racially and biologically undesirable members of society die. Problems of health and illness would be solved by the cultivation of the strong and the extirpation of the weak. Poverty and disease, according to this view, were the result of hereditary inferiority and the degeneration of human stock aggravated by the misguided ideals of welfare and egalitarianism. Before the arrival of the Nazis, this sort of "racial hygiene" was largely nationalist or meritocratic.[2] The Nazis made race the governing factor and substituted state compulsion for an earlier academic tendency toward voluntarism in matters of procreation, sterilization, and euthanasia. The Nazis also, unlike many earlier race hygienists, assumed that radical eugenic measures could be successful in countering dysgenic trends. The struggle for survival would now be one of the superior "Aryan" race against all inferior races. Victory of the relatively few superior humans would have to be absolute through the eventual extermination—and intervening enslavement—of the masses of inferior ones. Health and medicine in this brutal and anxious Nazi context naturally took on great importance. Not only did the German people have to be prepared—"hardened"—for the coming decisive struggles against their inferiors, they had to be "cleansed" of the inferior elements that had found their way into their ranks through centuries of inter-breeding, lax or indulgent governance, and the active racial conspiring of the Jews.

The Nazis also faced more prosaic—that is, real—problems in the realms of health and illness. Although Germany was a culture celebrated—by itself and others—for its collective obsession with cleanliness and was also a world leader in medical education and research, the health of large numbers of Germans in the early 1930s was not good. Economic inequality and the chronic illnesses and conditions associated with poor working and living conditions, particularly in the urban industrial centers, had produced a significant degree of morbidity in Imperial Germany before 1914.[3] The First World War added a huge number of physical and mental casualties among soldiers. The malnutrition and consequent illness on the German home front during the last three years of the war had affected the physical development of large numbers of children. The inflation of 1923 and the depression of 1929 likewise had significant health consequences, especially when added to earlier problems.[4] Not only were many people unable to afford good nutrition, medicine, visits to the doctor, or hospital treatment, but municipalities and states often lacked the funds to provide sufficient medical care or to improve sanitation and housing. Nazi group martial activities, especially among youth, often only exacerbated these conditions: In 1937, for example, military officials in Munich complained that barefoot marches undertaken—in any weather—by members of the Hitler Youth were, among other things, creating and aggravating foot conditions among draftees.[5]

The Nazi concern with health also built upon the longstanding process of the medicalization of modern society. The modernization of Germany since the late nineteenth century had brought with it "the extension of rational, scientific values in medicine to a wide range of social activities."[6] Doctors and medical care simply have become more important to more people (including themselves) during the modern period in the West. In Germany, this importance was enhanced by the state health insurance system that was erected beginning in the 1880s. Bismarck's aim in establishing this system was to bind the working class to the state by means of a paternalistic policy designed to subvert the power and influence of an autonomous socialist movement. As such, this policy was one extreme example of the use of medicine and health policy as an attempted means of social control by governing elites. Doctors themselves gradually built a reputation for caring and competence in the minds of their patients. Aided and abetted by pharmaceutical advances made by the burgeoning German chemical industry, for the first time doctors were able to diagnose, treat, and even cure illness.[7] Doctors parlayed their new expertise and influence into an increasingly aggressive campaign for professional autonomy and power, many of them often in conflict with a state health insurance system peopled with socialist physicians and bureaucrats and many of whom sooner or later became attracted to the National Socialists. The Nazis, for their part, purged the state health insurance system of political and "racial" enemies, that is, Socialists and Jews, cut benefits to save money and discourage use, and centralized the administration to eliminate the self-governing boards of the four types of sickness funds.[8]

But those Nazis who were most active and prominent in matters of medicine and health during the early years of the Third Reich were the inheritors of the natural health (*Naturheilkunde*) movement whose forces were more or less arrayed against the German medical establishment. Deputy Führer Rudolf Hess, agrarian Walter Darré, and Reich Physicians Leader Gerhard Wagner were the Nazi leaders of this movement. They urged a return to the land that would defy the crass and unhealthful industrialized world and reinvigorate the German body and the German spirit. In this spirit, the natural health movement praised the virtues of wholemeal bread (*Vollkornbrot*) and warned of the dangers of Coca-Cola as part of a national and racial campaign for national health (*Volksgesundheit*).[9] Modern industrial civilization, according to this view, had left the masses uprooted and mechanized, the effects of which, the proponents of natural health argued, could be traced in the high indices of physical and mental debilitation. Franz Wirz, a member of Wagner's Expert Advisory Council on Health, criticized the city worker's unhealthy breakfast of tea or coffee and pointed with approval to Hitler's ban on smoking in party offices. For dedicated Nazis, of course, Hitler himself—non-smoker, teetotaler, and vegetarian—served as the model of abstinence from the pollutions of modern life.[10]

Traditional "school medicine" (*Schulmedizin*), as it was called disparagingly by natural health proponents, was regarded by them as too scientific, rationalistic, and mechanical, too concerned with the manipulable parts of the human being as organism rather than as a whole person in tune with larger natural forces, and all in all too materialistic by fact and by fee. As part of the resultant ideological and political struggle with opponents and competitors within the state medical bureaucracy we will describe below, Reich Physicians Leader Wagner sought to mobilize proponents of natural health under his direction. This began on November 24, 1933, with the founding of the Reich Study Group of Biological and Natural Health Physicians.[11] This group was succeeded on May 24, 1935 by two groups, the Reich Study Group of Organizations for Life and Health Reform and the Reich Study Group for a New German Medicine. The first was under the direction of one of Wagner's deputies, Georg Gustav Wegener, and the other was led by Karl Kötschau. These organizations represented a mustering of Wagner's forces to foment fundamental change in the health sciences and their administration. As Wagner proclaimed:

> National Socialism is a renewing movement: It has never intended to be satisfied with a formal transformation of inner political relationships and the conquest of indefensible methods of governmental control.[12]

Although Wagner's statement reflected the vague subjectivity of Nazi "renewing," the basis for his attack on the retrenched medical bureaucracy was his advocacy of natural health in a highly nationalistic, racist, and anti-Semitic context. He mobilized the reform-minded medical journal *Hippokrates,* which had been founded in 1928 by, among others, racist holistic health reformer Erwin Liek, by making it the organ for Kötschau's Reich Study Group.[13] This journal thus joined *Ziel und Weg,* the organ of the Nazi Physicians League, and *Volksgesundheitswacht,* mouthpiece for the NSDAP's Expert Advisory Council on Health and edited by Bernhard Hörmann, director of the German Society for the Control of Abuses in the Health System. The Reich Study Group for a New German Medicine embraced those disciplines on the margins of the medical establishment: the Reich League of Nature Healers, the Society for Spas and Climatic Science, the Central Association of Homeopathic Physicians, the League of Hydropathists, the Reich League of Private Health Institutions, the Association of Anthroposophic Physicians, and the German General Medical Society for Psychotherapy.

But despite the mobilization of the psychotherapists under one Nazi banner in 1935, radical Nazi health reformers posed a serious threat to psychotherapy in the early years of the Third Reich. These particular Nazis associated any form of psychotherapy with psychoanalysis, the despised "Jewish science," while also rejecting almost all psychology out of hand as at best unnecessary for—and at worst an affront to—the Master Race. Psychoanalysis and much of psychology were regarded by many Nazis as another instance of the "hyperrationalized" culture of the Jew that was devoid of deeper feeling for nation, people, nature, and race. Psychoanalysis in particular could be painted as a distressing example of a Jewish obsession with disorder and conflict that was the sure sign for the Nazis of the racial degeneration spawned by the modern world of effete intellectuals.

The most vehement and pathological attacks along these lines were the turgid outpourings of the notorious "Jewbaiter of Nuremberg," Julius Streicher, Gauleiter of Franconia. Along with publishing the infamous *Der Stürmer,* Streicher was co-editor with Heinrich Will of *Deutsche Volksgesundheit aus Blut und Boden.* Beginning in 1933, this paper undertook to elucidate its concept of Nazi natural and racial health. The first issue that year introduced a continuing feature entitled "The Role of the Jew in Medicine" with a hysterical outburst against psychoanalysis, describing it as a Jewish "poisoning of the soul" (*Seelenvergiftung*) whose aim was to

> *remove the last ethical support* from the patient's soul in its battle over control of its instinctual life, and cast it down before the Asiatic world view, "Eat, drink and be merry, for tomorrow you die!" And that was Freud's *aim,* or perhaps his *assignment,* for he lined up dutifully with other Jewish endeavors *to strike the Nordic race at its most sensitive spot, its sex life.*[14]

Psychoanalysis was an especially suitable target for Streicher, not only because it allowed him to vent his bloody racist spleen against a prominent Jewish intellectual but because it also permitted him to exploit, as he did regularly in the pages of *Der Stürmer,* the subject of sex. The cartoon by Philippe Ruprecht (pseud. Fips) that accompanied the article on psychoanalysis features a typically caricatured Jew as a psychoanalyst (dressed inaccurately in a physicians' smock) and a blonde Aryan female patient complaining of headaches. Free associations include the word "knife," whereupon the analyst springs to the couch with his personal solution for the sexual frustrations arising from the woman's marriage.

Although not all the criticism of psychoanalysis was this extreme, it was commonly labeled a "foreign body within the German nation."[15] Psychoanalysis thus attracted the critical attention of the highest levels

"Oh, doctor, I'm having such terrible headaches."

"So, please lie down on the couch and say whatever comes into your mind."

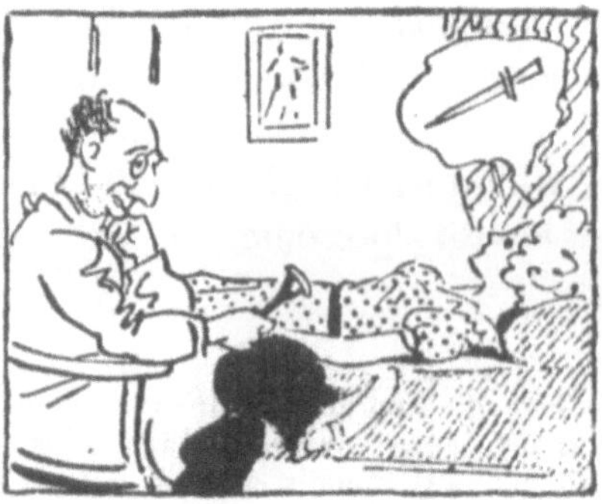

"Roast . . . . medicinal waters . . . blotter . . . handkerchief . . . knife . . ."

"Stop! Knife! That's it! The thought 'knife' manifests your sexual desires. Your headaches thus arise from the fact that you find no sexual gratification in your marriage. Hence it follows automatically how you can be cured . . ."

A Nazi View of "Jewish" Psychoanalysis

of Nazi officialdom. The Reich Chamber for Literature, which, under the direction of Propaganda Minister Joseph Goebbels, regulated literary production in the Third Reich, prepared lists of subjects deemed injurious to the *Volksgemeinschaft* and these included birth control, family planning, and psychoanalysis.[16] Freud himself remained a favorite object of scorn, vilified as a major representative of Jewish nihilism and entrepreneurship and accused of perverting the work of the Aryan German creators of "depth psychology"—Novalis, Carus, Schopenhauer, Goethe—by turning it into a business enterprise that thrived on a clientele of rich hysterics. Like Marx, Shaw, and Darwin, Freud was portrayed as part of the modern trend toward destroying what Nazis and their sympathizers regarded as the anthropological and historical ideal and reality of a heroic, soldierly man. In this view, psychoanalysis belonged to the overrationalized corruptions of late capitalism, its alleged obsession with sexual drives plaguing primitive peoples like the Jews making it a proper therapeutic method only in rare cases under strict psychiatric supervision. This particular critical concatenation singled out Schultz-Hencke and Groddeck as especially distressing examples of "psychological gangsterism."[17] The Nazis also seized upon the association of such figures as psychoanalyst Wilhelm Reich with the radical European left. Reich himself ended up in exile in Norway criticizing not only Carl Jung (see chapter 6) but the psychoanalysts for collaborating with the Nazis.[18]

There was little that psychoanalysts in Germany could do to counter such attacks save to try and keep a low profile. The many who were Jewish were of course effectively denied the right to speak as prelude (adopting the formulation of Raul Hilberg) to the denial of their right to exist as German citizens, their right to exist as psychoanalysts, and, ultimately, their right to exist at all. From 1933 on, the Berlin Psychoanalytic Institute reported attacks from Nazi party philosopher Alfred Rosenberg's Battle Group for German Culture. Three days before Hitler became Chancellor, Max Eitingon, founder and director of the institute, had visited Freud in Vienna and expressed his concern over the dismal course of political events in Germany. Such concern had been growing for some time in Germany and Europe, and intellectuals and professionals, among others, had begun emigrating as early as 1930 out of fear of fascism. Freud, like IPA president Ernest Jones, would, over the next five years, counsel submission to the exclusion of Jewish psychoanalysts in the interest of the preservation of at least some organized psychoanalytic presence in Germany and Austria. He thus advised Eitingon to hold out as long as possible, but the political success of the Nazis demonstrated that the future of the Berlin institute was in grave doubt. By April, a decree had been issued that prohibited the membership of foreigners in the executive of any medical society. Jews were defined as foreigners. By the end of May, Freud's works were being burned in the quadrangles of German universities. By November, the institute's executive consisted of only two members, both "Aryan," Carl Müller-Braunschweig and Felix Boehm. The number of psychoanalysts at the institute had dropped from around 65 to between 12 and 15, the number of candidates from 34 in 1932 to 18 in 1934, and the number of students fell from 222 in 1931 to 138 in 1932 and to 34 by 1934.[19] In a letter to Boehm on November 21, Eitingon resigned from the DPG and left Germany on the last day of 1933. A two-year-long hiatus then ensued, during which time the institute was allowed to function—more or less—without direct interference from the Nazi regime. Although a distinct pall hung over its activities, the educational work went on almost as before, only with a reduced number of participants. By the end of 1935, however, the repercussions from the proclamation of the Nuremberg Race Laws on September 15 of that year reached the DPG. An effort to save the society from dissolution took the form of the "voluntary" resignation of its few remaining Jewish members on December 1.

But the fate of the Berlin Psychoanalytic Institute and of the DPG was not to be that of psychotherapists in general in Nazi Germany. This was to be, as we shall see in chapter 4, the result primarily of the psychotherapists' own efforts to secure a safe place for themselves in the Third Reich. But their success in that respect was also a result of the struggle for power among individuals and groups in the field of medicine and public health. Nazi health propagandists and activists carried on a spirited battle with their adversaries within the medical establishment and the state medical bureaucracy. They also fought among themselves. The extreme radicals within the NSDAP—who wished to abolish the "materialistic" and "un-German" health profession and bureaucracy—would meet defeat by 1935. More moderate Nazi party reformers would largely fall by the wayside two years later. Of the former, Streicher was most dangerous to the psychoanalysts and psychotherapists since he saw all of established medicine as a Jewish conspiracy and condemned all psychologists as followers of Freud. Wagner, head of the party's Physicians League, was more restrained in his views, but he represented the threat of direct Nazi party control over all medicine including psychotherapy. Party activists and ideas ended up infiltrating the medical system in Germany in a tangle of accommodation, conflict, and opportunism. The combination of challenge to the establishment and the failure of any comprehensive institutional or programmatic reforms provided a rising but still marginal group like the psychotherapists with the opportunity to gain their own space and exploit both the Göring name and the nature of the service they could offer to the new regime.

Along with dangerous rhetoric and action from extreme party activists, the first years of the Third Reich saw a wild proliferation of organizations. At the center of this profusion of offices was Gerhard Wagner. Wagner had been leader of the NSDAP Physicians League since 1932. In 1934 Hess ordered Wagner to assume leadership of a unified party health organization, a province which had until then been—and would in the future be—claimed by Robert Ley, boss of the German Labor Front. In an effort to meet Hess's charge, by December Wagner had created the NSDAP Main Office for National Health, technically incorporating the health agencies of all party organizations except those of the SA and SS.[20] Wagner also headed the Expert Advisory Council for National Health and was NSDAP General Plenipotentiary for the Health System and Deputy for all University Affairs. As a result, Wagner was involved almost immediately after Hitler became chancellor in a competition with the health departments of the Ministry of the Interior for control over the administration of the country's health services. He also had to struggle against the claims made on health policy and administration by Reich Labor Leader Konstantin Hierl, Reich Labor Minister Franz Seldte in his capacity as supervisor of the national health insurance system, and DAF's Robert Ley, who would acquire a wide array of offices in his visionary scheme to extend National Socialist care and control into every corner of German life.

The rivalry with the Interior Ministry took on an almost comical form. During the spring of 1933, Wagner had established the first of his many Reich Study Groups, this one for Professions in Social and Medical Service. The Interior Ministry countered on November 20 by setting up a Reich Commission for National Health chaired by departmental head Arthur Gütt and Deputy Director Gustav Frey. Frey and Gütt also ran the State Medical Academy in Berlin, while Hans Reiter was director of the research activities of the Reich Health Office and Eduard Schütt presided over the Scientific Society of German Doctors in the Public Health Service. In 1934 Gütt became a ministerial director and head of the Interior Ministry's Division for National Health. Even when, during the early months of 1934, some rationalization of this confused and competing mass of sovereignties was attempted, the little accommodation that was achieved was tentative and cosmetic. It produced only agglutination and the persistence of party-state rivalry. On December 15, 1933, Wagner had announced that the Reich Study

Group for Professions in Social and Medical Service operated under the jurisdiction of the Interior Ministry and its chief, Wilhelm Frick, and was to be headed by a party man named August Fleck. As if the names of the participants were not easy enough to confuse, Fleck, in addition to being subordinate to Frick, was also a member of the party's Expert Advisory Council for Health and thus under Wagner's authority as well. Fleck's agency was located within the Reich Central Office of Health Leadership run by Fritz Bartels, an Interior Ministry department head who was Wagner's deputy in the Reich Physicians Chamber. The Reich Central Office was strongly oriented toward the NSDAP, with Bartels, Wagner, and Erich Hilgenfeldt, director of the NSV, the Nazi Social Welfare Organization, holding the key positions. Reiter was deputy director of the Reich Study Group for Public Hygiene under Bartels. According to *Der öffentliche Gesundheitsdienst* in 1935, the Reich Central Office constituted section two of the Reich Commission for National Health Service and included groups charged with combating various specific threats to national health such as drug addiction, tuberculosis, and cancer. Section one concerned itself with the tasks of national and racial preventive medicine (*Volkspflege*). However, in a schema published by Reiter in 1933 and reprinted by Frick early in 1934, the Reich Central Office buried the Reich Commission in an avalanche of organizations and capacities.[21]

With the promulgation of a law for the unification of the health services on March 30, 1935, the state medical bureaucracy launched an effective counteroffensive in service to its own prerogatives. In September of 1937 Interior Minister Frick happily confided in a letter to Heinrich Lammers, chief of the Hitler's chancellery staff, that from party headquarters in Munich Wagner was complaining of being shut out. Frick, with his own inclination for the bureaucratic and the statist, naturally felt that the duties of the state health administration had to be preserved from disruption from any source.[22] This was also the position the Reich chancellery adopted in the documentation it appended to the health services proclamation. In 1938 Wagner in desperation pressed for a policy that would have the party assume all new assignments in the field of medicine and health care, but the chancellery's response was firmly negative.[23]

While in fact the health services in Nazi Germany were never unified,[24] the Interior Ministry's defense of its authority in this realm marked an end to party attempts at radical changes in the administration and practice of health care. Changes would remain partial and incremental as Nazi ideals and personnel percolated into the system and, instead of sweeping it away, merely made it more redundant in a profusion of offices, jurisdictions, and fiefdoms. The first major casualty in the Nazi process of tempering its early rhetoric and blunting its ideologists' more extreme efforts at change in the realm of health and medicine was Julius Streicher, the gross corruptions of whose functions were by 1940 to deprive him of his party offices and power altogether. Streicher's *Deutsche Volksgesundheit aus Blut und Boden* had not been content in targeting just psychoanalysis or even just Jewish doctors as a group. The paper propagandized stridently during the two years of its existence for the virtues of the simple, clean life of the countryside, lamenting the "poisons" of modern civilization. Among these "poisons" were those allegedly pedalled by modern medicine. Inoculation was a favorite target, labeled, like so many other phenomena, a Jewish plot to sap the strength and vitality of the Aryan race. The German medical community responded to Streicher's views with almost unanimous distress, particularly in response to his attack on inoculation. In 1934 the Interior Ministry prohibited the dissemination of anti-inoculation propaganda and the following year Wagner declared that neither the NSDAP Physicians League nor the Main Office for National Health had any connection with *Deutsche Volksgesundheit aus Blut und Boden*.[25] Streicher and Wagner had already clashed over the question of possible restrictions on the "freedom to cure" enshrined in German law. Wagner wished to extend party control over all medical activities, while Streicher contended that moves to change the law were part of a Jewish conspiracy to destroy the German natural health movement.[26] By September 1935 the combined forces of Wagner's party offices and those of the Interior Ministry had succeeded in forcing Streicher's publication to fold in the process of joining one of Wagner's organizations, the Reich Study Group of Organizations for Life and Health Reform.

Streicher's capitulation demonstrated the importance of the medical mainstream in Nazi Germany, in particular doctors themselves. The new regime needed doctors to realize their biological aims and to serve their imperial ambitions. And the medical establishment, from private physicians to the staffs of university clinics and the ranks of the public health services, was eager to protect and advance its interests. The result was the early blunting of Nazi medical reform efforts.

Already in 1933, both Wagner and Hess, who was one of Wagner's patients and an enthusiastic supporter of natural medicine, were asserting that their statements and program proposals were not intended to bypass or prejudice traditional university medicine, but rather to expand the borders of medicine to include natural health theory and practice.[27] Four years later Wagner was constrained, as a result of protests in the press and from the medical profession, to "clarify" remarks he had made regarding his apparent intention to provide qualifying examinations for nonmedical healers in the party's own medical schools. His "clarification" emphasized the indispensability of a university education.[28]

By 1933 many doctors, especially younger ones whose careers had begun under the adverse economic circumstances following the First World War, supported National Socialism. The Nazis promised to lift doctors out of their economic difficulties and to rid the field of Jews and women. Such discrimination could be appealing to doctors on both ideological and economic grounds: no Jews or women would mean fewer competitors for scarce jobs as well as no Jews or women. Many conservative doctors, as we have already seen, also chafed under the restrictions of the corporate system of sickness funds administered by the national health insurance program. Before the First World War this had led doctors to form an aggressive corporate body of their own, the so-called Hartmannbund, to engage in union-like activities against the sickness funds such as work slowdowns and even strikes. But far from wishing to be classed as employees of the state, the great majority of doctors were desirous of achieving the legal status of profession. Since 1869, as a result of leadership from liberal free-market physicians in Berlin, doctors had been legally classified by the state as a trade rather than as a profession. But the growing bureaucratization of the health care system in Germany, the increasing technical sophistication of medicine, and—most importantly—the growing numbers of practitioners combined to produce significant momentum among doctors to achieve recognition as professionals. The advantages of free trade among doctors was limited to the very few, so the control over competition, standards, and fees offered by status as a profession became increasingly attractive to physicians.[29]

The Nazis delivered on their promise to get rid of Jewish doctors (though not, as it turned out from necessity, female doctors) and this, together with the passing of the Great Depression, provided enhanced job opportunities and incomes for "Aryan" physicians. In 1935 physicians' legal status was changed from that of a trade to that of a profession. At the same time, of course, the Nazis imposed political controls upon doctors that, when combined with a deterioration in educational standards and the perversion of professional ethics, represented a significant degree of what was in fact "deprofessionalization."[30] In August 1933 they created the Insurance Fund Physicians Association, which centralized the representation of 80 percent of the doctors who worked within the state health insurance system. In April 1936 the Reich Physicians Chamber assumed control over doctors in private and hospital practice under the Reich Physicians Ordinance of December 13, 1935, thereby dissolving the doctors' own corporate organizations.

Doctors are a major example of how professions in general in Nazi Germany, through varying combinations of their own initiative and compulsion by the regime, by and large displayed a functional unity in service to the Third Reich. Though this built in part upon the tradition in German professional organization of a strong role for the state, it would be a mistake to assume that this phenomenon was simply a matter of an unbroken tradition of German cultural and political authoritarianism. As we shall see in greater detail with the psychotherapists, professions, contrary to the happy assumption in the West, do not require a democratic environment in which to develop, perform, and flourish. Charles McClelland argues that there was no specifically German "fatal flaw" in this process of professionalization in Germany. Rather, corporatist characteristics inherent in the structure of modern professions combined with a series of economic disruptions and political reverses after the First World War to make National Socialism an attractive political option for many doctors. McClelland labels this process "interrupted professionalization" and not evidence for the inevitable evils of professionalization *per se* and also not peculiar to the German experience of it.[31] This interpretation differs somewhat from that of Konrad Jarausch who sees a problematic "neocorporatist" strain of professionalization across all the professions in Germany. This arose, according to Jarausch, out of a more general tradition of illiberalism and a bourgeois shift from liberalism to nationalism during the German Empire.[32] Michael Kater, on the other hand, has emphasized discrete qualities of the culture and history of modern Germany by concentrating on certain characteristics, such as political conservatism, anti-Semitism, militarism, and male chauvinism, which he argues were common among German doctors. When combined with the military disaster that befell the German Empire in the First World War and the economic and political crises that bedeviled the Weimar Republic after the war, these attitudes made many doctors receptive to the prejudices of the Nazis as well as to their promises.[33]

For their part, the Nazis were counting on the German medical community to help cultivate and police the new racial order. Psychotherapists, among others, were helped by this turn. Not only were the more threatening plans of Nazi reformers scotched, but the declared indispensability of traditional medicine—aided and abetted at Nazi urging by some natural health techniques—was affirmed. As we have seen, organized psychotherapy at this time in Germany was a movement comprised primarily of doctors and directed primarily at doctors. Like doctors in general, psychotherapists could offer the Nazis the type of practical, technical expertise they required in mobilizing and maintaining the human resources of a modern industrial society geared for rearmament and war. While natural health ideas and practices continued to exert some influence among doctors and Nazi functionaries and also contributed to the general racist climate in Germany, the chief medical roles in the program of Nazi racial hygiene—in the clinics, in the examining rooms, and in the extermination camps—were filled by university-trained physicians.[34]

Even natural health per se, once out of the hands of the more radical Nazi reformers, was not a threat to psychotherapy. In fact, German psychotherapists and the natural health movement shared two basic assumptions. The first was the proposition that the external environment powerfully affected a person's entire life. It followed that psychosocial engineering was viable not only on a hereditary basis under the new racial order—by breeding out congenital mental disorders—but that it could also be used for the proper structuring of the environment and the care of its inhabitants. That structuring incorporated certain values, which constituted the second assumption, that a purely rational, mechanistic approach to the health of the synergy of body and mind was insufficient in dealing with the natural ebb and flow of physical and psychological functions. Gerhard Wagner harped on the importance of appreciating the totality of the individual and the relationships between body and mind.[35] The care of a human being was not to be equated with the regulation of a machine, but was to incorporate a responsiveness to physical and psychological needs in a naturally elastic manner.

As a result, there was some mutual attraction and even some collaboration between psychotherapists and natural health activists and practitioners in the Third Reich. Psychotherapist Carl Haeberlin, from his post as physician at a sanitarium in Bad Nauheim, applauded the ostensible efforts of National Socialism to "win back the earth" and to reestablish the natural biological "rhythms of life" in the treating the whole person of mind and body.[36] For Haeberlin, the role of the physician was to take an active interest in the patient as a whole individual and to communicate with him or her on the basis of a shared community loyalty. The doctor would not only act as a healer but as a model of the healthy comrade in a common battle for the common good. The natural forces within each individual would thrive under, and unite with, the natural environment through the medication of a "people's doctor" (*Volksarzt*).[37] Healthy living and preventive medicine would allow the German people to flourish. The ability to maintain a natural order and rhythms of life, especially in disrupted circumstances, was celebrated by psychotherapists as one of the great strengths of Germans. For example, child psychologist Hildegard Hetzer observed among German refugees during the Sudeten crisis the importance to the well-being of children of their mothers maintaining a quiet, orderly, natural schedule of eating and sleeping.[38]

Psychotherapists in Germany also shared with the proponents of natural health a special disdain for university psychiatry. As we have seen, traditional nosological psychiatry in Germany stringently separated the individual's biological existence from the mysteries of his or her spiritual life. Psychotherapy and naturopathy both conceived of the unconscious as both biological and spiritual. In 1934 the new natural health hospital, the Rudolf-Hess-Krankenhaus in Dresden, included plans for a psychotherapeutic section under the direction of Alfred Brauchle, who had been a directing physician at Priessnitz Hospital in Berlin-Mahlow, the first natural health hospital in Germany.[39]

The high point of association between the psychotherapists under Göring came relatively early in the Third Reich, however. It occurred at the first and last congress of Wagner's Reich Study Group for a New German Medicine at Wiesbaden in 1936. Göring spoke on the theory of neurosis and Heyer on the dynamic unity of mind and body.

While these meetings were held in conjunction with those of the German Society for Internal Medicine, by 1936, as we have already seen, the Nazi movement for an alternative medical establishment was running out of steam.

The psychotherapists, too, were moving away from marginal health organizations allied with flagging Nazi party forces and toward the established bastions of the Nazified state health bureaucracy and medical profession. A month after the congress, the Göring Institute would be founded, providing a new and secure base for the protection and advancement of the psychotherapists' ideas and interests. The psychotherapists would eventually no longer feel compelled to associate their professional tenets and identity with the somewhat tenuous and sentimental nostrums prescribed by natural medicine. Hess Hospital's psychotherapist Alfred Brauchle himself would be the target of a representatively critical assessment by Heyer in the *Zentralblatt für Psychotherapie*. Brauchle's use of mass hypnosis and suggestion as a type of communal therapy (*seelische Gemeinschaftsbehandlung*) seemed to Heyer too casual and inflexible a psychotherapeutic device to be relied on so exclusively.[40] By early in the war, Cimbal would report to Göring from Bad Pyrmont that "the circle of natural medicine doctors is in a state of considerable disintegration."[41] Long before this in any case, as we shall see in the next two chapters, the psychotherapists would have courted and won other and more important allies and repelled other and more dangerous opponents in Nazi Germany.

Notes

1. Max Weinreich, *Hitler's Professors: The Part of Scholarship in Germany's Crimes against the Jewish People* (New York, 1946), p. 34.
2. Proctor, *Racial Hygiene,* p. 20.
3. Reinhard Spree, *Health and Social Class in Imperial Germany: A Social History of Mortality, Morbidity and Inequality,* trans. Stuart McKinnon and John Halliday (Oxford, 1988).
4. Gesundheitsamt Düsseldorf, Jahresgesundheitsbericht, February 28, 1933, Reg. Düsseldorf 54708, NWH; Peter Loewenberg, "The Psychohistorical Origins of the Nazi Youth Cohort," in *Decoding the Past: The Psychohistorical Approach* (New York, 1983), pp. 240–83.
5. Wehrwirtschafts-Inspektion VII, 1937, microcopy T-77, roll 248, frames 824–8, National Archives, Washington, D.C.
6. Paul Weindling, "Medicine and Modernization: The Social History of German Health and Medicine," *History of Science* 24 (1986): 277.
7. Edward Shorter, *Bedside Manners: The Troubled History of Doctors and Patients* (New York, 1985).

8. Peter Rosenberg, "The Origin and the Development of Compulsory Health Insurance in Germany," in Donald W. Light and Alexander Schuller, eds., *Political Values and Health Care: The German Experience* (Cambridge, Mass., 1986), p. 120; the four types of sickness funds were: local (*Ortskrankenkassen*), industrial (*Betriebskrankenkassen*), guild (*Innungskrankenkassen*), and miners' (*Knappschaftskassen*); see ibid., p. 112.
9. See, for example, Leonardo Conti, "Mehr Vollkornbrot! Aufruf zur Mitarbeit an der Vollkornbrotaktion," *Deutsches Ärzteblatt* 70 (1940): 310; "Coca-Cola, das grosse Fragezeichen," *Volksgesundheitswacht* 6 (1939): 127–8; and the request by the NSDAP Main Office for National Health for information on the possible deleterious effects of Coke and other soft drinks in *Deutsches Ärzteblatt* 70 (1940): 142. See also Rudolf Hess, "Arzt und Heilweise," in idem, *Reden* (Munich, 1938), pp. 259–62, the text of an address to the Twelfth International Congress of Homeopaths in Berlin on August 9, 1937; and Gerhard Wagner's introduction to Louis Grote and Alfred Brauchle, *Gespräche über Schulmedizin und Naturheilkunde* (Leipzig, 1935).
10. Franz Wirz, "Lebensbeanspruchung und Lebensgestaltung," *Hippokrates* 10 (1939): 627–31; see also Gustav Richard Heyer's review in *ZfP* 12 (1941): 358.
11. "Mit vereinigten Kräften vorwärts!" *Deutsche Volksgesundheit aus Blut und Boden* 3:12 (June 15, 1935): 5–6; and Karl Kötschau, *Zum nationalsozialistischen Umbruch in der Medizin*, p. 7.
12. Gerhard Wagner, "Neue deutsche Heilkunde," p. 419.
13. On Danzig surgeon Liek, see Kater, *Doctors Under Hitler*, pp. 227–30.
14. "Die Psychoanalyse des Juden Sigmund Freud," *Deutsche Volksgesundheit aus Blut und Boden*, 1:1 (August-September 1933): 15; italics in original.
15. Christian Jansenn, "Die Reform der Psychoanalyse durch C. G. Jung," in "Wider die Psychoanalyse," *Kritische Gänge: Literaturblatt der Berliner Börsen-Zeitung*, May 14, 1933, p. 2.
16. Dietrich Aigner, *Die Indizierung "schädlichen und unerwünschten Schrifttums" im Dritten Reich*, Sonderdruck aus dem *Archiv für Geschichte des Buchwesens* (Frankfurt a. M., 1971), pp. 937, 999–1000; see also Gudrun Zapp, "Psychoanalyse und Nationalsozialismus," p. 39.
17. Edmund Finke, "Siegmund Freud: Studien zum europäischen Nihilismus," *Deutsche Ostmark* 24 (1938): 45; see also H. Finck, "Volksgesundheit und Liebesleben," *Ziel und Weg* 4 (1934): 287–94.
18. *Zeitschrift für politische Psychologie und Sexualökonomie* 1 (1934): 59. The same political dynamics and difficulties applied among psychoanalysts in Austria: see Marie Langer, "Psychoanalyse in wessen Dienst?" *Neues Forum* 18 (1971): 39–42; Wolfgang Huber, *Psychoanalyse in Österreich seit 1933*, pp. 26–8, 17–81; and Muriel Gardiner, *Code Name "Mary": Memoirs of an American Woman in the Austrian Underground* (New Haven, 1983).
19. Käthe Dräger, "Psychoanalysis in Hitler Germany," p. 205; see also Uwe Henrik Peters, *Psychiatrie im Exil: Die Emigration der dynamischen Psychiatrie aus Deutschland 1933–1939* (Düsseldorf, 1992), pp. 11–19; and, on the entire period from 1910 to 1945, Lockot, *Die Reinigung der Psychoanalyse*, pp. 26–60. On Freud's ethically questionable stance, see Peter Loewenberg, "Foreword," in Geoffrey Cocks, *Treating Mind and Body: Essays in the History of Science, Profession, and Society* (New Brunswick, N.J., forthcoming).
20. Gerhard Wagner, Dienstanweisung Hauptamtes für Volksgesundheit der NSDAP, Munich, December 29, 1934, BDC: Parteikorrespondenz; Fritz Bartels, "Die Gesundheitsführung des deutschen Volkes"; and Dietrich Orlow, *The History of the Nazi Party*, pp. 67–70, 126, 149, 165.

21. "Der öffentliche Gesundheitsdienst," *Der Öffentliche Gesundheitsdienst* 1 (1935): chart following p. 326; and Fleck in *N.S. Gesundheitsdienst* 2 (1934): 1–3. See also Reichs- und Preussisches Ministerium des Innern, *Handbuch für das Deutsche Reich,* vol 46 (Berlin, 1936), pp. 132–3.
22. Frick to Lammers, September 1937, R 18, folder 5581. See also "Entwurf eines Gesetzes, betreffend Vereinheitlichung des Gesundheitswesens," II 1000a/28.10.33 IV, R 18, folder 5581, BA; and Heinz Spranger, "Übersicht über die Organisation und die Aufgaben der Reichsärztekammer," *Der Öffentliche Gesundheitsdienst* 2 (1936): 951.
23. "Vereinheitlichung des Gesundheitswesens—Begründung," October 1, 1934, R 43 II/717, BA, pp. 40–43. For the chancellery's position on Wagner's demands, see Aufzeichnung für die Besprechung über Fragen auf dem Gebiete des Gesundheitswesens am 18. Mai 1938, R 43 II/733, pp. 101–2. In 1937 the Foreign Ministry had complained to the chancellery that Wagner's attempts to coordinate health policy with Italy represented an intolerable party intrusion into the Reich's foreign policy: see Staatssekretär von Mackensen to Lammers, October 15, 1937, and Lammers to Haedenkamp, September 26, 1937, R 43 II/717. On the failure of "revolutionary foreign policy," see Martin Broszat, *Hitler State,* pp. 215–21.
24. See Michael H. Kater, "Doctor Leonardo Conti and His Nemesis: The Failure of Centralized Medicine in the Third Reich," *Central European History* 18 (1985): 299–325.
25. "Verbot impfgegnerischer Propaganda," *Reichs- Gesundheitsblatt* 9 (1934): 449–50; *Deutsches Ärzteblatt* 65 (1935): 133–4.
26. "Grundlagen einer Deutscher Volksgesundheit aus Blut und Boden. 12 Leitsätze," *Deutsche Volksgesundheit aus Blut und Boden* 1:1 (August-September 1933): 4; "Die Deutsche Gesellschaft zur Bekämpfung des Kurpfuschertums—eines der dunkelsten Kapitel der seitherigen Medizinal-Politik," *Deutsche Volksgesundheit aus Blut und Boden* 2:3–4 (February 1934): 20–24.
27. *Deutsches Ärzteblatt* 63 (1933): 685.
28. *Volksgesundheitswacht* 4 (1937): 256.
29. Charles E. McClelland, *The German Experience of Professionalization: Modern Learned Professions and Their Organization from the Early Nineteenth Century to the Hitler Era* (New York, 1991), pp. 78–87, 135–43, 180–85.
30. Konrad H. Jarausch, "The Perils of Professionalism: Lawyers, Teachers and Engineers in Nazi Germany," *German Studies Review* 9 (1986): 107–37.
31. Charles E. McClelland, "Modern German Doctors: A Failure of Professionalization?" in Berg and Cocks, *Medicine and Modernity,* pp. 81–97.
32. Konrad H. Jarausch, *The Unfree Professions: German Lawyers, Teachers, and Engineers, 1900–1950* (New York, 1990), pp. 22–4, 220–1.
33. Kater, *Doctors Under Hitler,* pp. 12–88.
34. Alfred Haug, *Die Reichsarbeitsgemeinschaft für eine Neue Deutsche Heilkunde (1935/36): Ein Beitrag zum Verhältnis von Schulmedizin, Naturheilkunde und Nationalsozialismus* (Husum, 1985), p. 90.
35. Gerhard Wagner, "Neue deutsche Heilkunde."
36. Carl Haeberlin, *Lebensrhythmen und Heilkunde: Entwurf einer biozentrischen ärztlichen Betrachtung* (Stuttgart, 1935).
37. Carl Haeberlin, "Lebensrhythmus und Lebensführung"; idem, "Aus der Praxis der Konstitutionstherapie," *Hippokrates* 5 (1934): 469–74. See also Vogt, "Die Behandlung nervöser und seelischer Krankheiten in Bad und Kurorten," in "Kongress für Psychotherapie in Breslau," p. 1066; Adolf Hoff, "Gesundungshäuser

für das deutsche Volk," *Hippokrates* 12 (1941): 435–7; and Walter Cimbal, *Naturgemässe Wege und Heilwege der Biochemie und Naturheilkunde* (Berlin, 1940).

38. Hildegard Hetzer, "Ordnung als eine Frage der Gesundheit," *Die Ärztin* 15 (1939): 56–7; see also Hetzer and Gertrud Noelle, "Lebensordnung und Lebensrhythmus im Kindergarten," *Zeitschrift für Kinderforschung* 47 (1939): 271–93; and Hetzer, *Kindheit und Armut: Psychologische Methoden in Armutsforschung und Bekämpfung,* 2nd ed. (Leipzig, 1937).
39. "Feierlicher Auftakt im Rudolf-Hess-Krankenhaus," *Ziel und Weg* 4 (1934): 447–9. In May 1941, after Rudolf Hess had flown to Scotland to try and make peace between England and Germany, the hospital was renamed the Gerhard-Wagner-Krankenhaus. See also Alfred Brauchle, "Seelische Naturheilkunde," *Volksgesundheitswacht* 1 (1934): 10–16; and idem, "Seelische Beeinflussung in der Gemeinschaft," *Münchener medizinische Wochenschrift* 87 (1940): 317–20.
40. Gustav Richard Heyer, review of Alfred Brauchle, *Seelische Beeinflussung in der Gemeinschaft: Ergebnisse aus der Gemeinschaftsarbeit von Naturheilkunde und Schulmedizin* (Leipzig, 1940), *ZfP* 14 (1942): 173; see also ibid., pp. 205–6.
41. Cimbal to Göring, June 25, 1941, Kl. Erw. 762/2, BA; see also Cimbal to Göring, December 5, 1940, ibid. See also Volker Roelcke, "'Zivilisationsschäden am Menschen' und ihre Behandlung: Das Projekt einer 'seelischen Gesundheitsführung' im Nationsozialismus," *Medizinhistorisches Journal* 31 (1996): 3–48.

4

Psyche and Swastika

Psychotherapists responded to the events of 1933 not only by defending their ideas and identity against both medical and political critics, but also by mounting an offensive designed to ride the wave of change that was apparently building to sweep over the German establishment. This response was strengthened by the fact that many psychotherapists believed, especially early on, that the new regime was a realization, or at least a means to a realization, of their own particular professional and cultural ideals. There was an accompanying satisfied conviction that the times were finally catching up with the revolutionary concepts that were in the process of challenging the traditional perspective on, and treatment of, the human psyche. Quite apart from explaining their motives, however, the ideals the psychotherapists expressed provided two critical elements in the development of psychotherapy as a profession during the Third Reich. The first was the contribution to a significant degree of unity among them that proved valuable during and after 1933 in seizing the opportunity for professional advance as well as in combating the dual threat that arose from Nazi health reformers and newly politicized opponents within the German medical establishment. The second element was the extent to which these ideals provided a mutually sympathetic link between leading members of the General Medical Society for Psychotherapy and various members and segments of the Nazi regime. Where psychotherapeutic ideas and rhetoric did not quite fit the apparent preferences of the Nazis, tactful alterations in form and content provided politically protective coloration.

For example, in a 1933 article Hans von Hattingberg celebrated "the incorporation of medical psychotherapy in these great events" which "move us in the spirit" of a dynamic and spiritually moving *Volksgemeinschaft.* With this sincere and strategic formulation, Hattingberg not only was able to suppress his own reservations about Nazi attacks on ideas but also to ignore the massive dangers implicit in his own Nazified appreciation of current events: "Therefore, we as doctors are able to say objectively that we cannot do without the work of that man (Freud), work which a politically aroused youth (from their standpoint quite correctly) burn."[1] But even such declarations of loyalty on the part of psychotherapists could meet with significant hostility from Nazi sources. Hattingberg's essay was one of a number of articles from the *Zentralblatt* from 1933 that were collected in a volume under Göring's editorship in a 1934 volume entitled *Deutsche Seelenheilkunde,* a book that was intended to present a new German psychotherapy (*neue deutsche Seelenheilkunde*) in the spirit of National Socialism. However, *Ziel und Weg,* the journal of the NSDAP Physicians League, reviewed *Deutsche Seelenheilkunde* most unfavorably. It was obvious from the essays contained in the volume, the reviewer wrote, that neither protestations of loyalty nor citations from the works of acceptable German authors on the subject of the unconscious could hide the fact that psychotherapy was still to a great extent dependent on the teachings of Jews Freud and Adler.[2] As this particular review perhaps indicates, the psychotherapists often faced various combinations of threats along these lines: a Nazi who hated Jews, a doctor who hated psychotherapy, or a Nazi doctor who hated Jews and psychotherapy.

Not only Freudians, therefore, had to adopt a defensive and opportunistic stance. Even psychotherapists sympathetic to the new regime had to protest their loyalty and that of their ideas in the face of Nazi criticism. That the new order was not a monolith is clear, as we will see below, from what was in fact a divergence of Nazi views on *Deutsche Seelenheilkunde.* But especially in the early years psychotherapists had to scramble to advertise not only their potential utility to the new regime but also the ideological compatibility of their ideas. Even as late as 1938, for example, *Ziel und Weg* criticized Hattingberg's *Über die Liebe* (1936) for its "perverse" notions of what love should be.[3] The psychotherapists' response to—and preemption of—such criticism often took the form of the "cosmetization" of language, that is, the appropriation of Nazi terminology in place of more ambiguous or objectionable wording. As we have seen, the association of their discipline with "Jewish" psychoanalysis was a real danger. After Freud's books had been burned at the end of May 1933, Göring wrote to Cimbal that the terms "psychoanalysis" and "individual psychology" would have to be dropped from the program of an upcoming conference; the latter, Adlerian term could perhaps be replaced by "applied character science."[4] But psychotherapists, among others, were also at an advantage in this regard since they could exploit Nazi manipulation and trivialization of such loaded ethnocentric words as *Seele* and *Charakter*.[5] For example, presumably to avoid such problems and to attract readers among the members of the heavily Nazified medical profession, Johannes Heinrich Schultz in 1936 altered the title of a handbook on psychotherapy designed for medical specialists and general practitioners, which had already appeared in four editions between 1919 and 1930, from *Die seelische Krankenbehandlung* to *Ziele und Wege der seelischen Krankenbehandlung,* so as to include a variation on the title of the Nazi journal *Ziel und Weg*. (Significantly, as we shall see, Schultz obviously felt secure enough by the time of the issuance of the next edition in 1943 to revert to the original title.) Even party membership was no guarantee of security from criticism, as any combination of ideology, professional competition, and personal conflict could generate potentially dangerous criticism. As we shall see below, the chief victim of this among the psychotherapists was Walter Cimbal, whose party membership apparently resulted in the creation of some powerful party enemies for him.

Individual psychotherapists of course had choices, choices revealing of the structural conditions under which they lived and worked. Responses to National Socialism in the medical profession as a whole ranged from emigration, particularly of course the forced emigration of Jews, to joyful collaboration. Most individual reactions, especially over time, fell somewhere in between. Psychiatrist Ernst Kretschmer opted for withdrawal into the relative backwaters of a university clinic. John Rittmeister, who returned from exile in Switzerland to become director of the Göring Institute's outpatient clinic, died in the resistance. There were degrees and styles of collaboration: Johannes Heinrich Schultz, always "correct," maintained a rigidly professional and apolitical profile while promoting psychotherapy in the context of his own militant German patriotism. Gustav Richard Heyer, possessed of a more volatile personality, joined the Nazi party in 1937 out of what seems a mixture of opportunism, some degree of ideological agreement, and an altruistic desire to effect the values inherent in psychotherapy. While perhaps only 5 percent of the members of the Göring Institute joined the party,[6] the percentage of party members among the leading psychotherapists of the day was much higher: Of forty-seven of these, seventeen, or around 36 percent, joined the NSDAP between 1930 and 1938 and only fourteen were not members of at least one of the auxiliary party organizations (*Gliederungen*) for doctors, social workers, teachers, and university students and professors.[7] Most of the party members joined in the rush of enthusiasm and opportunism that prevailed in early 1933 and thus fell into the heavily populated category of the "fallen of March" (*Märzgefallene*), or those who joined after the Nazi victory in the compromised national elections of March 1933. A few others joined in 1937, when party membership, after having been closed in 1934 to avoid further dilution by opportunists, was reopened to desirable classes of applicants such as bureaucrats and professionals.

The general enthusiasm of 1933 also had its special effect on "unpolitical German" tendencies among psychotherapists. Psychoanalyst Werner Kemper, for one, admitted that had he been "political," he might well have joined the Nazi party in 1933.[8] Enthusiasm could also be intensified by the fear used by the Nazis alongside propaganda to compel obedience. If not enthusiasm or trepidation, then patriotism—especially after 1939 and after the defeat at Stalingrad in 1943—could and did stifle criticism. From the beginning, moreover, Hitler's government could be conveniently regarded as legal. And though the bloody purge of Ernst Röhm's SA in 1934 might have raised questions about the continuing propensity to murderous violence on the part of the regime, the action also seemed to mark the defeat of party radicals.[9] The purge thus reinforced the equally convenient conviction of many Germans that if the Nazis were not to be temporary, at least their extreme rhetoric and behavior was. The perceived and propagandized image of Hitler being above politics also appealed to a large number of intelligent Germans distressed and disgusted by what they saw as the materialistic and ineffective experiment with Western democracy in the form of the Weimar Republic.[10] The Nazi party, its membership and support socially and politically heterogeneous, could be seen by contrast to represent a national rather than a purely political movement.[11] It might have made a difference had psychotherapists and other German professionals, intellectuals, and academics said "*nein*" or at least "*ohne mich*" ("without me"). And even had such actions not stopped or slowed Hitler, this would have been the right thing to do. Hardly any psychotherapists did this right thing, but what they did do reveals some striking and surprising features of the social history of Nazi Germany.

The opportunity not only for survival but also for professional development under the protection of the Göring name made any decision in favor of a higher morality even more difficult. The ideal of professional service to patients and society, reinforced by any number of small daily achievements in office and clinic, also obscured any individual contribution to larger, distant, and inexorable wartime inhumanities. Moreover, although the Nazis made much of the "coordination" (*Gleichschaltung*) of German society from the top down, the often chaotic nature of their governance and the vagueness of their programs permitted and even encouraged "autocoordination" from the bottom and middle up. As we will see in the next chapter, the psychotherapists displayed a significant degree of organizational initiative in the early months and years of the Nazi regime. Such a phenomenon indicates a degree of choice, which renders more individuals more culpable in terms of operational support for the Nazi regime. At the same time, it also meant that the psychotherapists, like other established and aspiring professionals in the Third Reich, exercised greater control over the practice and organization of their discipline. The result was, as we have mentioned before, a significant degree of functional unity of experts in service to the regime. This produced significant continuity with preceding and succeeding developments in Germany. And, once again, it demonstrates that modernization does not simply mean enlightened progress or that technical or professional performance requires a democratic system of politics.

With the exception of their exclusionary racial and political policies, the Nazis offered no genuine ideological criteria by which ideas, positions, or disciplines could be accepted or rejected. Indeed, once represented by someone with the ability to command attention, a discipline, group, or cause was invariably judged by both its inherent usefulness to the regime as well as advantage it offered to a Nazi patron or ally. This hardly means that Nazi ideals played no role in the functioning of the Nazi state. In fact, Nazi racism was both a cause of, and a complement to, the venal utilitarianism that was apparent within the bureaucracy of the Third Reich. Gross racial distinctions took the place of thought in the highest reaches of the Nazi universe and this racism permeated the society.[12] The racism of the Nazis, however, also imputed internal qualities to the "Master Race," thus opening the way for German psychotherapists to argue for the necessity of the professional cultivation of such characteristics. The Nazi belief in racial superiority based on inherent physical and psychological characteristics tended to disparage any sort of mere institutional reform as superficial and unnecessary. Nazi pragmatism was not a purely rational process of *Realpolitik* in the *absence* of ideology, but was in significant measure a *function* of incoherent and irrational racial fantasies. What had passed away after the first three or four years of Nazi rule was not the awful racism of Hitler and his cronies which eventually culminated in the Holocaust. Rather, the casualties in the Nazi takeover of the institutions of German government and society were the party activists, whose enthusiasms, feuds, and ambitions generated a blizzard of rhetoric, plans, and organizations in the first months and years of the Third Reich. Before they were eclipsed by war planners and Nazi technocrats, however, these party forces helped create an environment in which relative outsiders like the psychotherapists could make inroads on a shaken German establishment.

These dynamics supplemented the terror that for most Germans hovered only in the background by also encouraging doubt over not belonging to compelling movements of fellow countrymen, if not "racial comrades."[13] At the same time, the vectors of modern industrialism and consumerism combined with the Nazi destruction of traditional German social solidarities to produce an atomization of civilian society that in encouraging competition on the basis of productivity "foster[ed] the egotism of both individuals and institutions."[14] Most of these dynamics can be teased out of the following particularly naive and opportunistic observations from the ranks of physicians arguing for psychotherapy: Werner Zabel, later director of a natural health sanitarium in Berchtesgaden, went so far in 1934 as to aver that the new Nazi Ministry of Propaganda was an affirmation of the need for suggestive methods of psychotherapy on a national basis![15] Even those who were willing to act on their grave doubts about Hitler and the Nazis lived with laming illusion. Perhaps people who are dedicated to the treatment of mental illness are even more susceptible to such desperate hope: Georg Groddeck entertained to his death in 1934 that if he could just talk to Hitler, he could effect some change in the Führer.[16]

Beyond the vagaries of their initial reactions to National Socialism, in any case, the psychotherapists' idealistic and practical concern for professional survival, identity, and development was closely and advantageously linked with the cultural and philosophical values of the Romantic tradition in medicine that also informed much of what passed for philosophy in Nazi ranks. Matthias Heinrich Göring recalled in 1940 what he believed was the psychotherapeutic perspective that had been adopted and advertised by the new regime in 1933:

> The Reich Health Leader [Leonardo Conti] had at that time already expressed the view that the health and thereby the productivity of the individual was dependent on the physician viewing and treating him as a whole. To this whole as well belongs the unconscious in man. Our society sees as one of its principal assignments to call out to doctors, educators, and all fellow-countrymen who are concerned with human guidance, not lastly those in the armed forces and in the economy. Do not forget the unconscious! Do not think that you are grasping the whole man when you close your eyes to the unconscious![17]

It was with such rhetoric and such substance that psychotherapists in the first years of the Third Reich both parried criticism and promoted their discipline.

Fritz Künkel's response to the Third Reich was both typical and atypical for a man of his background. In 1920 Künkel had married a young Jewish woman named Ruth Löwengard. Although she died at the end of the decade, Künkel's reaction to Nazi rule was complicated by the three children their union had produced; he managed to get the children out of Germany only in 1938. It was this situation, coupled with his unpolitical nature, that, according to his son, prompted Künkel to advertise a certain enthusiasm for the ideals of the new regime in articles and books he wrote between 1933 and 1939. At the same time, however, Künkel's notion of "community" represented more than just a defensive or a rhetorical response to National Socialism. The second edition of *Grundzüge der politischen Charakterkunde,* which appeared in 1934, demonstrates, beginning with the word "political" in its title, the combination of satisfied—if oftentimes anxious—optimism and skillful pandering that characterized most of the early published work of psychotherapists in the Third Reich. In the introduction to the new edition, Künkel referred as follows to a discussion of the community as the fulfillment of individual lives that had appeared in the first edition of the book in 1931: "In some sections it has sufficed to substitute the present tense for the future one, since the formerly impending development has in the meantime been realized."[18] Men like Künkel could and did adopt an air of traditional moral and intellectual superiority toward a movement whose very rudeness confirmed the naïve impression and rationalization of such intellectuals that it was their ideas and influence that were coming to fruition and that would dominate crude political arrivistes. He joined the NSV and on at least one occasion, in 1933, pointed out to the authorities the crucial family affiliation of his official mentor Göring.[19] Künkel, unlike a number of his colleagues, did not express or manifest any explicitly anti-Semitic sentiments in his writing. His response to Hitler was of a more elevated nature born of fear for his children and some deeply held religious and professional beliefs. Still, what he had to say represented public support for the regime, whatever its actual effects on that regime or on people in general.

Ever since the First World War Künkel had proselytized vigorously the concept of the "we" relationship between individual and community as a sign of cultural maturity. With this perspective, he was particularly susceptible and responsive to Nazi exhortations about the necessity for a sense of collective and individual mission that would prove both the viability of the racial community and the character of each of its members. As a contemporary jurist put it, "[t]he idea of community, the idea of the 'we' as the totality of a people, comprises the political power of the Führer-state."[20] For Künkel, humanity had evolved from the primitive "we" of feudalism through individualism to the mature *Wir* of Germanic northern Europe. Following Rousseau, Künkel believed that a Führer embodied the will of the people not in any institutional manner but on an intuitive, organic basis. The function of psychotherapy, therefore, was to ensure the equation of health and loyalty; as Künkel wrote in 1934: "We are specialists in the management of transgression, and that means at the same time that we are specialists in the care of hypocrisy, of self-deception and treason against the *Volksgemeinschaft*."[21]

Künkel clearly drew some inspiration as well as advantage from the advent of National Socialism. He called in 1934 for the "we-ish [*wirhaften*] reconstruction of the German people,"[22] and in 1936, together with his wife, argued for the need to strengthen the national character to meet the demands of geography and history: "The German inherits all the heavy burdens that arise from the position of his fatherland in the middle of Europe, the indefensibility of his borders, and the peculiarity of his history."[23] As a former Adlerian, he believed this strengthening of character had to begin with the proper environment for the child, created first and foremost by the family and then by the school, with the assistance, if need be, of the psychotherapist or the educational counselor schooled in psychology and psychotherapy. The importance of emotional environment was a point stressed by all psychotherapists in the Third Reich, as we shall see in the next chapter, in their conflict with psychiatrists espousing and exploiting Nazi racial biology. For their part, the psychotherapists could exploit not only the general Nazi mobilization of experts in service to the state, but also the regime's interest in the active "care and control" (*Betreuung*) of the populace from childhood through school and into adulthood. In 1936 Künkel observed that neurosis actually thrived in advanced civilizations and among pure races, that it was thus the result of environment and not heredity. The family thus constituted the vital ground on which the continuing mental health and vitality of the nation could be built:

> The great decision as to whether this valuable human material will be rendered viable, valiant, and creative, or broken, cowardly, and sick, at the disposal of the state and the nation, as to whether the *Volk* will be rich in creative spirits or rich in hysterics and obsessive neurotics, this decision lies in the hands of the parents alone.[24]

Leonhard Seif, like his fellow Adlerian Künkel, was able to exploit the theme of community in the radically changed political circumstances of 1933. His contribution to Göring's 1934 edition of essays from the *Zentralblatt* was entitled "Volksgemeinschaft und Neurose" and was congruent with the Nazi insistence that the interests of the individual be subordinated to those of the community. Citing Nietzsche and Clausewitz, Seif declared that while politics created the institutional framework of a *Volksgemeinschaft*, pedagogy and psychotherapy would work to ensure the education of each child to his or her life tasks within the national community.[25] The consistent theme in Seif's work during the Third Reich was that "[e]ducation or psychotherapy is the task of forming a vital community [*Lebensgemeinschaft*], a 'we' relationship."[26] That Seif, however, saw the virtues of community in an ethically and practically wider context than that of the generally crabbed responses of psychotherapists to National Socialism is revealed at the end of his 1934 essay in *Deutsche Seelenheilkunde*: He cites not Nietzsche, Prinzhorn, or Clausewitz, but rather Kant on the formation of the true national community as a means toward the ideal world community. This was an invocation very much in the Enlightenment spirit of Seif's chief mentor, Adler, from whom he had by now drawn away.[27] Seif was not a party member, but was a member of the NSDAP Physicians League and the NSV, presumably as a means of ensuring the survival of educational counseling service in Munich.[28] As we shall see in chapter 10, his association with Adler would generate some criticism of him from high Nazi party offices.

Gustav Richard Heyer publicly greeted the advent of Hitler with enthusiasm. With typical personal and professional assertiveness, he declared in 1935: "How could health in the Germany of Adolf Hitler be contemplated without psychotherapy?"[29] Although he did not become a party member until 1937, colleagues remember him as a staunch supporter of the regime from the beginning, one of those who joined up out of conviction that the Nazis spoke to some deep sense of identity within the German people and nation. Among these, both Fritz Riemann, a Munich psychoanalyst, and Wolfgang Kranefeldt, a fellow Jungian who worked in Berlin from 1935 to 1942, recall Heyer as an enthusiastic Nazi who proudly wore a party lapel pin. Lucy Heyer-Grote, Heyer's first wife, claims, however, that Heyer became disillusioned with the Nazis and came to wear the pin on the inside of his lapel for use only when absolutely necessary. In general, though, Heyer, as recalled by his colleagues of the time, was a politically dangerous and combative individual, a characteristic that reportedly led to a potentially dangerous conflict in the early 1930s with one of his patients, Rudolf Hess.[30]

Both of Heyer's wives have claimed that Heyer was no racist. Heyer-Grote asserts that he joined the Nazi party only to work within it for improvement. Zoe Heyer maintains that her husband joined only after long reflection beginning as far back as 1930, and then, as with his approach to everything, did it wholeheartedly.[31] It is true that most intellectuals in Germany were probably too smart to believe in Nazi racist cant and in fact, were, as we have noted, busily overestimating their own influence while also rationalizing their actions. But at the same time we cannot ignore an intellectual and cultural heritage that incorporated, among other things, an ethnocentric and anti-Semitic bias. We also cannot ignore the willingness of such individuals as Heyer to engage in racist rhetoric out of whatever combination of conviction, fear, and opportunism. And we cannot turn a blind eye to the willingness even of intellectuals to be swept up in the popular excitement of the moment, a problem arguably at its worst during the interwar period in Europe.[32] As early as 1935, Heyer could write with both Jungian and Germanic fervor:

> We understand from Germany's most recent past what it is that the Führer appeals to: to fantasy, the emotions, to the irrational side of the people. And when we read his speeches and listen to them, what convinces, what carries us along, is not rational argument, but the image.[33]

Heyer's Jungian suspicion of the alleged materialism of psychoanalysis was certainly informed by anti-Semitic stereotypes. Such stereotypes made it easier for Heyer to dissociate psychotherapy from psychoanalysis in the Third Reich. In 1930 Heyer had written in an article in the *Münchener medizinische Wochenschrift* that Freud, while decisively influenced by the individualism of the era, had spearheaded the fight against medicine without a soul. Two years later, Heyer published the first edition of what was to become one of his major works, *Der Organismus der Seele,* and again acknowledged Freud's contribution: "Every confrontation with the venerable master demands a gesture of respect, appreciation, and admiration." The second edition, which appeared in 1937, however, displayed quite another stance: "Every confrontation with Sigmund Freud, each sharp criticism, nonetheless demands the acknowledgment of his historic contribution." Clearly Heyer understood the importance of Freud's work and the protection of the Göring name allowed him to express this grudging appreciation of psychoanalysis. But other references to Freud in the book are more ethically problematic: In 1932 Freud was a "master," but by 1937 he had been demoted to a "teacher"; his "sexual democracy" now constituted "psychological Bolshevism." While formerly Heyer had criticized Freud for a tendency to distort (*verzerren*) his intuition by "rational and concrete formulations," he now degraded Freud's intuition into "comprehension" and underlined the new and negative aspect he perceived by repeating it: "rationally and concretely indicated, or rather, distorted" ("*rational und konkretisch dar- bzw. entstellte*"). Heyer also simply eliminated a number of references to Freud, Adler, and other Jewish psychoanalysts and philosophers whose names had appeared in the 1932 edition. Heyer's treatment of Zionism also underwent a marked transformation. From being labeled "romantic-regressive," Zionism was now relegated to being part of a racial critique which suggested that it could solve the problem of Jewish rootlessness by establishing a Jewish homeland, a concept that, of course, also echoed the Nazi prewar aim of expelling the Jews from Europe:

> The Jew especially suffers from the unconnectedness of his blood—the "race"—with the soul of the spiritual world in which he lives. Zionism attempts a solution through the denial and abandonment of the latter, an experiment whose result is yet to be learned.[34]

In general, because of his philosophical orientation as well as his professional situation, Heyer was adept at using Nazi terms like *Brauchtum* ("custom") and *Betreuung* in order to deflect criticism and curry acceptance in the Third Reich.[35]

Of all the members of the psychotherapeutic community in Germany who had a chance at a career in the Third Reich, non-Jewish psychoanalysts, as we have seen, faced the most difficult challenge. Carl Müller-Braunschweig, one of the very few members of the Berlin Psychoanalytic Institute who remained active in the field in Nazi Germany, published a defense of psychoanalysis in a Nazi weekly in 1933, describing it as a technique which in the proper hands transformed weaklings and "asocials" into heroic and productive members of society.[36] In saying this, however, when and where he said it, Müller-Braunschweig was validating the same sort of language the Nazis used to describe the Jewish patients and practitioners of psychoanalysis.

Harald Schultz-Hencke, who had broken with the Berlin Psychoanalytic Institute late in the previous decade, used the revolutionary change (*Umbruch*) of 1933, as he himself described it, to systematize his own thought in a way he would describe fully and somewhat obscurely in 1940 in *Der gehemmte Mensch.*[37] His deviation from Freudian thought sought to unify the various schools of psychotherapy, but it did so in a way revealing of the continuities between certain of Schultz-Hencke's ideas and the ideals of the Nazi regime. In 1934 Schultz-Hencke wrote an essay for the *Zentralblatt,* which also appeared in *Deutsche Seelenheilkunde* later that year, entitled "Die Tüchtigkeit als psychotherapeutisches Ziel." The essay, echoing Müller-Braunschweig's arguments in both language and substance, argued that the goal of psychotherapy was to free the powers of fitness and proficiency within the individual, to allow patients to overcome the various physical and psychological inhibitions, and thus to allow them to lead productive and happy lives. This emphasis on therapy over analysis was in both the neo-Freudian and German Romantic traditions, but Schultz-Hencke, obviously responding sincerely to the ethos and opportunity of the hour, went further, contending that the achievement of this kind of psychological health was a duty each individual owed to his community and that its maintenance was the corresponding duty of the psychotherapist.[38]

For Schultz-Hencke in this 1934 essay, life goals were determined by ideology, not by science. In the case of psychotherapy, he defined health in terms of blood, strong will, proficiency, discipline (*Zucht und Ordnung*), community, heroic bearing, and physical fitness. Schultz-Hencke also took the opportunity in 1934 to criticize psychoanalysis for providing an unfortunate tendency toward the exculpation of the criminal. He faulted it, too, for the notion that religion was a product of the Oedipus complex, and that, as a discipline, it presumed to offer its own distinct pedagogy. All of these criticisms were particularly well received by one Nazi reviewer of *Deutsche Seelenheilkunde*. Schultz-Hencke also averred that psychoanalysis was the study of the inhibited individual, and consequently should be renamed desmology, its method that of desmolyse, from the Greek word for "chain."[39] Schultz-Hencke clearly saw an opportunity to deflect the type of criticism of those associated in Nazi minds with "Jewish" psychoanalysis to which, as we saw in chapter 3, he himself had been subjected. But he also saw the new regime as an opportunity to realize personal and professional ideals that had already been formulated and pursued. In doing this, he displayed neither pure opportunism nor simple conversion and continuing allegiance to Nazi views. In his case, as in Künkel's, perhaps the fact of physical disability or weakness played a psychological role in the evolution of the style and substance of an intellectual position that fed in unhealthy ways on the Nazi obsession with strength.

As we have already seen, Hans von Hattingberg greeted National Socialism with considerable enthusiasm in 1933. He did not join the NSDAP, taking only, in light of his ambition for a university teaching position, the prudent step of joining the Nazi University Lecturers League. He was also quite willing, out of both nationalism and professional opportunism, to place psychotherapy in service to the state. He expressed this lucidly in 1936 when, in comparing the "individualistic" liberal ethos of psychoanalysis to contemporary German psychotherapy, he claimed that "[t]oday state morality is more important to us than sexual morality."[40] By contrast, fellow psychotherapist Wladimir Eliasberg, who left Germany in 1933, soon warned the same year from Vienna that a profession had a responsibility to impose its standards on state policy and not vice versa.[41]

Like so many of his colleagues, Hattingberg's Romantic emphasis on the "religious" depths of the human psyche and his conservative nationalist perspective were stimulated by the advent of National Socialism. But in his enthusiasm for the new order, Hattingberg ignored the irrational and violent features of Nazi ideology. This was, to say the least, ironic, since in his January address in 1933 he had set his notion of spirit (*Geist*) against what he saw as a new and disturbing trend toward the elevation of instinct, the irrational, and the "blood."[42] Although his subsequent essay "Neue Richtung, Neue Bindung," which appeared in the *Zentralblatt* and in Göring's *Deutsche Seelenheilkunde* in 1934, was a relatively restrained restatement of his remarks to the Berlin Medical Society on January 11, 1933, as time went on Hattingberg became more radical in expressing a philosophy heavily influenced by the Romantic tradition in German psychology and by the applications he saw in the "new" Germany. This was, perhaps, a natural outcome of the freedom that he felt after 1933 to turn from criticizing the leaders of what he saw as an increasingly divided psychoanalytic movement to developing, like Schultz-Hencke, his own theory and practice.

Hattingberg's fellow independent Johannes Heinrich Schultz's response to National Socialism was typically measured. He was a member from 1933 to 1935 of only the innocuous Nazi Motor Corps for those who owned automobiles. And he did this, he said, only because of professional threats stemming from his first wife having been Jewish.[43] Schultz, however, was not without conservative nationalist cultural convictions that were in fact stimulated by the Nazi mobilization of Germany. In his professional concern with the psychological problems of individuals living in an industrial society, he tended to wax enthusiastic over the virtues of the natural life of strength and virtue within a national community. For Schultz, though, the issue was not the Romantic business of converting an urban society into a rural one, but the practical one of mobilizing medical resources to soothe and strengthen the mental resources of the population. It was both as a physician and a patriot that he wrote of the necessity for cooperation between educators and psychotherapists in strengthening German youth during the "nervous time" spawned by modern civilization.[44] And, as we shall see in chapter 9, his training as a psychiatrist would lead him during the war to echo Nazi policies for the "euthanasia" of those suffering from severe and "incurable" conditions.

Like Schultz, Werner Achelis was concerned about the deleterious effects on humans of modern civilization. Unlike Schultz, however, he joined the NSDAP in 1933 and was also a member of the Nazi Students League and the NSV.[45] His primary activity during the Third Reich was to propagate his own neoconservative critique of a materialistic Western civilization, and to celebrate the cultural revolution he saw sweeping the "new" Germany up into an ultimate "world-historical" role. Achelis saw the ravages of civilization everywhere, but he rejected Rousseau's "return to nature" as a counsel of pessimism and resignation. The alternative, he believed, was National Socialism: the acceptance of civilization's strengths (expertise, division of labor, organization) along with an accelerated development of the "natural forces" within the individual. For Achelis, the Nazi heroes of 1933 arrayed against the pernicious doctrines of 1789 represented a new ethic of human existence:

> In the contemporary battle cry of blood and soil, there exists . . . the great inspiration that there is only one way to recovery: back to nature, not in the original sense of Romantic flight from the world, or in the pseudo-realistic sense of an artificial reconstruction of relationships one construes to be natural, but in the sense of back to nature in ourselves![46]

Achelis posited a balance of rational and irrational to be struck within each individual and within the *Volk* as a whole through the unity of its members on a deep, unconscious level. It was this integral, abiding sense of community that would provide the resources for productive lives, which, in turn, would further the interests of the *Volksgemeinschaft*. While the demand for productivity and performance was for Achelis the cause of individual isolation, ruthless competition, and physical and mental disability in modern urban society, the same qualities within the Germanic racial community were celebrated as the result of shared cultural strengths. The rootedness of every person in the community would nourish the nation's productive capacities. Only depth psychology could illuminate and cultivate such processes through the expert yet empathic application of its therapeutic theory. And at the highest organizational level of the community, such therapeutic suggestion manifested itself as propaganda: "That after which propaganda strives is spiritual guidance. Existing natural impulses must be coordinated and blended."[47] For Achelis—naïvely—obedience and common interest were not to be achieved by coercion, but by applying shared values, values to be articulated by the government and embodied in a leader, whether family doctor or head of state.

Walter Cimbal was another psychotherapist who openly welcomed the new regime. He joined the party in March 1933; he told Göring later that year that he only waited that long because his wife was a leader in the democratic German People's Party (DVP) and was not sympathetic to the Nazis. He described himself in a letter to Göring as "unpolitical" but a "party man" (*Parteimensch*) who was heavily involved with the activities of the NSDAP. He claimed to have contacts in the medical bureaucracy at the Brown House, Nazi party headquarters in Munich. The head of Hitler's chancellery office, Heinrich Lammers, was an old student society friend ("*Bundesbruder*"). Cimbal boasted to Göring that he had always been a racist, was a Sudetenlander, and his two oldest boys were both in the SA and in medical school.[48] Given all of this, it was no surprise that his essay in *Deutsche Seelenheilkunde* in 1934 closed with a warm recommendation of Hitler's *Mein Kampf*.[49] In that same essay Cimbal depicted the German people as bound spiritually and historically to the land: "All of us as Germans are basically farmers to a certain degree. When we administer an office we cultivate it like the field on which our forefathers lived."[50] This sentiment exploited the Nazi emphasis, especially early on in the Third Reich, on the healthful "organic" basis of the German *Volksgemeinschaft*. In this context, Cimbal in turn emphasized the importance of the family as the basic productive and educational unit. While in fact the family would not only be supplemented but largely supplanted by the state in Nazi Germany,[51] Cimbal opportunistically argued that the state should cultivate the family and thus the psychological health of its most vital resource, its children.[52]

As we saw in chapter 3, Cimbal was one of those whose ideas and rhetoric to some extent anticipated Nazi tropes and trappings. But with the advent of the Third Reich, Cimbal, like other psychotherapists, was also constrained to "cosmetize" his terms and concepts in order to avoid association with "Jewish" psychoanalysis. This represented a mix of a great deal of new prudence, some old prejudice, and even older German Romantic holism. Cimbal spoke of psychoanalysis as a "dismemberment of the soul" (*Zergliederung der Seele*) to be avoided in psychotherapeutic settings: "A ground rule for all of these situations is that the psychological drilling machine [*seelische Bohrmaschine*] which had been formulated in the psychoanalytic method must be avoided."[53] It was an attack from a psychiatrist, however, that demonstrates the lengths to which Cimbal went to distance "German" psychotherapy from "Jewish" psychoanalysis and to win approval for himself and his discipline from the Nazi regime. In 1936 an article in *Der Öffentliche Gesundheitsdienst* painted Cimbal as a closet psychoanalyst trying to hide his allegiance to Freud by quoting from *Mein Kampf.* Cimbal's invention of such terms as "prenatal education" and "nordicization" of Jews through psychotherapy, the author complained, were designed to obscure a psychoanalytic emphasis on the malleable environment in place of immutable heredity.[54] The book in dispute was the second edition of *Die Neurosen des Kindes- und Jugendalters* (1935). Besides "coordinating" its language, Cimbal had expanded the first edition, which had appeared in 1931 and included a subtitle referring to learning difficulties. Most significantly, he added to the beginning a separate book published the year before which bore an advantageous title referring to character, race, and education (*Charakterentwicklung des gesunden und nervösen Kindes, ihre Beeinflussung durch Rasse und Erziehung*).

Cimbal's position was complicated, however, by his political difficulties. After the war he claimed that he joined the party in May 1933 in order to win an "amnesty" for his wife from political detention. Elisabeth Cimbal had been a politically active democrat who had generated a long list of enemies in the NSDAP. Chief among these was no less than the Gauleiter of Schleswig-Holstein, Hinrich Lohse. Given the significant Nazification among doctors, Cimbal's professional prospects became rather dim. By September he had been forced to resign his post at the University Hospital in Hamburg-Eppendorf. By 1938 Cimbal, together with his wife, had left Hamburg for a job at a sanitarium in Bad Pyrmont.[55] According to Cimbal after the war, his writings had always been "pacifistic" and "anti-fascist" while both he and his wife "between 1930 and 1945 moved ever more in active anti-fascist circles."[56] While it is clear that Cimbal was victimized by enemies within the Nazi establishment, his philosophical and professional proximity to Nazism is no less clear. Cimbal was one of those who, like psychotherapist Kurt Gauger (see chapter 6), discovered in the Third Reich that neither sincere nor insincere ideological agreement with the Nazis guaranteed political acceptance or professional success.

Like Cimbal, Carl Haeberlin also joined the Nazi party in 1933. He was also a member of the Nazi Physicians League and was one of those German psychotherapists whose work was inspired by the philosopher Ludwig Klages. Klages was a prominent figure in the turn-of-the-century revival of vitalism in Germany. Klages celebrated life and instinct over civilization and reason, seeing "mind as adversary of the soul" (*Geist als Widersacher der Seele*). Character for Klages was the innate but variable balance between spirit and soul in contrast to the modern emergence of the ego and the personality. Klages' life philosophy (*Lebensphilosophie*) was embraced by at least some Nazis as an affirmation of German cultural superiority.[57] Haeberlin believed that the work of Klages and Hans Prinzhorn was the foundation upon which a German psychology and psychotherapy could be established. In his essay for Göring's *Deutsche Seelenheilkunde* he used both Klages and Prinzhorn to support his contention that the Germanic triad of life, blood, and people was superior to the Western ideal of freedom, equality, and brotherhood. Like Prinzhorn, Haeberlin believed that Freud had to be transposed into a heroic German tradition: The concept of instinct must be accepted, but Freud's "analysis, destruction, reduction and devaluation of human deeds," what Haeberlin saw as a "logocentric" world view, had to be replaced by a "biocentric" ideal he saw at the center of Klages' thought.[58]

Beliefs such as these, of course, had little to do with the actual intentions or effects of National Socialism, but such rhetoric did allow for the forging of some significant alliances between the psychotherapists and agencies and individuals inside and outside of the Nazi party. In general, for the Nazis the state existed as an extension of what they regarded as nature, ensuring the well-being of its inhabitants for the purpose of cultivating their potential for its use.[59] Psychotherapy could contribute to this cultivation of a healthy spirit (*Gesinnung*), a term dear to the Nazi heart and for this reason singled out for mention by Achelis at the psychotherapeutic congress at Breslau in 1935.[60] The contribution to the psychological health of the race would be a vital complement to the fashioning of strong bodies within the Hitler Youth, the Reich Labor Service, the SA, and other party and government organizations.[61] The Nazis regarded the health services as a chief means to the preparation of the German people for war. In the words of Reich Physician Leader Gerhard Wagner, "[o]nly a people that is physically, spiritually, and mentally healthy and able to defend its right to existence with all available means will achieve a worthy and respected place in the world."[62] Health policy in this view was not so much a matter of care of the sick but of care of the healthy. Such a policy was the necessary complement to the Nazi campaign to eradicate the "useless eaters" of the "incurably" ill and insane along with the biological enemies of the Aryan race, most notably the Jews.

Psychotherapy, or as it was Germanically renamed during the first years of Nazi rule, *neue deutsche Seelenheilkunde,* had a role to play in this process. The psychotherapist was to be less of an analyst and more of an active agent of the community, leading his or her patients to healthy, productive lives. The partnership between doctor and patient was to involve the joyful exercise of authority on the part of the former and a willing subordination—what Prinzhorn had called "pedagogical love"—on the part of the latter. As one physician put it: "Despite the importance of analysis, spiritual guidance and the active cooperation of the patient represent the best way to overcome individual mental problems and to subordinate them to the requirements of the *Volk* and the *Gemeinschaft*."[63] Such psychological leadership (*Seelenführung*) demanded the psychotherapist's personal involvement in the dysfunction of the patient, a concern for the whole person, and a commitment to bring the patient into harmony with the community: "The personality is not a goal in and of itself; it is by nature linked to the community and is dependent in its functioning on its conformity to the demands of the community: profession, love, comradeship."[64]

This new officially enforced ethos was intended to constitute a clean break with the recent past in Germany. According to the Nazis, the German ideals of community had been dissolved under the Weimar Republic into crass and divisive social conflict. Conservative and Nazi critics labeled Weimar a "system" to reflect what they believed was its artificial and mechanical nature in opposition to the traditional organic German virtues of authority and community. In this view, medicine, overrun of course with Jews, had become beholden to materialism:

> In the Third Reich these limitations of the medical profession, "complexes of a bygone era," must fall away, for we see in the hysteria of the German people the biological sickness of a negative orientation of will under the Weimar system.[65]

In other words, given the proper Germanic environment of the Third Reich, the doctor and psychotherapist could concentrate on enhancing the physical and psychological strengths of a racially sound *Volk* instead of catering to the nervous afflictions imposed upon Germany by internal as well as external enemies after the First World War. Once again, we can detect the putative "advantage" on the human "supply side" in Nazi Germany to be won by the complementary ruthless exclusion of biological "inferiors" from the racial community. Johannes Neumann, a young member of the Göring Institute from Giessen, summed up the resultant task for psychotherapists in particular in Nazi Germany:

> The notion of *Volksgemeinschaft* demands a science which serves life. . . . The inevitable duty thus presents itself: the cure of neurosis and the cure of the times, to join genuine self-sufficiency with genuine community and to bring both into a right and true relationship with each other.[66]

In all of these ways the nature of the rising psychodynamic challenge to the physicalist psychiatric tradition in Germany gave the psychotherapists much of what they needed to escape Nazi persecution and, even more importantly for them, to exploit Nazi demands. But there would be no *neue deutsche Seelenheilkunde* in terms of theory or practice. The more radical Nazi voices among the psychotherapists like Achelis, Bilz, Cimbal, and Haeberlin would fade from prominence after the first years of the regime. It would be those psychotherapists who to one degree or another were associated with one or more of the major schools of thought who would exercise the greatest influence and authority during the Third Reich. This meant not a lesser, but a greater degree of collaboration with the Nazi regime, for the psychotherapists under Göring offered the Nazis much more than hortatory or ideological support. They successfully offered the Nazis the practical service of their discipline in pursuit of their own survival and professional development. Such a "technocratic" ethos in general played no small role in the racist and military excesses perpetrated by the Nazi regime. The psychotherapists were by and large insulated from these excesses by the nature of their work; their contribution to them was indirect in that they helped the society and regime function. They were divorced from any effective critical stance toward the regime by the opportunity given them by the nature of their expertise and the luck of their connection to the Nazi leadership. Their task, as they saw it and seized it, was to develop their discipline into a profession. This task would not go without significant challenge all through the Third Reich, as we shall see in the next chapter. This was due to their old foes, the university psychiatrists, who had staked their own strong biological claim in one of the darkest realms of Nazi racial hygiene.

Notes

1. Hattingberg, "Neue Richtung, Neue Bindung," pp. 98, 103.
2. *Ziel und Weg* 4 (1934): 464–7; see also Zapp, "Psychoanalyse und Nationalsozialismus," pp. 201–3, 212; and the review of *Deutsche Seelenheilkunde* by Heyer in *Hippokrates* 5 (1934): 432.
3. *Ziel und Weg* 8 (1938): 284; see also Zapp, "Psychoanalyse und Nationalsozialismus," p. 212.
4. Göring to Cimbal, August 6, 1933, Kl. Erw. 762/2.
5. Victor Klemperer, *Die unbewältigte Sprache: Aus dem Notizbuch eines Philologen "LTI"* (Darmstadt, 1966), pp. 279–80, 286–7.
6. Dräger, "Psychoanalysis in Hitler Germany," p. 208.
7. BDC: NSDAP-Zentralkartei. Eight of the psychotherapists were members of the NSV; seven of the Nazi Physicians League; five of the Teachers League; three each of the SA, the University Lecturers League, and the Motor Corps; two each of the Nazi Women's Organization and the Labor Front; and one each was a member of the Hitler Youth and the Student League.
8. Werner Kemper, interview with the author, November 28, 1973.
9. Franz L. Neumann, "Introduction," in Daniel Lerner, *The Nazi Elite,* Hoover Institute Studies, Series B: Elite Studies, No. 3 (Palo Alto, 1951), p. iv.
10. Ian Kershaw, *The "Hitler Myth": Image and Reality in the Third Reich* (Oxford, 1987).
11. Thomas Childers, *The Nazi Voter: The Social Foundations of Fascism in Germany, 1919–1933* (Chapel Hill, 1983); and idem, "The Middle Classes and National Socialism," in David Blackbourn and Richard J. Evans, eds., *The German Bourgeoisie: Essays on the Social History of the German Middle Class from the Late Eighteenth to the Early Twentieth Century* (London, 1991), p. 318.
12. Michael Burleigh and Wolfgang Wippermann, *The Racial State: Germany 1933–1945* (Cambridge, 1991). The centrality of racism to the Nazi movement and the Third Reich has led historians away from attempts to define Nazi Germany primarily in any other terms, such as class conflict; see Richard J. Evans, "In Search of German Social Darwinism: The History and Historiography of a Concept," in Berg and Cocks, *Medicine and Modernity,* pp. 55–79.
13. See, for example, Milton Mayer, *They Thought They Were Free: The Germans, 1933–1945* (Chicago, 1955), p. 194.
14. Michael Geyer, "The Nazi State Reconsidered," in Richard Bessel, ed., *Life in the*

Third Reich (Oxford, 1987), p. 59; see also Detlev J. K. Peukert, *Inside Nazi Germany*.

15. Werner Zabel, *Grenzerweiterung der Schulmedizin*, pp. 130–1.
16. Carl and Sylvia Grossman, *The Wild Analyst: The Life and Times of Georg Groddeck* (New York, 1965), pp. 194–5; see also Helmut Siefert et al., eds., *Groddeck Almanach* (Basel, 1986). Among early supporters of the Nazis, philosopher Martin Heidegger of Freiburg stands out in terms of such intellectually arrogant naiveté as well as in his commitment to certain ideals he saw embodied by National Socialism; see Dominick LaCapra, "Heidegger's Nazi Turn," in idem, *Representing the Holocaust: History, Theory, Trauma* (Ithaca, 1994), p. 142.
17. Matthias Heinrich Göring, "Eröffnungsansprache," in Rudolf Bilz, ed., *Psyche und Leistung*, p. 8.
18. Fritz Künkel, *Grundzüge der politischen Charakterkunde*, p. vi.
19. BDC: Kulturkammer.
20. Otto Kohlreutter quoted in Hubert Schorn, *Der Richter im Dritten Reich: Geschichte und Dokumente* (Frankfurt, 1959), p. 81.
21. Fritz Künkel, "Die Lehrbarkeit der tiefenpsychologischen Denkweisen," p. 238. See also Hans Alfred Grunsky, *Seele und Staat: Die psychologischen Grundlagen des nationalsozialistischen Sieges über den bürgerlichen und bolschewistischen Menschen* (Berlin, 1935), pp. 22, 65.
22. Künkel, "Die dialektische Charakterkunde als Ergebnis der kulturellen Krise," p. 84.
23. Fritz and Elisabeth Künkel, *Die Erziehung deiner Kinder*, p. 7.
24. Fritz Künkel, "Seelenheilkunde," p. 296. Künkel's interest in child development, shared professionally by his wife Elisabeth, is evidenced by the twelve editions (1930–32, 1954) of his study on adolescence, *Jugendcharakterkunde: Theorie und Praxis des Erwachsenwerdens* (Schwerin in Mecklenburg, 1930).
25. Leonhard Seif, "Volksgemeinschaft und Neurose," pp. 54, 60. Lene Credner, a member of Seif's circle, would later correctly even if cravenly define the interest of the Nazi leadership in what was known among the psychotherapists as psychagogy: "Our National Socialist state provides an example of this writ large: We are experiencing a conscious educational effort directed at the young unparalleled in history." Lene Credner, "Vererbung und Erziehungsberatung," in Seif, *Wege der Erziehungshilfe* (1940), p. 81. On psychagogy as an agent of fascist political conditioning of the masses, see Serge Tchakotine, *Le Viol des foules par la propagande politique* (Paris, 1939), a critique which is, however, limited by its Pavlovian perspective. See also George Frederick Kneller, *The Educational Philosophy of National Socialism* (New Haven, 1941). For a succinct dismissal of Nazi pedagogues Alfred Bäumler and Ernst Krieck, see Ringer, *Decline*, p. 442.
26. Leonhard Seif, "Erziehung der Erzieher," in idem, *Wege der Erziehungshilfe*, p. 32; see also Matthias Heinrich Göring, "Erfolgsmöglichkeiten der Psychotherapie"; August Hanse, "Ärztliche Seelenführung"; and Fritz Künkel, *Das Wir*.
27. Seif, "Volksgemeinschaft und Neurose," p. 60. See also "Dr. Leonhard Seif geboren 15.1.1866," *ZfP* 12 (1941): 321, wherein his differences with Adler are perhaps exaggerated by editors Göring and Bilz in the anti-Semitic spirit of a loyal Germanic psychotherapy; cf. Lene Credner, "Geleitwort zur Neuherausgabe," in Leonhard Seif, ed., *Wege der Erziehungshilfe: Ergebnisse und praktische Hinweise aus der Tätigkeit des Münchener Arbeitskreises für Erziehung*, 2nd ed. (Munich, 1952), pp. 8–9.
28. BDC: Parteikorrespondenz.
29. Gustav Richard Heyer, *Praktische Seelenheilkunde*, p. 113.

30. Matthias Heinrich Göring to Walter Cimbal, March 10, 1934, Kl. Erw. 762/2.
31. Zoe Heyer to the author, April 19, 1983; Lockot, *Erinnern und Durcharbeiten,* p. 162, maintains that Heyer was at first a convinced opponent of the regime and even considered leaving Germany until Jung convinced him to stay and try to change things from inside. Yet Lockot also notes that Heyer's opposition gradually turned to identification with National Socialism. Carl Müller-Braunschweig's son Hans claims that Heyer was often in uniform at the institute (see Zapp, "Psychoanalyse und Nationalsozialismus," p. 65), although he was not a member of any party organization that had a uniform. He was a member of the military reserve and served as a physician at the Greater Berlin Reserve Military Hospital beginning in 1942 (see chapter 11); Zoe Heyer, personal communication, March 1, 1983.
32. Julian Benda, *The Treason of the Intellectuals,* trans. Richard Aldington (New York, 1928).
33. Heyer, *Praktische Seelenheilkunde,* p. 80. Due to his training with, and partiality to, C. G. Jung, Heyer was often known and went by the name Carl Gustav Heyer: see Pongratz, *Psychotherapie,* pp. 259, 284.
34. Gustav Richard Heyer, *Der Organismus der Seele* (1932 and 1937), pp. 99, 100, 107, 108, 90–91, 81.
35. Gustav Richard Heyer, "Leben und Erkennen," p. 281.
36. Carl Müller-Braunschweig, "Psychoanalyse und Weltanschauung," p. 22,; see also idem, "Psychoanalyse und Weltanschauung," (1931): and pp. 102–16, the text of an address to the DPG in Dresden on September 29, 1930; and the criticisms of Müller-Braunschweig in Brecht et al., *"Hier geht das Leben auf eine sehr merkwürdige Weise weiter...,"* pp. 96–7; and Helmut Dahmer, "Kapitulation vor der 'Weltanschauung': Zu einem Aufsatz von Carl Müller-Braunschweig aus dem Herbst 1933," in Hans Martin Lohmann, *Psychoanalyse und Nationalsozialismus,* pp. 120–36.
37. Schultz-Hencke, Lebenslauf, p. 2.
38. Harald Schultz-Hencke, "Die Tüchtigkeit als psychotherapeutisches Ziel," p. 85; see also Zapp, "Psychoanalyse und Nationalsozialismus," pp. 129–65; and M. Kütemeyer, "Die Sprache der Psychosomatik im Nationalsozialismus," in W. Bohleber and I. Drews, eds., *"Gift, das du unbewusst eintrinkst... " Der Nationalsozialismus und die deutsche Sprache* (Bielefeld, 1991).
39. Schultz-Hencke, "Tüchtigkeit als psychotherapeutisches Ziel," pp. 85, 91, 95–7; and the review by R. Blum in *Ziel und Weg* 4 (1934): 466.
40. Hans von Hattingberg, *Über die Liebe,* p. 357.
41. Wladimir Eliasberg, *Arzt und Propaganda: ein Stück medizinische Soziologie aus der ärztlichen Wirklichkeit* (Vienna, 1936); "Sitzungsprotokoll vom 9.Dezember 1936," *ZfP* 10 (1937): 8.
42. Hattingberg, "Zur Entwicklung der analytischen Bewegung," p. 330.
43. Schultz, *Lebensbilderbuch,* p. 130; Cimbal to Göring, December 28, 1933, Kl. Erw. 762/2, BA.
44. Johannes Heinrich Schultz, "Seelische Schulung," p. 315; see also idem, "Der nervöse Zustand."
45. BDC: Reichsärztekammer and Parteistatistische Erhebung.
46. Werner Achelis, "Psychologische Zivilisationsbilanz," p. 60; see Werner Hollmann's review of Karl Pintschovious and Heinrich Zeiss, eds., *Zivilisationsschäden am Menschen,* in *ZfP* 14 (1942): 98–101. Achelis was inspired by Hans Blüher's work on the homosexual bonds uniting young men's association; on Blüher and the German Youth Movement as purveyors of a conservative and

nationalist etherealization of homosexuality, see George Mosse, "Nationalism and Respectability: Normal and Abnormal Sexuality in the Nineteenth Century," *Journal of Contemporary History* 17 (1982): 237, 240.

47. Achelis, "Psychologische Zivilisationsbilanz," p. 73.
48. Cimbal to Göring, August 15, 1933, Kl. Erw. 762/2; for his eldest son, see BDC: Parteikorrespondenz.
49. Walter Cimbal, "Aufgaben und Wege einer deutschen Seelenheilkunde," p. 117.
50. Ibid., p. 111.
51. On family demographics in Nazi Germany, see Richard Grunberger, *The 12–Year Reich,* pp. 235–50.
52. Cimbal, "Aufgaben und Wege," p. 111.
53. Walter Cimbal, *Naturgemässe Wege zum seelischen Gleichgewicht,* p. 137.
54. Gerhard Pfotenhauer, "'Aufnordnung' und 'vorgeburtliche Erziehung'—'Rassenhygiene' eines Psychoanalytikers," *Der Öffentliche Gesundheitsdienst* 2 (1936): 184–7.
55. Cimbal, "Familienchronik," pp. 110–13.
56. Ibid., p. 114; Personalakte Cimbal, Staatsarchiv Hamburg.
57. "Wir stehen zu Klages," *Wille und Macht* 6 (1938): 1–6.
58. Haeberlin, "Die Bedeutung von Ludwig Klages und Hans Prinzhorn," pp. 49, 39.
59. Hans-Dietrich Röhrs, "Biologischer Sozialismus," *Die Gesundheitsführung "Ziel und Weg"* 4 (1942): 181–8.
60. Werner Achelis, "Politische Schulung und die Frage der Gesinnungsschulung als rassenpsychologisches Problem," in "Kongress für Psychotherapie in Breslau," p. 1067; and Otto Curtius, "Kongress," p. 359. See also George Mosse, *Nazi Culture,* p. 349.
61. Buchholz, "Aufbau der Gesinnung und des Kameradschaftgeistes," in "Kongress für Psychotherapie in Breslau," p. 1067; and Curtius, "Kongress," p. 359.
62. Gerhard Wagner, "Der Weg zu einer neuen deutschen Heilkunde," p. 5.
63. August Hanse, *Persönlichkeitsgefüge und Krankheit,* p. 146; see the review by Werner Kemper in *ZfP* 12 (1941): 361–2.
64. Franz Brendgen, "Vegetative Stigmatisation und Neurose," p. 91.
65. Helmut Peil, "Über die Hysterie: Ein Beitrag zur Krise der Medizin," *Volksgesundheitswacht* 2 (1935): 6; see also J. Hobohm, "Der Nationalsozialismus als Überwinder des Zeitalters der Neurose," *Ziel und Weg* 4 (1934): 41–4.
66. Johannes Neumann, *Leben ohne Angst,* pp. 8, 172; see also ibid., pp. 142–3.

5

Psychiatry: Old Enemy in a New Reich

Traditional studies of the Nazi dictatorship have detailed the regime's ruthless and unified "coordination" of state and society. In the first decade after the war, some Western political scientists classified both Nazi Germany and Soviet Russia as totalitarian regimes that extended ideological control over all aspects of their respective societies. Other researchers, mostly historians, distinguished between the relative totalitarianism of the two regimes, generally arguing that the Soviet Union was much more totalitarian in its organization than its dictatorial rival and mate. In this vein of research, Nazi Germany was described, among other things, as a "dual state" in which party and state parceled out and vied for power. Subsequently, some historical work emphasized the relative influence of the state over the party while other studies analyzed the penetration of the state by Nazi personnel and ideals. As research into the domestic history of the Third Reich proliferated to match the earlier interest in its foreign and military policies, historians began to describe a less unitary regime. An analysis of various power bastions within the regime had in fact been anticipated during the war by study of the major economic centers of power in Nazi Germany. But the recent research emphasized a more pervasive pattern of "chaos" inside the political structure of the Third Reich, especially within areas more or less distant from the central diplomatic, military, and ideological interests of Hitler himself. These characteristics of the regime were labeled "feudal" or, more commonly, "polycratic." On the other hand, scholars have most recently documented the degree to which Nazi racial and totalitarian ideas and practices penetrated the society and polity of Hitler's Reich. Finally, new research into the social history of Nazi Germany has uncovered the striking degree to which events in various spheres were often initiated "from the bottom up" in response to the Nazi seizure of power "from the top down." All of these dynamics are evident in the history of psychotherapy in the Third Reich, as are certain distinct continuities in German history from before 1933 to 1945 and after.

As we have seen, psychotherapists in Germany were confronted in 1933 with a radically new political landscape filled with many dangers and some opportunities, but their major concern as a group, especially during the early years of the Third Reich, turned out to be an ongoing confrontation with their old nemesis, the psychiatrists. The reorganization of the patriotically renamed German General Medical Society for Psychotherapy between 1933 and 1936, which we will detail in this chapter, revolved primarily around the desire of the psychotherapists to avoid the imposition of any sort of control by a psychiatric establishment both newly aggressive and defensive as a result of the arrival of the Nazis. The first three years of the Third Reich would be years of intense political activity and initiative on the part of a number of psychotherapists in defense of their professional interests. This is ironic in at least two respects. The first irony is of course the practice of politics in a dictatorship; the face the Nazis showed to the world was of German political and popular unity in place of the corrupt democratic politics of the Weimar Republic. The reality of course was somewhat different: alongside unalloyed support for Hitler and Nazi terror against political opposition was a great deal of political maneuvering by representatives of various loyal bourgeois German interests. There was "coordination," however chaotic at times, but there was also a great deal of "autocoordination" as individuals and groups in competition with one another cut various sorts of deals with various officials and agencies to secure places or advance positions in the new order. The second irony—or, in light of the traditional model of the "unpolitical German," surprise—was the vigorous pursuit of interest politics by, among others, precisely those members of that idealistic German academic mandarin culture that was supposed to be so averse to the grubby material politics characteristic of the "shopkeeper mentality" allegedly so common in the modern West. But such disdain, to the extent it existed, was reserved for politics writ large, for the substitution of partisan interest for loyalty to the state. Professional politics was another matter, however, since by the twentieth century Germany had become a highly complex corporate industrial state that demanded the articulation and defense of organized interests.

Since the Nazis insisted on the importance of the "leadership principle" (*Führerprinzip*) in their reorganization of German state and society, the psychotherapists were confronted initially with a significant problem. The president of the General Medical Society for Psychotherapy, psychiatrist Ernst Kretschmer, was politically suspect in the eyes of the new regime. According to psychiatrist Oswald Bumke, a bitter foe of psychotherapy, Kretschmer said to him after the Nazi seizure of power in 1933: "'It's a funny thing with psychopaths. In normal times we render expert opinions on them; in times of political unrest they rule us.'"[1] Twelve years later, when the regime was in its death throes, the Nazi University Lecturers League rendered this judgment on Kretschmer:

> Seen from a National Socialist point of view, the National Socialist German University Lecturers League could never approve the hiring of Kretschmer, because on the basis of positive evidence we are of the opinion that he has never subscribed to National Socialist ideas.[2]

As a result of such mutual distrust, Kretschmer resigned as president of the General Medical Society on April 6, 1933, and entered a sanitarium for rest and treatment.[3] At the invitation of the executive committee, Vice President Carl Jung succeeded Kretschmer as president on June 21. In a letter to Johannes Heinrich Schultz of June 9 Jung had agreed to assume the post and named Heyer as his deputy.[4]

Since Jews were now forbidden to be members of the executive of any organization, the old executive committee of the General Medical Society was dissolved. Former executive committee members Wladimir Eliasberg and Arthur Kronfeld, both of whom were Jewish, resigned in courageously demonstrative fashion from the society entirely. Eliasberg moved from Munich to Vienna in 1933, fled to Prague in 1938, and to New York the following year. The Berliner Kronfeld emigrated to the Soviet Union where, upon the approach of German troops in 1941, he and his wife shot themselves. Although the number of Jewish members of the German General Medical Society for Psychotherapy of course declined precipitously after 1933, Jews were not officially banned from membership in the society until 1938, when Jewish doctors lost the right to practice medicine in Germany.[5]

Over the next few months the psychotherapists would struggle among themselves to reorganize in harmony both with the internal dynamics of the discipline and the various external forces which now impinged upon them. The internal dynamics included rivalry for leadership among the psychotherapists. Schultz, who was aligned with Kretschmer, and Kretschmer's representative in the General Medical Society, Friedrich Mauz, contested the Berlin psychotherapeutic leadership with Hattingberg, while Heyer in Munich attempted to capitalize on Jung's designation of him as his deputy in Germany.[6] The external forces, on the other hand, included various medical reformers within the Nazi party, the state health bureaucracy, and the psychiatrists, most significantly Ernst Rüdin, leader of the psychiatric section of the Society of German Neurologists and Psychiatrists, and Kretschmer. By September 15 the General Medical Society would become the German General Medical Society for Psychotherapy under the leadership of Matthias Heinrich Göring; by May 1934 the old society would become the International General Medical Society for Psychotherapy with its headquarters in Zurich under Carl Jung. The members of the international group would be organized by nation; the provisional governing committee of the German society included Cimbal as managing director, Haeberlin as vice president, and Hattingberg, Heyer, Künkel, Schultz, Schultz-Hencke, Seif, and Viktor von Weizsäcker.[7]

Göring had emerged early on as the likely leader for the psychotherapists. Because of his cousin Hermann he became the logical choice to negotiate on behalf of his colleagues with the various agencies of the party and state. The Göring family was close-knit and Matthias Heinrich's father Peter, the author of the family genealogy, had helped Hermann financially after the First World War. In 1935 Matthias Heinrich sat at the head table at the banquet following Hermann's sumptuous state wedding to actress Emmy Sonnemann.[8] According to Ernst Göring, during the Third Reich his father did not visit his powerful cousin often. He was there when the elder Göring needed him, but usually mention of the family name alone sufficed. Göring was also clearly the only compromise candidate among those vying for leadership within the General Medical Society following Kretschmer's resignation. According to Cimbal in a letter to Haeberlin of August 3, it was Hattingberg who suggested that Göring should take over leadership of what was in the course of the summer of 1933 already becoming a German group within the General Medical Society headed by Jung. Hattingberg argued that no one disliked Göring and that he was a Nazi party member.[9] Göring himself had been busy since the spring encouraging members of various regional groups of the Society for Individual Psychology to join with the other psychotherapists in a single German society. Göring headed the Wuppertal branch of the Adlerian society and, as he told his teacher Seif, since international organizations were frowned on by the government the future of individual psychology and the other psychotherapeutic schools in Germany could be secured only by the creation of a unified national body.[10]

Since the Nazi regime required that the heads of organizations be party members, Göring had agreed to join the NSDAP. As we have seen, he was firmly in the German Romantic tradition in medicine with all its concern and fascination with the individual, the internal, the unconscious, and the irrational. This inward orientation, coupled with his commitment to medical and religious rehabilitation and his conservative German patriotism, made it relatively easy for him to embrace National Socialism on what he thought were his own terms. He could therefore facilely join belief with opportunistic rhetoric, as in this early commentary on political and military discipline in the new Germany: "External drill does not suffice: the core of man must be grasped, as the Führer had repeatedly emphasized, and treated instinctively so that our subconscious is directed along the right path."[11] Göring affirmed the therapeutic necessity of the individual's integration into the community and, beyond that, the duty of the individual to remain healthy in service to his nation, his people, and his race. Psychotherapy, he asserted, was the means by which these ends could be attained in a stressful age when debilitating psychological conflict was more common than tuberculosis or cancer.[12] In responding to the urging of Cimbal, Haeberlin, and Hattingberg that he assume leadership of the German psychotherapists, Göring wrote to Cimbal:

> In the interest of our society I wish to accept your offer, because I am a National Socialist not in name only but wholeheartedly in the spirit of Adolf Hitler, because moreover I bear the name of the Prussian Minister-President and am related to him. Also in the interest of National Socialism I must not refuse, for I believe that we psychotherapists have a great mission in the new state. You yourself have already said something about this. I would simply like to add that we are called to educate children and adults in the right spirit.[13]

Göring obviously saw an opportunity in 1933 to put his ideas into effect. Part of the reason for his accepting the post of leader of the

German psychotherapists was his desire to unify the various schools of psychotherapeutic thought into some sort of Germanic psychotherapy. According to his son Ernst, Göring was a synthesist by nature, a characteristic that would be in harmony with his future role in protecting and promoting psychotherapy through the submersion of Freud and Adler. His criticisms of Freud would be both prelude and accompaniment to his exclusion of psychoanalysts Carl Müller-Braunschweig and Felix Boehm from any significant influence or authority within the society and the institute. But his toleration of the Freudians as a group, in line with a professional as well as a patriotic desire to unify psychotherapy, would gradually grow into interest and even some degree of grudging admiration for their work in the Göring Institute (see chapter 10). Although he pursued his personal vision, especially in the early years of the Third Reich, the result of the combination of his mild nature and his assignment was a general toleration for all points of view. Göring had neither the drive nor the intellect to produce a synthesis that had escaped much abler minds. And in terms of a combination of his own philosophical and psychotherapeutic views with those of National Socialism, such a synthesis was in any case illusory. During 1933 and 1934, for example, Göring designated Hitler's *Mein Kampf* as required reading for every psychotherapist, but few if any actually read it and there ensued no enforcement or sanction.[14] All in all, Göring's personal nature and intellectual limits corresponded to the predominant task of psychotherapists in the Third Reich under the protection of his name: the opportunistic mobilization of their expertise in service to the Nazi regime in pursuit of professional autonomy and development.

It is difficult to gauge the degree of anti-Semitism in Göring. At the fourth psychotherapeutic congress in 1929, he had indicated some philosophical problems with Freud.[15] His words and actions during the Third Reich leave no doubt over his condemnatory public stance then toward Jewish influence in his discipline. But what of his private attitude toward Jews themselves? Ernst Göring has recalled the many Jewish patients his father had and what mutual devotion existed between them and Göring. And yet in 1937 Göring would assert that between 1930 and 1933 only eleven Jews came to him and that he was unable to help any of them because of the "racial" difference.[16] With no real certainty, we can only speculate that such an odious claim might have exacted some sort of psychological toll on a man like

Göring, some thrashing about of a conscience amidst the tangle of ambition, fear, professional identity, and the philosophical hysteria mobilized by the Nazi regime. Anti-Semitism was an all-too-common adjunct to the aristocratic German traditions of which men like Göring partook, and the many brilliant Jews in medicine, especially those who dominated the elite and exclusive corridors of the psychoanalytic movement, could only have served to add professional jealousy to common cultural bigotry. At the same time, however, the association of such men as Göring with the Nazis did not derive from an uncomplicated and unconditional acceptance of National Socialism. Göring did not join the Nazi party in order to exercise his anti-Semitism; he joined as part of a process of professional necessity and national-cultural loyalty. It may or may not be true that before 1933 Göring had many Jewish patients with whom he was on excellent terms, but even dedicated anti-Semites, Hermann Göring among them, were known to cultivate relationships with "good" Jews (*Persiljuden*). In any case, whether or not Matthias Heinrich Göring was an anti-Semite before the advent of Hitler, a complex of personal and professional motives compelled him to advertise that he was after 1933. And, as we shall see, during the Third Reich he would also act like one on a number of occasions.

Apart from the lucky incursion of the Göring name, what is most notable about the early efforts of psychotherapists in Nazi Germany is the degree of initiative they took in responding to newly arranged dangers and opportunities. To be sure, some of this initiative stemmed from the very advantage of the tie to the emerging Göring satrapy at the top of the new regime. But what is as striking as the failure of higher morality—or any morality—in the face of Nazi designs and demands was the willingness and ability of individuals and groups not—unlike Jews and Communists—subjected to outright persecution to operate and shape the conditions of their service and obedience to the Nazi regime. Cimbal in particular in his early correspondence with Göring and Haeberlin stressed the need for making psychotherapy's case with the authorities and in seizing organizational initiative in dealings with the party, the state, and, especially during the first three years of the regime, their old enemy, the psychiatrists.[17]

Already in 1933 the psychotherapists understood very well what the stakes and issues were in the struggle against the psychiatric establishment. Künkel wrote to Göring in early August, citing the importance of avoiding internal strife in light of the "very favorable prospects" for psychotherapy.[18] A month later Cimbal expressed his view to Göring that Hitler's words at the party rally at Nuremberg that month demonstrated a point of view similar to that of German psychotherapists. At the same time, however, Cimbal noted that psychotherapy's future in Germany lay precisely with those who were psychologically weak, the self-indulgent, all those who needed to brought into the national community. Cimbal worried that association with these more problematical members of society might hold political dangers for psychotherapy. The solution, he thought, lay in the doctor's medical and political commitment to address the specific psychological difficulties arising from Germany's recent past.[19] In fact, the psychotherapists would exploit this approach in their confrontation with the psychiatrists, arguing that they could offer repair of essentially worthy German "stock"; the psychiatrists, as we shall see, would have to struggle against professional relegation to the sterilization and murder of "worthless" degenerated stock.

The immediate task for the psychotherapists, however, was to exploit the good professional fortune of the Göring name to establish their own organization. With Göring at the helm, the psychotherapists were in general spared the necessity of forging closer "political" ties with the Nazi regime. When Nazi articles and books on race were reviewed in the *Zentralblatt,* it was most often Göring who did the reviewing, displaying again the admixture of conviction, opportunism, and protectiveness that comprised his motives and actions as leader of his discipline in the Third Reich. Göring's name also meant that he and his colleagues were spared the task of constantly proving their allegiance to the Nazi regime. For example, while other psychotherapists were criticized in the party and professional media, Göring himself received uniformly favorable attention. Such was the case with his book on psychosomatic disorders, a highly technical work that was devoid of the Nazi rhetoric contained in those of his articles that German medical journals, prudently in part, now and again agreed to publish.[20]

It was also unnecessary for Göring to appear before his colleagues in an SA uniform, even though he was a member of the SA; Walther Poppelreuter, the director of the Institute for Clinical Psychology in Bonn, did not enjoy such a luxury.[21] Göring was not compelled to flaunt his name even had it been his nature to do so; he was content to use it. According to his son, he was of the opinion that if there were someone from whom he needed assistance, then that person should be approached directly rather than through channels, a tactic born of the forthright nature that, as we have seen, prompted his suspicions of the indirect methods of psychoanalysis. Of course, such an approach was made particularly effective by possession of the Göring name. As often as not, the name, along with his distinguished bearing and academic titles, won him at least a hearing, if not always success. It does not seem to have been the case that powerful Nazi individuals and organizations came to Göring in order to exploit his name in the constant jockeying for power that persisted within the hierarchy of the Third Reich. This did not mean, however, that the Göring Institute in particular was not used in the construction of bastions of power. Such attempts were made by Reich Physicians Leader Wagner, Labor Front Chief Ley, and Reich Health Leader Conti. On balance, it seems that the psychotherapists' chances for the survival and development of their profession after 1933 rested less on what the Göring name would bring them than on how far it would take them.

On August 7, 1933, Cimbal sent a letter to all members of the governing committee informing them they would meet (*Führertagung*) September 30 and October 1 in Bad Nauheim. This meeting would take the place of the congress that had originally been scheduled. There was too little time to plan a congress properly under the changed political conditions in Germany. Moreover, Cimbal noted, this smaller group would be sure not to contain disruptive or dangerous elements. The agenda for the meeting was the future direction of psychotherapy in Germany under the rubrics of Jung, Schultz, and the combination of individual psychology and psychoanalysis into *angewandte Charakterkunde*. Cimbal closed his communication with the news that Göring would be negotiating with the Prussian and Bavarian ministers of culture through the good offices of his cousin.[22] Göring did meet with his cousin during the second week of September and subsequently with Leonardo Conti, head of the Nazi Physicians League in Berlin, Hans Schemm, Bavarian minister of culture, and Walther Schultze, director of the Health Services Department in the Bavarian Interior Ministry. All of these meetings went well, Göring reported, Schultze's initial misgivings about individual psychology and psychotherapy being overcome by mention of Hermann Göring's patronage; Schemm agreed to provide schoolrooms in Munich for Seif's educational counseling services.[23]

Instead of the proposed meeting of psychotherapeutic leaders in Bad Nauheim at the end of September, however, the governing committee met at Künkel's house in the Charlottenburg district of Berlin on the evening of September 15. In attendance were Göring, Cimbal, Haeberlin, Hattingberg, Künkel, Schultz, Schultz-Hencke, and Seif. Göring reported that his cousin and Conti were well disposed toward psychotherapy because of what they saw as the great importance of "psychical influence" in society.[24] What is most striking about this meeting, however, is the fact that no officials of the government were in attendance. The psychotherapists—like other groups—were organizing themselves for the sake of their own professional purposes. Most of the issues discussed and decisions made at this meeting were thus continuous with ongoing concerns within the discipline although, to be sure, also within a loyal and controlled national profile. The German General Medical Society for Psychotherapy would constitute one of the national groups of the General Medical Society under Jung in Küsnacht/Zurich. All psychotherapists in Germany were to be members of this group and it would be registered as an association (*eingetragener Verein*, e.V.) in Wuppertal-Elberfeld. All lectures, courses, and advisory functions were to be under the supervision of physicians. Jung and Rudolf Allers of Vienna were to take over editorship of the *Zentralblatt* from Kretschmer and the journal, its publication suspended since the second number of 1933, would remain a publication of the international society. The German society would prepare its own special issue as a supplement to the *Zentralblatt*. Laypersons could participate in the congresses and become extraordinary members of the German Medical Society as long as they were sponsored by an ordinary member and approved by the executive committee.

Some old concerns, however, were now given greater urgency by the changed political conditions. It was now more important than ever that the psychotherapists control as much as possible what was said about them in the popular and professional press. Therefore, there would be no invitations for press coverage of the congress that was to take place the following April in Bad Nauheim in conjunction with the internists' congress in Wiesbaden. Advertising of the congress would be restricted to the members of the international society, other national member groups, and previous participants. Finally, there were discussions and decisions that directly reflected the political and racial demands of the new regime. All manuscripts, lectures, and reviews were to be submitted four weeks in advance and, in the case of addresses, presented without deviation from the text. Göring proposed that Jews could be members of the society, but could not serve on the executive committee. Jews would not be allowed to give lectures at Bad Nauheim, but they could participate in the discussions. In keeping with the "leadership principle" now mandatory in Germany and with the psychotherapists' own special reliance on Göring, certain tasks were reserved to Göring: He would be editor of all special numbers of the *Zentralblatt*. He would chair the congresses, name the lecturers, and censor the discussions. It was also his responsibility to name the regional officers of the society as well as to approve courses, lectures, and counseling services.[25]

The formal statutes of the society were worked out in the weeks following the September meeting. The first draft, drawn up by Cimbal at Göring's request to show to Conti and Gütt at the Interior Ministry,[26] swore unconditional loyalty to Hitler in its second article, but this was changed in the final draft to "the development of a psychotherapy in the spirit of the National Socialist world view" among four other, prosaic professional aims. Articles three and four concerned the leadership of the society, all of whom had to be of "Aryan descent." The president served at the pleasure of the Reich Minister of the Interior. Both drafts of the statutes, however, contradicted themselves by having the president name the executive committee and the executive committee (*Vorstand*) name the president; this, as we shall see, would delay the licensing of the association. The president also had the right to expel members of the society. The first draft further gave him the right to dissolve the society at any time, while the second draft left this to a two-thirds vote of the membership. In such a case, any remaining financial resources would be the responsibility of the Reich Interior Minister.[27]

These changes indicate not only a refinement of the organization's statutes, but also a firming of both the virtue and necessity of Göring's leadership. The dissolution of the society reserved to the president, presumably at the behest of higher authority, mentioned in the first draft was a sign of the psychotherapists' political anxieties, but its reservation to the membership in the second draft was not only prudent (why mention the unmentionable?), but also soundly based on their growing confidence that Göring would protect them. The absence of a provision in the second draft for the replacement of the president was another indication of Göring's indispensability; the very brevity of the statutes demonstrated his sufficiency in the often personalistic Nazi power system. Göring said in 1933 that the statutes would be published in the special edition of the *Zentralblatt* in 1934 dedicated to new German psychotherapy.[28] It is significant in just this regard that when *Deutsche Seelenheilkunde* appeared, the statutes were not included. It was also relatively immaterial what Hermann Göring thought about psychotherapy. The evidence on this is mixed. In 1933 Matthias Heinrich Göring wrote to his mentor Seif that to "have my cousin declare himself with respect to I[ndividual]. P[sychology]. has little point since he has much too much to do and anyway has little interest in psychology."[29] Apart from psychotherapist Göring's mood—or that of his cousin—at that juncture, he could have been speaking in confidential accuracy or trying to moderate expectations. It is most likely that Hermann Göring was motivated by family loyalty rather than commitment to his relative's discipline. Whatever the truth actually was, however, Göring never hesitated to advertise his cousin's deep interest in psychotherapy.[30]

One other, rhetorical, change also traced this same gradual trend in favor of enterprise over anxiety that characterized the evolution of psychotherapy in the Third Reich. In the December 1933 issue of the *Zentralblatt,* Göring published a hortatory version of the society's statutes in which he referred to himself as *Reichsführer*.[31] The first draft of the statutes simply referred to the "president" (*Vorsitzender*), but the second draft designated Göring as *Reichsleiter* (and the managing director as *Reichsgeschäftsführer*). This was not so much arrogance as anxious rhetorical imitation of Nazi symbols of power and they would disappear from psychotherapeutic organizational discourse early the following year for two reasons. The first reason was the growing confidence the psychotherapists had in Göring, in their organization, and in the services they could provide the regime. Professional capacity increasingly replaced political protestation. The second reason was that first Reich Physicians Leader Gerhard Wagner and then the Reich Interior Ministry, acting in accord with the regime's desire to limit the proliferation of inappropriate and grandiose titles with the words "*Reichs-*" or "*Führer*" in them, issued a directive stating that such terms were formal, legal ones not designed for general or casual use.[32] In 1938 the society's statutes duly dropped the prefix

"*Reichs-*" from the director's title.[33] Göring would simply be the *Vorsitzender* of the society and the *Direktor* or *Leiter* of the institute. Göring was elected by the executive committee as *Vorsitzender* and *Reichsleiter* in March 1934 and, after some delay because of the contradiction within the statutes, the statutes and the members of the executive committee—with the exception of Cimbal (see chapter 4)—were approved by the government.[34]

But the reorganization of the psychotherapists' own society was only one of the tasks they faced in the first year of Nazi rule. As we described earlier, psychotherapy was being both criticized and courted by Nazi party activists and, as we have just seen, agencies of the state health bureaucracy assumed a supervisory function over the new society. The major task for the psychotherapists, however, in the weeks, months, and years following the establishment of the German General Medical Society was to fend off various attempts by their old antagonists and rivals, the psychiatrists, to gain organizational control over psychotherapy. Sometime early in 1933 psychiatrist Ernst Rüdin was asked by the Reich Interior Ministry to dissolve the old psychotherapeutic society. According to Göring, Rüdin refused to do this, preferring instead to have the director of the German General Medical Society join the executive committee of the German Psychiatric Society.[35] Rüdin also hoped that Kretschmer might be willing to assume leadership of the new psychotherapeutic society, but Kretschmer himself had a different approach in mind, as he wrote Göring in early October:

> My interest in psychotherapy as a science and as a medical art is completely undiminished. My refusal to work further with the psychotherapeutic society in its earlier form had to do primarily with its organization, which made a strict, unified leadership impossible and which, in my view, was attempting to embrace too many diverse intellectual currents and special groups.
>
> As far as the present situation goes, I have at the behest of Rüdin and the psychiatric organizations close to him assumed leadership of a psychotherapeutic section of the German Psychiatric Society and hope in this way to bring psychotherapy a larger audience that up until now has kept its distance from it. It would not be possible for me also to lead the German group of the Psychotherapeutic Society that you have just reorganized and is in your good hands.[36]

At the urging of Walther Schultze, who at the time was with the Bavarian Ministry of Justice, Göring met with Rüdin in Munich in late September. Göring and Rüdin had known each other for twenty-five years and Göring was interested in his colleague's proposal that he join the executive of the psychiatrists' executive committee. Cimbal, Seif, and Heyer, however, weighed in strongly against any close organizational relationship with the psychiatrists.[37] Cimbal saw Kretschmer's proposal as particularly dangerous, given the new regime's preference for single centralized organizations.[38] Jung, too, expressed his view that the subordination of psychotherapy to psychiatry or neurology in Germany "would simply be a catastrophe."[39] Göring agreed with Cimbal that "we must not allow ourselves to be taken in tow by the old ossified psychiatrists,"[40] a remark that betrayed not only continuing professional anxiety but also a sense that psychotherapy's time had come with the passing of the old psychiatric paradigm. This confidence was also reflected in Göring's report of his visit while in Munich with one of psychiatrist Oswald Bumke's assistants, Gustav Störring.[41] While Bumke remained a strong critic of psychotherapy, Störring would become a member of the psychotherapists' governing board. If psychotherapy could make an appeal to the younger generation in the field, Göring felt, then there was reason to feel that events were running in their favor and passing the psychiatrists by.[42]

Rüdin was one of the very many prominent psychiatrists in Germany who collaborated eagerly with the Nazis from the very beginning. This collaboration began with the Law for the Prevention of Genetically Diseased Offspring of July 14, 1933. This law mandated the sterilization of those individuals suffering from a wide range of illnesses, which, in keeping with Nazi racial theory and the physicalist views of most psychiatrists, were defined as hereditary. These included schizophrenia, manic-depressive insanity, and alcoholism, among others. Rüdin was one of the three chief authors of the expert commentary on the law and editor of a companion volume that included an essay by Kretschmer on the heritability and racial danger of feeblemindedness.[43] So-called genetic health courts (*Erbgesundheitsgerichte*) were set up to evaluate such cases. Approximately 400,000 men and women were sterilized under this law, about 95 percent of these before the outbreak of the Second World War in 1939. As we shall see in chapter 9, Göring himself served on one of these courts. The radical decline in the number of compulsory sterilizations after 1939 was due to a number of factors, but the most significant was the establishment in that year of the even more radical "euthanasia" program. Under this program, by August 1941 more than 70,000 mental patients had been gassed. Ripples of public outrage brought an end to this centrally administered campaign, but the killings went on in asylums and hospitals by means of injections, poisonings, and starvation right up to the end of the war. Psychiatrists and doctors assumed the task of murdering mentally ill men, women, and children. In all, over 300,000 people died in this manner. It is important to note that the original act did not order doctors to murder these patients, it only empowered them to do so.[44]

There was significant support for this program among psychiatrists while prewar propaganda emphasizing the financial burden placed on society by hordes of mental patients created a significant degree of popular support for the medically supervised termination of "lives not worth living." Indeed, it was among the "reform psychiatrists" that the Nazis found some of their most willing collaborators. These psychiatrists sought to bring into the asylums active therapeutic methods that would break the old pattern of simply warehousing mental patients and describing their ailments. This led increasingly to distinctions between the "curable" and the "incurable." For the former, "work therapy" (*Arbeitstherapie*) was mandated. For the latter, who now constituted a growing proportion of long-term patients remaining in the asylums, the only option seemed sterilization. This thinking drew strength from the race hygiene movement, which stressed the hereditary nature of many disorders and urged strong prophylactic measures for the protection and improvement of the nation's racial stock. The July 1933 law, among other things, removed sterilization from the list of medical interventions prohibited by German law as "bodily injury."[45]

Rüdin was typical of such modern—even "progressive"—German psychiatrists. Urbane and charming, his closest collaborators and colleagues were not Nazi party leaders or functionaries but, according to colleague Walter Ritter von Baeyer, "liberal, critically engaged people who were skeptical about the hereditary health law and would rather have seen a program of voluntary rather compulsory sterilization."[46] For the psychotherapists, however, Rüdin and his colleagues were not only a threat to the autonomy and development of their discipline, they were a potential millstone. As Cimbal wrote to Göring on October 2, 1933, Rüdin's theory of heredity (*Vererbungslehre*) was incompatible with spiritual aspects of psychotherapy and there was every danger that association with the psychiatrists would lead not just to loss of autonomy but to destruction. This was so, Cimbal thought, because of what he termed the "Jewish" and materialistic basis of psychiatry.[47] Göring agreed with Cimbal that association with the psychiatrists had to be avoided, but also prudently and cravenly added that Adler had gone too far in ignoring the importance of heredity (*Erbmasse*).[48] At the same time, Cimbal worried about the NSDAP's commitment to hereditary biology and how that might lead, with the psychiatrists' help, to a widespread campaign of sterilization based on "hereditary fatalism" that not only would target the mentally feeble but also the gifted.[49]

On November 15, 1933, Göring met with Rüdin, Conti, and Arthur Gütt, chair of the Reich Commission for National Health, at the Interior Ministry in Berlin. Conti, who was Wagner's party deputy in Berlin, would become, as we shall see in chapter 8, an important ally of the psychotherapists since he was a political protegé of Hermann Göring. Discussions with Rüdin and Gütt resulted in a rejection of Kretschmer's proposal of a section for psychotherapy in the German Psychiatric Society. Göring would inform Kretschmer of this decision. Instead, it was decided that Göring would become a member of the executive committee of the psychiatric group within the just renamed Society of German Neurologists and Psychiatrists. He would also assume a like post in Gütt's Reich Commission for National Health. The short letter to Heyer in which Göring described the outcome of his negotiations at the Interior Ministry was a response to Heyer's long, anxious letter of October 18 in which he advised strongly against any formal association with the psychiatrists. Göring clearly felt that the dangers had been avoided, the necessary compromises made, and certain advantages won for the psychotherapists. In this, it seems, he was right, although the danger to psychotherapy from the ranks of psychiatry would by no means disappear. For the time being, however, the autonomy desired by the psychotherapists seemed to be assured through the continued existence of the German General Medical Society.[50]

This autonomy still had to be guarded. In December Göring and Cimbal corresponded anxiously about an invitation for the German General Medical Society to join another one of the Nazi party's health reform organizations, the Study Group of Practicing Biological Physicians. Both agreed that the party was a dangerous and unstable organization and that the offices of the Reich Interior Ministry were a much more secure harbor for psychotherapy.[51] Upon the advice of Rüdin and Gütt, Göring turned the invitation down. The head of the party organization, Hermann Griesbeck, responded that many psychotherapists were members of the organization and asked if Göring would be willing to assume leadership of them. Since psychotherapists in Munich were urging him to accept this charge, Göring agreed to do it. Apart from wishing to keep some distance from party organizations, Göring also confronted in this case the question of lay therapists. Many of the psychotherapists over whom he was now assuming nominal responsibility in Munich were not physicians and this raised the question of whether nonmedical psychotherapists would eventually become regular members of the German General Medical Society. Göring thought it very possible and the only problem was to avoid alienating the medical members of the society and physicians in general.[52] This was a particular aspect of a more general problem for the psychotherapists at the time. As Cimbal pointed out, most doctors expected Wagner's party reform efforts to fail and the psychotherapists had to avoid compromising themselves in the eyes of their medical colleagues. The trick, Cimbal thought, was to be associated with these party forces in such a way as to share credit for any success and avoid discredit in the event of failure.[53] Göring himself complained about the unscientific nature of Gerhard Wagner's Reich Study Group for a New German Medicine.[54]

Göring and Cimbal were also concerned about their relationship with the International General Medical Society under Jung in Zurich. This concern surfaced in connection with the planning for the seventh General Medical Society congress to be held in Bad Nauheim in May 1934. Jung, as we shall see in chapter 6, wished to help preserve and advance psychotherapy in Germany while also keeping his distance from the more obvious and objectionable concessions to Nazi ideology. It was for this reason that he, for example, would have nothing to do with the special issue of the *Zentralblatt* that Göring edited in 1934 under the obsequious title *Deutsche Seelenheilkunde*. Among the German psychotherapists there emerged the worry that if they lost their scientific and organizational ties abroad—and especially what they regarded as the special appeal an international figure like Jung had for the Nazi regime—they would have to seek closer ties with the Nazi party. And closer ties to the NSDAP would only drive foreigners further away, making the German psychotherapists even more dependent on the party in their ongoing struggle with the psychiatrists.[55] The congresses themselves were an important means of advancing the visibility and viability of psychotherapy in Germany precisely with regard to the danger posed by the German psychiatric establishment. A small—even tawdry—indication of this was the decision by Göring and Cimbal not to wear their Nazi party badges at the Bad Nauheim congress so as not to offend their foreign guests.[56]

The congress at Bad Nauheim marked the official establishment of the International General Medical Society for Psychotherapy. Jung held a three-year term as president as well as heading the Swiss contingent. The international society's statutes prohibited any single national member group from contributing more than 40 percent at an electoral meeting. This was designed, of course, to prevent domination of the society by the Germans.[57] The congress itself was, however, dominated by the Germans, as the eighth congress at Bad Nauheim in 1935 would be.[58] Göring opened and closed the congress with affirmations of loyalty to the Nazi regime and expressions of gratitude for the state's promotion of psychotherapy. In his opening address, among other things, he noted a close relationship with the Society for Racial Hygiene but also observed that, unlike that organization, the German General Medical Society allowed "non-Aryans" to be members, though not leaders.[59] These remarks clearly were designed as a concession, however faint and objectionable, to foreign opinion. Göring also outlined the dangers as well as the opportunities confronting psychotherapy in Germany:

> We know that there are still party members—and colleagues—who deny the necessity of psychotherapy, who assert that heredity is the only thing that matters and that education is unnecessary. Like the Führer, we claim that character can be developed and because of that psychotherapy is of the greatest importance. For psychotherapy, as Jung has emphasized over and over, is not just about curing sick people, but about making fit people who lack the correct attitude toward life.[60]

There were seventy-nine participants at the Bad Nauheim congress, of whom very few were Jews. Cimbal reported, however, that he had been criticized for some of the remarks made at the congress, particularly the prominent mention of Freud in Jungian Wolfgang Kranefeldt's paper.[61] Cimbal and Heyer also managed to turn back an attempt by a group of German Freudians and Stekelians to have the next congress held outside Germany.[62] For his part, Göring later that same May attended the congress of the German Psychiatric Society in Münster and upbraided the psychiatrists for criticizing psychotherapy and ignoring the wisdom of Adolf Hitler.[63] The psychotherapists also sought to expand their membership through the establishment of new regional groups, such as in Bonn and Darmstadt.[64]

During these years the psychotherapists also kept their distance from, as well as an eye on, the psychoanalysts. In the fall of 1933 Göring had expressed the desire to offer "even the old psychoanalysts the opportunity to say whether they could bring something to the new state."[65] He had in mind most prominently, however, Schultz-Hencke, who had some time ago broken with the DPG and the Berlin Psychoanalytic Institute. Göring obviously wished to include people like Schultz-Hencke in his group so that he could convince the authorities that even psychoanalysis could be exercised in the national spirit, thus further strengthening psychotherapy's claim to political reliability. But given the mutual hostility between the Nazis and the Freudian group in Berlin, the Göring psychotherapists also strove to keep their distance from the psychoanalytic society and institute. Early in 1934 Cimbal wrote angrily to Göring that Jung had sent him an announcement of lectures at the Berlin Psychoanalytic Institute that Carl Müller-Braunschweig had wanted published in the *Zentralblatt*.[66] Göring replied that the day was soon coming when the psychoanalysts in Berlin no longer would be able to operate freely and that of course the list of lectures could not be run in the *Zentralblatt*.[67] A couple of months later Göring reported to the NSDAP's Griesbeck that he would be checking the psychoanalytic institute's by-laws and financing as a result of public criticism of Jung by one of its members (see chapter 6).[68] By 1935 the psychoanalysts had been forced to drop "Berlin" from the institute's name and to change the name of their outpatient clinic from "*Poliklinik*" to "*Ambulatorium*" so as not to suggest any affiliation with city or state entities.[69] Finally, in early 1936 Göring was instructed by the NSDAP Expert Advisory Commission on National Health to render an expert opinion on the Psychoanalytic Institute as a prelude to its dissolution.

Following the International General Medical Society congress in Bad Nauheim in May and the German General Medical Society congress in Breslau in October 1935, the psychotherapists were once again approached by the psychiatrists. The Reich Interior Ministry, in its effort to centralize organizations as much as possible, proposed that the psychotherapists join the Society of German Neurologists and Psychiatrists. This proposal originated with Rüdin and was passed along by Herbert Linden. Göring rejected this proposal, pointing out that psychotherapy was related to all disciplines, especially internal medicine, and that he would in any case have to clear any such move with Reich Physicians Leader Wagner.[70] The executive committee of the German General Medical Society declared its willingness, however, to become part of a new umbrella organization, the Society of German Neurologists (Gesellschaft deutscher Nervenärzte). Hans Reiter, head of the Interior Ministry's Reich Health Office, who was friendly to psychotherapy, supported this option.[71] It was Reiter's office that would come to supervise the psychotherapists after the collapse of Wagner's Reich Study Group for a New German Medicine in 1937; and since neither the psychiatrists' proposal nor the psychotherapists' counterproposal was accepted, the psychotherapists ended up in a loose arrangement with the German Society for Internal Medicine.[72] All that came of the original clash of proposals was an agreement in the summer of 1936 to share knowledge, a process asserted to have begun at the August 1936 Frankfurt Congress for Neurology and Psychiatry.[73]

This same concern with disciplinary boundaries underlay the psychotherapists' contemporaneous consideration of the manner in which psychotherapy might in the future be constituted as an official medical specialty. One option was to have the specialty of *Nervenarzt* include psychotherapy, psychiatry, and neurology. This was an unlikely eventuality, however, given the differences among the three areas.[74] Even less likely was a specialty in psychotherapy itself, as Göring wrote to Jung on March 11, 1937: "Yesterday I heard that a medical specialty [*Facharzttitel*] in psychotherapy will definitely not be introduced in Germany."[75] A third option was supplementary certification (*Zusatzausbildung*) in psychotherapy. This would have the advantage of cultivating psychotherapy's ties to psychiatry, neurology, and internal medicine.[76] But no decision was ever reached in this regard during the Third Reich (see chapter 14). The same inconclusive results were obtained from the state authorities regarding coverage for psychotherapy under the health insurance program.[77]

The psychiatrists too were attempting to expand the boundaries of their capacities in the new state. One psychiatrist's argument in particular at this time caught the attention of the psychotherapists. The argument was that "neuroses, psychogenic, and hysterical reactions are psychopathic adjustment disturbances" which might as a result of future research be included under the sterilization law.[78] The psychotherapists apparently chose in this case to view the glass as half full, that is, that this point of view represented another possible opening for psychotherapy. Cimbal wrote to Göring that this essay was "utilizable" and that the author was willing to come to the 1935 Nauheim congress.[79] Göring agreed, saying that Franz Wirz, NSDAP chief administrator for University Affairs, had recommended that the psychotherapists cooperate with the race hygienists and hereditary biologists.[80]

As a result of the competition between two fields that were now growing increasingly distinct, the building of bridges also in effect meant the establishing of bridgeheads. This was particularly true for the psychotherapists. The first two congresses of the German General Medical Society for Psychotherapy, at Breslau in 1935 and Düsseldorf in 1938, had as their themes the possible areas of fruitful collaboration between psychotherapy and psychiatry. Both Robert Sommer and Breslau psychiatrist Johannes Lange gave papers on this subject at the 1935 meeting. Three years later Göring declared in his opening address at Düsseldorf: "We [psychotherapists and psychiatrists] cannot help our *Volk* by fighting, but only by trying to understand and come to friendly terms with one another."[81] But psychiatrist Hans Luxenburger of Munich gave a paper at Düsseldorf in which he made clear the claims that psychotherapy was now staking, whether inside the psychiatric establishment or outside of it, when he argued that psychotherapy could be used to attack neurotic elements in the personalities of even psychotic patients.[82] At the last congress held by the society, in Vienna in 1940, Vienna psychiatrist Otto Pötzl spoke on the need for psychiatrists and psychotherapists to cooperate in meeting the country's urgent demand for increased productivity by strengthening both the physiological and psychological elements that comprise human will.[83] But even this plea for patriotic cooperation only underlined the sovereignty the psychotherapists were now claiming from a position of considerable autonomous professional strength.

The first three years of the Third Reich were a period of some confusion, even chaos, as party, state, and segments of the private sector clashed and collaborated. This was also a period in which Nazi party forces staged an assault in many areas on the institutions of the German establishment. Individuals and organizations inside, outside, and alongside the German establishment launched initiatives in defense or pursuit of their interests. Given the newly energized struggle for medical sovereignty over mental illness, it is no surprise that in early

1936 Göring with some passion wrote to a young activist colleague in Berlin that he was, among other things, trying to use the party against the psychiatric establishment in the state health bureaucracy: "As you can see, I have struggled against a union with the psychiatrists. Without support from the Reich Health Leader, however, all struggle is in vain."[84] By 1936, however, this period of attempted "revolutionary" reorganization gave way to relative stabilization dominated by Nazified state bureaucracies and economic and military mobilization. In the field of psychotherapy, this transformation was dramatically underscored by the coincidence of two events in 1936. In April several psychotherapists, including Göring and Heyer, presented papers at the first and last conference (*Reichstagung*) of Gerhard Wagner's Reich Study Group for a New German Medicine in Wiesbaden. In May the German Institute for Psychological Research and Psychotherapy in Berlin was established under the formal supervision of the Reich Interior Ministry. Within a year Wagner's party health front had collapsed, while the Nazi state-sponsored Göring Institute was in the process of becoming an unprecedented institutional means of professional development for psychotherapy in Germany.[85] This institute also represented an end to the institutional advantage possessed up until that time by the state and university bastions of German psychiatry.

Notes

1. Oswald Bumke, *Erinnerungen,* p. 123.
2. Dozentenführer der Universität Tübingen Dr. Usadel to Rektor Stickl, January 6, 1945, BDC: Parteikorrespondenz.
3. Cimbal to Göring, September 3, 1933, Kl. Erw. 762/2; Kretschmer's son, Wolfgang, believes that Cimbal was speaking metaphorically about his father resting at a sanitarium. In the midst of all of this, the seventh congress of the General Medical Society for Psychotherapy, scheduled for Vienna in early September, was cancelled.
4. Carl Jung, *Letters,* p. 124; Robert Sommer remained as honorary president until his death in 1937.
5. Cimbal to Curtius, September 7, 1935, Kl. Erw. 762/2; Göring to Curtius, August 17, 1938, Kl. Erw. 762/2; Lockot, *Erinnern und Durcharbeiten,* pp. 60, 173; Ulrich Schultz-Venrath, "Ernst Simmel (1882–1947)—ein Pionier der Psychotherapeutischen Medizin?" *Psychotherapeut* 41 (1996): 110. The ban on Jewish membership applied to the Göring Institute since institute members also had to be members of the society: see Göring to Kogerer, March 15, 1938, Kl. Erw. 762/2. On the emigration of Goldstein and Lewin to the Netherlands and the United States, respectively, see Ash, *Gestalt Psychology,* pp. 282, 327–8.
6. Cimbal to Haeberlin, August 3, 1933, Kl. Erw. 762/2.
7. Matthias Heinrich Göring, "Mitteilung des Reichsführers der 'Deutschen

allgemeinen ärztlichen Gesellschaft für Psychotherapie'," *ZfP* 6 (1933): 140–1; and Walter Cimbal, "Bericht des Geschäftsführers," ibid., pp. 141–4.

8. Emmy Göring, *An der Seite meines Mannes* (Göttingen, 1967), chart following p. 110; see also Roger Manvell and Heinrich Frankel, *Hermann Göring* (New York, 1962), pp. 114–16, 268–9, and, on the clan gathering in Berlin in 1938, Willi Frischauer, *The Rise and Fall of Hermann Göring* (Boston, 1951), p. 148.
9. Kl. Erw. 762/2.
10. Göring to Seif, May 26, 1933, Kl. Erw. 762/2.
11. Göring, "Erfolgsmöglichkeiten der Psychotherapie," p. 227.
12. Matthias Heinrich Göring, "Die Kraft der Seele," p. 1076; see also idem, "Weltanschauung und Psychotherapie" (1936), p. 295, (1938), p. 1102; and idem, "Schlussansprache," in Otto Curtius, ed., *Psychotherapie in der Praxis,* p. 49. "Weltanschauung und Psychotherapie" was the text of an address given at the inaugural meeting of the Göring Institute membership and to the 1937 workshop of the German National Health League in Munich; see *Nationalsozialistische Bibliographie* 4:1/2 (January/February 1939), p. 64, entry 277. See also *Wiener medizinische Wochenschrift* 89 (1939): 723–4.
13. Göring to Cimbal, August 6, 1933, Kl. Erw. 762/2. His son Ernst recalls that Göring told him that he joined the party because he could not convince or coerce all the psychotherapists under his authority to do so. Whatever the truth of this, a combination of requirement, prudence, and conviction dictated Göring's action in this regard.
14. Göring, "Mitteilung des Reichsführers," pp. 140–1; and "Bericht über den VII. Kongress für Psychotherapie," *ZfP* 7 (1934): 133.
15. Cimbal, *Bericht,* p. 161.
16. Matthias Heinrich Göring, "Grundlagen der Psychotherapie," p. 1445.
17. See Cimbal to Göring, September 3 and December 28, 1933, Kl. Erw. 762/2.
18. Künkel to Göring, August 9, 1933, Kl. Erw. 762/2.
19. Cimbal to Göring, September 3, 1933, Kl. Erw. 762/2.
20. See the review of Göring, *Über seelisch bedingte echte Organerkrankungen,* in *Ziel und Weg* 9 (1939): 455–6; see also Zapp, "Psychoanalyse und Nationalsozialismus," p. 213; and Göring's reviews in *ZfP* 9 (1936): 297–8, 307–8; ibid., 10 (1938): 301.
21. Ulfried Geuter, "Der Leipziger Kongress der Deutschen Gesellschaft für Psychologie 1933," *Psychologie- und Gesellschaftskritik* 3 (1979): 9–10. Göring did, however, on at least one occasion express the intention to wear his SA uniform at an official function: see Göring to Wirz, March 25, 1935, Kl. Erw. 762/2. Professionals also attempted to appropriate the figure and image of Hitler himself as a political practitioner of their profession. See, for example, Dr. Stephen, "Adolf Hitler als Arzt des deutschen Volkes," *Volksgesundheitswacht* 2 (1935): 3–4; and Walther Poppelreuter, *Hitler der politische Psychologe* (Langensalza, 1934).
22. Cimbal, Rundschreiben, August 7, 1933, Kl. Erw. 762/2.
23. Göring to Cimbal, August 25, September 3, and October 1, 1933, Kl. Erw. 762/2; Cimbal, Bericht an die Berliner Konferenz über den augenblicklichen Stand der Verhandlungen für einen psychotherapeutischen Kongress und für die Fortführung der Gesellschaft, September 12, 1933, Kl. Erw. 762/2; and Cimbal and Göring, Protokoll der Gründungssitzung der "Deutschen allgemeinen ärztlichen Gesellschaft für Psychotherapie," September 15, 1933, Kl. Erw. 762/2; see also Seif to Göring, October 8, 1933, Kl. Erw. 762/2, thanking him for smoothing things over in Munich.

24. Cimbal and Göring, Protokoll der Gründungssitzung, p. 1, Kl. Erw. 762/2.
25. Ibid., pp. 2–4.
26. Göring to Cimbal, October 1, 1933, Kl. Erw. 762/2.
27. Satzungen der "Deutschen allgemeinen ärztlichen Gesellschaft für Psychotherapie," n.d.; Satzung der Deutschen allgemeinen ärztlichen Gesellschaft für Psychotherapie e.V., n.d., Kl. Erw. 762/2; see also Fritz Künkel, Denkschrift über die Stellung der psychotherapeutischen Forschungsgruppen, December 11, 1933, Kl. Erw. 762/2.
28. Matthias Heinrich Göring, "Mitteilung des Reichsführers," p. 141.
29. Göring to Seif, May 26, 1933, Kl. Erw. 762/2.
30. See, for example, Göring to Väth, April 8, 1936, Kl. Erw. 762/2.
31. Göring, "Mitteilung des Reichsführers," pp. 140–1.
32. Cimbal to Göring, January 21 and August 26, 1934, Kl. Erw. 762/2.
33. Göring to Otto Curtius, August 18, 1938, Kl. Erw. 762/2; see also Anton Sauerwald, Bericht, Vienna, March 21, 1938, in Huber, *Psychoanalyse in Österreich,* p. 241.
34. Hendricks to Göring, May 8, 1934, Kl. Erw. 762/2; Frey to Göring, April 27, 1935, Kl. Erw. 762/2; and Göring to Amtsgericht Wuppertal-Elberfeld, February 23, 1936, Kl. Erw. 762/2. Otto Curtius replaced Cimbal while Künkel was approved after investigation; see Göring to Cimbal, March 8, 1935, Kl. Erw. 762/2.
35. Göring to Cimbal, October 1, 1933, Kl. Erw. 762/2.
36. Kretschmer to Göring, October 6, 1933, Kl. Erw. 762/2. There was also some discussion of Kretschmer becoming honorary president of either the German or, along with Sommer, the International General Medical Society for Psychotherapy: see Cimbal, Bericht, September 12, 1933; Cimbal to Göring, October 2, 1933; Göring to Cimbal, October 7, 1933.
37. Göring to Cimbal, October 1, 1933, Kl. Erw. 762/2; Cimbal to Göring, October 2 and October 19, 1933, Kl. Erw. 762/2; and Heyer to Göring, October 18, 1933, Kl. Erw. 762/2.
38. Cimbal to executive committee, October 13, 1933, Kl. Erw. 762/2.
39. Jung to Göring, June 7, 1934, in Jung, *Letters,* p. 163; see also Jung to Gauger, April 16, 1936, Franz Jung.
40. Göring to Cimbal, October 7, 1933, Kl. Erw. 762/2.
41. Göring to Cimbal, October 1, 1933, Kl. Erw. 762/2.
42. Ibid.
43. Arthur Gütt, Ernst Rüdin, and Falk Ruttke, *Gesetz zur Verhütung erbkranken Nachwuchses* (Munich, 1934); Ernst Kretschmer, "Konstitutionslehre und Rassenhygiene," in Ernst Rüdin, ed., *Erblehre und Rassenhygiene im völkischen Staat* (Munich, 1934), pp. 184–93.
44. Gisela Bock, *Zwangssterilisation im Nationalsozialismus* (Opladen, 1986), pp. 230–46; Michael Burleigh, *Death and Deliverance: "Euthanasia" in Germany c. 1900–1945* (New York, 1994).
45. Hans-Walter Schmuhl, "Reformpsychiatrie und Massenmord," in Michael Prinz and Rainer Zitelmann, eds., *Nationalsozialismus und Modernisierung,* 2nd ed. (Darmstadt, 1994), pp. 239–66. A 1931 law regulating human experimentation in medical treatment and research was limited by German law protecting citizens from "bodily injury." Under the Nazis, these limitations fell away: see Geoffrey Cocks, "The Old as New: The Nuremberg Doctors' Trial and Medicine in Modern Germany," in Berg and Cocks, *Medicine and Modernity,* pp. 173–91.
46. Ludwig J. Pongratz, ed., *Psychiatrie in Selbstdarstellungen* (Berne, 1977), p. 17.
47. Kl. Erw. 762/2; see also Cimbal to Göring, October 19, 1933, Kl. Erw. 762/2.
48. Göring to Cimbal, October 7, 1933, Kl. Erw. 762/2.
49. Cimbal to Göring, July 22, 1934, Kl. Erw. 762/2. In this letter, Cimbal asserts that

"syphilis is the cause of every degeneration," a passage that Göring marked with an exclamation point and a question mark.
50. Göring to Heyer, November 19, 1933, Kl. Erw. 762/2.
51. Cimbal to Göring, December 16, 1933, Kl. Erw. 762/2; Göring to Cimbal, December 17, 1933, Kl. Erw. 762/2.
52. Göring to Gütt, January 10, 1934, Kl. Erw. 762/2; see also Seif to Göring, January 8, 1934, Kl. Erw. 762/2.
53. Cimbal to Göring, January 4, 1934, Kl. Erw. 762/2.
54. Göring to Meier, March 30, 1936, Kl. Erw. 762/2.
55. Göring to Gauger, March 10, 1936, Kl. Erw. 762/2.
56. Cimbal to Göring, February 20, 1934, Kl. Erw. 762/2; cf. Cimbal's eagerness to wear the badges (*Parteiabzeichen*) at least in closed meetings at the congress: Cimbal to Göring, August 26 and October 2, 1933, Kl. Erw. 762/2.
57. "Grundversammlung der Überstaatlichen Allgemeinen Ärztlichen Gesellschaft für Psychotherapie," *ZfP* 7 (1934): 134–8; and Jung to Poul Bjerre, January 22, 1934, in Jung, *Letters,* p. 135. The international society statutes made the president's decisions contingent upon the approval of the executive committee. See also C. G. Jung, *Civilization in Transition,* pp. 547–8.
58. Entwurf für den Aufbau des 8. psychotherapeutischen Kongresses in Bad Nauheim vom 11.-13. April 1935.
59. M. H. Göring, Eröffnungs-Ansprache anlässlich des allgemeinen ärztlichen Kongresses für Psychotherapie in Bad Nauheim 1934, p. 2, Kl. Erw. 762/3.
60. Ibid., p. 3; see also Hans von Hattingberg, "Fortschritte der Psychotherapie," *Fortschritte der Neurologie* 7 (1935): 85–105. Hattingberg did not attend the Bad Nauheim congress since he was in Ann Arbor lecturing at the University of Michigan.
61. Cimbal to Göring, August 4, 1934, Kl. Erw. 762/2; see also Wolfgang Kranefeldt, "Freud und Jung."
62. Cimbal to C. A. Meier, October 18, 1934, Kl. Erw. 762/2.
63. Diskussionsbemerkung, May 25, 1934, Kl. Erw. 762/2.
64. Karl Happich to Göring, June 27, 1934, Kl. Erw. 762/2; Göring to Happich, July 17, 1934, Kl. Erw. 762/2; Otto Zimmer to Göring, July 10, 1934, Kl. Erw. 762/2; Carl Gansen to Göring, November 26, 1934, Kl. Erw. 762/2; Hubert Kelter to Göring, February 26, 1935, Kl. Erw. 762/2.
65. Göring to Cimbal, September 6, 1933, Kl. Erw. 762.
66. Cimbal to Göring, January 21, 1934, Kl. Erw. 762/2.
67. Göring to Cimbal, January 23, 1934, Kl. Erw. 762/2.
68. Göring to Griesbeck, March 28, 1934, Kl. Erw. 762/2.
69. Lockot, *Erinnern und Durcharbeiten,* p. 344, n. 6.
70. Göring to Gauger, March 10, 1936, Kl. Erw. 762/2; Göring to Curtius, December 18, 1937, Kl. Erw. 762/2.
71. Reiter to Göring, March 14, 1936, Kl. Erw. 762/2; Göring to Curtius, March 28, 1939, Kl. Erw. 762/2.
72. Wagner and Göring, "Auflösung der Reichsarbeitsgemeinschaft für eine neue deutsche Heilkunde," *ZfP* 9 (1936): 258–9; *Hippokrates* 8 (1937): 1; Göring to Kretschmer, February 26, 1937, Kl. Erw. 762/2. Representatives of both Wagner and Reiter had attended the first congress of the German General Medical Society in Breslau in 1935.
73. "Tätigkeitsbericht 1935/36," p. 5.
74. Göring to Curtius, February 16, 1936.
75. Kl. Erw. 762/2. Göring had earlier learned that psychotherapists could not join the

new Reich Physicians Chamber as psychotherapists: see Heinrich Grote to Göring, March 5, 1936, Kl. Erw. 762/2.

76. Cimbal to Göring, August 4, 1934.
77. "Tätigkeitsbericht 1935/36," p. 4.
78. Hermann Hoffmann, "Die erbbiologischen Ergebnisse in der Neurosenlehre," in Rüdin, *Erblehre und Rassenhygiene,* p. 194.
79. Cimbal to Göring, February 2, 1935, Kl. Erw. 762/2.
80. Göring to Cimbal, February 24, 1935, Kl. Erw. 762/2. It is not known if Hoffmann attended the Nauheim or Breslau congress; he was not on the program of either gathering.
81. Matthias Heinrich Göring, "Eröffnungsansprache," in Otto Curtius, ed., *Psychotherapie in der Praxis,* p. 3.
82. Hans Luxenburger, "Die Indikation zur Psychotherapie der Neurosen vom Standpunkt der Erbbiologie aus gesehen," in Curtius, *Psychotherapie in der Praxis,* pp. 20–32.
83. Otto Pötzl, "Hemmung und Ermüdung," in Bilz, *Psyche und Leistung,* pp. 156–73; see also Huber, *Psychoanalyse in Österreich,* pp. 12–14, 29, 52, 131–2, and 175, n. 21.
84. Göring to Gauger, March 10, 1936, Kl. Erw. 762/2.
85. "Tätigkeitsbericht 1935/36," p. 5.

6

The Parvenu and the Patriarch

The founding of the Göring Institute in 1936 marked the eclipse of one of the noisiest outside agitators for a "new German psychotherapy," a young physician who literally emerged out of nowhere in 1933, Kurt Gauger. The institutionalization of psychotherapy in Germany also rendered superfluous the influence of C. G. Jung, whom the psychotherapists courted because of a fame and a psychology that conceivably could have been the basis for a German psychotherapy divorced from the common and damaging Nazi association of the field with Freud and the Jews. As it turned out, Matthias Heinrich Göring had no rival for leadership of the psychotherapists in Nazi Germany. The parvenu Gauger and the patriarch Jung both quickly receded into the lengthening professional shadow of the paterfamilias Göring.

To understand Kurt Gauger is to understand the real story of the Nazi "coordination" of psychotherapy in Nazi Germany. Gauger played an early and significant role in the affairs of psychotherapy under Hitler and he remained connected with the society and the institute up until the end. But his importance diminished rapidly as a result of the nature of Nazi governance, the professional advantages enjoyed by the psychotherapists under Göring's leadership, Gauger's own personal limitations and doubts, and the increasing emphasis placed by the Nazi regime on technical performance over ideological fidelity. To the degree psychotherapy in the Third Reich had been discussed in the traditional historical literature, it had been subsumed under the common rubric of *Gleichschaltung*: George Mosse in *Nazi Culture,* his useful early compendium of primary Nazi sources on various social and scientific subjects, includes portions of Gauger's book, *Politische Medizin.*

The words are fervent claims of allegiance to Hitler and National Socialism, and the implication of Mosse's selection is that these words tell us all we need to know about psychotherapy in the Third Reich. But the words, while revealing, do not even tell us even everything we need to know about Kurt Gauger as a psychotherapist and as a Nazi.

At the seventh congress of the General Medical Society in Bad Nauheim in 1934 quite a stir had been caused by the appearance of a young physician and psychotherapist in a dark beswastikaed uniform who had harangued the audience on the National Socialist revolution in medicine and psychotherapy. The words Kurt Gauger spoke on that day in May 1934 carried a certain malevolent weight, for at least some of his listeners believed that the dark blue of Gauger's SA Marine uniform was the even more intimidating black of the SS. His address, and its subsequent expansion into a book, constituted a wholehearted endorsement of National Socialism and a vitriolic attack on Western materialism. In terms of psychotherapeutic and philosophical content, Gauger's words displayed a relatively simplistic approach that was vaguely Jungian in derivation; he had been significantly influenced by the Jungian Heyer. Gauger also exploited for present political purposes the German psychotherapeutic emphasis on commitment to individual productivity and commitment to the national community: "The Third Reich has not inscribed happiness on its banners, but courage."[1] Gauger also chaired a discussion group at the congress on the incorporation of psychotherapy into the medical profession.[2] The eighth congress found him giving a lecture on ideals and character and in 1936 he addressed the inaugural meeting of the NSDAP task force on medical reform, taking as his topic the subject of conscience.

For psychotherapists in the early years Gauger loomed like Spenser's Archimago, seeming almost melodramatically useful but also dangerous, and all the more mysterious for his frequent invisibility. The psychotherapeutic leadership worried about his professional abilities, but concluded that a position and title within the German General Medical Society was worth what they perceived as his connections and power with the Nazi establishment in Berlin.[3] But Gauger's connections were largely a myth and that fact, compared with the magnitude of Göring's contacts and combined with his personal psychological struggles, would soon remove him from influence among the psychotherapists. Like Göring he was not a party man imposed on the psychotherapists from the outside. Indeed, his friend since boyhood,

Kurt Zierold, has recalled that Gauger was not personally acquainted with anyone in the party leadership, a significant handicap in an organization that depended so much on the importance of personal contacts. Even relatively obscure and politically ineffectual psychotherapists like the Blankenburg *Naturarzt* Strünckmann, who was a member of the Strasser circle in the old NSDAP and Jungian Richard Köster, who held the Gold Party Badge, were better connected.[4] In reality, Gauger was typical of the muddled idealist whose gamut ran from the pathological likes of Julius Streicher to scions of German culture like Martin Heidegger and Gerhart Hauptmann, all of whom, aside from the wide range covered by their individual moral transgressions, also ran afoul of the limits to revolution and substantive change in the Nazi blur of mobilization.

Kurt Emil Otto Gauger was born on March 10, 1899, in Stettin on the Baltic, the fourth of six children of school rector Albert Gauger. He graduated from the Kaiser Wilhelm Gymnasium there in 1917; he was drafted but did not see combat in the First World War. In March and April of 1920, he later claimed, he was a member of a Free Corps regiment in Stettin and subsequently was active within the ranks of the rightwing terror apparatus, Organisation C. Attending the universities of Greifswald, Leipzig, and Rostock, he majored in philosophy, psychology, and pedagogy, taking minors in comparative linguistics and history. He received a doctorate in philosophy in 1922 with a thesis on Eduard von Hartmann. Gauger spent the next three years at sea, traveling to North and South America, Japan, China, and, finally, Italy, where, like many Germans in fact and fantasy, he lingered to study under the lemon blossoms. In 1925 he returned to Germany and the following year took up medical studies at Berlin and Rostock. He was licensed as a physician on December 10, 1931, and established himself as a general practitioner and psychotherapist in November 1932.[5]

Gauger had first come into contact with psychotherapy in 1926. At the time he had become dissatisfied with his studies and sought help in Berlin from a Jungian psychotherapist, Mila von Prosch. It was she who inspired him to turn to medicine and become a psychotherapist. His friend Zierold had a contact on the scholarship commission and was able to procure funds for Gauger's medical education. Gauger then fell in with a psychotherapeutic circle around Werner and Waldtraut Achelis. He and Achelis grew to be close friends, even though, according to Zierold, his lowercase romantic inclinations led him to become Waldtraut Achelis's lover. He dedicated *Politische Medizin* to Werner Achelis, "a fellow worker in the construction of a German psychotherapy," a book to which Achelis was to write a "comprehensive cultural-political supplement," which in fact never appeared. Gauger was also a poet and prose fiction writer. His 1923 volume of poems, *Gotische Gedichte,* dedicated to Waldtraut Achelis, also displayed the uppercase Romantic bent that enabled him to establish and maintain a close working rapport with her husband, the Romantic philosopher Achelis. Gauger's poetry even accompanied the text of Achelis's *Principia Mundi* of 1930. He subsequently set up a psychotherapy practice in Berlin near the Kurfürstendamm, but he had trouble attracting patients and again sought out Zierold, who was director of the Film Evaluation Board. In this way he landed the job as director of the Reich Institute for Film and Illustration that would serve as his primary occupation during the Third Reich. Zierold also introduced Gauger to the woman who was to become his wife in 1935.

Gauger was short of stature and suffered from weak eyesight that caused him to squint continually. These conditions exacerbated a severe inferiority complex, compensation for which was, in Zierold's view, the primary source for Gauger's attitudes and actions toward Nazism and psychotherapy after 1933. Zierold maintains that Gauger was always seeking approval, reassurance, and praise, but that, because of his dependency on others, he succeeded only in sowing further doubt within himself. Gauger broke off his friendship with Zierold after the war, most probably, as Zierold surmises, because of the overwhelming sense of indebtedness he felt toward him. It is probable that feeling beholden to his friend threatened the tenuous feelings of superiority that Gauger periodically tried to utilize as a defense against the depression that was linked to his feelings of inferiority.[6] His claims and efforts to be well connected within the Nazi hierarchy were the chief expression during the Third Reich of such a sense of inferiority. His aggressive solicitation of Conti's influence for the benefit of psychotherapy was an exercise in just the sort of dependency Gauger was trying to deny by claiming the successful intercession of powerful figures such as Conti. There was more than exculpation in a long postwar letter to psychotherapists Wilhelm Bitter and Gottfried Kühnel that

> on my initiative and responsibility I sought out the then senior civil servant in the Interior Ministry and later Reich Physicians Leader Dr. Conti in order to "save

> what could possibly be saved" (C. G. Jung) which *I succeeded in doing*. *I* persuaded Conti to turn away from a prohibition that would have entailed unforeseeable consequences. No one stood by me at first. . . . I received the assignment from Conti to organize the psychotherapists, whereby I engaged Professor Göring as the best "cover" after I had personally sought him out at my own expense in Wuppertal.[7]

There was also no little degree of identification in Gauger with such powerful men as Conti and Jung in order to fulfill his own grandiose sense of himself, a grandiosity that was a defense against feelings of inner weakness and identity diffusion. Not surprisingly, this need contributed to utilitarian professional identification with Hitler himself:

> As inheritors of the individualistic epoch, we know much about individual conditions of mental illnesses. What we did not hear so much about, however, before Adolf Hitler, are the general conditions of the health of the soul.[8]

Even his postwar account of his joining of the Nazi party took the form not of exculpation but of the assertion of independence and initiative. He had joined the NSDAP on May 1, 1933, when his water sports club, Hochseesportverband Hansa e. V., had been coordinated by the Nazis. He became active as a physician with SA Marine Standarte 77 in Berlin:

> On my insistence my denazification papers contain the explicit finding that *I* became a party member for no particular purpose: not because of a position, for economic advantage or (the reason even many declared opponents of the regime sought party membership) because of civil service regulations, but rather as an *in*dependent private individual; without any compulsion; without any pressure; completely voluntarily! 1933![9]

Gauger's desperate search for affection and admiration found expression in the stories he wrote about the sea. In 1930 he wrote a novel that was published in 1940 as *Christoph: Roman einer Seefahrt*. This book was an attempted escape from his landlocked difficulties in dealing with a flagging career and professional identity in the midst of an economic slump that was very hard on young doctors. With a characteristically Gaugerian mix of guilt, aggression, egotism, and self-pity, his hero remarks that hard work brings nothing but pain: "'I know that it is a sin if one has bad luck and stands alone. No one could be more forsaken than I am.'"[10] Gauger himself was anything but forsaken. The year in which Gauger wrote these words saw him publish a work on psychotherapeutic method with his friend Achelis's Stuttgart publisher,

Püttmanns.[11] The novel, like his 1943 collection of short stories, was published by a subsidiary of the same firm, Kohlhammer, that published material from his friend Zierold's Office for Educational Films. Gauger dedicated the novel to Paul König, a dead sea captain and director for Norddeutsche Lloyd, to whom he declared his indebtedness for having been taught seamanship. The novel's protagonist, Christoph Fählmann, is a young doctor in the small town of Falkenberg. One of his patients comes to him with venereal disease and Christoph feels it his duty to tell her father, one of the town's leading citizens. He does this despite the fact that the girl, Grete Rickler, is of age. The story gets out and Grete's father is ruined by the scandal and Christoph is detained for questioning about his breach of medical confidentiality. Escaping the "revenge of a small town" full of intimate obligation, guilt, and regret, Christoph abandons his medical career to go to Hamburg and begin a life at sea. But once there he in despair throws himself into the Elbe River: "'The physician is dead and therefore Christoph Fählmann must also die.'"[12] Thus, even before he became a doctor and while surrounded by countless young physicians having a rough time making it in a crowded profession in the midst of the Great Depression, Gauger was fantasizing the worst about himself and his career.

Yet even as he is saying these words, Christoph has been fished from the Elbe by a group of sailors who take him in and quite literally nourish him. He tells them sorrowfully that he has no mother and during his first night aboard the steamer *Köln* he appears to the sailors in his sleep "like an infant."[13] Christoph becomes the ship's mascot and his physical stature, like Gauger's, expresses his relationship to the outer world:

> Hinrich gave him his huge sea boots which as a tillerman he no longer needed. Christoph had to put on three pairs of socks one over the other in order to get around in them. The work pants that Hinrich gave him had to be rolled up several times.[14]

The only hostile figure in this maudlin novel is a communist stoker who in the end hangs himself after failing in an attempt to kill Christoph. All the other seamen harbor great affection for Christoph, even to the point of open praise, which, according to Gauger, is not a trait of the seafarer. Christoph is mothered by these men through seasickness, a concussion, and heart palpitations: "I know now that I am one of the saved cases, Johann. There are particular people I have to thank for it. But that I have let myself be helped by these people is a matter of fate."[15] In these words there is not only indebtedness but invocation of fate (*Schicksal,*) which communicates self-pity and a compensatory desire for grandeur.

Gauger's activities on behalf of the psychotherapists, therefore, were motivated by deep conflicts, which established both the extent and the limits of his actions. His association with the Nazi party gave him the means by which he could seek to save his career as a physician. He was also a distant relative of Matthias Heinrich Göring. Gauger later claimed that he had been betrayed by Göring's collaboration with the Nazi regime in building an institute: his aim, he asserted, was the same as that of Jung, that is, to gather together and protect the psychotherapists.[16] In fact, however, the Nazi enthusiast as revealed by his strident words from 1933 to 1936 was simply passed over in the psychotherapists' rush for security and professional development under the Göring banner. His self-esteem once again damaged, Gauger resigned his post as honorary deputy director of the Göring Institute soon after its founding in 1936. He remained a member of the German General Medical Society and claimed during and after the war to have maintained a medical and psychotherapeutic practice, although his Reich Physicians Chamber file lists him as not being active as a physician. But it is not true that Gauger quit because of Göring's "coordination" of the psychotherapists. The Nazi coordination of German society had, after all, begun in 1933 with, among other things, Gauger's hortatory support. In 1937, moreover, Gauger listed his honorary position at the Göring Institute on an SA questionnaire.[17] He remained an SA doctor and from 1936 was enrolled with the Berlin police as an air raid physician (*Luftschutzarzt*) as well.

From 1934 on, Gauger's chief activity in the Third Reich was at the Reich Institute for Film and Illustration, which was under the authority of the Reich Education Ministry; in 1937 he became the institute's director.[18] This work provided his chief link to the psychotherapists. He produced a film on Heidelberg psychiatrist Ludwig Mayer's use of hypnotism which was shown at the ninth congress of the International General Medical Society in Copenhagen in 1937.[19] In 1935 Göring called a meeting at the film institute to present *Die Ewige Maske* (*The Eternal Mask*), a film on which Gauger had worked with director Werner Hochbaum and writer Leo Lapaire. The film was adapted from a novel by Lapaire and concerns a physician suffering from delusions. It celebrates the advance that psychodynamic therapy represented over the old psychiatric search for physical cause with its concomitant dismissal of the patient's own vital testimony. Produced by a Swiss-Austrian subsidiary of the German Tobis company, it starred Olga Tschechova and Mathias Wiemann, two prominent actors of the time. Gauger claimed after the war that Propaganda Minister Goebbels and the Nazi Physicians Chamber had forbidden the showing of the film but that he had showed it in defiance at the university in Berlin on May 31, 1935. Zierold does not remember it being banned, however, and there is no record of it among the blacklisted films of the Nazi period. In fact, it is listed as having been passed by the censors on October 12, 1935, premiering in Dresden on January 8, 1936, and in Berlin on March 3. The film even won a medal as the best psychological study at the biennial Vienna film festival.[20] In late 1941 Gauger was listed as the commentator for two films screened by the Göring Institute that "demonstrate the techniques of the destructive work of the Jewish spirit," a Soviet propaganda film, *The New Gulliver,* and Charlie Chaplin's *Modern Times*.[21] Finally, in 1942 Göring announced that both institutes would collaborate on the production of scientific films.[22] But Gauger was regarded with dislike and fear by most of the psychotherapists at the Göring Institute. Attendance at the 1935 showing of his film on psychotherapy was sparse, surely another blow to his self-esteem. Göring himself was most likely the lone moving force behind a favorable review of Gauger's "psychotherapeutic" novel in the *Zentralblatt* in 1942.[23]

Gauger's later career in the Third Reich was anything but smooth. His doubts about himself lingered or even grew. His collection of sea stories published in 1943 were all in the first person singular and contained elements of suicidal urges. One character in "The Beautiful Adventure" pretends to be a doctor in order to visit a dying friend, a strikingly morose *Doppelgänger* image of Gauger's ambivalence about his identity as a doctor.[24] Gauger also began to have doubts about the Nazis and his identification with them. Estranged from all but a few of the psychotherapists, he claimed to have fought successfully to keep his film institute from being swallowed up by the Propaganda Ministry. There is also evidence to suggest that he did protect "non-Aryans" and political opponents of the regime at his institute from 1936 on. In a sense, his failure as a major player in Nazi politics allowed him to do this. At the same time, as he himself argued, his membership in the party also gave him some leeway as far as the Gestapo was concerned.[25] While ignoring his own enthusiastic involvement in Nazi projects, Gauger touches on an important point about resistance (of much greater magnitude than his own) to Nazi—or any modern—tyranny: It involves a certain degree of integration into—and thus collaboration with—the very complex and extensive system it opposes.[26] One needs, as it were, a place to stand in order to make a stand. We shall see this more clearly in the case of psychotherapists in the Third Reich in the story of John Rittmeister in chapter 13. The psychotherapists, protected and successful under Göring, had the relative luxury of pursuing their professional aims and were less likely to have occasion or want to risk active resistance. At the same time, as we shall see, some small acts of humanity and resistance could stem from the exercise of professional duties. But these too were functions of a larger collaboration with, and technical contribution to, the energies and needs of the Nazi regime. If Gauger did more in opposition to the Nazis, it had more to do with professional failure than with success; if the psychotherapists as a group did less, it was primarily due to their success at professional development.

While parvenu Kurt Gauger imposed himself on the psychotherapists, patriarch Carl Jung was drafted by them to provide the protection and prestige they hoped his name would bring to their discipline in the Third Reich. Like Gauger, however, Jung and his reputation were rendered superfluous over time by the presence of the paterfamilias Göring. It seems unlikely that, had Göring not existed, Jung's fame, ideas, or efforts alone could have provided the psychotherapists in Germany much genuine protection, much less advantage. What Jung hoped was to make the old society formally international in nature and thus to protect psychotherapy, including of course the Jungian variety, from extinction in Germany. In the best of all possible German worlds, survival might even lead to the unification of the various schools of thought, thus subordinating the powerful and autonomous psychoanalytic movement to a more comprehensive psychotherapy more amenable to the Jungian point of view. In fact, after the establishment of the German Institute for Psychological Research and Psychotherapy in Berlin in 1936 seemed to herald just such a development, Jungian Otto Curtius reported that Jung was planning an institute in Zurich "after our Berlin model."[27] In any event, in a letter of November 23, 1933, to

Rudolf Allers, Jung concluded that "Göring is a very amiable and reasonable man, so I have the best hopes for our cooperation."[28]

The International General Medical Society for Psychotherapy was headquartered in Zurich. Jung held a three-year term as president of the international society as well as heading the Swiss group that came into existence in 1935. The statutes of the international society were adopted at the seventh congress of the old General Medical Society at Bad Nauheim on May 15, 1934.[29] As we have seen, these statutes attempted to counter the overwhelming weight of the German society: at the Bad Nauheim congress there were seventy-one German participants, two from Holland, a Swede, and a Swiss (Jung). On January 22, 1934, Jung had written to Poul Bjerre, who would become leader of a Swedish section of the international society in 1936, expressing his concern over just such an imbalance of power.[30]

Jung also claimed to be acting in the interests of the Jewish members of the international society. When Max Guggenheim of Lausanne objected to Jung's role in working with the psychotherapists in Germany, Jung responded that, among other things, he had enabled Allers, a Jew, to stay on as editor of the review section of the *Zentralblatt*.[31] Jung also inserted a circular letter in the December 1934 issue of the *Zentralblatt* which declared that the "international society is neutral as to politics and creed."[32] This separated membership in the international society from membership in any of the national groups within it, thus allowing German Jewish doctors to join the international society on an individual basis. But, as we have already seen, Jews could still be members of the German General Medical Society until 1938, when Jewish doctors lost the right to practice in Germany. Jung also intervened personally in the case of one his German Jewish followers, Gerhard Adler, who had been the subject of an anti-Semitic attack by Achelis at the German congress in Breslau in 1935.[33] According to Jung's son, Göring protected Adler while he was in Berlin and facilitated his eventual emigration to Switzerland in April 1936. While Adler disputes Göring's role, he has confirmed that Jung wrote Göring on his behalf.[34] For his part, Göring, as we shall shortly see, had every reason to cultivate Jung for the sake of psychotherapy in Germany. In 1934 he worked hard to get Jung to attend the Bad Nauheim congress and to advertise it in the *Zentralblatt*. In return, he promised to speak to Reich Physicians Leader Wagner about two issues of interest to Jung, the status of nonmedical psychotherapists and "the wishes of Dr. Adler."[35]

In a letter to Alphonse Maeder of Zurich on January 22, 1934, Jung wrote that Kretschmer had stepped down because matters had become too complicated and that he, Jung, would not have accepted presidency of the General Medical Society for Psychotherapy had it not been for the insistence of the Germans that no German could effectively assume a post in an international organization under the prevailing conditions in Germany.[36] There is no evidence that Jung forced Kretschmer's resignation in order to further his own designs and in his autobiography Kretschmer expresses no animus toward Jung.[37] The German psychotherapists' preference was determined not only by their desire for the protection they believed Jung's worldwide reputation would provide, but also by Jung's great popularity and respect among proponents of a new German psychotherapy that was ferociously opposed to Freudian theories. Thus, the genuine and justified anxiety that prompted German psychotherapists to engage Jung and motivated him to become involved in German affairs at this time also served for both Jung and his German colleagues as a cover both for concession to and enthusiasm for National Socialism. Moreover, the Germans' use of Jung was also in his interest in promoting analytical psychology, particularly at the expense of its archrival, Freudian psychoanalysis.

All of these motives were almost painfully evident when Jung was interviewed by one of his disciples, Adolf von Weizsäcker, over Radio Berlin on June 26, 1933, when Jung was in the German capital to give a seminar at the C. G. Jung Society there. Weizsäcker's first question concerned his mentor's perceptions of the differences between the German and the West European souls. Jung's response was that the primary distinction was the "youthfulness" of the German soul. He went on to stress the importance of appreciating the totality of the human organism, casting the greatest doubt on any psychology that, in a clear reference to Freud and Adler, respectively, reduced the individual to the sum of sexual drives or lust for power. It was this particular aspect of Jung's psychology, Weizsäcker agreed, that made it one of "vision," as opposed to the "intellectual basis" of Freudian and Adlerian psychology. In addition to his obvious awe of the master, Weizsäcker pursued his questions in the service of psychotherapy's place in the new Reich along the distinct lines established in his reverential introduction to the interview. There, among other things, he celebrated the fact that "Dr. Jung does not tear to pieces and destroy the immediacy of our psychic life, the creative element which has always played the decisive role in the history of the German mind."[38] As we shall see below, however, Jung was not simply being used. After the war Jung ruefully recalled this tone in a way that underlined the positive feelings he himself had about the political change represented by fascism:

> Our judgment would certainly be very different if our imagination stopped short at 1933 or 1934. At that time, in Germany as well as in Italy, there were not a few things that appeared plausible and seemed to speak in favor of the regime . . . . And after the stagnation and decay of the post-war years, the refreshing wind that blew through the two countries was a tempting sign of hope.[39]

Enthusiasm for Jung in Germany was not restricted to Jungians. Another student of Jung's, Wolfgang Kranefeldt, recalled that when he went to Berlin in 1935 to give a series of lectures on archetypes, he was received with great joy and admiration, especially by Göring, specifically because of his affiliation with Jung. The second issue of the *Zentralblatt* in 1935 was devoted to Jung's analytical psychology and many articles about Jung's psychology appeared in the journal between 1934 and 1936. The very next issue of 1935 published a commemoration of Jung's sixtieth birthday emphasizing his service to psychotherapy in Germany:

> In 1933 he assumed the presidency of the "International General Medical Society for Psychotherapy," taking on the difficult assignment of supporting a gravely threatened psychotherapy in its struggle for existence and at the same time preserving as far as possible international scientific relations.[40]

That German Jungians were not automatically trusted by the regime only increased the tendency to invoke Jung's name and presence as often as possible. In 1935, for example, a reporter for the *Deutsche Allgemeine Zeitung* wanted to write about Adolf von Weizsäcker's presentation at the German General Medical conference in Breslau. The editors turned the request down because they had been scared off by Achelis's attack on Gerhard Adler. Their conclusion was that "'Jung himself is certainly highly regarded at the top, but his followers are suspect and cannot be discussed.'"[41] Two years later, however, things had changed: In 1937 the *Deutsche Allgemeine Zeitung* published an admiring article about a young psychotherapy overcoming its infantile Freudian weaknesses under the maturing influence of Jung and his followers; the same month the *Kölnische Zeitung* published a similar article by Göring Institute Jungian Gustav Schmaltz.[42] Jung once again visited Berlin in September 1937, witnessed Mussolini's state visit to Germany, and earned the local C. G. Jung Society and the Göring Institute more than RM 2000 in proceeds from two lectures.[43]

For all these reasons, the German psychotherapists did everything they could to link Jung's name to their own activities. This again does not mean, as we shall see, that Jung did not have his own highly complicated and somewhat suspect personal, philosophical, and organizational motives for associating with the psychotherapists in Germany, but the Germans needed him more than he needed them. This is most strikingly evident in an event from Jung's first visit in 1933. According to Jung's close friend, Barbara Hannah, while Jung was in Berlin that year, the Duisburg Jungian Otto Curtius, whose brother Julius was a former chancellor, economics minister, and foreign minister from the DVP, persuaded Jung that Propaganda Minister Joseph Goebbels wished to see him. On being shown into Goebbels's office, it became apparent that Goebbels had extended no such invitation to Jung and that, on the contrary, had been told that Jung wished to see him.[44] Curtius (and/or Göring) clearly had thought that the meeting would be another potential plus for the profession they represented. The same motive of identifying German psychotherapy with Jung most likely accounted as well, at least in part, for Göring's proposal to Reichsführer-SS Heinrich Himmler in 1939 that the SS-Ahnenerbe fund a Göring Institute research project under Gustav Schmaltz on trees and forests as mythological symbols in dreams based on Jung's theories (see chapter 11).

More than one Nazi racial theoretician saw Jung's work as indispensable in providing rich material for the history and culture of a race:

> By means of this unconscious, one seeks to unlock an ancient spiritual heirloom, and the famous practitioner of depth psychology, C. G. Jung, goes so far as to maintain that within the unconscious lie deep spiritual strata whose disclosure even makes possible a "reconstruction of the prehistory" of cultures.[45]

But such views did not constitute ideological carte blanche from the regime for Jung's analytical psychology. The editor of the journal in which this 1939 article on depth psychology and race appeared felt compelled to add a note to the effect that while the essay was a welcome addition to a "yet open area of research," the author's assertion that heredity must be equated with the unconscious could not be endorsed without reservation. Nevertheless, the article was listed in the official Nazi bibliography edited by the chancellery's Philip Bouhler.[46] And during the war Nazi authorities made a distinction between Jungian depth psychology and Freudian psychoanalysis in allowing the importation of a new book by Jung.[47]

The regime itself displayed little scientific interest in Jung or his followers. It did, however, monitor their activities even outside of Germany. From 1935 to 1939, various government agencies gathered information on the annual Eranos conferences at Ascona in Switzerland. In 1936 the Reich Education Ministry refused to grant Germans permission to attend. The next year Göring arranged to have Eranos secretary Olga Fröbe-Kapteyn visit the Ministry to smooth the way for German participation. This intervention proved successful but by 1938 the Nazi Auslands-Organisation was objecting that there were lots of Jews at the meetings, that some of the topics were "politically conflictual," and that in general the whole organization seemed "mysterious." To resolve such doubts, a Ministry official asked Göring to have a report prepared on that year's meeting. On August 23, 1938 Olga von König-Fachsenfeld duly reported that she had heard nothing political at the conference, that the Swiss in particular seemed to have gone out of their way not to criticize Germany, and that while there were a number of Jews in attendance none was on the program. Permissions were given for Germans to participate in 1939 and in December of that year the German consulate in Locarno commented that while the participants at the meeting were certainly "different," the conferences did not seem to serve the interests of foreign powers, Jews, or Masons and that therefore Germans should be allowed to attend. The only restriction was to be that they could not address sessions where Jews were present.[48]

Jung's motives for his actions between 1933 and 1940 have been widely questioned and attacked. It is true that most of his protests about the course of events in Germany went exclusively into the ears and eyes of non-Germans, but perhaps this was only prudent given the German environment. And even though Jung corresponded with Gauger concerning the protection that the eager professional parvenu and party man might be able to provide for psychotherapy, he professed to be aghast at Gauger's book on "political medicine."[49] In 1935 he declared himself against naming Gauger as managing director of the

German society, preferring, not unselfishly, his follower Curtius.[50] Jung never became directly involved in the operations of the German General Medical Society or of the Göring Institute. Even his role in the protection of psychotherapy was ambiguous in effect. His claim to have succeeded in "tucking away Psychotherapy in a remote department where the medical Nazi boss could not reach it" is inaccurate.[51] Apart from the fact that Nazified state institutions were successfully fighting off party challenges, the equation of party with threat and state with opportunity (or at least protection) is far too simple a formulation. The Nazi preference for mobilization over reform, coupled with the conservative nationalism and Romantic medical orientation shared by party health ideologues and by most German psychotherapists, made the party far less of a threat than it might have appeared at the time. And, as we have seen already, Göring was the key player in these machinations, not Jung.

The starting point for criticism of Jung is the introduction he contributed to the resuscitated *Zentralblatt* of December 1933.[52] There he wrote that, in his capacity as editor, he saw his purpose as the clarification of various teachings, theories, and practices within a political context even though psychotherapy itself had nothing to do with politics. But Jung's ambiguous embrace of forces, symbols, races, and elites led to the same sort of relativism that had paralyzed German intellectuals of the nineteenth and twentieth centuries. In general, his statements of the Nazi era exhibited a fairly distinct disdain for what he saw as a shallow and mechanical democracy in its denial and denigration of the awesome depths of the human soul and the soul's unique and dynamic cultural, national, and racial manifestations.[53] Jung had observed in his radio interview with Weizsäcker in 1933 that "every movement culminates organically in a leader."[54] Europe could not, he said, understand Germany because it was not in the same situation and did not share the same historical and psychological experiences. He endorsed Hitler's constant assertion that the individual must have the courage to go his own way, thereby ignoring the totalitarian aspirations of Hitler's regime. In the same manner, in his introduction to the *Zentralblatt,* Jung found a formulation that fit both his own anthropological tendency toward national and racial characterization as well as the practical demands of the moment: "Genuinely independent and perceptive people have for a long time recognized that the difference between Germanic and Jewish psychology should no longer be effaced, something that can only be beneficial to the science."[55]

Jung's words, and the fact that they were published alongside Göring's call to the Nazi colors, caused an international furor. Jung later claimed that Göring's essay was to have been published only in the special German supplement to the *Zentralblatt* and that it was only by accident that it had appeared in the "international" journal.[56] Perhaps Jung was thinking of what was to become "Die nationalsozialistische Idee in der Psychotherapie," Göring's introductory essay to *Deutsche Seelenheilkunde,* and did not anticipate the strident pro-Nazi rhetoric of Göring's little communication, but surely he should have been—and probably was—aware that his remarks would be placed within a framework of loyalty to the Nazi cause in a journal that, while under Jung's editorship, was published and printed in Germany as the main public vehicle for the German psychotherapists. This was especially so in light of his German colleagues' efforts to associate his name, person, and theory with themselves.

Regardless of their context, however, Jung's observations were objectionable in and of themselves to many, as they seemed to support the official anti-Semitism of the Nazi government. In February 1934, Gustav Bally, a former Berlin psychoanalyst who had been forced to emigrate to Switzerland because of "anti-state activities," attacked Jung's future credibility as editor of a periodical subservient to the Nazi regime. Bally pointed to what he considered the damning emphasis Jung had placed on the supposed distinctions between Jewish and Germanic science, a common theme among Nazi intellectual apologists. At best, Bally concluded, Jung was unwittingly abetting National Socialism.[57] One result of Bally's criticism was Göring's assurance to the Nazi party's Hermann Griesbeck that "my deputy" Kurt Gauger would look into the finances and by-laws of the Psychoanalytic Institute in Berlin.[58] For his part, Jung replied to Bally by citing his "disappointment" at the publication of the Göring pledge of allegiance to Hitler in the *Zentralblatt* and by noting that he was president not of the German society but of the international society. Furthermore, Jung cautioned,

> [a]s conditions then were, a single stroke of the pen in high places would have sufficed to sweep all psychotherapy under the table. That had to be prevented at all costs for the sake of suffering humanity, doctors and . . . science and civilization.[59]

Jung's use of the past tense in 1934 is indicative of how his perception of the danger to psychotherapy had changed. This could evidence rueful reappraisal on the basis of a guilty conscience and/or an honest sense of having accomplished something positive in terms of the protection of psychotherapy. It is also an indication of the growing security won by the psychotherapists, a security Jung was probably trying to enhance by making a public distinction between "then" and "now." This would not only justify, to himself at least, his ongoing involvement with affairs in Germany, but also the policy adopted by the psychotherapists under Göring.

In response to Bally's objection to his distinction between German and Jew, Jung denied that he was making any value judgments and rejected the assertion that he had only recently and strategically begun emphasizing racial and cultural differences among peoples. It is clear in this instance, however, that he was attempting to use his own particular psychological view, with its criticism of the materialism of Freud's perspective and the rootlessness of modern Jewish culture, to protect psychotherapists in Germany. In an essay in the *Zentralblatt* in 1934, Jung again sought to distinguish between the Jewish and the "Aryan" unconscious, claiming that Freud "did not know the German soul, and neither do any of his blind adherents. Has not the shattering advent of National Socialism, upon which the world gazes with astonished eyes, taught them better?"[60]

The basis for Jung's and the German psychotherapists' concern, of course, was the association in Nazi minds of all psychotherapy with psychoanalysis. But these fears also built upon earlier professional disagreements and cultural prejudices. For example, in 1936, when the DPG anxiously approached the C. G. Jung Society in Berlin with a proposal for merger (see chapter 7), Jung advised against it. In a letter to Kurt Gauger, Jung observed:

> I must know that I have a strong man in this affair, otherwise I fear that an undermining psychology will be promoted under the cover of my name. As you know, I am no absolute anti-Freudian zealot [*Freudfresser*], rather I acknowledge the correctness of a number of Freudian statements with respect to the special structure of neuroses and most especially their sexual aspect. However, these things must be taught in a positive philosophical context so that they cause no public harm.[61]

Jung refers earlier in the letter to the anti-Christian orientation of the psychoanalysts ("these people"), making it clear that deep philosophical differences, too easily exploitable under National Socialism, underlay the more pragmatic considerations of the day. Jung had expressed himself in similar fashion two years before in a letter to Kranefeldt:

> As is known, one cannot do anything against stupidity, but in this instance the Aryan people can point out that with Freud and Adler, specific Jewish points of view are publicly preached and, as can likewise be proved, points of view that have an essentially corrosive character. If the proclamation of this Jewish gospel is agreeable to the government, then so be it. Otherwise, there is also the possibility that this would not be agreeable to the government...[62]

On the other hand, by 1936 Jung was contemplating National Socialism in general with a more critical eye:

> The impressive thing about the German phenomenon is that one man, who is obviously "possessed," has infected a whole nation to such an extent that everything is set in motion and has started rolling on its course to perdition.[63]

These words are from Jung's essay "Wotan," which Göring Institute Jungian Lucy Heyer-Grote claimed to have used in psychotherapy with comforting effect on patients who were opponents of the Nazi regime. It was a work that anticipated Jung's September 1939 judgment that "Hitler is reaching his climax and with him the German psychosis."[64] In the realm of psychotherapy itself, earlier that same year Jung himself turned down a request from the editor of the *Zeitschrift für Rassenkunde,* Egon Freiherr von Eickstedt of Berlin, to write an article on contemporary racial problems.[65] Two years before, Jung had been appalled to learn from C. A. Meier, managing editor of the *Zentralblatt,* that Göring had written for publication there a short review of official Nazi party philosopher Alfred Rosenberg's *Der Mythus des 20. Jahrhunderts* (1930). In a letter to Göring of November 16, Jung suggested that the book be passed over in silence and in fact the review did not appear, perhaps a sign that Jung and Meier could exercise some influence over what appeared in the journal's pages.[66]

Jung's role in the affairs of psychotherapy in Germany diminished significantly once the German psychotherapists established their institute in May 1936. His major preoccupation from 1936 to 1940, when he resigned as president of the International General Medical Society, was with the international congresses and the controversies surrounding them. The controversies mostly had to do with the attempts of the Germans to assert their numerical dominance within the international society. This political dominance had emerged at the 1934 congress in Bad Nauheim. The original seventh congress scheduled for Vienna in April of 1933, which had been postponed because of the poor economy and the Nazi seizure of power, was to have featured, among others, Anna Freud, Paul Schilder, and Charlotte Bühler. The Vienna congress would have represented not only a broadening of the thematic concerns of the General Medical Society but also a diversification of the national origins of its members, a significant evolution away from the original almost exclusively German membership. Now, with the emergence of the Nazis, the trend seemed to be toward the original pattern of German dominance even as the organization became officially international in nature. The Danish group, under J. H. van der Hoop, had been the first national group to form in 1934 and this was the basis of the proposal to hold the eighth congress in Copenhagen. This, as we saw in chapter 5, was scotched by the Germans, largely as a result of the Nazi government's refusal to allow German participants a sufficient amount of foreign exchange. However, the founding of the Göring Institute in 1936, which gave the German psychotherapists a more secure base of operations, combined with the Nazi regime's desire to cultivate—and exploit—European contacts, along with the increase in the number of national groups in the International General Medical Society, resulted in the ninth international congress in 1937 being held in Copenhagen.[67] Poul Bjerre, leader of the Swedish group that had formed in 1936, had, with Göring's support, proposed that the theme of the congress be "Race and Depth Psychology." Neither Jung ("too controversial") nor the Nazi government ("too soon") were in favor of this and the proposal was rejected. In Copenhagen the formation of an English section of the international society was formalized, with Göring opposing without success the naming of Erich Strauss, a Jew, as one of the group's leaders.[68]

The tenth, and last, congress was held in Oxford in the summer of 1938. The Austrian national group, which had formed in 1936, had been collapsed into the German group as a result of the Nazi annexation of Austria in March. Again the Germans had pushed for the congress to be held in Germany, and again because of foreign exchange restrictions. By the time of the congress, moreover, the Nazi regime had stepped up its persecution of the Jews, effectively banishing them from German professional life. As we have already seen, the German General Medical Society had as a result changed its statutes so as to ban Jews from being members. Göring was forced by the German Foreign Office to refuse the money from the international society offered to the seven divisional directors of the new German institute since Jews from other countries were being allowed to participate in the congress. Jung had earlier assured Strauss, the English president, that the statutes of the international society with regard to membership were still in force. As it turned out, ten of the German participants in the congress were Jews and were not included among the thirteen participants mentioned in the *Zentralblatt*.[69] At the congress, in exchange for an assurance from Jung that the next international congress would take place in Germany (Göring had in mind Vienna[70]), Göring agreed that Hugh Crichton-Miller should become vice president of the international society. Jung subsequently wrote to Göring that this compromise had thrown a good light on the Germans in the face of "certain Jewish intrigues."[71]

But no congress was held in 1939 and relations between Jung and Göring progressively soured. On September 2, 1939, Jung complained to Hugh Crichton-Miller of Göring's "simple psychology" and "general inability" when Göring interpreted Jung's suggestion of van der Hoop for his successor as president as an anti-German stratagem. Göring at the time was attempting to redress what he saw as the growing imbalance within the society in favor of national groups from democratic countries. At the Oxford congress Jung had even asked Ira Wile, an American member of the international society, about the possibility of the formation of a national group from the United States.[72] After the congress, Göring wrote colleague Edgar Herzog that he had met with Nazi officials and that "it would be very good if the authoritarian states were to join the international society so that the liberalistic states would not maintain superiority."[73] Göring succeeded in July 1939 in having national groups from Hungary, Italy, and Japan organized. Jung's response to this was an attempt to resign as president of the international society. He was induced to stay on until these groups had actually been accepted into the international society. Negotiations dragged on into the following year and since the additions represented a strengthening of German influence through the recruitment of two Axis partners and a revisionist Balkan state, Jung saw no reason to continue purely as a figurehead president. Following a meeting of delegates from Germany, Italy, Sweden, Switzerland, and Hungary in September 1940 in Vienna and the refusal of Poul Bjerre to succeed Jung as president, the international society was placed for the duration of the war under German direction and its headquarters were moved from Zurich to Berlin.[74] Göring, who had been co-editor of the *Zentralblatt* with Jung since 1936, now became its sole editor-in-chief. Officially, it remained the journal of the international society, but, in Göring's words, in order to ensure a "strict execution" of its "care and control," Rudolf Bilz took over as managing editor from Otto Curtius and C. A. Meier.[75] By the end of 1940 Göring wrote to Meier that in the "transvaluation of all values" that had now been accomplished in Germany and in Europe, neither Jung nor Crichton-Miller had any authority left.[76]

Such a detailed historical and institutional context helps in this case to counteract the tendency among psychoanalysts, and nonhistorians generally, to focus on individuals, especially on the "great" in history and especially in a time, the first half of the twentieth century, when the world was seemingly dominated by larger-than-life figures, both benevolent and malevolent. Clearly, the significance of individuals, such as Freud or Jung—or Hitler—should not be underestimated, but too often forays into recent history by psychoanalysts in particular have slighted proper historical method and exhibited both an ahistorical concern with the anecdotal and, even more troubling, the prejudgments that come with partisanship. The latter problem is especially acute when it comes to debates between Jungians and Freudians, camps divided by deep philosophical differences, differences that became manifest during the period in Europe between the two world wars. Anti-Semitism of course bulked large in European life in those years and thus unavoidably played a role in the intramural clashes within the psychoanalytic movement. These general philosophical differences and the specific tradition of anti-Semitism also naturally played a part in the reception and use of Jung and Jungian psychology in Germany between 1933 and 1940.

In December 1933 Jung became the editor of the society's journal, the *Zentralblatt für Psychotherapie,* which was published in Germany by Hirzel Verlag of Leipzig. The journal, like the international society as a whole, was dominated by the large and newly aggressive German group that had formed the bulk and center of the old society. It was in this journal that Jung published his observations on the distinctions between German and Jewish psychology alongside calls by Göring to the Nazi colors. While Jung's words here betrayed some ethically dubious habits of mind, Jung's opponents have often reduced these pronouncements to proof of unalloyed anti-Semitism and wholehearted collaboration with the Nazis. Such a view, however, ignores Jung's increasing disaffection toward the Nazis and his desire to protect psychotherapists in Germany from dangerous Nazi equations with so-called "Jewish" psychoanalysis. Any dissection of Jung's motives and actions, therefore, cannot be based simply on a recitation and critique of his words in the *Zentralblatt,* as has most recently been attempted by Jeffrey Masson.[77] By 1940, in any case, as we have seen, Jung had resigned as president of an international society rendered moribund by war and had likewise left the editorship of the journal to a now estranged Göring and his collaborators.

While Jung's critics must be more attentive to historical detail and to multiple and evolving motives on Jung's part, his defenders must be more candid about the disturbing ambiguities in his thought, especially with regard to Jews. As Paul Roazen has rightly observed, "just as Jung shared sexist prejudices toward women, it would not be surprising for him to have uncritically adopted many traditional stereotypes about Jews."[78] There have been any number of ways in which insufficiently critical admirers of Jung have attempted to render harmless his expressions of such views in connection with the Third Reich. The first is simply to ignore the problem in accounts of professional development.[79] A second, and more common, strategy has been to deny that Jung thought or acted in an anti-Semitic fashion. This was the approach of the earliest of the postwar Jungian apologists.[80] The third approach is to argue simplistically that Jung made mistakes rather than acting out of evil intent. These sources quote Jung's postwar reflections on Nazism to trace the growth of his doubts, beginning with his "Wotan" essay of 1936, in "working through" ambivalent and hostile feelings.[81]

Another, and largely overlooked, means of rendering Jung's statements less ambiguous and questionable is through their alteration in translation. For example, in his 1934 *Zentralblatt* essay Jung twice uses the adjective "*arisch*" in discussing "Aryan" psychology. In the translation by R.F.C. Hull in the Bollingen Series of Jung's collected works, the German adjective "*arisch*" is capitalized and placed in quotation marks.[82] In the original, however, the word appears in the lower case and without quotation marks. The translator might argue that current usage demands the quotation marks or that they indicate what Jung really meant or would have said later on, but proper historical inquiry demands fidelity to the primary source. At the time, to be sure, the word "Aryan" was used often and without quotation marks. The word occurs regularly, for example, in Freud's correspondence, as Peter Gay has shown in his recent biography.[83] Of course, the important matter is what the word meant to its user and in the case of Jung's *Collected Works* one tends to think that the editorial decision was designed to cosmetize and thus alter the historical picture. The same is true of the translation of a footnote to a speech given by Jung in Vienna in November 1932 that was published in 1934 as part of a book entitled *Wirklichkeit der Seele*. The note is to the following text:

> . . . the great liberating ideas of world history have sprung from leading personalities and never from the inert mass . . . . The huzzahs of the Italian nation go forth to the personality of the Duce, and the dirges of other nations lament the absence of strong leaders.[84]

The note itself in the original German reads: "*Seitdem dieser Satz geschrieben wurde, hat auch Deutschland seinen Führer gefunden.*"[85] The translation reads, incorrectly: "After this was written, Germany also turned to a Führer." The latter verb construction implies a neutrality or even a disparagement on Jung's part and a resignation or desperation on the part of the Germans not expressed by the original language. The translation should read: "Since this sentence was written, Germany too has found its leader." The Jungian cultural specificity of the pronoun is missing in the Hull translation, as is the positive connotation of discovery in "has found" that corresponds to the endorsement of strong leaders found in the text, a theme to which Jung returned in his 1933 interview on Radio Berlin.[86]

Jung, as we have seen, did not involve himself unilaterally in the domestic affairs of Nazi Germany. He was in fact sought out by psychotherapists there who felt his association and endorsement would add luster to their bid for professional autonomy from then dominant nosological psychiatry and dissociate them from Freud in the eyes of the regime. The German Jungians in particular, as we have seen, were of course eager to promote Jung for generally defensive as well as specifically partisan purposes. So though Jung could hardly have been averse to the advancement of his school of thought at the expense of that of Freud, he was involved in a project that he could rightly claim served the survival of psychotherapy in general. Should he have anticipated the extent to which psychotherapy could contribute to the repressive aims of National Socialism? Should he not have weighed more carefully the effects his words and actions in support of events in Germany had on both the victims and the victors in the Third Reich?

Jung's abiding emphasis on the unique collective experiences and memories of the world's cultures, nations, and races provided inspiration for various individuals and groups in Nazi Germany. While Freud and his theories were officially disapproved and thus, when used, cloaked in Aesopian language, Jung's ideas were often evaluated positively in Nazi literature. This is not to say that in fact Jung's ideas and those of the Nazis were identical, only that such identifications could be and were effected. And while, as Robert Proctor has noted in his recent book on medicine in Nazi Germany, Jung never went on from differentiation to denigration in his cultural relativism, Nazi "racial anthropologists" and physicians sought to elucidate the pernicious peculiarities of "Jewish" science and culture in ways, while of course more crude and vicious, similar to contemporaneous musings by Jung.[87]

Göring and others had originally hoped to use Jung and his followers at the institute in Berlin, individuals such as G. R. Heyer, Wolfgang Kranefeldt, and Olga von König-Fachsenfeld, as a major resource for the construction of a non-Freudian "German psychotherapy." Although this fascistic spirit pervaded the institute, neither a "German psychotherapy" nor Jung's theories by themselves in fact played a predominant role in the psychotherapists' activities. The various practical demands assumed by the psychotherapists in applying and advertising their therapeutic expertise in the realms of German society, industry, and the military took precedence over the more abstract and less pragmatic characteristics of Jungian psychology. Already in 1939, Göring was complaining to Curtius that the Jungians in Berlin were receding into the organizational background of his institute.[88] Curtius responded that while Jung's thought was close to National Socialism and that Hitler himself would understand Jung very well, Jung's psychology tended toward the theoretical rather than the practical and "still lacked a practical method of instruction."[89] Still, Jungian themes continued to be applied to the events and rigors of the time. In 1943, for example, the *Zentralblatt* published an article dealing with the asserted healing power of the symbols of mother earth and father heaven from the ancient German religion of nature, powers supposedly helpful in strengthening the "feminine" sphere of the home as a refuge for the returning soldier; this article was also listed in the official Nazi bibliography.[90]

By 1939 Jung, his ideas, and his followers were not an important issue for the Nazis. By that time as well Jung and Göring, as we have seen, were at odds over German domination of the international society and Jung had already for some time been casting a more critical eye over the Nazi phenomenon. The significance of Jung's experiences during these years seems to lie less in the degrees of overt prejudice on his part than in the various suprapersonal dynamics his words and deeds engaged. Anti-Semitism was endemic in European society but particularly in the German lands where strong nationalism was aggravated by the proximity of the Slavic world and by the migration of *Ostjuden* into Germany and Austria. The traditional elites in Germany remained closed to Jews. As historian Fritz Stern has put it in describing the homogeneity of the officer corps in contrast to that of France: "In Germany there was no Dreyfus Affair because there was no Dreyfus."[91] The medical profession was particularly anti-Semitic due to the pervasiveness of Social Darwinist, eugenic, and racist theorizing and, after 1918, as a result of economic pressures that increased jealousy and resentment of the many prominent and successful Jewish physicians in Berlin and other large cities. Thus, the Nazis could appeal to doctors and other professionals on the basis of an interlocking grid of nationalism, corporate self-interest, and anti-Semitism.

European anti-Semitism was not usually racist in the Nazi sense. The interwar fascist movement capitalized on a more general cultural movement against materialism that often caricatured Jews as lacking "spirituality." Historian George Mosse has shown how pervasive this caricature was, citing as one example the late nineteenth-century Swiss historian Jacob Burckhardt who, while not close to the nascent *völkisch* movement, fulminated against the decline of aesthetics and civilization as evidenced by the machinations, among others, of venal Jews.[92] Jung never expressed himself in quite so direct a fashion, but did share the widespread concern about the deterioration of spiritual values that, among other things, led him to see in the fascist mass movements of the 1920s and 1930s elements of what he and other intellectuals called liberation. This philosophical stance cultivated degrees of anti-Semitism inherited from the culture, the intensity of which varied with time and event. It must be said that Jung broke from these notions in a way that suggests a dialectic of prejudice and tolerance within him that was ultimately resolved in favor of the latter. This is not to agree, however, with the argument of Wolfgang Giegerich that all along Jung was purposefully engaging the shadow of racial prejudice in order to extirpate it.[93] Such a judgment naively ignores the plurality of motives and conditions present in any human action, a number of which we have explored in the case at hand. Such a rationalization also turns a blind eye to the negative effects of Jung's lack of vigorous early criticism of Hitler and the possible legitimacy for the regime created in the minds of many or some through Jung's association with it, whatever protective professional capacity he effected or intended.

Jung's outlook also proved to be problematic in a more general way. Although the Nazis exploited modern technical and material resources, including medicine and psychotherapy, they also built their power on yearnings for the mysterious and the transcendent. In this respect, we can recall with profit German Freudian John Rittmeister's critique of Jungian psychology's lonely and exalted exclusivity in contrast to Freud's more "democratic" interest in common human struggles. Jeffrey Masson has seen this same orientation in Jungian therapy as a function of the denial of collaboration with Nazism:

> the essence of the defect of Jungian psychotherapy is the attempt to avoid touching on those issues that are most concrete, most real, most related to the body and to a specific moment in history.... Jung could not afford to urge his patients to examine their pasts, for he needed to avoid thinking about his own past, tainted as it was by collaboration with the Nazis.[94]

Even though, as we have seen, Jung's "collaboration with the Nazis" was not as straightforward as Masson believes, there is a dynamic in Jung's case that is philosophically and morally problematical. But it is to be seen the other way around: The same airy approach to human experience manifest in Jungian therapy that Masson sees as caused by collaboration with the Nazis was, rather, one of the historical factors that led Jung to rhetorical and organizational flirtation with the Nazis. The case of C. G. Jung and psychotherapy in Nazi Germany, therefore, reveals the perils of fascination among those who because of their position, privilege, and prominence must maintain an especially critical, rational, and ethical distance from destructive enthusiasms, recognizing the crucial difference between saying "This is amazing" and saying "This is wrong."

Notes

1. Kurt Gauger, *Politische Medizin,* p. 27; see also the noncommittal review of Gauger's book in *Der Öffentliche Gesundheitsdienst* 1 (1935): 618–19; and the excerpt in George Mosse, ed., *Nazi Culture,* pp. 215–27.
2. "Bericht über den VII. Kongress für Psychotherapie," *ZfP* 7 (1934): 129.
3. Cimbal to Göring, October 21, 1934, Kl. Erw. 762/2.
4. Lockot, *Erinnern und Durcharbeiten,* pp. 68, 84, 186; Strünckmann, like Cimbal, ran afoul of party rivalries, in his case association with Gregor Strasser, a former pharmacist, who was murdered in the Nazi purge of June 1934.
5. BDC: Reichsärztekammer; and Kurt Gauger, Lebenslauf, Berlin, June 27, 1938, BDC: Kulturkammer; see also the curriculum vitae in idem, "Über den Einfluss des Duodenalsaftes auf die Zuckervergärung" (Inaugural dissertation, Berlin, 1932).
6. See Sigmund Freud, "On Narcissism: An Introduction" (1914), in idem, *Collected Papers,* trans. Joan Riviere (New York, 1959), 4:30–59; and Heinz Kohut, *The Analysis of the Self* (New York, 1971). In 1935 Gauger gave a paper at the international congress in Bad Nauheim on ideals and character; in 1936 he addressed the NSDAP conference in Wiesbaden on conscience. Both topics demonstrate his preoccupation with self-esteem:

   It would not surprise us if we were to find a special institution in the mind which performs the task of seeing that narcissistic gratification is secured from the ego-ideal and that, with this end in view, it constantly watches the real ego and measures it by that ideal. If such an institution does exist, it cannot possibly be something which we have not yet discovered; we need only to recognize it . . . our conscience. (Freud, "On Narcissism," p. 52)
7. Gauger to Bitter and Kühnel, May 9, 1955, pp. 8, 9; italics in original.
8. Kurt Gauger, "Psychotherapie und politisches Weltbild," p. 167; see also idem, *Politische Medizin,* p. 17; and Mosse, *Nazi Culture,* p. 218.
9. Gauger to Bitter and Kühnel, p. 7; italics in original.
10. Kurt Gauger, *Christoph: Roman einer Seefahrt* (Stuttgart, 1940), p. 52.
11. Kurt Gauger, *Der richtige Atem: Begriff, Technik und seelischer Hintergrund* (Stuttgart, 1930).
12. Ibid., p. 60. The sacrificial Christ imagery is apparent in the protagonist's Christian name. Gauger was a Lutheran who under the Nazis switched to the officially approved "believer in God"; see BDC: Reichsärztekammer and Kulturkammer. Christoph's family name is also revealing since in pronunciation and spelling it translates as a mix of "failed" (*fehlen*) and "able" (*fähig*) "man."
13. Ibid., p. 100.
14. Ibid., p. 109.
15. Ibid., p. 253.
16. Gauger to Bitter and Kühnel, p. 9. Gauger claimed to have visited Jung in Zurich, but Jung's son recalls no such visit.
17. BDC: SA. He dropped mention of this association the following year (BDC: Kulturkammer), although he was still listed on the governing board of the Göring Institute as late as 1942: Kl. Erw. 762/2.
18. Herbert Rudolf, "Der Film im Unterricht," *Völkischer Beobachter,* February 15, 1938, p. 5.
19. Göring to Jung, March 4, 1937, Kl. Erw. 762/2; Kurt Zierold, *Der Film in Schule und Hochschule,* 3rd ed. (Stuttgart, 1938), 137–45; Oluf Bruel, "Bericht über den ix. Internationalen Ärztlichen Kongress für Psychotherapie in Kopenhagen, 2.-4.

Oktober 1937," *ZfP* 10 (1937): 135; see also Ludwig Mayer, *Die Psychotherapie des praktischen Arztes* (Munich, 1939); and "Tätigkeitsbericht 1940," p. 3.

20. Alfred Bauer, *Deutscher Spielfilm Almanach 1929–1950* (Berlin, 1950), pp. 273–4; Gauger also claimed to have worked on another film, *Light Cavalry,* in the summer of 1935; BDC: Kulturkammer.
21. Rundschreiben, November 22, 1941, Kl. Erw. 762/4.
22. "Jahresbericht 1941 des Deutschen Institutes für Psychologische Forschung und Psychotherapie und Hinweise für die Weiterarbeit anlässlich der Mitgliederversammlung am 28 März 1942," *ZfP* 13 (1942): 63.
23. *ZfP* 14 (1942): 228–9.
24. Kurt Gauger, *Herz und Anker: Seemannsgeschichten* (Stuttgart, 1943), pp. 82–8.
25. Gauger to Bitter and Kühnel; Gauger claimed that the building at Kleiststrasse 10–12 housing his film institute was funded by a friend of the conservative resistance movement, former Prussian finance minister Johannes Popitz.
26. Michael Geyer, "Resistance as Ongoing Project: Visions of Order, Obligations to Strangers, and Struggles for Civil Society, 1933–1990," in idem and John W. Boyer, eds., *Resistance against the Third Reich, 1933–1990* (Chicago, 1994), pp. 338–9.
27. Curtius to Göring, May 31, 1937, Kl. Erw. 762/2.
28. Jung, *Letters,* p. 112. Ernest Jones, president of the International Psycho-Analytical Association, had a similar opinion of Göring: "I found Göring a fairly amiable and amenable person . . . ": Jones, *Sigmund Freud,* 3:187. Some of this impression may have sprung from hope that things for psychoanalysis might not be so bad as they seemed; in 1936 Jones wrote to Anna Freud: "It was easy to get on excellent terms with Göring who is a very sympathetic personality"; quoted in Lockot, *Die Reinigung der Psychoanalyse,* p. 52, n. 66.
29. "Grundversammlung der Überstaatlichen Allgemeinen Ärztlichen Gesellschaft für Psychotherapie," *ZfP* 7 (1934): 134–8. The statutes of the international society, in contrast to those of the German society, made the president's decisions contingent upon the approval of the executive committee.
30. Jung, *Letters,* p. 135.
31. Ibid., p. 156. Allers was anti-Freudian and had converted to Catholicism: see Rudolf Allers, "Die neue Zeit und die Heilerziehung," *Der Christlíche Ständestaat,* March 4, 1934.
32. Jung, *Civilization in Transition,* p. 546. In December 1944 the Analytical Psychology of Zurich adopted a secret agreement that limited the number of Jews who could be members. This limit seems to have been in effect unofficially since the 1930s and was only made official in 1944. This act seems to have arisen from concern over the large number of Jewish refugees in Switzerland and the fear that the small group would be overwhelmed with Jewish members. There was also some fear of a German invasion of Switzerland, although this restriction lasted until 1950. It is also probably accurate to say that this action reflected the irrational forces of the time as well as the systemic anti-Semitism extant in Europe. See Aryeh Maidenbaum, "Lingering Shadows: A Personal Perspective," in Aryeh Maidenbaum and Stephen A. Martin, eds., *Lingering Shadows: Jungians, Freudians, and Anti-Semitism* (Boston, 1991), pp. 296–9.
33. Achelis, "Gesinnungsschulung als rassenpsychologisches Problem," in Curtius, "Kongress," p. 358.
34. Gerhard Adler, personal communication, September 3, 1980.
35. Göring to Jung, March 12, 1934, Kl. Erw. 762/2; Jung also lectured in Berlin in

1934; see Werner H. Engel, "Thoughts and Memories of C. G. Jung," in Maidenbaum and Martin, *Lingering Shadows*, p. 262.

36. Jung, *Letters*, pp. 136–8.
37. Ernst Kretschmer, *Gestalten und Gedanken*, pp. 133–6; Ellenberger, *Discovery*, p. 740, n. 57; see also Jung, *Letters*, p. 161.
38. C. G. Jung, "An Interview on Radio Berlin," in idem, *C. G. Jung Speaking*, p. 60; Jung also gave a seminar in Berlin in 1934: see Engel, "Thoughts and Memories of C. G. Jung," pp. 261–72.
39. Jung, *Civilization in Transition*, p. 205; on the elitism inherent in Jungian psychology of the time, see Hans Dieckmann, "C. G. Jung's Analytical Psychology and the *Zeitgeist* of the First Half of the Twentieth Century," in Maidenbaum and Martin, *Lingering Shadows*, pp. 167–75.
40. Otto Curtius and C. A. Meier, "Prof. Dr. C. G. Jung zum 60. Geburtstag," *ZfP* 8 (1935): 146.
41. Otto Curtius to Olga Fröbe-Kapteyn, n.d., Franz Jung; Adolf von Weizsäcker, "Heilerziehungsberatung," in Curtius, "Kongress," p. 365. In early 1939 Göring complained to Jung about a foreign rumor that Weizsäcker was Jewish; see Göring to Jung, January 28, 1939, Kl. Erw. 762/2.
42. Paul Feldkeller, "Geist der Psychotherapie," *Deutsche Allgemeine Zeitung*, October 9, 1937; Gustav Schmaltz, "Die Sprache des Unbewussten," *Kölnische Zeitung*, October 19, 1937, Reichsministerium für Wissenschaft, Erziehung und Volksbildung (hereafter REM) 2954, Zentrales Staatsarchiv, Potsdam.
43. Abrechnung der Vorträge Prof. Jung 28./29. September 1937, Kl. Erw. 762/2; on Mussolini's visit, see Gerhard L. Weinberg, *The Foreign Policy of Hitler's Germany: Starting World War II, 1937–1939* (Chicago, 1980), pp. 279–83. Jung also met with Göring in Wiesbaden in April 1936 on the occasion of the joint meeting of the Reich Study Group for a New German Medicine and the German Society for Internal Medicine; see Jung to Göring, March 5, 1936, Kl. Erw. 762/2. On the Jungians in Munich and Berlin, see Käthe Bügler, "Die Entwicklung der analytischen Psychologie in Deutschland," in Michael Fordham, ed., *Contact with Jung: Essays on the Influence of His Work and Personality* (Philadelphia, 1963), pp. 33–5.
44. Barbara Hannah, *Jung: His Life and Work*, p. 211. Franz Jung also recalls this incident. It is possible, of course, that Göring had a hand in this. Hannah *thinks* it was Curtius but is not absolutely certain (p. 211n). She also implies that Curtius (or whoever) saw a chance that Jung might have been able to "cure" Goebbels of his obvious neuroses (p. 211n), but the more likely, or at the very least the more compelling, motivation was the protection of psychotherapy by using Jung.
45. Alfred A. Krauskopf, "Tiefenpsychologische Beiträge zur Rassenseelenforschung," p. 362.
46. Ibid., pp. 362n, 368; *Nationalsozialistische Bibliographie* 4:5 (May 1939), p. 35, entry 131.
47. Aktennotiz, March 4, 1943, MA 116/6, Institut für Zeitgeschichte.
48. REM 2797, Zentrales Staatsarchiv.
49. Jung, *Letters*, p. 184; see also idem, "Votum C. G. Jung," *Schweizerische Ärztezeitung für Standesfragen* 16 (1935); and idem, "Contribution to a Discussion on Psychotherapy," in Jung, *Civilization in Transition*, pp. 557–60. Cf. his professed admiration for Göring's book on psychosomatic medicine: Jung to Göring, June 29, 1937, Franz Jung.
50. Jung to Heyer, May 20, 1935, Franz Jung.

51. Jung to Parelhoff, December 17, 1951, quoted in Paul Roazen, *Freud and His Followers* (New York, 1973), p. 293.
52. No issues of the journal appeared between February and December while the psychotherapists were reorganizing their affairs. This stemmed from political prudence as well as from the fact that the *Zentralblatt,* which since 1929 had appeared in twelve slim issues a year, had a small subscribership that concerned its publisher, Hirzel Verlag of Leipzig; from 1934 until 1944 the journal appeared six times year; see Cimbal, Bericht über die Besprechungen zwischen Herrn D. Curtius, Herrn Dr. Hüthig und den Unterzeichneten betreffen die Möglichkeiten einer Neugründung des Zentralblattes für Psychotherapie, November 18, 1935, Kl. Erw. 762/2; and Proctor, *Racial Hygiene,* p. 324.
53. On the dangers and possibilities of the psychology of nations, see Andrew Samuels, "National Socialism, National Psychology, and Analytical Psychology," in Maidenbaum and Martin, *Lingering Shadows,* pp. 177–209.
54. Jung, "Interview on Radio Berlin," p. 65.
55. C. G. Jung, "Geleitwort," *ZfP* 6 (1933): 139; and "Editorial (1933)," in Jung, *Civilization in Transition,* pp. 533–4; my translation.
56. Jung, *Letters,* p. 146; see also Göring, "Mitteilung des Reichsführers der Deutschen allgemeinen ärzthchen Gesellschaft für Psychotherapie," *ZfP* 6 (1933): 140–1; and Cimbal to Göring, February 20, 1934, Kl. Erw. 762/2.
57. Gustav Bally, "Deutschstämmige Psychotherapie," p. 2. Jung was widely criticized for this position: see B. Cohen, "Ist C. G. Jung 'gleichgeschaltet'?" *Israelitisches Wochenblatt für die Schweiz,* March 16, 1934; and Jung to Cohen, March 26 and April 28, 1934, in Jung, *Letters,* pp. 154–5, 159–60; see also pp. 156–72.
58. Göring to Griesbeck, March 28, 1934, Kl. Erw. 762/2.
59. C. G. Jung. "Zeitgenössisches," *Neue Zürcher Zeitung,* March 13 and 14, 1934, p. 1; and "A Rejoinder to Dr. Bally," in Jung, *Civilization in Transition,* p. 536.
60. C. G. Jung, "Zur gegenwärtigen Lage der Psychotherapie," pp. 9–10; and "The State of Psychotherapy Today," in Jung, *Civilization in Transition,* p. 166; my translation.
61. Jung to Gauger, May 14, 1936, Franz Jung. Franz Jung argues that *Freudfresser* should be translated as "Freudian zealot," a point of view adopted in the first edition of this book. Although it is true, according to some native-speaking German language scholars, that the term can—or even should—be so translated, it seems clear now that the context of the letter and that of the general situation at the time makes it certain that Jung meant "anti-Freudian zealot."
62. Jung to Kranefeldt, February 9, 1934, quoted in Mortimer Ostow, "Letter to the Editor," *International Review of Psycho-Analysis* 4 (1977): 377.
63. C. G. Jung, "Wotan," *Neue Schweizer Rundschau,* March 1936; and in Jung, *Civilization in Transition,* p. 185.
64. Jung to Hugh Crichton-Miller, September 2, 1939 (original in English), in Jung, *Letters,* p. 276.
65. Jung to Eickstedt, July 3, 1939, in Jung, *Letters,* p. 272; see also Egon Freiherr von Eickstedt, *Grundfragen der Rassenpsychologie* (Stuttgart, 1936).
66. Jung, *Letters,* p. 238; and C. A. Meier, personal communication, July 12, 1980; see also Göring to Cimbal, February 24, 1935, Kl. Erw. 762/2. The psychotherapists believed they had a contact with Rosenberg since psychoanalyst Felix Boehm was Rosenberg's fraternity brother (*Korpsbruder*); see below, chapter 8, and Göring to Curtius, October 11, 1938, Kl. Erw. 762/2.
67. Matthias Heinrich Göring, "Internationale allgemeine ärztliche Gesellschaft für

Psychotherapie," *Deutsches Ärzteblatt* 67 (1937): 1099. The Göring Institute, too, attracted some prewar international contacts, including at least two psychologists from the United States: see Richard Schmiechen, *Changing Our Minds: The Story of Dr. Evelyn Hooker* (film, Intrepid Productions, 1992).
68. Lockot, *Erinnern und Durcharbeiten*, pp. 262–7, 286–90; REM 2954, Zentrales Staatsarchiv, Potsdam.
69. Hans von Hattingberg, "Bericht über den X. Internationalen ärztlichen Kongress für Psychotherapie in Oxford," *ZfP* 11 (1939): 1–6.
70. Göring to Kogerer, July 15, 1938, Kl. Erw. 762/2.
71. Jung to Göring, October 6, 1938, Kl. Erw. 762/3.
72. C. G. Jung and C. A. Meier, "Protokoll der Delegiertenversammlung der International Allgemeinen Ärztlichen Gesellschaft für Psychotherapie anlässlich des Internationalen ärztlichen Kongresses für Psychotherapie in Oxford am 31. Juli 1938, 15,30 Uhr, in Balliol College," *ZfP* 11 (1939): 8; Göring to Syûzô Naka, October 3, 1938, Kl. Erw. 762/3.
73. Göring to Herzog, September 13, 1938, Kl. Erw. 762/3; see also Satzung der Japanischen allgemeinen ärztlichen Gesellschaft für Psychotherapie, n.d., Kl. Erw. 762/3. Göring was also interested in having a group from Yugoslavia formed; as for the Hungarians, he assured Karl Haedenkamp, Reich Physician Leader Wagner's deputy for foreign affairs, that even though most Hungarian psychotherapists were Freudians, the "purely Jewish instinct in psychoanalysis" was not influential there: Göring to Haedenkamp, March 16, 1939, Kl. Erw. 762/3.
74. M. H. Göring "Aktuelles," *ZfP* 12 (1940): 193–4.
75. Göring, "Bericht," p. 5; idem, "Bericht der internationalen Gesellschaft," *ZfP* 13 (1941): 1; and "Jahresbericht 1941," p. 74. Jung was editor-in-chief of the *Zentralblatt* from 1933 to 1940, and Göring from 1936 to 1944; managing editors were Cimbal (1933–34), Meier and Curtius (1934–39), Bilz and Meier (1940), and Bilz (1940–44).
76. Göring to Meier, October 9, 1940, and December 11, 1940, Kl. Erw. 762/3.
77. Jeffrey Moussaieff Masson, *Against Therapy: Emotional Tyranny and the Myth of Psychological Healing* (New York, 1988), pp. 94–123.
78. Paul Roazen, *Freud and His Followers* (New York, 1985), p. 292; see also idem, "Jung and Anti-Semitism," in Maidenbaum and Martin, *Lingering Shadows*, pp. 211–21.
79. H. Buder, "Der Zeitraum von 1933 bis 1945 und der Zeit nach dem Kriege," in Fordham, *Contact with Jung*, pp. 33–5.
80. Ernest Harms, "Carl Gustav Jung—Defender of Freud and the Jews" (1946), in Maidenbaum and Martin, *Lingering Shadows*, pp. 17–49.
81. James Kirsch, "C. G. Jung and the Jews: The Real Story," (1982), in Maidenbaum and Martin, *Lingering Shadows*, pp. 17–49; cf. the critique of this "working through" thesis by Richard Stein, "Jung's 'Mana Personality' and the Nazi Era," in ibid., pp. 89–116; and a critique of Jung's emotional status in Jay Sherry, "The Case of Jung's Alleged Anti-Semitism," in ibid., pp. 117–32.
82. C. G. Jung, "The State of Psychology Today," *The Collected Works of C. G. Jung* (Princeton, 1953–79), 10:165–6.
83. Peter Gay, *Freud: A Life for Our Times* (New York, 1988), pp. 205–39.
84. C. G. Jung, "The Development of Personality," *Collected Works*, 17:167–8.
85. C. G. Jung, "Vom Werden der Persönlichkeit," in idem, *Wirklichkeit der Seele* (Zurich, 1934), p. 180n.
86. On other liberties with translation, see Jay Sherry, "Case Not Proven," *San Francisco Jung Institute Library Journal* 14:2 (1995): 17–23.

87. Proctor, *Racial Hygiene,* pp. 162–3.
88. Göring to Curtius, February 2, 1939, Kl. Erw. 762/2.
89. Curtius to Göring, February 8, 1939, Kl. Erw. 762/2.
90. Frederik Adama van Scheltema, "Mutter Erde und Vater Himmel in der germanischen Naturreligion," *ZfP* 14 (1943): 257–77; *Nationalsozialistische Bibliographie* 8:6/8 (June/July/August 1943), p. 120, entry 51.
91. Fritz Stern, "The Burden of Success: Reflections on German Jewry," in idem, *Dreams and Delusions: The Drama of German History* (New York, 1987), p. 108.
92. George L. Mosse, *Germans and Jews: The Right, the Left, and the Search for a "Third Force" in Pre-Nazi Germany* (New York, 1970), pp. 57–60.
93. Wolfgang Giegerich, "Postscript to Cocks," *Spring* 10 (1979): 228–31.
94. Masson, *Against Therapy,* p. 123.

7

Institute and Profession

The establishment of the German Institute for Psychological Research and Psychotherapy in 1936 marked the true beginning of the rather exceptional process of professionalization that psychotherapists experienced in the Third Reich. This unprecedented institutionalization of psychotherapy in Germany allowed the psychotherapists for the first time to exercise de facto control over the training and practice of their discipline. This control was not legally exclusive since psychotherapy could be taught and practiced outside of the Göring Institute, but the institute did represent a central locus for the discipline during the nine years of its existence. The creation of the institute also opened the door to increasing levels of funding from various agencies of the state and the military. While the German General Medical Society remained a "purely scientific" organization without any legal professional capacities,[1] the Göring Institute constituted an entity that put professional meat on the bones of a scientific society. In order to ensure this status, Göring insisted on the complete independence of the institute from society and its status as a national group within an international body.[2]

The creation of the institute came out of movement from several directions and it began, oddly enough, with the increasingly besieged psychoanalysts. On February 18, 1936, Felix Boehm met with a representative of the Medical Division of the Ministry of the Interior, possibly Herbert Linden or his deputy. Boehm was one of only two remaining members of the executive committee of the Psychoanalytic Institute in Berlin and he was representing the DPG's request for continued licensure. The Medical Division was of the opinion that psychoanalysis would not be forbidden, since it was a useful therapy. This pragmatic view was shared within the Nazi party as well. At a meeting with psychotherapists on April 26, 1936, Reich Physicians Leader Wagner's deputy, Franz Wirz, noted that he and the party were not so much opposed to psychoanalysis as to its practice by Jews, saying: "We all know that the Wassermann reaction [a diagnostic test for syphilis] was discovered by a Jew. But no one in Germany would be so foolish as no longer to make use of this reaction."[3] Under no circumstances, however, could the government allow the official existence of an institution dedicated to the teachings of Freud. But the ministry also believed there was a solution to this problem.

The solution lay with the psychotherapists under Göring. It was precisely at this time that Göring was attempting to establish a psychotherapeutic outpatient clinic in Berlin. Göring had apparently approached the Jungians in Berlin about cooperation in this venture, but he was apparently encountering significant funding difficulties and this particular project in the end went nowhere.[4] The Interior Ministry, however, had suggested to Boehm that the psychoanalysts combine with the other psychotherapeutic groups in Berlin in a common institute. The Medical Division reasoned that by such a merger the remaining non-Jewish psychoanalysts would acquire the necessary sanction to continue their work and the other psychotherapists would gain the use of the Psychoanalytic Institute's offices and clinic, located at Wichmannstrasse 10. Boehm reported back to the Medical Division on March 18 that the DPG was willing to accept this arrangement. In line with what we have observed above concerning the initiative taken by the psychotherapists in organizing their affairs under the new regime, even the psychoanalysts apparently saw these maneuvers as much an opportunity as a means of protection.[5] They felt that their expertise and institutional resources would give them a certain practical predominance in the new institute, something that in fact to a certain degree they would eventually achieve. Apparently the psychoanalysts took it upon themselves to approach the C. G. Jung Society in Berlin with the proposal for merger—seemingly as if it were their idea—and Jung instructed Eva Moritz, the president of the Jungian Society in the German capital, to get in touch with Gauger to make sure that the "anti-Christian" Freudians not assert themselves over the other psychotherapeutic schools.[6]

The Interior Ministry, which, like the NSDAP, seemed in all of this to be much less afraid of the psychoanalysts than the psychotherapists, wrote to Göring in Wuppertal with the proposal for a common institute embracing the DPG, the C. G. Jung Society, and Künkel's Study Circle for Applied Characterology. Details were worked out at the April 26 meeting with Wirz and Göring, a ministry representative, and two university psychiatrists. The founding of the institute followed in May with Göring as director and psychoanalyst Boehm as secretary.[7] In November Göring moved to Berlin and addressed the first meeting of the membership on "Weltanschauung und Psychotherapie."[8] The German Institute for Psychological Research and Psychotherapy began functioning with the winter semester 1936–37 on October 1 in its new building at Budapesterstrasse 19. Like the German General Medical Society, it was a registered association. Its statutes were administered by Herbert Linden in the Medical Division of the Interior Ministry who also became a member of the governing body of the institute. Linden was a psychiatrist by training and during the winter semester of 1939–40 would give a course at the institute on racial and biological hygiene (see Appendix 1). Although Linden was a member of the body responsible for assessing and promoting the progress toward unifying the various theories of the three schools of psychotherapy gathered at the Göring Institute, by all accounts this function was actually controlled by Göring and the other psychotherapists on the board.[9] In all of its manifestations and limitations, this goal and others remained a professional and not a governmental responsibility. This was not just a function of the identity of Göring, but of the Nazi preference for the security of a functional unity of experts over the complexities and uncertainties of genuine institutional change.

Aside from the routine details required by its formal supervision of the Göring Institute and some continuing negotiations over questions of professional certification and licensure, the Interior Ministry, like the NSDAP, did not figure prominently in the organizational affairs of psychotherapy in the Third Reich. The ministry's major involvement seems to have ended, in fact, with the establishment of the institute, the solution to the problem of the remaining psychoanalysts, and the securing of Göring to supervise the psychotherapists. Indeed, as the government's chief representative of the medical establishment, the various medical departments of the Interior Ministry continued to entertain no official notion of medical psychology apart from traditional university and clinical psychiatry. In 1939 Werner Achelis, the director of the Göring Institute's public relations department, decried the "materialistic" state medical bureaucracy that continued to refuse to recognize the advances of the past twenty years, advances that had, in his sincere and strategic view, culminated in National Socialism.[10] The involvement of official agencies with the Göring Institute, as we shall see, would primarily be a result of the psychotherapists' own search for funding, especially with the onset of war in 1939.

The Göring Institute was funded by various means and to varying degrees in the course of its existence. From 1933 to 1936, German psychotherapists had supported the German General Medical Society out of their own pockets, just as they had since 1926. This was no easy task given the relatively poor financial condition in which many of the psychotherapists found themselves, something which spurred the psychotherapists to argue for the inclusion of psychotherapy in the state health insurance system.[11] The maintenance of an institute, even with the "loan" of the teaching and treatment facilities of the former Berlin Psychoanalytic Institute, was an even more daunting proposition. In the fall of 1936 Göring wrote to Jung that the Jungians in Berlin were hesitant about joining the institute for financial reasons. Göring stressed the importance of finding outside funding for the institute in attracting and retaining qualified members.[12] Although the institute from its founding in 1936 received some money from the Labor Front, until the outbreak of war it was primarily self-supporting. Ernst Göring claims that his father spent a great deal of his own money to keep the institute going during the first three years of its existence.

The Göring Institute, for all the unique features incumbent upon its establishment and maintenance, is significant as an example of the process of professionalization in modern Germany to and through the Third Reich. This is the case in two fundamental ways: (1) the similarities and differences between professional development in Germany (and continental Europe) and in Britain and the United States; and (2) the realities of professional behavior in Nazi Germany. As to the first, the traditional Anglo-American model of professionalization has stressed the reality and desirability of professional autonomy from state sponsorship or control. It is the practitioners themselves who organize, practice, and regulate their profession for the benefit of their clients in terms of expertise and standards. This autonomy also allows the professionals themselves to benefit from control of the market for their services. This can take the form of a classic liberal free market, but more often has evolved into varying means and degrees of market control such as restricting external competition through licensure and internal competition through restrictions on the number of practitioners. The German (and Continental) tradition of strong state claims on education, law, commerce, and health offers a different model of professionalization, but one that has reminded Western scholars that even in Britain and in the United States the modern bureaucratic state has been a necessary part of professional development. This does not mean that the state, even in Germany, has determined the process of professionalization. Research into the history of the professions in Germany has to some extent supported recent studies in German social history, which reveal the surprising degree of organizational initiative and autonomy "from below" of groups advancing and defending their ideas and interests within a complex industrial society and economy. As we have already seen, this process was evident among psychotherapists from the earliest years of the Third Reich.

Integration into the state system of education and health insurance compensation was the ultimate goal of the psychotherapists at this time. In terms of achieving these ends, their record was dismal. Not only did they face significant established opposition, but their very success in establishing themselves in various occupational realms also aggravated the problem of differentiating themselves from other professions, especially medicine, and of finding a disciplinary identity among the numerous fields scattered between medicine and psychology. Coupled to this was the chronic theoretical and practical disunity among psychotherapists concerning the cause, nature, and treatment of psychological disorders, an equally chronic division over the question of lay therapy, and disagreement over the form of professional licensure. Without such differentiation and concomitant unity, psychotherapy could never achieve licensure by the state as a profession. Only one of their number won a post (and a minor one at that) teaching psychotherapy at the university level. Although they made some inroads among private insurers (see chapter 9), they failed to have psychotherapeutic treatment included under the state health insurance scheme. Furthermore, the medical offices of the Reich Ministry of the Interior never acknowledged an autonomous psychotherapy, remaining firmly in the hands of traditional university psychiatry. Professional development along such lines would come only in the postwar successor states.

But the extralegal nature of the Nazi regime made such formal victories superfluous for the short term, because the Göring Institute received de facto recognition as the center for psychotherapy through the support of various agencies of the regime, the military, and industry. Moreover, such autonomy prevented absorption by official state and university psychiatry, allowing psychotherapists the freedom to set standards for training, including the trademark "training analysis," and practice. It was this very fear of domination by established psychiatry that in 1943 occasioned the Göring Institute's decision not to affiliate with the medical faculty of the Friedrich Wilhelm University in Berlin.[13] The therapists' small numbers also spared them the market difficulties experienced by larger and more developed professions such as lawyers and doctors in general. (The decline in competition for scarce good jobs was a major reason why doctors and lawyers welcomed the expulsion of Jews from their professions and why lawyers welcomed the concomitant Nazi banning of women from the ranks of lawyers and judges.) And it was only during the war that rival psychiatrists attempted to compete with the psychotherapists by introducing electroshock and drug therapy into German asylums.[14] This was done to meet heightened Nazi demands for productivity from members of the "Master Race," to try to limit the growing competence of the Göring Institute (which by 1945 would have 290 members, 215 training candidates, and, before the war shut most of them down, branches in several cities), and to escape the professional blind alley of the murder of mental patients suffering from "hereditary" disorders. In 1944 an article in Joseph Goebbels's prestige paper *Das Reich* accurately reported the de facto professional status of psychotherapy in the Third Reich:

> Psychotherapy . . . has made great strides in the last decade and in Germany has been visibly acknowledged by the state through the recent elevation of the German Institute for Psychological Research and Psychotherapy (in Berlin) to a Reich Institute in the Reich Research Council.[15]

The initiative of the psychotherapists under Göring exploited the realities of Nazi governance. *Gleichschaltung*, the process by which individuals and groups were "coordinated" in service to the regime, was not simply imposed from above by a monolithic totalitarian state but was to a great extent self-imposed from below by various groups defending their interests and seeking their places in the new order. Göring, as we have seen, was not forced on the psychotherapists by

Nazi officials either within the party or state medical bureaucracy, but was drafted by anxious and opportunistic colleagues who rightly saw him as a valuable means of protection and promotion. And, as we have just seen, even the founding of the institute in 1936 resulted from a combination of Göring's own efforts to mobilize Adlerians, Jungians, and various independents and the desire of the Ministry of the Interior to close down the "Jewish" Psychoanalytic Institute in Berlin. State authority and power were of course not absent from these transactions, but organizational initiative from outside the government, particularly when it came from patriotic and solidly bourgeois experts, often received the regime's sanction at the expense of those within the Nazi party who called for radical and violent overthrow of traditional elites and institutions. In general, below the bloody arenas of Hitler's *grosse Politik,* there was a signal lack of unified direction from the regime with regard to specific reforms or programs; far more typical was the building of satrapies and the clash of interest groups.[16] This process of "incomplete" revolution provided opportunities for certain old and new groups to advance their interests, creating a significant degree of functional unity among experts in service to the regime in place of and alongside of Nazi rhetoric about the ethnic German *Volksgemeinschaft.*[17]

The Third Reich seemed to offer a chance for specific professions to improve their situation, such as doctors who resented the corporate system of sickness funds under the national health insurance program and sought to change their status from that of a trade to that of a profession.[18] The Nazis also appeared to offer the possibility for the "reprofessionalization" of such professions as teachers and lawyers, who had been disadvantaged during the Weimar Republic. However, the long-term trend under National Socialism was one of "deprofessionalization" through the deterioration of educational standards, the perversion of professional ethics, and the assertion, however chaotic, of ideological and governmental control.[19] Had the Nazis won their war, it is likely that such a trend would have intensified, although some countervailing pragmatism might have protected technical professions.

The psychotherapists without Göring (who turned sixty in 1939) almost certainly would have shared a fate even beyond the general deterioration of standards, the loss of students and practitioners, and the laming material demands of mobilization and war they in fact experienced. The protection afforded by the Göring name and its bearer's relatively unassertive nature and modest intellectual gifts, along with the sterility of any concept of a "German" psychotherapy and the Nazis' countervailing short-term pragmatism, allowed for a significant degree of theoretical and practical autonomy for psychotherapists. At the same time, however, they compromised professional ethics for personal and professional gain, beginning with the exclusion of Jewish colleagues and patients between 1933 and 1938. As we will see in chapter 9, individual psychotherapists could protect patients from the Nazis, and psychotherapy offered in general a relatively humane option to a deadly Nazified psychiatry. But at the other extreme existed the possible betrayal of patients who expressed disloyal or defeatist sentiments. This constituted a violation of that confidentiality that, while not unqualified in a lawful society, is the indispensable basis for trust in a psychotherapeutic relationship. Though allegedly protecting some mental patients from being sent to asylums where they faced the possibility of murder, for example, Göring also participated in evaluating such patients (see chapter 9) and was also not willing to endanger his position or his institute by supporting two colleagues' protests against the "euthanasia" program.[20]

It is therefore manifestly *not* the thesis of this book that Nazi Germany provided a positive environment for the practice of psychotherapy, for the advancement of science, knowledge, and human services in general, or that psychotherapists in the Third Reich were unsung heroes and martyrs. It *is* the thesis of this book, however that the Third Reich witnessed not only the survival but also the professional and institutional development of psychotherapy in Germany. Psychotherapy *as an institutional and professional* entity fared better under National Socialism than might have been expected and has been assumed. This continuity with preceding and succeeding developments in the field occurred alongside the destruction of individual careers, the compromise of professional, private, and public ethics, and within the general malaise that settled over human affairs under Hitler. The history of psychotherapy in the Third Reich is significant in terms of its morally and intellectually ambiguous accommodation to the established powers in Nazi Germany, on both the individual and collective levels, in pursuit of professional and institutional status. Neither psychotherapy in particular nor professions in general were structurally immune to the idea and practice of service to the Nazi regime.

Compared with other academic groups, such as scholars of classical antiquity, who were not touched at all by the Nazis, or with those historians under Walter Frank who erected a full-blown Nazi institute for history, the psychotherapists occupied a middle ground of collaboration.[21] Antiquarians were of little or no use to the Nazis, while historians in general could be lured or compelled to change the results of their work to suit the new political order. Psychotherapists served the Nazi state, too, but essentially by means of the technical exercise of the established methods of their expertise. On the margins of the German medical establishment, their status and degree of organization really gave them little to lose and, with the presence of Göring, a great deal to gain. The intellectual heritage of their discipline, moreover, gave them the appearance and some substance of ideological harmony with National Socialism. The presence of powerful enemies in both party and state inspired solidarity and minimized public differences over doctrine. Such solidarity, by way of contrast, did not exist within the physics community, which split over the issue of "Aryan" vs. "Jewish" physics and was considerably damaged as a result (see chapter 10). The contrasting nature of psychotherapy and physics also made a "German" psychotherapy, however objectionable in terms of the universal humanitarian goals of science and medicine and however limited in therapeutic effect by its own goal of adjusting patients to a repressive social and political order, much less inherently ridiculous than an "Aryan" physics. Finally, there was the cautious "cauterization" of contacts with other disciplines and professional groups that was especially prevalent during the first years of the regime. This arose out of fear of being associated with a group that might not pass the Nazi litmus test for loyalty or being subordinated to one that had. Such intramuralism gave the psychotherapists the chance to organize themselves, submerge their own professional differences as much as possible, and initiate their own contacts under the protection and advantage of the Göring name. As we have seen, the Nazis shook up the German establishment enough to allow a marginal group like the psychotherapists to advance themselves organizationally. But the Nazis, aside from their policies of war and racial extermination, did not change Germany to the degree that they necessarily posed a revolutionary threat to any group apart from their obvious political enemies. The psychotherapists were therefore not in danger simply because they might not meet certain strict ideological standards in the eyes of this or that Nazi leader or organization.

Because psychotherapists in Germany, like those throughout the world, still have not achieved full professional status, their experience in the Third Reich hardly represents a resolution of the critical problems of professional definition that continue to face the field. Psychotherapy everywhere still lacks clear definitional and disciplinary boundaries, embracing as it does so many theories and practices scattered across the fields of medicine and psychology and throughout the social sciences and humanities as well. In Germany, this theoretical and practical diffusion was aggravated after 1933 by the attempt of the newly organized psychotherapists to protect and extend their professional control over the entire field of medical psychology. This would result in a short-term gain along with some long-term benefits in terms of broadening the influence of their discipline. But the process was anything but clear-cut given both the complicated recent history of the medicine of the mind in Germany and the political confusions occasioned by the new Nazi regime.

Indeed, given the flux in the fields of German psychotherapy and psychiatry we have already described, there was, not unexpectedly, a significant degree of uncoordinated initiative, especially just after the Nazi seizure of power. For example, in June 1933 Kurt Delius, a Dortmund neurologist and psychiatrist and member of the General Medical Society who would also join the Göring Institute, drafted an expanded list of services for his practice. He used medicine's status then as a trade to broaden his practice under German commercial law in anticipation of general commercial and insurance reform. While psychoanalytic treatment had been included in the Prussian and German commercial rate system since 1925, Delius's list of services included eleven types of psychotherapy, including "genuine psychoanalytic (psychocathartic, individual psychological) treatment."[22] For the emerging psychotherapeutic leadership, this action was clearly too much too soon. Göring wrote to Cimbal that Delius's proposal was too complicated.[23] No doubt Göring and his colleagues, aside from their interest in moving psychotherapy away from the legal status of a trade to that of a profession, worried about the reaction of their psychiatric and party opponents to such an ambitious move. On the one hand, it might increase moves by either the party or the state psychiatric establishment to rein in the psychotherapists. On the other hand, particularly since Delius stressed his experience as a *Facharzt* in neurology and psychiatry, it might represent a means for reform psychiatrists to define psychotherapy as a psychiatric preserve. More generally, such commercial freedom was also a challenge to the evolution of professional controls over training and practice. Control over the field of psychotherapy was necessary not only for immediate political reasons, but to prevent the sort of uncontrolled quackery that gave the opponents of an autonomous psychotherapy powerful ammunition. Delius himself as a neurologist and psychiatrist would not be a problem in this regard, but leaving the field open to commercial exploitation from any source clearly was not in the interest of an aspiring profession.

Because the history of psychotherapy in Third Reich, however, is the history of a certain degree of professionalization, we must briefly situate this history in the context of the history of professions in general. The earliest studies of the professions were as idealistic as they were formalistic. According to the standard definition, a profession is distinct from a business occupation in that "the professional does not work in order to be paid as much as he is paid *in order that he may work*."[24] The standards for professional status include: a systematic theory, a course of higher education, professional responsibility based on a code of ethics, formal professional associations, and community acknowledgment of the profession's authority. Professionalization was thus seen as part of the progressive modernization of society until critical postwar sociologists began debunking the myth of unalloyed service in favor of a strong critique of professional pecuniary self-interest.[25] The historian, however, will also "think of occupations as falling somewhere along a continuum of professions"[26] and will be concerned with change and continuity over time. The historian will also want to know more about how professional development is affected, even defined and determined, by external agencies.

By the above criteria, psychotherapy can appear to be well developed as a profession. In her analysis of the professional development of psychotherapy in the United States, however, Gertrude Blanck compares four more specific criteria in medicine and psychotherapy: differentiation from other professions, evolution of a system of education, development of professional organizations centralized on a national level, and legal recognition in the form of licensure.[27] Blanck found that there are three directions in which psychotherapy might evolve: as a branch of medicine, as a branch of psychology, or as a separate entity. At the present, there seem to be trends in all three directions.[28] According to Blanck, psychotherapy is not yet sufficiently distinct from either medicine or psychology to be judged a profession in its own right and this is the most crucial difficulty it faces in the way of professionalization.[29]

Both psychiatrists and clinical psychologists claim psychotherapy as an integral part of their operations, the former most often concerned with profound mental disturbances such as schizophrenia and the latter with less severe behavioral problems.[30] The major obstacle to psychotherapy's evolution into a separate, fully fledged profession, however, has been its subordination to the medical profession. Medicine, until very recently, has tended to become all-embracing in its claim to the cure of human illness and attempts of subsumed disciplines to assert their independence have produced substantial conflict.[31] In Germany, as we have seen, nosological and descriptive psychiatry by and large responded to the challenge of psychotherapy and psychoanalysis with a vigorous defense of its neurological foundations. At the same time, reform psychiatrists claimed psychotherapeutic capacity as part of their established professional realm, increasingly, however, in competition with extramural claims, most prominently that of the General Medical Society, on the practice of psychotherapy.

The psychotherapists at the Göring Institute, as a result of the history of their discipline and of the demands placed on it by the Nazi regime, retained a broader perspective on the healing of psychological disorders. Neurosis, the battleground for psychotherapists, was a more comprehensive category than those including the more disabling disorders with which psychiatrists were usually involved. Since neurosis was largely a category of psychological illness, it also transcended the traditional medical emphasis on discrete physical repair. Its very nature made it not only a function of the patient's experiences and (mis)perceptions, but of the entire life context of the patient, involving his or her emotional relationships with family, friends, and the community at large. Added to this was the growing emphasis in medical and public health circles and, especially after 1933, in government on the desirability and necessity of prevention, rehabilitation, and productivity. This emphasis reflected a variety of concerns ranging from progressive commitment to the betterment of individuals and society to more problematic fiscal, political, and military considerations.

All of these factors, however, raised the question of whether psychotherapy should be restricted to physicians. What the Germans called *grosse* psychotherapy, the highly sophisticated theories of the functioning of the unconscious and of the dynamic relationship between mind and body, was close to traditional psychosomatic medicine. This could be the basis for a psychotherapeutic specialization within medicine. Psychoanalysis, though, highly complex and technical in its own right, did not require a medical education for its practice. Psychoanalysts, especially in the United States, have remained divided on the question of lay analysis, but the whole revolutionary thrust of the Freudian movement was toward the expansion of psychology into the therapeutic realm claimed by medicine. For psychotherapy in general, the question remained, however: Should psychology be monopolized by doctors or should doctors be included among psychologists? Compromise on the issue of what academic qualifications the psychotherapist, psychoanalyst, or psychologist should possess rested in Germany in the 1930s and 1940s on medical supervision of nonmedical therapists in order to ensure that no physical ailment has been overlooked. The other major category of psychotherapeutic technique also posed a threat to the exclusive therapeutic claims of the medical profession. *Kleine* psychotherapy included all those systematic and unsystematic psychological theories and techniques designed to ease mental suffering on the conscious level. To some degree or other, every doctor knowingly or unknowingly attempts this, but the question again was: Are the qualities of common psychological sense, empathy, and the ability to comprehend and use various psychological methods in a therapeutic context beyond the layperson? Some even argued that it was precisely the doctors who were too technically educated and oriented to appreciate the human nuances necessary for successful psychotherapeutic intervention.

The original aim of most of the doctors in the General Medical Society for Psychotherapy was and continued to be the promotion of training in psychotherapy for every physician. This was opposed to entrusting such work only to the specially trained psychotherapist, the expertise of the psychiatrist, or the basic good sense supposedly cultivated—or at least not vitiated—among general practitioners in the course of medical training. This was in part a tactical decision. As we have seen, the chances for a medical specialization in psychotherapy remained small and such a specialization in any case might result in psychiatric domination of the field. There was also the question of adequate facilities for such training and of the demand for it among physicians. In Germany in the 1930s the actual and perceived need for psychotherapy was heightened by the psychotherapists' own pursuit of their professional ambitions among the competing agencies of the regime and the regime's own desire to mobilize all capacities for the further "hardening" of a warrior people. Among other things, this aggravated the shortage of physicians interested in or trained in psychotherapy.

With this, the issue of nonmedical therapists again came to the fore. Göring himself argued that the great need for psychotherapy among the German people demanded at least the temporary utilization of lay therapists. The need was so great, Göring averred, that even the shortage of physicians to supervise these therapists should not prevent their deployment.[32] As we shall see in chapter 9, the Nazis were anything but averse to the idea that psychotherapy might be necessary to overcome years of "degeneration" among a German populace exposed to the pernicious effects of modern "Jewish" democratic and communist social influences. Most Nazis were also pragmatic enough to acknowledge that biological measures could not eliminate the need, at least not right away, for physical and psychological maintenance of even the "Master Race." Indeed, there was some conviction among Nazi race theorists and policymakers, prodded in this respect by psychotherapists, that highly developed races—like thoroughbred horses and expensive automobiles—would necessarily be more sensitive and, especially in meeting the higher challenges incumbent upon the racially superior, more subject to psychological distress and therefore more in need of the continuous sophisticated maintenance of fine psychological tuning. Psychotherapists were not as vulnerable on this score as the psychiatrists, who worried that the Nazi leadership would see them as superfluous once the mentally degenerate had been eliminated from the race (see chapter 8). In this sense, as Henry Friedlander has put it, "the psychiatrists faced the dilemma of what to do once they had killed all their patients."[33]

But the psychotherapists did have to worry, among other things, about the association of their discipline with quackery. As noted above, German law allowed the free practice of medicine and there were many "cures" for mental distress to be had from any number of settled or ambulant practitioners who advertised freely in the papers. Physicians in general, as exponents of scientific medicine, looked down upon nonmedical healers, even if some doctors were committed to varying degrees of natural health and homeopathic medicine. Psychotherapists saw the training and medical supervision of nonmedical practitioners not only as a way to grow in numbers, but a means of controlling the practice of lay therapy. This way they could ultimately preempt and control all nonmedical psychotherapy or, failing that, at least avoid a damaging association with those who were not under their control. As we will see in chapter 8, this issue would come to a head during the Third Reich and the psychotherapists would by and large avoid the dangers incumbent in both the problem and its solution.

The second of Blanck's criteria for professional status is the evolution of a system of education. In the case of medicine generally, this has involved five distinct stages: from individual practice to the establishment of an apprentice system; from the private seminar to the institute; and, finally, integration into a university system. When psychotherapy is measured against these, its various schools, especially psychoanalysis, can be found to have passed through all but the last stage. Accomplishing this last step has been particularly difficult in Germany, where the faculties of the universities were securely entrenched behind a massive glacis of knowledge, tradition, prestige, and power. The first official state teaching commission (*staatlicher Lehrauftrag*) for psychotherapy was granted by the medical faculty of the Friedrich Wilhelm University in Berlin to Hattingberg in August 1933. That appointment evidences the growing influence of organized psychotherapy in Germany during the 1920s and early 1930s, primarily under the aegis of the psychotherapists' General Medical Society. It was also anticipatory of the more general professional opportunity that was presented by the conjunction of National Socialism with the person of Göring. For the most part, however, the universities remained closed to psychotherapy. Hattingberg in 1933 had won only the right to offer courses in psychotherapy in Berlin and even his promotion in 1940 was only to that of an unsalaried honorary professor.[34] Heyer in Munich, in spite of strenuous efforts, was frustrated in his attempts to win any sort of position there.[35] At the same time, affiliation with the universities carried with it the danger of loss of professional autonomy through the imposition of psychiatric control over psychotherapy and, later, as we shall see, the competition offered by academic psychologists.[36]

The resistance and threat presented by alternative sources of training in the universities to the independent professional status of psychotherapy was obviated to a significant degree by the essential fulfillment by psychotherapy in the Third Reich of Blanck's third criterion, the centralization of a professional organization on a national basis. Building on the foundation laid down by the General Medical Society, the Göring Institute achieved this centralization, if imperfectly, for the nine years of its existence from 1936 to 1945. The institute's more tangible significance to the professionalization of psychotherapy in Germany beyond 1945, however, lay in its more basic function as a means for survival during that violent and destructive era, the opportunity it occasioned for some degree of constructive communication among the various schools of psychotherapeutic thought, its role as an organizational model for postwar institutions, and its operation as an entity for research, training, and practice, however compromised by dictatorship and war. Many of the leading psychologists and psychotherapists in both postwar German republics received their training or were professionally active at the Göring Institute.

Blanck's fourth criterion, legal recognition of the profession through licensure, has not yet been met by psychotherapy in Germany. The licensing of a profession restricts the performance of a particular set of practices to those so licensed. Certification, on the other hand, restricts only the use of a specific title to those who have met certain prescribed standards of training. A pertinent German example of the latter is the title of certified psychologist (*Diplom-Psychologe*), introduced as a result of the demand for psychologists by the Reich's military and by the combined professional efforts of university psychologists and the Göring Institute in 1941.[37] Licensing of psychotherapists and psychologists has always been a difficult issue for a number of inherent reasons. In the practice of *kleine* psychotherapy, it is hard to determine exactly what functions the psychotherapists or psychologist performs that are not performed to varying degrees by other professions. While *grosse* psychotherapy is much more specialized, its independent application has generally been restricted to physicians, so that a successful professional delineation has not yet emerged. Finally, the endemic conflicts among psychotherapists, psychoanalysts, and psychologists have also stood in the way of establishing standards that might be used to formulate a unified theory or build a professional structure. Nazi Germany saw no resolution of these difficulties or any tangible fiscal acknowledgment of professional status through the systematic inclusion of psychotherapists in the state's health insurance scheme. However, as a result of the government support that was eventually afforded the Göring Institute through the German Labor Front, the Reich Research Council, and other organizations, coupled with the absence of any significant professional competition in training or practice, psychotherapy in the Third Reich achieved a significant degree of de facto licensure.

One other model of professionalization has been applied to professions under fascist governance. According to this view, professions were affected in such a way as to "have been forced into patterns which, from the standpoint of modern Western society, are somewhat in between public service and professions . . . the three patterns of business, professions and public service merging into one."[38] This model for professions under fascism, while partly accurate, is an ideal type which does not take account either of the traditional role of the state in professionalization in Germany (and the West) or the complexities of state and society in the Third Reich. The institutionalization of what Timasheff calls state-inspired "solidaristic motivation" was only imperfectly perpetrated in the Nazi style of highly structured lawlessness. At the fountainhead, Hitler's administrative ignorance and disinterest resulted in almost random gushings of his—often interpreted—will through the outlets of various persons and organizations. Coursing from the Führer's juvenile artistic temperament and his political sense of divide and rule, the countercurrents and eddies of the feudal tributaries that comprised the mainstream of Nazi leadership diluted the already thin gruel of the movement's ideas. The Nazi aim of *Gleichschaltung* more often meant conformity than revolution.[39] Hitler, bent on his aims of territorial conquest and racial extermination, considered Germany a projectile to be angrily hurled, not an institutional entity to be carefully constructed. This combination of compulsion and chaos, arising from the intellectual and organizational flabbiness of Nazi structures and affairs, allowed psychotherapy under the protection of the Göring Institute to work in a number of different directions in service both to the regime and the profession. Psychotherapy, caught up in the (failed) Nazi campaign to strengthen the nation's health—a campaign that exploited the profession's own tendency toward emphasizing the prevention and cure of widespread neurosis—became an officially sanctioned profession in the "new" Germany. But this was not something essentially new in the history of the professions in Germany; as we have seen, the initiative displayed by the psychotherapists in offering their expertise to the Nazi regime stemmed primarily from ongoing ideas, ideals, and ambitions.

Thus, with arriviste confusion on the one side and traditional skepticism and hostility on the other side, psychotherapy forged its way between the prejudices of both party and state in a drive to achieve professional autonomy. In so doing, the psychotherapists derived whatever advantage they could from each side but relied fully only on the protection of the seigniorial Göring name and on their confidence in the marketable expertise of its practitioners. For his part, Göring was able to steer the psychotherapists safely between the Charybdis of swirling party radicalism and factionalism and the Scylla of stony state resistance. By the time Ernst Kretschmer reassumed the presidency of the General Medical Society for Psychotherapy after the war, the substantially broadened field of psychotherapy had received a decided professional boost, even given the great task of organizational and ethical reconstruction that would be required of it in the moral and physical rubble left by Hitler's Reich and Hitler's war. Although some specific reforms, directly or indirectly relevant to psychotherapy, issue from the Nazi era, the development of psychotherapy as a profession owes nothing to National Socialism in terms of direct systematic sponsorship or reform. But the Third Reich served as part of a conduit, however warped, for certain elements of modernization.[40] At the same time, the Nazis transformed German society simply by shaking the tree.[41] The history of psychotherapy in the Third Reich shows that this shaking reached into the branches of the German medical profession.

Notes

1. Protokoll der Gründungssitzung, p. 4, Kl. Erw. 762/2.
2. Göring to Curtius, February 14, 1938, Kl. Erw. 762/2.
3. Felix Boehm, "Bericht über die Ereignisse von 1933 bis zum Amsterdamer Kongress im August 1951," p. 303. The fact that Boehm is the source for both of these claims does not alter the fact that the attitude he reports fits with the overall pattern of Nazi policy in this field. Wirz's choice of example, a test for syphilis, was perhaps consciously or unconsciously a choice related to his own prejudices against Jews and the common Nazi association of Jews in general, and psychoanalysis in particular, with corrupt sexuality.
4. Jung to Gauger, May 14, 1936, Franz Jung.
5. Lockot, *Erinnern und Durcharbeiten,* p. 188.
6. Ibid.
7. "Tätigkeitsbericht 1935/36," p. 5.

8. Göring to Jung, May 31, 1936, Franz Jung; C. G. Jung et al., "M. H Göring," p. 194.
9. "Tätigkeitsbericht 1937," p. 201; Göring, "Bericht," p. 2.
10. Achelis, "Psychologische Hygiene," p. 251.
11. "Tätigkeitsbericht 1935/36," p. 4.
12. October 26, 1936, Kl. Erw. 762/2.
13. Göring to Sergius Breuer, October 2, 1943, German Captured Documents/Reichsforschungsrat, reel 107, folder 12850, Administrative correspondence of the Department of Psychology and Psychotherapy, Jan. 1943–Dec. 1944, ALSOS RFR 260, Library of Congress, Manuscript Division, Washington, D.C; and see below, chapter 11.
14. Karl-Heinz Roth, "Leistungsmedizin: Das Beispiel Pervitin," in Fridolf Kudlien, ed., *Ärzte im Nationalsozialismus* (Cologne, 1985), p. 173.
15. Heinrich Goitsch, "Heilwege für die erkrankte Seele," p. 8.
16. Peter Hüttenberger, "Nationalsozialistische Polykratie," *Geschichte und Gesellschaft* 2 (1976): 419–42.
17. Konrad H, Jarausch, "The Crisis of German Professions, 1918–1933," *Journal of Contemporary History* 20 (1985): 394.
18. Michael H. Kater, "Professionalization and Socialization of Physicians in Wilhelmine and Weimar Germany," *Journal of Contemporary History* 20 (1985): 677–702.
19. Konrad H. Jarausch, "The Perils of Professionalism: Lawyers, Teachers, and Engineers in Nazi Germany," *German Studies Review* 9 (1986): 107–37.
20. Frederic Wertham, *A Sign for Cain: An Exploration of Human Violence* (New York, 1966), pp. 178–9; Klaus Dörner, "Nationalsozialismus und Lebensvernichtung," *Vierteljahreshefte für Zeitgeschichte* 15 (1967): 143; Robert Jay Lifton, *The Nazi Doctors: Medical Killing and the Psychology of Genocide* (New York, 1986), pp. 83, 85–7, 91.
21. Volker Losemann, *Nationalsozialismus und Antike: Studien zur Entwicklung des Faches Alte Geschichte 1933–1945* (Hamburg, 1977); Helmut Heiber, *Walter Frank und sein Reichsinstitut für Geschichte des neuen Deutschlands* (Stuttgart, 1966).
22. Ergänzungen zur Adgo und Preugo für das Gebiet des Facharztes für Neurologie und Psychiatrie, September 1933, p. 4; Lockot, *Erinnern und Durcharbeiten,* p. 205.
23. Göring to Cimbal, October 9, 1933, Kl. Erw. 762/2.
24. Ronald A. Pavalko, *Sociology of Occupations and Professions* (Itasca, Ill., 1971), p. 21; italics in original.
25. Konrad H. Jarausch, "The German Professions in History and Theory," in Geoffrey Cocks and Konrad H. Jarausch, eds., *German Professions, 1800–1950,* pp. 9–10.
26. William J. Goode, "Encroachment, Charlatanism and the Emerging Profession: Psychology, Sociology and Medicine," *American Sociological Review* 25 (1960): 902–14.
27. Gertrude S. Blanck, "The Development of Psychotherapy as a Profession," pp. 160–1.
28. Ibid., pp. 229–37.
29. Ibid., pp. 241–4.
30. Goode, "Encroachment," p. 910.
31. Blanck, "Psychotherapy as a Profession," p. 160; Goode, "Encroachment," pp. 903, 910.
32. Göring to Wirz, May 28, 1938, Kl. Erw. 762/3.

33. German Studies Association Conference, Washington, D.C., October 4, 1985.
34. Hattingberg, Lebenslauf, p. 3, BDC: Reichsschriftumskammer; Friedrich Wilhelm Universität, Personal- und Vorlesungsverzeichnis, Trimester 1941, p. 39.
35. Heyer to Jung, n.d., Franz Jung.
36. Mitchell G. Ash, "Academic Politics in the History of Science: Experimental Psychology in Germany, 1879–1941," *Central European History* 13 (1980): 255–86.
37. See Geuter, *Die Professionalisierung,* pp. 309–51; and below, chapter 10.
38. N. S. Timasheff, "Business and the Professions in Liberal, Fascist and Communist Society," in Howard Vollmer and Donald Mills, eds., *Professionalization,* p. 60.
39. Broszat, *Hitler State,* pp. 43–4, 284, 348–9; see also Robert Koehl, "Feudal Aspects of National Socialism," *American Political Science Review* 54 (1960): 921–33.
40. David F. Crew, "General Introduction," in idem, ed., *Nazism and German Society, 1933–1945*, pp. 23–8.
41. David Schoenbaum, *Hitler's Social Revolution.*

8

The First Göring Institute, 1936–1939

While the 1933 statutes of the German General Medical Society for Psychotherapy were comprised of a good deal of anxious rhetoric, the 1936 statutes of the German Institute for Psychological Research and Psychotherapy e.V. reflected a calmer and more assured professional outlook. They outlined four aims of the new institute: (1) the creation of "German" psychotherapy and psychology through the unification of the existing schools of thought; (2) the maintenance of an outpatient clinic; (3) the establishment of advisory boards, especially in the field of education; and (4) the training of medical and nonmedical psychotherapists.[1] Articles 4, 5, and 6 called for a director, a secretary, a treasurer, and a governing board. Besides Göring and Linden, the governing board consisted of representatives of three groups gathered within the institute: Künkel and Edgar Herzog for the Künkel (Adler) group, known opportunistically and defensively as the *Gemeinschafts-psychologen*; Moritz, Kranefeldt, and Adolf von Weizsäcker for the Jungians; and the psychoanalysts Boehm, secretary of the institute, Müller-Braunschweig, the institute's treasurer, and Schultz-Hencke. Also serving on the board at its inception were three members who were close to the Jung faction: Achelis, Curtius, society secretary, and Gauger as deputy director; Schultz and Hattingberg sat for the independents. Members who subsequently served on the board were Bilz, Johanna Herzog-Dürck, Maria Kalau vom Hofe, Werner Kemper, Rittmeister, Julius Schirren, and August Vetter.

In addition to its major work in treatment, training, and advisory functions, the Göring Institute also operated as a parent organization for affiliated groups of psychotherapists in other German cities. By

1937 there were four of these: in Düsseldorf under Fritz Mohr, Seif's Munich Work Group for Community Psychology, a group in Stuttgart, and another in Wuppertal. In 1939 the groups would become official branches of the Göring Institute as a result of the expansion and reorganization that was made possible by the advent of DAF supervision and funding (see chapter 10). The groups in Düsseldorf and Wuppertal were combined into a Rhineland branch, although they remained organizationally separate. The Stuttgart branch under Georg Roemer, a board member of the Society of German Neurologists and Psychiatrists, became known as the branch for Württemberg and Baden and in 1940 the Seif and Heyer groups in Munich would combine under Seif's direction into a formal and united Bavarian branch that was by far the most active center for psychotherapy in the Third Reich outside of Berlin. The Austrian branch in Vienna under Kogerer, however, was merely vestigial and, like the Düsseldorf and Wuppertal groups, was barely active after the outbreak of war. In May 1941 Göring himself assumed leadership of the Stuttgart branch through the designation of "commissars" Paul Beetz and Gustav Graber. In 1942 Curtius was put in overall charge of the Munich group, with Seif remaining head of educational counseling. In 1943 a group under Josef Meinertz in Frankfurt am Main became an official branch and by 1944 only it and the Munich and Stuttgart groups were still functioning.

In 1937 the Göring Institute and its branches claimed 128 members. Among these were 60 doctors, 25 academics (those with a university degree), 43 nonacademics, and 3 patrons. Ten of the doctors were women, as were 9 of the 25 academics and 39 of the 43 nonacademics. In 1938 membership increased to 154, of whom 78 were doctors, 28 were academics, and 48 were nonacademics. By September 30, 1939, the Göring Institute had 188 members: 87 doctors (16 women), 33 academics (10 women), and 58 nonacademics (49 women). The number of patrons had increased to 10 and of the total membership exactly half, or 94, were in Berlin. Membership in 1940 stood at 88 doctors (17 women), 39 (12) academics, 61 (52) nonacademics, and 16 (4) patrons, for a total of 204 (85), 97 of whom were gathered in Berlin. The last published statistics show that in 1941 membership was at 240, of whom 100 (22 women) were doctors, 42 (29) were academics, and 80 (64) nonacademics. There were now 18 supporting members, or patrons, and 118 of the members were in Berlin. Subscriptions to the *Zentralblatt* had increased during the year from 303 to 380, including 10 new foreign subscribers to bring their total to 51. This was noted as being remarkable for wartime. Less remarkable and more distressing, however, was the inevitable loss of members to military service: 26 in 1940 and 43 by the following year.[2]

The growth of the institute's membership compared favorably with membership in the General Medical Society before 1933, which had reached a peak in 1931 with 479 members. This is particularly so given the much greater professional commitment and capacity demanded by institutional affiliation. It is also likely that the old society would sooner or later have been riven with splits, especially along the lines of more traditional psychiatrists like Kretschmer and those who favored a more autonomous development for psychotherapy. At the time of the institute's founding, the society counted 210 members; by the time it disappeared from the public record in 1941 this number had increased to 291.[3]

Finances were tight for the first three years of the Göring Institute's existence; all the teachers and administrators served without pay.[4] The shortage of funds was almost pathetically underlined in the institute's report for 1937. There it was reported that a committee to oversee the library had not yet been named since there was no money with which to buy books. Some of the wounds in this regard were self-inflicted. The psychotherapists had inherited the Psychoanalytic Institute's library, but from 1938 on at the latest, Freud's works were kept under lock and key by Göring in a so-called "poison cupboard" (*Giftschrank*). Contributions of books were made by, among others, Hattingberg, Heyer, Schultz, Schultz-Hencke, and "to our joy also C. G. Jung."[5] This latter, celebrated event was most likely the result of an institute request for copies of his collected works.[6] Moreover, during 1937–38 only one volume of six issues of the *Zentralblatt* appeared. Although C. A. Meier has maintained that this was a result of his editorial policy of quashing "Nazi nonsense" before publication, it is more likely that the journal's difficulties stemmed primarily from a lack of income, aggravated by the disruptions occasioned by Nazi rule. Franz Jung has recalled that the International General Medical Society, whose organ was officially the *Zentralblatt*, experienced problems with the publisher, S. Hirzel of Leipzig, over the small subscribership to the journal. In 1935 the society was even looking into the possibility of changing publishers.[7] It was precisely this shortage of money, according to

Ernst Göring, that prompted the psychotherapists to seek closer ties with the Robert Ley's wealthy German Labor Front.

In spite of these difficulties, between 1936 and 1939 the Göring Institute managed to make headway on at least three of the four basic aims it had outlined for itself in its statutes. The other, the creation of a "German" psychotherapy through the unification of the three major schools and the independents, remained as illusory as it was—particularly in the context of Nazism—morally objectionable. Even here, as we shall see, there was some communication and cooperation across sectarian boundaries that was not without some professional value; at the same time, however, the separate groups and individuals also tended to forge their ways as well. From the beginning, however, the institute did treat patients, train psychotherapists, and perform advisory functions, especially in education, in accordance with the aims laid down in the statutes. While we will look more closely at the treatment of patients in chapter 9 and at some specific aspects of the institute's curriculum and advisory functions in subsequent chapters, in this chapter we will outline the basic structure and operations of the outpatient clinic, the institute's advisory work, and its training system.

The outpatient clinic had originated with the old DPG under Eitingon and Simmel in 1920. When the Göring Institute took it over in 1936, its stated purpose was fourfold. First, it was to serve, as before, as a people's clinic (*Anstalt für mittellose Volksgenossen*), hence its name, *Polikinik,* from the Greek *polis* for "city." It was also to be a methodological laboratory for psychotherapists and students, thereby serving an educational and a scientific function within the institute as well as constituting a medical facility.[8] The clinic began its operations on October 15, 1936, with a staff of 52 institute members and 15 candidates, each under the supervision of an instructor. Patients were regularly referred to the clinic for internal medicine at the Charité Hospital, which was under the direction of Friedrich Curtius, brother of the institute's Otto Curtius.[9] In the first year, as reported by Boehm, who was in charge of statistics and the recording of the histories of the clinical cases (catamnesis), 412 patients were seen. Of these, 136 were under continuing care; 38 more were being continued in treatment as former patients from the old psychoanalytic institute, bringing the total to 174. Of these, 31 patients were taken into private treatment, the small honoraria that would result being apportioned to younger colleagues. Patient complaints ranged from psychoses, epilepsy, and idiocy (49 of which cases were determined from the outset to be unsuited for psychotherapeutic treatment) to alcoholism, depression (the largest single category), "organ neuroses," sexual disorders and perversions, character disorders, anxiety neuroses, compulsion neuroses, hysteria, and what in contemporary psychotherapeutic practice are often called "problems in living," mostly difficulties at school or work.[10]

The next year, 1937, saw 259 patients come to the clinic for the initial consultation for purposes of evaluation for treatment. This evaluation was made jointly by Boehm, Göring, and Schultz. Among these patients were 13 homosexuals, a category we will examine in chapter 11. Overall, 110 were either deemed unsuited for therapy, did not return for treatment, were cured or substantially improved in one session, or broke off treatment prematurely, while 58 were continuing treatment at the clinic. Forty-three cases were being handled in private practice and 52 cases had been continued from the previous year, 10 in private treatment. No statistics for 1938–39 were published, but the following year the clinic handled 144 cases. In 1941, out of 464 people who visited the clinic, 260 were referred for treatment and of these 181 continued with it. Boehm also offered in his report for that year a cumulative evaluation of the work of the clinic from 1936 through 1941. Of the 641 cases handled, 17 for various reasons (death, departure, military service) were without result, 60 were designated as untreatable, 118 remained unchanged, 136 somewhat improved, 140 improved, 137 substantially improved, and 33 cured.[11] According to Werner Kemper, who became director of the outpatient clinic in 1942, approximately 80 percent of the patients were from the middle classes, 10 percent were workers, and 10 percent were from the upper class.

Every full member of the institute was required to have at least one clinical patient under continuing treatment, and every candidate had to carry at least two clinical cases to conclusion under the control of his or her training therapist. Since each candidate was required to have a patient continuously under treatment for the duration of training, one or more additional cases could be handled under the control of someone other than the candidate's training therapist. This proved to be an important source of income for the candidates, since each psychotherapist was guaranteed RM 6 (about $1.50) per hour, any difference between the required honorarium paid by the patient being made up by the institute. The honorarium was a necessary part of the treatment not only in terms of giving the patient a financial stake in getting better, but also for the patient's coming to terms with the role of money in psychic life. Candidates were allowed to keep their honoraria while institute members retained only the minimum fee for clinical patients. Therefore, the predominance of bourgeois patients was significant in terms of the institute's finances, since honoraria were based on the ability to pay, beyond the psychotherapeutic maxim of the necessity of sacrifice. Boehm pointed out that the institute's providing of funds for the often financially strapped candidates was also necessary in order not to prejudice the candidates' conscious and unconscious attitudes in favor of clinical patients of comparatively substantial means.[12]

Kemper has estimated that around 50 percent of all the cases treated in the outpatient clinic were handled by various modes of short-term therapy, what he called "focal therapy" (*Fokaltherapie*). This corresponded to the traditional advocacy by a large number of psychotherapists in Germany at the time for those methods that would best address the widespread incidence of neurosis in modern society and also appeal to doctors in their busy practices. The short-term orientation, as we have seen, was also compatible with the Nazi emphasis on the efficient enhancement of national health. Indeed, Göring had more than one reason in 1939 for selecting the psychoanalyst Gerhard Scheunert, a student of Therese Benedek, to direct the operations of the clinic. Scheunert's interest and expertise was in short-term therapies and their efficacy not only in treating patients efficiently and effectively but in thereby offering a solution to the problem of time and expense that prevented psychotherapy's inclusion in the state health insurance system (see chapter 9). One of the purposes of the initial consultation between a prospective patient and the directors of the clinic was to determine which method, applied by which psychotherapist, would be most effective for a given case.[13] Furthermore, the guidelines for the outpatient clinic stipulated the means by which auxiliary methods of treatment, such as breathing exercises, music, and movement therapies, or autogenic training, could supplement a continuing treatment. Reports on the progress of treatment were to be submitted after six weeks, six months, and one year, and they were to avoid terms that were peculiar to a particular psychotherapeutic orientation.[14] This requirement, it was maintained, greatly facilitated the filing of private insurance claims. This stipulation also prevented the usage of politically provocative Freudian terminology as well as serving the ostensible aim of uniting psychotherapeutic thought and practice.

The work of the outpatient clinic was directed toward the goals of serving impecunious patients and validating psychotherapy's claim to medical and professional status. The guidelines for the clinic did mention the need for the proper *Weltanschauung* on the part of both patient and therapist, excluding thereby those who did not measure up to the requirements of the 1935 Nuremberg Race Laws. This of course meant Jews, a gross violation of general and medical ethics we shall discuss in chapter 9. Concessions to Nazi racism, however, were also part of a defense against the dangerous psychiatric charge that the Göring Institute was attempting to treat incurable congenital mental illness, something that an addendum to the clinic's diagnostic schema promised would not be done.[15] It also represented another attempt to unify the theory and practice of psychotherapy in Germany. The schema (see Appendix 3) came out of a committee consisting of Göring, Achelis, Boehm, Hattingberg, Herzog, Heyer, Kemper, Kranefeldt, Müller-Braunschweig, Rittmeister, Schultz, and Schultz-Hencke, and therefore represented at least temporary theoretical consensus and compromise on the nature of neurosis and its treatment. In his report of 1940 Schultz noted the controversies regarding these issues that had marked the work of the committee and that affected the work of the outpatient clinic in both positive and negative ways. But he also characteristically concluded that the intellectual fermentation taking place was also a sign of professional growth and necessary for the productive development of the clinic as a weapon in psychotherapy's fight for survival and recognition:

> The outpatient clinic is our weapons forge. That sometimes there are metal fragments and sometimes hammers clash may be somewhat disturbing to you . . . but it is necessary. We desperately need that. You are perhaps not entirely clear about how threatened even today your whole existence as psychotherapists is.[16]

The third aim of the Göring Institute as delineated in its statutes was the establishment of advisory boards for the active application of psychotherapeutic expertise to problems facing society. On November 1, 1939 the educational counseling service (*Erziehungshilfe*) that had been functioning under Fritz and Elisabeth Künkel since 1938 as an undifferentiated operation of the outpatient clinic was expanded into a formal subdivision of the clinic under the direction of Olga von König-Fachsenfeld, a student of Heyer's from Munich. Its function was to bring psychotherapeutic assistance to young people who were having difficulty in school or whose difficulties at home became manifest at school. König-Fachsenfeld was replaced in 1942 by Gottfried Kühnel, a student of Kretschmer's who ran a home for psychopathic patients in Berlin. König-Fachsenfeld went to Stuttgart to become managing director of the Württemberg-Baden affiliate of the institute and run the educational assistance program there with Jutta von Graevenitz and Wilhelm Laiblin. The educational counseling clinic in Berlin treated and advised children of fifteen years of age and younger, along with their parents. Between November 1, 1939, and February 1, 1941, 116 cases were handled; and from January 1 to December 31, 1941, 129 cases were handled. Diagnoses ranged from idiocy to brain damage to various types of neurotic behavior, but the single greatest number, according to König-Fachsenfeld, suffered from school problems stemming from a disrupted family environment. Therapies included play therapy for children and toddlers (with the child acting out conflicts through drawing, puppetry, pretend-school, toy selection, etc.), family therapy, and auxiliary modes such as gymnastics and music, as well as group therapy and individual treatment and counseling. The average duration of treatment, according to figures drawn up by Julie Aichele of Berlin, was six months for children under ten years of age and a year for those over ten.[17]

Elisabeth Künkel estimated that about 50 percent of the children who came to the Göring Institute were incapable of integrating themselves into the community, but that only approximately 6 percent were hereditarily disordered and therefore untreatable through psychotherapy.[18] It was the disposition of these latter cases, König-Fachsenfeld has recalled, that brought the shadow of Nazism directly into the children's clinic (*Kinderpoliklinik*). The children could be sent to "safe" homes or asylums; in milder cases the institute would advise bringing the child in for treatment as a protective device. NSV child psychologist Hildegard Hetzer has made similar claims for protecting children from the SS during the war at Posen in Poland (see chapter 11, note 29). There is much that we do not know for certain about the fates of many such children. Whatever the motives of various psychotherapists, decisions no doubt were made that involved varying degrees of concession and/or agreement with the brutal Nazi policies toward those they defined as "hereditarily damaged." Another category König-Fachsenfeld recalled were children emotionally torn by state demands to inform on their parents.

The educational counseling clinic's contact with state authority, however, usually came in the more benign form of cooperation with various agencies involved with educational and family matters. All educational counseling services were under the direction of the municipal youth office. In many if not most cases, the psychologists and psychotherapists at the Göring Institute were dealing with the same civil servants and social workers with whom they had worked as individual therapists before the Nazis took power. Between October 1939 and May 1940, for example, of the children being treated at the Berlin clinic 23 percent had been referred to the Göring Institute by city, state, or party organizations (e.g., NSV), 28 percent by physicians, 10 percent by teachers, and 39 percent by parents and others.[19]

The institute also sought to publicize the work of other agencies in this field. The Berlin Transport Works operated two convalescent homes for children, as did the local Public Youth Authority with its Center for Special Psychological Care.[20] The Göring Institute was also in contact with the Nazi youth organizations, the Hitler Youth and the League of German Girls, with Josephine Bilz, wife of Rudolf Bilz, active as a physician with the Hitler Youth. The subdivision for educational counseling also published a series of pamphlets written by its members on various topics related to child psychotherapy and educational psychology. By 1941 three members of the Göring Institute had been put in charge of private homes for disturbed children (*Heilerziehungsheime*): in Berlin under Adelheid Fuchs-Kamp; in Schwallenberg, southeast of Bielefeld, run by Karoline Schmidt and Modesta Thimme; and in Beuren bei Nürtingen in Württemberg under Julie Aichele. Cooperation between these institutions and the Göring Institute was overseen by Adolf von Weizsäcker.[21]

A similar affiliated operation in Vienna reported a significant degree of participation from the local NSV: 53 kindergartens with 1546 children; 84 day nurseries (*NSV-Horten*) with 3024 children; a juvenile justice assistance program run by the NSV, handling 2422 cases; and 11 counseling offices, which between November 1939 and April 1940 reportedly conducted 839 consultations in 459 hours. These facilities, however impressive in terms of numbers, were more custodial than psychotherapeutic and only supplemented the municipal programs begun after World War I. Three psychologists and 19 social workers were active within the Vienna programs. From January 1, 1939, to March 31, 1940, 2302 children, 75 percent of whom were of school age, were attended to. The counselors registered their concern about the fact that only 41 percent of the children were living with their natural parents. The greatest number of children (31.5 percent) were brought for help by their parents; the police referred 20.5 percent, the schools 18 percent, the courts 6 percent, and the NSV only 2 percent. Potential delinquency (34 percent) and school problems (23 percent) headed the list of complaints, a further breakdown in terms of psychological dynamics not being given. In the realm of prevention through supplemental education outside the home, it was pointed out that by the end of March 1940 Vienna was running 301 kindergartens and 159 day-care centers for 5590 preschoolers and 3274 schoolchildren.[22]

A significant adjunct to the Göring Institute's interest in and support of educational counseling in Vienna was the presence there of psychoanalyst August Aichhorn. According to Ernst Göring, König-Fachsenfeld, and Kemper, Aichhorn was highly regarded by Göring, lectured in Berlin in 1938, and was protected by Göring; in 1939 Aichhorn, along with Vienna colleague Heinrich von Kogerer, attended Göring's sixtieth birthday celebration in Berlin.[23] Göring, of course, had studied with Seif and Künkel and was very interested in child psychotherapy and delinquency. Alice Lüps, a relative of his, was also active in the field. Aichhorn himself had been a schoolmaster and worked with delinquent children at reformatories outside Vienna at Ober-Hollabrunn and St. Andrä. Anna Freud had been impressed with Aichhorn's work and suggested he undertake psychoanalytic training. After completing his training in Vienna, he had published his most famous work, *Verwahrloste Jugend,* on delinquent youth in 1925, to which Sigmund Freud himself contributed a foreword. Its perspective was that if a child had an unsatisfactory relationship with a parent, that child would later have difficulties in establishing relationships with other people. In 1932 Aichhorn retired to private practice (one of his analysands was the future American psychoanalyst Heinz Kohut[24]). He also established a Child Guidance Service for the Vienna Psychoanalytic Society. One reason he stayed in Vienna after the Nazis took over in 1938 was his son's imprisonment in Dachau for anti-German nationalist activity.[25]

It was at the Göring Institute affiliate in Munich—near Dachau—that what had come to be known as "psychagogy" was most enthusiastically pursued under the grandfatherly aegis of Leonhard Seif. In all, between 1922 and 1939 Seif's center had held 1221 counseling sessions with 470 families, 2.6 sessions per family. The only other figures available were published for the year 1941, when the number of counselings numbered 93 for 66 families.[26] It is impossible to say what may have played a larger role in the diminishing number of counselings per family; an increasing efficiency on the part of the therapists, the Nazi emphasis on speed over depth, or various disruptive environmental influences on families during wartime. In any case, with the formal link to the Göring Institute and, earlier in 1936, with the Bavarian Popular Education Chancellery, the work of Seif's groups with various party and governmental agencies increased.[27] These included the NSV, the Assistance Service for Mother and Child, the Youth Assistance Program, the DAF Women's Office, the Reich Mothers Service in the German Women's Welfare Service, the party's organizations for teachers, the Hitler Youth, and the League of German Girls.[28] The emphasis throughout remained on short-term suggestive methods, family therapy, play therapy, various auxiliary methods, and the general encouragement of social prevention of child neuroses and difficulties through the maintenance of sound educational practices and environmental standards at home and in school. Seif's institute also sponsored work on hereditary disorders under psychiatrist Lene Credner, paralleling the work done by Hans Luxenburger in his own practice in Munich.[29]

In 1940, following discussions between Göring and the Reich Criminal Police Office, a second subdivision of the outpatient clinic was established. It would deal with matters of criminal psychology under the direction of psychoanalyst Marie Kalau vom Hofe. Kalau vom Hofe had done her training analyses with Sandor Radó in 1925 and later under Müller-Braunschweig. She came to the institute in 1937 to do work in another of Göring's fields of particular interest, forensic psychiatry. Since 1926 Kalau vom Hofe had been pursuing work in this field at the Charité and at Berlin Police Headquarters on the Alexanderplatz. She saw her new assignment as twofold: first, to further the participation of the psychotherapeutic and psychoanalytic point of view in the criminal justice system for the benefit of those charged with crimes who were suffering from treatable mental illnesses; and, second, to promote psychotherapy as a profession. She cautioned, however, that in both instances the opposite of what was desired by psychotherapists would occur if extravagant claims were made about the healing power of psychotherapeutic methods. During 1940 the criminal psychology division handled fifty-three cases, described as primarily involving compulsive thieves as well as a broad range of sexual offenders: one case of bestiality, two pedophiles, three exhibitionists, two sadists, and eleven homosexuals (nine male, two female). Children were also treated: one fifteen-year-old boy for cruelty to an animal and a six-year-old girl for repeated thefts of baby carriages. Kalau vom Hofe reported that in one particular case that involved an exhibitionist, the court of appeals had followed the advice of the institute's expert opinion on the case by recommending psychotherapy. The institute's success in treating this small number of offenders, however, was far less than satisfactory. Of the seventy-three cases investigated in 1941, only six underwent therapy.[30] There is no record of the fate of the others.

The fourth of the institute's aims was the training of psychotherapists. Article eleven called for the creation of a training committee, which came to be made up of Göring, Schultz, Künkel, Müller-Braunschweig, and Adolf von Weizsäcker. From the beginning, the committee insisted that each candidate's own analysis or therapy (*Lehranalyse*, *Lehrbehandlung*) was an indispensable part of training. It was this aspect of psychotherapeutic practice that traditional psychiatrists found most objectionable.[31] By requiring a training analysis, the aspiring profession thus clearly indicated the direction it was taking in its institutionalization under Göring's leadership and protection. This requirement would be a point of conflict after the war between psychiatrists under Kretschmer in the reestablished General Medical Society and representatives of the various psychodynamic groups coming out of the Göring Institute. A generation later, young psychoanalysts would criticize an alleged lack of rigor in both the quantity and quality of the training analyses of psychoanalytic candidates as a result of wartime conditions and the loss of so many skilled Jewish psychoanalysts.[32]

In addition to the training analysis, the institute stipulated a theoretical course of study and practical experience that would extend over a minimum of two years (see Appendix 2). Medical candidates were required to take courses in psychology, philosophy, and ethnology, while nonmedical candidates had to take instruction in anatomy, physiology, biology, and psychiatry. The training therapy could be undertaken at any branch of the Göring Institute on the approval of Göring and the local director, but at least one year of the theoretical course work and the entire practical segment for full training as a psychotherapist had to take place in Berlin. One semester, or under special circumstances two semesters, of the theoretical portion could take place at one of the branches of the institute. The cost of a two-year course of study ran between RM 3000 and RM 4000 and subsequent membership in the institute required that the applicant be at least thirty years old and have five years of professional experience. The institute also required continuing education, which included practical orientation to the various modes of theory and treatment, the continuous treatment of one clinical patient, participation in seminars, attendance at institute or university lectures, participation in scientific meetings, and, where possible, further work in the outpatient clinic or one of its subdivisions.

The institute also reserved the right to steer the choice of location for its candidates' practices in the interest of both the profession and its patients in the equal distribution of psychotherapists throughout Germany. Although the curriculum was claimed to lay "special weight . . . upon a fundamental and thorough knowledge of heredity and racial research,"[33] the total of all the hours of instruction actually offered in these subjects between 1936 and 1945 reached only thirty-one (see Appendix 1). And while we cannot ignore the pervasiveness of racist thinking in Nazi Germany in general and among psychotherapists in particular, it is likely that such perspectives were secondary to the psychotherapists' ambition in their own courses to promote the subject of their newly professionalizing discipline.

According to article 7 of the statutes, the institute offered only two categories of membership, ordinary (*ordentliche*) and supporting (*fördernde*). While membership in the German General Medical Society required a degree in medicine, however, at the Göring Institute any fully trained psychotherapist could be a member, regardless of whether he or she was a physician.[34] Beginning in 1940, moreover, a third category, that of extraordinary (*ausserordentliche*) membership, was added. The necessity for such a change arose from what was claimed to be the large number of nonacademic candidates at the institute who sought training to supplement their professional work. For the most part, these were teachers and those practicing orthopedic gymnastics, and the great majority were women. In response to this demand, and in an attempt to increase it, the psychotherapists in 1939 instituted a program under the direction of Künkel and through his deputy Herzog for "consulting psychologists" (*beratende Psychologen*), stressing the importance of such training for professionals in large organizations but in general for those whose work "involves intercourse with people, the psychological widening and deepening of which seems desirable (e.g., doctors, jurists, clergymen, teachers, plant foremen, social workers, youth counselors, etc.)."[35]

Although the name "consulting psychologist" was dropped in 1941 in favor of the more general designation "extraordinary membership," the aim of the program remained the same: to provide at minimum a year-long course of study in psychotherapy for those who wished to incorporate a psychotherapeutic perspective into their own professions, including a training analysis, but excluding the practical aspect of a "control analysis." The original title of "consulting psychologist" probably was considered too presumptuous, especially in light of the rather modest number of candidates the program attracted, and was probably the product of an early and perhaps too provocative proselytizing zeal. In 1938 there were sixteen candidates and in 1939 fifteen, all seeking training to supplement their primary professions. In 1940 there were nine candidates and twenty-seven in 1941; by then there were also twelve extraordinary *members* of the institute. Women continued to outnumber men in this category. Extraordinary membership did not carry with it the right to practice psychotherapy or to advertise with the title "extraordinary member of the German Institute for Psychological Research and Psychotherapy."[36]

As with institute membership, the number of candidates in all categories increased over the years. In 1937 there were 42, including 26 candidates for regular membership: 16 doctors and 10 academics from nonmedical fields, exactly half of them women. The next year there were 47 candidates, including 17 doctors and 13 academics; in 1939, a total of 49 (19 doctors, 15 academics). By 1939 the number included 18 advanced candidates (*Praktikanten*) who had begun their control cases in the clinic under the supervision of their training therapist. In 1940 the candidate total had risen to 59, including 25 *Praktikanten*: 25 doctors (20 men, 5 women) and 25 candidates for the title of "attending psychologist" (*behandelnde Psychologe*), comprised of 14 academics (9 men, 5 women) and 11 nonacademics (1 man, 10 women). (On attending psychologists, see chapter 10.) The last year for which we have statistics, 1941, showed a significant increase in the number of training candidates—from 59 in December 1940 to 110 in December 1941. Candidates for ordinary membership numbered 83 (38 doctors and 45 attending psychologists). Twenty-seven of the doctors and 19 of the attending psychologists were men. Seven candidates that year had been drafted into the armed forces and one had died in the fighting.

The place of women in the field of psychotherapy both reflected and refracted a larger social reality under Nazism. Except among those without academic degrees, women were in the minority among candidates and practitioners at the Göring Institute. They were most often active as therapists in education or more generally with children. In these respects, the position of women reflected the conditions in the traditional German patriarchy that were aggravated by the misogynist Nazi regime. In particular, this status also reflected the tradition in German medicine and public health that "theory and research were to be reserved for men, and the domestic application of those theories became women's work."[37] At the same time, however, there were female physicians and academics training and working as psychotherapists in the Third Reich. This was in part due to the nature of psychotherapy as a "nurturing" interpersonal process distinct from the increasingly technical and impersonal practice of medicine that had always been dominated by males. It was also in line with the trend just before and during the Second World War toward the increased admission of women into medical schools to compensate for the drafting of male doctors into the military.[38] Had the Nazis won their war, such gains would likely have been reversed, although it is difficult to imagine a victorious Third Reich ever at peace with itself or with the outside world: A permanent state of military emergency born of a persistent state of innate psychological and ideological aggressiveness and ever more potential victims would likely have maintained a pragmatic demand for labor and expertise destructive of—or at least competitive with—Nazi misogynist ideals and practices. In the event, however, women in psychotherapy by and large represented a significant part of the special mix of oppression and opportunity offered women by National Socialism.[39]

In addition to the newly established operations of the Göring Institute, the psychotherapists in the three years before the outbreak of war in 1939 were involved in three major events, one ongoing and two episodic. The ongoing event, at which we look next, was their consistently troublesome relationship with the university psychiatrists. While there were attempts at some cooperation, the relationship in the last three years of the prewar period, as we shall see, continued to be characterized mostly by hostility, suspicion, and conflict. The two episodic events were of no less significance. The first, in 1938, was a result of the annexation (*Anschluss*) of Austria. This resulted in the destruction of the Vienna Psychoanalytic Society, Institute, and Press and the expansion of Göring Institute operations into what came to be called the Ostmark region of greater Germany. The other episode was the reorganization of the Göring Institute itself in the course of 1939. This was in part the result of Göring's desire to enhance his control over the affairs of psychotherapy in Germany by bringing to Berlin men and women from the provinces whom he liked and trusted. There was also a significant shift within the party's health apparatus that brought to power within the Interior Ministry an individual, Leonardo Conti, who was friendly to a psychotherapy practiced under the Göring name. The final reason for the reorganization of the institute in 1939 was affiliation with the Labor Front for the sake of the money it could bring to the support of the institute's operations. This affiliation, together with closer wartime ties with the military, especially Hermann Göring's Luftwaffe, would be the basis for the expansion of the institute's capabilities and influence during the early years of the Second World War.

The psychotherapists' newly won institutional status only hardened their position against the attempts by the psychiatrists to exert some control over them. As we saw in chapter 5, there was some contact and cooperation between the two camps, but even these efforts were increasingly distinguished by the assumption, especially on the part of the psychotherapists, of a formal scientific and organizational distinction between psychotherapy and psychiatry. Of course, the very gains made by the psychotherapists required some cooperation. For example, in 1937 the Society of German Neurologists and Psychiatrists, reversing an earlier stand, declared their desire to join the Society for Internal Medicine, the umbrella society that included the General Medical Society for Psychotherapy.[40] Such ententes were always double-edged: cooperation could mean cooptation, the extension of one field into that claimed by the other. At the same time, for the psychotherapists, distinction also served the political end of not impinging upon the dangerous territory of the Nazi sterilization and "euthanasia" of those mental patients deemed hereditarily and thus incurably defective. The Göring Institute required courses in psychiatry for all nonmedical candidates, but not for medical candidates. This corresponded to the psychotherapists' emphasis on the relationship of psychotherapy to all medical specialties. While it was assumed that medical candidates regardless of specialty would have some basic knowledge of psychiatry, the institute welcomed psychiatrists as candidates only on a par with other medical backgrounds. In the same dualistic spirit of cooperation and differentiation, patients were regularly referred to the Charité, to the clinic for internal medicine under Friedrich Curtius, or to Karl Bonhoeffer's neurological and psychiatric clinic (as well as to psychologist Erich Jaensch's Institute for Constitutional Research).[41] For the pragmatic psychotherapist Schultz it was this strategic recognition of the limits of psychotherapy, among other things (see chapter 9), that inspired him in 1936 to admire and praise the 1933 sterilization law.[42]

Psychiatrists, as we have seen, were not uniformly hostile to the young profession. Psychiatrist Ernst Speer, who after the First World War had established a psychotherapeutic sanitarium in Germany at Lindau on Lake Constance, was one of the few psychiatrists to be a member of the institute. In addition, psychiatrists like Lange, Luxenburger, and Bonhoeffer retained an interest and a respect for the work of the psychotherapists at the Göring Institute. In the 1920s, Bonhoeffer had even attempted to gain a professorship at Berlin for psychoanalyst Carl Müller-Braunschweig.[43] Pötzl provided facilities at the psychiatric clinic of the University of Vienna beginning in 1938. Even such virulent critics of psychotherapy such as Oswald Bumke and the rabid Nazi Max de Crinis could act in accordance with traditional professional standards to fellow members of the academic club. According to Ernst Göring, Bumke helped a group of psychotherapists obtain a lecture hall at the University of Munich after it had suddenly become "unavailable" during the political turmoil of 1933. De Crinis supported and worked with one of his students, the Stuttgart Jungian Wilhelm Bitter, and, according to August Vetter, had a collegial relationship with Hattingberg at the University of Berlin. In 1942 one of de Crinis's students, Gertrud Veit, a Nazi party member and a physician with the League of German Girls, began a training analysis at the Göring Institute with Elisabeth Lambert, becoming a *Praktikantin* in 1943.[44]

Another advantage for the psychotherapists was the fact that the Nazi regime was drawn to psychotherapy because it avoided the distasteful psychiatric diagnosis of hereditary taint among members of the "Master Race" (*Herrenvolk*). The same psychological fears of weakness, contamination, and degeneration that drove Nazis to try and root out the "racially inferior" also predisposed them to wish for as few of these elements as possible in the German populace.[45] So the practical virtues of human repair and improvement the psychotherapists offered constituted the comforting confirmation of German racial superiority. The psychotherapists were able to turn these dynamics against the psychiatrists, as Heyer did in 1935 by pointedly criticizing "official psychiatry with its therapeutic nihilism."[46] And as late as 1943 Hattingberg argued before the Kaiser Wilhelm Society that in the majority of mental cases, even when viewed from a genetic viewpoint, it was not a question of what the Nazis termed "life not worthy of being lived" (*lebensunwertes Leben*) or what Justice Minister Franz Gürtner even more crudely called "useless eaters," but of "people who can at least be brought to live normal lives, and sometimes extremely productive lives, once they are freed from their inhibitions."[47] Hattingberg was echoing the assertion by colleague Achelis, among others, that psychotherapy, unlike psychiatry, was not in the business of treating hopeless psychopaths but in treating precisely the healthy, civilized individual.[48] Such claims also of course further distanced "German" psychotherapy from association with the alleged "Jewish" psychoanalytic preoccupation with degenerate hysterics and similar worthless beings.

There were signs of concern within the psychiatric establishment that its role had to be expanded. This was a newly intensified response to the psychodynamic challenge raised most significantly by Freud at the turn of the century but now, ironically and tragically, given new and evil form by the Nazi insistence on "negative eugenics." Ernst Rüdin warned in 1939 that ignorant optimism based on simplistic notions about race and heredity threatened to undermine the practice of psychiatry.[49] At a psychiatric congress in 1941, Carl Schneider concluded a session on the psychotherapy of psychoses on a note of concern that the political leadership might limit the role of psychiatry to the sterilization and "euthanasia" of the congenitally diseased. If this were to be the case, Schneider worried, once these tasks were completed, psychiatry would be superfluous: "Should not eugenics, racial improvement, and other measures taken by the state be able to so free the *Volk* from the social, moral, and economic burden of the insane that psychiatry will no longer be needed at all?"[50] Schneider proposed that psychiatrists respond to such a challenge by reaffirming the biological basis of all mental life and the improbability of the easy and quick solution to the problem of biological engineering. Among other things, Schneider pointed out the continuing influence worked by the environment, even if endogenous and exogenous psychoses should somehow be eliminated. But an assured future awaited psychiatry, he warned, only if it acknowledged the totality of the human organism, addressed itself to psychological disturbances of all kinds, and immersed itself "in the religious, philosophic, and mythic ideas of the whole *Volk*."[51]

Although some psychiatrists eventually tried to distance themselves from the Nazi attack on mental patients (see chapter 9), it is still a shame that the great majority of psychiatrists did not share the same active concern for the victims of Nazi psychiatry as they did for their science. But neither the political nor the professional environment encouraged such concern for the human objects of state medicine. There is evidence of some psychiatric resistance to the Nazi campaign of the sterilization and murder of mental patients, but such instances were relatively rare.[52] More important for most psychiatrists were the now strong competing claims of the Göring psychotherapists. The tradition of reform psychiatry offered some room for maneuver here. For example, psychiatrist Johannes Bresler advocated what he opportunistically and ambitiously termed "national psychotherapy." Bresler believed that some psychotherapeutic work was possible with "incurable" psychopaths and on the collective plane postulated the therapeutic value of the "national will" (*Volkswille*) in responding to a "national" psychotherapy.[53] In adopting this and similar positions, psychiatrists recognized the importance of the "supply side" of the Nazi demand for racial purity. Even the SS had taken the time and the trouble to note that the aid that had in the past been given to "asocial" individuals would under the new order go to mother and child in the prophylactic spirit of the therapeutic *Volksgemeinschaft*. It was, according to the SS, the state's duty to foster a health sense of "life management" (*Lebensführung*).[54] One SS report, citing psychotherapist Walter Cimbal, argued that doctors should no longer be on the defensive but should rather take the offensive not only in eliminating the weak but in repairing and enhancing the strong.[55] And in October 1944 Hitler's secretary, Martin Bormann, complained in a letter to

Reichsführer-SS Heinrich Himmler in the latter's capacity as Minister of the Interior that the Ministry's offices of public health (*Gesundheitsämter*) should return to their accustomed duty of "positive" work in promoting the health of the populace and not be restricted to the "thankless" tasks of eliminating the weak. To this end, Bormann wrote, the overall control in such matters of the NSV should be strengthened in accord with Hitler's decree of August 22, 1944, on the "racial mission" of the Nazi welfare program.[56]

The psychiatrists of course were anything but defenseless. In spite of the type of Nazi and psychiatric protestation cited above, the regime relied on a willing psychiatric establishment to do its dirty work. By 1944, when Bormann was writing out of whatever complex of motives to Himmler about "positive" eugenics, the Nazis had issued the draft of a law designed to systematize and broaden the reach of a psychiatric police force to embrace in deadly fashion all those deemed "asocial":

> Those persons are asocial [*gemeinschaftsunfähig*] who on the basis of a hereditarily determined and therefore irremediable mental disposition are not in the position through their personal, social, or national behavior to fulfill the minimum demands of the *Volksgemeinschaft*.[57]

With its strident emphasis on youth, health, and activity, National Socialism had almost made illness of any sort a crime against the state. Pure blood and healthy sexual relations were to be the guarantors of a superior race. Racial biology was given precedence over human psychology. In 1937, for example, the *Monatsschrift für Kriminalpsychologie* became the *Monatsschrift für Kriminalbiologie*.[58] This view was also propagandized to the masses. In 1941 the Tobis production of Wolfgang Liebeneiner's *Ich klage an!* appeared on movie screens all over Germany. The film concerns a doctor's mercy killing of his wife, a pianist suffering from multiple sclerosis. The real killing, done secretly from September 1941 onward after some public protest earlier in the war, also served as a test bed for the Final Solution.[59]

Aside from scientific disagreement and professional territoriality, then, it was such fundamental political issues as we have just described that added force to the maneuvers and conflicts between psychotherapists and psychiatrists in the first years following the establishment of the Göring Institute. Just as the psychotherapists tried to do to them, psychiatrists did not hesitate to exploit the new political environment in their attacks against the psychotherapists. Even a psychiatric ally of the psychotherapists like Hans Luxenburger, presumably out of a mix of prudence and conviction, could assert to his colleagues in psychiatry that the teachings of Freud and Adler remained "Jewish" no matter how much "German" camouflage or decoration was applied.[60]

In the years leading up to the war, however, probably the most visible psychiatric critic of psychotherapy was Otto Bumke. Even though an anti-Nazi, Bumke exploited the prevailing atmosphere to professional advantage by pointing out the debt of "German psychology" to "Jewish" psychoanalysis.[61] This provocative association was made in the 1938 second edition of a book originally published in 1931. The title of the book alone, *Psychoanalysis and Her Children,* now effected a dangerous equation for German psychotherapists as "children" of Freud. Bumke's abiding criticism of psychoanalysis and psychotherapy was based on the old nineteenth-century psychiatric notion of the untouchable psyche, which charged that any attempt "to reduce the psyche to its humble and primitive elements"[62] was at best irreverent. Bumke denied the existence of the unconscious, railed against the dilettantism he saw as inherent in psychotherapy, and in his 1938 book offered a sweeping condemnation of the entire field by targeting the "Germanic" darling of the field at the time, C. G. Jung: "Thus does Jung commit the same mistake as before him Freud and even earlier Charcot and Bernheim and many others had: he believes everything that his hysterical patients tell about the innocence of their conscious."[63] Bumke also did not hesitate to sponsor a dissertation on psychoanalysis and criminality written by a member of a Nazi study group that was investigating "Jewish influence" in psychiatry and psychology.[64]

It is no surprise, therefore, to find the psychotherapeutic leadership complaining in 1938 about the "unbelievable attacks" from one of Bumke's assistants at a meeting of the Nazi University Lecturers League.[65] Göring's reaction was to invite the offender, Max Mikorey, to speak at the psychotherapists' Düsseldorf congress. Göring had already made sure that the congress did not coincide in time or place with that of the psychiatrists "so that we are not so closely associated with the psychiatrists."[66] As for Mikorey, the idea was to "bracket" him with three psychotherapists (Fritz Mohr, Schultz-Hencke, and Schultz) in a discussion of the treatment of neurosis by psychotherapy.[67] Mikorey's presentation was not included in the conference volume but was supposed to be published in the *Zentralblatt*; it never appeared.[68] Subsequent direct contact with Bumke through Hattingberg appeared to Göring to lead nowhere and Göring's own attempt to engage Kretschmer to write a friendly article on psychiatry and psychotherapy for the *Zentralblatt* also failed.[69] Göring apparently felt there was some hope for Mikorey, although he later commented that Mikorey seemed to think that military service was a cure for neurosis.[70]

During 1938 the psychotherapists and the psychiatrists were also dueling in the pages of the Nazi party newspaper, the *Völkischer Beobachter*. This had begun in 1937 with an article in the Munich edition about the meeting at which Mikorey had made his intemperate remarks about psychotherapy. In response, Göring was determined to use his cousin's good offices to have an article on psychotherapy placed in the *VB*.[71] The upshot of this determination was most likely the interview with Göring that appeared in the national Berlin edition of the paper on May 14, 1939, under the striking title "The Earliest Childhood Influences Also Determine the Shaping of Life."[72] In the meantime, however, the psychotherapists had to deal with another attack from the psychiatrists in the pages of the party paper, this time a critical report on the Düsseldorf congress, which concluded in extremely dangerous fashion:

> In his concluding remarks Kemper of Berlin pointed to the unchanged existing gulf between the "depth psychologists," as the earlier Freudian psychoanalysts now call themselves, and the hereditary biological principles expressed by Luxenburger, Enke, and Mikorey. It seems to me that in spite of all efforts at reconciliation this is probably an unbridgeable ideological antithesis.[73]

Göring wrote Curtius in frustration and some anger: "Unfortunately, Mr. [Dr.] Hannemann has thrown a big monkey wrench into the works [*kräftig quergeschossen*], although at the congress he acted as if he supported all our work."[74] This time Göring sought to use Felix Boehm's fraternity connection with Nazi party philosopher Alfred Rosenberg to publish a response.[75] Göring had already complained to the editors that no announcement of the Düsseldorf congress had been published in an earlier listing of other congresses.[76] As a result of this complaint, a small report on the Düsseldorf congress appeared in the Berlin edition of the *VB* the same day as Hannemann's critical evaluation in the Munich edition.[77] Göring's response to Hannemann appeared on December 3 in the *VB* under the headline "Deutsche

Seelenheilkunde" and with a subtitle that left no doubt as to the Nazi bona fides of "German psychotherapy": "A German Area of Science that Lay Almost Completely in Jewish Hands." Göring prominently mentioned a telegram from Hitler in response to one from the psychotherapists expressing their loyalty to the Führer on the occasion of the congress, quoted approvingly from *Mein Kampf,* and briefly praised hereditary biology. Once again directly using prejudice to professional advantage, he also decried the former influence of Jews in depth psychology. The main emphasis in the piece, which made it into the official Nazi bibliography, was the newfound unity among psychotherapists in Germany in service to society and state.[78]

In the midst of this wrestling match with the rival psychiatrists and in line with the same need and desire to divorce their discipline from association with Jews, the psychotherapists participated in the destruction of psychoanalysis in Vienna, the city of its birth. In March 1936 the SD seized the stocks of books at the central warehouse of the International Psychoanalytic Press in Leipzig.[79] By May, as we have seen, the Berlin psychoanalysts had their institute taken over by the psychotherapists. The Reich Physicians Decree of September 13, 1935, effective April 1, 1936, gave the Interior Ministry the power to prevent the practice of medicine by anyone on the basis of "national unreliability"; only those of German blood could hold administrative positions.[80] This was prelude to the exclusion of Jews from medical practice. On June 14, 1937, Hitler explained to Bormann the particular importance of moving against Jewish doctors: "The Führer regards the cleansing of the medical profession as far more important than, for example, of the bureaucracy, since in his opinion the duty of the physicians is or should be one of racial leadership."[81] A subsequent decree sent down from Berchtesgaden on July 25, 1938 expanded on the Nuremberg Race Laws of 1935. The state medical licensing of Jews would end on September 30 and Jews would be barred from state medical examinations after December 31.[82] The German General Medical Society for Psychotherapy promptly banned Jews from membership and a year later the Göring Institute prohibited the training and, save in emergency, the treatment of Jews. Most of the Jewish psychoanalysts in Germany had escaped already abroad, although fifteen would die in the Nazi concentration camps. Remarkably, Karl Landauer, who before the war had fled only to Amsterdam, and some others managed to provide psychotherapy inside Bergen-Belsen.[83]

The *Anschluss* of Austria in March 1938 spelled the end of the Vienna Psychoanalytic Institute. Göring, at the suggestion of the Freudians in his institute, sent Müller-Braunschweig to Vienna in the hope of incorporating the institute and the publishing house there into his own institute. Max Schur, Freud's personal physician, has recalled that the psychoanalysts in Vienna learned from Müller-Braunschweig that there allegedly was sharp division among the Nazi leaders as to their fate. The more radical faction around Goebbels and Himmler wanted to "throw the whole group in prison. Göring, under the influence of his psychiatrist cousin, was in favor of moderation."[84] The moderate view, with the support of a German Foreign Office concerned about international protest over rough handling of Freud, won out, but M. H. Göring's plans for inheriting the Vienna institute fell through. One of the reasons for this was that a letter from Müller-Braunschweig to Anna Freud was intercepted by the Gestapo. In the letter Müller-Braunschweig expressed his unconditional loyalty to her father's work and contradicted Göring by expressing the hope that the institute in Vienna could maintain its own separate existence, not only in order to ward off Nazi influence but also to avoid the consequences of the longstanding rivalry between analysts in Berlin and Vienna.[85] Müller-Braunschweig also sought, as he had in 1933, to distance psychoanalysis in Germany from its Jewish associations by proposing to the party's Franz Wirz the founding of a *Deutsche Zeitschrift für Psychoanalyse*.[86] When Göring was informed of the letter, he pronounced it a betrayal of his intention to preserve the Vienna institute. Both Anna Freud and Müller-Braunschweig were interrogated by the Gestapo and Göring consequently denied Müller-Braunschweig the right to teach or to publish. According to Ernst Göring, however, his father managed to persuade the Gestapo to allow Müller-Braunschweig to keep his psychoanalytic practice, including a training analysis for Ernst himself.[87] Göring also prohibited Felix Boehm, who had also been involved in the negotiations about Vienna, from providing training analyses, although he was permitted to retain his private practice.

In Austria, brownshirts ("Their heels, like spades on the floor"[88]) had invaded Freud's office already on March 15. Anton Sauerwald, a surgeon and member of Reich Physicians Leader Wagner's staff, was assigned by the Nazis to supervise the liquidation of the Vienna institute, press, and clinic. At a meeting of the directorship of the Vienna institute on March 20, 1938, attended by Sauerwald, Jones, Anna Freud,

Paul Federn, Müller-Braunschweig, and others, it was decided that the institute would become part of the DPG with the simultaneous exclusion of all "non-Aryan" members. After the exclusion and the resignation of some non-Jewish members in protest, of the thirty-six analysts in Vienna, only two, Wilhelm Sölms and August Aichhorn, remained. Sauerwald, although a dedicated anti-Semite, had studied chemistry at the University of Vienna under Josef Herzig, a lifelong Jewish friend of Freud's, and claimed to hold great respect for the founder of psychoanalysis. It is reported that Sauerwald consequently concealed the fact of Freud's foreign bank account until Freud had left Austria on June 4 and thus was able to refuse Nazi demands that any such money be handed over to them.[89] August Beranek, since 1935 the technical director of the Vienna institute's publishing house, presided over the actual destruction of the institute, joined the NSDAP, and moved to Berlin as a bookseller. The Austrian psychoanalytic society was officially dissolved on August 25, leaving behind only a study group connected with the Göring Institute. Göring appointed psychiatrist and neurologist Heinrich von Kogerer as leader, announcing that the "stronghold of Jewish psychotherapy . . . has fallen."[90]

In Germany proper, in the wake of Nazi attacks on the Jewish community in November during the "Night of Broken Glass," the DPG itself lost its status as a registered association (as did the C. G. Jung Society), becoming the Göring Institute's "Arbeitsgruppe A," although its private meetings were allowed to continue. Freud's works, which up until that time could still be purchased in Germany even if they were not to be openly displayed, were formally banned. The institute's copies, as we have noted, came under Göring's "protective custody," although apparently private copies circulated freely among the members.[91] Psychoanalytic terminology was also replaced: the "Oedipus complex" became the "family complex" and "psychoanalysis" became "developmental psychology." These moves, made out of fear, did, however, correspond with the institute's aim in transcending divisions among psychotherapists. The Adlerians became "Arbeitsgruppe B" and the Jungians "Arbeitsgruppe C," while the maintenance of even a camouflaged Freudian group indicated the indispensability of psychoanalytic theory to the field. But the public life of psychoanalysis per se was over. Dietfried Müller-Hegemann, a student of Schultz-Hencke's at the Göring Institute, recalls a fitting image for the events of 1938. In the foyer of the institute a staring contest had ensued for two years between opposing portraits of Sigmund Freud and Adolf Hitler, recalling the confrontation between portraits of Beethoven and Hitler described in Günter Grass's *The Tin Drum*: "Hitler and the genius, face to face and eye to eye. Neither of them was very happy about it."[92] But in 1938 it was finally adjudged that Freud had lost, and he, though unblinking, was taken down. Finally, when in 1939 Danish society president Oluf Brüel proposed an obituary in the *Zentralblatt* for Freud, who died in September, Göring demanded that any such obituary be cleared through him and in no case would a picture be published.[93] In the end, there was not even an obituary.

By 1939, in any case, Göring felt he had more important things to worry about. The prospect of enhanced status, increased responsibilities, and greater funding prompted Göring to reorganize his institute through a reshuffling of personnel and posts. Public political loyalty in form of Nazi party membership played a role in these maneuvers alongside personal preference and professional expertise. Göring wanted party member Curtius to become the new managing director to succeed Hilde Strecker, who since 1936 had watched over the relatively modest funds of the original institute. Curtius, however, declined, suggesting Hans Meyer-Mark, whom Göring rejected because he was half-Jewish and not a doctor.[94] Göring ended up settling for someone who was neither a doctor nor a party member: industrial psychologist Felix Scherke, informally assisted by Meyer-Mark, became managing director. Göring summoned Heyer from Munich to direct the program for attending psychologists (see chapter 10) and chose yet another party member, Achelis, to head up the literature section. Schultz would run the division for continuing medical education, while Hattingberg and Schultz-Hencke were responsible for science and research. The outpatient clinic, which up until that time had been run by the triumvirate of Göring, Boehm, and Schultz, was given over to psychoanalyst and party member Gerhard Scheunert. But Scheunert was in the army and so Schultz was appointed as his deputy, leaving the direct supervision of the clinic—ironically, as we shall see in chapter 13, given Göring's desire for public Nazi "political correctness"—in the hands of John Rittmeister.

The psychotherapists also suffered other losses in personnel. Fritz Künkel had been placed in charge of the consulting psychologists through his deputy, Edgar Herzog. In 1939 Künkel had embarked on another of his frequent foreign lecture tours, this time to the United

States. He had first visited America in 1936 and was attracted by its "frontier culture." He was also unhappy about the political situation in Germany and when war broke out in September he elected to stay in the United States.[95] Elisabeth Künkel continued to operate a private clinic at her summer home east of Berlin which during the war provided inpatient treatment for referrals from the Göring Institute.[96] Another early stalwart of the psychotherapeutic movement, Walter Cimbal, had already fallen prey to diabetes, depression, and his many enemies inside the party and the medical profession and in 1940 dropped his membership in the society and institute altogether.[97] Curtius remained as secretary of the German General Medical Society for Psychotherapy until 1940, retiring to Schliersee in Bavaria in 1944. He had become secretary in 1937 after replacing Cimbal as managing director in 1935, but the latter office had been eliminated now that the institute handled finances. Haeberlin became Göring's deputy for the society in 1937, but resigned in 1939.

But other individuals and forces outside the Göring Institute were rising on the eve of war to occasion the expansion of the psychotherapists' capacities in service to the Third Reich. The first of these individuals and forces were Robert Ley and the Labor Front, whose operations involving psychotherapy we will study in some detail in chapter 10. Ley was driven by a grandiose vision of a national-racial work and welfare state in service to the Führer as well as by a desire to extend his personal control over as much of German state and society as possible. In both of these aims he was frustrated, in great measure due to the influence of Hermann Göring and the Four-Year Plan for the mobilization of the German economy for war and conquest:

> Göring's priorities of higher production and wage stability tended to work against Ley's populist support of higher wages and general perks for the workers. Under the pressure of Göring, then, the DAF evolved after 1938 increasingly into an agency for the mobilization and social control of labor and less and less its advocate. The war would complete the transformation.[98]

In early 1939 Göring had empowered Ley to develop a plan for reformed health care and old-age insurance in keeping with the aims of the Four-Year Plan. This was the entrée for the psychotherapists into the generous funding available from the DAF and from German industry. In February Matthias Göring was planning to use the occasion of a family baptism to speak to Hermann about the "transformation"

(*Umgestaltung*) of the institute: as he put it to Curtius, the failure of the Education Ministry to solicit the psychotherapists' views on the reform of medical education "is one of the reasons why I am now going to turn to the Four-Year Plan and the DAF."[99]

The psychotherapists were also able to exploit a sudden acceleration in the turn of control of medical affairs away from the NSDAP and toward the Ministry of the Interior, a turn that also brought them further individual fruit from the Göring tree in the person of new Reich Health Leader Leonardo Conti. On March 25, 1939, Reich Physicians Leader Wagner, seriously ill since 1938, died. His death came a month after the promulgation of the Health Practitioners Law (Heilpraktikergesetz), which marked the end of party attempts at fundamental reform of the health care system. What reform there would be would be effected under the aegis of the medical departments of the Interior Ministry. This involved expanding state supervision over the practice of medicine and shortening the course of medical study so that more doctors under greater centralized control could be produced more quickly for service to the racial state. This exhortative ethos of control over reform found dramatic expression in the Health Practitioners Law. This law, which (shorn of the racial requirements) is still law in Germany, ended the freedom to cure that had existed in Germany since 1871. According to the Nazi health leadership, such a "liberal-democratic" policy had merely served as a license for Jews to swindle gullible Germans. Under the new law, the government would closely supervise the training of all medical personnel, including officially approved health practitioners. This represented a compromise between the proponents of natural health and traditional university medicine, but one that gave professional preference to regular physicians and organizational power to the Interior Ministry instead of to the NSDAP.[100]

This compromise was part of the eclipse of the early party activists we described in chapter 4. The halcyon days of 1933 had passed and Wagner had become one of those "old fighters" (*Alte Kämpfer*) who were overshadowed and left behind by Hitler's courting of new supporters in the anterooms, boardrooms, and barracks of German society. The somewhat patronizing words written by Martin Bormann in a 1944 introduction to a volume of Wagner's speeches underlined the anachronism of such noisy attempts at overturn and change: "The speeches are characteristic of the stormy period of development after the revolution."[101] The book was edited by one of Bormann's political protégés and Wagner's successor, Leonardo Conti. Conti had become director of the party's Main Office for National Health on April 22, 1939, and immediately festooned himself with the brand new Nazi neologism of Reich health leader. On the recommendation of Interior Minister Frick, Conti was also named by Hitler to replace Wagner as Reich Physicians Leader. At the same time he became a state secretary in the Interior Ministry, an occasion on which an editorial in *Der Öffentliche Gesundheitsdienst* stressed the importance of "the united direction of party and state health organizations" under the Ministry's direction.[102]

Conti had impeccable credentials as a party man. Born Leonardo Ambrosis Georges Giovanni Conti in Lugano, Switzerland, he claimed to have debated Communist leader Karl Liebknecht in 1919. He had participated in the Kapp Putsch against the Weimar Republic in 1920, and from 1921 to 1923 he was a member of the rightist student group Wikingbund. In 1923, while studying at Erlangen in northern Bavaria, he joined the SA and later in Berlin became chief for SA Standarte V "Horst Wessel." He joined the party in 1927 and the same year helped establish the SA medical corps. Two years later he was involved with Bormann and Wagner in the reform of SA insurance, and in 1930, as Wagner's overseer (*Gauobmann*), had become head of the Nazi Physicians League in Berlin.[103] By the critical year of 1934, however, Conti was rapidly falling away from Wagner and the SA and into the more elite and establishment realms of the SS and the Ministry of the Interior. Although there exists no evidence of a major or official feud between Conti and Wagner, there are significant indications that, aside from competing ambition, the two acted out the traditional animosity that played between SA and SS, between party and state, between Munich and Berlin.[104]

When, as Reich Health Leader, Conti had to prepare the edition of Wagner's speeches in 1944, it was Bormann, a patron of both Wagner and Conti, who produced the regulation praise that was in order for the dead Reich Physicians Leader. Much earlier, Conti had warned of the ultimately abortive Stennes Putsch bubbling up out of the SA, and four years later he was reaping the vengeful rewards of the aftermath of the Röhm Putsch. Conti was charged by Reich Physician of the SA Emil Ketterer with repeating, or even originating, the rumor that Ketterer had been found in bed with Röhm on the night of June 30, 1934, the so-called "Night of the Long Knives." Conti also allegedly had drawn Wagner into the affair by claiming that Wagner was protecting Ketterer, a friend of Erwin Villain, whom Wagner had recommended for a post over Conti's objections. Conti denied having said that Ketterer had been found in bed with Röhm. What he had said, he maintained, was only that Ketterer had been in the same house as Röhm on June 30 and was therefore unfit.[105]

It was in fact Conti's skirmish with Villain before the Röhm Putsch that showed more clearly and violently where the lines of sovereignty and loyalty were being drawn in the struggle for power over the administration of the medical affairs of the Reich. Villain was the Nazi boss of the Greater Berlin Physicians Association and Wagner's agent (*Vertrauensmann*) in Berlin. Wagner had demanded the naming of Villain to the presidency of both the physicians chamber and court of honor for Berlin. Conti, as the responsible official in the Prussian Interior Ministry, had recommended to the minister-president of Prussia, Hermann Göring, that this appointment not be made, citing what Conti regarded as Villain's personal deficiencies. Göring accepted Conti's recommendation. Upon hearing a report of all of this from Wagner, Villain wrote Conti, challenging him to a duel with sabers. Göring forbade Conti to accept the challenge, but the affair did not end there.

Villain's desire to exact what he regarded as satisfaction from Conti for this affront took the form of a physical assault by Villain on Conti in Munich on the night of March 4, 1934. Villain was arrested, and what ensued was almost a farcical exercise of opposing interests and influences. Ketterer managed to have Villain freed into his custody, but Göring had Villain arrested again in order to bring him back to Berlin. The Bavarian Minister of the Interior, Adolf Wagner, then had Villain released. Ketterer hid the fugitive in the alpine village of Partenkirchen where, under the official protection of the SA, he resisted all attempts at arrest and transport to Berlin after he had been found by a public prosecutor sent to Munich from Berlin. At this juncture, Reich Interior Minister Frick and Reich Justice Minister Gürtner involved themselves in the case, and Villain finally agreed to return to Berlin under the supervision of Berlin SA leader Karl Ernst to stand trial. All the while Villain remained on active duty with the SA and was even awarded its dagger of honor. Despite attempts by the SA to have the trial aborted and a clumsy attempt by Ketterer to influence the court while it was in session, Villain was convicted of assault and sentenced to eight months in prison. He filed an appeal, while an SA court of honor convened by Röhm found Conti in contempt of the SA.[106] Any effects of such prosaic and petty proceedings were eclipsed, however, by the June 30 purge of the SA by Hitler at the urging of Göring and Himmler. Villain was one of the victims.[107]

Although in 1935 Wagner himself declared his belief that Conti was innocent of wrongdoing in the Ketterer and Villain affairs,[108] this declaration must be viewed as an expression of resignation rather than rapprochement. The tide had already turned from SA brown to SS black. After Wagner's death, Conti set about assembling all capacities and prerogatives concerning health and medicine within his offices at the Interior Ministry. Conti was a teetotaler and a nonsmoker, but his relatively moderate views on the need for natural health practices aided and abetted by the burgeoning achievements of the German drug industry (see chapter 12) made him a more attractive ally for the medical establishment than the radical Wagner and his noisy cronies.[109] In 1942, for example, Conti would clash with the archdabbler Himmler over state regulation of "people's doctors,"[110] insisting that the Interior Ministry must have control over their activities.

Conti's first task on being named Reich Health Leader was to install men loyal to him at key positions in the state medical bureaucracy. Conti himself replaced Arthur Gütt as state secretary while Kurt Blome supplanted Wagner's deputy, Fritz Bartels. These appointments were made by Hitler on Frick's recommendation. On March 30, 1940, Conti announced the dissolution of the Reich Central Office of Health Leadership, which under Bartels had been a bastion of party health activities within the Interior Ministry. The surviving Reich Commission for National Health Service was to be bound closer than ever to the Ministry and on April 12 Reiter's Reich Health Office was also placed more firmly under Ministry control. Interior Ministry bureaucrats Robert Cropp and Herbert Linden were named to direct the activities of the Reich Commission, and close cooperation was proclaimed between it and the party's Race Political Office.[111]

These moves gutted what was left of the party's health apparatus, leaving it with only the broad but insubstantial direction of the racial consciousness of the nation as part of overall healthfulness. Conti also moved against the DAF, first by becoming a state secretary in the Labor Ministry and thereby assuming authority over the management of national health insurance. Ley protested to Hess that this made

Conti his own superior, because as state secretary in the Interior Ministry he already controlled the Panel Doctors Association of Germany, which represented doctors participating in the state medical insurance program, and the Reich Physicians Chamber. Such a monopoly prejudiced DAF efforts in the sphere of what Ley called social politics and in general compromised the role of the NSDAP.[112] Previously, Ley had separated the DAF's Office for National Health from the party's Main Office for National Health in an attempt to retain some sovereignty in the medical field, but Conti in the meantime had acquired formal control over DAF health activities through the creation of a new DAF office, Fachamt Gesundheit, under his direction. He also installed his choice, Werner Bockhacker, as director of another Labor Front organization, the Office for Health and National Care, and moved Bockhacker's offices from the party city of Munich to the seat of the Reich government in Berlin.[113]

Conti eventually fell prey to hierarchical intrigue and his plans to centralize the Reich health system failed.[114] But, in contrast to the coarser brutes carrying SA knives, Conti had the lean and hungry look of the smooth, intelligent, ambitious SS man. As such, his activities on behalf of the Interior Ministry at the expense of party organizations delighted Frick, who was "at heart a civil servant who abhorred wild and uncontrollable actions by undisciplined party members."[115] Frick's campaign for control of the Reich's internal affairs had met with early success since he possessed in the Interior Ministry a sophisticated base of operations from the beginning in 1933. By the time party forces began to organize effectively in 1934, Frick, in the interest of the "seizure of society's strengths,"[116] was able over the next five years to check and to repel them.

Most disturbing, of course, had been the threat of SA under Röhm who had pressed for a soldier's state, not so much in the spirit of a genuine "second revolution" but in a chaotic demand for state aid, for the spoils of victory in monthly checks. The brownshirts were "desperados in search of a pension."[117] By contrast, Conti was to Frick a shining example of the process begun in 1933: to subordinate the party to the state by way of ordained party-state unity. The key element in the state's victory—in fact a partial and Pyrrhic victory—was the channeling of party influence through the state ministries and their bureaucracies. In the field of health, the legal basis for this was the legislation that decreed the unification of Germany's health care system.

What Conti represented, therefore, was the creation of an SS "'col-lateral state,'" which "gradually penetrated existing institutions, undermined them, and finally began to dissolve them."[118] This process was accelerated by the conflicts of interests and political confusions that had existed within the state bureaucracy since the First World War.[119] Frick himself fell prey to Reichsführer-SS Himmler in large bites: Himmler's assumption of control over all police forces in 1936 and his acquisition of the post of Interior Minister in 1943. These were only major instances in a constant process whereby the Third Reich lost the characteristics of a state as it degenerated into a jumbled agglomeration of action centers, plenipotentiaries, and various and sundry deputations of the only thing that consistently counted in Nazi Germany: loyalty, real or apparent, to Hitler. Conti's collection of offices and capacities inside the Interior Ministry constituted not a unification of the health system, but the construction of a personal realm of power and authority that perversely capitalized on the state's earlier efforts to centralize and rationalize the health bureaucracy.

Both the party and the state were gradually submerged in a "series of undulating layers of influence, operating simultaneously above, below, and parallel"[120] to each other. This constituted Hitler's law and governance of a besieged fortress and was a signal element in the opportunity for psychotherapists in the Third Reich to organize themselves and operate professionally. It was a result of the superficial nature of the Nazi transformation of Germany that initially gave the appearance of efficiency, unanimous popular and institutional acquiescence, and coherent and aggressive plans for reform. The Nazi concern with mobilizing expertise and avoiding disruptive reform—along with the pervasiveness of personal loyalties and feuds—filled the racist vacuum that constituted Nazi ideas.[121]

More specifically, Conti had ample reason to appreciate the Göring name. As we have already seen, Conti had benefited from the support of Hermann Göring, his boss as head of the Prussian Ministry of the Interior, in his struggle with the SA in 1934. But Conti's ties with the Göring bastion in Prussia had a longer history. In December 1930 Conti had been a member of SS-Gruppenführer Kurt Daluege's staff in Berlin when Daluege was assigned to Hermann Göring in Göring's capacity as Reich Commissar for the Prussian Interior Ministry. It was Göring's assignment to rid the Prussian police administration of all politically unreliable officials. Daluege was to become one of his chief operatives in the short struggle with Himmler for control of the police and the Gestapo.[122] On February 13, 1933, Göring delegated Conti to rid the medical profession of Jews and Marxists; on January 12, 1934, he named him Prussian state councilor for life.

Conti's success under Hermann Göring's aegis, a success that was to continue under Frick after the Prussian and Reich Interior Ministries were fused during 1934–35,[123] reached its peak in 1939. That year it was Göring who resolved the tug-of-war between Munich and Berlin over the succession to Wagner's post by naming Conti as Reich Health Leader.[124] Göring's liking for Conti certainly would not have been diminished by an earlier decision Conti allegedly made. In 1940 Matthias Heinrich Göring publicly celebrated the fact that in 1933 Conti "was consulted by the Prussian Minister-President for his opinion on whether our society should continue on in existence."[125] Although elder cousin Göring's reconstruction of the events understandably implied that this consequent decision was based on the proper consideration of scientific merit and *völkisch* value, it would be fatuous to ignore Conti's political motivation for having rendered a positive evaluation of the General Medical Society for Psychotherapy. Ernst Göring has recalled that his father often mentioned Conti's name, although he feels that Conti was ambivalent about psychotherapy. Kemper also recalls one Conti visit to the institute. Conti was convinced of the importance of early childhood as a basis for good adult health. This stemmed in great measure from his mother's leading role in the midwifery movement in Germany.[126] If, however, Conti was ambivalent about psychotherapy and if Göring exaggerated his role given the former's powerful status by 1940, then there is all the more reason to emphasize the political in Conti's favorable decision in 1933.

By the outbreak of the Second World War the Göring Institute had achieved the status of formal supervision from the state through the offices of the Medical Division under Herbert Linden. It had also won additional security from the same source in the person of Leonardo Conti. The war—and preparations for war—brought the institute money from the Labor Front and from the military, in particular Hermann Göring's Luftwaffe. As we have seen, many structural and suprapersonal forces contributed to these developments, but what united and magnified these forces to the material benefit of psychotherapists in the Third Reich was the professional accident of Matthias Heinrich Göring. It was not so much what Göring brought to the psychotherapists but what he enabled. It is in this sense that Otto Curtius was right when he wrote to Göring on March 10, 1939: "You have truly served as a deus ex machina."[127]

Notes

1. "Tätigkeitsbericht 1937," pp. 204–5.
2. "Jahresbericht 1940," p. 2; "Jahresbericht 1941," p. 63; for a list of the members, see Lockot, *Erinnern und Durcharbeiten,* pp. 352–4.
3. Mitgliederliste der Deutschen allgemeinen ärztlichen Gesellschaft für Psychotherapie [c. 1936], Kl. Erw. 762/2.
4. Herbert Gold, "Auch die ersten Kindheitseinflüsse bestimmen die Lebensgestaltung," p. 5.
5. "Tätigkeitsbericht 1937," pp. 202–3.
6. Boehm to Jung, December 4, 1936, Kl. Erw. 762/2.
7. Cimbal, Bericht über die Besprechungen zwischen Herrn Dr. Curtius, Herrn Dr. Hüthig und dem Unterzeichneten betreffen die Möglichkeiten einer Neugründung des Zentralblattes für Psychotherapie, November 18, 1935, Kl. Erw. 762/2. According to Göring, Hirzel complained about long delays in the editorial work from Zurich: see Göring to Poul Bjerre, November 12, 1940, Kl. Erw. 762/3.
8. Johannes Heinrich Schultz, "Poliklinische Aufgaben und Pflichten," pp. 12–13.
9. "Tätigkeitsbericht 1938," pp. 4–6.
10. "Tätigkeitsbericht 1937," pp. 204–5.
11. "Jahresbericht 1941," pp. 65–7; and Felix Boehm, "Erhebung und Bearbeitung von Katamnesen," p. 20.
12. Felix Boehm, "Polikinische Erfahrungen," p. 7; see also Reichsintitut für Psychologische Forschung und Psychotherapie im Reichsforschungsrat, Richtlinien der Poliklinik, pp. 2, 8–9.
13. Boehm, "Poliklinische Erfahrungen," p. 75; Gerhart [sic] Scheunert, "Über Psychotherapie Kurzbehandlungen," pp. 218–20.
14. Richtlinien der Poliklinik, pp. 4–5.
15. Klinisches Diagnosen-Schema der Poliklinik und Psychodiagnostischen Abteilung, in Reichsinstitut für Psychologische Forschung und Psychotherapie im Reichsforschungsrat, Richtlinien der Poliklinik, p. 15.
16. Johannes Heinrich Schultz, "Vorschlag eines Diagnosen-Schemas," pp. 99–100; see also ibid., pp. 157–60, and Klinisches Diagnosen-Schemas, pp. 11–15.
17. Olga von König-Fachsenfeld, "Erziehungshilfe"; idem, "Arbeitsplan für Erziehungshilfe," in Matthias Heinrich Göring, ed., *1. Sonderheft des Deutschen Instituts für Psychologische Forschung und Psychotherapie,* pp. 23–7; Elisabeth Künkel, "Die Bedeutung des Spieles in der Erziehungshilfe," in ibid., pp. 56–8; and Gerdhild von Staabs, "Spieltherapie beim Kleinkind," in ibid., pp. 59–60. See also Göring, "Bericht," p. 4.
18. Elisabeth Künkel, "Zur Auswertung der Erfahrungen in der Erziehungshilfe des 'Instituts' in Berlin," in Matthias Heinrich Göring, ed., *Erziehungshilfe,* p. 14.
19. Olga Freiin von König-Fachsenfeld, "Die Erziehungshilfe in Berlin," in Göring, *Erziehungshilfe,* p. 12; see also idem, "Erziehungshilfe," *Die Ärztin* 17 (1941): 350–2. *Freiin* means "baroness." On psychologists in the NSV, see Geuter, *Die Professionalisierung der deutschen Psychologie,* pp. 406–14.
20. See Else Wildfang, "Erziehungshilfe der Berlin Verkehrsbetriebe (BVG)," in Göring, *Erziehungshilfe,* pp. 18–19; and Adelheid Fuchs-Kamp, "Sozial Betreute Kinder im psychotherapeutischen Heim," in ibid., pp. 25–7.

21. Adolf von Weizsäcker, "Heim-Erziehung," p. 95; Pongratz, *Psychotherapie,* p. 207; see also Weizsäcker, "Die tiefenpsychologische Behandlung von Kinderneurosen," versus Hans Eyferth, "Kinderpsychotherapie und Heilerziehung," *Zeitschrift für Kinderforschung* 49 (1941): 143–51.
22. F. Winkelmayr, "Die Erziehungshilfe in der Stadt Wien," in Göring, *Erziehungshilfe,* pp. 22–4; see also Richard Seyss-Inquart, "Aus der psychotherapeutischen Praxis in der Anstalt für Erziehungsbedürftige Kaiser-Ebersdorf in Wien," *ZfP* 14 (1942): 129–49; and Otto Schürer von Waldheim, "Arbeitstherapie als Mittel zur Besserung verwöhnter Jugendlicher," *ZfP* 13 (1941): 208–19. Richard Seyss-Inquart was the elder brother of Austrian Nazi Artur Seyss-Inquart; see Wolfgang Rosar, *Deutsche Gemeinschaft: Seyss-Inquart und der Anschluss* (Vienna, 1971), pp. 15–16.
23. Göring to Curtius, April 17, 1939, Kl. Erw. 762/2; Huber, *Psychoanalyse in Österreich,* pp. 61–7, 242–46.
24. Heinz Kohut, *The Curve of Life: Correspondence of Heinz Kohut, 1923–1981,* ed. Geoffrey Cocks (Chicago, 1994), pp. 8, 47–59.
25. On Aichhorn's career in general, see George J. Mohr, "August Aichhorn," in Franz Alexander et al., eds., *Psychoanalytic Pioneers* (New York, 1966), pp. 348–59. See also August Aichhorn, *Verwahrloste Jugend, die Psychoanalyse in der Fürsorgeerziehung: Zehn Vorträge zur ersten Einführung* (Leipzig, 1925); and the letter from Göring to August Sauerwald reprinted in a postwar newspaper article in which Göring expresses the hope that this book can be spared from banning through the removal of Freud's foreword: Karl Hans Heinz, "Sigmund Freud's braunes Leid," *Neues Österreich,* October 13, 1948, p. 3, Thomas Aichhorn. Aichhorn's namesake was a strongly Catholic member of Austrian fascist Engelbert Dollfuss's Fatherland Front and spent a year in Dachau; Ernst Federn, personal communication, August 9, 1982. See also Anna Freud, "August Aichhorn, July 27, 1878–October 17, 1949," *International Journal of Psycho-Analysis* 32 (1951): 51–6. Aichhorn himself was a Christian Socialist but, according to his Jewish psychoanalytic colleague, Hermann Nunberg, not an anti-Semite; see Nunberg, *Memoirs, Recollections, Ideas, Reflections* (New York, 1969), p. 20.
26. "Auszug aus der Statistik der Beratungsstelle," in Seif, *Wege der Erziehungshilfe,* pp. 209–11; "Jahresbericht 1941," p. 76.
27. "Dr. Leonhard Seif, geboren 15.1.1866," *ZfP* 12 (1941): 322; Lene Credner, "Geleitwort zur Neuherausgabe," in Leonhard Seif, ed., *Wege der Erziehungshilfe: Ergebnisse und praktische Hinweise aus der Tätigkeit des Münchener Arbeitskreises für Erziehung,* 2nd ed. (Munich, 1952), pp. 8–11.
28. Kurt Seelmann, "Vorbedingungen für die Errichtung einer Erziehungsberatungsstelle," in Seif, *Wege der Erziehungshilfe,* pp. 117–27; Margarete Krause-Ablass, "Auswirkungen auf NS-Mutterdienst," in ibid., pp. 293–5; see also Hildegard Hetzer, "Die Zusammenarbeit von Kindertagesstätte und Erziehungsberatung der NSV-Jugendhilfe," *Nationalsozialistischer Volksdienst* 9 (1942): 133–8.
29. Lene Credner, "Die körperliche und erbbiologische Untersuchung," in Seif, *Wege der Erziehungshilfe,* pp. 140–50; Göring, "Bericht," p. 1.
30. Marie Kalau vom Hofe, "Kriminalpsychologie"; "Jahresbericht 1941," pp. 70–1; see also Göring, "Kriminalpsychologie," in Gustav Kafka, ed., *Handbuch der vergleichenden Psychologie,* vol 3: *Die Funktion des abnormen Seelenlebens* (Munich, 1922), pp. 155–229.
31. "Tätigkeitsbericht 1937," p. 202; former psychoanalytic members of the Göring

Institute use the term "training analysis," while the official term at the time was "training treatment." The latter term was designed to divorce "German" psychotherapy from "Jewish" psychoanalysis, although the former term was the original and more felicitous term for the student's own psychotherapeutic experience at the start of training. For that reason, the term "training analysis" is used in this account.

32. Ulrich Schultz-Venrath, "Der Missbrauch von Geschichte als transgenerationelles Traumatisierungsphänomen," p. 398. This argument is partially weakened through its ad hominem aspect; see also Lockot, *Erinnern und Durcharbeiten,* p. 200.
33. Deutsches Institut für Psychologische Forschung und Psychotherapie e.V. in Berlin, Richtlinien für die Ausbildung, p. 5; see also ibid., pp. 4–6; and the yearly lists of courses in the institute's (Ankündigung der) Veranstaltungen; for the same phenomenon in psychology, see Geuter, *Die Professionalisierung der deutschen Psychologie,* pp. 205–9.
34. "Tätigkeitsbericht 1937," p. 203.
35. Deutsches Institut für Psychologische Forschung und Psychotherapie, Richtlinien für die Ausbildung, p. 2; Göring, "Bericht," pp. 3, 5.
36. Deutsches Institut für Psychologische Forschung und Psychotherapie, Richtlinien für die Ausbildung, pp. 1, 7–8; Edgar Herzog, "Arbeitsplan der Abteilung 'Beratende Psychologen'," in Göring, *1. Sonderheft,* pp. 12–15; and Göring, "Bericht," pp. 3, 5.
37. Stacey Freeman, "Medicalizing the Nurse: Professional and Eugenic Discourse at the Kaiserin Auguste Victoria Haus in Berlin," *German Studies Review* 18 (1995): 433; see also ibid., p. 432, and Young Sun Hong, "Femininity as a Vocation: Gender and Class Conflict in the Professionalization of German Social Work," in Cocks and Jarausch, *German Professions,* pp. 232–51.
38. Proctor, *Racial Hygiene,* pp. 128–9.
39. Adelheid von Saldern, "Victims or Perpetrators? Controversies About the Role of Women in the Nazi State," in Crew, *Nazism and German Society,* pp. 141–65.
40. Lockot, *Erinnern und Durcharbeiten,* pp. 255, 361, n. 10.
41. "Tätigkeitsbericht 1937," p. 205.
42. Johannes Heinrich Schultz, "Das Leib-Seele Problem in der Heilkunde," p. 292; see also idem, "Psychopathie und Neurose," *Forschungen und Fortschritte* 17 (1941): 228–9.
43. Dührssen, *Ein Jahrhundert Psychoanalytische Bewegung,* pp. 82–3, 144.
44. Veit to Felix Scherke, June 27, 1943, Kl. Erw. 762/6.
45. Klaus Theweleit, *Male Fantasies: Women, Floods, Bodies, History,* trans. Stephen Conway (Minneapolis, 1987).
46. *Hippokrates* 6 (1935): 801.
47. Hans von Hattingberg, *Neue Seelenheilkunde,* pp. 42–3.
48. Achelis, "Psychologische Zivilisationsbilanz," p. 81; see also Scheunert, "Über Psychotherapie Kurzbehandlungen," p. 206, n. 2; and Schultz, *Lebensbilderbuch,* p. 131.
49. Martin Gumpert, *Heil Hunger!,* pp. 43–4.
50. Carl Schneider, Schlussbemerkungen, p. 3.
51. Ibid., p. 6; see also Ostmann, "Völkische Psychiatrie," *Deutsches Ärzteblatt* 63 (1933): 164–5.
52. Dirk Blasius, "Psychiatrischer Alltag im Nationalsozialismus," in Detlev Peukert and Jürgen Reulecke, eds., *Die Reihen fast geschlossen: Beiträge zur Geschichte des Alltags unterm Nationalsozialismus* (Wuppertal, 1981), pp. 367–80.

53. Johannes Bresler, "Gibt es nationale Psychotherapie?" *Psychiatrish-Neurologische Wochenschrift* 42 (1940): 12–14.
54. Der Höhere SS- und Polizeiführer in Frankreich/SS Führer im Rasse- und Siedlungswesen, Gedanken über eine SS-mässige Fürsorge: Fürsorge und Weltanschauung, n.d., BDC: SS-Führer.
55. E. Abigt, "Zur Ertüchtigung des Hochzuchtmenschen," ms., n.d., Microcopy T-175, roll 17, frames 881–8, National Archives.
56. Bormann to Himmler, October 1944, R 18, folder 2983, BA.
57. Reichsleitung des Rassenpolitischen Amtes der NSDAP, Richtlinien für die Beurteilung der Erbgesundheit des RMdI 18.7.40, quoted in Ernst Illing, "Asoziale Jugend," *Medizinische Zeitschrift* 1 (1944): 24.
58. Hans Reiter, "Dem neuen Jahrgang zum Geleit," *Monatsschrift für Kriminalbiologie* 28 (1937): 1–2.
59. Henry Friedlander, *The Origins of Nazi Genocide: From Euthanasia to the Final Solution* (Chapel Hill, 1995).
60. Hans Luxenburger, "Rückblick auf die wissenschaftlichen Sitzungen der II. Jahresversammlung der Gesellschaft Deutscher Neurologen und Psychiater in Frankfurt am Main, 22.-25. VIII 1936," *Deutsche medizinische Wochenschrift* 62 (1936): 1702; see also Zapp, "Psychoanalyse und Nationalsozialismus," pp. 218–20.
61. Oswald Bumke, *Die Psychoanalyse und ihre Kinder,* p. 2; see also idem, "Über Psychoanalyse," *ZfP* 3 (1930): 650–4; and Decker, *Freud in Germany,* pp. 164–5.
62. Zilboorg, *A History of Medical Psychology,* p. 497.
63. Bumke, *Die Psychoanalyse und ihre Kinder,* p. 116; see also Ulfried Geuter, "Der Leipziger Kongress der Deutschen Gesellschaft für Psychologie 1933," *Psychologie- und Gesellschaftskritik* 3 (1979): 7–25.
64. Adolf Stelzle, *Das Verbrechen in der Auffassung der Psychoanalyse* (Dachau, 1940), p. 24; *Nationalsozialistische Bibliographie* 7:11/12 (November/December 1942), p. 14, entry 63.
65. Göring to Haeberlin, February 5, 1938, Kl. Erw. 762/2.
66. Göring to Curtius, December 18, 1937, Kl. Erw. 762/2.
67. Curtius to Göring, July 22, 1938, Kl. Erw. 762/2; Fritz Mohr, "Die Behandlung der Neurosen durch Psychotherapie," in Curtius, *Psychotherapie in der Praxis,* pp. 48–67. Mikorey too worried about "Jewish influence" in criminal psychology in particular: see Stelzle, *Das Verbrechen in der Auffassung der Psychoanalyse,* pp. 21–2; and Max Weinreich, *Hitler's Professors: The Part of Scholarship in Germany's Crimes Against the Jewish People* (New York, 1949), p. 40.
68. Curtius, *Psychotherapie in der Praxis,* p. 67.
69. Göring to Curtius, March 28, 1939, Kl. Erw. 762/2; Göring to Kretschmer, December 21, 1938, Franz Jung.
70. Göring to Curtius, May 22, 1939, Kl. Erw. 762/2.
71. Göring to Curtius, December 18, 1937, Kl. Erw. 762/2.
72. Gold, "Auch die ersten Kindheitseinflüsse bestimmen die Lebensgestaltung."
73. Karl Hannemann, "Seelenheilkunde und politische Führung," p. 12.
74. Göring to Curtius, October 11, 1938, Kl. Erw. 762/2.
75. Ibid.; Curtius to Göring, October 18, 1938, Kl. Erw. 762/2.
76. Göring to *Völkischer Beobachter,* August 25, 1938, Kl. Erw. 762/2; and *Völkischer Beobachter* to Göring, September 2, 1938, Kl. Erw. 762/2.

77. "Neue Wege der Heilkunde: 2. Tagung der Deutschen Gesellschaft für Psychotherapie in Düsseldorf," *Völkischer Beobachter,* October 2, 1938, p. 5.
78. Matthias Heinrich Göring, "Deutsche Seelenheilkunde"; *Nationalsozialistische Bibliographie* 4:1/2 (January/February 1939), p. 64, entry 276.
79. Jones, *Sigmund Freud,* vol. 3, p. 188.
80. *Reichsärzteordnung* (Berlin and Vienna, 1944).
81. Heinrich Lammers, Ergebnis des Vortrages beim Führer am 14. Juni 1937 in Gegenwart von Reichsleiter Bormann, R 43, II (Medizinalwesen) 733, p. 43, BA. On at least one occasion Hitler remarked to Wagner that of all academics doctors were the most important to the state: see Hans-Dietrich Röhrs, *Hitlers Krankheit: Tatsachen und Legende* (Neckargemünd, 1966), pp. 71–2.
82. "Wortlaut der 4. Verordnung des Führers und Reichskanzlers zum Reichsbürgergesetz," *Reichsgesetzblatt* (1938): 679–80; see also Geoffrey Cocks, "Partners and Pariahs: Jews and Medicine in Modern German Society," *Leo Baeck Institute Yearbook* 36 (1991): 165, 167.
83. J. Tas, "Psychical Disorders Among Inmates of Concentration Camps," *Psychiatric Quarterly* 25 (1951): 679–90. M.H. Göring, "Bericht über die Tatigkeit der Internationalen Allgemeinen Ärztlichen Gesellschaft für Psychotherapie und Ihrer Landesgruppen in den Jahren 1939 und 1940," *ZfP* 13 (1941): 5.
84. Max Schur, *Freud: Living and Dying* (New York, 1972), p. 496.
85. Dührssen, *Ein Jahrhundert Psychoanalytische Bewegung,* p. 177.
86. Lockot, *Die Reinigung der Psychoanalyse,* pp. 113–14.
87. See also Carl Müller-Braunschweig, "Forderungen an eine die Psychotherapie unterbauende Psychologie," *ZfP* 11 (1939): 168–76; and an interview in the popular press: Charlotte Köhn-Behrens, "Wer ist denn nun hysterisch?," *Berliner Illustrierte Nachtausgabe,* August 22, 1939, in Brecht, *"Hier geht das Leben,"* p. 162.
88. Ellen Hinsey, "The Stairwell, Berggasse 19, Vienna," in idem, *Cities of Memory* (New Haven, 1996), pp. 35–8; see also Peter Gay, *Freud: A Life for Our Time* (New York, 1986), pp. 622–3.
89. Jones, *Sigmund Freud,* 3:217–26; see also Ronald Clark, *Freud: The Man and the Cause* (New York, 1980), p. 510; Anton Sauerwald, Bericht, Vienna, March 21, 1938; Gerhard Maetze, "Psychoanalyse in Deutschland," in Dieter Eicke, ed., *Die Psychologie des 20. Jahrhunderts,* vol. 2: *Freud und die Folgen* (I), (Zurich, 1976), p. 1171; and Huber, *Psychoanalyse in Österreich,* pp. 52–6.
90. *Münchener medizinische Wochenschrift* 85 (1938): 1095; see also Reichskommissar für die Wiedervereinigung Österreichs mit dem deutschen Reich, Stab Stillhaltekommissar für Vereine, Organisationen und Verbände, to Polizeidirektor Wien, August 25, 1938, Sigmund-Freud-Gesellschaft, Vienna.

    Richard Sterba, one of the few non-Jewish members of Freud's circle in Vienna, has a more critical view of Müller-Braunschweig's role in the German takeover of the Vienna Psychoanalytic Society: see Richard F. Sterba, *Reminiscences of a Viennese Psychoanalyst* (Detroit, 1982), p. 165. Sterba does report, however, that Müller-Braunschweig wanted him to return from Basel to help conduct the operations of the Vienna society, a recollection that is in line with Müller-Braunschweig's reported desire to maintain a psychoanalytic presence in the Austrian capital. Ernest Jones, according to Sterba (pp. 163–4, 165–6) had also wished him to remain in Vienna because, as Sterba later learned from Helene Deutsch's autobiography, Jones wanted the psychoanalytic movement to be headquartered in London with Sterba as the representative in Vienna who would be "racially" acceptable to the Nazis and thus able to perpetuate its existence there: see Helene Deutsch, *Confrontations with Myself: An Epilogue* (New York, 1973), p. 170; see also Huber, *Psychoanalyse in Österreich,* pp. 54–5.

On the efforts of a number of foreign colleagues to help Austrian psychoanalysts in escaping from Austria after the *Anschluss,* see Walter C. Langer, and Sanford Gifford, "An American Analyst in Vienna During the *Anschluss,*" *Journal of the History of the Behavioral Sciences* 14 (1978): 37–54; see also Kohut, *The Curve of Life,* pp. 8–12, 64–5, 207–8.

Kogerer's wife was half-Jewish. As a result, his party membership of May 1, 1938, was suspended on May 27 and revoked in September. On December 14, 1941, however, Kogerer was granted a special dispensation (*Gnadenent scheid ung*) by Hitler and eventually reinstated in the party; BDC: Parteikorrespondenz; see also Heinrich von Kogerer, *Psychotherapie* (Vienna, 1934).

91. Lohmann and Rosenkötter, "Psychoanalyse in Hitlerdeutschland," pp. 80–1; Pongratz, *Psychotherapie,* p. 41. Gerhard Scheunert recalls that he did not receive his subscription to the *Internationale Zeitschrift für Psychoanalyse* during 1934 and 1935, but began receiving it again after the DPG had been assimilated by the Göring Institute. In 1938 the institute expressed the hope that some of the books from the forty-five crates that the SD had taken from the International Psychoanalytic Press in Leipzig and Vienna would be given to the institute's library. It is not clear whether this happened: see "Tätigkeitsbericht 1938," p. 4. It was the institute's understanding, apparently a correct one, that the books were not to be destroyed: see Huber, *Psychoanalyse in Österreich,* p. 179, n. 27. Werner Kemper claims that all but two copies of each book taken from the press were destroyed: see Pongratz, *Psychotherapie,* p. 276. In a postwar account Schultz-Hencke reported that he was asked to send a list of the fifteen most important psychoanalytic works; everything was pulped except for some sold in Switzerland for foreign exchange and fifteen copies of each book kept by the Gestapo: see Sechster protokollarischer Bericht, June 13, 1945, pp. 1–2, Kl. Erw. 762/7.
92. Günter Grass, *The Tin Drum,* trans. Ralph Manheim (New York, 1961), p. 116. According to Lockot, Müller-Hegemann is speaking of the psychoanalytic institute from 1934 to 1936; Lockot, *Erinnern und Durcharbeiten,* p. 351 n. 6. This is possible, although Müller-Hegemann was not a member of the Berlin Psychoanalytic Institute, joining the Göring Institute in 1937. Would the psychoanalysts have opposed these portraits in their institute? Would Freud have occupied such a place of "honor" opposite Hitler in the Göring Institute for almost two years? Given the jarring nature of the image, it is perhaps appropriate that this issue remains unclear, perhaps even apocryphal.
93. Göring to Jung, November 9, 1939, Franz Jung; Jung to Göring, November 18, 1939, Kl. Erw. 762/2.
94. Göring to Curtius, February 2, 1939, Kl. Erw. 762/2.
95. Elisabeth Künkel to Reichsschriftumskammer, November 18, 1939, BDC: Kulturkammer; John Kunkel, "The Life of Fritz Künkel," p. 3. Künkel's fascination with the American West was widely shared in Germany and Europe: see Ray Allen Billington, *Land of Savagery, Land of Promise: The European Image of the American Frontier* (New York, 1981).
96. Matthias Heinrich Göring, Rundschreiben, April 8, 1942, Kl. Erw. 762/4.
97. Jung to Göring, June 4, 1936, Franz Jung; Cimbal to Göring, June 12, 1937, and Curtius to Göring, April 13, 1939, Kl. Erw. 762/2; Cimbal to Göring, July 17, 1940, Kl. Erw. 762/3; Cimbal, "Familienchronik," p. 112.

98. Ronald Smelser, *Robert Ley: Hitler's Labor Front Leader* (Oxford, 1988), p. 257.
99. Göring to Curtius, February 2, 1939, pp. 2, 3–4, Kl. Erw. 762/2.
100. "Gesetz über die berufsmässige Ausübung der Heilkunde ohne Bestallung (Heilpraktikergesetz)," *Reichsgesetzblatt* (1939): 251–2, 259–62; Bernhard Hörmann, "Kampf der Gefahr!" *Volksgesundheitswacht* 3 (1936): 3; Rudolf Ramm, *Ärztliche Rechts- und Standeskunde,* pp. 59–63; the article by Health Practitioner Leader Ernst Kees, "Wer fällt unter das Heilpraktikergesetz?" *Deutsches Ärzteblatt* 69 (1939): 275; Johannes Heinrich Schultz, "Die Aufhebung der Kurierfreiheit," ibid., pp. 151–7; and Kurt Blome, *Arzt im Kampf: Erlebnisse und Gedanken* (Leipzig, 1942), pp. 295–303; for Achelis's obsequious review of Blome, see *ZfP* 15 (1943): 58.
101. Martin Bormann, "Vorwort," in Leonardo Conti, ed., *Reden und Aufrufe Gerhard Wagners,* p. iii; see also Röhrs, *Hitlers Krankheit,* pp. 80, 126.
102. *Der Öffentliche Gesundheitsdienst* 5 (1939): 313; *Deutsches Ärzteblatt* 69 (1939): 321.
103. Leonardo Conti, Fragebogen für kommunalpolitische Fachredner der Partei, Berlin, January 25, 1938, BDC: SS-Führer.
104. Röhrs, *Hitlers Krankheit,* p. 64. Röhrs was Conti's representative in Munich and with the Reich Physicians Chamber.
105. Akten des Obersten Parteigerichts I. Kammer: Conti 4339–34, November 1934, BDC: Oberstes Parteigericht; see also Emil Ketterer, SA-Führerfragebogen, Munich, May 22, 1935, BDC: SA and Reichsärztekammer. On the Stennes Putsch, see Heinz Höhne, *The Order of the Death's Head: The Story of Hitler's SS,* trans. Richard Barry (New York, 1970), p. 66. The SS was originally part of the SA and Conti's membership in the SS dated from 1927: BDC: SS-Führer.
106. Übersichtsdarstellung der Ereignisse im Falle Villain, Berlin, March 12 and June 2, 1934, BDC: Oberstes Parteigericht; and Das Landgericht, 13. grosse Strafkammer, Beschluss, Berlin, April 23, 1934, BDC: Oberstes Parteigericht; see also Donald M. McKale, *The Nazi Party Courts: Hitler's Management of Conflict in His Movement, 1921–1945* (Lawrence, Kans., 1974).
107. Villain's party membership card notes with grim bureaucratic nonchalance that he had left (*ausgetreten*) the party on June 30, 1934, BDC: NSDAP-Zentralkartei. According to Siegfried Ostrowski, Villain was particularly brutal in his actions toward Jewish doctors. Ostrowski also reports as common knowledge among physicians that Villain had assaulted Conti with his riding crop, as well as the widespread assumption that, as a result, Villain had died in the melée of June 30 at Conti's hands; see Ostrowski, "Zur Lage der Berliner Jüdischen Ärzteschaft unter dem Hitlerregime von 1933—Ende August 1939," p. 9, File 01/16, Yad Vashem Archives, and published as: "Vom Schicksal Jüdischer Ärzte im Dritten Reich: Ein Augenzeugenbericht aus den Jahren 1933–39," *Bulletin des Leo Baeck Instituts* 6 (1963): 313–51. On Villain versus the psychoanalysts in Berlin, see Brecht, *"Hier geht das Leben,"* pp. 99–100. On Adolf Wagner, see Edward N. Peterson, *The Limits of Hitler's Power,* pp. 163–4, 166–8.
108. Wagner to Reichsleiter Gusnier, January 24, 1935, BDC: Oberstes Parteigericht.
109. See Leonardo Conti, "Gesundheitsführung—Volksschicksal," March 28, 1942, text of an address to the NSDAP Main Office for Health, BDC: SS-Führer.
110. Michael H. Kater, *Das "Ahnenerbe" der SS 1933–1945: Ein Beitrag zur Kulturpolitik des Dritten Reiches* (Stuttgart, 1974), p. 100; see also Jill Stephenson, *The Nazi Organization of Women* (Totowa, N.J., 1981), pp. 46–9.
111. *Deutsches Ärzteblatt* 69 (1939): 561; "Das Gesundheitswesen von Partei und

Staat," *Deutsches Nachrichtenbüro,* April 1, 1940, p. 1; and R 18, folder 5583.

112. Ley to Hess, December 12, 1939, R 18, folder 5572. Ley had been asking Hess to ensure the DAF's sovereignty over the health field: see Ley to Hess, June 3, 1939, BDC: Parteikorrespondenz Franz Wirz.
113. *Reichsband: Adressenwerk der Dienststellen der NSDAP* (1939), pp. 377–8; see also Smelser, *Robert Ley,* p. 275; and Marie-Luise Recker, *Nationalsozialistische Sozialpolitik im Zweiten Weltkrieg* (Munich, 1985), pp. 121–7.
114. A protégé of Bormann's, Conti was nevertheless supplanted by Bormann's arch-enemy Karl Brandt; Conti hanged himself on October 6, 1945, while awaiting trial at Nuremberg; see Burton C. Andrus, *I Was the Nuremberg Jailer* (New York, 1969), pp. 87–8; and Airey Neave, *On Trial at Nuremberg* (Boston, 1978), p. 76.
115. Orlow, *History of the Nazi Party,* p. 53.
116. Broszat, *Hitler State,* pp. 348–9.
117. Joachim Fest, *The Face of the Third Reich,* p. 147.
118. bid., p. 117; see also Albert Speer, *Infiltration,* trans. Joachim Neugroschel (New York, 1981).
119. Jane Caplan, *Government Without Administration: State and Civil Service in Weimar and Nazi Germany* (Oxford, 1988).
120. Orlow, *History of the Nazi Party,* p. 488.
121. Broszat, *Hitler State,* pp. 348–9.
122. Höhne, *Death's Head,* pp. 63, 67–9, 76–7; Broszat, *Hitler State,* p. 65.
123. On Conti, see "Lebenslauf und Amtseinführung," *Deutsches Ärzteblatt* 69 (1939): 324–5.
124. Röhrs, *Hitlers Krankheit,* pp. 126–7. Michael Kater (*Journal of the History of Medicine* 41 [1986]: 372) has objected to this partisan Nazi source for Conti's appointment by Göring, but such information is not a function of Röhrs's Nazism or allegiance to Conti and is thus probably reliable; Kater, moreover, acknowledges Göring's patronage of Conti: see Kater, *Doctors Under Hitler,* p. 24.
125. Matthias Heinrich Göring, "Eröffnungsansprache," in Bilz, *Psyche und Leistung,* p. 8. Psychoanalyst Franz Baumeyer recalls that Conti's deputy, Franz Bunz, was at an early meeting of psychotherapists and government officials; see "Stadtrat Dr. med. Bunz 50 Jahre," *Deutsches Ärzteblatt* 69 (1939): 391. It is likely that Hermann Göring made it clear that he expected Conti to approve the psychotherapists or that he did not have to make it clear. It is also possible that Conti had already learned of the Göring psychotherapists from Gauger (see chapter 6).
126. Leonardo Conti, "Die Bedeutung der Wissenschaft, insbesondere der kinderärztlichen, in der Gesundheitsführung," *Deutsche medizinische Wochenschrift* 68 (1942): 53–9; idem, "Geburtshilfe und Hebammenwesen in Deutschland," *Deutsches Ärzteblatt* 68 (1938): 4–8, 26–9; Kater, *Doctors Under Hitler,* p. 26.
127. Kl. Erw. 762/2.

Fritz Künkel

John Kunkel

Leonhard Seif

S. Hirzel Verlag

Gustav Richard Heyer

Lucy Heyer-Grote

Harald Schultz-Hencke

Gisela Krichhauf

John Rittmeister
Eva Hildebrand

Hans von Hattingberg
S. Hirzel Verlag

Johannes Heinrich Schultz
Georg Thieme Verlag

Walter Cimbal
Berlin Document Center

Ernst Kretschmer

Georg Thieme Verlag

Matthias Heinrich Göring

S. Hirzel Verlag

Hermann Göring's Wedding, 1935: Matthias Heinrich Göring marked with arrow at upper left; (1) Field Marshal von Mackensen; (2) State Secretary Meissner; (3) Count Rosen, brother-in-law of Göring's first wife; (4) Reich Minister Rust; (5) Deputy Führer Hess; (6) War Minister von Blomberg; (7) Reich Bishop Müller; (8) Foreign Minister von Neurath.

Staatsbibliothek Berlin

Carl Gustav Jung
S. Hirzel Verlag

Kurt Gauger
Berlin Document Center

Gerhard Wagner

Leonardo Conti
Bundesarchiv

Werner Kemper
Gisela Krichhauf

Max de Crinis
Berlin Document Center

Göring Institute Executive Committee, c. 1940: (L-R) Heyer, Kemper, Schultz-Hencke, von König-Fachsenfeld, Achelis, Rittmeister, Herzog-Dürck, von Hattingberg, Göring, Schultz, Scherke, Boehm, Bilz, Müller-Braunschweig.

9

Patients and Psychotherapy: Neurosis in Nazi Germany

In 1940 German emigré homeopath Martin Gumpert published a little book entitled *Heil Hunger! Health under Hitler.* It was the purpose of the book, the author noted in his foreword, to reveal "to American readers that dictatorship is a sickness which drives all concerned to inevitable physical breakdown; that freedom is the first condition for the biological advancement of the individual and of the social group."[1] Gumpert observed that Nazi attempts to mobilize the health of the German populace were "opposed to the fundamental tenets of all civilized health welfare work, the substance of which is that care and consideration are the essential presuppositions of social achievement."[2] In general, he argued that what could be witnessed in Nazi Germany was a "general nervous breakdown which hangs like a dark cloud over Germany."[3] Other contemporary emigré sources, such as the international medical journal published in Prague by socialist physicians and the reports of socialist agents inside Nazi Germany, also detail the deleterious effects of the Nazi disruption of the German health care system for political, racial, and military purposes.[4]

It is the case that the Third Reich presided over a general deterioration of the health of the German people. This was due to a number of factors. As we have already noted, the health of the population in general had suffered significantly from major crises since 1914. Moreover, the benefits of modern medicine and health care policy in the twentieth century had only gradually begun to affect the urban and rural masses. The Nazis worsened things by purging the medical profession of many of its best practitioners for political and racial reasons. They also set about reducing health insurance benefits for purposes of the mobilization of financial and human resources for war. While in the peacetime years of the Third Reich rates of tuberculosis and venereal disease declined and the birthrate climbed, other illnesses, such as diphtheria and scarlet fever, increased from 1933 to 1939. Industrial accidents also grew significantly in number, especially during the war. The war of course only further worsened matters as the home front was stripped of physicians called to military service, the Allied bombing raids disrupted health and health care in the large cities, nutrition suffered, and soldiers and slave laborers from the East brought dysentery, typhus, and spotted fever into the Reich.[5] Even then, as a result of the mobilization of emergency health services, the exploitation of European foodstuffs, and the ruthless Nazi segregation of slave labor, widespread malnutrition and epidemics like those experienced during the First World War did not occur.[6]

It is more difficult to assess any change in the incidence or nature of mental illness in the Third Reich. Gumpert's argument, echoed by Lockot, that dictatorship itself is a sickness that by its very presence occasions physical and mental breakdown among its denizens has greater moral than empirical force.[7] It is certainly true that many in Germany—and in Europe—had their well-being and their lives destroyed by Nazism and for such people physical and mental affliction became the order of the day. The rate of suicide, for example, increased significantly in the 1930s, although the ongoing effects of the Depression would have to be added to the direct and indirect effects of the new political order on this statistic.[8] It is also true that the stories of the victims and their suffering are the most important to emerge from the Nazi era. But what of those who were not targets of the regime? What of the many supporters of Nazism? What about those Germans who were, or came to be, ambivalent about National Socialism? It is a sobering fact that the vast majority of people were able to accommodate themselves in various ways—and often enthusiastically even at the end—to Hitler's regime.

We have recently learned much about the ways in which the Nazis managed to appease and appeal to vast segments of the German population. The Nazis used both the stick and the carrot in regulating German society. Workers, for example, had their unions taken away and could be threatened with incarceration in a "work/re-education camp," but the Nazis also propagandized effectively among workers for the future benefits of consumerism and the "honor of labor."[9] The figure of Hitler himself was a major integrative influence among Germans of all classes.[10] While sooner or later and to one degree or another almost all Germans were victimized by the Nazis, most were also accomplices of the regime. For example, it is true, as Gisela Bock has argued, that women were victimized as a group by the Nazis, but it is also the case most German women also both by intent and effect supported the regime.[11] This often took the form of performance of maternal duties in the home.[12] But women also experienced some degree of social and occupational mobility as a result of the Nazi shake-up and mobilization of traditional society. This could take the form of increased public and private employment in industry and service occupations or even, as we saw in chapter 8, unprecedented opportunities in professions such as medicine. Young girls often found the League of German Girls an opportunity to break out of stifling family environments and exercise capacities for service and leadership that would serve some expectation and achievement of postwar occupational autonomy.[13] These gains of course did not constitute systematic advancement or equality with males and women continued to suffer from subordination in the work place as well as from the increased physical dangers common to all workers at the time. Among all Germans, the middle classes were the most indulged, although, as we have seen in the case of the professionalizing psychotherapists, even here the Nazis "promoted the most productive sections of the *Mittelstand* at the expense of its more marginal elements."[14]

In general, what occurred under National Socialism was a fragmenting of society through the destruction of old solidarities from the top of German society to the bottom. While the rhetoric of the racial *Volksgemeinschaft* could provide some "symbolic capital" in making people from all classes at times feel like they were part of a greater—or the greatest—whole, the demands of the Nazi regime for productivity created an environment of individual competitiveness in line with the Nazi emphasis on hierarchy. Among workers, the unemployment of the Depression made most of them grateful just to have a job. At the same time, rearmament demanded skilled workers who were in short supply. The result was an increasing wage differential between skilled and unskilled workers which only aggravated the tendency to think in terms of individual advancement instead of class solidarity.[15] The combination under National Socialism of individual interest and initiative with brutal political constraint is grimly dramatized by the fact that the Gestapo was most often prompted to action against individuals by the denunciations of other individuals.[16] The war cut both ways by increasing patriotism in two forms, the thrill of victory and then the threat and agony—especially from the East—of defeat. The total collapse of support for Nazism at the end and after the war was in part a function of the very socially dissolutive tendencies the Nazis had unleashed and exploited.

In order to determine the incidence and social place in it of common mental illness, therefore, it is necessary to disaggregate as much as possible the society of Nazi Germany. This is exactly the point made by psychologist Bruno Bettelheim in his commentary on a book of dreams collected in Germany between 1933 and 1939. The dreams, collected by a journalist who left Germany in 1940, are those of people who for one reason or another found themselves in degrees of opposition to the Nazi regime. Not surprisingly, the dreams manifest anxiety and conflict; moreover, some, the author admits, have been consciously or unconsciously retouched in the telling.[17] But what of the dreams of those who to one degree or another supported the regime? Of those many who were ambivalent about the regime or whose views changed over the twelve years of Nazi rule? And what is the relationship among the personal, the social, and the political in these dreams?[18] We simply do not have enough data to offer conclusive and comprehensive answers to these questions.

But our increasing knowledge of the social history of the Third Reich suggests that for most people, particularly before the war brought significant and multiplying burdens to almost everyone, the overt political pressures of the regime only hovered in the backgrounds of their lives. For most, psychological problems stemmed from the immediate circumstances of their lives. The very danger associated with the discussion of "politics" at the time only strengthened the tendency to focus on personal matters. And among the patients seen by psychotherapists at the Göring Institute there were very few Jews or others who were directly endangered by the regime.[19] Occasionally, there would be a tacit understanding between therapist and patient of skepticism if not opposition to the regime. On the other hand, there were reports of Hitler appearing in dreams as a strong and beneficent father figure.[20] Finally, it is also the case that neurosis in general, as a quantitative and qualitative balance of psychological forces in the context of a life, could also enhance function under specific and even demanding circumstances. For example, an obsessive-compulsive personality often makes a good bureaucrat, that is, someone who has to be concerned with detail and order. Because what is strength is also weakness, psychological trouble for the dedicated bureaucrat would come precisely along the neurotic fault line of obsession and compulsion and not just be the result, wholly or in part, of generalized "stress."

Another question arises at this juncture: Is it possible under a dictatorship to have the trust necessary for a psychotherapeutic relationship? This is a particularly acute problem in psychoanalysis, which operates under the rule ("the basic rule") that the patient must never censor his or her thoughts. Although there are no known cases of it, there was also the fear among psychotherapists in general, and psychoanalysts in particular, that any given patient could be a secret policeman or simply a private citizen who might inform on the therapist. Just being a psychoanalyst posed special dangers in spite of the protection of the Göring name. Gustav Graber of Stuttgart, for one, was told by his secretary, who also worked at the state Ministry for Education, that the Gestapo kept an eye on him simply because he was an analyst. The same was true for Alexander Mitscherlich in Heidelberg. It is likely that both the quantity and quality of psychoanalysis and psychotherapy was diminished by the conditions set by the Third Reich.[21] For example, Carl Müller-Braunschweig was able only with great difficulty to carry through an analysis with a patient who had at first refused to speak freely for fear of divulging military secrets.[22] Gerhard Scheunert, though, had a general staff officer in psychoanalysis and the analysis failed to reach any depths because, among other things, the officer used the need to protect state security as a defense against personal insight.[23] This is not to say, however, that psychoanalysis and psychotherapy could not be practiced, even successfully, in Nazi Germany. Although any number of people could have been dissuaded by the official and unofficial ties of the Göring Institute to the Nazi hierarchy from seeking help there, society under National Socialism was much less efficiently tied to a totalitarian yoke than had earlier been assumed. Furthermore, especially among the bourgeois clientele and professional staff of the Göring Institute, there were a great number of shared social and ideological values. Göring himself was not regarded by the psychotherapists as a dangerous Nazi, known familiarly as "Papi" and "Father Christmas," and the institute was in fact not run in jackboot fashion.[24] Finally, the nature of the psychotherapy offered by the institute was usually of the short-term variety that focused on the addressing of immediate problems rather than an extensive plumbing of psychological and philosophical depths that might dredge up potentially dangerous sentiments. All in all, psychotherapists in the Third Reich served the regime not by ferreting out racial and political enemies, but by helping their patients get back to work.

We must also remember that the Nazis encouraged psychotherapy not only because of the Göring imprimatur, but because their aims and ideals demanded it. Not only did they need psychotherapy for pragmatic reasons, but also because their racial policy was primitively Manichean. The ruthless Nazi racial division—of worthwhile life on the hand and worthless life on the other—accounted for why the Nazis never utilized the asylum as a repository for political opponents, as the Soviets so notoriously did, whereby simply and systematically "protest against society can be explained away as a neurotic symptom."[25] Such a perspective, in spite of its essential violation of general and medical ethics, implies, like all manner of authoritarian and totalitarian effort at mind control, the possibility and desirability of correction. To be sure, many under such a system are simply locked forever in a savage and sad parody of medical care, but the distinction here between Nazi and Soviet methods helps to illuminate a heretofore unexamined sphere of public and professional life in the Third Reich. Whatever the similarities between Nazi Germany and Soviet Russia, their ideologies are fundamentally dissimilar. Marxism, in its materialism, is inherently rational and looks to scientific strategies—in this case, a psychiatry originally based on Pavlovian psychology and more recently characterized by an organic chemical bias—to build and secure a well-ordered egalitarian society.[26] National Socialism, for its part, had no ideology worthy of the name. It was a movement founded on a charismatic rather than an ideological basis.[27] For the Nazis, "feeling with the blood" was sufficient reason for letting the blood of their enemies flow freely. Unlike the Soviets, the rational determinism of whose psychiatric system in theory excluded no one save a very few completely hopeless cases from treatment or from inclusion in the socialist order, the Nazis embraced an exclusionary hierarchical biological and racial determinism that robbed psychiatry of any officially recognized reparative function at all.

But while psychiatry under National Socialism was therefore assigned a defensive role by the irrational Nazi concern with racial biology, psychotherapy could exploit the complementary Nazi desire to exert "care and control" over the deep-seated irrational elements of superior will and character possessed by the biologically superior racial stock that comprised at least a plurality of the people living in Germany.[28] This was precisely the division of labor within the general mobilization of medicine made clear on one occasion by the Interior Ministry's Hans Reiter to a 1940 meeting of child psychiatrists.[29] Aside from those psychiatrically defined cases of genetic disorder already in asylums, and flagrant cases of "inborn" homosexuality and other officially deviant behaviors among those labeled "asocials"—who were to be eliminated through sterilization and murder—the Nazis could not apply a racial-biological standard to "Aryans" who exhibited lesser, and more common, neurotic conflict. By ideological as well as psychological definition, mental disorder within the "Master Race" could not be genetic or essentially organic. It followed that, given the proper guidance of an innate German will, any such mental distress a member of the German *Volksgemeinschaft* suffered was correctable.

This division of labor, however, was not perfectly defined. There was in Nazi thought and policy, and in popular perceptions and fears of it, a certain fluidity of boundaries between health and illness. This was particularly the case in the realm of mental illness, where diagnoses could in the Nazi environment be as fatal in their ambiguity as in their determinativeness.[30] Such fear of the consequences of Nazi racial policy necessarily crossed class boundaries and thus was a generalized phenomenon in German society under Hitler. The law designed to prevent the reproduction of so-called "degenerates" spawned in the population what the Reich Interior Minister called "an almost psychotic fear."[31] The wartime program to kill off mental patients broadened this fear. Families worried—with good cause—that sending a grandparent to a rest home could result in that person's death.[32] This trend most likely would have been aggravated had the Nazis won the war, for they would then have had the opportunity to turn to the complete "cleansing" of the German body biologic. It was in 1944, after all, that the regime drafted a law designed to deal finally and ruthlessly with all those deemed to be incapable of contributing to the racial community (*gemeinschaftsunfähig*). Such dynamics only made the psychotherapists' efforts more important for their patients as well as for their professional ambitions. At the same time, however, the psychotherapists' record with their patients in the Third Reich, however, is not without ambiguities and even outrages.

Although various modes of psychotherapy were used in private practice by German psychotherapists and by physicians and laypersons throughout the Third Reich, the work of the approximately fifty psychotherapists of the Göring Institute's outpatient clinic alone provides a significant sample of the methods used to treat various neurotic conditions. Most, but not all, of these methods were short-term therapies, varying in type and scope depending on the school of thought to which the particular psychotherapist belonged, but also reflecting the basic neo-Freudian therapeutic turn as well as the common professional and governmental emphasis on what was construed as effective social service. While analyses at the old Berlin Psychoanalytic Institute usually lasted about a year (200–250 hours) and had as their aim a fundamental reordering of the patient's life, the therapies usually offered at the Göring Institute were oriented toward restoring the ability to work. This neo-Freudian emphasis, which also drew strongly from the more general German Romantic tradition in medicine and psychology, "eliminates all the reservations with which Freud hedged the therapeutic objective of adjustment to an inhuman society."[33] The resultant emphasis, whether under democracy or dictatorship, is on the healthy, happy sublimation of businessman, worker, or administrator. This throws into sharp relief the observation that "one of the attractive features of the earliest psychoanalytic viewpoint was its respect for disability and failure"[34] in contrast to therapeutic concern with distinction and success. While neo-Freudian psychoanalysts retained a faith in reason that facilitated their critique of a wide range of social oppression based on a respect for the individual, in Germany after 1933 the combination of aspects of a Romantic ideology, as well as a corporatist tradition in culture and profession (see chapter 16), combined with both structural constraints and professional opportunities to aggravate among psychotherapists an emphasis on the service of both patient and therapist to the prevailing system and ideology.[35]

According to a clinic survey in 1940, of 170 patients unable to work for almost two years, 159 had their capacity to work fully restored after 75 sessions, while the other 11 needed only 41 sessions.[36] It was certainly the case that the screening of patients for admittance was designed to protect the institute (and perhaps also the patients) from failure to treat successfully more complicated and possibly "hereditarily incurable" disorders. Once a prospective patient had been diagnosed (often in collaboration with experts in psychiatry and internal medicine at the Charité) by means of an interview, a physical examination, and appropriate psychological tests, the form of therapy would be chosen.[37] This choice depended on the severity of the neurotic symptoms, a measure that was usually taken by means of Schultz's four categories. Schultz claimed that 50 percent of all neuroses could be handled through the application of various methods of *kleine* psychotherapy, sometimes in groups.[38] His four types of neuroses and the requisite treatment reflected this view: exogenous alien neuroses (*exogene Fremdneurosen*) resulting from a hostile environment and requiring only advice and the improvement of external conditions; physiogenic border neuroses (*physiogene Randneurosen*), which were the product of "bad habits" suggested by the patient's life context and which could be eliminated through *kleine* psychotherapy, that is, concerned consultation with a therapist and perhaps a change in environment; psychogenic layer neuroses (*psychogene Schichtneurosen*), which, comprising around half of all neuroses, were disturbances at one or more levels of the patient's instinctual or affective life and had to be dealt with through the use of *kleine* and/or *grosse* psychotherapy; and characterogenic core neuroses (*charakterogene Kernneurosen*), which demanded depth treatment of the whole of the patient's character.[39]

According to Rittmeister, the methods in general included "depth psychological treatment," such as, according to Kemper, classical terminable psychoanalysis with the analysand free associating in a supine position and the analyst seated behind or alongside the patient's head. Less rigorous and time-consuming was consultation with a "depth psychologist," wherein both patient and therapist would assume a more "active" posture seated facing each other. This more active, egalitarian, and present-centered orientation also animated group therapy sessions, educational counseling in which children and their parents were involved, and the application of hypnosis, autogenic training (autohypnosis), along with nerve end massage (for writer's cramp), gymnastics, breathing exercises, and voice therapy.[40] Autogenic training was developed by Schultz during the 1920s as a means of treating the stress of modern urbanized life through relaxing blood and muscle through concentration. Schultz had been inspired by yoga, but he made a sharp distinction between it and his own system of self-hypnosis.

Yoga, after all, required an exacting posture as a prerequisite to the proper level of concentration, an inappropriate means of relaxation for the harried, burdened man of Western industrial civilization.[41]

These various short-term methods comprised a vast range of interpersonal relations, something in line with the psychotherapists' aim to extend their professional boundaries as widely as possible and with public demands for efficient means of maintaining and restoring human productivity. For example, during the war Fritz Mohr of the institute's Düsseldorf affiliate published an example of the use of the simple power of suggestion. It concerned a mother who had lost the ability to lactate after witnessing the deaths of a number of children in an English bombing raid. Mohr told her to think of secreting on the basis of the unity of body and mind and thereafter, despite day and night bombing, she was able to function normally. Mohr concluded:

> This case certainly does not reveal anything that is at all new for us psychotherapists, but it does illustrate how a relatively simple mode of psychotherapy that is accessible to every doctor can perform worthwhile *völkisch* work.[42]

Mohr's example was also in full consonance with the Nazis' insistence on breastfeeding, a process whose biological function was linked in the Nazi mind with a crucial psychological dimension, as demonstrated by the propaganda slogan "*Stillfähigkeit ist Stillwille*" ("The ability to nurse is the will to nurse").[43]

The vigorous proselytizer Schultz was the most systematic and imperial in this process. According to Schultz, inexpensive, short-term therapy included advice (*Beratung*), discussion (*Aussprache*), instruction (*Belehrung*), enlightenment (*Aufklärung*), encouragement (*Ermutigung*), reassurance (*Beruhigung*), hardening (*Abhärtung*), exercise (*Übung*), and prohibition (*Verbot*). These, he advised, were all methods of general psychotherapeutic guidance that could be used as rational, conscious therapy by any doctor without intensive psychotherapeutic training. It followed for Schultz that the simpler methods could also be utilized by trained laypersons. Available as well were more sophisticated suggestive procedures like hypnosis, autogenic training, and psychocatharsis.[44] Schultz drew his emphasis on active modes of psychotherapy, what he called collectively rational waking therapy (*rationale Wachtherapie*), from nineteenth-century internist Ottomar Rosenbach and neurologists Paul DuBois and Oskar Vogt.

According to Schultz, both psychoanalysis and psychiatry failed to appreciate the holistic nature of the human being, the former by ignoring the biological and the latter by ignoring the psychological. He rejected the psychoanalytic view that all humans (and thus civilization) were riven with internal conflict. The didactic aim of Freudian psychoanalysis favored knowledge over healing, he observed, and was thus prejudicial to a therapeutic synthesis within the shared values of a community. As he put it in 1944: "*Neue deutsche Seelenheilkunde,* on whose construction our institute now labors, has broken radically with this bias."[45] Drawing on the Gestalt perspective of Viktor von Weizsäcker, Schultz argued that neurosis was a function of particular social faults and it was the task of psychotherapy to understand the individual as a subject in all of his or her individual physical, psychological, and social complexity. Schultz appreciated the psychoanalytic emphasis on the laborious process of rationally overcoming conflicts. He always stressed the necessity of balancing psychotherapeutic empathy (*Menschenkenntnis*) with scientific rigor. Schultz thus regarded analysis as a valuable tool in the cure of some layer and core neuroses.[46] But he thought in general that psychoanalysis was too expensive and time-consuming to be effective as a means of treating the great majority of psychological disorders. As for psychiatry, Schultz believed that even disorders attributed to heredity, which comprised a portion of these core neuroses, were curable through psychotherapy, for they were not matters of incurable physical decay but of difficulties buried deep within the physiological/psychological character structure.[47]

Gerhard Scheunert, Göring's first choice for director of the outpatient clinic, was a psychoanalyst specializing in short-term therapeutic methods. He also advocated the use of hypnosis and autogenic training, the latter, he found, being especially helpful for insomniacs. He also approved of the so-called Happich method of light hypnosis and autogenic training. This was a meditation exercise in which the patient could divest the self of rational/intellectual defenses. In this mode of psychotherapy, childhood imagoes would be recreated by "walking," first to a stream bank in an open field, from the meadow to a mountain, and then through a forest to a chapel. Unlike Schultz, who was interested in active modes of suggestive psychotherapy, Scheunert not surprisingly explored the short-term application of the "passive-contemplative" approach of psychoanalytic free association. He described a number of cases in which only three or four hour-long sessions were sufficient to reveal the outlines of the primary psychological conflict. One of these cases concerned a young man who wished to become engaged but felt he could not because of longstanding impotence discovered through a series of unsuccessful liaisons with prostitutes. Therapy revealed a tremendous guilt over onanism that stemmed primarily from a tyrannical pietistic father. This revelation, according to Scheunert, resulted in the cure of the patient's impotence.[48]

Klaus Wegscheider, practicing in Berlin-Schöneberg, was, like Scheunert, motivated in great measure by a desire to shorten the duration and expense of psychotherapy in order to allow the many doctors practicing under the state medical insurance system to practice psychotherapy. These many doctors received only very small fee-for-service payments and none at all for psychotherapy specifically. Any psychotherapy had to be paid for out of the lump sum payments and these payments lasted only six months.[49] Since 70 percent of patients were covered by state health insurance, for the great majority of physicians any psychotherapy would have to be performed over a very short term and within the flow of general medical practice. Wegscheider therefore placed a pragmatic emphasis on suggestion, hypnosis, and autogenic training. Also like Scheunert, however, he advocated psychocatharsis (a release of pent-up emotions). Moreover, Wegscheider was a proponent of "functional" psychotherapy, the scheduling of short periods of psychotherapy alternating with periods of no treatment. The advantage of this system was that it met the requirements of limited insurance coverage, eased the patient load on the physician, and—making a virtue of a necessity?—forced the patient to come to grips with life problems during each interim.[50] Wegscheider was a student of Kretschmer and so emphasized Kretschmer's theory that particular body types have particular character structures. This approach reflected a view of neurosis that tended to stress stimuli rather than motives. It was up to the physician to understand the affective manifestations of physical tone and type and not up to the patient—as in psychoanalysis—to "work through" unconscious conflict. This approach was advantageously congruent with doctors' traditional hierarchial view of their relationship with patients. As Wegscheider put it, "the patient performs, the doctor directs."[51]

The Göring Institute endeavored to have psychotherapy included in both the public and private health insurance systems in Germany, but succeeded only in making inroads with private carriers (*Ersatzkassen*), which offered more services for higher premiums and covered about 30 percent of those insured. The psychotherapists argued that such coverage was in the interests of patients, society in general, and would also save money in the long run through the prevention of more serious and expensive mental and physical complaints. Psychotherapy would also allow many to lead productive lives who otherwise would have to be pensioned or go onto the public welfare roles.[52] In 1938, as a result, the institute was engaged in conversations with various public and private insurance authorities.[53] In 1943 the institute signed an agreement with the central economic group (*Wirtschaftsgruppe*) for private life and health insurance carriers whereby the group would submit to its members a plan for coverage of psychotherapeutic services.[54] Under this arrangement, according to Kemper, psychotherapists at the Reich Institute (see chapter 13) saw patients insured for up to 100 hours of psychotherapy.[55] The institute also won a contract with the association of private carriers for white collar employees (*Angestellte*) for coverage of treatment by attending psychologists.[56] In the implementation guidelines for this contract, Göring made the following stipulation: "The admission of patients is to be handled with the greatest caution. Only socially and biologically valuable patients with positive prospects for a successful cure over the short term may be treated."[57] It is difficult to determine the exact proportion of racist rhetoric to racist conviction in this statement. What is clear, however, is the convergence of professional, financial, and political interests in the speedy dispatch of psychological disorders for the sake of individual and social productivity.

There were two fundamental problems standing in the way of psychotherapeutic services being fully integrated into the state health insurance system. The first was that there was disagreement among various agencies about the desirability of this. As we saw in chapter 1, the Reich Insurance Office had in 1926 declared that neurosis was a psychological disorder, not a physical illness meriting compensation under the established regulations. This position was reconfirmed by the Nazi bureaucracy in 1939.[58] The Reich Supreme Court, on the other hand, tended to regard neurotic sequelae to an accident (*Unfallneurosen*), even in the presence of neurotic predisposition, as a common phenomenon deserving of compensation. Under National Socialism, however, the lower courts increasingly regarded neurotic reactions to trauma as a sign of abnormality and deviance. The plaintiff was most often designated a slacker of sound body who simply wanted damages or a pension. Physicians providing expert testimony in such cases were also constrained by the Nazi ethos of productivity.[59] The Supreme Court's old liberal attitude was markedly out of step with the new regime, which had little use for the judiciary anyway. Ironically, now that the psychodynamic point of view was a significant one among doctors, the old medical consensus dating from 1891 that neurosis was a "true illness in the medical-biological sense"[60] was broken and psychotherapists had to battle both the insurance bureaucracy and the Nazi regime to establish psychogenic conditions as worthy of compensation and treatment.

It was of course treatment that the psychotherapists emphasized, in line with their campaign for professional status. But this confronted the second fundamental problem standing in the way of full participation in the health insurance system, the simple fact of bureaucratic territorialism and immobilism. Göring, in an address in 1938 to the Reich Insurance Office, had pointed out that people whose neuroses rendered them unable to work constituted a great financial burden for society through lost productivity and higher social welfare outlays: for higher civil servants (*Beamte*) through an increased demand on state and private pension funds and, for employees (*Angestellte*) and laborers (*Arbeiter*), public welfare. Insurance compensation for psychotherapeutic care, would, he argued, to a great extent lift this burden from state and society. Göring also insisted that psychotherapy was cheaper and more effective than institutional care. A proper understanding of the psychological and biological nature of the unconscious and its treatment, Göring concluded, would lead not only to timely and thrifty treatment of neuroses but would also contribute to what he described as the regime's interest in the prevention of illness from the earliest ages.[61] Unfortunately for Göring, however, the Reich Insurance Office, in typical bureaucratic fashion, was more concerned about its procedures, precedents, and finances than it was about the burdens on other segments of the government or society in general. Any change, moreover, would have to take place in slow bureaucratic time and amid the crippling difficulties thrown up by the Nazis' war.

Much less benign were cases involving patients targeted for destruction by the regime. In chapters 11 and 12 we will investigate three categories of patients—homosexuals, men and women suffering from impotence and frigidity, and soldiers—Göring Institute psychotherapists studied and treated with support from outside agencies. But the institute also confronted on an individual basis "non-Aryan" patients and prospective and actual patients possibly suffering from "hereditary" mental disorders. Although in the wake of the expansion of the Nuremberg Race Laws in 1938 the institute banned the treatment of Jews, some psychotherapists continued to treat Jewish patients and train Jewish students. On December 11, 1939, Göring issued a directive complaining about such violations and reminding institute members that such activity was illegal.[62] According to Julius Schirren, a young Jewish woman was privately trained up until 1939 and during the war had handled some cases outside the institute.[63] Another former member of the institute has asserted that a Jungian psychotherapist, Gerda Walter, had even been assigned to treat Jews, although it seems unlikely that this "official" assignment continued after 1938 or 1939. The designation of a Jungian was ideologically prudent as well as consistent with the psychotherapists' early stated aim to build much of "German" psychotherapy on a Jungian basis. But had there been repercussions from this, the therapist being a Jungian likely would not have helped matters, either in terms of a specious and useless argument for "converting" Jews or of avoiding the necessity of simply breaking off the therapy. Finally, in 1943, Kemper, the new director of the outpatient clinic, devised an evaluation form that included Erich Jaensch's officially approved racial character types together with a question as to the patient's racial background. Kemper's argument that this was just a formality only underscores the fact that especially by 1943 such a "formality" was cruelly superfluous. How many Jews or Russian prisoners of war were likely to be coming in for treatment? Aside from general trepidation and concern for the institute's continued prosperity, a likely reason for the introduction of this particular form was as part of damage control following the arrest of previous outpatient clinic director Rittmeister on charges of espionage (see chapter 13).

Partly from conviction and partly from prudence, moreover, leading psychotherapists had for some time been expressing doubts about the efficacy of "race-mixing" in psychotherapeutic practice. Both Göring and Jung, for example, had asserted that psychoanalysis was a creation of the Jewish mind for the Jewish mind and that race was a determining factor in any psychotherapeutic situation.[64] For some it followed that a therapeutic alliance could not be formed between an "Aryan" and a Jew. The only direct attempt to deal with the issue of race and psychotherapy beyond sloganeering protestations of allegiance to the Nazi regime, however, had been a paper presented to the Austrian section of the International General Medical Society on December 1, 1936. The most unusual thing about this paper was that its author, Erwin Stransky, was (by birth) Jewish, a fact that he presented to his audience as assurance that he was meeting the issue squarely. His purpose, he declared, was to deal with questions of race and psychotherapy in a completely objective fashion and his essay, which appeared in the *Zentralblatt* in 1937, does display a rigorous rationality. But the long involved formulations and sentences also betray a psychological tension that perhaps supports Wladimir Eliasberg's judgment that Stransky, born a full Jew and then baptized when he was an adult, "became the typical *persecute persecutor*."[65] It was also the case, however, that Stransky, his strong German nationalism to no avail, was under the pressure faced by all Jews under Nazi domination: Three years later he would attempt to engage Göring's support for his emigration, but Göring's inquiry with the Reich Interior Ministry was without success.[66] Stransky's paper itself examined the question of the therapeutic alliance between "Aryan" and Jew and the "Aryanization" of psychoanalytic theory. He concluded that the documented successes of such racially mixed doctor-patient relationships were due to the "deghettoized" or "ariotropic" nature of the Jewish physician or to the natural social subordination of the Jewish patient. Both of these alleged phenomena derived from Jewish experiences in the predominant "Aryan" racial culture. As for the utility of Freudian and Adlerian doctrine, Stransky cited the work of Jung, Göring, Künkel, and others as proof that in the proper racial hands even Jewish thought could be beneficial to non-Jewish practitioners and patients.[67]

While the alleged problems involved with psychotherapy by and for Jews were rendered academic by the central dark reality of Nazism, the issue of the diagnosis and treatment boundaries between psychotherapy and psychiatry remained very real. As we have already seen, the psychotherapists were at some pains not only to expand their competence at the expense of their rivals, the psychiatrists, but also to wall off their practice from the increasingly psychiatric dead end of sterilization and "euthanasia." They had nothing to do directly with the emptying of the asylums, including now doubly doomed Jewish mental patients. All Jews who had been institutionalized were weeded out and required to be lodged at the Berndorf-Sayn sanitarium in Coblenz.

After that facility was taken over in 1942 by the SS-Lebensborn (see chapter 11), the patients were sent to the Jewish Hospital in Berlin, which was under the nominal authority of Leo Baeck's Reich Association of Jews in Germany. According to its director of neuropsychiatry, Hermann Pineas, "selections" were regularly made among these patients by the Nazis for transport to the extermination camps in Poland.[68]

But the psychotherapists were anything but completely segregated from Nazi psychiatric outrages in general. There was even some approval of it expressed by leading psychotherapists, chief among whom in this respect was Johannes Heinrich Schultz. This approval in Schultz's case was a function of his broad background in psychiatry and neurology, the rigorously rational comprehensiveness of his thought patterns, and his opportunistic desire to expand and protect psychotherapy. At the same time, however, his espousal of forced sterilization and "euthanasia" under Nazi auspices was also another distressing example of the complementary relationship between healing and killing in the Third Reich.[69] It is no exculpation, but rather a necessary historical elaboration, to point out that all of these motives were always present in Schultz's published thoughts on this subject and were in line with some of what we have already identified as "progressive" thinking in psychiatry (see chapter 1). This was true in even the most infamous of these in a long essay on the construction of a differential diagnostic scheme for the Göring Institute outpatient clinic. In the context of a remark about the severely retarded cases illustrated in a famous book by Wilhelm Weygandt—an adult's "brain . . . smaller than that of a newborn"[70]—Schultz seconds the view of psychiatrist August Hoche about the "'destruction of life not worth living'" and goes on to "express the hope that the insane asylums [*Idiotanstalten*] will soon transform and empty themselves in this way."[71] Schultz argues, rationally and protectively, that psychotherapy can do nothing in such cases and that the only—and admirable—alternative to Hoche's approach is institutional care (*Fürsorge*). Such a sentiment fit well with its equally opportunistic complement, the cultivation—with the help of psychotherapy—of the most valuable members of society. As Schultz put it in 1942:

> A person's first six years, which usually lie beyond his conscious recall, are of decisive importance for his character development, a further contribution to the axiom that has been militantly assured today in Germany for the first time: that the family is the irreplaceable nucleus of the organic *Volk*.[72]

The active, as opposed to the rhetorical, involvement of Göring Institute psychotherapists in decisions regarding forced sterilization and "euthanasia" of mental patients is not well documented. Göring's son claims that his father acted on behalf of a number of psychiatric patients who were threatened by the regime with sterilization and death, allegedly using his authority and influence to have them placed in the Bodelschwingh asylum at Bethel, near Bielefeld in the Ruhr. It is possible to give some credence to son Göring's claim for his father. The director at Bethel, Karsten Jasperson, was one of the few psychiatrists to resist Nazi demands to sterilize and kill asylum inmates, something which not surprisingly angered the regime.[73] Psychiatrists who had originally supported Nazi legislation sought to distance themselves, either before or after the war, from the sterilization and murder of mental patients. Kretschmer, who himself had contributed published words to this campaign for racial hygiene, claimed after the war that while Ernst Rüdin publicly supported forced sterilization, he did so only because he was helpless in the face of Nazi insistence.[74] There apparently was in fact some official displeasure with Rüdin: When in 1941 the SS research society Ahnenerbe approached Rüdin's psychiatric institute to aid in its research in racial biology, SD chief Reinhard Heydrich killed the offer with the judgment that Rüdin was not acceptable for membership in the SS.[75] Bumke made the same claim of helplessness for himself.[76] Even Karl Bonhoeffer, while condemning medical killing after the war (see chapter 15), wrote in 1934 of psychiatrists' obligations under the Nazi sterilization law.[77] On the other hand, according to Viktor Frankl, Otto Pötzl of Vienna tried to protect him and a number of Jewish and non-Jewish patients who were in danger of sterilization or death.[78]

But the psychotherapists, too, had in fact a more complicated relationship to the Nazi assault on "hereditary" mental illness. It was the declared policy of the institute to prohibit psychotherapists from providing private evaluations for hereditary health courts.[79] This policy likely was motivated by the desire to avoid a situation in which the diagnostic deck would be stacked in favor of psychiatrists and in which psychotherapists would be courting official disfavor. This same concern was behind Göring's caution that psychotherapists giving expert testimony for the military or industry could provide diagnoses only and not conclusions as to the fitness of an individual for service or work.[80] Göring, who taught a course in forensic psychiatry at the institute, stressed the necessity of exhaustively filling out that section of an evaluation calling for psychological diagnosis, something Göring said psychiatrists did not do. This would ensure, Göring hoped, that the court would not confuse a neurotic with a "psychopath" and that, as in compensation cases, psychotherapy would be mandated in the case of the former.[81] This point of view was of benefit to those who, by whatever margin, were designated as neurotic and in need of therapy. But it also necessarily involved a concession to the existence of others who would not be spared the full and often fatal extent of Nazi law. Göring apparently had at least one chance to represent this position himself within the hereditary health court system: The one case that has surfaced involving Göring ended with a denial of a request for sterilization of a twenty-five-year-old woodworker because of feeblemindedness.[82] There is in this decision not only the general concession—and contribution—to the powerful reality of Nazi policy, but also that mixture of intellectual arrogance and misplaced charity that can be part of the modern expert's nature. Göring could, and certainly did, justify and rationalize any decision in such a circumstance on the basis of what was on balance in the best long-term interests of the patient and of society. Under the press of professional ambition, personal prestige, and the racist communal ethic of the time, consistent or even occasional concern for individual patients—and for whole categories of the mentally ill—had little relevance.

In the Nazi environment most slippery slopes, if not becoming moral chasms, became slimy slopes. This was certainly the case with the issue of medical confidentiality. In December 1942 Hitler decreed that medical confidentiality would no longer apply to cases involving treason or danger to national security.[83] The confidential nature of what transpires between patient and therapist, although not unqualified even in a lawful society, is of course a sine qua non of psychotherapeutic treatment. According to Jungian Wolfgang Hochheimer, Göring demanded just such a suspension of medical confidentiality at a meeting of the full membership of the institute. Hochheimer's own inquiries after the war elicited from some of those present that the demand was met with a silence that for many constituted a mix of disagreement and fear of certain colleagues who were party members. Psychoanalysts Käthe Dräger and Gerhard Maetze recalled that Göring in the fall of 1944 broached the subject of Hitler's order, but took no action when it was overwhelmingly rejected by the members of the institute.

In any case, in the absence of agents provocateurs among the patients, enforcement of this edict was impossible. The inclusion of the phrase "in special cases" in Conti's own communication of the order to regional party medical officials constituted an attempt by Conti to pitch an unqualified Hitler order that he knew would be impossible to enforce and would receive a mixed reception among medical personnel. Implementation of this decree would rest with individual physicians and psychotherapists or with assistants and secretaries, who were also legally bound by medical confidentiality.[84]

There was in fact at least one case at the Göring Institute of adherence to Hitler's order. During the war a court assigned Jungian psychotherapist Marianne Stark to provide an expert opinion on a thirteen-year-old learning disabled delinquent. Stark established a rapport with the young boy and learned that he had been stealing rifles from military depots. She convinced him to let her hide the weapons with the—rather extraordinary—promise that she would return them to him when he was eighteen. Stark, however, could not keep the weapons in her own house, because she was also hiding a family of Jews. So she gave the rifles to Göring. In the meantime the boy had been arrested on a minor charge. Göring was called to testify and, in violation of medical confidentiality, revealed the existence of the weapons cache. According to Stark, Kalau vom Hofe, director of criminal psychology at the Göring Institute, rendered a severe diagnosis of the boy as a "psychopath" and he was sentenced to a long prison term, which was subsequently reduced to a year. But the boy ended up at the notorious Hadamar asylum in the state of Hesse. Stark managed to use contacts in diplomatic circles to prevent the killing of the boy, but he had already been injected with tuberculosis bacilli in a human experiment and died in 1947.[85]

At the very least, this case demonstrates the awful consequences in Nazi Germany of not assuming the worst. Göring's violation of a medical confidence between a therapist and a patient and between two colleagues was in and of itself an unethical act. It destroyed the therapeutic alliance between Stark and the boy and eventually destroyed the boy's life. Göring no doubt felt that the private stockpiling of weapons in wartime went beyond delinquency to treason, since even in the absence of evidence of intent to use the weapons their loss constituted harm to the national defense. Any such harm to the Nazi war effort, not to mention use of the weapons against the regime, would have of course been morally justified in effect even absent intent. But appreciation of that was clearly beyond Göring's capacities and sentiments at the time. It is all but certain that the chief motivation on Göring's part, aside from protecting his institute, was patriotic outrage over such an act during wartime rather than unalloyed allegiance to National Socialism. For Göring, as for most Germans, the war was a matter of the nation at risk, a conviction that submerged most if not all of any reservations he may or may not have had about the regime. There is no evidence that Göring or Kalau vom Hofe knew, much less recommended, that the boy be sent to Hadamar to become a test animal. But that only returns us to the grave matter of unintended rather than unanticipated consequences. The very fact that Göring and other psychotherapists claimed on occasion to have acted on behalf of patients in danger obviously meant they were aware of the danger to patients declared to be "psychopathic," "asocial" or "an enemy of the people" (*Volksfeind*). While this reminds us once again of the often complementary nature of resistance and collaboration—and thus of good and evil—in the Third Reich, it also underlines the unrelenting gravity of almost every decision made or not made under such a regime.

At the other end of the spectrum of patients, the Göring Institute often dealt with the psychological problems of Nazis and their families. Since incurable hereditary degeneracy could not be openly entertained as a possible cause of personal psychological difficulties within the Nazi racial elite, psychotherapy was an ideological as well as practical choice. For example, during 1942 Göring was involved in the clandestine case of the seventeen-year-old daughter of an SS regimental commander who had been killed in battle. In February General of the Waffen-SS Karl Wolff, Himmler's chief of staff, wrote to Göring with the request that he examine the girl, then lodged in a Bodelschwingh home, in order to determine the cause of her disturbed behavior, most notably her compulsive lying. Wolff also mentioned that the paternal grandparents wished to deprive the girl's stepmother of the guardianship stipulated in her husband's will. Himmler, with indulgent organizational loyalty and typical petty bourgeois sentimentality, was said by Wolff to desire the fulfillment of the fallen man's wishes.[86] Himmler reportedly felt that a psychotherapeutic examination would establish the basis for a legal dismissal of the grandfather's complaint against the stepmother. The Berlin district court agreed with the plan to have the girl examined by Göring and opined that following the receipt of Göring's report, the grandfather's complaint would be voided.[87] The girl was duly examined by Göring beginning in early March and continuing into the summer and the results of the investigation were sent to Himmler on July 30. Interviews had also been held with the girls' stepmother, grandfather, and grandmother.

The actual analysis of her family and personal history was carried out by Kalau vom Hofe in her capacity as a criminal psychologist and the findings did indeed tend to prejudice the grandparents' case. The girl came from a broken home; her parents had divorced when she was only four. Kalau vom Hofe took pains to point out the tensions within the family that would have affected the infant's development from birth. According to the stepmother, the original mother was to blame for the breakup of the first marriage and had taken the child to live with her grandmother. But she subsequently placed the girl in a home where she remained for the next eight years. The girl recalled that during this time she saw less and less of both her mother and her maternal grandfather. She was apparently a difficult ward from the beginning and was ten years old by the time her paternal grandparents took any interest in her. At twelve she joined her father and his new wife, but difficulties persisted and she was in and out of homes while the conflict within the family over what to do with her steadily became more acute.

The child's father had always shown great affection for her, but professional obligations and the fact that he was living with his sister prevented him from taking care of her before he remarried. Kalau vom Hofe, prudently avoiding explicit psychosexual analysis, expressed the opinion that the conflict over custody of the child stemmed from the father's early childhood, which was dominated by an exaggerated fixation on his mother and also on his unmarried sister, with whom he was later to live. Neither woman wanted to let him go and the girl's paternal grandmother found it intolerable that the stepmother should take possession of her son's only child. The effect of this familial struggle on the girl was to reduce her to a mere legacy of her dead father and to increase her isolation from love and affection. Small of stature, shy, and suffering from partial hearing loss in her right ear, the girl resorted to asocial behavior toward those figures of authority with whom she came into contact. Kalau vom Hofe was quick to maintain, however, that there was no evidence of hereditary illness: The child's lack of genuine personality development and of relationships with other children and with adults was the result of her infantile and childhood experiences.

Kalau vom Hofe advised that the girl be placed in a home where she could receive psychotherapeutic care over an extended period of time.[88] Göring subsequently recommended that the girl should live with a family in Munich and undergo psychotherapeutic treatment there. Since the girl's problems were curable rather than hereditary, the cost of her accommodation and schooling were to be covered by the SS orphan pension fund. Moreover, the Reichsführer's office assured Göring that Himmler would contribute an additional amount—around RM 50 per month—toward the cost of psychotherapy.[89] Wolff reported to Göring that he was quite in agreement with the institute's determination that the girl's mental distress originated from environmental influences and not from hereditary taint.[90] Such relief as Wolff may have felt over this diagnosis is hardly surprising, though there is no evidence that Göring and Kalau vom Hofe had to tailor either the diagnosis or their recommendations to suit their professional and political advantage. At the same time, one cannot ignore in all of this the corrosive effect on objectivity of brutal dictatorial authority.

By mid-September, in any case, it was necessary for Göring to change the location of the patient's residence and treatment. The girl was now to live with pedagogue Wilhelm Laiblin in Stuttgart and to be treated by the Jungian Jutta von Graevenitz. Göring also suggested that the grandparents not be informed of the girl's destination until she had settled in.[91] But the girl did not go to Stuttgart, but ended up at the Waldhaus Sanitarium near Tübingen in the care of Auguste Marzinowski. Apparently there was difficulty all along the line in finding a place for her, but Himmler was willing to double his contribution to the girl's treatment.[92] It is possible that fear of the SS prompted hesitation and perhaps even refusal on the part of some members of the Göring Institute to assume responsibility for her therapy. Whatever the causes, what is striking in this shuffling of the patient from place to another is the repetition of one of the circumstances identified by Kalau vom Hofe as responsible for her psychological difficulties, perhaps another indication of the damaging effect of political realities on psychotherapeutic care in the Nazi dictatorship.

Psychotherapists also confronted some of the mental casualties peculiar to the brutal Nazi order. Lucy Heyer-Grote had in therapy a

Norwegian SS man torn between his desire to provide his parents with the extra rations that came with his SS posting and his guilt over the atrocities he witnessed in the East. Marianne Stark had the same experience in her control analysis with a young German who joined the SS because of the impressive uniform and the effect it had on his girlfriend.[93] Schultz had a psychosomatic case of uncontrollable trembling from a patient who had executed Polish civilians.[94] Indeed, there is evidence that in general the SS had to be concerned about the psychological effects of the mass shootings of civilians on the men carrying them out; this was one major reason for the choice of gas chambers for the Final Solution.[95] Several of the SS commanders in charge of the mass killings in the East had to quit; perhaps the most notable case of this kind involved Major-General Erich von dem Bach-Zelewski,

> who was taken to the SS hospital in Hohenlychen, suffering from a nervous breakdown and congestion of the liver. Haunted by his guilt, he would pass his nights screaming, a prey to hallucinations. Dr. [Ernst] Grawitz, the [h]ead SS doctor, reported to Himmler: "He is suffering particularly from hallucinations connected with the shootings of Jews which he himself carried out and with other grievous experiences in the East."[96]

Most often, however, psychotherapists dealt with the less direct effects of Nazi inhumanity. In Munich, for example, they treated secretaries from the "Brown House," the Nazi party headquarters and individuals from all walks of life and stations in society, some of whom suffered from silence in the face of monstrosities, but more often were confronting quotidian psychological problems as well as personal and familial loss. Gumpert even claims that many Nazis went to Jewish doctors primarily for psychological reasons, that is, so they could vent their complaints about the regime without fear of reprisal.[97]

The Göring Institute psychotherapists also came into contact with some of the psychological difficulties suffered by members of the Nazi leadership. It was rumored within the institute that Göring was involved in the treatment of his cousin's morphine addiction. Pedagogue Otto Haseloff, who shared quarters with Schultz-Hencke during the last year of the war, claims that the Reich marshal was consulting Schultz-Hencke because of addiction to morphine and the methamphetamine Pervitin (see chapter 12).[98] Likewise, Reich Health Leader Conti and high Labor Front officials were supposedly undergoing therapy at the institute. According to a former member of the institute, in the autumn of 1944 Göring learned that Nazi judge Roland Freisler's wife Marion wished to be treated for severe depression. No one at the institute was willing to have anything to do even with the family of the infamous inquisitor of the People's Court. Before any possible difficulties stemming from the institute's reluctance could be manifested, however, Freisler himself was killed in a bombing raid on Berlin on February 3, 1945.[99] This case, like the case of the daughter of the SS officer discussed above, reveals another ambiguous aspect of the nature of psychotherapy under authoritarian rule. What is the therapist's, and in general the doctor's, duty under the Hippocratic oath when it comes to treating the perpetrators of evil, or the people who sustain them at home and at work? To be sure, the psychotherapists in this case were, as far as we know, simply protecting themselves while their overall service to the regime showed that they were quite willing for the sake of their profession and for any number of other reasons to help Germans and Nazis get back to health and to work.

But more usual than the refusal to treat was the willingness of the psychotherapists to exercise their professional capacities and contacts. Wilhelm Bitter even became involved in the secret wartime diplomacy that resulted from top-level Nazi concern over the mental soundness of Adolf Hitler himself. Such concern was nothing new. In 1938 Berlin psychiatrist Karl Bonhoeffer was involved in a resistance plan to declare Hitler insane, a scheme that was abandoned when the Munich conference on Czechoslovakia and the Sudetenland gave Hitler European sanction for his actions. In the autumn of 1939, Carl Jung received a telephone call from Munich from one of Hitler's doctors, requesting Jung to come to Berchtesgaden to render a psychiatric evaluation of the Führer.[100] Bitter's involvement came in 1943 as part of a well-documented sequence of events. By that year the reversal of Nazi military fortunes had begun to prompt a certain amount of scuttling about in the upper reaches of the Nazi leadership in search of a way out of the closing trap. Himmler and his SD foreign intelligence chief, Walter Schellenberg, came up with a plan to abandon western Europe in return for an armistice on that front that would allow Germany to prevent the Russians from conquering the Continent, a major concern of Churchill's. Bitter became a party to the plot because he had some close contacts in Geneva with the British government. Psychiatrist Max de Crinis, Bitter's academic mentor, was also a close friend of

Schellenberg's and had shared in some of Schellenberg's espionage adventures. After Foreign Minister Joachim von Ribbentrop had suffered from disturbed behavior following a kidney disorder, de Crinis had rendered a psychiatric evaluation of von Ribbentrop at Schellenberg's behest. In Schellenberg's latest scheme, de Crinis provided a diagnosis of Hitler that declared the Führer as unbalanced, perhaps from Parkinson's disease. It was hoped that the psychologically disabled Hitler would be "paralyzed" by the plotter's proposal of an armistice in the West. Himmler even had Conti attend a meeting on the subject and Conti left behind at his death a medical opinion on Hitler's condition. In any case, the plan fell apart when Hitler at its mention did not. Bitter came under suspicion as a defeatist and was forced to emigrate to Switzerland in the summer of 1943.[101]

Psychotherapist Erika Hantel's professional involvement with members of the Nazi elite was more direct. Expressing her fascination with the psychological dynamics of the Nazis, she sought a position as a psychotherapist at a so-called "biological sanitarium" in Berchtesgaden. This institution was run by Werner Zabel, a cancer specialist and a former senior staff physician at the Rudolf-Hess-Krankenhaus, who held great admiration for C. G. Jung. Heyer had recommended Hantel and she served at the sanitarium during 1940 and 1941. Zabel's sanitarium was run according to the tenets of natural medicine. The cook there, a Hungarian named Konstanze Manzialy who specialized in vegetarian dishes, subsequently was taken on by Hitler and the Führer himself once saw Zabel for treatment of a gastrointestinal disorder.[102] Hantel, in the terminology in vogue at the sanitarium, provided "heart massage" (autogenic training and *kleine* psychotherapy) and other psychotherapeutic methods for a number of inhabitants and functionaries from Hitler's retreat on the nearby Obersalzberg who would often trail down exhausted after Hitler's late-night and early-morning monologues. These psychotherapeutic sessions were sporadic and generally only atmospheric adjuncts to rest and relaxation, but among those with whom Hantel had professional contact in this manner were Hitler's secretary, Martin Bormann, and Hitler's architect, Albert Speer.

Bormann, Hantel recalls, was extremely nervous and anxious. Air rattling in the pipes in Hantel's office reportedly irritated him to the point that she had to have the pipes fixed. Given Bormann's position, such a disposition was not surprising. Whatever his own character deficiencies, his job could only burden him further:

> Hitler's authority in the Third Reich rested upon his undisputed claim to omnipotence and omniscience. Bormann did not challenge the first, but sought to control the second. The feat alone required immense energy and perseverance. Daily life with Adolf Hitler even in the years of military success was mentally and physically taxing. Hitler had already settled his routine of turning night into day.[103]

While Hantel found Bormann extremely primitive and skittish, she perceived Speer as lost in planning architectural monumentalities. Speer, whose uncle Ernst was a member of the Göring Institute, has denied every being under the care of a psychotherapist, recalling only that Zabel was an old school friend of his and that he was treated for a kidney ailment at the sanitarium.[104] Whatever the actual truth of the matter, it is the case that the minor nature of this kind of occasional psychotherapy, especially as part of a treatment for a physical disorder, could allow it to pass from memory. Even Hantel's own account of her contact with Speer leaves room for doubt about its frequency and intensity. And as with Schultz's failed autogenic treatment of film director Leni Riefenstahl in 1942,[105] there clearly were inherent and situational limits to the effectiveness of psychotherapy. Hantel, in any case, saw fewer and fewer patients after the German invasion of Russia in June 1941, when pressing military business often kept the Führer and his entourage in Berlin and at his various military headquarters. It is to the ever more dynamic and portentous history of the Göring Institute during Hitler's war to which we now turn in the next four chapters.

Notes

1. Martin Gumpert, *Heil Hunger!*, p. v.
2. Ibid., p. 16.
3. Ibid., p. 41; see also Gumpert, *Hölle in Paradies: Selbstdarstellung eines Arztes* (Stockholm, 1939), pp. 241–2.
4. See *Internationales Ärztliches Bulletin Jahrgang I-VI (1934–1939) Reprint*, Beiträge zur Nationalsozialistische Gesundheits- und Sozialpolitik 7 (Berlin, 1989); Proctor, *Racial Hygiene*, pp. 148, 213, 262–4, 267; and *Deutschland-Berichte der Sozialdemokratischen Partei Deutschlands (Sopade)* (Salzhausen, 1980).
5. Kater, *Doctors Under Hitler*, pp. 41–53.
6. Foreign Office and Ministry of Economic Warfare, "Public Health," (London, 1944), pp. 229–56G, Wiener Library, London; United States Strategic Bombing Survey, Morale Division, Medical Branch Report, *The Effect of Bombing on Health and Medical Care in Germany* (Washington, D.C., October 30, 1945), pp. 30–94, 263.
7. Lockot, *Erinnern und Durcharbeiten*, p. 212.

8. Gumpert, *Heil Hunger!*, pp. 41–5; Cimbal to Haeberlin, August 3, 1933, p. 4, Kl. Erw. 762/2.
9. Crew, "General Introduction," in idem, *Nazism and German Society*, pp. 7–9.
10. Ian Kershaw, *The "Hitler Myth": Image and Reality in the Third Reich* (Oxford, 1987), pp. 253–69.
11. Gisela Bock, *Zwangssterilisation im Nationalsozialismus: Studien zur Rassenpolitik und Frauenpolitik* (Opladen, 1986).
12. Claudia Koonz, *Mothers in the Fatherland: Women, the Family and Nazi Politics* (New York, 1986).
13. Dagmar Reese, "Emanzipation oder Vergesellschaftung: Mädchen im 'Bund deutscher Mädel'," in Hans-Uwe Otto and Heinz Sünker, eds., *Politische Formierung und soziale Erziehung im Nationalsozialismus* (Frankfurt am Main, 1991), pp. 203–25.
14. Crew, "General Introduction," in idem, *Nazism and German Society*, p. 19.
15. Tilla Siegel, "Wage Policy in Nazi Germany," *Politics and Society* 14 (1985): 1–51.
16. Robert Gellately, *The Gestapo and German Society: Enforcing Racial Policy, 1933–1945* (Oxford, 1990).
17. Charlotte Beradt, *The Third Reich of Dreams*, trans. Adriane Gottwald (Chicago, 1968), p. 11.
18. "An Essay by Bruno Bettelheim," in Beradt, *Third Reich of Dreams*, pp. 151–70.
19. See, for example, Gustav Richard Heyer, *Menschen in Not*, passim.
20. Lockot, *Erinnern und Durcharbeiten*, pp. 213–14.
21. On psychoanalysis, see Arthur Feiner, "The Dilemma of Integrity"; Gerard Chrzanowski, "Psychoanalysis: Ideology and Practitioners," pp. 492–3; and Rose Spiegel, "Survival of Psychoanalysis in Nazi Germany." On Mitscherlich, Werner Bohleber to Peter Loewenberg, May 29, 1996.
22. Regine Lockot, personal communication, April 30, 1980.
23. Michael Rutschky, "'Wir wollen da wieder anfangen, wo wir '33 hatten aufhören müssen': Das Berliner Psychoanalytische Institut."
24. On the affectionate fun poked at Göring in the unofficial institute humor magazine, see Lockot, *Erinnern und Durcharbeiten*, pp. 337–8, n. 8; on Kemper's evaluation of Göring's personality and leadership style, see Pongratz, *Psychotherapie*, p. 287.
25. Philip Rieff, *Freud: The Mind of the Moralist*, 3rd ed. (Chicago, 1979), p. 243.
26. Boris M. Segal, "The Theoretical Bases of Soviet Psychotherapy," *American Journal of Psychotherapy* 29 (1975): 503–23; David Joravsky, *Russian Psychology: A Critical History* (Oxford, 1989), pp. 230–7.
27. Joseph Nyomarky, *Charisma and Factionalism in the Nazi Party* (Minneapolis, 1967); Hans Buchheim, *Totalitarian Rule: Its Nature and Characteristics*, trans. Ruth Hein (Middletown, Conn., 1968), pp. 35–6.
28. Nazi eugenicist Fritz Lenz theorized that only 30 percent of the population was worthy of being protected from forced sterilization; see Bock, *Zwangssterilisation*, p. 112.
29. "Bericht über die 1. Tagung der Deutschen Gesellschaft für Kinderpsychiatrie und Heilpädagogik," *Zeitschrift für Kinderforschung* 49 (1941): 4; see also *Deutsche Wissenschaft: Arbeit und Aufgabe* (Leipzig, 1939), pp. 101–48.
30. Bock, *Zwangssterilisation*, pp. 303–5.
31. R 18/5585, BA.

32. Christa Wolf, *Patterns of Childhood,* trans. Ursule Molinaro and Hedwig Rappolt (New York, 1980), pp. 149, 195–8.
33. Herbert Marcuse, "Critique of Neo-Freudian Revisionism," in idem, *Eros and Civilization: A Philosophical Inquiry Into Freud* (Boston, 1955), p. 257.
34. Paul Roazen, *Erik H. Erikson: The Power and Limits of a Vision* (New York, 1976), p. 172. It was precisely the most radical social and political theoreticians in the Freudian movement who finally lost out to the psychoanalytic conservatives and liberals with the advent of Hitler: see Russell Jacoby, *The Repression of Psychoanalysis: Otto Fenichel and the Political Freudians* (New York, 1983), p. 77.
35. See, for example, Erich Fromm, "The Social Philosophy of 'Will Therapy'," *Psychiatry* 2 (1939): 233; Martin Birnbach, *Neo-Freudian Social Philosophy* (Stanford, 1961); and Isabel V. Hull, "The Bourgeoisie and its Discontents: Reflections on 'Nationalism and Respectability'," *Journal of Contemporary History* 17 (1982): 255–7.
36. Boehm, "Erhebung und Bearbeitung von Katamnesen," pp. 18–19; Lockot, *Erinnern und Durcharbeiten,* pp. 216, 217; see also Lockot, p. 218, for a tabulation of psychoanalytic and psychotherapeutic cases at the two Berlin institutes from 1920 through 1941.
37. For a list of diagnoses from the two Berlin institutes from 1920 through 1940, see Lockot, *Erinnern und Durcharbeiten,* pp. 219–20.
38. See Johannes Heinrich Schultz, *Neurose, Lebensnot und ärztliche Pflicht,* a collection of essays from the *Deutsche medizinische Wochenschrift.*
39. Johannes Heinrich Schultz, "Praktischer Arzt und Hypnose"; Hattingberg, *Neue Seelenheilkunde,* pp. 44–5; and Fritz Künkel, "Das Hausarzt und Psychotherapie."
40. Rittmeister, "Der augenblickliche Stand der Poliklinik," pp. 90–3.
41. Johannes Heinrich Schultz, *Das autogene Training, konzentrative Selbstentspannung: Versuch einer klinischpraktischen Darstellung,* 5th ed. (Leipzig, 1942); idem, *Übungsheft für das autogene Training,* 5th ed. (Leipzig, 1943); see also Kretschmer, *Gestalten und Gedanken,* pp. 179–92.
42. Fritz Mohr, "Brief an eine durch Fliegerangriff stillunfähig gewordene Mutter," p. 1016; see also Heyer, *Menschen in Not,* pp. 101–3.
43. Erik H. Erikson, "The Legend of Hitler's Childhood," in idem, *Childhood and Society,* 2nd ed. (New York, 1963), p. 30.
44. Johannes Heinrich Schultz, "Über kleine Psychotherapie," p. 72; see also idem, "Die Bedeutung primitivaktiver Methoden in der Psychotherapie mit besonderer Berücksichtigung der Behandlung Alkoholkranker," *ZfP* 9 (1936): 193–200. Beyond their practical medical aims and effects, however, such processes are common to the "political re-education" that occurs in totalitarian systems: coercion, exhortation, therapy, and realization; see Robert Jay Lifton, *Thought Reform and the Psychology of Totalism* (New York, 1961), pp. 458–61.
45. Johannes Heinrich Schultz, "Über tiefenpsychologische Kurzbehandlungen," p. 29.
46. Schultz, *Psychotherapie,* pp. 101–6.
47. Ibid., pp. 41–62.
48. Scheunert, "Über psychotherapeutische Kurzbehandlungen," pp. 208–9, 213–14.
49. Ibid., p. 219; Wegscheider, "Psychotherapie bei Kassenpatienten," p. 57.
50. Klaus Wegscheider, "Psychotherapie bei Kassenpatienten," pp. 61–7.
51. Ibid., p. 65; see also Kretschmer, *Gestalten und Gedanken,* pp. 180–1; and

Schultz, *Lebensbilderbuch,* p. 160.

52. Matthias Heinrich Göring, "Die Bedeutung der Neurose in der Sozialversicherung," p. 43. This was a lecture given on February 2, 1938, at the Reich Insurance Office. Göring subsequently sent three copies of the address to the Reich Insurance Office for dissemination to the relevant officials: see Göring to Senatspräsident, February 13, 1938, R 89/15115, BA.
53. "Tätigkeitsbericht 1938," p. 4.
54. Abkommen zwischen dem Deutschen Institut für Psychologische Forschung und Psychotherapie und der Wirtschaftsgruppe Lebens- und Krankenversicherung, January 1, 1943, Kl. Erw. 762/4.
55. Harald Schultz-Hencke, Zweiter protokollarischer Bericht, May 30, 1945, p. 13, Kl. Erw. 762/7.
56. Ausführungsbestimmungen zu dem Vertrage zwischen dem Deutschen Institut für Psychologische Forschung und Psychotherapie und dem Verband der Angestellten-Krankenkassen e.V.. n.d., Kl. Erw. 762/4.
57. Ibid.
58. Eghigian, "Bürokratie und das Entstehen von Krankheit," pp. 221–2.
59. Wilhelm Schmitz and Gerhart Schramm, "Unfallneurose und Reichsgericht," *Münchener medizinische Wochenschrift* 86 (1939): 1387–90.
60. Göring, "Bedeutung der Neurose," p. 36.
61. Ibid., pp. 36, 43, 46–7, 48, 49–50; see also the discussion of Göring's paper in *ZfP* 11 (1939): 50–6; and Eghigian, "Bürokratie und das Entstehen von Krankheit," p. 220.
62. Kl. Erw. 762/4.
63. Kl. Erw. 762/6. Schirren does not say whether the woman was a full Jew or not, a matter of some importance in the deadly Nazi scheme of things.
64. For another expression of this view, see Heinrich von Kogerer, "Spezielle klinische Prognose und Psychotherapie," in Curtius, *Psychotherapie in der Praxis,* p. 118.
65. Ladislas Farago, ed., *German Psychological Warfare,* p. 270; see also Decker, *Freud in Germany,* pp. 245–6; and Freud, *Freud/Jung Letters,* p. 247. On Stransky's paper, see Zapp, "Psychoanalyse und Nationalsozialismus," pp. 105–6.
66. Lockot, *Erinnern und Durcharbeiten,* pp. 179, 181–2.
67. Erwin Stransky, "Rasse und Psychotherapie," pp. 23–4, 27. Viktor Frankl, a Viennese colleague of Stransky who survived two years in Theresienstadt, argued that psychotherapy could never represent a world view, but that a world view could serve as a means of therapy; see Viktor E. Frankl, "Zur geistigen Problematik der Psychotherapie," *ZfP* 10 (1937): 8, 33–45; Huber, *Psychoanalyse in Österreich,* pp. 31–2; and Frankl, *From Death-Camp to Existentialism: A Psychiatrist's Path to a New Therapy,* trans. Ilse Lasch (Boston, 1959). In his forthcoming NYU dissertation historian Timothy Pytell argues that Frankl's essay betrays a naive, flirtatious, and possibly opportunistic ambiguity concerning fascism; see also Viktor Frankl, "Seelenärztliche Selbstbesinnung," *Der Christliche Ständestaat,* January 30, 1938.
68. Hermann Pineas, personal communication, June 25, 1981; see also "10. Verordnung zum Reichsbürgergesetz 4. Juli 1939," *Reichsgesetzblatt* (1939): 642–3; "Aufnahme jüdischer Geisteskranker in Heil- und Pflegeanstalten," *Reichsgesetzblatt* (1941): 37–8; and *Reichsgesetzblatt* (1942): 906; and Raul Hilberg, *The Destruction of the European Jews* (Chicago, 1961), pp. 122–4, 303–4.

69. See, for example, Tübinger Vereinigung für Volkskunde, *Volk und Gesundheit: Heilen und Vernichten im Nationalsozialismus* (Tübingen, 1982); and Kölnische Gesellschaft für Christlich-Jüdische Zusammenarbeit, *Heilen und Vernichten im Nationalsozialismus* (Cologne, 1985).
70. Schultz, "Vorschlag eines Diagnosen-Schemas," p. 113.
71. Ibid.; see also p. 123; and Lockot, *Erinnern und Durcharbeiten,* p. 221.
72. Johannes Heinrich Schultz, *Die seelische Gesunderhaltung unter besonderer Berücksichtigung der Kriegsverhältnisse,* p. 48. This sentiment was the basis for Schultz's positive and craven review of Nazi judge Roland Freisler's book on divorce law; see *ZfP* 11 (1939): 122.
73. Klaus Dörner, "Anstaltsalltag in der Psychiatrie und NS-Euthanasie," in Johanna Bleker and Norbert Jachertz, eds., *Medizin im "Dritten Reich",* 2nd ed. (Cologne, 1993), pp. 175, 181; Microcopy T-1021, Roll 11, frame 29, National Archives.
74. Kretschmer, *Gestalten und Gedanken,* p. 158.
75. Michael H. Kater, *Das "Ahnenerbe" der SS 1935–45: Ein Beitrag zur Kulturpolitik des Dritten Reiches* (Stuttgart, 1974), p. 206.
76. Bumke, *Erinnerungen,* pp. 145–6. There was also some reservation within the Reich Interior Ministry: see Broszat, *Hitler State,* pp. 292–3, n. 57.
77. Karl Bonhoeffer, *Die psychiatrische Aufgaben bei der Ausführung des Gesetzes zur Verhütung erbkranken Nachwuchses* (Berlin, 1934).
78. Pongratz, *Psychotherapie,* pp. 191–2. On Frankl's experimental surgery on Jewish attempted suicides, see V.E. Frankl, "Pervitin intrazisternal," *Ars Medici* 32 (1942): 58–60. I am grateful to Timothy Pytell for this citation.
79. Matthias Heinrich Göring, "Abfassen von Zeugnissen und Gutachten," p. 35.
80. Ibid.
81. Ibid., p. 36.
82. Erbgesundheitsgericht Gera Beschluss vom 21. Mai 1937, R 18/5585, Rep. 320, #585, H. 1: Staatssekretär Pfundtner, 117–18, BA; Lockot, *Erinnern und Durcharbeiten,* pp. 224–5.
83. See Hitler's order of December 23, 1942, to doctors, health practitioners, and dentists as articulated in: Leonardo Conti, Führerordnung über Aufhebung der Schweigepflicht in besonderen Fällen, January 9, 1943, Conti file 213, BDC: Reichsärztekammer.
84. Kl. Erw. 762/6.
85. Lüdger Hermanns and Ulrich Schultz, "Interview mit Marianne Stark-Henning."
86. Wolff to Göring, February 4, 1942, BDC: Personalakten Prof. Göring; and Fitzner to Wolff, February 5, 1942, BDC: Personlakten Prof. Göring; see also Microcopy T-175, Roll R76, folder 107, National Archives. On Himmler, see Hans Peter Bleuel, *Sex and Society in Nazi Germany,* pp. 201–7; and Peter Loewenberg, "The Unsuccessful Adolescence of Heinrich Himmler," *American Historical Review* 76 (1971): 612–41; see also Bericht, January 16, 1942, BDC: Personalakten Prof. Göring; and Wolff to Amtsgericht Berlin, February 4, 1942, BDC: Personalakten Prof. Göring.
87. Amtsgerichtsrat Dannenberg to Himmler, February 28, 1942, BDC: Personalakten Prof. Göring.
88. Matthias Heinrich Göring and Marie Kalau vom Hofe, Fachärztliche Stellungnahme, July 30, 1942, BDC: Personalakten Prof. Göring; and Fitzner to Göring, September 14, 1942, BDC: Personalakten Prof. Göring.
89. Fitzner to Heckenstaller, August 6, 1942, BDC: Personalakten Prof. Göring; and Heckenstaller to Fitzner, September 2, 1942, BDC: Personalakten Prof. Göring.

90. Wolff to Göring, September 7, 1942, BDC: Personalakten Prof. Göring.
91. Göring to Fitzner, September 11, 1942, BDC: Personalakten Prof. Göring.
92. Fitzner to Wolff, October 28, 1942, BDC: Personalakten Prof. Göring.
93. Hermanns and Schultz, "Interview with Marianne Stark-Henning."
94. Ellen Bartens, personal communication, July 1, 1984.
95. Raul Hilberg, "The Nature of the Process," in Joel E. Dimsdale, ed., *Survivors, Victims, and Perpetrators: Essays on the Nazi Holocaust* (Washington, D.C., 1980), pp. 16–35; idem, *Perpetrators Victims Bystanders: The Jewish Catastrophe, 1933–1945* (New York, 1992), pp. 55–64; see also below, chapter 10.
96. Heinz Höhne, *The Order of the Death's Head: The Story of Hitler's SS*, trans. Richard Barry (New York, 1969), p. 363. Himmler was also treated for a nervous stomach disorder at Hohenlychen: see Helmut Heiber, ed., *Reichsführer! Briefe an und von Himmler* (Munich, 1970), pp. 130–3.
97. Gumpert, *Hölle im Paradies*, pp. 251–2; see also Kater, *Doctors under Hitler*, p. 190.
98. Lockot, *Die Reinigung der Psychoanalyse*, p.p. 240–1, n. 25. A Freudian "slype" in Lockot's book renders Pervitin "Pervertin."
99. Gert Buchheit, *Richter in roter Robe: Freisler, Präsident des Volksgerichtshofes* (Munich, 1968), pp. 274–5.
100. Jung, *Letters*, p. 405n. Bonhoeffer's activities in 1938 were related to the author by Klaus Hoppe. See also Robert G. L. Waite, *The Psychopathic God: Adolf Hitler* (New York, 1977), pp. 349–56.
101. Pongratz, *Psychotherapie*, p. 46n; Walter Schellenberg, *The Schellenberg Memoirs*, ed. Louis Hagen (London, 1956), pp. 86–7, 90–1, 112, 265, 284, 391, 438, 440; and Felix Kersten, *The Kersten Memoirs 1940–1945*, trans. Constantine Fitzgibbon and James Oliver (New York, 1957), pp. 165–71; On similar squirmings in 1945, see Höhne, *The Order of the Death's Head*, pp. 571–2. Barbara Hannah reports that Jung was involved in a plot, which she places in the summer of 1942, involving a German psychiatrist and some Swiss psychiatrists. Since the plot and its outcome are similar to that recounted by Bitter and Schellenberg, it is likely that it was the same one described by those sources for 1943; see Hannah, *Jung*, pp. 273–4.
102. Glenn Infield, *Eva and Adolf* (New York, 1974), p. 147.
103. Orlow, *History of the Nazi Party*, p. 335.
104. Albert Speer, personal communication, August 31, 1979.
105. Leni Riefenstahl, *A Memoir* (New York, 1992), p. 282.

10

The Second Göring Institute, 1939–1942

In 1941 the official in-house journal of Robert Ley's German Labor Front, *Der Hoheitsträger,* ran an article on the social and economic importance of the cultivation of psychological health. The article, which would be listed in the *Nationalsozialistische Bibliographie,* spoke in particularly glowing—if also grammatically and rhetorically tortured—terms of the work of the Göring Institute:

> The "German Institute for Psychological Research and Psychotherapy" in Berlin, which, under the direction of Professor M. H. Göring, a relative of the Reich Marshal, operates in continued close touch with official agencies, has for years endeavored with success to train capable, practical psychologists and to place the fruits of recent depth psychological research and characterology at the service of a farseeing spiritual *Volkshygiene.* Since this important institute also operates an outpatient clinic, every fellow German, including those of modest means, is urged to take personal advantage of the blessed achievements of contemporary psychotherapy and characterology.[1]

These words of praise reflected a collaboration between the Labor Front and the Göring Institute that arose both from the DAF's bureaucratic imperialism and its boss's ambivalent organizational relationship with Hermann Göring. The Labor Front assumed formal supervision over the Göring Institute on September 30, 1939. While friction would eventually develop between the institute and the DAF, the psychotherapists' search for adequate funding was over. It was DAF money that allowed the institute to create divisions for the training of attending and consulting psychologists in 1939 and to amalgamate them with the training of physicians into an overall training division under Heyer in 1940. All attending psychologists, whose training we will investigate below, were required to be members of the Labor Front.[2] By 1940 the institute had expanded to ten divisions: administration (Göring), management (Scherke), literature (Bilz/Achelis), *Weltanschauung* (Achelis), training (Heyer), criminal psychology (Kalau vom Hofe), educational counseling (König-Fachsenfeld), expert opinion and catamnesis (Boehm), outpatient clinic (Schultz), and there were plans for a division for industrial psychology. As a result of this growth, the institute had to take on fourteen new employees, including two domestics, bringing the total in 1940 to sixteen; in 1941 the number of employees climbed to nineteen. By the summer of 1941 the institute had also completed a move from its expanded offices at Budapester Strasse 29, which it had occupied since April 1, 1937, to still larger premises at nearby Keithstrasse 41. Ernst Göring recollected that his father, parsimonious by nature, felt compelled to halve the salaries proposed by the DAF and rejected the provision of automobiles for official use of the institute's directors. At the 1940 German General Medical Society congress Göring expressed a justified appreciation to the Labor Front, an organization that in 1939 took in RM 539 million, more than three times the income of the NSDAP itself: "Herr Dr. Ley has recognized how important depth psychology is, not only in medicine but for all segments of life, especially the economy. He has made it possible for our institute to be well financed, for which we thank him most heartily."[3]

In 1939 the psychotherapists also published a special issue of the *Zentralblatt* containing essays selected from that year's volume that reflected their new organizational affiliation and orientation. The four articles all had in common a concern with the application of psychotherapy to social and industrial problems: Scheunert on short-term therapy, Göring's essay on psychotherapy and insurance (see chapter 9), and two new contributors, Hans Kellner and Hans Meyer-Mark, on the factory physician and psychotherapy and neurosis and the economy, respectively. The institute was not starting from scratch in this endeavor, however. Industrial psychologists like Meyer-Mark, Felix Scherke, August Vetter, Erika Hantel, and Gustav Schmaltz were already professionally active within industrial circles and with the help of the Göring name they established working relationships with various large firms. Scherke, who came to the Göring Institute by way of the Institute for Consumption Research in Nuremberg, had especially extensive contacts, including with the huge dye trust, I. G. Farben.[4]

Vetter, who headed the Göring Institute's psychological testing division in the outpatient clinic from 1939 to 1945, became a consultant for I. G. Farben in 1940 through an arrangement made by his eminent teacher and friend, Gustav Kafka.[5] The firm even sent Vetter to Sweden in 1942 to give a series of lectures on German diagnostic testing. Meyer-Mark cultivated, according to Hantel, a number of important industrial contacts, particularly in textiles.[6] Hantel herself, who had studied with Heyer in Munich, Viktor von Weizsäcker at Heidelberg, and Ernst Jaensch at Marburg, was a consultant, along with Wilhelm Bitter, at the Robert Bosch electrical works in Stuttgart during 1939 and from 1942 until the end of the war she was chief psychologist at the Arado aircraft works in Brandenburg-Neuendorf just west of Berlin.[7] Schmaltz, a member of the Düsseldorf affiliate, was himself the owner of a machine tool factory and was prominent within a modest segment of the industrial leadership of the Ruhr. He was director of the Technical Group for Woodworking Machines of the Economic Group for Mechanical Engineering.[8]

The relationship of the Göring Institute to the Labor Front arose from more than joint technical interest in industrial psychology and the Nazi bias toward harnessing expertise to expedite Hitler's policies. The Labor Front, like the Nazi movement and regime as a whole, placed an inordinate emphasis on the power of political conviction, the national will, and the consequent mission of party organizations to educate the people in the spirit of heroic sacrifice for the state. Where education failed, of course, terror or the pervasive threat of terror, would be used. This was particularly the case with the German working class, which Hitler and the Nazis regarded as a major contributor to Germany's decline in the twentieth century. The perceived collapse of the home front as the cause for German defeat in the First World War obsessed Hitler in particular. He wanted at all costs to avoid a repeat of it in the course of his war for world domination. The Nazis tried to preempt wartime rebelliousness on the part of the workers over wages, working hours, or trade union autonomy by using a fusion of terror, racial rhetoric, and the sop—or promise—of consumer goods even far into the war. There is evidence to suggest that the Nazis were also aiming for a total war economy that sacrificed living standards. Even before the war, it seems that living standards were declining for most Germans and that consumer goods varied widely in quality and quantity.[9] Moreover, as we have already seen, the Nazis could rely on a certain degree of working-class quiescence and even support. Nevertheless, while in the latter stages of the war the Nazis opted increasingly for terror, in 1939 and 1940 at least there was a real, though only partially successful, attempt to reproduce the perceived utopia of the patriotic solidarity of 1914 by both material and psychological means.

Ley's Labor Front was at the forefront of this effort. Beyond the social anodyne of the Strength through Joy (Kraft durch Freude) program—modeled on fascist Italy's Dopo Lavóro—with its cruises, vacations, and unfulfilled promises of Volkswagens, however, there was also cynical rhetoric and false assurances papering over Hitler's designs for aggression.[10] The Labor Front itself, a far cry under Ley from even the shallow "National Socialism" of the departed Strasser brothers, emphasized "adjustment" (*Ausgleich*) over "struggle" (*Kampf*), reflecting the typical fascist striving after a superficial and hierarchic harmony of classes in place of the sharp, issue-oriented uncertainties of genuine social change.[11] Ley did attempt throughout the war to formulate policies that would create a postwar social welfare state for the "Master Race."[12] But these unrealized plans ran up against the greater Nazi emphasis—even necessarily within the DAF itself—on military conquest and industrial productivity. They also foundered from the beginning of the Third Reich on the byzantine power struggles within the Nazi leadership and the resistance of employers and the state bureaucracy.[13]

Between 1936 and 1939 Ley and the DAF plumped for industrial productivity as part of a campaign against Minister of Economics Hjalmar Schacht, a sharp critic of Ley. Schacht rightly saw that Ley's offensive was based on the political considerations of personal power and the mobilization of labor, not on sound economics. Ley was in a rather strong position since the unemployment that had plagued Germany in the early 1930s had given way to shortage of labor, especially among skilled workers. Ley could thus use a demand for higher wages and better working conditions as a means to solidify DAF control over the labor force. He moved quickly to extend his realm and his power. Most significantly, he sought to ally with Hermann Göring, who as Plenipotentiary for the Four-Year Plan was emerging as the overseer of the war economy Schacht so strenuously opposed on fiscal grounds.[14] The DAF chief saw in Göring's incipient ascendancy in the economic realm a wedge by which that sector of German life could be pried loose from its traditional moorings and brought under the care and control of National Socialism as administered by the Labor Front. For example, the increased demand for skilled industrial labor occasioned by Germany's remilitarization prompted the Labor Front to try to gain control over the training of young workers. This intruded directly into one of the spheres of competence exercised by Schacht's ministry. Schacht went straight to Göring to complain, and then to Hitler, whom Ley had temporarily swayed in his direction. The upshot was that although Schacht prevented the DAF from taking complete control of vocational training, he was unable to force the closure of the Labor Front office for such matters in general.

Göring was unwilling to accommodate Schacht in this regard because the director of the DAF's Office for Vocational Training and Works Management, Karl Arnhold, had convinced him that his program would accelerate the training of apprentices and alleviate a scarcity of skilled labor that by 1937 had become especially worrisome.[15] At the end of 1936 Arnhold's office by its own count supervised over 400 training workshops, with an additional 150 under construction. These workshops were staffed by about 25,000 instructors and had been visited by approximately 2.5 million workers.[16] The Labor Front also introduced occupational preference guides (*Berufsfindungsmethode*) into schools and youth groups to steer individuals toward appropriate jobs, thus ostensibly avoiding later problems of maladjustment and supplementing the professional education programs built into the factories themselves. Arnhold claimed that by 1940 four million men and women had voluntarily taken part in these programs.[17]

The Göring Institute would come to work closely with Arnhold's office not only because of Ley's desire to attach himself parasitically to the Göring edifice but also as a direct consequence of Hermann Göring's admiration for Arnhold's work.[18] Arnhold was an engineer by training and a professor at a technical college in Dresden. In 1926 he had founded the German Institute for Industrial Training, or DINTA. DINTA was sponsored by German heavy industry under the leadership of Albert Vögler, chairman of the board of newly created German steel cartel, Vereinigte Stahlwerke. The Nazis coordinated DINTA, renaming it the German Institute for National Socialist Technical Industrial Research and Training and in 1936 Arnhold became head of the Labor Front's vocational training office. By 1940 he was also ministerial director of the division for Vocational Training and Productivity in the Economic Ministry, an office established under now Reich Marshal Göring's Four-Year Plan. In these capacities Arnhold was able to continue with the work he had begun before 1933. In establishing DINTA, he had given organizational expression to his concern over the shrinking profits of German industry in spite of all the reorganization, rationalization, and beckoning internal and external markets of the latter half of the 1920s. The reason for this lag, according to Arnhold, was twofold. First was the materialism of workers encouraged by a socialist government and the trade unions. Second were employers more concerned with technology and finance than with leadership. What was needed in the factory, Arnhold argued, was a sense of community, of joy in one's creative and productive labor, as well as discipline and a sense of duty. Education, recreation, and martial order at work and play were the things that would restore German productivity, Arnhold thought.[19]

These ideas were in line with Vögler's emphasis on the "human factor" as a challenge to nineteenth-century materialism, liberalism, and Marxism. Such an outlook, especially when Arnhold placed it in the context of 1919, "as we confronted the task of overcoming the material advantage of other nations through the quality of German men,"[20] was very attractive to those within the Nazi party and the Labor Front who thought in terms of racial and national character and comradeship (*Kameradschaft*). In sponsoring DINTA's program of vocational training, which by 1933 was operating in over 350 industries in Germany, Arnhold, who was not a party member, called for an end to the patriarchal factory system in favor of an industrial brotherhood of management and labor. Rationalization, whether in the Western capitalist style of Frederick Jackson Taylor's motion studies or in the Soviet style of Stakhanovism, could never, he believed, achieve the productivity lying dormant within the blood of the "soldierly" German *Volk*.[21] At the same time, Arnhold's emphasis on technical interventions also reflected the influence Western, and especially American, technocratic ideas had on German industry before and after 1933.[22]

Robert Ley was alluding to Arnhold's work when he maintained that health was 90 percent of the social question, that productivity was the sign of health, and that war was the test as well as the assurance of Germany's struggle for existence.[23] His widely purveyed contention put an enormous emphasis not only on the physical resources of the German working population, but on its putative psychological strengths as well. The proper combination of worker and machine, for one thing, rested on an understanding of the human psyche, an accurate assessment rendered more attractive to the Nazis through its trust in the qualitative powers of German will over and above the harder and more tangible coordinates of technology and numerical superiority. Beyond its general avoidance of the issues of social conflict and class interest, it was this apparent solution to some of the labor problems facing Germany's rearmament program that moved Hermann Göring to praise Arnhold's activities at the inaugural meeting of the Reich Defense Council, which he chaired, on November 18, 1938.[24]

In addition to conferences with the DAF Office for Health and Popular Protection, the Göring Institute worked closely with Arnhold's Office for Vocational Training and Works Management. For example, the institute's program for consulting psychologists reportedly was established in consultation with Arnhold's DAF organization.[25] During 1939 and early 1940 there were also a number of lectures given at the institute by industrial psychologists, including one by party member Albert Bremhorst, who headed the DAF Office for Vocational Training and Works Management while Arnhold was serving in the military.[26] Heyer could thus accurately boast that the "DAF has recognized that the economy as well is constituted by men with souls."[27] Meyer-Mark, echoing Heyer, proclaimed the necessity of psychotherapy taking the place of religion in maintaining the spiritual strength of the populace in order to guarantee a healthy economy.[28]

Arnhold himself was typically more prosaic in an address to the third and last congress of the German General Medical Society for Psychotherapy in Vienna in 1940. He outlined three necessary components of industrial psychology in the Third Reich: the political environment, psychotherapy, and psychological hygiene and psychotechnology.[29] This congress, with papers by society representatives from Italy, Japan, and Sweden and participants, it was claimed, from Chile, Denmark, China, Switzerland, and Hungary,[30] was dedicated to the theme of "Psyche and Productivity." The Japanese presenter, Nikiti Okumura, was unable to attend because the Soviets refused him a visa to travel through Russia.[31] Aside from comprising part of the Axis alliance within European psychotherapy, the Japanese work on the psychotherapeutic applications of Eastern philosophy, particularly the "Morita system" of rest, encouragement, and work, constituted an area of longstanding interest for the German psychotherapists.[32] The congress also marked an effort at cooperation between German psychotherapists and Italian pedagogical psychologists with an address by Ferruccio Banissoni of the University of Rome. Banissoni's appearance in Vienna paved the way for formal meetings between Italian and German psychologists and psychotherapists in Rome and Milan in June 1941. The eighteen-member German delegation was led by psychologist Oswald Kroh and included three military psychologists as well as Göring and Hattingberg. The meetings were presided over by Agostino Gemelli, president of the branch for applied psychology of the Italian National Council for Research.[33] In his report to the Reich Education Ministry, however, Kroh complained that psychology in Italy was held back by the tradition of idealistic philosophy in the universities; the only route for psychology was through medicine.[34] Out of these meetings was supposed to come an international congress for psychology in Rome in 1942 dedicated to industrial psychology, which in the end never took place.[35]

In 1941 the DAF Office for Vocational Training and Works Management founded its own Institute for Work Psychology and Work Pedagogy. The DAF institute projected a 7 to 8 percent increase (with a maximum of 20 percent in exceptional cases) in productive capacity in the cases handled. Preventive efforts were the task of three Reich Schools for Work Guidance: at Windlingen outside Vienna, at Augustusburg near Chemnitz, and in Berlin, which together, according to DAF figures, had trained a total of 1725 workers by 1938.[36] But while morale and productivity among German workers in general remained relatively high both before and during the war, the Labor Front's efforts in this regard could not begin to compensate for the acute physical and psychological strain on German labor. The Göring Institute was also directly involved in these efforts, however. Its division for industrial psychology planned to establish a study group to develop characterological tests for the DAF institute and actually collaborated in the practical application of such testing in three large industrial concerns near Berlin. In addition, with the help of Meyer-Mark, Arnhold had set up a model textile factory that employed an industrial psychologist from the Göring Institute.[37] During the war Göring proposed a research project on the psychology of foreign workers, especially those from eastern Europe, a subject of concomitant interest within the DAF.[38] Finally, drawing upon their own contacts in industry, the psychotherapists as late as 1944 planned a conference on industrial psychology at an I. G. Farben leisure hostel (*Freizeitheim*) near Heidelberg.[39]

The industrial psychologists of the Göring Institute brought to this realm their emphasis on repair of the productive individual in his or her specific work environment. Their view was that, in the event of a problem, work assignments were not to be gratuitously changed or work loads immediately lightened; psychologists, employers, and Nazi rulers also agreed, of course, that a pension was only to be a last resort. The cause of the difficulty was to be examined through the personal as well as the professional involvement of the psychologist in the individual's problem. According to the psychologists, most accidents were not the result of inadequate workplace safety measures but rather due to an improper inward orientation on the part of the injured worker. Education and testing therefore had to supplement therapy and counseling. This approach, with its emphasis on productivity and rehabilitation, underlined the responsibility of the individual to the state and also served the aims of industrial management by putting the burden of healthy and safe performance on the individual worker. The Hermann Göring Works in the former Austria were supposed to be particularly advanced in having applied this policy to prevention and rehabilitation.[40]

During the war, Ernst Kretschmer even weighed in from semi-retirement in Marburg with a pitch for his theory of constitutional personality types. In an article in a regional newspaper in 1944, Kretschmer argued that the DAF had the right idea in fitting the individual worker to the job by means of psychological evaluation. He noted that while race was a relevant factor in measuring human potential, character types cross racial lines. The Japanese, Kretschmer observed, were a particularly good example of this fact. The DAF itself had in fact discovered this in its own studies of foreign workers in Germany.[41] Kretschmer concluded that it is crucial for a society to do the same for its healthy members as its sick ones, that is, to engage actively in diagnosis, prognosis, and treatment.[42] Around the same time, one of Kretschmer's close colleagues at Marburg published a similar piece insisting on the duty to health and productivity.[43] These views were in line with Nazi policy even late in the war when threats against shirkers were accompanied with calls for the psychological cultivation of the will to work.[44] They were also in harmony with requests like the one Göring received from Conti for articles from psychotherapists on "psychological hygiene" for the daily press.[45]

The same pragmatic and productivist concern with the psychological dynamics of will and work was behind DAF involvement in the establishment of training for nonmedical "attending psychologists" at the Göring Institute. The term itself was first used in 1938, but questions about the legal and professional status of such lay psychotherapists had emerged with the founding of the institute in 1936. Numerous extended discussions were held with the party's Bernhard Hörmann on whether nonmedical psychotherapists should be regarded as health practitioners. It was finally decided, however, that they would be organized as an independent branch of the DAF Office for National Health. The Interior Ministry had also taken part in these deliberations and had determined that the psychologists should be included under the law governing medical assistants. This solution was satisfactory to the psychotherapists, since they regarded the official recognition, control, and practice of lay psychotherapy as necessary to the growth of the profession within medicine and to society's maintenance of mental health. They also did not wish to see the psychologists shunted off into the still suspect realm of natural medicine.[46] The passage of the Health Practitioners Law in 1939 still led to some confusion among psychotherapists, however. Both August Aichhorn and Lucy Heyer-Grote applied for registration as health practitioners, even though Aichhorn opined that his duties did not place him under the authority of the law since as an attending psychologist and a member of the Göring Institute he practiced in close cooperation with physicians.[47]

Because the psychotherapists at the Göring Institute also insisted that the work of the attending psychologists be supervised by physicians, the application by the Interior Ministry of the law governing medical assistants was preferable in terms of both professional standards and status.[48] This particular issue, as we shall see in chapter 14, was to be another postwar point of controversy between the psychiatrists around Kretschmer and the psychotherapists emerging from the ruins of the wartime institute. In any case, because of the war no official guidelines for attending psychologists were issued by the Interior Ministry. In the interim the psychologists were to follow the general guidelines for physicians laid down in the law in 1937. Although by 1941 attending psychologists belonged to the DAF's Special Office for Free Professions, any genuine professional status in the form of the establishment of a set of professional regulations (*Berufsordnung*) was not regarded by the Interior Ministry as important to the war effort.[49]

But the ministry also exempted attending psychologists, "as members of a health profession," from war work.[50] The ministry requested only that the Göring Institute stop accepting women for training as attending psychologists so that they could be spared for more important work as youth leaders and operating room nurses.[51] This whole process revealed not only the conservative medical bias of the Interior Ministry's perspective but a general ministerial concern with arrangement and order in place of reform or any wrestling with substantive issues.

The Interior Ministry had also stipulated that attending psychologists must have a university degree, but that in cases where exceptional professional performance and experience (e.g., state-approved teachers) were in evidence, applicants without degrees could receive ministerial permission for admission to the training program.[52] All nonmedical ordinary candidates received special training in medical subjects and also undertook a training analysis of at least 150 hours; extraordinary candidates had only to complete at least 100 hours of their own psychotherapy or psychoanalysis. On completion of training, the title of "attending psychologist" was conferred on the basis of temporary guidelines set down by the Interior Ministry. In addition to having to work with a physician in practicing as a psychotherapist, the attending psychologist was not permitted to prepare expert opinions or to appear in court as an expert witness. The institute, however, declared its readiness to supply experts for these purposes in cases in which attending psychologists were involved. The psychologists were permitted to place their title on their doorplates and stationery and, in appropriate instances, to place there as well their affiliation with the German Institute for Psychological Research and Psychotherapy. Like physicians, attending psychologists were prohibited from advertising and were sworn to maintain professional confidentiality.[53] And, as we saw in chapter 9, the institute had succeeded in arranging some private insurance coverage for psychotherapy carried out by attending psychologists. This formal expansion of psychotherapy outside the ranks for physicians was part of a general trend. In every year of its existence for which there are statistics (1937–41) except 1938, nonmedical members outnumbered physicians at the Göring Institute and by 1941 nonmedical candidates for certification as attending psychologists outnumbered medical candidates.

Even greater progress was made on the question of state certification of academic psychologists. On June 16, 1941, the Education Ministry issued instructional guidelines and ordinances for the training and state examination for a diploma in psychology. The certification of psychologists followed from the efforts of academic psychologists to promote the field as well as from the demand for applied psychology in industry and the armed forces. As the psychotherapists sought control of all practitioners in the realm of medical psychology, a number of leading academic psychologists complemented this effort and sought to exploit the prestige of the Göring Institute. Both Göring, who in 1941 became an editor of the *Zeitschrift für angewandte Psychologie,* and Heyer participated in a series of discussions about developing the standards for certification of psychologists. These discussions took place at the Göring Institute and included prominent university psychologists such as Oswald Kroh of Munich, editor of the *Zeitschrift für Psychologie,* Phillip Lersch of Cottbus, and Friedrich Sander of Jena. General Hans von Voss and army psychologist Max Simoneit were also involved, along with DAF representatives Albert Bremhorst and Carl Alexander Roos, Walter Stets from the Labor Ministry, and educational psychologist Arthur Hoffmann of Cottbus.[54]

The new regulations, retroactively in force from April 1, 1941, required students seeking certification as psychologists to be examined in the general psychology of the conscious and unconscious life of the individual and the community; in developmental psychology; in characterology and hereditary psychology; in the psychology of expression (*Ausdruckspsychologie*); in "biological-medical auxiliary sciences"; and in philosophy and ideology.[55] The applicant was further required to complete an internship at one of a number of types of approved institutions. Included in the list were homes and educational advisory boards run by the NSV, primary and secondary schools, advisory boards connected with the state labor exchange, training and apprenticeship facilities in industry and trade, psychological installations of the Labor Front, reformatories, psychotherapeutic advisory boards, psychiatric and related clinics, racial hygiene advisory boards, and geopolitical institutes.[56] A few certified psychologists sought postgraduate specialization in medical psychology at the Göring Institute.[57] The institute did not require the degree for its nonmedical candidates, but did prefer it over other university degrees and considered making it a requirement.[58]

The regulations for state certification of psychologists did not go without challenge, however. The fact that a capacity for medicine was included in the examinations reflected the ignorance and rhetoric that characterized much of the Nazi attempt to mobilize Germany's resources. Awed by experts and guided as well by their own designs for Germany, the Nazis thought and acted in a broad manner that was, in this case, agreeable to both the academic psychologists and the psychotherapists. But the arrogation of a medical function for psychologists aroused a storm of protest from psychiatrists, who were apparently taken by surprise by the breadth of professional capacity spelled out in the new regulations. Max de Crinis, with the support of colleagues Ernst Rüdin, Otto Wuth, Paul Nitsche, and Oswald Bumke, launched a counterattack from inside the Education Ministry itself. Through de Crinis psychiatrists and neurologists protested that they could not be expected, as the regulations envisioned, to teach, examine, and present patients to mere laypersons. More important, the psychiatrists asserted, they could not countenance the official creation of a group of half-educated medical dilettantes.[59] As a result of this campaign, in 1942 Education Minister Bernhard Rust, in an unpublished directive, quietly deleted from the regulations the adjective "medical" in the phrase "biological-medical auxiliary sciences," struck out the provision for practical experience on psychotherapeutic advisory boards and in psychiatric clinics, and removed the words "psychiatrist" and "neurologist" from the composition of the examination committees.[60]

With the exception of medicine, it is difficult to determine exactly what "biological auxiliary sciences" might have meant, but it is clear that the psychiatrists triumphed in formally divesting the certified psychologist to any claim to the practice of scientific medicine as the psychiatrists understood it. The requirement for medical capacity could be quietly dropped from the regulations since they contained no specific provisions concerning the *practice* of psychology in medicine. Neither the bureaucrats nor the academic psychologists were ready for the licensing of full clinical psychologists because from the beginning both were more concerned with the application of psychological methods and expertise in education, industry, and the military than with the more daunting task of confronting the medical profession in a battle over the educational and professional standards for the practice of medical psychology. As a result, on March 22, 1943, the Education Ministry announced the recognition of four areas of specialization for certified psychologists: educational psychology, vocational psychology, industrial psychology, and business psychology.[61]

Even though the Göring Institute insisted on medical supervision of nonmedical psychotherapists under the 1939 Interior Ministry regulations governing medical assistants, psychiatrists like de Crinis saw this as a wide breach in the walls surrounding the practice of medicine. Through this breach would pour the great unwashed of ill-trained medical personnel. As if there had not been ample reason to do so before, the academic psychiatrists now regarded the operations of the Göring Institute and the suddenly aggressive and successful efforts of the university psychologists as a dangerous precedent that boded ill for the future direction of psychology in medicine. By 1944, de Crinis would have to change tactics to meet this threat. Instead of insisting, as he did in 1941, that psychiatrists and neurologists be relieved of the duty of helping train psychologists, de Crinis would propose providing such candidates with courses in psychiatry and psychopathology. In other words, when faced with the *fait accompli* of a significant degree of official recognition for psychologists, psychiatrists were forced to launch a professional counteroffensive rather than continue to rely purely on the defensive advantage of an established position. In recommending this course to his medical opposite number in the Interior Ministry, Gustav Frey, de Crinis seemed to be worried specifically about renewed efforts by the Education Ministry to give psychologists some measure of legally recognized competence in psychotherapy: "No dilettantism," he wrote Frey, "can be tolerated in this field. This would be the case if—as intended—a share of psychotherapy (depth psychology) were to be handed over to the psychologist."[62] By no means, de Crinis continued, should certified psychologists have anything to do with medicine—that is, with the practice of psychotherapy. Furthermore, it was his firm opinion that expert testimony from psychologists should not be introduced in court cases alongside the extant testimonial capacity of psychiatrists. With an eye to exploiting the wartime decline in interest on the part of the military in applied psychology (see chapter 12), de Crinis also pointed out that the actual need for certified psychologists was so small that all the fuss over professional recognition on the part of "these so-called practical psychologists" was groundless.[63]

De Crinis's concerns testify to the flux within the realms of medical psychology endemic to the era and to the power and influence of the

Göring Institute. In the long run, as we shall see in chapter 14, the 1941 regulations would help lead to a professional advantage for university psychologists. Even before the war there was evidence of debate between German psychotherapists and psychologists over the relative therapeutic virtues of medical and psychological training.[64] There was also some concern expressed over the competition represented by academic psychologists to the psychodynamic approach of the psychotherapists.[65] In any case, in this way as well the Göring Institute represented the most significant challenge to psychiatry's increasingly tattered claim to sovereignty over the medical treatment of mental disorders. This was dangerously clear to de Crinis and his colleagues, and the collaboration on pragmatic grounds of university psychologists like Kroh with the Göring Institute only underscored this fact. Whatever the guidelines for medical assistants and for the certification of psychologists did or did not say with respect to the practice of medicine, established psychologists at the Göring Institute like Hantel, Heyer-Grote, and Kurt Seelmann, among others, exercised a largely independent competence in psychotherapy that made them seem anything but mere medical assistants. In addition, as we have seen, the role of psychology in education was also intimately related to the psychotherapeutic care of children, as the 1943 specialization guidelines indicated through the inclusion of therapeutic pedagogy.[66]

The psychiatrists were also constrained to continue the organizational dance with the psychotherapists in which both partners struggled to lead. In 1940 psychiatrist Paul Schröder of Leipzig founded the German Society for Child Psychiatry and Medical Pedagogy as a companion organization to the older Association for the Care of Juvenile Psychopaths. The founding of this new group had two purposes. The first, mirrored clearly in the names of the new and old organizations, was to help psychiatry escape from the literal dead end of Nazi eugenics. The second purpose was to assert psychiatric control over realms of repair claimed by an autonomous psychotherapy. Schröder himself had been an early advocate of psychoanalysis becoming one of the psychiatrist's tools. At the first congress of the new society he combined both purposes in his observation that the traditional interest of psychiatrists in the boundaries shared by medicine with education and therapy had been given an added urgency by the Nazi concern with productivity.[67] The Society of German Neurologists and Psychiatrists, for its part, tried to gather both groups under its wing so as to reassert the primacy of psychiatry in general in the field of mental health and medical therapeutics. In the spring of 1941 Rüdin, the president of the society and head of its psychiatric division, sought, together with the Interior Ministry's Herbert Linden, to organize a meeting in Munich on the subject of psychotherapy. Besides Rüdin, the participants were to include Göring, Kretschmer, Schultz, and de Crinis. The meeting apparently never took place, but a conference earlier in the year in Berlin showed that the old-school psychiatrists who ran the Society of German Neurologists and Psychiatrists felt themselves increasingly threatened by the psychotherapists' monopolistic claim to therapeutic competence. At this meeting of May 10 chaired by Herbert Linden of the Ministry of the Interior, Göring and Rüdin squared off, with the former arguing that psychotherapy was related to all medical disciplines, especially internal medicine and pediatrics, and the latter asserting that psychotherapy was a matter for psychiatrists.[68] The correspondence from the planning of the Munich meeting also displayed the same disagreements and tensions. Rüdin, noting his conversations with Göring, stressed to a Berlin associate that psychiatry must spare no effort to remain in charge of medical psychotherapy. In light of this necessity, Rüdin went on, the society had to tread carefully in the conflict between Kretschmer and Göring over the direction the professional affairs of psychotherapy should take (see chapter 5).[69]

Rüdin obviously hoped that his society would grandly incorporate all the professional groups dealing with psychotherapy. As a first step in such a process, he proposed the holding of joint congresses. The first of these gatherings of psychotherapists, psychologists, psychiatrists, and neurologists was planned for 1941 in Würzburg. Rüdin remarked that Kretschmer, who referred to the psychotherapists under Göring as "the remains of a psychotherapeutic society," could help reliably introduce psychotherapy into the university curriculum and direct the affairs of psychology and constitutional pathology within the psychiatric society. Rüdin also assured Nitsche that, as members of the executive committee, Göring and Kretschmer could keep undesirable psychotherapists out of the Society of German Neurologists and Psychiatrists.[70] Nitsche, the managing director of the society from 1935 to 1939, responded that the organization of discussions of psychotherapy at the 1941 congress must give witness to the "unconditional preponderance" of the psychiatric point of view.[71] The plans for the Würzburg congress, which never took place because of wartime exigencies, specified that the gathering was open only to physicians. The sessions on its basic theme of psychotherapy were indeed structured in such a way as to make it appear that the treatment and cure of mental disorders were a task that was exclusive to the psychiatric profession. Following a first day to be devoted almost nostalgically to military psychiatry and brain injury, Carl Schneider of Heidelberg was to report on the therapy of endogenous psychoses; five psychotherapists from the Göring Institute were to lecture in the context of reports on suggestion and training by Kretschmer and Schultz. But these presentations were to be buried among contributions from twenty-seven psychiatrists and neurologists.[72]

The German Society for Child Psychiatry and Medical Pedagogy was also to hold its own, second, congress in Würzburg in October, on the heels of the psychiatrists' gathering. The timing was the result of an agreement between Rüdin and Schröder, both of whom were concerned about the growing number of nonmedical members of Schröder's group. In July Rüdin had averred darkly to Linden that Göring was seeking to take over Schröder's society in order to leave the psychiatrists without an organizational or professional claim to therapeutic capacity. In Vienna in 1940 Göring had in fact announced that the first congress of the German Society for Child Psychiatry and Medical Pedagogy was being held jointly with the third congress of the German General Medical Society for Psychotherapy.[73] The truth of the matter is difficult to determine, since the Schröder psychiatrists and teachers met on September 5, the psychotherapists on the sixth and seventh. The official report of the former group made no mention of the psychotherapists' congress, a silence that revealed the Schröder group's desire to avoid being overshadowed or coopted by an aggressive organization of practitioners they considered their professional inferiors.[74] Göring's announcement, on the other hand, seems to evidence precisely the motive ascribed to Göring by Rüdin.

Thus, it was primarily professional rivalry with newly mobilized psychotherapists that inspired Rüdin's loyal May 1941 assertion to Hans Reiter, the president of the Interior Ministry's Reich Health Office and a friend to the Göring psychotherapists, that the efforts toward a common congress of the three groups represented an efficient and *völkisch* attempt at unifying group resources for the "care and control of the central nervous system" (*"Betreuung des Zentralnervensystems"*).[75] Certainly, in any case, numbers at least were in the psychiatrists' favor. The Society of German Neurologists and Psychiatrists counted around 800 members as against the much smaller number of organized psychotherapists and child psychiatrists. But the psychotherapists under Göring were not vulnerable on this score. The German General Medical Society had met for the last time in 1940, but even before then, with the wartime infusion of money from the Labor Front, the Göring Institute had become the locus of the psychotherapists' unprecedented professional status and capacity.

The early war years accelerated the trend toward the pragmatic for psychotherapy in the Third Reich. While the war brought radicalization of measures against national and racial enemies, the most vile of which was the Holocaust, for psychotherapists and others engaged in "productive" and "curative" tasks the war years brought increased demands from the regime and from themselves for results rather than rhetoric. Since National Socialist values in any case had always rested within the nimbus of subjectivity and shared experience, the tendency toward controlled manipulation, exploitation, utility, and mobilization spared practical and technical disciplines whose devaluations required much more than generally short-lived, half-hearted, and intellectually impoverished attempts at "Aryanization." Hitler's Germany demanded obedient productivity and judged a discipline in the end by its usefulness within the context of vague notions of inherent German racial superiority. As Alan Beyerchen has shown in the case of physicists, what ultimately concerned the Nazis was political opposition, not professional debate. The failure of "Aryan physics" was based on the inability of its proponents within the physics community to show Nazi leaders that their aims had practical benefits and that professional opposition to their theories and programs was a threat to the development of physics as a practical profession in service to the Reich. Indeed, what became clear was that the opposite was the case. The Nazis therefore contented themselves with tirades against "Jewish physics" and, as elsewhere, forcing Jews from their posts.[76]

In such an environment of technical supply and demand and amid the organizational superfluity of the Nazi state, party ideologues, as we have already seen in the case of Julius Streicher and Gerhard Wagner, were usually passed over. For example, in 1939 Kurt Seelmann, a young teacher and member of Seif's Adlerian circle in Munich, was being considered for promotion to the rank of senior master (*Hauptlehrer*), a rank he achieved in 1940. In the course of deliberations within the government and the party, the regional party education office produced an evaluation on May 19, 1939, that gushed approval.[77] Two years later, however, Seelmann was the subject of a more critical evaluation by an agency of the NSDAP. In 1941 the German Popular Education Service was planning a series of nationwide lectures on the preservation of mental health (*"seelische Gesunderhaltung"*) and Seelmann was to be one of the participants. The German Popular Education Service was a semi-independent part of the DAF's "Strength Through Joy" program that competed in modest fashion with Goebbels's propaganda empire. As early as 1935 Ernst Göring had given lectures on psychotherapy for this agency. However, on July 28, 1941, Alfred Rosenberg's NSDAP office for the oversight of "cultural-political" activities in Berlin requested the party leadership in Bavaria to evaluate Seelmann's suitability for such a role.[78] The response from Munich has not survived, but we might well assume that, as in the case of Seelmann's promotion, Bavaria, with traditional independence—or, from the Prussian point of view, a peculiarly particularistic and uniquely boorish and beery Bavarian cussedness—protested that there were no subversives active within its borders.[79] In any case, the final recommendation of the Rosenberg office on August 15, 1941 to the DAF agency was that Seelmann should not be invited to participate. Although, in the opinion of Rosenberg's office, there were no obvious political liabilities apparent in Seelmann's background (a member of the party affiliate for teachers, he had inquired about party membership),[80] his professional associations were suspect:

> He was . . . already working during the Weimar period with Leonhardt Seiff [*sic*], the Munich representative of Freudian-Adlerian psychoanalysis. He directed an educational counseling clinic that was abolished after the taking of power, since operations were conducted by the rule of individual psychology and psychoanalysis. Today the aforementioned Dr. Seiff has switched to *"Gemeinschaftspsychologie."* It is to be assumed, however, that Seelmann is still as before a prisoner to the former way of thinking.[81]

This example shows the persistence of Rosenberg's Nazi ideological fervor long after it had ceased even to appear to mean much of anything in many instances. Seelmann recalls that even though he had to be careful in delivering lectures occasionally monitored by Nazi informants, up to 1943 he regularly spoke in Munich and elsewhere in Germany for the German Popular Education Service and other groups.

Furthermore, the assertion that Seif's "Freudian-Adlerian" educational counseling clinic had been abolished in 1933 was inaccurate. As the evaluation itself admits, Seif had merely "switched" to "community psychology," a judgment that implies as much camouflage as artifice and so implicitly acknowledges a continuity of thought and action in spite of the Nazi seizure of power. The only genuine change in the clinic's status was its affiliation with the German General Medical Society for Psychotherapy in 1933, its association with the Göring Institute in 1936, and its combination with Heyer's group into a formal branch of the DAF institute in 1939. Seif himself had been cleared in like manner to Seelmann by the Nazi Teachers League and by the party's Main Office for National Health.[82] Moreover, a book of which Seif was the senior author and which described the operations of his educational counseling clinic was included in the Nazi bibliography.[83] All of this transpired in January of 1941, the same year in which Seelmann was being written off as an agent of Jewish thought by Rosenberg's organization. And in 1942 Seelmann published his first book, *Kind, Sexualität und Erziehung,* and it too was included in the Nazi bibliography. The book was essentially a popular guide to the prevention of psychological disorders through the proper parental, medical, and educational guidance of children by means of an understanding of childhood sexual development. The tiny abstract in the bibliography provided a final revealing utilitarian counterpoint to Rosenberg's ideological condemnation of Seelmann and Seif:

> This work stems from the experiences of the medical-psychological counseling office of the Munich *Nervenarzt* Dr. L. Seif and his associates and therefore champions the theoretical principles of that school. Without giving credence to the content in all its details, the book may be recommended as a practical aid for parents and educators.[84]

Like Seelmann's book, two books by Johannes Heinrich Schultz also included in the Nazi bibliography were also practical guides, one for the general public and the other for the general medical practitioner. *Geschlecht, Liebe, Ehe* (1941) was similar to Seelmann's work in content as well as form and the bibliography praised it for its "cautious introduction" to sex, love, and marriage in the context of race and nature (*Erbgebundenheit*).[85] *Die seelische Gesunderhaltung* (1942), based on a Schultz address to the press in January 1941, was recommended as a sound set of principles and guidelines for the practicing physician.[86] In this book as well Schultz in typical fashion once again took the opportunity to set firm—and professionally protective—limits to psychotherapy in conjunction with praise for Nazi eugenics.

Schultz, as we have observed before, was the prototype of the in-house pragmatist. As such, he was in his element during the war when the practical demands—and resultant financial support—for psychotherapy were reaching a peak. He was known around the institute as "*der kluge Hans*" ("the clever fellow") and it was typical of Schultz's continual balancing of personal and professional interests that he never joined the Nazi party but remained only a candidate (*Anwärter*) for membership. While he published regularly in the medical press, the two books of his included in the Nazi bibliography were published by firms—Reinhardt and Mittler—whose lists consistently toed the Nazi line. Moreover, they were printed in Gothic, or Germanic, script (*Bruchschrift*), a sure sign during the Third Reich of public devotion to the Nazi spirit. Both books, however, also promoted the professional work of the Göring Institute in the style of Schultz's longstanding commitment to an ecumenical balance between medicine and psychology. Schultz was everywhere in print on behalf of psychotherapy, most notably perhaps in 1943 in Goebbels's aspiring highbrow weekly paper, *Das Reich,* in 1943.[87] He was also the institute's director for continuing medical education, a means for proselytization among physicians. He had been active in the affairs of the Berlin Academy for Continuing Medical Education since 1924 and was an editor of an international journal for continuing medical education. In 1944 the academy in Berlin, where Schultz, Göring, Schultz-Hencke, and Hattingberg had lectured, listed a workshop on psychotherapy to be conducted by Schultz.[88]

But the single most striking indication of the trend toward the useful at the Göring Institute was the fate of what had enthusiastically been labeled "new German psychotherapy" in Article 2 of the Göring Institute's statutes. Of course, even such aims, to the small extent they were attained, were not just ideological in terms of the creation of a "German psychotherapy," they were also inherently practical in terms of promoting cooperation among psychotherapists for purposes of political protection and professional advance. Article 9 called for monthly meetings of all members of the institute, during which papers would be presented and discussions held on the unification of the three major schools of thought as well as on the cultivation of relationships with neighboring disciplines. Article 9 also required occasional meetings of each study group, the Adlerian, the Jungian, and the Freudian, to which members of the other groups would be invited to hear presentations on the host group's work. During 1936 the psychoanalytic group held three such meetings, at which in turn Luise Mitscherlich, Karen Horney, and Felix Schottlaender spoke. The Jungians presented a series of public lectures, two of which, as we saw in chapter 6, were given by Jung himself. The monthly meetings were called "triseminars," (*Dreier-Seminare*) since they were conducted by three instructors, one from each group (see Appendix 2). These were intended to vitiate and then eliminate the differences among the separate schools of thought. This was to be done in the rhetorical and substantive context of professional service to state and community, as Mohr put it at the Düsseldorf congress in 1938:

> In order that we may, as nearly as possible, attain this goal, to lead the many inherently valuable people back into our *Volksgemeinschaft* as active and sound members, to protect the healthy from illness and thus on the whole to contribute to *Volksgesundheit,* requires basic cooperation and not theoretical conflict.[89]

In 1938 a common training program was established to replace the separate curricula formerly maintained by the Freudians, Adlerians, and Jungians. This program was designed to produce a generation of psychotherapists who would be unencumbered by the prejudices and narrow perspectives of the past. Almost every veteran of the Göring Institute acknowledges that some good came from such enforced cooperation. In late 1944, for example, Freudian Kemper spoke to Jungian Schirren of the "balance of power" at the institute that had been upset with the departure of Heyer.[90] Of course no genuine unification ever came close to being realized. Göring, for all his nativist, parochial, and religious enthusiasm for a German psychotherapeutic consensus, had neither the vision nor the personality to carry through such an ambitious—indeed illusory—plan. Ironically, too, his very success in protecting and advancing psychotherapy did not allow him to pursue ideological or scientific purity. The autonomy of the institute granted by the Göring name meant that he did not have to exercise the broad censorship powers granted him within the society and the institute. At the same time, the very professional position attained by the psychotherapists meant that he could not risk political damage from outside forces through purges and expulsions.

According to Kemper, Göring ignored provocative remarks, as when at an institute meeting in 1942, Schultz-Hencke, in response to a questioning of his loyalty to the government by a psychotherapist who was a member of the Nazi party, declared that he was no National Socialist and would never be. Schultz-Hencke was further compromised—though not endangered—within the institute by a Jewish wife, as was the case for at least two other colleagues, August Vetter and Ludwig Zeise, who had Jewish wives.[91] According to secretary Ellen Bartens, around twenty to twenty-five Jews and half-Jews worked at the institute. Göring also apparently ignored the fact that Käthe Bügler, one of Heyer's students, was half-Jewish. As we have already seen, he apparently intervened on behalf of Müller-Braunschweig in the Vienna imbroglio of 1938 and he allegedly did the same for a Munich member of the institute who was accused by the Gestapo of child molestation in the treatment of several cases of bed-wetting. Göring also tolerated the possibly perilous fact for the institute that the director of the Vienna section of the institute was married to a half-Jew and in 1939 had been deprived of his Nazi party membership as a result. This in fact was not all that an anomalous event in Nazi Germany: Kogerer was granted a dispensation by Hitler and allowed to regain his party membership in 1941.[92]

The crippling loss of practitioners suffered by the psychoanalysts initially gave an advantage to the two other groups whose theories and representatives were supposed to form the core of a new German psychotherapy. But the loyalty to a school of thought that was cultivated by the intense personal and therapeutic nature of the training analysis helped render the curriculum as somewhat of a smorgasbord. Added to this was the notorious individuality of the psychotherapists and their often strident conflicts and feuds over doctrine and method. Käthe Dräger, who received her training in psychoanalysis at the Göring Institute, has recalled the pervasive feeling among the students that the triseminars were most often a windy waste of time and that it was more important to pursue one's professional training instead of tilting at professional windmills. Even Göring himself observed obliquely that in the triseminars the trend was not toward genuine unification of competing theories but rather toward a continuing process of communication that bore only the rudiments of true synthesis:

> [S]pecial value is placed during these evenings on simple formulations and the avoidance of technical terms such as Oedipus complex, Künkel's psychological concept of a "vicious circle" [*Teufelskreis*] and anima. I believe that—apart from

> our lectures—we have these seminars to thank for the fact that our young members and candidates can grow beyond the orthodox schools and can recognize the good as well as the partiality of these orientations.[93]

Apart from the triseminars, there was one other major attempt at a theoretical and practical synthesis of psychotherapeutic thought. This was a forty-one-page manuscript, "Thesen zur Neurosenlehre," written chiefly by Hattingberg, director of the research division, in late 1939 or early 1940. This draft document remained an amalgam of general German Romantic medical notions informed by professional opportunity in service to the Nazi state: neurosis was a disruption of the natural rhythm of the human organism and its active relationship with the whole; the family unit was to remain the basic expression of a natural balance and psychological well-being; the role of the psychotherapist was to be not that of a passive analyst in the Freudian tradition, but that of a spiritual guide; any member of the community who did not actively share in the collective *Weltanschauung* would eventually become unworthy and superfluous; and the healthy, productive individual would exercise virtues and ideals determined by his or her race, community, and own character acting in harmonious concert: "The healthy, perceptive person sees his honor in remaining true to his *Volk* and to himself."[94]

But this project was lamed from the start by what Hattingberg claimed was the poor response from institute members to his questionnaire regarding progress made in developing a common vocabulary and theory.[95] Although Kemper expressed amazement at how theoretically neutral the document appeared from his postwar perspective, these theses were not simply a nonprovocative theory of neurosis or, as Kemper maintained, intended simply as protection from the Nazis.[96] Hattingberg, at least in part, believed that psychotherapy had to respond to the *völkisch* assignment set it by the state through actually achieving the unification of theory and practice in psychotherapy. Not surprisingly, therefore, the unpublished manuscript also bore the distinct stamp of Hattingberg's own ideas. It is also further evidence of the sort of offhand and superficial synthesis that occurred under Göring's leadership in the Third Reich. This synthesis derived from Göring's outlook and character as well as from the eclecticism that prevailed within the general and specific intellectual traditions shared by German psychotherapists and psychoanalysts. Aside from their inherent conceptual limitations, the Göring Institute's half-baked theses toward a unified theory of neurosis, like the triseminars, floundered amid its members' more immediate professional interests and obligations, responsibilities that were given an even greater urgency with the onset of war and the institute's sudden wealth. Added to this was a perceptible dimming of the bright theoretical and political enthusiasm that had emanated from the early proponents of a "German" psychotherapy.

The *Zentralblatt* also reflected the wartime (re)turn to the practical demands of the discipline. In 1935, out of a combination of fear and loyalty, the titles of the journal's review categories had been changed from the technical to the Germanic: "Psychotherapie" became "Seelenheilkunde," "Psychologie" was changed to "Seelenkunde"; and "Physiologie" was rendered "Körper-Seelenhaushalt." At the end of 1936 the *Zentralblatt* became the official organ of the Göring Institute with Göring as co-editor. As a result, the category of "Psychoanalyse" disappeared and psychoanalytic works, when they were reviewed, appeared under "Depth Psychology" ("Tiefenpsychologie"). In the same year "Erbbiologie und Rassenkunde" was added. In 1939, however, the titles introduced in 1935 reverted to the originals and the only change after that came in 1941 with an expansion of the review categories that honestly reflected the institute's activities and the interests of psychotherapists dating back to the inception of the journal (e.g., child psychiatry, philosophy, ethnology, "unity of body, soul, and spirit"). While psychoanalysis did not reappear as a review category, psychoanalytic works continued to be reviewed, as with a long and positive review of neo-Freudian Karen Horney's *New Ways in Psychoanalysis* (1939). Even during the 1930s, more or less fair and sober reviews of works by Freud, Theodor Reik, Anna Freud, Ernest Jones, and Richard Sterba appeared, but in general orthodox Freudian works were ignored or dismissed. An example of the latter was this succinct critical eructation from Schultz on Sandor Lorand's article, "Hypnotic Suggestion" (1941): "Orthodox psychoanalytic gossip."[97] It was again a work of Horney's, *The Neurotic Personality of Our Time* (1937), that attracted the longest and most positive review, by Edgar Herzog. Even psychoanalyst Müller-Braunschweig, who was still officially *persona non grata,* published a long review of Josef Meinertz's *Psychotherapie: Eine Wissenschaft!* (1939) in 1941. Jung's Swiss associate, C. A. Meier, who had been ousted from his position as managing editor in 1940, published a review of Henry V. Dicks's *Clinical*

Studies in Psychopathology (1939) in 1942. And the institute's own Freudians of course could rely on proprietarily positive reviews, as in Schultz's praise for Kemper's study of sexual dysfunction in women placed immediately after his smug dismissal of Lorand.

What was true of psychotherapy's professional profile toward the outside was even more the case within the Göring Institute itself. The most significant indication of this was the growing influence of Freudians in the institute's work and the declining effect of the projected amalgam of Jungian and Adlerian concepts that were to have been the bedrock of a departure from "Jewish" psychoanalysis. Like other therapeutic means in the field, where Freud worked, Freud was used. Ernst Kris, a psychoanalyst who had fled from Austria, observed during the war that the German army and the Ministry of Propaganda incorporated a psychoanalytic perspective in their psychological work, unconcerned that Freud's works had been publicly burned in 1933. To be sure, Kris was making the general and partisan point that no psychology in the twentieth century could dispense with Freud. But the army did, as we shall see, refer to Freud. And although there is no evidence for any enthusiasm on the part of Goebbels for Freud, we do know that in 1940 Göring announced the existence of contacts with the Propaganda Ministry and, according to Johanna Herzog-Dürck, there was at least one institute meeting with representatives of Goebbels's ministry.[98]

The Freudians had of course been forced to sacrifice a great deal in order to have been allowed the protection of the Göring Institute. First, there was the expulsion and emigration of their many Jewish colleagues and it was the DPG that had originally provided the new institute with the building, the equipment, the library, the clinic, and at least some of the expertise necessary to utilize them. Freudians also assumed important roles in the institute. The large number of courses given by Freudians Schultz-Hencke and Kemper stood in revealing contrast to the fewer and fewer courses offered by such early fervent ideologues as Achelis, Bilz, Hattingberg, Heyer, and other, lesser lights (see Appendix 1). To be sure, the latter were involved in helping run the institute, the handling of private and clinical patients, and the business of research and publication. Heyer in particular was influential as director of training. But Freudians Schultz-Hencke and Kemper were also powerful influences.[99] As the years passed, Julius Schirren, Heyer, and Hattingberg, among others, continued to entertain various versions of the earlier and enthusiastically promoted Jungian tradition and continued to wield an influence on the course of study, but their importance bore no resemblance to that previously envisioned in terms of the value of Jung's "anthropological" depth psychology for a truly Germanic psychotherapy. At the same time, the departure of Fritz Künkel for America in 1939 left the Adlerians at the institute without their most dynamic representative.

This trend was not just the result of the relative merit and efforts of individuals, however. As will be exemplified in chapter 11, the somewhat mystical and contemplative orientation of Jung's thought was less useful than the neo-Freudian everyday therapeutic concerns of the psychoanalysts at the institute. The Jungians themselves often displayed this same detachment from the more mundane "real" world. When Göring was reshuffling the institute's administration in 1939, he complained to Otto Curtius that the Jungians in Berlin were not interested in assuming leadership positions.[100] Curtius replied that while Jungian thought would be appealing to Hitler himself, it tended to be theoretical rather than practical and also lacked a practical means of instruction.[101] Jung's teachings were largely relegated by virtue of their philosophical and religious orientation to the cultural realm, which held less immediate significance for the practical aims of Nazi policy and the psychotherapists' own professional goals. The psychoanalysts, spurred by peril as well as by opportunity, were particularly visible and active in the running of the outpatient clinic. And, like the other two "working groups," the Freudians kept up their own regular series of meetings and lectures.[102] Even Göring himself, who had been one of those most bitterly opposed to "Jewish psychoanalysis," gradually came around to tolerating and even accepting psychoanalysis by virtue of its theoretical and practical contributions to the work of his institute. According to Kemper, Göring's wife Erna, who had been a strong and dangerous defender of a Nazified psychotherapy, also came to appreciate and even admire psychoanalysis. She had been trained as a nurse and had met Göring while serving as an operating room nurse in Coblenz.[103] She was also a party member and a member of the Nazi Women's League, the Red Cross, and the NSV.[104] But she was analyzed by Kemper, during which sessions she allegedly passed on information from her husband regarding colleagues who were in proximate or immediate danger from the authorities.[105]

The initial war years, therefore, brought not only the reorganization and enrichment of the Göring Institute. They also witnessed an ongoing trend toward the pragmatic and functional unity in support of the regime in individual and collective pursuit of professional advancement. In spite—or rather because—of these developments, psychotherapists in the Third Reich also continued to confront competition and criticism from the German psychiatric establishment. But such opposition was as much an indication of the psychotherapists' professional success as a reminder of their limits. Their value to the Nazi regime as politically protected experts was to be evident, as we shall see in the next chapter, even on a most dangerous problem in the dark realm of the SS.

Notes

1. Friedrich Schulze-Maier, "Gesundheitspflege der Seele," p, 26; *Nationalsozialistische Bibliographie* 6:7/8 (July/August 1941), p. 31, entry 194.
2. Deutsches Institut für Psychologische Forschung und Psychotherapie, Richtlinien für die Ausbildung, p. 7.
3. Göring, "Eröffnungsansprache," in Bilz, *Psyche und Leistung,* p. 7. The old e.V. would continue to carry out small administrative duties under the direction of Secretary Boehm and Treasurer Müller-Braunschweig through the secretarial and bookkeeping offices, respectively of the new "DAF-Institute": "Jahresbericht 1940," p. 1; see also "Jahresbericht 1941," p. 62. On the inadequacy of the Budapester Strasse offices, see Göring, "Bericht," p. 4; and on DAF finances, see Timothy W. Mason, *Arbeiterklasse und Volksgemeinschaft: Dokumente und Materialen zur deutschen Arbeiterpolitik 1936–1939* (Opladen, 1975), p. 83; and Smelser, *Robert Ley,* pp. 161–2.
4. Felix Scherke, Lebenslauf, Berlin, November 4, 1936, BDC: Kulturkammer; Schultz, *Lebensbilderbuch,* p. 134.
5. August Vetter, "Testverfahren als Hilfsmittel der Psychologischen Diagnostik," *ZfP* 14 (1942): 41–6.
6. See Hans Kellner, "Querschnitt durch die wichtigsten körperlichen und seelischen Krankheiten bei weiblichen Textilarbeiterinnen," June 24, 1940, N 5 I/21, BA.
7. For case studies out of her experience during this time, see Erika Hantel, *Verborgenes Kräftespiel*; and Heyer, *Menschen in Not,* pp. 50–9.
8. *Wer Leitet? Die Männer der Wirtschaft und der einfachen Verwaltung* (Berlin, 1941), p. 100.
9. Eleanor Hancock, *The National Socialist Leadership and Total War, 1941–5* (New York, 1991), pp. 1–26.
10. Mason, *Arbeiterklasse,* pp. 1–16.
11. Broszat, *Hitler State,* pp. 145–6, 151; see also Schoenbaum, *Hitler's Social Revolution,* pp. 73–112.
12. Marie-Luise Recker, *Nationalsozialistische Sozialpolitik im Zweiten Weltkrieg* (Munich, 1985).
13. Matthias Frese, *Betriebspolitik im "Dritten Reich": Deutsche Arbeitsfront, Unternehmer und Staatsbürokratie in der westdeutschen Grossindustrie, 1933–1939* (Paderborn, 1991).

14. R. J. Overy, *Goering: The "Iron Man"* (London, 1984).
15. Mason, *Arbeiterklasse,* pp. 123–42; see also R. J. Overy, "The German Pre-War Aircraft Production Plans: November 1936–April 1939," *English Historical Review* 90 (1975): 792–3.
16. Mason, *Arbeiterklasse,* p. 93; Arthur Schweitzer, *Big Business in the Third Reich* (Bloomington, 1964), pp. 179–94; see also Willy Müller, *Das soziale Leben im neuen Deutschland,* pp. 164–9; and Otto Marrenbach, ed., *Fundamente des Sieges: Die Gesamtarbeit der deutschen Arbeitsfront von 1933 bis 1940,* 2nd ed. (Berlin, 1941), pp. 278–92.
17. Karl Arnhold, *Leistungsertüchtigung,* pp. 28–55.
18. Matthias Heinrich Göring, Antrag zur Errichtung und Finanzierung eines Reichsinstituts für Psychologische Forschung und Psychotherapie an der Universität Berlin, July 30, 1943, p. 1, RFR 107/12850, German Captured Documents/Reichsforschungsrat, Library of Congress.
19. Robert Brady, *The Spirit and Structure of German Fascism* (New York, 1937), pp. 161–74; Smelser, *Robert Ley,* pp. 189–92; Frese, *Betriebspolitik,* pp. 15–23, 125, n. 33; Franz Neumann, *Behemoth: The Structure and Practice of National Socialism* (New York, 1942), pp. 429–31; and Rolf Seubert, *Berufserziehung und Nationalsozialismus: Das berufspädagogische Erbe und seine Betreuer* (Weinheim, 1977), pp. 59–138; Joan Campbell, *Joy in Work, German Work: The National Debate,* 1800–1945 (Princeton, 1989), pp. 351–81; Viktor von Weizsäcker, "Über den Begriff der Arbeitsfähigkeit," *Deutsche medizinische Wochenschrift* 57 (1931): 1696–8; J. Ronald Shearer, "Talking About Efficiency: The German Experience in the Nineteenth and Twentieth Centuries," *Central European History* 28 (1995): 483–506; and Kathleen Canning, "Feminist History after the Linguistic Turn: Historicizing Discourse and Experience," *Signs* 19 (1994): 368–404.
20. Karl Arnhold, "Umrisse einer deutschen Betriebslehre," in idem, *Der Deutsche Betrieb,* p. 24.
21. Arnhold, *Leistungsertüchtigung,* p. 12; on DINTA, see "Arbeitswissenschaft im Dienst der Volksgemeinschaft," *NS Sozialpolitik* 1 (1934): 235–9.
22. Mary Nolan, *Visions of Modernity: American Business and the Modernization of Germany* (New York, 1994); Siegfried Jaeger, "Zur Herausbildung von Praxisfeldern der Psychologie bis 1933," in Mitchell G. Ash and Ulfried Geuter, eds., *Geschichte der deutschen Psychologie im 20. Jahrhundert: Ein Überblick* (Opladen, 1985), pp. 96–103.
23. E. Gründger, "Die Sicherung der Schaffenskraft: Aufbau und Aufgaben des DAF Amtes für Volksgesundheit," *Monatshefte für N.S. Sozialpolitik* 7 (1940): 9–11.
24. Mason, *Arbeiterklasse,* p. 918.
25. Edgar Herzog, "Arbeitsplan der Abteilung 'Beratende Psychologen'," p. 12; and Göring, "Bericht," p. 1.
26. Hans von Hattingberg, "Forschung und Bücherei," *ZfP* 14 (1942): 9. Arnhold reassumed his post until November 26, 1942, when Herbert Steinwarz took over. Arnhold claimed after the war that he had resigned his post because of personal differences with Ley; see Gerhard P. Bunk, *Erziehung und Industriearbeit: Modelle betrieblicher Lernens und Arbeitens Erwachsener* (Weinheim, 1972), p. 259, n. 3. Bremhorst could recall no dispute between Arnhold and Ley, while another of Arnhold's colleagues saw his dissociation from Ley as a prudent move in expectation of a Nazi defeat: Ulfried Geuter, personal communication, May 30, 1981. Whatever the truth with regard to

Arnhold's motives, it is reasonable to suppose that disenchantment and disillusionment with the increasingly flabby and stumbling Labor Front influenced his decision.

27. Gustav Richard Heyer, "Aus der psychotherapeutischen Praxis" (1940), p. 556.
28. Hans H. Meyer-Mark, "Neurotiker der Wirtschaft," p. 246.
29. Karl Arnhold, "Psychologische Kräfte im Dienste der Berufserziehung und Leistungssteigerung," in Bilz, *Psyche und Leistung,* pp. 105–27; see idem, "Arbeitspsychologie."
30. Bericht über den 3. Kongress für Psychotherapie, n.d., Kl. Erw. 762/2.
31. "Aktuelles," *ZfP* 12 (1940): 193; "Tätigkeitsbericht 1940," p. 4.
32. Nikiti Okumura, "Japanische Psychotherapie und Zen," in Bilz, *Psyche und Leistung,* pp. 183–205; Sohei Morita, "Der Begriff der Nervosität," *ZfP* 12 (1940): 38–53; Syûzô Naka, "Die Psychotherapie in Japan," in Curtius, *Psychotherapie in der Praxis,* pp. 144–7; and Werner Becker, "Die Psychotherapie in Japan," *Psychiatrisch-Neurologische Wochenschrift* 43 (1941): 60–1.
33. Matthias Heinrich Göring, "Aktuelles," *ZfP* 13 (1941): 130; see also Ferruccio Banissoni, "Leistungssteigerung durch psychische Energieentfaltung," in Bilz, *Psyche und Leistung,* pp. 128–55.
34. Kroh to Reichserziehungsministerium, June 25, 1941, REM 2954, Zentrales Staatsarchiv, Potsdam.
35. Göring, "Eröffnungsansprache," p. 9.
36. Marrenbach, *Fundamente des Sieges,* p. 272; see also Müller, *Das soziale Leben,* pp. 100, 159–69; Arbeitswissenschaftliches Institut der Deutschen Arbeitsfront, *Jahrbuch* (Berlin, 1937), pp. 376–84; and Der Reichsorganisationsleiter der DAF, ed., *Organisationsbuch der NSDAP* (Munich, 1937), pp. 205, 234–8.
37. Karl Arnhold, *Wege zur Leistungssteigerung in der Textilindustrie* (Berlin, 1942), p. 55; see also "Jahresbericht 1941," p. 74.
38. Reichsministerium für Volksaufklärung und Propaganda to Hermann Göring, April 22, 1943, RFR 107/12850; Smelser, *Robert Ley,* p. 271.
39. Matthias Heinrich Göring to Karl Brandt, February 18, 1944. BDC: Parteikorrespondenz Heyer.
40. F. Gl., "Das Arbeitspsychologische Institut der DAF," *Betriebsführer und Vertrauensrat* 9 (1942): 117–18; Friedrich Koch, "Über Arbeitsneurosen," *Münchener medizinische Wochenschrift* 86 (1939): 1161–4; and Neumann, *Behemoth,* pp. 298–303; see also Kurt Lachmann, "The Hermann Göring Works," *Social Research* 8:1 (February, 1941): 24–40.
41. Smelser, *Robert Ley,* p. 271.
42. Ernst Kretschmer, "Konstitution und Leistung," *Westfälische Landeszeitung,* August 20, 1944, microcopy T-78, roll 190, frames 1866–7, National Archives.
43. Willi Enke, "Seelenheilkunde und Gesundheitspflege," *Mülhauser Tagblatt,* August 18, 1944, microcopy T-78, roll 192, frames 6053–4, National Archives.
44. Adolf Friedrich, "Der Rhythmus der betrieblichen Entwicklung," *Völkischer Beobachter,* April 7, 1944, p. 6.
45. Matthias Heinrich Göring, Rundschreiben, July 22, 1943, Kl. Erw. 762/4.
46. "Tätigkeitsbericht 1937," p. 203; Göring, "Bericht," p. 1; "Gesetz zur Ordnung der Krankenpflege," *Reichsgesetzblatt* (1938): 1309–15; and Robert Cropp, Rundschreiben, March 18, 1943, in Dührssen, *Ein Jahrhundert Psychoanalytische Bewegung,* p. 180.
47. Aichhorn to Polizei Präsidium, Abt. V, Wien, March 28, 1939, Thomas Aichhorn; *Amtsblatt des Polizeipräsidiums in Wien* 2:6 (March 15, 1939): 3; cf. below, chapter 12, on the contentious issue of medical supervision of attending psychologists.

48. Achelis, Rundschreiben an alle Behandelnden Psychologen, July 7, 1939, Kl. Erw. 762/4; Edgar Herzog to Göring, September 11, 1938, Kl. Erw. 762/3.
49. "Jahresbericht 1941," p. 65.
50. Matthias Heinrich Göring, Rundschreiben, March 27, 1943, Kl. Erw. 762/4.
51. RMdI IV e 1684/43–3836, June 21, 1943, Kl. Erw. 762/6.
52. Deutsches Institut für Psychologische Forschung und Psychotherapie, Richtlinien für die Ausbildung, p. 1.
53. Ibid., p. 7; "Jahresbericht 1941," p. 65; and "Richtlinien für das Arbeitsgebiet 'Behandelnde Psychologen'," n.d., Thomas Aichhorn.
54. "Jahresbericht 1941," p. 65; Oswald Kroh, "Bedeutsamer Fortschritt in der Psychologie," *Zeitschrift für Psychologie* 151 (1941): 1–32; Schultz's review of Kroh in *ZfP* 14 (1942): 89–91; Gustav Richard Heyer, "Ausbildungs- und Berufsfragen," in "Jahresbericht 1940," p. 11; and Geuter, *Professionalisierung der deutschen Psychologie,* pp. 326–8; see also Kroh, "Missverständnisse um die Psychologie," *Deutschlands Erneuerung* 27 (1943): 21–37; Walter Stets, "Freiheit der Berufswahl," *Das Reich,* December 13, 1942, p. 6; and Arthur Hoffmann, "Erziehungs-Psychologie—Aufgaben und Wege," *ZfP* 13 (1941): 177–207. Hoffmann's essay was the text of a report given at the Munich branch of the Göring Institute on June 19, 1941.
55. "Diplomprüfungsordnung für Studierende der Psychologie," *Deutsche Wissenschaft, Erziehung und Volksbildung* 7 (1941): 256.
56. Ibid., p. 258.
57. Wolfgang Hochheimer, personal communication, September 30, 1981.
58. Matthias Heinrich Göring, Bericht, August 24, 1941, Kl. Erw. 762/3.
59. Nitsche to Rüdin, July 17, 1941, and Rüdin to de Crinis, July 21, 1941, microcopy T-1021, frames 424–7, National Archives; and Wuth to Bumke, February 23, 1942, H 20/480, BA-MA; Bumke to Wuth, February 27, 1942, H 20/480, BA-MA; and Wuth to Bumke, March 3, 1942, H 20/480, BA-MA.
60. Der Reichsminister für Wissenschaft, Erziehung und Volksbildung an die Unterrichtsverwaltungen der Länder mit Hochschulen (ausser Preussen), die Herrn Vorsteher der nachgeordneten Reichs- und Preussischen Dienststellen der Wissenschaftsverwaltung, August 20, 1942, R 21, folder 469, BA.
61. Oswald Kroh, "Zum Ausbau der Prüfungsordnung für Diplom-Psychologen," *Zeitschrift für Psychologie* 155 (1943): 1–16.
62. De Crinis to Frey, July 11, 1944, R 21, folder 475, BA.
63. Ibid.
64. Erich Tiling and Max Simoneit, "Der Psychiater auf der Psychologischen Prüfstelle," *Der deutsche Militärarzt* 3 (1938): 509–14, 4 (1939): 201–5, 205–6. Tiling was a neurologist and friend of Felix Boehm who became a member of the Göring Institute in 1940: see Lockot, *Die Reinigung der Psychoanalyse,* p. 109.
65. This was probably part of Kemper's wartime concern about the "balance of power" at the institute: see Kemper to Julius Schirren, November 16, 1944, B 339/43, BA.
66. Kroh, "Zum Ausbau der Prüfungsordnung," p. 12; on the evolution of these regulations, see Geuter, *Die Professionalisierung der deutschen Psychologie,* pp. 241–5, 267–9, 326–89, 416.
67. Paul Schröder, "Kinderpsychiatrie und Heilpädagogik," *Zeitschrift für Kinderforschung* 49 (1941): 11–12.
68. Protokoll der Sitzung mit der Psychiatrischen Gesellschaft unter Vorsitz von Ministerialrat Linden am 10.4.41., pp. 1, 2, 4, Kl. Erw. 762/2; see also Aktennotiz

über Besprechung Professor Göring mit Min.Rat Linden am 11.XI.40, Kl. Erw. 762/2; and Friedrich Mauz to Bernhard Rust, September 27, 1937, REM 2954, Zentrales Staatsarchiv.

69. Rüdin to Nitsche, February 6, 1941, microcopy T-1021, roll 11, frame 368, National Archives; on the problems in arranging the Munich meeting, see Rüdin to Linden, March 28, 1941, ibid., frame 366.
70. Rüdin to Nitsche, February 6, 1941, frame 369.
71. Nitsche to Rüdin, July 25, 1941, microcopy T-1021, roll 11, frame 434, National Archives. In 1941 eight of the eleven members of the society's board were psychiatrists; the other three were neurologists: see Bericht, August 6, 1941, ibid., frame 459. Still Rüdin worried about the threat to psychiatry even from neurology: see Rüdin to Linden, July 24, 1941, ibid., frames 450–1.
72. Tagesordnung, ibid., frames 512–15; see also frames 507 and 474. Besides Schultz, the psychotherapists on the program were Gottfried Kühnel, Hattingberg, Mohr, Schultz-Hencke, and Rittmeister. Schultz had also lectured at the 1939 Wiesbaden congress; see ibid., frames 522–3. It is significant that while twenty-two medical journals carried notices about the 1941 congress, the *Zentralblatt für Psychotherapie* did not; see ibid., frame 508.
73. Göring, "Eröffnungsansprache," p. 9.
74. See Göring's review of the Schröder group's published report on the meeting in *ZfP* 13 (1942): 382–3.
75. Rüdin to Reiter, May 23, 1941, microcopy T-1021, roll 11, frame 386; see also ibid., frames 387–94, 450–1. Schröder died unexpectedly in the early summer of 1941 and Rüdin was actively involved, through correspondence with Reiter and Linden, in the selection of his successor in order to ensure, as he put it to Linden, that child psychiatry did not "slip away" from psychiatry; see ibid., frames 387–91. See also Lockot, *Erinnern und Durcharbeiten*, pp. 258–61.
76. Alan Beyerchen, *Scientists under Hitler: Politics and the Physics Community in the Third Reich* (New Haven, 1979), pp. 205–7.
77. BDC: Parteikorrespondenz; Kurt Seelmann, personal communication, October 15, 1980; see also Seelmann, Lebenslauf, Munich, November 1, 1942, BDC: Parteikorrespondenz.
78. BDC: Parteikorrespondenz.
79. On Bavaria and the Reich, see Peterson, *Limits of Hitler's Power*, pp. 149–233.
80. Gauleitung München-Oberbayern to Julius Streicher, May 19, 1939, BDC: Parteikorrespondenz.
81. BDC: Parteikorrespondenz. Seif had been a member of the young avant-garde that had supported Freud against the assaults of the medical establishment; see Ellenberger, *Discovery*, pp. 805–6.
82. BDC: Parteikorrespondenz.
83. *Nationalsozialistische Bibliographie* 5:12 (December 1940), p. 20, entry 114; see also Göring's review in *ZfP* 13 (1942): 310.
84. *Nationalsozialistische Bibliographie* 8:4/5 (April/May 1943), p. 23, entry 164; see also Seelmann to Reichsschriftumskammer, November 1, 1942, BDC: Parteikorrespondenz. Seelmann said he did not know he needed a special permit to publish the book; all he had done originally was send a copy through Göring to the Propaganda Ministry.
85. *Nationalsozialistische Bibliographie* 7:7/8 (July/August 1942), p. 32, entry 165.
86. Ibid., 7:3/4 (March/April 1942), p. 28, entry 149.
87. Johannes Heinrich Schultz, "Leistung und Psyche."
88. "Berlin Akademie für ärztliche Fortbildung," *Deutsches Ärzteblatt* 74 (1944):

181–2; see also Johannes Heinrich Schultz, "Rundschau: Psychotherapie"; idem, "Was kann die Psychotherapie in der Behandlung des Hochdruckes leisten?" *Zeitschrift für ärztliche Fortbildung* 41 (1944): 305–8; and idem, "Arbeitsplan für ärztliche Fortbildung," in Göring, *1. Sonderheft,* pp. 6–8. On a series of lectures Schultz gave at the Berlin Medical Society, see *Deutsches Ärzteblatt* 73 (1943): 151.

89. Fritz Mohr, "Die Behandlung der Neurosen durch Psychotherapie," p. 67; see also "Tätigkeitsbericht 1937," p. 201; and Künkel, "Psychotherapie: Eine Übersicht," pp. 1363–4. For the text of her address to the DPG in 1936, see Karen Horney, "Das neurotische Liebesbedürfnis," *ZfP* 10 (1937): 69–82.
90. Kemper to Schirren, November 16, 1944; Pongratz, *Psychotherapie,* pp. 270, 277.
91. Baumeyer, "Zur Geschichte der Psychoanalyse in Deutschland," p. 217; Pongratz, *Psychotherapie,* p. 318; Dührssen, *Ein Jahrhundert Psychoanalytische Bewegung,* p. 182.
92. BDC: Parteikorrespondenz; see also Heinrich von Kogerer, *Psychotherapie* (Vienna, 1934); and Kohut, *The Curve of Life: Correspondence of Heinz Kohut, 1923–1981* (Chicago, 1994), p. 290 n. 1. See also Kurt Seelmann, "Ein Fall von Bettnässen," in Göring, *Erziehungshilfe,* pp. 66–8.
93. Göring, "Bericht," p. 2. Thirteen triseminars took place in 1936–37, while during 1938–39 there were sixty-two scientific meetings including triseminars; see ibid., p. 3; and "Tätigkeitsbericht 1937," p. 201. For a summary of the postwar debate over the triseminars, see Zapp, "Psychoanalyse und Nationalsozialismus," pp. 42–3; and for Kemper's argument that the differential analysis of specific case studies was a valuable part of these meetings, see Pongratz, *Psychotherapie,* pp. 277–8.
94. Deutsches Institut für Psychologische Forschung und Psychotherapie, "Thesen zur Neurosenlehre," p. 28.
95. Hattingberg, "Forschung und Bücherei," pp. 4–5; see also idem, "Arbeitsplan der Forschungsabteilung," in Göring, *1. Sonderheft,* pp. 16–20; and idem, "Die Willensstörung in der Neurose," p. 33.
96. Werner Kemper, personal communication, March 2, 1974.
97. *ZfP* 14 (1943): 300.
98. Johanna Herzog-Dürck, personal communication, April 28, 1980; see also Göring, "Allgemeines" (1940), p. 3. On Kris, see Frederick Wyatt and Hans Teuber, "German Psychology Under the Nazi System," pp. 235–6; and Farago, *German Psychological Warfare,* p. 33.
99. Dührssen, *Ein Jahrhundert Psychoanalytische Bewegung,* pp. 181–2.
100. Göring to Curtius, February 2, 1939, Kl. Erw. 762/2.
101. Curtius to Göring, March 10, 1939, Kl. Erw. 762/2.
102. Arbeitsgruppe A des Deutschen Instituts für psychologische Forschung und Psychotherapie, Bericht über die wissenschaftliche Tätigkeit von Oktober 1939 bis März 1942, March 23, 1942, Kl. Erw. 762/4; for a list of psychoanalytic meetings and topics from 1935 to 1944, see Baumeyer, "Zur Geschichte der Psychoanalyse in Deutschland," pp. 211–15.
103. Peter Göring, *Vorarbeit zu einer Geschichte der Sippe* (Munich, 1911), p. 321.
104. BDC: Parteistatische Erhebung 1939 and Parteikorrespondenz.
105. Baumeyer, "Zur Geschichte der Psychoanalyse in Deutschland," p. 209.

11

The SS, the Wehrmacht, and Sexuality

The Nazis held extremely strong, inflexible, and erroneous views on human sexuality. In Nazi ideology, there reigned an absolute distinction between male and female, an inviolable division of sexual roles, and an unassailable hierarchy of men over women. For the Nazis, men were to be workers and warriors while it was the job of women to conceive, bear, and raise children. It was the duty of all racially fit men and women to produce racially fit children in order to guarantee the survival and eventual global domination of the "Master Race." Anyone, male or female, who failed to fulfill this duty was subject to correction, persecution, or exclusion from the racial community. For both ideological and demographic reasons, therefore, there was no room in the Nazi world view—or in the Nazi world—for those men and women who did not fit these narrow sexual stereotypes. According to Nazi race theory, any deviation from the heterosexual norm represented biological degeneration and was thus an impediment to the preservation and cultivation of the racial community. So, in addition to being unproductive, such individuals as homosexuals were marked by nature, as it were, for destruction by a state committed to the illusory aim of racial purification. Yet the very inadequacies of Nazi theory, the inefficiencies of Nazi governance, and the pressures of mobilization and war contributed to a search for ways not only to kill homosexuals but to "cure" those designated by medical experts as treatable. Both the SS and the Wehrmacht availed themselves of a variety of experts in confronting the problems generated by their political and military reliance on human beings much more complicated in their sexuality than the prevailing ideology could allow.

German and Western society as a whole had of course long condemned homosexuality as abnormal. Paragraph 175 of the German Penal Code prohibited homosexual activity and paragraphs 42 and 51 provided for the institutionalization and medical treatment of what was regarded as a mental disorder. In 1930 many, if not most, German psychiatrists supported the abolition of paragraphs 51 and 175.[1] They did so out of a pragmatic concern that lawyers and judges were increasingly—and destructively—interfering in a medical matter. But in Germany the medical profession, like the bourgeoisie as a whole, also by and large saw homosexuality as a widespread threat to the social order. Despite a vigorous movement at the turn of the century for the liberalization of views and laws regarding private sexual behavior, birth control, and abortion, in Germany as elsewhere an established nineteenth-century conservative social tradition declared, eventually in racist terms, the abnormality and degeneracy of such attitudes and practices. This anxious bourgeois concern with order and respectability linked itself with a nationalism that celebrated the subordination of private interests to those of the state. In Germany this trend led to a strengthening of a cultural preference for hierarchical and authoritarian ideals of community rooted in the immutable biological laws of nature as opposed to the liberal, individualistic, and materialistic urban civilization spawned by the Industrial Revolution.[2] The attitude of German physicians toward homosexuality was also conditioned by their scientific conviction that it was an analyzable and treatable disorder. This prompted them to favor treatment over punishment while at the same time it bolstered the prevailing cultural bias that saw homosexuals as a problem to be solved. The professional ambitions of psychotherapists, especially during the Third Reich, strengthened this general medical propensity to offer solutions to such "problems."[3]

The Nazi regime expanded the laws against homosexuality and sent thousands of homosexuals to their deaths in concentration camps. But many more homosexuals avoided such persecution since, unlike most Jews and communists, they were not usually easily identifiable.[4] Furthermore, even though during the war Hitler had declared the death penalty for homosexual activity in the SS and the police while the party and Nazi youth groups had from the beginning expelled overt homosexuals from their ranks,[5] the Nazis were constrained by the pervasiveness of homosexual behavior in the populace, especially among adolescents, to seek medical assistance in dealing with this problem. Their aims were pragmatic in the sense that they wished to exploit as many socially and sexually productive individuals as possible; they were ideological insofar as the Nazis strove to use the power of biology to overwhelm perversions supposedly cultivated by a decadent and materialistic civilization. Crude and sadistic experiments in the camps were one result. These aims also drew upon the Nazis' desire to exert technical control over all aspects of life, as well as the deep psychological need of many Nazis to assert, out of "their own personal agony of armor-plated self-discipline,"[6] a masculine identity against everything internally and externally construed as soft or feminine.

That this threat was deeply and personally felt was also due to the fact that homosexuality was anything but unheard of among the Nazis themselves. SA leader Ernst Röhm (see chapter 8) was only the most prominent homosexual in Nazi ranks. In 1932 psychiatrist Bumke had even written to Munich publisher Johannes Lehmann about the danger to Germany's youth if homosexuals such as Röhm should assume power. Lehmann purportedly showed the letter to Hitler, who dismissed it with an affirmation of his loyalty to Röhm.[7] Göring Institute psychoanalyst Franz Baumeyer claimed that many high-ranking Nazis sought help from psychotherapists for problems linked to homosexuality, echoing colleague Müller-Hegemann's view that the institute generally and continually served a desperately conflicted Nazi leadership. Seelmann recalls attending a meeting of the German General Medical Society for Psychotherapy in 1934 concerning the Röhm affair and in 1943 Boehm solicited reports from institute members on the successful treatment of sexual disorders with the observation that such cases were of particular importance for the advancement of psychotherapy.[8] Although hard evidence of Nazi patronage of the Göring Institute for treatment of homosexuality is lacking, it is clear that the Nazis, for both practical and ideological reasons, looked to psychotherapists, among others, to deal with homosexuals. The Nazis naturally endeavored to avoid publicity, especially to quiet parents' fears, and to blame the incidence of homosexuality on Weimar youth groups. They also stressed the need for prevention and education through counseling and medical attention. The Nazis were constrained to distinguish between homosexuals per se, whom they declared to be biologically degenerate, and the susceptibility of Aryan adolescents of good stock and breeding to "blunders" (*Pubertätsentgleisungen*).[9] The psychotherapists, therefore, were busily engaged in research and practice on the subject, particularly in the realms of adolescent and forensic psychology. Kalau vom Hofe treated a number of youths whom the Hitler Youth and the League of German Girls had referred for homosexuality, including many who had gotten into trouble with the police.[10] In a number of cases, she claimed, long-term psychoanalysis was used in treating them. Ernst Göring also confirmed that the Nazi youth organizations made use of the institute and that cases of homosexual behavior were regularly referred to it.

The psychotherapists of course were only too eager to prove their professional competence in this particular area, in particular drawing upon the work of Hattingberg, Schultz, Boehm, Kalau vom Hofe, Mohr, and Kemper.[11] Once again, Freudians were prominent in this particular arena, confirming not only the ongoing pragmatism of the institute and the regime but the continuing caricature, according to Kalau vom Hofe, of psychoanalysis in the minds of the Nazi authorities. In early 1938 an institute survey conducted by Boehm announced that since 1923 some 60 psychotherapists now at the Göring Institute had treated or extensively counseled 510 homosexual patients. Of these, it was reported that 341 had been cured, that is, had undergone a lasting change in their sexual preference. In 1944 Schultz claimed that by 1939 the Göring Institute could report the private and clinical cure of 500 homosexuals.[12] Boehm presented the 1938 figures in the context of a critical review in 1940 of a book written by psychiatrist Rudolf Lemke, in which Lemke argued that the root cause of homosexuality was a congenital disposition, making it a disorder whose effects could by alleviated by psychotherapy, but which itself could never be cured by psychological means.[13] In 1944 Schultz was arguing in opposition to a similar point of view in the military.

The SS, as the putative Nazi racial elite, was especially concerned with issues of sexuality, procreation, and "perversion." The increasingly pragmatic stance and competence of the Göring Institute outlined in the preceding chapter would be the basis for much of the psychotherapists' collaboration with Heinrich Himmler's SS. We have already seen in chapter 9 how Himmler was involved in the institute's treatment of the daughter of one of his minions. This was in spite of the fact that Himmler had a distinct and ignorant disdain for psychiatry in general. In this vein, he made what seems to have been a direct reference to the position and strategy of the Göring psychotherapists in a discussion of homosexuality in 1940: "'They're a trade union for pulling people's souls to pieces, headed by Freud, their Jewish honorary president—though they may quietly disown or supersede him for their own ends.'"[14] At the same time, Himmler did not hesitate to affirm portions of the psychoanalytic point of view in particular in erecting the SS-Lebensborn for the procreation and cultivation of a master race:

> Ignoring the obvious contribution which a Jew, Sigmund Freud, had made to his analysis, Himmler asserted that sex was natural and that in establishing artificial restrictions on sexual relations society created the unhealthy conditions which currently threatened Germany.[15]

It was precisely this muddled thought process that allowed the SS to become involved in two special areas of institute research we will presently describe, one on homosexuality and the other on psychogenic sterility, supported by other agencies of the state (see chapter 13).

The psychotherapists' contacts with the especially dark domain of the SS were varied. Göring's eldest son, Peter, had joined the SS in 1935 and served in it as a physician.[16] Göring himself had apparently met with Himmler at least twice and claimed that both Himmler and SS Chief Physician Ernst Grawitz had expressed personal interest in the work of the institute.[17] According to König-Fachsenfeld, Werner Achelis was on the staff as a psychotherapist at Hohenlychen, Karl Gebhardt's Waffen-SS orthopedic hospital and sanitarium near the Ravensbrück concentration camp north of Berlin. Achelis's position is not surprising given the importance attributed there to the necessity of psychological adjustment for those who had lost limbs and suffered from other severe medical problems.[18] Göring himself, according to his son Ernst, prepared expert opinions on cases at Hohenlychen and there is documentary evidence of Göring's physical presence at Hohenlychen on at least one occasion.[19] August Vetter recalls that Göring and Hattingberg once asked him to prepare some lectures on any subject he chose to give to a group of SS men. Such an inspirational series of conclaves apparently never took place, but that the Göring Institute and the SS had associations with one another is clear.

It is also clear that at least some of the initiative in developing these contacts rested with the psychotherapists. In 1939, after having received some copies of the SS journal *Germanien* from editor Otto Huth, Göring wrote directly to Himmler, suggesting a research topic for the SS-Ahnenerbe, which fostered ancestral research and under whose auspices the journal was published. The topic Göring proposed was for the project titled "Forest and Tree in Aryan-Germanic Spiritual and Cultural History"; his proposal was entitled "Forest and Tree in Dreams" and included Göring's observation that "in dreams from the collective unconscious (C. G. Jung), forest and tree often play a large role."[20] It is interesting and perhaps relevant that this Ahnenerbe project was in part funded by the Reich Forestry Office, which was formally under the direction of Hermann Göring. In any case, M. H. Göring proposed Gustav Schmaltz as the author of such a study. Himmler passed Göring's letter along to Walter Wust, curator of the Ahnenerbe, but the forest and tree project was never completed. In the meantime, however, two of the officials involved in the appraisal of Göring's proposal had recommended acceptance, three had advised against undertaking it on financial grounds, two had abstained, and the director of the project had concluded that there were other, more important themes to be taken up with the limited funds available.[21]

Another member of the institute, Eckart von Sydow, who was a member of the Freudian group and a friend of Felix Boehm, also sought to enlist the financial support of the Ahnenerbe in 1939. He wished to travel to Africa to study native plastic arts in southern Nigeria. A professor of philosophy at the University of Berlin, Sydow had previously undertaken two trips to the area, one in 1936 on a grant from British sources and another during 1937–38 under the sponsorship of the DFG. He was also a party member, even though one of his early works on primitive art was on the Nazi index of prohibited books. The Ahnenerbe turned Sydow down and he applied once again to the DFG, which in May 1941 granted him further funds for research into the native sculpture of southern Nigeria.[22] From these studies, Sydow published an article of which the SD spoke approvingly. The SS security service noted to the Ahnenerbe that Sydow's conclusion that the continuation of paganism in southern Nigeria would preserve these arts corresponded to the SD's notion of a successful German colonial policy there. It was decided that more information on Sydow would be gathered to see if he might be suitable for research on the plan.[23]

Aside from such individual involvements, the Göring Institute was also connected with SS projects on the related problems of procreation and homosexuality. Unlike the "cultural" activities of the SS we have just described, these sexual and "racial" issues attracted greater resources. They also engaged a wider spectrum of psychological expertise, including Freudians like Kalau vom Hofe and Kemper, from the Göring Institute. Once again we witness a technical and pragmatic aspect to Nazi policy that, in the case of the psychotherapists, underlined a growing psychoanalytic capacity in, and contribution to, the work of the Göring Institute. While the Jungians might be recommended for work on such things as trees in dreams, others, especially Freudians, got the call when it came to sexual matters. This was particularly marked in the case of SS concern over the psychological elements of infertility and homosexuality. Under Hitler, heterosexual activity, like health, had become a duty. Masturbation was said to result in the loss of valuable *völkisch* sperm and to lead to weakness and even homosexuality, paths to be avoided by entrance into the Hitler Youth, where the body could be hardened and the character strengthened.[24] A vigorous population policy had always been an integral part of the National Socialist program. Germany, along with the rest of Europe, had suffered a decline in the birthrate during the twentieth century. The Nazis, as the beneficiaries of the waning of the Great Depression, did achieve an increase in the rates of marriage and birth, but hardly one of staggering proportions. The war naturally arrested any continued improvement, although the rates did not fall as drastically as they had during the First World War. The Nazis encouraged large families, celebrated the traditional roles of women as wives and mothers, and criticized the "Jewish-inspired" feminist movement for its alleged destruction of the home in its opposition to large families.[25] For racially pure women, the Nazis banned abortion. In 1941 the Interior Ministry prohibited the manufacture and/or sale of contraceptives and abortion paraphernalia.[26]

The Nazis also looked to the medical profession to abolish physical and psychological hindrances to procreation. As early as 1936 both the Labor Ministry and Interior Ministry had declared that social health insurance would cover the cost of curing both physiogenic and psychogenic infertility in women, as it was in the interest of preserving the new *Volksgemeinschaft*.[27] For its part, the SS formed a study group to evolve a "positive" population policy. This group was dominated by medical experts in "racial biology": Carl Clauberg of the Institute for Reproductive Biology in Königshütte, Gunther von Wolff of Berlin, and Günther K. F. Schultze of Greifswald. In line with this assignment, Schultze participated in a conference on sterility at the Berlin Medical Society, while Wolff produced a manuscript on infertility in women that Himmler thought quite good. Himmler recommended, however, that its publication be put off until after the war, when it could, he wrote, be "psychologically still much better constructed."[28] It is likely that Himmler was referring both to the form and the content of the piece since, as we shall presently see, the SS would engage psychological experts in this work. A recourse to psychology was also consistent with the project's focus on women, whom the Nazis regarded as not only physically but also psychologically weaker. Especially when it came to sex, the Nazis for their own psychological and ideological reasons also preferred to emphasize female rather than male dysfunction to an extent beyond even the generally larger proportion of female medical disorders in this category due both to biological and cultural construction.

The SS concern with the psychological dynamics of human procreation was manifested most prominently within the SS-Lebensborn (Spring of Life). The Lebensborn was designed to secure the coming Aryan generations by enabling and encouraging racially desirable women to bear children. This was to be accomplished by providing communal homes for such women and their infants. The first Lebensborn home for such mothers and children was established at Steinhöring near Munich in 1936. Eventually there were to be ten such homes in Germany and another ten scattered across occupied Europe. More consistent with SS cruelty, the Lebensborn also appropriated "Aryan" children from all over Europe for placement with German families. With this latter project there was, naturally but anything but humanely, a concern with problems of psychological fitness and adjustment among the kidnapped children. Since 1934 Hildegard Hetzer had worked in Berlin for the Association for the Protection of Children from Exploitation and Abuse and for the NSV Jugendhilfe. In early 1942 the NSV sent Hetzer to Posen in the annexed "Reichsgau Wartheland" territories of Poland. Although she has denied it, it is possible she knew of, or even participated in, psychological examinations of such children for the NSV and Lebensborn.[29]

The Lebensborn was also necessarily involved in sponsoring work in the arena of sexual dysfunction. In a letter to its administrative director Max Sollmann, medical director Gregor Ebner maintained that medical efforts to restore organic capacity for sexual performance through surgery and hormonal therapy had failed, and that to cure sterility "a conversion of the whole organism must be accomplished."[30] Ebner enclosed a report from an SS Lebensborn doctor in The Hague, touting the effectiveness of solar-heated mudbaths in creating the sense of well-being necessary for fertility and sexual activity among both males and females. This doctor, named Meyer, also asserted that primitive peoples, like asocials and the feeble-minded, had a higher birthrate than civilized peoples. It seemed to him that the higher the mental development, the more likely a disturbance in procreative ability. Like Himmler, Meyer was interested in natural medicine. He decried the evils of modern civilization that disrupted the natural rhythm of the human organism. But he went further by arguing that such disturbances were often psychologically determined and only aggravated by the perils of contemporary life. Mudbaths alone, then, were not enough:

> At the same time psychological influence must be utilized . . . . I have experienced cases in which the frigidity of a woman under such treatment, namely healthful nutrition, open-air gymnastics, a regulated daily schedule in combination with hypnosis was in a short time . . . much improved.[31]

At least one member of the Göring Institute had a direct, if brief, association with the Lebensborn. In 1942 Erika Hantel published an article in the national edition of the *Frankfurter Zeitung* on the wartime lessons to be learned from the homes for women founded by the medieval priest Lambert le Buégne. The first of these homes was established in Liège in 1148 for the protection of women widowed by the Crusades, unmarried mothers, older single women, and other widows. Hantel saw instructive parallels to Germany in 1942 that were not restricted simply to the care of women whose husbands had died at the front. The medieval homes stressed the preservation of "motherly" qualities, something that Hantel—in line with the thinking of colleagues Achelis, Hattingberg, and Schultz on the proper balance of male and female within individuals—thought compelling in a wartime society that required women to replace men at the workbench, in the office, and on the assembly line. Although the Nazis never effectively mobilized women for such work, Hantel believed that before women were mobilized to exercise masculine qualities, a solid basis of womanhood had to be cultivated and made conscious, not rashly sacrificed to production schedules and war alarums. In this, she wrote, lay the future of the nation and the race.[32] It is relevant to our theme of pragmatism in this chapter to note that a similar essay on German soldiers returning home by a Jungian member of the institute did not lead to the type of professional solicitation that ensued for the industrial psychologist Hantel.[33] While this in part had to do with the fact that the Jungian piece was published in the *Zentralblatt* and not in a national newspaper, it also had to do with the less practical application of Jungian mother and father archetypes to pressing demands.

According to Hantel, Himmler, who was dissatisfied with the coverage of the Lebensborn in the *Völkischer Beobachter,* read the article. Knowing through Göring she was a psychologist, he decided that she should write an article about the Lebensborn. It was probably not just the general subject matter of the original article or the professional manner of its analysis that appealed to Himmler, but rather Hantel's positive references to the traditional roles of women. In any case, Hantel was contacted by Himmler's press chief, Hans Johst, and ordered in November 1942 to see Sollmann at Lebensborn headquarters in Munich. Heyer accompanied her and she was accommodated at the sumptuous Hotel Vierjahreszeiten. Sollmann offered her RM 10,000 to undertake the assignment, but she expressed reservations, saying that she was not a party member and that her husband was regarded as politically untrustworthy by the regime. In addition, although she did not mention it to Sollmann, Hantel had already visited one of the Lebensborn homes and found it a "psychological horror" with too much work and too little medical attention. Hantel was rescued by events: the battle for Stalingrad and the resultant military disaster precluded further interest in the project on the part of the SS. Hantel was left, she claimed, with at least one striking Nazi psychosexual irony, however. During her interview with Sollmann, he allegedly confessed to being under pressure from Himmler because of his failure to carry out another assignment, to impregnate a woman.

The SS was even more concerned about homosexuality. In the words of one SS essay, a homosexual was a "homunculus and therefore excluded from the laws of life."[34] In 1940, however, Himmler's masseur recommended to him medical treatment for young boys manifesting homosexual tendencies. Himmler reportedly replied: "That's splendid, Herr Kersten, I will nominate you as my advisor on homosexual matters. The Hitler Youth has already taken up something like that, but nothing has yet been done for a fundamental solution to the problem."[35] Despite the evident sarcasm in his "appointment" of Kersten, we know that Himmler did take a strong interest in matters of homosexuality in Germany in general and in the SS in particular. This concern ranged from musings on the possible correlation of lefthandedness and homosexuality to his thoughts that it was a perversion related to espionage, sabotage, and evasion of military service. But Himmler also acknowledged the desirability of attempts at the cure of homosexuality, even though he was dubious about the outcome. The turn of the war's tide, in any case, dissolved what little official commitment he may have had to a medical approach to the problem. On November 15, 1941, Hitler decreed the death penalty for homosexual members of the SS.

The SS, however, pursued its own reparative and curative efforts in the form of sadistic and futile biological experimentation. The Danish physician Carl Vaernet, for one, was retained by the SS with an annual stipend of RM 10,000 to test his method of curing homosexuality through the implantation of artificial sex glands. Vaernet, working in Prague with prisoners from the Buchenwald concentration camp, claimed success for his efforts. One patient, a fifty-five-year-old theologian, had since the age of twenty-two been unable to have heterosexual relations because of what Vaernet reported as "anxiety," and had forthwith become a homosexual. After the operation, Vaernet asserted, the patient began to have dreams accompanied by erections of sexual intercourse with women. He was sleeping better and his bouts of depression had disappeared. There was one problem, however. The patient's religious convictions prevented him from visiting a brothel in order to test his new capacity.[36]

The SS also had contact with the Göring Institute concerning the treatment of homosexuals. Göring, Schultz, and Kalau vom Hofe worked on an individual basis with the SS on this matter. Late in the war, Kalau vom Hofe recalled, she treated four homosexuals who, in keeping with an SS policy for those convicted of "habitual crimes," had been released from concentration camps and were being held at the Berlin-Charlottenburg jail.[37] Kalau vom Hofe also claimed to have made every effort to avoid having homosexuals she treated in the criminal psychology division of the Göring Institute sent to concentration camps. This could be accomplished by having such patients placed for treatment as inpatients in a hospital.[38] Schultz had concerned himself with the treatment of homosexuality since 1937. Schultz characterized only a small minority of homosexuals as congenital and thus untreatable while most had become homosexuals and were thus treatable with depth psychology.[39] Schultz's relationship with the SS was anything but politically and ethically unproblematic. In 1943 Himmler brusquely rejected the proposal of Martin Brustmann, a consulting physician for the SS Race and Settlement Main Office with connections to M. H. Göring, for a wartime therapeutic program for homosexuals. According to Himmler, every human resource had to be committed to the struggle for survival, not wasted on unproductive and degenerate homosexuals. Although the SS continued to work with Göring for expert evaluation of homosexuals, the Reichsführer's animus, expressed in a letter to SS security chief Ernst Kaltenbrunner, also fell on Schultz, who, in collaboration with the now discredited Brustmann, had rendered at least one expert opinion on a case of homosexuality about which Himmler was personally concerned.[40]

This case involved an SS man sent by his family to the Göring Institute after having been threatened with execution by his superiors. Such an instance was naturally a particularly appalling problem for the SS. On the one hand, as Hitler had ordered, the thing to do was to carry out the death penalty. On the other hand, it was ideologically and organizationally tempting to try and demonstrate that such individuals were treatable and thus not "real" homosexuals in the racial and biological sense who had somehow slipped past the gatekeepers of Hitler's elite. Schultz proposed, and apparently in this case carried out, a radical test of the effectiveness of psychotherapy in curing such homosexuals: The patient had to perform sexual intercourse with a female prostitute in front of a panel of experts.[41] Outrage at such a procedure must be tempered by the possible truth of Schultz's claim that this was done, successfully, to save this man's life. It is not known whether other such "performances" took place, but once again we have evidence of the ethically and practically ambiguous conjunction of good and evil under Nazism. By saving a life in such a manner—while also advancing professional therapeutic claims—Schultz and the institute were abetting the whole deadly Nazi system that condemned thousands of similar cases to persecution and death. The same dynamic obtained in the case of a cook at the Göring Institute who was let go because of homosexuality.[42] Let go where? And to what extent was the intent and the effect the protection of the individual as well as of the institute?

Another, final, question must be asked about such an activity as

Schultz's: Was this in fact not a singular instance (among others?) by which Schultz attempted to save a life, but a standard procedure (among others?) by which homosexuals were systematically assigned to treatment or sent to a concentration camp? This is the argument of a recent article in the German newsweekly *Der Spiegel*. The article cites Schultz's praise for Nazi eugenics to buttress the assumption that Schultz must have been involved in sending homosexuals to concentration camps.[43] But this account is an exaggeration of a newspaper article by a psychiatrist published ten years earlier in which it is implied that the 500 homosexuals Schultz in 1944 claimed as "cured" were those "saved" by such a method and that others must have "failed" the performance test.[44] Schultz's words in favor of Nazi eugenics were anything but harmless in intent and effect, but words and actions cannot simply be equated. Based on the scant evidence of such instances we have, the ethical and institutional dynamics involved are more complicated than the sensational branding of Schultz as a Nazi in the conventional sense allows. If Schultz or anyone else at the Göring Institute was involved in the systematic condemnation of homosexuals to death, then that evidence has yet to be uncovered. The relevant questions specific to the available evidence are: To what extent did Schultz and others approve of, and in what ways contribute to, the sterilization and murder of "incurable" mental patients and homosexuals? To what extent were their actions governed by other interests under the constraints of unassailable Nazi power? What happened to those homosexuals who were designated by psychotherapists as untreatable?[45] Even in these cases motives were complex: in general, to maintain credibility with the regime for the sake of individual and collective professional interest and for the sake of those who "could be saved" commensurate with a variable mix of professional, national, and ideological convictions. By the same token, we cannot accept the exculpatory argument that such actions were taken merely "to save what could be saved." That asserts an unalloyed opposition to the Nazi regime's policies that was simply not the case. Aside from wartime loyalty to the nation, there existed among psychotherapists, as we have seen, the pressure of burgeoning professional interests as well as a tradition of "progressive" support for eugenics. The support proffered the Nazi regime by the psychotherapists at the German Institute for Psychological Research and Psychotherapy issued not just from unalloyed ideological fanaticism and cynical opportunism. The critical alloys, as we have already seen, were the product of the broader and deeper historical conditions under which psychotherapy developed before as well as after 1933.

Psychotherapists and psychiatrists in the military also confronted each other directly over homosexuality. It was during the Second World War that Western military establishments in general first medically stigmatized homosexuals. As we shall see in chapter 12, psychotherapists had greater influence in the Luftwaffe, while the army medical services remained firmly under the control of the psychotherapists' psychiatric antagonists. According to Werner Kemper, it was the Luftwaffe that first suggested that the Göring Institute establish a research project on homosexuality.[46] The one recorded instance of a meeting between Matthias Heinrich Göring and Hermann Göring occurred on September 25, 1942, and the subject noted in the Reich marshal's appointment calendar was homosexuality.[47] The result was that the army (and navy) and the air force ended up with different policies on homosexuality. Beginning in 1942 the Wehrmacht grappled with the problem of homosexuality and in so doing engaged contending institutional and professional forces in the fields of criminology, medical psychology, and forensic medicine. At the center of the controversy, not surprisingly, were the contending views and interests of psychotherapists and psychiatrists. The psychotherapists maintained that the vast majority of homosexual cases had psychological origins and could therefore be treated and cured. The psychiatrists, by contrast, argued that homosexuals suffered from a hereditary disorder and advocated punishments for repeat offenders ranging from imprisonment to castration to death.

In 1942, in the case of an officer convicted of homosexual activity, Hitler decreed that since he had been judged to have a hereditarily defective disposition, he must be punished and not be permitted—as he had requested in his appeal for leniency to the Führer—to rehabilitate himself in combat. This decision was passed down from Hitler's headquarters as a precedent, but one that left unanswered a number of important questions. As a result, the Armed Forces High Command sought the views of the Ministry of Justice, the Gestapo, the Criminal Police, and the army psychiatrists. There were a variety of opinions, making it clear that a unified policy would have to be negotiated. The Ministry of Justice, the Gestapo, and the psychiatrists essentially agreed that adult homosexuals were suffering from an incurable hereditary defect, but that homosexual incidents among adolescents might often be the result of pubertal difficulties and/or seduction by a "true" adult homosexual. The psychiatrists warned against discharging homosexuals from the armed forces because this might encourage simulation among "normal" soldiers wishing to escape the front. Only the Criminal Police distinguished between hereditary and environmental homosexual disorders. They pointed out that many homosexuals released into the Wehrmacht from preventive detention had not subsequently engaged in homosexual conduct. In any case, there was not enough room in the concentration camps, the Criminal Police argued, so the armed forces would have to construct their own detention facilities. Since, in the view of the Criminal Police, not all homosexuals were incurable, there was hope that treatment could help to solve the problem. This approach arose from the working relationship between the Criminal Police and the Göring Institute through the psychotherapists' attempts out of the offices of the Reich Air Ministry "to reintegrate such people into the racial community" instead of filling up concentration camps.[48]

On May 19, 1943, Field Marshal Keitel, chief of the Armed Forces High Command, issued guidelines on punishment (including death) for homosexual activity. There were three categories of perpetrators: those congenitally afflicted or suffering from an untreatable drive, onetime offenders (particularly victims of seduction), and those in whom a hereditary disposition was uncertain.[49] On June 7, 1944, the Luftwaffe health service published its own directive. This fourteen-page document emphasized that not every man who committed a homosexual act was a homosexual, that most homosexuals did not manifest a hereditary disposition (*Hang*) but rather a desire (*Trieb*) acquired in life, and that a majority of the latter—and some of the former—could be cured with psychotherapy.[50] The battle lines had been drawn. On December 9, 1944, de Crinis expressed his unconditional opposition to the Luftwaffe guidelines in a letter to the Army Medical Service Command.[51] That the army stood by the 1943 policy is evidenced by the conclusions of a commission studying the use of expert medical opinions in the implementation of those guidelines on December 15, 1944. The fact of the membership in this group of psychoanalyst Felix Boehm, who was a member of the Göring Institute, underlined the limits of the psychotherapists' influence in the army, though also the extent of their collaboration with Nazi brutality.[52]

As with certain of Schultz's words and actions with respect to the "treatment" of homosexuals, Boehm's participation in the army decision underscores once again in grim fashion the ethical problems generated and confronted by psychotherapists in the Third Reich. The cardinal elements of this situation reflected the more general conditions of the development of psychotherapy in Germany both before and after the Nazi seizure of power. These elements may be summarized as follows. The efforts of psychotherapists and psychoanalysts to "cure" homosexuals represented: (1) an attempt to enhance and protect professional status; (2) a desire to "help" the "sick"; (3) support for the regime's insistence on a productive populace; (4) an alternative to the policies of punishment, imprisonment, castration, and extermination carried out by psychiatrists, the SS, and the military; and (5) a resultant lack of resistance to overall Nazi persecution of homosexuals and thus, as in other matters and in general, degrees of participation in an inhuman system.

Notes

1. Arthur Schindler, "Die Umfrage der *Deutschen medizinischen Wochenschrift* betreffend den Satz 175 StGB," *ZfP* 3 (1930): 68–70; see also Ernst Kretschmer, *Psychiatry,* pp. 177, 262–5; and James D. Steakley, *The Homosexual Emancipation Movement in Germany* (New York, 1975), pp. 9–10, 13, 21, 30–40, 84–5, 106, 110–11.
2. George L. Mosse, *Nationalism and Sexuality: Respectability and Abnormal Sexuality in Europe* (New York, 1985).
3. Fritz Mohr, "Einige Betrachtungen über Wesen, Entstehung und Behandlung der Homosexualität," pp. 1, 13, 16, 17, 19, 20; Hattingberg, *Über die Liebe,* pp. 67–82; Harald Schultz-Hencke, "Über Homosexualität," *Zeitschrift für die gesamte Neurologie und Psychiatrie* 140 (1932): 300–12; Johannes Heinrich Schultz, "Bemerkungen zur Arbeit von Th. Lang über die genetische Bedingtheit der Homosexualität," ibid. 157 (1937): 575–8; Heyer, *Menschen in Not,* pp. 212–18; Herbert Linden, "Bekämpfung der Sittlichkeitsverbrechern mit ärztlichen Mitteln," *Allgemeine Zeitschrift für Psychiatrie* 112 (1939): 405–23; Schultz's review essay in *ZfP* 12 (1940): 180–3; and Claudia Schoppmann, *Nationalsozialistische Sexualpolitik und weibliche Homosexualität,* pp. 117–42.
4. Richard Plant, *The Pink Triangle: The Nazi War Against Homosexuals* (New York, 1986), p. 52; Burkhard Jellonek, *Homosexuelle unter dem Hakenkreuz: Die Verfolgung von Homosexuellen im Dritten Reich* (Paderborn, 1990).
5. BDC: Reichskartei-Warnkartei.
6. Peukert, *Inside Nazi Germany,* p. 169.
7. Bumke, *Erinnerungen,* pp. 163–6.
8. Felix Boehm, Rundschreiben, March 12, 1943, Kl. Erw. 762/4.
9. "Sonderrichtlinien: Die Bekämpfung gleichgeschlechtlicher Verfehlungen im Rahmen der Jugenderziehung," *Arbeitsrichtlinien der Hitler-Jugend* 4/43, Berlin,

June 1, 1943, p. 6, R 22, folder 1196, BA; see also Jugendführer des Deutschen Reiches, ed., *Kriminalität und Gefährdung der Jugend: Lagebericht bis zum Stande vom 1. Januar 1941* (Berlin, 1941), pp. 87–120; Hans Büsing, "Erfahrungen mehrjährigen jugendärztlicher Tätigkeit im Rahmen eines ländlichen Gesundheitsamtes in Hinblick auf die Neuausrichtung der HJ-ärztlichen Tätigkeit," *Der Öffentliche Gesundheitsdienst* 6 (1940): 405–20; and Peter D. Stachura, *The German Youth Movement 1900–1945* (London, 1981), pp. 132, 161–2.

10. There was no specific law against female homosexuality and most Nazis were for psychological and practical reasons more concerned about male homosexuality since their sexism assumed pliable heterosexuality on the part of women. Some Nazis, however, favored extending the laws against homosexuality to cover women on the belief that lesbians could "pollute" society and prove an impediment to a rise in the birthrate; see Schoppmann, *Nationalsozialistische Sexualpolitik*, pp. 250–3.
11. Ibid., pp. 143–57.
12. Johannes Heinrich Schultz, Anweisung für Truppenärzte über Erkennung und Behandlung von abnormen seelischen Reaktionen (Neurosen), p. 18.
13. *ZfP* 14 (1942): 123.
14. Felix Kersten, *The Kersten Memoirs 1940–1945*, trans. Constantine Fitzgibbon (New York, 1957), p. 58.
15. Larry V. Thompson, "Lebensborn and the Eugenics Policy of the Reichsführer-SS," *Central European History* 6 (1971): 56–7; see also Michael H. Kater, *Das Ahnenerbe der SS 1933–1945: Ein Beitrag zur Kulturpolitik des Dritten Reichas* (Stuttgart, 1974), p. 205.
16. Peter Göring, R.u.S.-Fragebogen, Potsdam, March 27, 1938, BDC: SS-Unterlagen and Parteistatistische Erhebung 1939.
17. Collection Himmler, Box 1, reels 37A and 38A, Terminbücher, entries for January 10 and December 18, 1939, Hoover Institution.
18. William Telling, "Reconditioning the Maimed," *The Listener* 18 (1937): 1003; Karl Gebhardt, "Allgemeines zur Wiederherstellungschirurgie," *Zentralblatt für Chirurgie* 63 (1936): 1570–6; idem, "Erziehungsfragen im Behandlungsgang versicherungspflichtiger Kranker," *Deutsche medizinische Wochenschrift* 63 (1937): 736–8; and idem, "Erziehungsfragen im Behandlungsgang," in idem, ed., *Behandlung der Knochen- und Gelenktuberkulose nach den Erfahrungen von Hohenlychen vom November 1933 bis 1938* (Leipzig, 1939), pp. 57–62.
19. Göring to Rostock, May 31, 1944, BDC: Parteikorrespondenz Heyer.
20. Göring to Himmler, May 10, 1939, BDC: SS-Führer; NS 21, folder 336/C 1, BA.
21. Gilbert Trathnigg to Wust, July 11, 1939, NS 21, folder 336/C 1, BA; Himmler to Göring, May 27, 1939, BDC: SS-Unterlagen; see also Gustav Schmaltz, "Einige Bemerkungen zur Praxis der Psychotherapie," *ZfP* 10 (1938): 141–9.
22. Eckart von Sydow to "Das Ahnenerbe," e.V., June 26, 1939, BDC: SS-Unterlagen; DFG-Registratur, BDC: Personakten von Sydow; and BDC: Parteistatistische Erhebung 1939; see also Hans-Martin Lohmann and Lutz Rosenkötter, "Nachtrag zu unserem Beitrag 'Psychoanalyse in Hitlerdeutschland'," p. 81. Sydow was born in 1885 in Dobberpfuhl, joined the party in 1933, and was also a member of the Nazi University Lecturers League and the NSV; see also Paul Kühne, "Dr. Felix Boehm: Ein halbes Jahrhundert psychoanalytischer Geschichte" (1958), in Boehm, *Schriften zur Psychoanalyse*, p. 313.
23. Franz Alfred Six to Wolfram Sievers, June 24, 1942, BDC: SS-Ahnenerbe; see Eckart von Sydow, "Zukunftsaussichten der negerischen Kunst," *Koloniale Rundschau* 33 (1942): 26–31.

24. Peter Johannes Thiel, "Die Selbstbefleckung (Onanie!)," *Deutsche Volksgesundheit aus Blut und Boden* 2 (1934): 10; see also Bleuel, *Sex and Society*, p. 23.
25. John Knodel, *The Decline of Fertility in Germany 1871–1939* (Princeton, 1974); Richard Korheer, *Gebürtenrückgang: Mahnruf an das deutsche Volk* (Munich, 1935); "Die Fruchtbarkeitszunahme des deutschen Volkes," *Deutsches Ärzteblatt* 72 (1942): 118–19; and Erich Nehse, "Die Frauenfrage vom eugenischen Standpunkt aus betrachtet," ibid. 63 (1933): 704–5. On women in the Third Reich, see Gisela Bock, *Zwangssterilisation im Nationalsozialismus: Studien zur Rassenpolitik und Frauenpolitik* (Opladen, 1986), pp. 141–78; Claudia Koonz, *Mothers in the Fatherland: Women, the Family and Nazi Politics* (New York, 1987); Mosse, *Nazi Culture*, pp. 39–47; Bleuel, *Sex and Society*, pp. 34–7, 54–68, 76–85, 120–7, 148–73; Grunberger, *The 12–Year Reich*, pp. 251–66; and Jill Stephenson, *Women in Nazi Society* (New York, 1975).
26. "Polizeiverordnung über Verfahren, Mittel und Gegenstände zur Unterbrechung und Verhütung von Schwangerschaften vom 21. Januar 1941," *Die Gesundheitsführung "Ziel und Weg"* 3 (1941): 7.
27. F. Rott, "Die Unfruchtbarkeit der Frau als Krankheit im Sinne der Reichsversicherung," *Reichs-Gesundheitsblatt* 11 (1936): 738–42; "Beiseitigung der Unfruchtbarkeit bei Frauen," *Deutsches Ärzteblatt* 67 (1937): 833; see also G. Haselhorst, "Weibliche Sterilität," *Deutsches Ärzteblatt* 65 (1935): 1259–61.
28. Himmler to Grawitz, June 8, 1942, BDC: SS-Führer; Günther von Wolff, "Weibliche Unfruchtbarkeit: ihre Ursachen und die Möglichkeiten ihrer Verhütung" (Berlin, n.d.), BDC: SS-Führer; see also Grawitz to Himmler, May 25, 1941, BDC: SS-Führer; Helmut Heiber, ed., *Reichsführer! Briefe an und von Himmler* (Munich, 1970), pp. 151, 159–60, 170–71; and Günther K. F. Schultze, "Der gegenwärtige Stand der Bekämpfung der weiblichen Unfruchtbarkeit," *Deutsche medizinische Wochenschrift* 68 (1942): 997–1002, 1027–32.
29. Hetzer's claim to have protected children from the SS in Poland (see chapter 8), unless it refers to other or general SS activities, would seem to contradict at lest her claim not to have known anything about the "Germanization" of children in the East. See Hildegard Hetzer, Lebenslauf, June 13, 1943, BDC: Kulturkammer; Geuter, *Die Professionalisierung der deutschen Psychologie*, pp. 410–12, 511–12 n. 18, 571; and Georg Lilienthal, *Der "Lebensborn e.V.": Ein Instrument nationalsozialistischer Rassenpolitik* (Stuttgart, 1985), pp. 206–16, 219–21, 225. On Hetzer's contact with the Göring Institute, see *ZfP* 14 (1942): 9. Cf. the probably inaccurate account in Marc Hillel and Clarissa Henry, *Of Pure Blood*, trans. Eric Mossbacher (New York, 1970), pp. 183–198. Ethologist Konrad Lorenz was apparently involved in a similar capacity in Posen: see Ute Deichmann, *Biologists Under Hitler*, trans. Thomas Dunlap (Cambridge, Mass., 1996), pp. 185, 193–7; and Rudolf Hippius et al., *Volkstum, Gesinnung und Charakter: Bericht über psychologische Untersuchungen an Posener deutsch-polnischen Mischlingen und Polen, Sommer 1942* (Stuttgart, 1942), p. 12; see also *ZfP* 13 (1941): 120–2; Rudolf Bilz, *Lebensgesetze der Liebe*, pp. 5–6, 11, 30, 77–8, 81, 83, 90–2; and Josephine Bilz, *Menschliche Reifung im Sinnbild: Eine psychologische Untersuchung über Wandlungsmetaphern des Traums, des Wahns, und des Märchens*, *ZfP* supplement no. 5 (Leipzig, 1943), pp. 46 n. 1, 70.
30. Ebner to Sollmann, March 6, 1944, NS 19/202, folder 1152, BA. On Lebensborn, see Bleuel, *Sex and Society*, pp. 161–6; and Lilienthal, *Der "Lebensborn e.V."*
31. Dr. Meyer, "Vorschläge zur Behandlung und Heilung der Empfängnisunfähigkeit der Frau und der Zeugungsunfähigkeit des Mannes," The Hague, n.d., pp. 11–12, NS 19/291, folder 1152; on Himmler and natural health, see Felix Kersten, *The*

Kersten Memoirs, pp. 38–51; Kater, *Das "Ahnenerbe" der SS,* pp. 99–100; and Fest, *Face of the Third Reich,* p. 100.

32. Erika Hantel, "Beginenwesen—ohne Romantik," *Frankfurter Zeitung,* October 24, 1942; and in idem, *Brücken von Mensch zu Mensch,* pp. 90–4.
33. Frederik Adama van Scheltema, "Mutter Erde und Vater Himmel in der germanischen Naturreligion," *ZfP* 14 (1943): 257–77, which was, however, listed in *Nationalsozialistische Bibliographie* 8:6/8 (June/July/August 1943), p. 10, entry 51.
34. "Homosexualität und Kunst," *Das Schwarze Korps,* March 11, 1937, p. 6; see also Bleuel, *Sex and Society,* pp. 23–4, 96–101, 118–19, 217–25; Heinrich Himmler, *Geheimreden 1933 bis 1945,* ed. Bradley F. Smith and Agnes F. Peterson (Frankfurt am Main, 1974), pp. 93–104, 120; Hans-Georg Stümke and Rudi Finkler, *Rosa Winkel, Rosa Listen: Homosexuelle und "Gesundes Volksempfinden" von Auschwitz bis Heute* (Reinbek, 1981); and Claudia Schoppmann, *Zeit der Maskierung: Lebensgeschichten lesbischer Frauen im "Dritten Reich"* (Berlin, 1993).
35. Kersten, *Memoirs,* p. 59; Schoppmann, *Nationalsozialistische Sexualpolitik,* pp. 157–62.
36. Vaernet to Himmler, October 30, 1944, BDC: SS-Führer; see also Schoppmann, *Nationalsozialistische Sexualpolitik,* pp. 160–2.
37. Martin Broszat, "The Concentration Camps 1933–45," in Helmut Krausnick et al., *The Anatomy of the SS State,* trans. Richard Barry et al. (New York, 1968), pp. 446–7; Pierre Seel, *I, Pierre Seel, Deported Homosexual: A Memoir of Nazi Terror,* trans. Joachim Neugroschel (New York, 1995), pp. 46–52.
38. Lockot, *Erinnern und Durcharbeiten,* p. 225.
39. Schultz, "Vorschlag eines Diagnosen-Schemas," p. 145; and idem, Anweisung für Truppenärzte, p. 19.
40. Heiber, *Reichsführer!,* pp. 271–3; microcopy T-175, roll 55, frames 0024–27, National Archives; Schoppmann, *Nationalsozialistische Sexualpolitik,* pp. 158–60; see also Heiber, *Reichsführer,* pp. 55, 199–200; Kersten, *Memoirs,* pp. 56–64; Himmler, *Geheimreden,* pp. 97–8; Heinz Höhne, *The Order of the Death's Head: The Story of Hitler's SS,* trans. Richard Barry (New York, 1970), pp. 142–3; Jellonek, *Homosexuelle unter dem Hakenkreuz,* pp. 171–5; and Schultz, "Zur Psychologie der Perversionen."
41. Ellen Bartens, personal communication, July 1, 1984; Lockot, *Erinnern und Durcharbeiten,* pp. 225–6. Bartens was a secretary at the Göring Institute whom Schultz allegedly told about this case. One wonders why Schultz would share such information with a secretary unless it was to plant a postwar alibi for his work with the SS. Boehm's secretary, Grete Mittelhaus, has given the same account; Claudia Schoppmann, personal communication, July 27, 1994.
42. Lockot, *Erinnern und Durcharbeiten,* p. 226.
43. "Bluthaftes Verständnis," *Der Spiegel,* June 27, 1994, p. 183ff.
44. Ulrich Schultz, "Autogenes Training and Gleichschaltung aller Sinne," *Die Tageszeitung,* June 20, 1984; Ulrich Schultz-Venrath, personal communication, August 21, 1994.
45. For an example of one case dangerously designated as "feeble-minded," see Schoppmann, *Nationalsozialistische Sexualpolitik,* p. 160.
46. Werner Kemper, personal communication, February 20, 1974.
47. Microcopy T-84, roll 6, frame 5303, National Archives; see also below, chapter 13.
48. Vortragsvermerk für Herrn Feldmarschall, August 12, 1942, p. 2, H 20/479, BA-MA.

49. H 20/474, BA-MA.
50. Ibid.; cf. Geoffrey G. Giles, "'The Most Unkindest Cut of All': Castration, Homosexuality and Nazi Justice," *Journal of Contemporary History* 27 (1992): 56.
51. H 20/479. BA-MA. The copy of the Luftwaffe directive in H 20/474 had been received by the consulting army psychiatrists on November 11, 1944, and is heavily marked with marginalia, mostly agitated exclamation points and question marks.
52. H 20/474, BA-MA. Cf. Franz Seidler, *Prostitution, Homosexualität, Selbstverstümmelung: Probleme der deutschen Sanitätsführung, 1939–1945* (Neckargemünd, 1977), pp. 213–21, which by ignoring the institutionalized disagreements between Wehrmacht psychotherapists and psychiatrists leaves the apologetic impression that by 1944 there was agreement on the less brutal Luftwaffe guidelines regarding homosexuality. Seidler also fails to mention the 1944 commission report on the army policy. The German navy, too, took a progressively more brutal line against homosexuality with the outbreak of war in 1939 and with the Wehrmacht policy change in May 1943. There is also evidence, according to historian John Fout, that working-class homosexuals in Germany before and after 1933 were more systematically and harshly prosecuted than homosexuals from the middle classes.

12

Psychotherapy and War Neurosis

The Göring Institute's greatest single capacity during the war naturally was service to the military. The German army, stung by its defeat in the First World War and under the material constraints of the Treaty of Versailles after 1918, turned after the war in part to the discipline of psychology to enhance the qualitative selection and cultivation of soldiers' attitudes and aptitudes. In 1936, for example, Karl Pintschovious of the Reich War Ministry observed that courage was impulsive action, while mental endurance, embedded within a strong character structure, was what was needed in complicated and prolonged modern wars. This endurance was a matter of complex internal operations against the anxiety that invariably accompanied participation in battle.[1] In April 1929, in the face of some persistent skepticism among more traditional military officers, Hans von Voss and Max Simoneit had established a department of psychology in the War Ministry. Preparation for war, from this psychological point of view on the lessons of the First World War, involved the psychotechniques of finding the right man for the right job, sustaining morale, acclimating troops to the stresses and strains of mechanized warfare, heightening efficiency, improving the relationship between officer and enlisted man, and preventing war neuroses. This approach coincided with that of many front-line officers who saw war as "machine based and industrial" and with that of many new staff officers who emphasized efficient modern management and planning.[2] The Nazis encouraged this technical interest in psychology through their inchoate preoccupation with race and will and their appreciation for the military value of psychological suggestion, power, and surprise. Nazi propaganda about racial comradeship and the weeding out of disruptive social and "racial" elements also contributed to the systematic evaluation of "character" as a basis for efficient and loyal military performance and to effect more comradely relationships between officers and men.[3] As a result, by 1942 the Central Psychological Laboratory in Berlin comprised twenty divisions and supervised the operations of seventeen army and two naval testing stations. It employed around 200 psychologists and drew on the work and resources of institutes and universities throughout Germany. After 1940 Voss and Simoneit were provided with partial use of Strassburg University in order to study the psychological problems brought about by war. The Luftwaffe, too, mobilized psychologists.[4]

According to Kemper, the Göring Institute assisted the army psychologists at the War Ministry in preparing national psychological profiles as a part of a campaign of psychological warfare. Foreign countries subjected to such analysis included the Soviet Union, the United States, Great Britain, France, and Czechoslovakia. The study on France, by way of illustration, stressed the French heritage of racial prejudice (!) as represented in the works of Gobineau and de la Rocque and suggested that this prejudice might be exploited by propaganda to produce friction between French soldiers of different races.[5] Psychological warfare was perceived in the broadest possible terms. In the words of Luftwaffe officer Friedrich von Cochenhausen, director of the German Society of Military Politics and Military Sciences, in an introduction to a bibliography on psychological warfare compiled by the Göring Institute's Felix Scherke, "spiritual conduct of war is, seen psychologically, the art of collective *Seelenführung*."[6] Psychological warfare was therefore a matter of an exploitable understanding of one's enemies as well as of one's own people and army. This bibliography, though fragmentary, illustrated this broad scope since it includes such works as: Harold Lasswell's *Propaganda Technique in the World War,* José Ortega y Gasset's *The Revolt of the Masses,* Gustave Le Bon's *Psychology of the Crowd,* Hitler's *Mein Kampf,* and Freud's *Group Psychology and the Analysis of the Ego.*

Naturally, the major sphere of military psychology in which the German psychotherapists were most active was the study, diagnosis, and treatment of war neuroses. The purpose of the psychological research carried on by Voss and Simoneit and of the reforms made in the selection, training, and care of the soldier and officer was not only to increase effectiveness but to decrease the propensity for mental breakdown under the alternate terror and boredom of warfare by instilling unity, purpose, and community feeling.[7] There is little doubt that the incidence of maladaption and disabling neurosis was reduced by this kind of professional application. While old-line officers often saw a disparity between psychology and military discipline, such psychological methods augmented the German army's traditional expertise in welding human beings into an efficient military instrument. But the psychologists knew that prevention could not be absolute and that therefore a capacity for treatment would also be necessary. In 1936 Pintschovious had somewhat boldly—and inaccurately—declared that National Socialism was in close touch with psychoanalytic thought by way of Friedrich Nietzsche and Richard Wagner. The strengthening of the will and the curing of anxiety, he concluded, were, through the work of Adler and Künkel in particular, the responsibility of psychotherapists.[8]

The reintroduction of conscription in 1935 did confront the German military with some extreme cases of mental disorder. The combination of improved screening techniques and the more brutal ongoing effects of the hereditary health law of 1933 reduced the number of psychopathic personalities at the medical inspection stations and in the services. Such cases at any rate comprised a maximum of 10 percent of the population as a whole.[9] Johannes Heinrich Schultz, in another advertisement for his profession in opposition to the prevailing psychiatric view in the army, thought it of paramount importance that men suffering from neuroses were not simply dismissed as congenitally malformed.[10] Even in its severest forms, echoed one military psychologist, neurosis was a product of human interaction with the environment and required treatment that could lead to substantial improvement or even full recovery.[11] Military psychiatrists would not in fact be overwhelmed, as they had been in the First World War, by cases of "war neurosis," in particular hysteria. This was due not only to better selection and prevention measures in the military but also to the "slower" outbreak of the war and the change in the nature of warfare from static trench warfare to a war of movement; only during the so-called "Sitzkrieg" of the winter of 1939–40 did the strain peculiar to life in the trenches manifest itself to even a noticeable degree.[12] The new war, however, brought its own demands and costs: for example, there was an increase in headaches due to the speed and change occasioned by mechanized war.[13]

The psychotherapeutic point of view on war neuroses was not restricted to prevention, treatment, and rehabilitation, however. In his comparative assessment of psychopathological casualties in the two world wars, Luftwaffe medical officer Gustav Störring opined that the Nazi regime had instilled in its people the idea for which and the will with which to fight. It was Störring's view that this, along with the changed conditions of warfare and greater preventive "care and control" over soldiers' free time, had resulted in a significant decline in war neuroses as compared to the First World War.[14] Such an emphasis on human will not only harmonized with Nazi ideology, it revealed the traditional and now timely stress psychotherapists laid both on the patient's *capacity* to recover but also on the patient's *responsibility* to recover. This therapeutic and professional ethos fit dangerously well with uncompromising and brutal Nazi demands for allegiance and performance. But such measures and conditions could not eliminate neurosis in the military. At the beginning of the war, psychosomatic complaints predominated, but by the end of 1943 psychogenic disorders were on the rise.[15] The social composition of patients also changed from the First World War, reflecting not only social change but the war fever among the highly educated in 1914: While 56 percent of all cases of war neurosis in the first war came from the ranks of academics and intellectuals, in the second war 56.5 percent of cases came from the middle classes.[16]

Once the war was underway it was, not surprisingly, Hermann Göring's Luftwaffe in which psychotherapy attained a significant degree of organizational and functional status. In 1939 a branch office for psychotherapy was established in the Reich Air Ministry at Knesebeckstrasse 46/47 in Charlottenburg not far from the Göring Institute.[17] Both Schultz and Göring were reserve air force medical officers and Schultz worked on Luftwaffe matters through Major Otto Brosius at the Air Ministry.[18] Hantel remembers accompanying Göring to the ministry on one occasion when he commented on how nice Hermann looked in the huge portrait of him in the entry hall. According to Ernst Göring, his father was so highly regarded in the air force that he alone among all reserve medical officers achieved the rank of major (Oberstabsarzt) and was the only man serving in the German armed forces allowed to wear a beard. Whatever the accuracy and significance of these bagatelles, it is logical to assume that the family name opened many doors in the Luftwaffe in particular; by 1944

Göring himself had been promoted to lieutenant-colonel (Oberfeldarzt).[19] It was in fact the elder Göring who, again according to his son, suggested the institutionalization of psychotherapy in the Luftwaffe, although it never achieved major status in the Luftwaffe medical service.[20] Nevertheless, the Luftwaffe as a new, relatively independent, and Nazified branch of the armed forces did not have as strong a psychiatric tradition in its medical service as did the army and the navy, so there was a comparative willingness on that score as well to work with the Göring Institute.

The psychotherapists were involved in a wide range of activities within the Luftwaffe. One of these was the study and treatment of suicide. The institute was officially charged with investigating the psychodynamics of attempted suicide, cowardice before the enemy, desertion, and insubordination.[21] Many German psychotherapists and psychoanalysts had extensive experience with thoughts and acts of suicide among their patients, acts that had negatively affected the public and professional reception of psychotherapy in the 1920s.[22] And of course such phenomena did anything but disappear under National Socialism.[23] In fact, suicide was an especially acute problem in Nazi Germany among both civilians and soldiers, particularly because of the generalized and justified fear of harsh punishment for perceived failure or dereliction. In 1942 Störring allowed as how the suicide rate in the armed services might go up over that of the First World War because of the more than amply justified fear of harsh punishment upon being branded a "parasite on the nation" (*Volksschädling*).[24] According to Hantel, in August 1944 Heyer was treating an army general who had lost his voice and who eventually committed suicide.

It was also the Luftwaffe, as we learned in the preceding chapter, that was allegedly the first to request that the institute establish a research project on homosexuality, a claim perhaps buttressed by the recorded meeting of the Göring cousins on the subject in 1942 at the time, as we shall see in the next chapter, when the institute was moving into the RFR. Hattingberg's son, Immo, a psychosomaticist and psychotherapist, did psychological research with the Luftwaffe and in 1944 the RFR was funding a research project by a surgeon at the Aviation Research Institute in Munich on increasing flying fitness through tests, exercises, drugs, and psychotherapy.[25] A number of high-ranking Luftwaffe officers attended seminars and practica at the Göring Institute on short-term therapy designed to improve the handling of their men. According to Ernst Göring, an air force officer could receive up to two years' leave to undertake course work in psychotherapy. In addition, according to institute members Fritz Riemann and Eva Hildebrand, Luftwaffe personnel frequented the outpatient clinic. One Air Ministry officer even suggested that since Luftwaffe personnel were on the average younger and better educated than their peers in the army and the navy, neurosis could represent a greater problem for the air force.[26] The chief of the Luftwaffe medical services, Erich Hippke, cautioned against confusing pubertal difficulties among young Luftwaffe auxiliaries with psychopathy.[27]

The Luftwaffe, also at the urging of Göring, set up a number of official psychotherapeutic installations in the field, a measure which the army never adopted. Luftwaffe medical officers regularly trained at the Göring Institute for service at these stations.[28] Psychological strain, Luftwaffe doctors believed, was particularly prevalent among flying personnel. Fighter pilots awaiting scrambles and long-range reconnaissance personnel could be susceptible to the types of hysterical reactions common to long periods of waiting that had characterized much of the symptomatology in the First World War. Psychologically astute selection and training could not guarantee flyers against the psychic consequences of wartime air duty, and the experiences of the First World War had shown the desirability of early detection and treatment of "psychic morbidity." Therefore, not only did the flight surgeon have to be especially alert for signs of neurosis or "fatigue," but also needed to be trained to deal with such problems. It was the task of the so-called medical observation stations to conduct both psychological and physiological examinations.

The first such stations were established in 1940 at Luftwaffe hospitals in Cologne, Brussels, and Paris. These hospitals were all near advance units easily accessible by rail. Each station was staffed by an internist, a physician with psychotherapeutic training in addition to a background in neurology and psychiatry, and "a medical assistant with special training." After five days of observation, sick fliers were either returned to their units or referred to a hospital for treatment or to a hostel for recuperation under a regimen of psychotherapy, autogenic training, hypnosis, physical therapy, exercise, hydrotherapy, and relaxation. In 1940 as well special sections for such cases were established at the Luftwaffe hospital in Halle-Dölau and at a convalescent home in Oberschreiberhau. By 1943 larger medical observation centers were also in place at Luftwaffe hospitals in Brunswick, Frankfurt am Main, Munich, and Vienna. There were medical observation stations in Paris-Clichy, Brussels, Athens, Minsk, Cracow, Pleskau, and Oslo. Between 50 and 180 fliers from front-line fighter, bomber, reconnaissance, and transport units and from training schools and rear areas were examined monthly at the centers and between 20 and 40 a month at the stations.[29] In 1944, the Luftwaffe also established a special reserve anti-aircraft battery in Dortmund for members of the air force suffering from psychogenic disorders.[30]

According to Immo von Hattingberg, there were few purely psychogenic disturbances among the patients seen by Luftwaffe doctors. This was due, he asserted, to the improved selection procedures used by the military, better training and organization of medical personnel, and diagnoses of fatigue that would otherwise have been cursorily defined as psychogenic. Genuinely serious psychogenic cases were referred as outpatients to the Göring Institute, although such a recourse was rare since, according to Hattingberg, those cases requiring extended psychotherapeutic treatment were written off for reassignment to the Luftwaffe. For the same reason, Hattingberg notes in his postwar description of Luftwaffe medical care for the American air force, psychoanalysis was abandoned by the Luftwaffe after an early trial. Such an intensive and extensive treatment, it was felt, demanded a freedom for readjustment in the patient's external life that was impossible given the tense demands that came with combat flying duty.[31] More generally within the Luftwaffe medical service, moreover, neurologists and psychiatrists tended to avoid "the therapeutically and administratively troublesome category of psychoneurosis."[32]

Göring's own younger son Ernst was employed as a psychotherapist by the Luftwaffe. Probably as a result once again of the family name, his activity was unique and experimental. Ernst had taken his medical examinations in 1938 and began his training at his father's institute in 1939. That year he also served at the Charité clinic for internal medicine and received his doctorate from the University of Munich with a thesis on childhood enuresis. The young Göring was also an avid horseman who was a member of the SA Riding Corps. Because he had found that riding relieved him of the tremendous stress and anxiety that had accompanied his medical exams, he decided that horseback riding could be used as a means of psychotherapy. It was this insight that no doubt inspired the book review his father wrote for the *Zentralblatt* on international equestrian competition and its instructive expression of will and of the feeling between man and horse.[33] Göring *fils,* like Göring *père,* had studied with Leonhard Seif, but his early interest and training in gymnastics, combined with his work in medicine and psychotherapy, coalesced with his love for horses into a method he came to call "riding therapy" (*Reittherapie*). The junior Göring served a year in the Luftwaffe and in 1940 was given charge over the psychotherapy ward of the Luftwaffe hospital in Brunswick. His assignment was to rehabilitate pilots who were "flown-out" (*abgeflogen*). Göring recognized that the pilot of an airplane is especially susceptible to stress primarily because he is always alone, even in a multi-place aircraft, in the exercise of his duties and skills. Göring worked at Brunswick during 1940 and into 1941, but then was transferred to the 1st Nightfighter Group at Venlo in Holland. The stress on the nightfighter pilots was particularly severe and it was here that he was able to put his idea of riding therapy into practice. He procured horses from local residents—including from the woman who was to become his wife—and soon those pilots who could no longer get up in their Messerschmitt Bf 110s were getting up on horses as a major part of a program of rehabilitation.[34] The demands of the straining Nazi war machine by 1942 were such, however, that this and other kinds of psychotherapy became a luxury the Wehrmacht could no longer afford. In late 1942 Göring was reassigned to work as a regular doctor with a Luftwaffe field division on the Russian front.[35]

Psychotherapists were also confronted with the use and abuse of the amphetamine Pervitin in the Luftwaffe. Pervitin was the German name for a slightly more potent methamphetamine form of the central nervous system stimulant Benzedrine that had been approved for use in the United States in 1937. Despite much debate among medical experts, including psychotherapists, over their effectiveness and effects, the use of stimulants such as caffeine and methamphetamines like Pervitin was extensive, especially in the Luftwaffe.[36] On October 25, 1941, in fact, the Luftwaffe medical service ordered that Pervitin be among the drugs to be kept under lock and key.[37] There was even some experimentation with Pervitin in psychotherapy and psychiatry, but its efficacy, especially in an outpatient setting, proved distinctly limited.[38] Pervitin, like drugs in general, was in high demand in Nazi Germany. Novelist Heinrich Böll, in the memoirs of his young adulthood in Nazi Germany, reports almost becoming addicted to Pervitin.[39] As we saw in chapter 9, Hermann Göring allegedly also was addicted to the drug and even Hitler himself was dosed with it by his quack physician Theodor Morell.[40]

The sudden demand for drugs was a function of two phenomena. The first of these was the growing medical and popular dependence on pharmaceuticals, which for the first time became widely available—and aggressively marketed—in the West during the 1930s. As early as 1936 an alarmed city medical director in Oberhausen in the Ruhr referred to a generalized "hunger for drugs" ("*Arzneihunger*").[41] In 1941 the SD was complaining about the deleterious flood of advertising ("*Reklameflut*") issuing from the drug companies.[42] And the demand for pharmaceuticals would only grow with the suffering and shortages multiplying over the course of the war. The second phenomenon was that the Nazi regime, despite a campaign by Conti against the use of Pervitin in particular, sought to encourage prescriptions to heighten productivity, not only for Pervitin but for a similar drug, Phosphyll, known as the "workingman's Pervitin" due to its high rate of use among armaments workers.[43] In the midst of this pharmacological flurry of activity, one pharmacologist, referring to what he called the productivist "Americanization" of the world, rather boldly—and accurately—labeled these stimulants "the chemical whip."[44]

German psychotherapists also functioned in one other sphere of Luftwaffe concern: the impact of air attacks on civilian morale. In a speech in Berlin in 1937, Hermann Göring had declared that defense against air attack (*Luftschutz*) was not just a matter of mounting fighter aircraft, flak batteries, detection devices, and early-warning systems, but of preparing the populace for the psychological challenges of air raids.[45] Schultz was the primary moving force behind the Göring Institute's role in attempting to maintain general mental health and productivity under the strain and disruption of all aspects of enemy raids. In a lecture to the Berlin Medical Society on January 1, 1940, and to the German General Medical Society for Psychotherapy on February 7, Schultz discussed the psychological effects of blackouts. He explained that darkness was the perfect atmosphere for what he termed "distortion neurosis" (*Entstellungsneurose*), the conviction that within a threatening environment "something could happen." Such mental processes were a threat in and of themselves to others and they could be eliminated or minimized only by psychotherapeutic intervention. Blackouts could also be turned to advantage, Schultz volunteered, by allowing the city dweller to achieve harmony with natural phenomena and to commune in the darkness with the inner self and the community, whence issued the true strength of the nation. Under Schultz's direction, therefore, the institute issued a pamphlet on the "do's" and "don'ts" of blackout conduct. This effort engaged the collaboration of Achelis, Hattingberg, Kemper, Meyer-Mark, and others.[46] Schultz also translated the Reich Marshal's prewar imperatives into the psychotherapeutic conception of the air-raid shelter community (*Luftschutzraumgemeinschaft*) where the mettle of the German *Volk* would be tested and, given the proper psychotherapeutic advice and assistance, hardened. The experience of the common danger, Schultz asserted, would draw the bonds of community tighter and provide a therapeutic environment in and of itself for those whose will was flagging.[47] While these measures paled in the face of the massive bombing campaign carried out by the British and the Americans and little organized psychotherapeutic care was available, the negative effects on the mental health of those who survived the bombing were, however, generally not severe.[48]

It was of course Matthias Heinrich Göring who had the most to do with the affairs of psychotherapy in the Luftwaffe. He travelled in occupied Europe not only in pursuit of his duties as director of the institute but also in service to the Luftwaffe. In November and December of 1940 he toured the eastern occupied territories and then inspected air force installations around Germany and in Paris and in Oslo, also consulting with psychotherapists in France, Norway, and Holland.[49] As we have already seen in chapter 10, he went to Rome in June 1941 as part of a delegation of industrial and military psychologists. In August of that same year he travelled to Sofia, Bulgaria, to discuss the deployment of German-trained psychotherapists with the Bulgarian air force. Göring also consulted there on the "psychotechnology" of special weapons and took the opportunity to explore the possibility of a Bulgarian national member group of the International General Medical Society for Psychotherapy.[50] Göring returned to Paris in November 1943 accompanied by Luftwaffe physician Gustav Störring and industrial psychologist Felix Scherke. Here too he busied himself on behalf of his institute and the General Medical Society. He gave a lecture entitled "The Foundations of Psychotherapy" for the local German Institute to a French audience at the Maison de la

Chimie.[51] Göring and Scherke also met with psychoanalyst René Laforgue and two work physiologists. Out of this meeting came a report on the political situation in France that commented on the attitudes of the French working class and concluded, with astounding insight, that the Germans had made a lot of psychological errors in dealing with the French![52] Laforgue was a provisional member of the International General Medical Society and had proposed a member group from France which, together with a group from Norway, Göring planned to recognize after the war.[53]

Göring and the psychotherapists faced much less professional opportunity in the other branches of the Wehrmacht. There is no record at all of psychotherapists on duty with the navy, and the army medical services were dominated by the old-school psychiatrists who managed to defend their position there with much greater success than in the civilian realm. Psychotherapists who were conscripted as medical personnel into the army were lost to the profession for that period. The best that Göring (and Schultz) could do was to minimize the length of military service by appeal to the authorities on the basis of the medical importance to the war effort of the Göring Institute. Göring managed to use his influence to get Kemper released from his military obligation after a short "guest appearance" in order that he might continue as director of the outpatient clinic.[54] Schultz likewise prevented the conscription of psychoanalyst Fritz Riemann until 1943.[55] Schultz-Hencke served part-time at a military hospital during 1942 and 1943.[56] Heyer volunteered for army medical duty and served as an internist at the Greater Berlin Reserve Army Hospital from early 1942 to 1944. Never hesitant to voice a complaint, he protested to Hitler's headquarters that the menial and mundane routine of his assignment was an insult to his professional standing and military rank as well as a disservice to the state.[57]

The turning of the war's tide in 1942 from blitzkrieg and victory to attrition and defeat not only increased the number of mental casualties among German soldiers, it arrested the earlier organizational momentum established by psychology and psychotherapy in the military. In 1942 the Reich War Ministry disbanded its Psychological Section and its journal *Soldatentum* and the army eliminated its psychological testing stations.[58] The growing casualty list demanded more physicians and the Nazi preoccupation with quality and character turned, as the number and power of Germany's enemies multiplied, to a reliance on quantity based on a now last-ditch belief in inherent racial superiority. The biological certainties of Nazi racism had always been fundamentally impatient with the niceties and ambiguities of academic psychologists. This ethos merged with the traditional skepticism of many in the military toward the fancy theories of psychologists and the soft indulgence of psychotherapists. In the army there would be a return to an emphasis upon battlefield operations and the leadership of men and cultivation of character by unit commanders.[59] Similarly, in the Luftwaffe psychological research and the use of applied psychology were phased out in 1942.[60] Here disagreements between psychologists and the High Command over particular cases as well as the desperate need for pilots helped lead to this change.[61] According to one rumor at the time, Hermann Göring himself was supposedly angry about a negative psychological evaluation of one of his nephews.[62] The Göring Institute's work was also affected: for example, a research project on personality development and psychotherapeutic training funded by the RFR in 1944 was designated as less urgent than research into the physiology of high-altitude flying and crashes due to pilot error.[63] That the German navy only partially disbanded its psychological services was most likely due to the more generalized specialist training in technical capacities required in that branch of the service.[64]

But while the psychological infrastructure in the military was being dismantled, at the same time the increase in psychological disorders in the military also produced a demand for psychotherapeutic expertise.[65] The very lack of an official status in the army also allowed the Göring Institute to escape the institutional fate of the psychologists. This brought psychotherapists once again into direct conflict with their psychiatric rivals. It did not revolve so much around the psychiatrists' complete rejection of psychotherapeutic methods, since there was a wide range of views on technique among psychiatrists and about how they should be applied and by whom.[66] Moreover, some psychiatrists who were members of the Göring circle served in the Wehrmacht medical corps and many injuries and illnesses incurred in military service carried with them psychological sequelae.[67] The psychiatrists were compelled by their new competitors and the possible recurrence of the psychological casualties experienced in the First World War to declare their exclusive knowledge of the uses and limits of psychotherapy.[68] They had a strong position in the Wehrmacht medical services, particularly in the army, and jealously guarded it, especially when the problem of "war neuroses" brought with it a strengthened challenge from the psychotherapists under Göring.

The first line of defense for the psychiatrists was to minimize the problem of neurosis. While, as we have seen, the problem was not as great as it had been in the First World War, the change in the nature of the war along with the turning of the military tide against Germany resulted in an increase in the incidence of psychological disorder among German troops. A quarterly report from a psychiatrist attached to Army Group D in France in 1944 claimed that "the so-called war-neurotic question up until now has not been a problem."[69] Conceding that the possible demoralization following the recent Normandy invasion was not reflected in the accompanying statistics, he nonetheless declared that his experience told him there would be no appreciable jump in cases of neurosis.[70] There was in general evidence of an ebb and flow in the statistics of mental casualties, depending on the intensity of the fighting,[71] but at what level rested on how various complaints were diagnosed and what level of "psychogenic disorders," as they came to be called, was regarded as critical.[72] In the 1944 report out of France, for example, the largest classification was that of "constitutionally abnormal," a category open in any number of cases to psychotherapeutic reinterpretation, especially since 78.85 percent of them were ambulatory and included "asocials," "mental failures," and those suffering from "hysterical superimpositions."[73] As for therapy, the psychiatrists claimed great success for the new electroshock treatment; Friedrich Panse of the reserve hospital at Ensen near Cologne was the leading exponent of this practice.[74]

On the other hand, army internists suspected that the growing number of chronic stomach disorders included a large percentage of psychosomatic cases. In July 1943 the first of a number of "stomach battalions" was established to deal with the problem not only by means of medication and diet but also by "education" to duty and efficiency (*Leistungsfähigkeit*) as well as referral to psychiatrists.[75] Even among army psychiatrists opinions could vary. A quarterly report from the eastern front for the second quarter of 1944 emphasized the importance of "*seelische Führung*" in providing for the "healthy maintenance of the powers of mental resistance."[76] This psychiatrist, attached to the Fourth Panzer Army, complained that haphazard replacements reduced psychic will and disrupted the organic unity of the formations for which the German army had long been famous.[77] With continuing Russian breakthroughs, moreover, instances of panic among the troops were on the rise.[78] There is evidence, furthermore, that the stalling of the German offensive in Russia in the winter of 1941–42 had produced the type of trench warfare that, along with heavy losses destroying unit coherence, could spawn neurosis.[79] The fighting in the East was particularly savage, a result primarily of Nazi racial policy and propaganda. At least one German psychiatrist argued that this fact, coupled with the distance from home and the consequent paucity of leaves, would lessen the chance of breakdowns among men too preoccupied with fighting for their lives, far from any reminders of home.[80] Heyer, from a broad psychocultural perspective, worried that German soldiers in the East, far from their roots in Germany, might, as a result of "spatial-racial russification," lose those characteristics that made them soulfully dynamic.[81]

The clash between psychiatrists and psychotherapists of course was not confined to scientific debate, but had significant institutional dimensions as well. Otto Wuth, consulting with the Academy for Military Medicine in Berlin, and Oswald Bumke, the consulting psychiatrist for the Wehrmacht's Seventh Military District in Munich, agreed in an exchange of letters in 1942 that unless the war lasted a very long time, those suffering from war neuroses or battle fatigue (*Kriegszitterer*) would not be a problem for the military. Should this happen, however, both Wuth and Bumke thought it professionally prudent to have such cases referred to psychiatric colleagues who were practiced in the use of hypnosis and other auxiliary "active" modes of psychotherapy. In being specific about such an eventuality, Wuth and Bumke were clearly attempting to head off a possible further expansion of the psychotherapists' competence in the now professionally competitive field of medical psychology. Wuth allowed as how three cases in Berlin had been sent for hypnotic therapy to the psychotherapeutic group around the more trustworthy Schultz, but both psychiatrists agreed firmly that if any of these cases were handled "analytically," it would be a "catastrophe."[82] While the use of the adverb "analytically" marked a prudent and sincere distancing from psychoanalysis, by 1942 psychiatrists were much less concerned with attacking "Jewish" psychoanalysis than defending themselves against the Göring psychotherapists in general. Wuth also noted that unlike in the First World War the Nazi party leadership offered an avenue for appeal to "nondoctors" for cases of "war neurotics."[83] Wuth was obviously anxious about the leverage the psychotherapists enjoyed within the Nazi leadership and in civilian society as a whole. For Wuth, the party was a place where psychotherapists could impress nonmedical people unable to understand the scientific complexities of psychiatry and who often resented the traditional university elites. In addition, Wuth could distrust the party's general desire to control matters and probably suspected that on the issue of war neurotics it would often prefer to hear the therapeutic optimism of the psychotherapists. Thus, for orthodox psychiatrists the stakes in the battle over control of military were high indeed. In a letter dated October 25, 1944, to the Army Medical Service Command Max de Crinis, like Wuth associated with the Academy for Military Medicine, stressed the importance of maintaining "scientific control in the army" over mental cases requiring therapy.[84] Although his concern about the danger of such men being released from civilian hospitals if discharged from the Wehrmacht was frequently expressed among psychiatrists, de Crinis's emphasis on the army as a bastion of scientific reason also embodied his oft-expressed concern over the competition offered psychiatry by the dilettantish psychotherapists under Göring.

The debate in the military over the word "neurosis" also displayed the professional struggle going on between psychiatrists and psychotherapists in the military. On June 30, 1944, the head of the Wehrmacht Health Services issued a directive outlining the various terms to be used in place of "neurosis." Terms like "war neurotic," "war trembler," and "war hysteric" were forbidden.[85] The term to be used instead was "abnormal mental reaction." Purely psychological disorders became "abnormal experiential reactions" and psychosomatic problems "psychogenic (experience-conditioned) functional disorders." With some justification, it was claimed that the term "neurosis" was vague and overused, but for psychiatrists it was equally true that its use was associated with, and gave credence to, a psychodynamic view of the mind to which a physicalist psychiatry was opposed. For many psychiatrists and Nazis, moreover, the work recalled the vexing problems of the last war and smacked of medical indulgence of cowardly malingerers. Many psychiatrists of the old school, encouraged by Nazi racial theory, divided those cases not diagnosable or treatable by psychiatric methods into true "psychopaths," or those hereditarily defective, and malingerers, those consciously feigning illness to shirk duty. For psychiatrists in general, neurosis could fall into either category.[86] Psychiatrists also argued that psychotherapeutic methods, whatever their past successes, consumed too much time and expense given the pressing demands of the war.[87] In spite of their promotion of short-term methods dedicated to swift readjustment and enhanced productivity, psychotherapists were vulnerable on this score, especially amid the hysteria generated among the Nazis by the worsening war situation.

In the last years of the war Nazis resorted to a typical mixture of propaganda and terror to combat any slackening of will and performance. The implementation of the Total War program in 1943 represented not only a marshalling of Germany's material resources but its "spiritual" resources as well. In the military this took the form of the deployment of political commissars called National Socialist Leadership Officers (NSFO). From November 28, 1943, these took the place of the army organization dedicated to the cultivation of morale that had been set up after the First World War in response to the army's collapse in 1918. This so-called Wehrgeistige Führung had always manifested an interest in academic and medical psychology. In early 1943, for example, Karl Arnhold gave a series of lectures for the organization on the working relationship between industrial and military psychology.[88] There was a carryover of personnel into NSFO ranks and a number of these officers had received training at the Göring Institute: One, a psychiatrist, produced a manual on the subject dedicated to Matthias Heinrich Göring as the "spiritual father of this work."[89] But the new repressive orientation represented by political surveillance at the front only aggravated the stress and breakdown now more common because of the gradual disintegration of an army in defeat. As the previously cultivated Nazi and military ideal of organic comradeship among officers and men confident of success was replaced by the reality of political commissars in the midst of retreat and devastation at the front and at home, the morale and mental health of soldiers could only suffer.

The mounting desperation of the Nazi regime during the last two years of the war fostered an environment of punishment. "Difficult" soldiers were often simply sent to the front. According to Müller-Hegemann, such incorrigibles, when not dispatched to prison or a concentration camp, were often relegated to mine-clearing duties or assigned to a penal unit. While the Waffen-SS was particularly harsh along these lines, this was the case in the Luftwaffe as well.[90] Psychiatrists attempted to exploit this environment by charging psychotherapists and psychologists as not only being "soft" in terms of scientific rigor but also in terms of the necessity now for more stringent discipline for malingerers and slackers. This was part of a larger campaign against patients and doctors in general who were not living up to the demands of total war: "In every case the doctor awakens in the patient the conviction that the demand for relief from an assignment is justified, and is driven into neuroses which, as with the pension neurotic of peacetime, never release their hold."[91]

Individual psychotherapists found themselves involved in cases of soldiers, sailors, and airmen in trouble with military authorities because of alleged or actual psychological problems. Adolf Martin Däumling, a physician and psychologist who served at the Göring Institute from August 21, 1944, to January 31, 1945, had been given the assignment of evaluating Luftwaffe officers who faced charges of high treason and cowardice before the enemy. According to Däumling, the institute provided expert psychotherapeutic testimony regarding the officer's state of mind.[92] The assignment was typical of the type of work the institute was increasingly called upon to do in the last years of the war insofar as it involved a mixture of both personal and professional concerns for the mediation of judgment in such cases. Kalau vom Hofe confirms the heavier wartime caseloads that descended on the psychotherapists in Berlin and recalls that a great deal of her own work was with Boehm, who was in charge of the Göring Institute's subdivision for evaluations. Boehm himself was apparently involved in a representative case of the type we are describing. As we saw in chapter 11, Boehm had a less admirable role to play in the military policy on homosexuality, but he was given personal credit by Eva Hildebrand, John Rittmeister's widow, for saving the life of her second husband. This of course was a typical pattern in Nazi Germany (and under any repressive regime); "saving what could be saved" involved single cases, often friends and acquaintances, while sacrificing groups of anonymous people. In 1944 Heinz Hildebrand was on trial for making remarks injurious to the fighting spirit of the people and Boehm was assigned by the court to prepare an expert opinion on him. Boehm determined that Hildebrand was suffering from a mental disturbance and thus was not responsible for his actions; as a result, according to his wife, Hildebrand, a soldier, was sent to prison instead of being executed.

In general, according to Kemper, institute psychotherapists during the latter stages of the war became adept at the so-called "back-and-forth game" (*hin-und-her Spiel*). A number of the directors of military clinics in the Greater Berlin area were former students of members of the institute and it often happened that a patient in danger of being punished as a malingerer or a traitor, or simply of being sent back to the front, would instead be shuffled back and forth between hospital and institute for evaluations, tests, and treatment. Diagnoses would conflict—a not uncommon phenomenon anyway—or were delayed until the military and the government, still more or less impressed by medical expertise and exasperated by medical bureaucracy, lost track of, and interest in, the case. Those who were allegedly protected in this way included a demoted major and an infantry general who were kept at a military reserve hospital.[93] Gerhard Maetze recalled that psychoanalyst Dietfried Müller-Hegemann, a communist active in the underground, was particularly skilled at holding men out of combat for as long as possible.[94] Kemper asserted after the war that between 100 and 200 patients in Berlin were saved in this manner. In 1944 Nazi doctor Otto Nitzsche, without mentioning the Göring Institute or any other organization by name, complained loudly in the medical press over such treasonable activity.[95] Of course, such incidents must be placed against the background not only of functional psychotherapeutic support of the Nazi regime but also in the context of all the cases not seen or turned away by the Göring Institute. These, for reasons of professional reputation, individual conscience, and likely outcome, remain in the shadows. The psychotherapists could rationalize their behavior not only in terms of "saving what could be saved" (including themselves and their profession), but also because their transgressions in this regard were mostly ones of omission. Other agents, such as psychiatrists, could be relied upon to perform the actual destructive work in such cases.

Notes

1. Karl Pintschovious, *Die seelische Widerstandskraft im modernen Krieg,* pp. 13–56; see also Wladimir Eliasberg, "German Philosophy and German Psychological Warfare," *Journal of Psychology* 14 (1942): 207.
2. Michael Geyer, "The Past as Future: The German Officer Corps as Profession," in Cocks and Jarausch, *German Professions, 1800–1950,* p. 196.
3. Farago, *German Psychological Warfare,* pp. ix-x; John Laffin, *Jackboot: The Story of the German Soldier* (London, 1965), pp. 154–9, 166–7, 176–7, 180–1.
4. Farago, *German Psychological Warfare,* pp. 13–33; Ulfried Geuter, personal communication, May 5, 1981; see also Max Simoneit, *Deutsches Soldatentum 1914 und 1939* (Berlin, 1940); and Geuter, *Die Professionalisierung der deutschen Psychologie,* pp. 180–6, 255–67, 390–429.

5. Generalstab des Heeres, "Propagandamöglichkeiten in der Farbigenarmee Frankreichs," Völkerpsychologische Untersuchungen Nr. 8, H 1/661, BA/MA; and microcopy T-78, roll 440, National Archives.
6. Felix Scherke and Ursula Vitzhum, eds., *Bibliographie der geistigen Kriegsführung* (Berlin, 1938), p. 10; see also William Ebenstein, *The Nazi State* (New York, 1943), p. 108.
7. Heinrich Wietfeldt, *Kriegsneurose als psychisch-soziale Mangelkrankheit* (Leipzig, 1936), pp. 12–13, 25.
8. Pintschovious, *Die seelische Widerstandskraft,* p. 24.
9. Simon, "Das Problem der Psychopathen in der Wehrmacht," *Der deutsche Militärarzt* 3 (1938): 33–5.
10. Schultz, Anweisung für Truppenärzte, p. 20.
11. A. Eichberg, "Der nervöse Mensch als Soldat," *Der Truppendienst* 4 (1939): 329–31; cf. the somewhat grudging acknowledgment of psychotherapy's usefulness in Werner Villinger, "Psychiatrie und Wehrmacht," *Münchener medizinische Wochenschrift* 88 (1941): 437–43.
12. Hummel, "Vergleichende Untersuchungen," p. 23.
13. Gustav Störring, "Die Verschiedenheiten der psychopathologischen Erfahrungen im Weltkriege und im jetzigen Kriege und ihre Ursachen," p. 28; Hummel, "Vergleichende Untersuchungen," pp. 39–41.
14. Störring, "Die Verschiedenheiten der psychopathologischen Erfahrungen," pp. 26, 27.
15. Lockot, *Erinnern und Durcharbeiten,* pp. 227–8.
16. Hummel, "Vergleichende Untersuchungen," p. 43. On this response of university-bound students to the outbreak of war in 1914, see Erich Maria Remarque's *All Quiet on the Western Front* (1929).
17. Schultz, *Lebensbilderbuch,* pp. 135–6; Matthias Heinrich Göring to Friedrich Falkenberg, June 7,1940, Kl. Erw. 762/2; Göring to Georg Ekimoff, May 8, 1941, Kl. Erw. 762/3.
18. Schultz, *Lebensbilderbuch,* p. 136; see also Otto Brosius, "Methode und Auswertung Kurzer zum Zwecke des Menschenerkennens durchgeführter Aussprachen," *Soldatentum* 4 (1937): 130–4; and Lockot, *Erinnern und Durcharbeiten,* p. 210.
19. Wolfgang Driest, *Richtlinien über Menschenführung in der Truppe,* p. 4; Pongratz, *Psychotherapie,* p. 290.
20. Heinrich Knoche, *Die Entwicklung und Organisation des Sanitätswesens der deutschen Luftwaffe 1935–1945* (Freiburg, 1974); and Heinz Knoche, personal communication, December 22, 1982.
21. Richard Donnevert, Aktenvermerk über die Besichtigung des Reichsinstitutes für Psychologische Forschung und Psychotherapie im Reichsforschungsrat; Berlin W.62, Keithstr.41, December 3, 1944, p. 1, RFR 107/12850, and Scherke to Kemper; see also A. Bingel, "Psychiatrie in der Luftfahrtmedizin," in Kretschmer, *Psychiatry,* pp. 276–88; and Heinrich Lottig, "Neurologische und psychologische Erfahrungen aus der Luftfahrtmedizin," *Fortschritte der Neurologie* 11 (1939): 441–54.
22. Cimbal, "Gründungsgeschichte," p. 8.
23. Gustav Schmaltz to Julius Schirren, January 9, 1943, B 339/42, BA.
24. Störring, "Die Verschiedenheiten der psychopathologischen Erfahrungen," p. 27. During the Second World War, the Wehrmacht handed down more than 50,000 death sentences and executed between 5000 and 6000 soldiers for desertion: Manfred Messerschmidt and Fritz Wüllner, *Die Wehrmachtjustiz im Dienste des Nationalsozialismus: Zerstörung einer Legende* (Baden-Baden, 1987).

25. RFR 110/13080t, German Captured Documents/Reichsforschungsrat, Library of Congress; Immo von Hattingberg, Fragebogen, August 19, 1939, BDC: Parteikorrespondenz. Hattingberg had joined the Nazi party in 1930, had left in 1932, and rejoined in 1940.
26. P. Würfler, "Zum Verständnis der Neurose, auch im Hinblick auf militärische Verhältnisse," *Der deutsche Militärarzt* 4 (1939): 124–8.
27. Erich Hippke, Anweisung für die Truppenärzte über gesundheitliche Betreuung der jugendlichen Lw-Helfer und Lw-Helferinnen; see also Schultz, Anweisung für Truppenärzte, p. 20.
28. See, for example, the questionnaire of Hans Suchner, November 6, 1942, Kl. Erw. 762/6.
29. Immo von Hattingberg, "Medical Care for Flying Personnel," pp. 1060–3, 1067.
30. Anweisung für Truppenärzte Einzelordnungen Nr. 11, December 6, 1944, p. 4. RL 4 II/304, BA-MA.
31. Hattingberg, "Medical Care for Flying Personnel," pp. 1063–4, 1068.
32. Leo Alexander, *Neuropathology and Neuropsychiatry, Including Encephalography, in Wartime Germany* (Washington, D.C., n.d.), p. 30.
33. *ZfP* 10 (1938): 186; Clemens Laar (pseud.), . . . *reitet für Deutschland: Carl Friedrich von Langen: ein Kämpferschicksal* (Hanover, 1936).
34. BDC: Reichsärztekammer and Parteikorrespondenz; see also Hattingberg, "Medical Care for Flying Personnel," p. 1060; and Bingel, "Psychiatrie in der Luftfahrtmedizin," pp. 283–5.
35. The resultant shortage of doctors on the home front even caused some Nazi leaders to consider the employment of Jewish doctors to treat German patients: see Geoffrey Cocks, "Partners and Pariahs: Jews and Medicine in Modern German Society," *Leo Baeck Institute Yearbook* 36 (1991): 191–205.
36. Oberkommando der Luftwaffe, Leistungsteigernde Mittel bei der Luftwaffe, August 31, 1944, H 20/345, BA-MA; for the debate over Pervitin, see G. Lehmann et al., "Pervitin als Leistungssteigernde Mittel," *Arbeitsphysiologie* 10 (1939): 692–705; O. Graf, "Über den Einfluss von Pervitin auf einige psychische und psychomotorische Funktionen," ibid., pp. 680–91; and W. Heubner, "Pharmakologisches über Pervitin," *Deutsche medizinische Wochenschrift* 70 (1944): 517–19. The same was true of the armed forces of other nations during the Second World War: see Lester Grinspoon and Peter Hedblom, *The Speed Culture: Amphetamine Use and Abuse in America* (Cambridge, Mass., 1975), pp. 18–19, 40–5.
37. Luftwaffensanitätsabteilung der 11. Flak Division, May 15, 1943, microcopy T-321, roll 17, frame 631, National Archives.
38. Johannes Heinrich Schultz, "Pervitin in der Psychotherapie," *Deutsche medizinische Wochenschrift* 70 (1944): 519–21; Helmut Selbach, "Probleme um die Pervitinanwendung in der Psychiatrie," ibid., 521–4.
39. Heinrich Böll, *What's To Become of the Boy? Or: Something to Do with Books*, trans. Leila Vennewitz (New York, 1984), pp. 73–4.
40. Leonard L. Heston and Renate Heston, *The Medical Casebook of Adolf Hitler* (New York, 1979), pp. 82, 86.
41. Auszug aus der Niederschrift über die 7. Sitzung der Rheinischen Arbeitsgemeinschaft für Wohlfahrtspflege am 4. Juli 1936 im Kreissparkassengebäude zu St. Goar, RW 53/445, NWH.
42. Meldungen aus dem Reich, February 20, 1941, microcopy T-175, roll 260, frame 3286, National Archives.
43. F. Mörchen, "Phosphyll," *Deutsche medizinische Wochenschrift* 61 (1935): 598–

9; Hans Brack, "Die Phosphyll-Behandlung," *Die medizinische Welt* 9 (1936): 1847–9; Armin Bauer & Co. to Reichsgesundheitsamt, June 9, 1943, R 86, folder 3996; and Kroll AG to Reichsgesundheitsamt, November 14, 1944, Reichsgesundheitsamt to Kroll AG, December 5, 1944, R 86, folder 3990, BA.

44. F. Eichholtz, "Ermüdungsbekämpfung: Über Stimulantien," *Deutsche medizinische Wochenschrift* 67 (1941): 55, 56; on Conti, see Hans-Dietrich Röhrs, *Hitlers Krankheit: Tatsache und Legende: Medizinishe und psychische Grundlagen seine Zusammenbruchs* (Neckargemünd, 1966), pp. 96–104.
45. Heinrich Grunwaldt, "Über die psychischen Bedingungen des Luftschutzes," p. 39.
46. Johannes Heinrich Schultz, "Seelische Reaktionen auf die Verdunkelung."
47. Schultz, *Die seelische Gesunderhaltung*, pp. 31–4.
48. United States Strategic Bombing Survey, Morale Division, Medical Branch Report, *The Effect of Bombing on Health and Medical Care in Germany* (Washington, D.C., October 30, 1945), pp. 101–5.
49. Kirst[?] to Otto Curtius, November 25, 1940, Kl. Erw. 762/2.; Bericht von Prof. M. H. Göring über Besprechungen mit Psychotherapeuten in den besetzten Gebieten, n.d., Kl. Erw. 762/3; Aktennotiz Besprechung Professor Göring mit Dr. van den Hoop and Professor Rümke in Amsterdam am 21.XI,1940, n.d., Kl. Erw. 762/3. See also Hans Reiter's desire for contacts with even unfriendly occupied countries, with the exception of the military Generalgouvernement of occupied Poland, on matters of health: Rundschreiben an die medizinisch-wissenschaftlichen Gesellschaften, May 15, 1941, Kl. Erw. 762/2.
50. Göring to Georg Ekimoff, July 7 and November 13, 1941; Göring, Bericht, n.d., Kl. Erw. 762/3.
51. "Les conferences de l'Institut allemand," *Oeuvre,* November 19, 1943, PC 5, reel 102, Wiener Library, London.
52. Bericht über Besprechungen zwischen Prof. Carrel, Dr. Ménetrier und Dr. Laforgue einerseits und Prof. Göring und Dr. Scherke and[e]rerseits vom 17.-20.11.43 in Paris; Zusatz zu dem Bericht über die Besprechungen zwischen Professor Carrel, Dr. Ménetrier, Dr. Laforgue einerseits, Professor Göring und Dr. Scherke andererseits vom 17.-20. 1943 in Paris; and Schultz to Mentzel, December 17, 1943, RFR 107/12850; and in Alain de Mijolla, "Documents Inédits: Les Psychanalystes en France durant l'Occupation Allemande, Paris, Novembre 1943," *Revue Internationale d'Histoire de la Psychanalyse* 2 (1989): 463–73.
53. Laforgue to Göring, September 9, 1940, Kl. Erw. 762/3; Göring to Laforgue, January 1, 1941, Kl. Erw. 762/3; also involved in the affairs of the International Society during the war was French psychoanalyst René Allendy: see Göring's report included with Robert Cropp, Reichsinnenministerium, to Reichserziehungsministerium, October 19, 1937, REM 2954; and Alain de Mijolla, "La Psychanalyse et les Psychanalystes en France entre 1939 et 1945," *Revue Internationale d'Histoire de la Psychanalyse* 1 (1988): 167–223. See also Statuten der schweizerischen Gesellschaft für Praktische Psychologie, July 1942, Kl. Erw. 762/3, the statutes for the Swiss group of the International Society.
54. Pongratz, *Psychotherapie,* p. 260.
55. Ibid., pp. 360–1.
56. Schultz-Hencke, Lebenslauf, BDC: Parteikorrespondenz, p. 3.
57. Heyer to Hasselbach, December 29, 1943, BDC: Parteikorrespondenz; and BDC: Reichsärztekammer. Scheunert, by contrast, in 1993 asserted that his service as an army doctor protected him from the possible consequences of his doubts about the Nazi party: Scheunert to Nedelmann, p. 3.

58. Geuter, *Die Professionalisierung der deutschen Psychologie,* p. 390.
59. Martin van Creveld, *Fighting Power: German and U.S. Army Performance, 1939–1945* (Westport, Conn., 1982), pp. 132–6.
60. Bingel, "Psychiatrie in der Luftfahrtmedizin," p. 276; Geuter, *Die Professionalisierung der deutschen Psychologie,* p. 390.
61. D. Russell Davis, *German Applied Psychology,* B.I.O.S. Trip Nr. 2084 (London, n.d.), pp. 5–6.
62. Geuter, *Die Professionalisierung der deutschen Psychologie,* pp. 391, 394.
63. Werner Osenberg, Recherche Nr. 31, June 4, 1945, FD 545/46, Box S243, Speer Collection, Imperial War Museum, London. The Göring project was rated more highly, however, than ones on breast milk, medicinal soils, and the psychology of Eastern European peoples.
64. Geuter, *Die Professionalisierung der deutschen Psychologie,* pp. 390, 402–3.
65. Alexander, *Neuropathology and Neuropsychiatry,* p. 13.
66. Günter Elsässer, "Erfahrungen an 1400 Kriegesneurosen (Aus einem neurologisch-psychiatrischen Reserve Lazarett des 2. Weltkrieges)," in E. K. Cruickshank, et al., eds., *Psychiatrie der Gegenwart: Forschung und Praxis: Soziale und Angewandte Psychiatrie* (Berlin, 1961), 3:696.
67. Heinrich von Kogerer, Auszug aus einem Erfahrungsbericht (über die Zeit vom November 1941 bis Februar 1942), microcopy T-78, roll 188, frames 228–9, National Archives.
68. Max de Crinis, Miltärärztliche Akademie, October 26, 1944, H 20/464. BA-MA.
69. Beratender Psychiater beim Heeresgruppenarzt D, Vierteljährlicher Erfahrungsbericht für die Zeit vom 1.4. bis 30.6.1944, Paris, July 10, 1944, pp. 1–2, H 20/122, BA-MA.
70. Ibid., p. 2.
71. Beratende Psychiater beim Heeres-Sanitätsinspekteur, Auszugsweise, n.d., H 20/464. BA-MA.
72. Oberkommando der Wehrmacht, Chef des Santitätswesens, August 24, 1944, H 20/835. BA-MA. See also microcopy T-78, roll 183, frame 3999. National Archives.
73. Beratender Psychiater beim Heeresgruppenarzt D, Vierteljährlicher Erfahrungsbericht 1944, p. 2.
74. Friedrich Panse, Auszugsweise Abschrift, March 15, 1944, H 20/464.
75. *Bericht über die 4. Arbeitstagung der Beratenden Ärzte vom 16. bis 18. Mai 1944 im SS-Lazarett Hohenlychen* (n. p., n. d.), pp. 206–10; see also Rolf Valentin, *Die Krankenbataillone: Sonderformationen der deutschen Wehrmacht im Zweiten Weltkrieg* (Düsseldorf, 1981).
76. Dr. Wilke, Beratender Psychiater beim Armeearzt Panzer A.O.K. 4—i.A. Heeresgruppenarztes Nord-Ukraine, Erfahrungsbericht über die Zeit vom 1. April bis 30. Juni 1944, p. 5, H 20/122.
77. Creveld, *Fighting Power,* pp. 91–4; Henry Dicks, Psychological Foundations of the Wehrmacht, Directorate of Army Psychiatry Research Memorandum Nr. 11/02/9a (1944), Wiener Library; Robert Schneider, "Military Psychiatry in the German Army," in Richard A. Gabriel, ed., *Military Psychiatry: A Comparative Perspective* (New York, 1986), pp. 119–46.
78. Wilke, Erfahrungsbericht, pp. 5–7.
79. Omer Bartov, *Hitler's Army: Soldiers, Nazis, and War in the Third Reich* (New York, 1991).
80. Richard Jung, "Einleitung zur Kriegspsychiatrie," in Cruickshank, *Psychiatrie der Gegenwart,* p. 570.

81. Gustav Richard Heyer, "Zur Psychologie des Ostraumes," *Zeitschrift für Geopolitik* 19 (1942): 309–15. Heyer's essay was analyzed by an undetermined Nazi organization concerned with the East and praised as a cultural jeremiad but also criticized for its unsupported generalizations about the Russian character: see microcopy T-84, roll 294, frames 872–8, National Archives; and Michael Burleigh, *Germany Turns Eastward: A Study of Ostforschung in the Third Reich* (Cambridge, 1992).
82. Wuth to Bumke, February 23, 1942, H 20/480; Bumke to Wuth, February 27, 1942, H 20/480; and Wuth to Bumke, March 3, 1942, H 20/480.
83. Otto Wuth to Hans Bürger-Prinz, April 24, 1942, H 20/464.
84. H 20/464.
85. OKW Chef W. San Nr. 3696/44 HS In/Wi G Ib vom 30. Juni 1994, cited in Schultz, Anweisung für Truppenärzte, p. 2; *4. Arbeitstagung,* p. 276. In Driest's *Richtlinien über Menschenführung,* the word "neurosis" appears in its second edition of 1944 only a few times and always in quotation marks.
86. Immo von Hattingberg argued after the war that this was not a matter of political prohibition but of scientific advance: Hattingberg, "Medical Care for Flying Personnel," p. 1063. In fact it was both, although the psychiatric seconding of this ban was less apparent in the Luftwaffe.
87. Max de Crinis to Heeres-Sanitätsinspekteur, December 4, 1944, H 20/464.
88. Oberkommando des Heeres, Unterlagen zur wehrgeistigen Führung der Truppe, no. 2 (January 1943), H 34/21, BA-MA; and microcopy T-77, roll 135; see also Volker R. Berghahn, "NSDAP und 'Geistige Führung' der Wehrmacht 1939–1945," *Vierteljahreshefte für Zeitgeschichte* 17 (1969): 17–72.
89. Driest, *Richtlinien Über Menschenführung,* p. 4.
90. *Luftwaffeverordnungsblatt* no. 1209 (1943): 636; see also Otto Paust, "Gegen jeder Kriegspsychose," *Das Schwarze Korps,* August 25, 1938, p. 1.
91. Otto Nitzsche, "Kriegswichtiges in der ärztlichen Praxis," p. 170.
92. Adolf-Martin Däumling, personal communication, August 18, 1980.
93. Anonymous to Kemper, July 14, 1964; Pongratz, *Psychotherapie,* p. 291.
94. For Müller-Hegemann's own account, see Jochen Köhler, *Klettern in der Grossstadt: Volkstümliche Geschichten vom Überleben in Berlin 1933–1945* (Berlin, 1979), pp. 139–40, 246–8.
95. Nitzsche, "Kriegswichtiges in der ärztlichen Praxis," p. 169.

13

Reich Institute

The year 1942 marked a grim and momentous juncture in the history of the Second World War. It was a year that witnessed the turning point of the war against fascism in Europe. It was also the year in which the Nazis launched the Final Solution against the Jews of Europe. The same characteristics of 1942 may be said to apply to the history of psychotherapy in the Third Reich. In this regard, 1942 marked the beginning of a momentous turn in the political and material fortunes of the Göring Institute. This was the result of a move away from an increasingly flabby Labor Front into an exceedingly well-funded Reich Research Council that was coming under the supervision of Hermann Göring. The same year, however, also witnessed the eruption of the single greatest threat to the continued existence of the institute in Nazi Germany: the arrest of one of the institute's department directors on charges of espionage for the Soviet Union. The two events were crucially linked, the political disaster contributing a powerful impetus to the professional opportunity. What is more, as we will see in the following chapters, the figure and fate of John Rittmeister would become an important flashpoint for postwar conflict among German psychoanalysts and represents an important instance of our theme of the nature of "resistance" in the Third Reich.

On September 26, 1942, psychoanalyst John Rittmeister, director of the Göring Institute outpatient clinic, and his wife Eva were arrested by the Gestapo on charges of espionage. The Rittmeisters were accused of being members of the so-called "Red Orchestra" (*Rote Kapelle*), a spy network inside the Luftwaffe that was supplying the Soviet Union with highly confidential information. The group was headed by Harro Schulze-Boysen, an officer in the Air Ministry's intelligence branch. Schulze-Boysen himself had been arrested on August 30 when the Gestapo began a sweep of the organization's hideouts in Berlin. The arrests shook the institute to its core since, aside from the seriousness of the charges themselves, the association in the minds of the authorities and of the institute's professional opponents of treason, Bolshevism, and psychoanalysis constituted a volatile mixture dangerous to the future of organized psychotherapy in Germany.

Rittmeister was one of the leading young Freudians at the Göring Institute. In 1937, against the advice of friends, he had returned to his native Germany from Switzerland to work at the Göring Institute. He had been working at a Swiss sanitarium, but was forced to leave Switzerland because of alleged communist activities.[1] That very year he also apparently finished a paper highly critical of the Jungian point of view.[2] Rittmeister opted to return to Germany in order, as he put it in his prison diary on January 24, 1943, to seek a wife and a professional position in his homeland.[3] At the institute in Berlin he entered a training analysis with Kemper and in 1939 was named to direct the operations of the outpatient clinic. He also became involved with a group of young students and professionals who were part of a left-wing resistance and espionage organization, one of whose members, an aspiring actress named Eva Kneiper, he married in July 1939.[4] Rittmeister was led onto the path of resistance to the Nazis by his longing for a "new humanism" to take the place of what he saw as the crass and heartless culture of the West. He considered himself to be a pessimist by nature. To save himself from despair over a world devoid of meaning, he wrote in prison on January 13, 1943, he threw himself into "social eudaemonism and optimism" and fought "mysticism . . . solipsism and skepticism" for the sake of working for a realistic and realizable social good.[5]

Rittmeister was not the only anti-Nazi or even the only socialist at the Göring Institute. Dietfried Müller-Hegemann, a student of Schultz-Hencke's, for one, was a modestly active communist during the Third Reich. Freudian Käthe Dräger distributed anti-fascist materials as a member of the communist underground and was sent as punishment to teach in Poland in 1942. Dräger returned to Berlin in 1944 upon Göring's intervention at the urging of Müller-Braunschweig, who argued that the institute needed more instructors.[6] But Rittmeister's philosophical and political convictions made him a restless critic of the status quo at the institute and in Germany. The results ranged from the "snub" that the Jungian Wolfgang Kranefeldt remembers receiving from Rittmeister to Rittmeister's successful but ultimately tragic search for comrades within the secret salons of opposition in Nazi Berlin. The students with whom he associated were convinced that reading and discussion would lay the foundation for a campaign to convince the German people to change their form of government.[7] It was this group that came into fatal contact with Schulze-Boysen in 1942 and became part of his apparatus. Rittmeister and his circle apparently did not share the activist politics of Schulze-Boysen's operatives and allegedly knew little or nothing of their espionage activities, although Rittmeister himself did help Schulze-Boysen compose anti-Nazi leaflets.[8] Rittmeister and his wife denied the charge of high treason on account of espionage, but he was condemned to death in January 1943 and was executed at Plötzensee Prison in Berlin on May 13, 1943.[9] His wife was sentenced to a term of imprisonment.

Rittmeister's arrest, trial, and execution naturally aroused the anxiety of his colleagues at the Göring Institute. Fear of the Gestapo was part of everyday consciousness in the Third Reich even before the strain of war on the Nazis intensified the search for traitors, malingerers, and scapegoats. Would Rittmeister's predicament draw censure and reprisal down on the institute and its members? This fear must have tempered any personal and collegial concern for Rittmeister and his wife. Added to this was the conviction on the part of a number of psychotherapists that the issue in the Rittmeister case was not Nazi oppression but treason in wartime. The result was that many regarded Rittmeister with a mixture of patriotic indignation, anxious and angry resentment, and some pity. It was certainly out of some such combination of motives that Schultz, according to Kemper, approached Gauger, who was still regarded as having some contacts within the regime, to ask—fruitlessly—what might be done.

Rittmeister's arrest did not necessarily mean that the psychotherapists as a group would suffer at the hands of the Gestapo, although, as we will see, at least one professional antagonist tried to use his own Nazi credentials to discredit the Göring Institute over the Rittmeister affair. At the time, the level of anxiety, naturally enough, was quite high, and postwar accounts may have further exaggerated the degree of danger as a means of expressing sympathy, whether genuine or retroactively feigned, for a victim of the Nazis as well as identifying with him post hoc as an endangered opponent of the regime. But whatever their sympathy for their colleague, the psychotherapists were also concerned, of course, for their own personal safety and for the survival and integrity of their institute and profession. Göring was rightly the focus of the psychotherapists' hopes during this crisis, as a number of them have since affirmed. The feeling among them after the war was that Göring had saved the institute from destruction simply by virtue of who he was. This is probably an exaggeration. It is clear, however, that the degree of Göring's concern about the matter led him to take steps to practice vigorous damage control.

Göring met with the Reich Marshal on September 25. As we saw in chapter 11, the officially recorded subject of the conversation was the German Penal Code Statute defining homosexuality as a crime. Whether or not a discussion of homosexuality was in fact a camouflage for discussion of the Rittmeister affair is impossible to determine. But given the fact that Rittmeister's arrest was to occur the very next day, we might at least suppose that the issue came up since the Gestapo had been arresting members of Schulze-Boysen's group for almost a month. It is possible, therefore, that Matthias Göring was making a last-minute plea for Hermann's intercession or, at the least, discussing the implications for the institute of Rittmeister's impending arrest. The Göring family concern over the matter went even deeper, however. Schulze-Boysen himself had been able to obtain his position at the Luftwaffe Research Office in spite of his previous left-wing activities and arrests because his wife was the daughter of an aristocratic friend of Hermann Göring. It is thus certain that the affair sent shock waves through the entire Göring family. Matthias Heinrich Göring knew of Rittmeister's sympathies and associations, though apparently not of the links to the Red Orchestra.[10] It is possible, therefore, that August and September of 1942 at the Göring Institute were months of shared anxiety, or even of warnings and appeals. From former institute members we know that rumors were flying about the institute before as well as after Rittmeister's arrest. Although Kemper would not say, his psychoanalytic sessions with Erna Göring and her alleged confidences may well have concerned Rittmeister before and during this period of crisis.

Kemper, Schultz's secretary Ellen Bartens, and Ernst Göring have all claimed that Göring sought out his cousin to discuss the possibility of doing something for Rittmeister. The record of the meeting on September 25 might therefore be confirmation of testimony to discussion of the topic. No matter what the accuracy of this scenario might be, however, it is all but certain that the Göring cousins would have met at some time or other for no other reason than the coordination of damage control. In fact, there is evidence to suggest that Göring sought out his cousin not so much—if at all—to do something *for* Rittmeister as to do something *about* him. Especially given the repugnant and dangerous charge of high treason in wartime, we may assume that Matthias Heinrich Göring was from the beginning more concerned about his institute than he was about Rittmeister. Moreover, on the basis of Ernst Göring's recollections, it seems that Rittmeister and his wife were compromised to the degree of having aroused the patriotic wrath of the institute's director. A final element was that another member of the Red Orchestra, student and pianist Helmut Roloff, was also close to the Görings, having as a youth spent a year as a member of the elder Göring's household. One of the radio transmitters used by the group was found in Roloff's grand piano; another transmitter had been dumped into the Spree River. According to Roloff, who survived, Göring had interceded with his cousin on his behalf at Rittmeister's expense by claiming that Rittmeister had hidden the transmitter in the piano without Roloff's knowledge.[11] However, Rittmeister's wife has maintained that Roloff was not a member of Rittmeister's group and that she and her husband were not even acquainted with him.[12]

We have already noted that many of the members of the institute apparently saw things in much the same light as Göring, particularly in view of the threat to themselves, their institute, and their work. In addition, it is possible, though not likely, that Matthias was called on the carpet—not likely because Hermann, of course, was even more vulnerable to criticism and embarrassment than his cousin. After all, the spy ring had thrived within a Luftwaffe that had long since begun to lose its luster for Hitler and had become grist for the mills of avaricious and vengeful rivals of the Reich Marshal within the Nazi hierarchy. Whatever the actual situation, Göring's stock with Hitler sank lower and lower, for on the heels of this scandal came the Luftwaffe's failure at the impossible task of supplying the surrounded German Sixth Army in Stalingrad. Göring, with typical bravado and in an attempt to regain some favor, had boasted that his planes could supply the trapped soldiers. A further burden was the growing Allied air offensive against German cities and industry. In sum, Hermann

Göring could hardly have been either in the mood or the position to do anything for Rittmeister, even if his cousin had asked him to.

It is true that Rittmeister was granted the dubious respect of being guillotined instead of hanged and that his wife was imprisoned briefly instead of being sentenced to death. Hitler, foreshadowing the punishment he would ordain for the conspirators in the assassination plot against him of July 20, 1944, had insisted on strangulation by rope and death sentences for the wives of those condemned in the first round of Red Orchestra trials in December 1942. It is probable, however, that the Rittmeisters' fate as two comparatively minor figures in the case was the result less of Göring family influence than of the waning of the intensity of Hitler's desire for revenge and the less vengeful, if hardly indulgent attitude of the presiding Luftwaffe judge on the Reich Court Martial, Manfred Roeder.[13] We have no evidence of any investigation or action launched against the Göring Institute by the authorities—or squelched by the Reich Marshal—as a result of this affair. The only changes at the institute were the formal dissolution of the Freudian Arbeitsgruppe A, the requirement that all scientific meetings take place at the institute, and the further camouflaging of the Freudians' meetings under the innocuous title of "Evening Lectures on Casuistry and Therapy."[14] But the Göring family was seriously concerned and institute members believed then and believed later that it was the Göring name that protected them so that the institute could survive and prosper. There can be no doubt, though, that the Rittmeister affair provided another powerful incentive for Matthias Heinrich Göring to seek closer ties to his cousin's still expanding war empire for the sake of political protection as well as financial support and security. Before Rittmeister was dead, in fact, the psychotherapists' would be anchored securely to leeward of Hermann Göring's still bulky isle of power, wealth, and influence.

The psychotherapists, while grateful for—and reliant upon—DAF funding, had been chafing under the growing organizational disarray of the DAF. They were also unhappy about the potential for party interference in their affairs, a danger now certainly magnified by the Rittmeister crisis. This fear of Nazi organizations, even weakened as the NSDAP had been by the growth of extraparty entities, was not an idle one: As late as December 1944, an inspection report by a deputy Gauleiter sent to the RFR concluded that the institute was overfunded and underutilized.[15] More important was the fact that despite its great wealth and organizational reach, during the war the German Labor Front was in chaotic decline. Ley himself "spent most of his days in an alcoholic stupor,"[16] his plans for a productive racial welfare state confined to increasingly irrelevant paper. Even before the war Hermann Göring had correctly if also a bit jealously pointed to the fat accumulating around the Labor Front and suggested to a Wehrmacht audience that the DAF "should produce more strength and less joy."[17] The wartime troubles of the DAF only increased the psychotherapists' desire to obtain other sources of support outside of party organizations and within the seemingly more secure and stable environment of state scientific agencies. This would involve several steps in several different directions at once, the first of which were taken in 1942 and which culminated in the creation of the Reich Institute for Psychological Research and Psychotherapy inside Hermann Göring's empire of state authorities in 1944.

In 1942 Matthias Heinrich Göring sought to have his institute affiliated with the Kaiser Wilhelm Society, a request that was apparently turned down, although it may have resulted in some funding.[18] The Kaiser Wilhelm Society had been founded in 1911 to support scientific research independent of the obligations of a university position. After the First World War, an Emergency Association of German Science was set up to fund and coordinate research endangered by the nation's financial and political crises. Later renamed the German Research Association, the DFG embraced universities, academies, and societies like the Kaiser Wilhelm Society, and was funded by government and private industry. The Nazis of course conducted a racial and political purge of all these institutions and then vigorously supported their work in pursuit of their own aims.[19] On March 16, 1937, Bernhard Rust, minister of science and education, established the Reich Research Council in cooperation with Hermann Göring's Four-Year Plan. The task of the Reich Research Council was to sponsor research and development in technology and the natural sciences. Officially, the RFR was the natural science branch of the DFG, since the latter had been established by law and the former only by administrative decree.[20]

Army General Kurt Becker was appointed president of the RFR and served in that capacity until his death by suicide in 1940, whereupon Rust himself assumed the post for the next two years. By 1942, however, Minister of Armaments Albert Speer had become convinced that the war could be won only if a new and devastating weapon were developed. Albert Vögler, president of the Kaiser Wilhelm Society, called Speer's attention to the neglected field of nuclear fission, complaining that the Education Ministry and the RFR lacked the requisite energy under the alcoholic Rust to encourage and fund vital research. Speer recommended to Hitler that Hermann Göring be appointed head of the RFR, "thus emphasizing its importance."[21] For his deputy, Göring chose Rudolf Mentzel, an SS officer and since 1936 president of the DFG. Werner Osenberg, head of Mentzel's planning office, was given the task, along with Göring's own technical advisor Fritz Görnnert, of revitalizing the war-related work of the Reich Research Council. Its resources grew to gargantuan proportions as funds from Göring's vast holdings flowed into the RFR from the Reich Office for Economic Construction to the tune of thirty to forty million Reichsmarks a year. In 1943 a special *Kriegsetat* was established to provide another fifty million Reichsmarks annually.[22]

As director (*Fachspartenleiter*) of the Medical Division of the RFR Göring appointed the eminent surgeon Ferdinand Sauerbruch, who had headed the same division in the "old" Reich Research Council. Sauerbruch had earlier been appointed a state secretary by Göring in appreciation for his treatment of ailing Weimar President Paul von Hindenburg. Sauerbruch had a particular interest in aviation medicine, but after the war expressed strong reservations about psychotherapy to Schultz-Hencke and characterized the Göring Institute as mere "window dressing."[23] Sauerbruch and the Reich Marshal were hardly close, but the confluence of interest and acquaintanceships in this particular corner of Hitler's Reich made Sauerbruch an appropriate administrative link between the RFR and the Göring Institute, a capacity confirmed by the institute's former managing director, Felix Scherke.[24] The formal association of the Göring Institute with the Reich Research Council, in any case, dated from Hermann Göring's assumption of the RFR's presidency.

Typically for the Third Reich, however, the exact organizational relationship between the psychotherapists and the RFR took some months to work out. On January 6, 1943, Hermann Göring had given his approval for the creation of the Reich Institute for Psychological Research and Psychotherapy in the Reich Research Council.[25] During almost all of 1943, however, the possibility of an affiliation of the new Reich Institute with the Friedrich Wilhelm University in Berlin was explored and then rejected. This proposal seems to have come from

Rust.[26] It has all the markings of an attempt by Rust to retain or regain some of the power that had been taken away from him by the intercession of Speer and Göring in the realm of wartime scientific research. Rust had also always been frustrated by state (*Land*) controls over education and probably saw Göring's new institute as a means to insert an independently and richly funded Reich wedge into the university in Berlin.[27] Everyone involved was against the idea: the deans of the medical and philosophical faculties, the rector of the university, and Matthias Heinrich Göring himself. Göring did not want to be affiliated with either the philosophical or medical faculties since he felt that the pedagogy and practice of psychotherapy would not be ready for inclusion in the university curriculum for about ten years.[28] This stance reflected the concern that a jejune university psychotherapy would just be taken over by psychiatry. It would be better to wait for such a big move and in the interim make small inroads, as in Göring's contemporaneous but fruitless pursuit of the establishment of an academy for national and colonial psychology or of a like teaching position (*Lehrstuhl*) at the University of Göttingen.[29]

From the springtime on, however, Göring concentrated on the central task of garnering financial support from the Reich Research Council, an entity which under his cousin's influence would be more receptive to his efforts than the more traditional hard science—and nonfamilial—Kaiser Wilhelm Society. In his application Göring delineated seven tasks for psychotherapy crucial for the war effort. Two of these, Göring claimed, had been singled out by Reich Health Leader Conti as decisive for the war effort: the psychological care and control of the industrial work force; and the fight against juvenile delinquency. Five other tasks were listed as important to the war effort: homosexuality; psychopathology and neurosis among racially sound members of the populace; the psychopathology of addictions; psychology and fertility in marriage; and depth psychological expert opinions.[30] For all of this work Göring requested a year's budget of RM 176,400.[31] There was grumbling within and without the RFR about the high level of funding for the relatively few patients that were seen, but the spoken conclusion was that the previous and projected work of the institute merited support. The unspoken conclusion, of course, was that Hermann Göring's cousin had a special family claim on the resources of the Reich Research Council. This consideration was reflected in Mentzel's summary of university objections to affiliation of the Reich Institute.

Among these was the—also unexpressed—observation that Matthias Heinrich Göring was well along in years and that there was uncertainty about who would succeed him.[32] Presumably to no one's surprise, by the end of 1943 Göring's institute was granted annual funding from the RFR: RM 318,000 for the period from November 1, 1943, to March 31, 1944; and RM 880,000 for the fiscal year April 1, 1944, to March 31, 1945.[33]

According to Scherke, the new Reich Institute also received funding from the compensation fund of the DAF, from the city of Berlin, and from the Reich Air Ministry.[34] This generous funding allowed the institute to maintain itself in good professional fashion right up until the end of the Third Reich even in the midst of wartime cutbacks and shortages. Müller-Hegemann has recalled the contrast between the Göring Institute, where nothing was lacking, and the common privations elsewhere due to the war. Göring received a monthly salary of RM 1500. There were now four main department heads (Heyer for training, Kemper for the clinic, Kühnel for educational counseling, and Schultz for research) and each had a monthly salary of RM 1000. The directors of what were now eight subdivisions were paid RM 500 a month: literature (Bilz), statistics and evaluation (Boehm), marriage counseling (Hattingberg), archive (Heyer), forensic psychiatry (Kalau vom Hofe), educational aids and curricula (Müller-Braunschweig), industrial psychology (Scherke), and testing (Vetter).[35] Full-time staff also received RM 500 and participation in special research projects brought an additional RM 500 monthly. All this was in addition to whatever members earned from private practice, something that, according to Ernst Göring, was a source of considerable income straight through to the end in 1945.

The reorganization of the institute reflected the reemphasized priorities that had helped Göring win RFR funding. The new department for educational counseling was a function of the RM 38,100 total designated for January 1944 to March 1945 to fund the study and treatment of child developmental problems (RM 20,100) and the fight against juvenile delinquency (RM 18,000). The new subdivision for marriage counseling reflected the RM 9000 allotted for fertility in marriage. The RM 18,000 for work on productivity, along with the RM 4500 for study of the psychology of workers from France and the RM 6600 for a like study of workers from the East, presumably went to the subdivisions for industrial psychology and testing. The very pragmatic orientation toward assistance to Nazi military and racial aims was mirrored not only in the dropping of the division for ideology under Achelis, but also in the change of the division for criminal psychology into one for forensic psychiatry: Kalau vom Hofe, as we saw in chapters 8 and 11, was increasingly busy with cases of homosexuality, for which the new budget allocated RM 7200. This work involved not so much psychological research, but the working confrontation with courts, police, and rival psychiatrists. The research department under Schultz would supervise research not only on these topics but also on those listed on the psychology of the British people (RM 6000), race and psyche (RM 6000), and criminal psychology and psychopathology (RM 8100). The enlargement of the outpatient clinic described by Dräger was made possible by means of an allocation of RM 15,000 for "Basic Research" (*Quellenforschung*).[36]

The creation of the Reich Institute for Psychological Research and Psychotherapy was made official on January 1, 1944.[37] As such, it was a political harbinger of sorts. For all his power and wealth, Hermann Göring's stock had been falling with Hitler ever since the Luftwaffe's failure at Dunkirk and in the Battle of Britain. His sybaritism and ostentation further weakened his political clout. The Total War program, announced in February 1943 by his rival Goebbels in the wake of the defeat at Stalingrad, posed a potentially grave threat to Göring's fat empire. That same month, for example, SA cadres at Goebbels's urging smashed in the windows of the gourmet restaurant Horcher, one of the Reich Marshal's favorite Berlin haunts.[38] Although a concerned Göring prevented the closing of the restaurant, more serious inroads could be anticipated. Beginning in late 1943 and continuing throughout 1944, therefore, Göring made efforts to shore up his bastions of strength, wealth, and influence. By October 1944 all institutes and groups that were members of the RFR had the prefix "Reichs-" added to their official titles. According to Kurt Zierold, the redesignation was intended to draw public limits for the purveyors of total war in their fervent rallying of the Germans for the final desperate battle against their many enemies.[39]

Matthias Heinrich Göring took the opportunity of the reorganization of his institute in 1944 to take care of some of his own nagging and pernicious political business. At the beginning of the year Vienna psychoanalyst August Aichhorn was named an extraordinary member of the new Reich Institute and in March Berlin psychiatrist Viktor

Emil Freiherr von Gebsattel was sent by Göring to Vienna, ostensibly to discuss the establishment of an outpatient clinic there. Gebsattel had been a member of Freud's circle in Vienna before the First World War, but had turned to an anthropological-existential-religious depth psychology under the influence of Ludwig Binswanger, Erwin Strauss, and Eugène Minkowsky that was in accord with his own Roman Catholicism. Once he got to Vienna, however, Gebsattel, apparently by mutual agreement, replaced Aichhorn, who was acting director of Vienna operations in the absence of Heinrich von Kogerer, who was in the army. Allegedly the real reason for Gebsattel's dispatch to Austria was to get him—and the Reich Institute—out of the line of possible fire stemming from Gebsattel's contacts with the conservative German resistance movement.[40]

Although the now old German Institute for Psychological Research and Psychotherapy remained in official existence until the end of the Third Reich, the psychotherapists under Göring were no longer simply members of a registered association or simply affiliated with a party organization like the DAF, rather they were now part of a state institute entitled to legal status. This status was in the process of being formalized amidst the chaos of the collapsing Reich, but was never legally confirmed. Erna Göring discovered that after the war, when she was denied a widow's pension by the West German government on the grounds that the Reich Research Council had itself never been fully incorporated and thus had not been included under the requisite public assistance regulations.[41]

The incipient status of the Reich Institute in 1944, however, was why Göring lost no time in seeking in February of that year to have bestowed on both Heyer and Schultz-Hencke the title of full professor under the state civil service system of ranks. In the case of Heyer, who had been a university lecturer in internal medicine at Berlin since December 1939, Göring asserted to Karl Brandt, Hitler's personal physician and newly appointed General Commissar for Public Health Services, that aside from a record of longstanding scholarly achievement and service as a university lecturer, Heyer merited the title of professor as director of a major division of a Reich Institute.[42] In pushing Heyer for this post, Göring was in part perhaps trying to make up for Heyer's feeling that before the war Göring had obstructed his career.[43] He was of course also aware of the fact that both he and Schultz had become professors by means of university teaching and that Hattingberg had won the post of honorary professor in 1940. But his chief motivation was that he obviously regarded the Reich Institute as an official state institution, to be staffed, like a university, by full and associate professors who were salaried civil servants under the auspices of the Interior Ministry. As a further step in the direction anticipated and charted by Göring, the RFR in July 1944 granted the institute a formal research commission in psychology.[44] And in November, Göring, no doubt hopeful that Germany's military fortunes might begin to match those of his institute and the RFR, requested RM 880,000 for the fiscal year 1945–1946.[45]

While the transformation of the Göring Institute into a Reich Institute in the Reich Research Council enhanced the wealth and status of psychotherapy in the Third Reich, rivals and enemies still danced around the margins of this little—and short-lived—professional empire. Chief among these was Max de Crinis, whom we have encountered before and will encounter again. During the war de Crinis emerged as the most outspoken and influential Nazi within the German psychiatric establishment. He would make his presence felt in the evolution of the Reich Institute, in the political fallout from the Rittmeister affair, and in the battle over war neuroses. De Crinis had been a psychiatrist at the University of Graz in Austria. He had fled his homeland in 1934 after the failure of the local Nazi putsch against the government of Engelbert Dollfuss and had become director of the psychiatric clinic at the University of Cologne. It was rumored within the Göring Institute that de Crinis had been forced to flee Austria because he had been involved in the coup attempt. A party member since 1931, de Crinis joined the SS in 1936 and in 1939 replaced the politically discredited Bonhoeffer as psychiatric director of the Charité. Shortly after his appointment in Berlin, in a revealing act, de Crinis had the bust of the former illustrious psychiatric director of the Charité, Carl Westphal, removed from its position at the entrance to the psychiatric wing of the hospital. De Crinis believed—wrongly—that Westphal was Jewish and engaged the daughter of the Viennese psychiatrist Theodor Meynert, de Crinis's teacher and Freud's nemesis, to find a bust of her father to replace Westphal's.[46] It was also in 1939 that de Crinis became active in the operations of the SS Race and Settlement Main Office; by 1941 he had also taken over the post of medical director in the scientific office (Amt W) of Rust's Ministry of Science and Education.[47]

De Crinis, like his mentor Meynert, was opposed to any attempts to instill what he regarded as "speculative philosophy" into medicine. He saw the whole "crisis in medicine" movement as a Jewish conspiracy to destroy the sound biological and scientific bases of modern psychiatry. For de Crinis, psychotherapy was to be only an adjunct method to a nosological and physiological science.[48] At the same time, as we saw in chapter 10 concerning the training of academic psychologists, de Crinis and his cronies had been thrown on the defensive by the professional advances made by psychotherapists and psychologists. As for the psychotherapists in particular, de Crinis was also painfully aware of the temporary trump card of Göring. The resultant tension between criticism and circumspection in his forays on psychotherapy in the Third Reich was evident, for example, in his commentary on the possible affiliation of the Göring Institute with the University of Berlin in 1943. Knowing that his letter would be seen by Hermann Göring's RFR staff, de Crinis began by expressing his interest in the establishment of the Reich Institute and his respect for Göring's serious scientific intentions. But he then observed that the employment of lay psychologists was inappropriate, that psychotherapists had no monopoly on the protection of the mental health of the German people, that the Charité clinic saw many more patients than the Göring Institute, and that therefore the amount of money foreseen for the psychotherapists was out of all proportion to the contribution they made relative to that of psychiatrists. He concluded, however, by saying that these criticisms by no means meant that he was opposed to the founding of a Reich Institute.[49]

De Crinis also emerged as the chief opponent to Göring's campaign in early 1944 for a full professorship for Heyer. As we have seen, the Jungian Heyer had long been in the front ranks of those who opposed the materialistic basis of traditional German psychiatry. In Munich after the First World War he had begun to interest himself in the synergy of mind and body, conducting experiments on stomach secretions, which, he argued, displayed evidence of psychosomatism. In his 1935 book, *Praktische Seelenheilkunde,* Heyer excoriated materialistic medicine in general—its dead facts, machines, apparatuses, and commercial excesses—all of which contradicted the idea of the physician as bound closely to patient, people, and God. The "new Germany" would, he had noted confidently, hasten the end of such a materialistic outlook.[50] He was also a strong defender of the lay practice of psychotherapy. As director of the Göring Institute program for attending psychologists De Crinis abhorred, Heyer, in a classic period double entendre, argued that anyone under the proper medical supervision could be a *Heiler* (healer).[51] For all these reasons, de Crinis, in a letter to Paulus Rostock of Brandt's medical staff at Hitler's headquarters, insisted that Heyer should not be named a full professor but only an unsalaried titular professor. De Crinis seized the opportunity to place his negative judgment in the context of a threatening observation about the Göring Institute as a whole without, however, criticizing Göring himself:

> The activity of the Institute for Psychological Research and Psychotherapy has satisfied me neither scientifically nor politically. Confidentially, I should like to note that a year ago one of their most zealous collaborators was executed on account of espionage. Of course Professor Göring cannot be held responsible for this, and I emphasize expressly that I have the greatest confidence in Professor Göring in every way. Herr Heyer is not so scientifically important as he is depicted by Professor Göring, and in a review of Heyer's last book (*Praktische Seelenheilkunde*) I pointed to his inconsequential and unscientific approach to the question of body and mind.[52]

Equally dangerous was his observation that the institute had not abandoned the "speculative and philosophical dogma" of Jewish Freudianism, which lacked a sound scientific and racial basis:

> The Reich Institute for Psychological Research and Psychotherapy has unfortunately not given up the Jewish orientation of Freudian psychoanalysis, and German psychiatry will in the near future find it necessary to move against this degenerate phenomenon that continues to wear a puny national cloak.[53]

In the event, Heyer was not named full professor.[54] But the greater significance in this conflict belongs to de Crinis's almost schizophrenic distinction between Göring and psychotherapy. He was clearly skittish about taking on the Göring name and empire. He was also certainly willing to bide his time until the elderly Göring passed from the scene: at least one—and probably widely shared—view from within the Science and Education Ministry was that the psychotherapists' institute was assured of existence only for as long as Göring remained its director.[55] He may also have felt, with some justification, that Göring was a somewhat pliable personality with strong links to the psychiatrists who could be manipulated or at least relied upon to restrain some of the more radical voices among the psychotherapists. At the same time, de Crinis worried mightily about the trend toward lay therapy, especially in light of evidence that attending psychologists at the Göring Institute were in fact not under the control of physicians as stipulated by Interior Ministry regulations.[56] He argued that such training efforts (which were under Heyer's direction) were scientifically and medically unsound, so much so, he claimed, that the Wehrmacht and the Luftwaffe had stopped using such personnel altogether as a result of a number of bad experiences with them.[57]

The opposition of de Crinis and others of course did not prevent the Göring Institute—now a rich Reich Institute—from pursuing and expanding its professional capacities. Most of these were connected with the military, as we have seen in chapter 12, but the psychotherapists were also, as we have seen in chapters 9 and 10, continuously engaged by civilian agencies as well. One of these psychotherapeutic capacities in particular was even accelerated during the war. According to Kemper, there was a "rudimentary" research project underway at the Göring Institute on the problems of psychogenic infertility. We have already seen how the SS was involved in such research that engaged one psychotherapist in a peripheral manner. Likewise, at the beginning, work on this topic at the institute was primarily a matter of the professional interests of a number of members rather than any one in particular. Schultz and Hattingberg, for example, were interested in the psychological dynamics involved in the preservation of the natural family unit and proper social milieu as guarantors of productive male and female sexuality. With the establishment of the Reich Institute, as we saw above, Hattingberg would expand this interest as director of a well-funded subdivision for marriage counseling. The general—and professionally promotional—psychotherapeutic position was that health and fertility could be assured only if the mistake of lumping all the unproductive sexual perversions and disorders into the category of psychopathy were avoided. According to Schultz in a typical formulation, two-thirds of all such problems were psychogenic in nature. Therefore it was development and therapy, and not racial and biological exclusion, that would provide the *Volksgemeinschaft* with the highest possible percentage of useful members.[58]

Reich Health Leader Conti was particularly interested in this matter. This stemmed not only from his mother's leadership in the midwifery movement, but from his worry about the dysgenics of war. Conti, echoing the concern of early race hygienist Alfred Ploetz and the antiwar stance of the Monist League before 1914, anguished that in wartime the fittest die at the front while the less fit and the unfit burden already strained medical services at home.[59] The only solution would be to promote the conception and birth of as many healthy children as possible. To this end, Conti formed a task force on "Assistance by Childlessness in Marriage."[60] The Göring Institute was among those entities to respond to this initiative by increasing their work on the psychological dimensions of the problem. Werner Kemper was the psychotherapist most involved with the issue, as psychogenic frigidity and the psychobiology of sexual dysfunction had long been interests of his. He claimed that his book on frigidity, *Die Störungen der Liebesfähigkeit beim Weibe* (1942), was requested by perusal by Hans Karl von Hasselbach, one of the Hitler's physicians at the Führer's headquarters and there is documentary evidence that Hasselbach had been sent the book.[61] Between 1942 and 1944 there was a great deal of discussion and debate among physicians and psychotherapists over the cause and cure of infertility and sterility. The resultant medical literature almost uniformly stressed the importance of psychological factors in sexual matters, from deep childhood traumata to the adverse effect that the incessant propaganda for more children could have on the psychological disposition to sexual performance and procreation.[62]

Since neither the Göring name nor the activities of the psychotherapists could do anything to alter the course of the war itself, however, the Reich Institute had to carry on its operations under increasingly difficult circumstances. The ranks of members and candidates were thinned by call-ups for military service, casualties from the bombing, and emigration from an ever more disrupted Berlin. The number of courses offered at the Göring Institute declined significantly as a result. Kemper and others recalled how treatment of patients became ever more difficult because of the accelerating breakdown of transportation and communication in the city. A good portion of the institute's administrative operations were moved out of Berlin southeast to Saxony with the onset of day and night bombing in late 1943. Scherke took the business office, the industrial psychology division, and the publicity office to Madlow near Cottbus, while the library and the photo archive resided in Görlitz.[63] The affiliates of the institute fared as poorly. As early as 1941 the Düsseldorf group had to suspend operations because bombing raids made it impossible to meet at night.[64] By

1944 only three branches—in Munich, Stuttgart, and Frankfurt am Main—were still in existence, although it was noted that some training was available in Düsseldorf and Vienna. But by the winter of 1944, following destruction of the Munich institute Akademiestrasse offices on July 13, Seif had retired to the position of honorary president and the Frankfurt branch had been reduced to occasional sessions by invitation only.[65]

The *Zentralblatt* also ceased publication with the first thin issue of volume 16 in 1944. The *Zentralblatt* had been one of the relatively few journals approved for continued publication under the rationalization measures for medical research decreed by Paulus Rostock in 1943.[66] The combination of the low number of subscriptions and the air attacks on Leipzig that disrupted publisher Hirzel's operations spelled the end of the journal. The vulnerability of Leipzig to bombing had been underlined for the psychotherapists early on, when the entire stock of the new edition of Kemper's book on female infertility had been lost in the destruction of Thieme Verlag's warehouse in a 1942 raid.[67] In a raid in early 1944 on Berlin, Heyer lost all the copies of his published papers and from temporary exile at Rosenheim in Upper Bavaria placed an ad in the last *Zentralblatt* requesting copies from colleagues.[68] In the last months of the war the capital of Hitler's shrinking Reich edged closer and closer to complete chaos. Göring, in full panicked patriotic cry, branded both Scherke and Schultz as defeatists as the Russians closed in on the German capital. Scherke in February allegedly refused a Göring order to return the management of the institute to Berlin.[69] According to Schultz, he incurred Göring's wrath when he pointed to the futility of Göring's plan for institute members to serve as psychological advisors to the last German units defending Berlin.[70] With or without the benefit of last-ditch psychological advice, of course, the Germans were doomed, and in the waning days of April 1945 the Göring Institute came to its combustible end.

Notes

1. Ludger Hermanns, "John F. Rittmeister und C. G. Jung," pp. 138–9; see also Manfred Schultz, "Dr. John Rittmeister: Nervenarzt und Widerstandskämpfer" (Medical dissertation, Wilhelm Humboldt University, 1981).
2. John F. Rittmeister, "Voraussetzungen und Konsequenzen der Jungschen Archetypenlehre" (c. 1937); see also Hermanns, "Rittmeister und Jung," p. 137; and above, chapter 2.

3. John F. Rittmeister, Tagebuchblätter aus dem Gefängnis, p. 23. In light of Rittmeister's strong communist beliefs and his subsequent association with Soviet spies, it is not illegitimate to speculate whether his many travels before the war ending with his expulsion from Switzerland had anything to do with clandestine communist operations in Europe.
4. Heinz Höhne, *Codeword: Direktor: The Story of the Red Orchestra,* trans. Richard Barry (London, 1971), p. 127.
5. Rittmeister, Tagebuchblätter, p. 64.
6. Lockot, *Die Reinigung der Psychoanalyse,* p. 196.
7. Höhne, *Codeword: Direktor,* p. 127.
8. Ibid., pp. 132, 134, 136.
9. Ibid., p. 203.
10. Hans-Joachim Seeberger, personal communication, July 29, 1985.
11. Lockot, *Erinnern und Durcharbeiten,* p. 86.
12. Eva Hildebrand-Rittmeister, personal communication, April 15, 1983.
13. Höhne, *Codeword: Direktor,* pp. 182, 202.
14. Pongratz, *Psychotherapie,* pp. 267, 279.
15. Richard Donnevert, Aktenvermerk über die Besichtigung des Reichsinstitutes für psychologische Forschung und Psychotherapie im Reichsforschungsrat, Berlin W.62, Keithstr. 41, December 3, 1944, pp. 1–2; Donnevert to Mentzel, December 3, 1944, RFR 107/12850.
16. Orlow, *History of the Nazi Party,* p. 418; see also Albert Speer, *Inside the Third Reich: Memoirs,* trans. Richard and Clara Winston (New York, 1970), pp. 254–5.
17. Timothy W. Mason, *Arbeiterklasse und Volksgemeinschaft: Dokumente und Materralen zur deutschen Arbeiterpolitik 1936–1939* (Opladen, 1975), p. 129.
18. Anon. Ministerialrat Klingelhofer, June 23, 1942; and DFG-Registratur 1942, BDC: Personalakten Prof. Göring.
19. Kristie Macrakis, *Surviving the Swastika: Scientific Research in Nazi Germany* (New York, 1993).
20. Kurt Zierold, *Forschungsförderungen in drei Epochen* (Wiesbaden, 1968), pp. 215–24; see also Alan D. Beyerchen, *Scientists under Hitler: Politics and the Physics Community in the Third Reich* (New Haven, 1979), pp. 155–6.
21. Speer, *Inside the Third Reich,* p. 225; "Erlass des Führers über den Reichsforschungsrat vom 9. Juni 1942," *Reichsgesetzblatt* (1942): 389.
22. Zierold, *Forschungsförderungen,* pp. 225–6, 251–2.
23. Harald Schultz-Hencke, Fünfter protokollarischer Bericht, June 11, 1945, p.7, Kl. Erw. 762/7; see also idem, Zweiter protokollarischer Bericht, May 28, 1945, p. 9, Kl. Erw. 762/7; Ferdinand Sauerbruch, *Master Surgeon,* trans Fernand G. Renier and Anne Cliff (New York, 1954), pp. 227–8, 237; and Zierold, *Forschungsförderungen,* pp. 220, 224. At the time, Conti, to be sure from some bureaucratic jealousy, expressed uncertainty over Sauerbruch's fitness to pass judgment on psychotherapy: Conti to Mentzel, June 23, 1943, RFR 107/12850.
24. Scherke to Kemper, October 20, 1970, Werner Kemper.
25. Sergius Breuer to Matthias Heinrich Göring, January 6, 1943, RFR 107/12850.
26. Dekan Grapow an Rektor der Universität, January 13, 1943, asks the rector to speak against the affiliation to the Reich Science Minister, i.e., Rust. It is also significant that correspondence to and from Rust is not included in this file since he was no longer involved in RFR affairs, having been supplanted by Göring's man Mentzel.
27. Peterson, *Limits of Hitler's Power,* pp. 53–4.

28. Dekan Grapow to Rektor der Universität, RFR 107/12850.
29. Mentzel to Ludolf Haase, June 15, 1943; and Haase to Mentzel, June 16, 1943, RFR 107/12850.
30. Göring, Antrag zur Errichtung und Finanzierung eines Reichsinstituts, July 30, 1943, p. 4, RFR 107/12850; on delinquency, see Der Jugendführer des Deutschen Reiches to Mentzel, April 9, 1943, RFR 107/12850; and Peukert, *Inside Nazi Germany,* pp. 156, 162, 163, 222, 225–7, 230.
31. Kostenvoranschlag für den Etat zur Durchführung besonderer kriegsentscheidender bzw. kriegswichtiger Fragen auf dem Gebiete der seelischen Gesundheitspflege, July 30, 1943, RFR 107/12850.
32. Mentzel to Görnnert, December 17, 1943, RFR 107/12850.
33. Hermann Göring to Matthias Heinrich Göring, December 16, 1943, RFR 107/12850; DFG Registratur 1943, BDC: Personalakten Prof. Göring.
34. Scherke to Kemper.2
35. Baumeyer, "Zur Geschichte der Psychoanalyse in Deutschland," p. 218. Kemper led the training division in late 1944 when Heyer left Berlin: see Kemper to Schirren, November 16, 1944, B 339/43, BA.
36. Deutsches Institut für Psychologische Forschung und Psychotherapie, Entwurf Etataufstellung für den Reichsforschungsrat vom 1.I.1944 bis 31.III.1944 und die vier Vierteljahre des folgenden Etatjahres, November 6, 1943, RFR 107/12850; Dräger, "Psychoanalysis in Hitler Germany." p. 210.
37. "Reichsinstitut für Psychologische Forschung und Psychotherapie," *Deutsches Ärzteblatt* 74 (1944): 60.
38. Willi Boelcke, ed., *The Secret Conferences of Dr. Goebbels: The Nazi Propaganda War 1939–43,* trans. Ewald Osers (New York, 1970), p. 326; on Göring's style of leadership, see Peterson, *Limits of Hitler's Power,* pp. 72–6; and Albert Speer, *Infiltration,* trans. Joachim Neugroschel (New York, 1981), pp. 40, 115–16.
39. Zierold, *Forschungsförderungen,* pp. 248–53. The rivalry between Goebbels and Göring also did not prevent the publication of laudatory articles on the Göring Institute in Goebbels's *Das Reich* in 1943 and 1944: see above, chapter 7, note 15, and chapter 10, note 87.
40. Huber, *Psychoanalyse in Österreich,* pp. 66–8, 191, n. 35; see also Viktor von Gebsattel, *Not und Hilfe: Prologomena zu einer Wesenslehre der geistig-seelischen Hilfe* (Colmar, 1944).
41. Luise Albertz, Deutscher Bundestag Petitions-Ausschuss Vorsitzende, to Erna Göring, December 6, 1956, Ernest Göring.
42. Göring to Brandt, February 18, 1944, BDC: Parteikorrespondenz Heyer; and Göring to Paulus Rostock, Der Bevollmächtige für das Sanitäts- und Gesundheitswesen (Medizinische Wissenschaft und Forschung), March 18 and May 31, 1944, BDC: Parteikorrespondenz Heyer. Conti was increasingly bypassed in health affairs, in particular by Brandt. In 1944, perhaps in an attempt to retain a tie to the Göring empire, Conti awarded Matthias Heinrich Göring the Badge of Honor for German Racial Cultivation, second class; see *Deutsches Ärzteblatt* 74 (1944): 99; and *Die Gesundheitsführung "Ziel und Weg"* 6 (1944): 107; see also Conti to Mentzel, June 23, 1943, RFR 107/12850.
43. Heyer to Jung, March 31, 193[7?], Franz Jung. In 1932 Jung spoke positively of Heyer's "aggressive temperament"; C. G. Jung, *Letters,* p. 113. Göring's son Ernst clashed with Heyer at the University of Munich.
44. DFG Registratur 1944, BDC: Personalakten Prof. Göring.

45. Göring to Rudolf Mentzel, November 17, 1944, RFR 107/12850.
46. De Crinis to Sergius Breuer, September 6, 1940, Universität Berlin: Psychiatrische/Nervenklinik Charité 1941/4, Geheimes Staatsarchiv, Berlin/Dahlem.
47. R 21, folders 475–6, Amt W: Medizinische Fakultäten und Gesellschaften, Medizinalstudium, Fachzeitschriften, Psychologie (Handakten Prof. de Crinis) 1942–1945, BA. De Crinis poisoned himself on May 1, 1945: see Werner Forssmann, *Experiments on Myself: Memoirs of a Surgeon in Germany*, trans. Hilary Davies (New York, 1974), p. 240.
48. Max de Crinis, Denkschrift (n.d.), BDC: Korrespondenz Wi; see also Tagung der Dekane der med. Fakultäten im Reichserziehungsministerium, May 6, 1941, pp. 17–20, BDC: Korrespondenz Wi Rudolf Mentzel.
49. Max de Crinis to Dekan der Medizinischen Fakultät, September 11, 1943, RFR 107/12850.
50. Heyer, *Praktische Seelenheilkunde*, pp. 58, 82.
51. Gustav Richard Heyer, "Bericht über die Ausbildung der Behandelden Psychologen," in Göring, *1. Sonderheft*, pp. 9–11.
52. De Crinis to Rostock, April 3, 1944, BDC: Personalakten des Prof. de Crinis.
53. Ibid. Kemper claimed this was proof of the known influence of psychoanalysts at the Göring Institute, but it indicates only that de Crinis was condemning psychotherapy as a whole by associating it once again in the minds of the authorities with Freud.
54. Rostock to Brandt, April 15, 1944, BDC: Parteikorrespondez Heyer.
55. Anon. to Ministerialrat Klingelhöfer.
56. Donnevert, Aktenvermerk über die Besichtigung des Reichsinsituts, p. 2.
57. De Crinis to Gustav Frey, July 11, 1944, R 21, folder 475.
58. Johannes Heinrich Schultz, "Seelische Gründe der Unfruchtbarkeit," p. 22; see also Fritz Mohr, "Die seelischen Faktoren bei der Entstehung und Behandlung der Unfruchtbarkeit der Frau," *ZfP* 7 (1934); 208–20.
59. Leonardo Conti, "Stand der Volksgesundheit im 5. Kriegsjahr," p. 15, Reg. Aachen 16486, NWH. This was the text of a secret speech given in Breslau in 1944.
60. "Anordnung Reichsgesundheitsführers—Arbeitsgemeinschaft 'Hilfe bei Kinderlosigkeit in der Ehe,'" *Reichs-Gesundheitsblatt* 17 (1942): 761.
61. Heyer to Hasselbach, December 29, 1943, BDC: Parteikorrespondenz. Kemper's book was reprinted in 1943, 1967, and 1972.
62. Werner Kemper, "Der seelische Anteil an der Sterilität"; D. Kleff, "Das Problem der Sterilität," *Deutsches Ärzteblatt* 72 (1942): 368–70; H. Stieve, "Nervös bedingte Unfruchtbarkeit," *Deutsches Ärzteblatt* 74 (1944): 3–8; and A. Meyer, "Über die seelischen Ursachen der unfreiwilligen weiblichen Sterilität," *Deutsches Ärzteblatt* 74 (1944): 219–25.
63. Göring, Rundschreiben, September 10, 1943, Kl. Erw. 762/4; Donnevert, Aktenvermerk über die Besichtigung des Reichsinstitutes, p. 1.
64. Curtius to Göring, January 14, 1941, Kl. Erw. 762/2.
65. Reichsinstitut für Psychologische Forschung und Psychotherapie im Reichsforchungsrat, Ankundigungen der Veranstaltungen des Sommer-Semesters 1944, pp. 16–20; and idem, Ankundigung der Veranstaltungen des Winter-Semesters 1944/45, pp. 16–20.
66. Der Bevollmächtige für das Sanitäts- und Gesundheitswesen/Der Beauftragte für medizinische Wissenschaft und Forschung, Medizinische Zeitschriften, die nach dem 1.I.1944 bestehen bleiben sollen, Berlin, n.d., p. 4, R 18, folder 5572.
67. Pongratz, *Psychotherapie*, p. 290; and Heyer to Hasselbach.

68. *ZfP* 16 (1944): 73; see also Pongratz, *Psychotherapie,* pp. 285–6, and Kemper to Schirren, November 16, 1944.
69. Johannes Grunert, "Zur Geschichte der Psychoanalyse in München," p. 883.
70. Schultz, *Lebensbilderbuch,* p. 139.

14

Reconstruction and Repression

Even though the Reich Institute for Psychological Research and Psychotherapy in the Reich Research Council was reduced to rubble in the final days of the Third Reich, its history goes far beyond 1945. This is the case for two fundamental reasons. The first reason is that the history of the Göring Institute forms an indispensable part of the continuity in the professional development of psychotherapy in modern Germany. Indeed, in the terminology of evolutionary biology, the Göring Institute comprised an episode of sudden accelerated advance as described by the theory of "punctuated equilibrium." That is, evolution, like history, is not just a steady trend of events, but is punctuated by relatively abrupt episodes of development. The second reason is that the treatment of this history took on distinct and important forms in both East and West Germany after the Second World War. This was due to the controversial—and hence repressed—nature of psychotherapy's role in the Third Reich. When this repression was lifted, as we shall see in chapter 15, this history took on a number of revealing forms that reflected not only advances in historical inquiry but also professional positions linked to the twentieth-century development of the discipline of psychotherapy, a history of which the Göring Institute was an important part. In this reworking of historical memory, the Göring Institute therefore became a means to its own history.

There were thus two equally fundamental dynamics to the history of psychotherapy in the German lands in the first three decades after 1945. The first was the reconstruction of a professional capacity developed chiefly between the ends of the two world wars. The second, coincident with the first, was widespread repression among psychotherapists in both East and West Germany of the true nature of the history of their discipline in the Third Reich. Both of these dynamics served continuity in the professional development of psychotherapy in Germany in the twentieth century. Just as was the case in 1933, the year 1945 marked a bridge and not a break in the history of an increasingly multifaceted field of competing professional expertise. The destruction of the Göring Institute did not mean the end of psychotherapy in Germany, for it had provided enough exposure, organization, training, and practice for the nascent profession to propel it into autonomy. Psychotherapy in the Third Reich had achieved de facto recognition as a profession from the state as well as unprecedented—and generous—financial support. The abrasion worked by the Nazi years and their passing ultimately stripped German psychotherapeutic thought of the *völkisch* tendencies exploited and articulated by National Socialism. This abrasion also burnished the no less ethically problematic commitments to professional development and the practice of psychotherapy in the arguably confluent interest of patient and society. This practical capacity was in particularly acute demand just after the war amid the physical and spiritual wreckage of an occupied and divided Germany. It was also in harmony with the social service ethos called "demostrategy" pervading European governments which in mobilizing for total war had confronted the political necessity of addressing the many material problems facing their societies.[1] Finally, such professional pragmatism served the task of repressing the recent Nazi past, a task served in turn by the more general trend in both postwar German republics to reconstruct—each in its own terms—a stable, conservative political and social order.[2]

Professional developments in the connected realms of psychiatry, psychotherapy, psychoanalysis, and psychology as a whole in the postwar era, particularly in West Germany, also displayed two major features. The categories that the original General Medical Society for Psychotherapy used during the interwar years to describe its scientific aims and professional ambitions are useful in describing the status of organized psychotherapy after the Second World War. In 1925 the General Medical Society had articulated both a "foreign policy" and a "domestic policy" for psychotherapy in Germany. In the realm of its "foreign policy" after the Second World War in divided Germany, psychotherapy experienced further significant progress toward professional status and integration into the public and private health care systems. The reindustrialization of both German states demanded the psychological services offered by willing groups of aspiring professionals inside and outside of medicine.[3] As a result of this success as well as of its recent history, psychotherapy's "domestic policy," again especially in the Federal Republic of Germany, was marked by competition, conflict, and compromise among contending groups of practitioners.

This nature of this professional postwar reconstruction and its collective repression of the immediate past was dramatically reflected in the founding of the journal *Psyche* in 1946. The journal was the brainchild of psychoanalyst Alexander Mitscherlich, who from 1937 on had wintered the Nazi regime in Heidelberg and who with his wife Margarete Nielsen would become a leading psychoanalytic critic of the postwar German denial of the Nazi past.[4] The initial advertisements for the journal claimed that *Psyche* was the only German publication carrying on the tradition of earlier journals that had been forced to cease publication by the Nazis. Mitscherlich himself had stressed that in no way was the new journal a successor to the old *Zentralblatt*, which had been the chief—indeed only—journal for psychotherapy in Germany between 1933 and 1944.[5] At the same time, however, *Psyche*'s self-described aim, like that of the *Zentrablatt*, was to provide a forum for all schools of *grosse* psychotherapy. Although the content of *Psyche* was unencumbered by the political and ideological strictures of the Nazi years, its concerns had thus traveled the professional bridge built over and through the Third Reich by the Göring Institute, a fact ignored in its editors' assertion of a clean break and a new start. In fact, of the twenty-nine contributors listed in the advertisement, eight had been members of the Göring Institute, including one who was director of the outpatient clinic and another who was a member of the Nazi party, as well as at least two others who had trained at or otherwise been associated with the institute. Over time, moreover, the focus of the journal shifted to reflect the growing divisions among psychotherapists in West Germany. In 1966, *Psyche*, in the words of its subtitle, was transformed from *A Journal for Depth Psychology and Anthropology in Research and Praxis* to one for *Psychoanalysis and Its Applications*. This recreated the original organizational and theoretical split between psychoanalysts and psychotherapists in Germany between the wars that had been autocratically and superficially papered over during the Third Reich and which emerged in the 1950s as a major instance of differences in theory and praxis among psychotherapists and psychologists in West Germany.

The fate of individual psychotherapists from the Göring Institute varied widely. According to Kemper, Göring had died of typhus in a Russian detention camp at the end of July.[6] Also according to Kemper, Erna Göring, after being turned away by Kemper and others in Berlin, sought refuge with former Reich Youth Leader Baldur von Schirach and his wife in Bavaria. In 1948 she attempted to become a member of the new institute there but was turned down not only because of her Nazi past but because of her incomplete training.[7] Ernst Göring went his own way as a psychotherapist, devoting himself after 1969 primarily to riding therapy in a small town in the southwestern German state of Baden-Württemberg. His elder brother Peter remained a pediatrician until his death in 1979. Other leading psychotherapists of the preceding era were already gone. Künkel had remained in America, where he was on a lecture tour, with the outbreak of war in 1939. In 1947, with her two children, Elizabeth Künkel joined her husband. Künkel had become a popular speaker and writer in the United States, fusing his religious impulse with the doctrine of self-improvement à la Norman Vincent Peale, a combination that proved to be appealing to general audiences.[8] Künkel founded a short-lived clinic in Los Angeles and died there in 1956.[9] Hattingberg had died unexpectedly of pneumonia early in 1944.[10] His son Immo, who had served with the Luftwaffe as a physician specializing in psychosomatic disorders, practiced at the Teutoburger Wald sanitarium at Bad Rothenfelde in West Germany.[11] Werner Achelis showed up at a DPG meeting in 1950, but, because he had been regarded as one of the most dangerous Nazis at the Göring Institute, he remained excluded from the professional affairs of the field until his death in 1982.[12] Walter Cimbal served in 1945 as a physician in Lower Silesia for German refugees and expellees from the East, returned to Hamburg in 1947, published a short article in 1963 on the history of psychotherapy in Germany (see chapter 1, note 42), and died in 1964.[13] Erwin Stransky, the Jewish psychotherapist who before the war had publicly characterized and critiqued the alleged differences between "Jewish" and "Aryan" psychotherapy, survived the war. In 1950 he presented a talk at the founding of a regional group of the Austrian Society for Mental Hygiene. He quoted Kretschmer on the tendency of psychopaths to rule in times of trouble (see chapter 5) and pointed to the political dangers of suggestibility and "emotional contagion." As for the future of psychotherapy, he noted the importance of seeking the assistance of psychologists and Christian clerics but also asserted that therapy was a matter for physicians.[14]

Kurt Gauger was almost uniformly shunned. According to Kemper, psychoanalyst Alexander Mitscherlich, and his friend Kurt Zierold, Gauger suffered from hysterical blindness after the war as a depressive reaction to the collapse of his ideals. His constitutionally weak eyes had, however, already suffered damage in a fire at his film institute in 1943 and later commentators have seen his troubles after the war not just those of a suddenly bereft Nazi but of a misguided idealist who lost his Nazi faith long before 1945 (see chapter 6). This slight reevaluation of Gauger is reflective in part of a more general critique of psychotherapists and psychoanalysts at the Göring Institute (see chapter 15) who explicitly or implicitly projected onto Gauger alone the more general phenomenon of their professional collaboration with the Nazi regime. Gauger was in fact cleared of complicity by the de-Nazification courts, although these proceedings cannot be regarded as anywhere near a full or accurate accounting of the complex phenomenon of collaboration. When he applied for a job in 1948 with the Labor Welfare Agency in Lower Saxony, however, the Society for Psychotherapy in Berlin recommended that he not be hired.[15] Gauger subsequently established a psychotherapeutic practice, first in Munich and then in Düsseldorf, and had referrals of patients from Wilhelm Bitter and Gottfried Kühnel.[16] He otherwise isolated himself from his former friends and colleagues; according to Zierold, who no longer saw him after the war, Gauger apparently died in Düsseldorf in 1959.

Gustav Richard Heyer and Otto Curtius were denied membership in the C. G. Jung Society after the war because of their Nazi party membership.[17] Jung himself rejected Heyer's protestations of political innocence and unalloyed loyalty to Jung.[18] Johannes Heinrich Schultz was likewise marginalized to a significant degree. Schultz remained in professional association with Kretschmer because of the latter's interest in hypnosis as an auxiliary psychotherapeutic method and founded the German Society for Medical Hypnosis on June 22, 1959, as the West German section of the International Society for Clinical and Experimental Hypnosis.[19] Together with Heyer, Schultz also founded a quarterly journal "for active clinical psychotherapy" in 1956 in cooperation with other former members of the Göring Institute including

Fritz Mohr of Düsseldorf, August Vetter of Munich, and Klaus Wegscheider of Kassel as well as psychiatrist Gustav Störring of Kiel and naturopath Louis Grote. Heyer and Schultz also both published postwar versions of earlier works now divested of their encomiums to National Socialism.[20] Heyer died in 1967 and Schultz in 1970.

Psychotherapists as a group had to defend themselves from accusations of collaboration hurtling across disciplinary lines in fields of medicine and psychology now made more competitive as a result of wartime demand and development for such expertise. In 1949 Wilhelm Bitter and the managing director of the German Society for Psychology, Albert Wellek, clashed sharply at a meeting in Würzburg over a widely disseminated pamphlet prepared by university psychologists that sought to discredit Jung's analytical psychology. Wellek responded to subsequent criticism of German psychology for its collaboration with the Nazis by racial characterologists Ferdinand Clauss, Hans F. K. Günther, and Erich Jaensch by insisting that psychologists had come nowhere near the degree of collaboration exhibited by Jung and the psychotherapists.[21]

Not surprisingly, it was the younger and less ethically and politically burdened psychotherapists and psychoanalysts—or those perceived as such—who were engaged in the most important organizational, practical, and theoretical work of the continuous development in the field. The older and more prominent psychotherapists had by and large passed their professional peaks by 1945 and their more or less swift decline into relative obscurity was only hastened in some cases by the thoroughly noxious nature of Nazism that made heroes only of its victims. Among the younger veterans of the Göring Institute there were fewer Nazi party members than among the older activists and leaders of the psychotherapeutic movement between the wars. During the war, interest in joining the Nazi party declined significantly among the academic and professional elites because of some disillusionment with a corrupt and criminal regime as well as the professional opportunities available elsewhere in industry and the applied sciences to those with technical training.[22] For psychotherapists, there had been the added protection of the Göring name that made party membership even less of a necessity. Finally, as the war went badly for Germany, there was a growing appreciation of the fact that party membership would spell a distinct disadvantage with the passing of the Third Reich.

It was the Freudians Kemper and Schultz-Hencke who emerged right after the war as the chief operatives for psychotherapy in Berlin. Kemper by the autumn of 1945 was giving an extension course in Berlin-Charlottenburg on psychotherapy, the lectures from which he published as a book, *Die Seelenheilkunde in unserer Zeit,* in 1947. More significant was the collaboration between Schultz-Hencke and Kemper in establishing an outpatient clinic in the ruins of the city to care for patients from the Göring Institute and to treat new patients emerging from the rubble of the war. Schultz-Hencke located a partially bombed out school near his apartment in the vicinity of the Fehrbelliner Platz and it was there that he, Kemper, and a few other psychotherapists and psychoanalysts practiced beginning in 1945. On April 29, 1946, the insurance authority in Berlin, the Versicherungsanstalt Berlin, agreed to underwrite the psychoanalysis and psychotherapy by both medical and nonmedical practitioners within what was now officially named the Central Institute for Psychogenic Illnesses. Kemper assumed the post of director while Schultz-Hencke supervised the programs for research and mental hygiene. The institute, which in fact operated only as a clinic, was housed in a wing of a former barracks on the Papestrasse and it was soon staffed by former members and students of the Göring Institute. The guidelines for the institute declared that only fully trained psychoanalysts could serve as directors of the various divisions, but the Central Institute nonetheless became a collecting point for all medical and nonmedical psychotherapists in Berlin. Insurance money not only allowed these people to practice, it provided for the expansion of the clinic to include a division for child therapy.[23] Not surprisingly, there was some early and ongoing criticism from physicians about the continuing employment of nonmedical practitioners. One member of the health administration in Berlin, referring to the wartime institute as "a pure Himmler affair," observed that for this reason the Göring Institute was a millstone around the necks of those trying to establish the proper relationship between doctors and medical assistants.[24]

The original permission for the clinic to function as an official entity was given by Ferdinand Sauerbruch, who had been placed in charge of Berlin's health administration by the Russians. Schultz-Hencke reported on May 15, 1945, that "the Russians are actively interested in psychotherapy."[25] Of course, this had to do with the fact of great demand for psychological counseling services in the shattered city: After all, as Schultz-Hencke himself observed a month later, the Soviets had dissolved the Russian psychoanalytic society in 1936.[26] In the immediate postwar period, however, psychotherapists from all the occupied sectors of Berlin took part in meetings, including one in the Soviet zone on November 22–23, 1946, attended by eighty-five psychiatrists and neurologists from East Berlin and Kemper and Schultz-Hencke from the West. The theme of both Kemper's and Schultz-Hencke's remarks was that disputes among the various schools of psychotherapeutic thought had to be overcome. This view found favor among those who were conceiving of psychotherapy in a Marxist context, in great measure because of its challenge to the dominant psychoanalytic position in the field. Kemper and Schultz-Hencke subsequently participated in the first scientific meeting of psychiatrists and neurologists from throughout Germany in the Soviet sector of Berlin on May 27–29, 1949, and both were charter editorial board members of *Psychiatrie, Neurologie und medizinische Psychologie.* This journal was founded in 1949 as the declared successor to Oskar Vogt's *Zeitschrift für Hypnotismus* (1895–1902; 1902–42: *Journal für Psychologie und Neurologie*). Vogt was the founder of modern hypnotic medicine and was a major source of inspiration for East German psychotherapists who found a congruence between Marxism and Vogt's tradition of rational, suggestive medical psychology. There was also great interest in Schultz's autogenic training.[27] Marxists set this tradition against what they regarded as the Western bourgeois values embodied in the passive analytical method, Freud's notion of the individual in fundamental conflict with society, and the Romantic indulgence of the irrational embodied the nineteenth-century German psychotherapeutic tradition. As a "neo-analyst," however, Schultz-Hencke was granted a teaching commission at the Humboldt University in the Russian sector of Berlin on September 20, 1949; Kemper had turned down the offer of a similar post the year before.[28]

The Central Institute constituted a clinic and not a full psychotherapeutic institute, but contemporaneous moves were afoot to establish full institutional status. In 1946 Kemper presided over a gathering of psychotherapists who came to be called the Berlin University Lecturers Committee. It was this body that evolved into a registered association (e.V.), the Institute for Psychotherapy, on May 9, 1947. The Central Institute, while retaining its own organizational identity, became the outpatient clinic of the new institute. It was Kemper's aim in particular to continue the tradition of the old Göring Institute in which members of all psychotherapeutic schools of thought worked together. Given the present division of Germany into military zones of occupation, regional centralization such as that represented by the 1946 and 1947 Berlin institutes seemed the only alternative. This had been decided in the last two meetings of the executive committee of the Reich Institute at the end of 1945 and in March 1946.

But the organizational—and, more importantly, the financial—legacy of the Göring Institute was anything but uncomplicated. Comptroller Felix Scherke, who had managed the institute from Cottbus since late 1943, had moved away from the advancing Red Army to Niederaudorf on the Inn River in upper Bavaria early in 1945. Göring had wanted Scherke to return to Berlin, but on April 1, 1945, direction of the institute's affairs was delegated to Otto Curtius in Schliersee south of Munich. In August Curtius resigned as director in favor of Max Steger while Scherke remained managing director. Scherke had moved to Munich with control over around RM 100,000 from the Reich Institute account. On February 8, 1946, the American military occupation government in Munich approved the operation of the Institute for Psychological Research and Psychotherapy. The monies left in Berlin had disappeared and the psychotherapists there claimed those in Munich for themselves. But by August the Munich institute was recognized as the legitimate successor to the Reich Institute and thus entitled to the remaining funds. This decision was made on the basis of the official recognition of the institute by American and Bavarian health authorities and of the fact that a good number of psychotherapists from the old institute—a.o., Riemann, Scherke, Johanna Herzog-Dürck, Alice Lüps, Adolf Däumling, Friedrich Seifert, Ludwig Zeise, August Vetter—were active in Munich from September 1945, a time when Berlin was only just getting to its devastated feet. Subsequently, the Berliners brusquely rejected a demand from Munich that they place their institute under Munich's authority.[29]

Psychotherapists in other parts of Germany were also organizing themselves. In September 1947 Gottfried Kühnel called a meeting at Bad Pyrmont of representatives of all disciplines having to do with psychological care. Out of this meeting came the Study Society for Practical Psychology under Gustav Störring. In 1948 Jungian Bitter founded an association in Stuttgart for physicians and clergymen and, together with psychoanalysts Felix Schottlaender and Hermann Gundert, established the Stuttgart Institute for Psychotherapy, which was funded by the state and city. At Lindau on Lake Constance psychiatrist Ernst Speer in 1950 held the first of what were to become annual meetings on psychotherapy.[30] Psychoanalyst Alexander Mitscherlich had returned to Germany from exile in Switzerland in 1937 to help a colleague in trouble with the authorities, had been arrested, and spent his time as an assistant to Viktor von Weizsäcker at Heidelberg under Gestapo surveillance. In 1947, as we have seen, Mitscherlich founded *Psyche,* a journal for applied psychoanalysis and in 1950 he and von Weizsäcker, with the support of the Rockefeller Foundation, would establish the first psychosomatic division within a German university clinic at Heidelberg.[31]

The formal organizational culmination of these early efforts to rebuild the professional community of psychotherapists constructed during the Third Reich came with the establishment in September 1949 of the German Society for Psychotherapy and Depth Psychology in Brunswick. The DGPT was only an umbrella organization that had arisen out of a meeting called by Bitter in March 1949. At this meeting were representatives of the major depth psychological groupings in Germany at the time: Carl Müller-Braunschweig for the Freudians, Gustav Schmaltz for the Jungians, Leonhard Seif for individual psychologists, Ernst Michel for the followers of Künkel, Schultz-Hencke for the "neo-analysts," and Mitscherlich representing the psychosomatic group around Weizsäcker. The society's first task was to compile a list of psychotherapists who had trained at the Göring Institute. It turned out that fewer than a hundred of the total number of 300 were presently living in West Germany. The organization's first congress was held in Brunswick in 1950; by 1964 it embraced the reestablished DPG, the German Psychoanalytic Union (DPV, see below), and the German Society for Analytical Psychology; by 1972 the DGPT would have 700 members.[32]

This formal unity, however, belied an ongoing disunity among psychotherapists after the war that was also prelude and accompaniment to significant differences with academic psychologists and psychiatrists. The first great division in psychotherapeutic ranks occurred among the psychoanalysts. On October 16, 1945, the DPG was refounded under the leadership of Müller-Braunschweig. Since the DPG, however, did not have the wherewithal to support an institute, beginning in 1947 its candidates received their training at Kemper's Institute for

Psychotherapy. But differences surfaced immediately between the two organizations. Müller-Braunschweig was opposed to the short-term therapies that predominated at the institute's outpatient clinic as a result of the requirements of city health insurance. The institute, as we have already observed, was also catholic in its recruitment of practitioners and training of candidates. Kemper even succeeded in attracting some of the Jungians, Wolfgang Kranefeldt and Julius Schirren among them, to join his institute; the Jungians' own institute, formed by the group around Käthe Bügler, closed in 1949.[33] The biggest problem in the way of continuing collaboration between the DPG and Kemper's group, however, was the presence at the institute of Schultz-Hencke, who had assembled around him an influential group committed to "neo-analysis," which, among other things, claimed to have reconciled Freudian and Jungian theory.[34] Schultz-Hencke's position was further strengthened in 1948 with the departure of Kemper to establish a psychoanalytic society, institute, and clinic in Brazil. Kemper had left because he was afraid for his family's safety in the increasingly threatening cold war climate in Berlin and would not return until 1967.[35]

Müller-Braunschweig came into open and bitter conflict with Schultz-Hencke, who in December 1945 had advanced twenty-nine theses toward overcoming the divisions in psychotherapy, took over the direction of the Institute for Psychotherapy from Kemper in 1948, and who would die an untimely death in 1953. The two men clashed publicly in 1949 at the International Psycho-Analytic Congress in Zurich. Because of this open split, the DPG was admitted to membership in the IPA only on a provisional basis. Müller-Braunschweig redoubled his efforts to steer the DPG in an orthodox direction, but on June 10, 1950, he and five others—divided equally between medical and non-medical psychoanalysts—secretly founded the German Psychoanalytic Union (DPV). On December 3, 1950, Müller-Braunschweig, Gerhard Scheunert, Käthe Dräger, and a few others seceded from the DPG. In 1951 the IPA withdrew provisional recognition from the DPG and granted full recognition to the DPV.[36] The split between orthodox psychoanalysis and the "neo-analysts" more closely associated with the work done during the Third Reich was now fully established.

The DPV opened its own Karl Abraham Institute in 1951, although it continued to receive some patients from the Central Institute for Psychogenic Illnesses for its training candidates to treat.[37] The Abraham Institute also lacked the funding for supporting training analyses enjoyed by the Schultz-Hencke institute through its agreement with the Berlin insurance carriers.[38] However, other psychoanalytic institutes would follow: the Sigmund Freud Institute in Frankfurt am Main in 1964, the Michael Balint Institute in Hamburg in 1974, and the Alexander Mitscherlich Institute in Kassel in 1985. In Austria, August Aichhorn revived the Austrian Psychoanalytic Union. By the time Aichhorn died in 1949, the Vienna Work Group for Depth Psychology had been founded, the psychiatric clinic at the University of Vienna was using short-term psychotherapeutic methods, and work in Aichhorn's field of psychopedagogy was going on.[39] The succeeding years, however, were chiefly characterized by competition and conflict between the DPV and the DPG. The DPG, under the leadership of Schultz-Hencke, Franz Baumeyer, and Felix Boehm, carried on the more eclectic tradition of therapy and theory that had characterized the old General Medical Society for Psychotherapy, the neo-Freudians in general, and the practices at the Göring Institute. In 1954 Boehm and others founded the *Zeitschrift für Psychosomatische Medizin* as the DPG's official journal, and in 1967, similar to the change in *Psyche,* it would add the word "psychoanalysis" to its title as part of its professional claim in the field. *Psyche* was by now steadily moving away from its original eclectic position and toward a position in harmony with that of the DPV and the IPA. This orientation was made clear when in 1963 *Psyche* published an essay highly critical of Schultz-Hencke's "neo-analysis," placing it in the shadow of the unsavory political legacy of the Göring Institute.[40]

The General Medical Society for Psychotherapy itself was refounded on September 11, 1948, at a congress of neurologists and psychiatrists at Marburg/Lahn by Ernst Kretschmer and Gottfried Kühnel.[41] Kretschmer, who led the group, held the same view of psychotherapy as he always had, that is, that it should be the province of physicians trained in psychiatry and neurology. As before, Kretschmer rejected the necessity of the training analysis that was the centerpiece of training for the psychoanalysts and other psychotherapists.[42] He wished to restrict the training of psychotherapists to the university medical faculties, a realm into which few psychotherapists or psychoanalysts had found entry: Fritz Mohr was honorary professor at the medical academy in Düsseldorf, Viktor von Gebsattel taught psychotherapy as a university lecturer in neurology at the University of Freiburg where Immo von Hattingberg was a lecturer and clinical assistant, while stepsister Marlies von Hattingberg worked at the medical clinic at the University of Munich.[43] The reconstituted General Medical Society was therefore at the forefront of early postwar psychiatric resistance to the type of psychotherapy proposed by various depth psychologists and psychoanalysts who had emerged from the Göring Institute and the prewar psychotherapeutic and psychoanalytic movements.

Kretschmer was in a very strong position to advance his views. Unlike many of his psychiatric colleagues, he was unencumbered by past affiliation with the Nazi regime. Although, as we have seen, he did add his voice both to the Nazi eugenics program (chapter 5) and to the German war effort (chapter 10), he was regarded both before and after 1945 as someone not in sympathy with National Socialism. An example of the former was his failed candidacy for the chair in psychiatry and neurology at Tübingen University early in 1945 (see chapter 5).[44] Kretschmer's politically unobjectionable status in the eyes of the occupation authorities was evidenced through his editorship of a scientific review of wartime German psychiatry for the Office of Military Government for Germany in 1948. Kretschmer naturally used this opportunity to promote the work of psychiatrists and neurologists and to ignore that of the psychotherapists at the Göring Institute.[45]

As president of the General Medical Society and editor of its journal, *Zeitschrift für Psychotherapie und medizinische Psychologie,* founded in 1951, Kretschmer joined issue early on with professional opponents on vital matters of the organization, legal recognition, and training of psychotherapists. He viewed the course taken by the psychotherapists under Göring as inimical to the interests of a scientific medical psychotherapy. In the summer of 1948 Kretschmer was called on by the several West German state physicians chambers (*Ärztekammer*) to serve as an expert witness on the question of the regulation of psychotherapy. Kretschmer was highly critical of the recommendations of the chambers under their president Carl Oelemann, recommendations that had been worked out with the cooperation of psychotherapists Bitter, Weizsäcker, and others. He declared himself against the establishment of special psychotherapeutic training institutes, against the training analysis, and against the training of attending psychologists. Between 1948 and 1950 Kretschmer succeeded in fending off the demands of the independent psychotherapists, for he enjoyed the powerful support of the majority of the neurologists and psychiatrists in West Germany. Bitter, as his opposite number in this dispute, was forced to agree to the stipulation that his institute in Stuttgart would receive funding from the government only if it agreed to train no nonmedical candidates. Even a letter from C. G. Jung to Baden-Württemberg Finance Minister Edmund Kaufmann was to no avail in the face of the powerful front of neurologists and psychiatrists Kretschmer had assembled. Since the financial situation of the psychotherapists in Stuttgart was precarious, they were compelled to accede.[46]

Thus, by 1951 there was a panoply of organizations concerning themselves with psychotherapy. In 1951 Walter Seitz, head of the outpatient clinic at the University of Munich and director of the Institute for Psychological Research and Psychotherapy in the Bavarian capital, published a useful overview of the field. Seitz observed that there were four groups of psychotherapists in West Germany in the early postwar period. The first, to which Seitz himself belonged, espoused "classical depth psychology" and found its chief organizational expression in the DGPT under the honorary chairmanship of Viktor von Weizsäcker. Training in psychotherapy and depth psychology for this group rested on two fundamental prerequisites: a specific talent and self-understanding gleaned through a training analysis. Seitz argued that in spite of all the disagreements among psychotherapists and psychoanalysts, there was unity on these two points and a resultant commitment to cooperate in the interest of the profession's development. Although Seitz typically made no mention of psychotherapy in the Third Reich, it is clear that the Göring Institute had contributed in no small measure to this postwar orientation, for it had been vigorously and effectively affirmed in the face of the powerful professional opposition it encountered from the medical establishment during the Third Reich.

These psychotherapists, Seitz observed, also affirmed the training of nonmedical candidates and required (as had the curriculum of the Göring Institute) that such candidates have completed a university education in the human sciences. Nonmedical psychotherapists were to be supervised by physicians and a full physical examination was to be conducted by the physician before a patient was turned over to a lay therapist. Seitz went on to contend that the current need for both medical and nonmedical psychotherapists was especially acute in the postwar period. He estimated that around one million neurotics, as well as those who were suffering from psychosomatic illnesses, were in need of care in West Germany and there were only about 200 practitioners of *grosse* psychotherapy in the whole country at the time. He remarked that any potential danger that lay therapists might overlook an organic illness or incipient psychosis was far outweighed by the danger of what Seitz saw as the medical profession's continued underestimation of the effects of the unconscious mind on the genesis and persistence of physical ailments.

It was these nonmedical "attending psychologists" who comprised the second group Seitz described as challenging the medical establishment in the realm of medical psychology. Since 1941 many of these practitioners had been identified by the designation of Dipl. Psych. awarded to graduates of German universities with a degree in academic psychology who had gone on to receive training in psychotherapy and clinical psychology. Seitz rightly perceived that the medical profession would eventually face a greater challenge from this group to its asserted—but now tattered—sovereignty over the field of medical psychology than from any other psychotherapeutic group. This was so, he thought, because of the greater number of university psychologists and their greater influence for being part of the powerful university establishment in West Germany. Once again unmentioned by Seitz was the contributing factor that autonomous psychotherapists no longer possessed the power and influence granted them by the unified and well-funded organizational basis of the Göring Institute. As we shall see, psychologists have indeed become a powerful professional interest group in West Germany since the war.

A third group, according to Seitz, was paradoxically powerful in a supposed age of enlightenment and amid the social demand for expertise. These were the so-called "wild" psychotherapists who had been included under the 1939 Health Practitioners Law and who in fact represented, among other things, ongoing popular skepticism toward modern scientific medicine. Seitz argued, echoing earlier psychoanalytic condemnations of non-Freudian "wild" psychoanalysts, that both the medical profession as well as all "serious" psychotherapists had to be on guard against this menace to the health of the people and to the status of the medical and psychotherapeutic professions. Quackery, he said, threatened the prestige of medicine in the eyes of the populace and that of psychotherapy in the eyes of more traditional physicians. Seitz emphasized what he saw as the professional status of psychotherapy in and of itself, standing between the large body of physicians on the one hand and the large group of psychologists on the other. Psychotherapy for Seitz was a health profession and as such it belonged in the realm of medicine rather than in the humanities or social sciences, in the clinic rather than in the seminar room. But Seitz was opposed to the more restrictive position on this issue of the fourth group of postwar psychotherapists, that is, those gathered under Kretschmer's mantle in the revived General Medical Society. For these practitioners, as we have seen, psychotherapy was to remain the province of university psychiatry.[47]

The very variety of psychotherapeutic positions in postwar West Germany, however, was testimony to the fact that the renewed attempt to confine psychotherapy to psychiatry was not the defense of an established position but rather a response to an opposite reality. Not only was psychotherapy not confined to psychiatry, it was no longer even confined to medicine. Both the social, political, and economic demand for psychological expertise and the institutional lobbies of its practitioners had permanently expanded the disciplinary base of medical psychology. Even the much more recent surge in biochemical research and treatment in the realm of mental illness has not reversed the long modern trend toward the mutual expansion of psychology and medicine. While traditional nosological psychiatrists maintained university positions and trained students, this oldest of the old guards had been thrown on the defensive by their murderous collaboration with the Nazis. They fought what was in fact a rearguard action, most infamously as experts in compensation cases for psychic damage from Nazi persecution whereby they denied claims on the basis of claimants' hereditary disposition (*Anlage*).[48] Even those psychiatrists who used psychotherapy found the professional tide running strongly against them. This was clear as early as 1946 when Kurt Schneider at Heidelberg was unable to prevent the naming of psychoanalyst Mitscherlich to a chair for psychotherapy.[49]

In an early test of strength in 1949, Kretschmer and Bitter came into conflict over the legal status of attending psychologists. Kretschmer was opposed to the 1939 decision of the Reich Interior Ministry that had placed attending psychologists under the 1938 law governing medical assistants. He felt that even in consultation with a physician such practitioners exercised an independent therapeutic capacity well beyond the far more restricted and closely supervised activities of nurses and other auxiliary medical personnel. In this, as we have seen,

Kretschmer was absolutely correct. He argued that attending psychologists already practicing should be placed under the authority of an expanded Health Practitioners Law (see chapter 8) and that in the future all practice of psychotherapy be reserved for licensed physicians.[50] Bitter and other psychotherapists rightly saw this suggestion as a step toward the prohibition of lay psychotherapy and psychoanalysis and fought successfully against it.[51] In West (and East) Germany the law would eventually mandate not only that nonmedical practitioners be assigned to cases by physicians but that such physicians be trained in "depth psychology."[52] Only in the military did the old guard maintain some superiority: While military psychology remains established within the West German armed forces, psychotherapy is seldom used in the medical service and psychologists work under the supervision of a psychiatrist.[53] Aside from this, the belated postwar attempt to restrict the practice of psychotherapy to physicians had been decisively turned back.

The ongoing disciplinary expansion of the field was also reflected on the organizational level. The General Medical Society for Psychotherapy had held its first congresses after the war in combination with those of the old Society of German Neurologists and Psychiatrists, the succeeding General League of Neurologists, and the German Society for Psychiatry and Neurological Medicine. But by 1955 Kretschmer's organization and the DPGT, under Alexander Mitscherlich, had agreed to a common program for introducing a supplementary certification in psychotherapy for medical doctors. This specialization in psychotherapy was adopted by the executive board of the West German Federal Physicians Chamber in 1956 and the following year at Baden-Baden the General Medical Society, the DGPT, and the German Society for Psychiatry and Neurological Medicine settled on a course of training in psychotherapy and psychoanalysis for doctors. The General Medical Society itself prospered: in 1964, the year Kretschmer died, the society numbered 445 members. Walter Theodor Winkler, since 1941 a student and colleague of Kretschmer's at Marburg and Tübingen and his successor as president of the General Medical Society, boasted in 1956 of the progress made by medical psychotherapy. But this progress was anything but simply along the lines of the relatively narrow path of professional development for psychotherapy Kretschmer advocated. As the postwar proliferation of autonomous and nonmedical psychotherapists demonstrated, the independent and disciplinarily inclusive path taken by the Göring psychotherapists was of decisive significance. Even some of Kretschmer's assistants had secretly undertaken training analyses with former Göring Institute lay therapist Auguste Marzinowski in Tübingen.[54] Winkler also asserted that the great postwar activity in the field constituted a "rebirth of psychotherapy" because of the reconstruction of international scientific dialogue interrupted by dictatorship and war.[55] This was true as far as it went, but the notion of "rebirth" served to dismiss the lines of professional continuity laid down by psychotherapists in the Third Reich. As we shall see in chapter 15, this failure to acknowledge the recent history of the field represented an active repression of unpleasant ethical truths. But it also represented a conscious political strategy that was in this case undermined by its own documentation: Of the 71 authors in the field Winkler listed in the bibliography of his article, 30 had been members of the Göring Institute (e.g., Bilz, Boehm, Gauger, Hantel, Heyer, Kemper, Müller-Braunschweig, Schultz) and at least 11 others had been active in the field during the Third Reich.[56]

Psychotherapy also continued to make gains in the realm of public policy. By 1962 the Federal Physicians Chamber recognized the official status of psychotherapy by approving a fee schedule for psychotherapeutic services. By the mid-1960s, despite objections from a number of psychiatrists and neurologists who desired stricter university clinic control over the teaching and use of psychotherapy, an approved list of clinics and institutes for such training was worked out by a committee composed of representatives of the three allied societies. In 1970 medical psychology, medical sociology, and a practicum in psychosomatic medicine became required subjects for medical students.[57] In the same year private insurance companies adhered to the decision of the West German government three years before to include psychotherapy in the national health insurance program. In 1976 treatment of chronically neurotic patients was added. There had been resistance among psychoanalysts to such insurance coverage on the grounds that insurance payments could not take the therapeutic place of the patient's own financial investment in his or her psychoanalysis. This reluctance, combined with more recent concerns about rising health insurance costs, led to a decision in 1992 to exclude long-term psychoanalysis from the list of services covered by public health insurance.[58]

In the process of all these advances the relations between the General Medical Society and the DGPT grew closer. Beginning in 1965 they held joint congresses.[59] In acknowledgment of the general trend and consistent with its efforts to promote psychotherapy against intransigent psychiatrists and neurologists, the General Medical Society was compelled to abandon its traditional stand against nonmedical psychotherapists and against the training analysis. In 1970 the West German government explicitly included nonmedical psychotherapists and psychoanalysts in the national health insurance program and the training analysis has remained a required part of training in officially approved psychotherapeutic and psychoanalytic institutes in the Federal Republic.[60] A change in the statutes of the society in 1975 provided for the extraordinary membership of nonmedical psychotherapists and psychoanalysts. The General Medical Society also sought to strengthen its ties to general practitioners by forming, in 1969, a study group for "general psychotherapy." This led to the founding in 1973 of the German Balint Society dedicated to the development of Michael Balint's "patient-centered therapy." Along with the Medical Society for Autogenic Training and Hypnosis and the Association for Continuing Psychotherapeutic Education, the Balint Society became a corporate member of the General Medical Society.[61] The psychoanalysts in particular, as we will see in greater detail in chapter 15, were also growing in numbers and influence. The old guard of the DPG and the DPV, represented by Boehm and Müller-Braunschweig, respectively, who both died in 1958, had been succeeded by a younger generation of students from the war years. Schultz-Hencke had been succeeded as head of the Institute for Psychotherapy in Berlin in 1953 by Franz Baumeyer and he in turn by Annemarie Dührssen in 1965, who had received her training under Schultz-Hencke at the Göring Institute.

The influence of academic psychologists in psychotherapy and psychoanalysis was also increasing, as Seitz had pointed out in 1951. In 1976 the regulations governing national health insurance were changed to require a university degree in psychology for nonmedical psychotherapists. By 1977, 5800 such degrees had been granted. This change was a signal advance for the psychologists since up until that time other academics such as sociologists, teachers, and ministers could qualify for certification upon completing postgraduate training in psychotherapy.[62] The Göring Institute had only recommended the degree of Dipl. Psych. for nonmedical candidates. This was due to the fact that such candidates were few in number then and the psychotherapists needed as many candidates as possible from a variety of disciplinary background in their professional struggle with university psychiatry. The Göring psychotherapists, however, also appreciated the eventual competition represented by academic psychologists and for that reason as well wanted to cultivate their ties to other disciplines essential to psychotherapy in their traditional Romantic conception of it.

The potential for conflict between psychotherapists and psychologists was realized in 1980 when the West German government was planning to designate behavioral therapy (*Verhaltenstherapie*) as a therapeutic mode so as to encourage its application by psychotherapeutically qualified physicians. Psychologists objected to this on the grounds that behavioral therapy was based on learning psychology and other psychological theories and that doctors equipped only with the supplementary certification in psychotherapy or psychoanalysis would therefore not possess the necessary knowledge to use it. According to this view, only psychologists with the degree of Dipl. Psych. should be allowed to practice it.[63] Clinical psychologists, beyond their professional desire not to be defined purely as a subspecialty of medicine, were obviously concerned about the traditional claims made on the realm of applied psychology by the medical profession. This was especially so since most psychotherapists and psychoanalysts in Germany had come out of the medical field. In order to meet the challenge from "popular" psychotherapy and to encourage the use of *kleine* psychotherapy among general practitioners, these practitioners have continuously promoted their belief that psychotherapy cannot be divorced from medicine.[64] At the same time, given the curative omnivorousness of the medical profession everywhere and its historically strong positivistic orientation in Germany, psychotherapists and psychoanalysts themselves have always been concerned about medical monopolization of psychotherapy.

This concern had been at the heart of the opposition psychotherapists, psychoanalysts, and psychologists have expressed to the creation of a formal medical specialization in psychotherapy. Such a designation might, it has been argued, undercut the ideal that every physician should be schooled in psychotherapy in order to improve his or her treatment of patients as whole human beings. It might also allow the medical profession to establish its own exclusive standards and regulations for the training and practice of psychotherapists. These were the criticisms levelled at the introduction in West Germany in 1970 of a required clinical course in psychosomatic medicine.[65] And, most distressing for psychoanalysts and most psychotherapists, such a development might mean the sacrifice of the training analysis.[66] Such concerns have prevented the implementation of unified legislation, a West German government draft law for which appeared in 1978, governing both medical and nonmedical psychotherapists.[67]

In 1978, however, West German doctors approved more extensive requirements for supplementary certification (*Zusatzbezeichnung*) in psychotherapy and introduced a like specialization in psychoanalysis. In 1992 full specialization in psychotherapy (*Facharzt für Psychotherapie*) was approved by the medical community in the newly united Germany. These new regulations for physicians were the result chiefly of the efforts of the General Medical Society to ensure a future supply of well-qualified psychotherapists. Bavaria was the first state to implement its own version of the guidelines in 1993 and the other states followed in 1994. Typical for the federal structure of Germany and in line with the German particularistic tradition of state's rights in such matters as education, the regulations differ in some ways from state to state.[68] The specialization embraces theoretical instruction in all of the major approaches in the field: depth psychological psychotherapy, psychoanalytic psychotherapy, cognitive-behavioral methods, and various supportive and group therapies. The training overlaps most closely, however, with psychosomatic medicine and places a corresponding emphasis on medical diagnosis and practice: For example, twenty of the forty patients handled in the clinical portion of the training must be suffering from psychosomatic illnesses.[69] In addition to theoretical and practical training, though, a "self-experience" (*Selbsterfahrung*), the classic psychoanalytic training analysis, is also required.

Reform psychoanalysts such as Annemarie Dührssen regard this specialization as the culmination of the professional development of psychoanalysis (see chapter 15). But these regulations in fact represent not only the progress psychotherapy in general has made in achieving recognition from and integration into the health establishment in Germany, they also demonstrate the necessity for compromise among the various interest groups in the now very crowded, competitive, and even contentious field of medical psychology. In light of this law, many psychiatrists are even more concerned about the further compromising of their earlier monopoly on treatment of mental disorders.

Moreover, the competing claims of academic psychologists and psychotherapists in the field persist in this legislation: Students have the choice between specializing in cognitive-behavioral or depth psychological psychotherapy. And while there is theoretical instruction in psychoanalytic methods, clinical training in psychoanalysis is excluded. This exclusion arises from two considerations. The first is the desire of the psychoanalysts to retain the exclusivity of the supplementary specialization in psychoanalysis approved in 1978. The second is the psychoanalytic insistence on a longer period and frequency of treatment, 250 hours versus the 150 hours required by the 1992 guidelines. At the same time, however, the psychoanalysts benefit from the requirement of a "self-experience," or personal analysis, for both the supplementary certification in psychotherapy and psychoanalysis and for specialization in psychotherapy. While the "self-experience" can be along the lines of a psychoanalytic training analysis or of behavioral therapy, this requirement has so far meant a monopoly for psychoanalytic institutes since cognitive-behavioral therapy has only the theoretical rudiments of such training. A personal analysis within the confines of behavioral theory makes little sense since there is no conception of the unconscious from which resistances manifest themselves and no transference whereby the patient projects feelings onto the analyst.[70] On the other hand, the training analysis has been reduced from the traditional 250 to 150 hours, as it was at the Göring Institute during the war.[71]

In addition to these ongoing compromises and conflicts, there are, more generally, limits to the expansion of depth psychological influence in medicine in Germany. Continuing medical education for practicing physicians requires neither self-experience nor supervised therapy. Still only a minority of medical students choose supplementary certification or specialization in psychotherapy. A survey taken in 1993 among students at the psychosomatic clinic of the University of Bonn revealed that 14 percent had undertaken specialized training in psychosomatic medicine and psychotherapy, 11 percent had undergone therapy, 7 percent wanted to undergo therapy, 6.7 percent were planning on specializing in the field, and 62 percent desired only to keep up with the literature.[72] Presently, around 2000 physicians in Germany are active in the area of psychosomatic medicine and psychotherapy.[73] And of course the distinction and division between medical and nonmedical psychotherapists persists.

The proponents of medical specialization in psychotherapy in Germany included many colleagues from the new eastern provinces of the Federal Republic. Their presence after 1990 significantly augmented the forces in favor of specialization in psychotherapy within the now united German medical establishment. These physicians had been the beneficiaries of such specialization, first in combination with other fields (e.g., psychiatry/neurology, internal medicine, general medicine, gynecology) and later on its own, in the Democratic Republic since 1978.[74] Psychotherapy in East Germany from 1949 on reflected the different political and social conditions obtaining there. East German doctors in general demonstrated a high degree of appreciation for psychological dimensions of illness as compared to their colleagues in other East Bloc satellites.[75] This was probably due to the legacy of a medical establishment not present—with the possible exception of Czechoslovakia—elsewhere in the less developed countries of Eastern Europe. It was also due to the development of psychotherapy during the Third Reich and the sweeping away in the Soviet zone of occupation of many of the traditional bastions of authority, including those in the universities and the field of medicine. By and large, however, the field as a whole found a more congenial atmosphere in the West. Dietfried Müller-Hegemann was one of the few psychotherapists to settle in East Germany after the war and he eventually emigrated because he found that the authorities were not sympathetic to the type of analytically oriented individual psychotherapy he wished to pursue.[76] Psychoanalysis, of course, was viewed as an intolerably bourgeois creation unsuited for a socialist society, but the emphasis on the positive relationship of the individual to the environment that had been so prominent among German psychotherapists was particularly attractive to the builders of the new state in East Germany. Psychotherapy was incorporated into the medical establishment in the Democratic Republic without the squabbles among the various traditional antagonists and competitors that was continued in the Federal Republic. This was due to strong state sponsorship and the absence of representatives of traditional psychiatry in the purged ranks of the university medical faculties in East Germany. In line with socialist ideals, group therapy was heavily promoted. The group ideal extended to training and practice. There was no training analysis, but instead a so-called "self-experience community" consisting of approximately 120 hours of small-group meetings and around 50 hours of large-group sessions.[77]

The first outpatient clinic had been established in 1950 in Berlin and training and clinical facilities were gradually introduced into the universities and municipalities. During the early 1950s, however, most therapists continued to receive their training at the institute established by Kemper and Schultz-Hencke. Practice was based largely on Schultz's autogenic training and some application of Pavlovian theory. There was also a strong emphasis on short-term therapy to meet what was described as the overload of patients. These efforts and others culminated in the founding in Leipzig on June 10, 1960, of the Society for Medical Psychotherapy of the German Democratic Republic. The erection of the Berlin Wall in August of 1961 intensified the trend to make psychotherapy useful to the state. In 1963, in collaboration with the resolution adopted by the Sixth Party Congress of the ruling Social Unity Party on the accelerated construction of socialism, psychotherapists became even more active in incorporating psychotherapy into a socialist system newly and vigorously committed to mobilizing its citizens' talents and energies for achieving high social productivity in industry, agriculture, and international sport. This included the training of clinical psychologists as psychotherapists along roughly the same lines as in Nazi Germany after 1939 and in West Germany after 1949.[78] The role the Göring Institute played in this process was more indirect than in the case of psychotherapy in the Federal Republic. Still, its influence was acknowledged—at least in deed if not in word—in the Democratic Republic. As we have seen, both Kemper and Schultz-Hencke provided early assistance to the building of an organized psychotherapeutic competence in the Russian sector of Berlin. As in the West, psychotherapists who trained at the Göring Institute, like Alexander Mette of Weimar and Kurt Höck of Berlin, were important figures in the evolution of psychotherapy in East Germany after the war. Mette was the founder and editor-in-chief of *Psychiatrie, Neurologie und medizinische Psychologie,* the leading East German journal in the field.[79]

In sum, amidst the suffering and chaos of the immediate postwar period, the chilling fears of the cold war, and the exertion and exhilaration of subsequent professional reconstruction and advancement, psychotherapists in both postwar German successor states had little time and even less desire for hard reflection on the crucial history of their discipline in the Third Reich. The very success of the Göring Institute in providing a continuous line of professional development in psychotherapy helped postwar practitioners repress knowledge of the institute's morally problematic existence. By the 1970s, however, older psychotherapists, their profession the labor of memory, had come to that time of life prime for reflection on the past. New generations inside and outside of the field had come to critical political and professional age. Abroad, the subject of psychotherapy in the Third Reich became the property of historians.[80] Particularly among young psychoanalysts in West Germany, questions had begun to be asked and answers had begun to be elicited. The age of reconstruction and repression was coming to an end. The age of rebellion and remembrance had arrived.

Notes

1. Gordon Wright, *The Ordeal of Total War 1939–1945* (New York, 1968), p. 246.
2. See, for example, Robert G. Moeller, *Protecting Motherhood: Women and the Family in the Politics of Postwar West Germany* (Berkeley, 1993), especially pp. 71–2.
3. Horst-Eberhard Richter, *Die Chance des Gewissens,* pp. 212–29.
4. Alexander and Margarete Mitscherlich, *The Inability to Mourn: Principles of Collective Behavior* (1967), trans. Beverley R. Placzek (New York, 1975).
5. Mitscherlich to Kranefeldt, November 28, 1947, quoted in Lockot, *Die Reinigung der Psychoanalyse,* pp. 160–61.
6. Pongratz, *Psychotherapie,* p. 277. It was also reported that Göring had committed suicide in Breslau just after the war in Europe ended; Walter Cimbal to Theodor Winkler, January 21, 1957, Georg Cimbal.
7. Grunert, "Zur Geschichte der Psychoanalyse in München," pp. 886–7.
8. See, among many others, Fritz Künkel, *God Helps Those . . . Psychology and the Development of Character* (New York, 1931). Rittmeister, "Der augenblickliche Stand der Poliklinik," p. 92, incorrectly names the Künkels as heads of the outpatient clinic's subdivision for educational assistance: see "Berichtigung," *ZfP* 12 (1940): 273.
9. *New York Times,* April 2, 1956, p. 23.
10. "Aktuelles," *ZFP* 16 (1944): 1.
11. Immo von Hattingberg, "Untersuchungen zum ärztlichen Verständnis der Angst beim Herzinfarkt," *Medizinische Klinik* 60 (1965): 1113–7, 1150–3; idem, "Die Aufgaben der Rehabilitationsbehandlung in der Sozialmedizin," *Münchener medizinische Wochenschrift* 108 (1966): 426–30.
12. Lockot, *Die Reinigung der Psychoanalyse,* p. 252; Schultz-Hencke, Zweiter protokollarischer Bericht, May 26, 1945, pp. 6–7, Kl. Erw. 762/7; Hildegard Achelis, personal communication, May 2, 1983.
13. Senat der Freien und Hansestadt Hamburg, Staatsarchiv, personal communication, August 7, 1985.
14. "Verein der Ärzte im Steiermark," *Münchener medizinische Wochenschrift* 92 (1950): 566; Huber, *Psychoanalyse in Österreich,* pp. 131–2.
15. Gauger to Bitter and Kühnel, May 9, 1955, p. 1.
16. Ibid. See Kurt Gauger, *Die Dystrophie als psychosomatische Krankheitsbild* (Munich, 1952); idem, *Psychotherapie und Zeitgeschehen: Abhandlungen und Vorträge* (Munich, 1954); and idem, *Dämon Stadt* (Düsseldorf, 1957).

17. Hannah, *Jung*, p. 289n.
18. Jung, *Letters*, p. 406.
19. Pongratz, *Psychotherapie*, p. 323n; Friedrich Domay, *Handbuch der Deutschen Wissenschaftlichen Gesellschaften* (Wiesbaden, 1964), p. 543; and Schultz, *Lebensbilderbuch*, p. 161.
20. Schultz, *Geschlecht, Liebe, Ehe* (1951); Heyer, *Praktische Seelenheilkunde* (1950); Heyer, *Der Organismus der Seele* (1951).
21. Albert Wellek, "Deutsche Psychologie und Nationalsozialismus," *Psychologie und Praxis* 4 (1960): 177–82.
22. Michael H. Kater, *The Nazi Party: A Social Profile of Members and Leaders, 1919–1945* (Cambridge, Mass., 1983), pp. 132–5, 266–8.
23. Pongratz, *Psychotherapie*, pp. 64, 294–9, 303–6; Dräger, "Psychoanalysis in Hitler Germany," p. 212; and Dührssen, *Ein Jahrhundert Psychoanalytische Bewegung*, p. 200.
24. Schultz-Hencke, Vierter protokollarischer Bericht, June 7, 1945, pp. 3–5, Kl. Erw. 762/7.
25. Schultz-Hencke, Erster protokollarischer Bericht über den Verlauf der Gründung des Instituts für Psychotherapie, May 21, 1945, p. 2, Kl. Erw. 762/7.
26. Schultz-Hencke, Fünfter protokollarischer Bericht, June 12, 1945, p. 11, Kl. Erw. 762/7.
27. Kurt Höck, "Psychotherapie in der DDR," p. 7; see also idem, "Entwicklung und Aufgaben der Psychotherapie in der DDR."
28. Lockot, *Die Reinigung der Psychoanalyse*, p. 242; Pongratz, *Psychotherapie*, p. 326.
29. Grunert, "Zur Geschichte der Psychoanalyse in München," pp. 881–5; Lockot, *Die Reinigung der Psychoanalyse*, pp. 91–2.
30. Pongratz, *Psychotherapie*, pp. 46–9, 56–7, 65–6, 309.
31. Lockot, *Die Reinigung der Psychoanalyse*, pp. 131–76; Mitscherlich also worked with Schottlaender before parting with him over Schottlaender's growing affinity for Schultz-Hencke's "neo-analysis": see ibid., 126–31, 264–75.
32. Pongratz, *Psychotherapie*, pp. 59–63, 303; Domay, *Handbuch der Deutschen Wissenschaftlichen Gesellschaften*, pp. 543–50; and Hans Thomä, "Some Remarks on Psychoanalysis in Germany," pp. 685–8.
33. Lockot, *Die Reinigung der Psychoanalyse*, pp. 111–12, 123–5. As early as March of 1946 Schirren had given two radio addresses on psychotherapy over the American radio station in Berlin: see B 339/60, BA.
34. Richter, *Die Chance des Gewissens*, pp. 67–75.
35. Pongratz, *Psychotherapie*, pp. 326–9.
36. Lockot, *Die Reinigung der Psychoanalyse*, pp. 208–61.
37. Dührssen, *Ein Jahrhundert Psychoanalytische Bewegung*, p. 213.
38. Richter, *Die Chance des Gewissens*, p. 72.
39. Huber, *Psychoanalyse in Österreich*, pp. 71–172.
40. Helmut Thomä, "Die Neo-Psychoanalyse Schultz-Henckes," *Psyche* 17 (1963/64): 44–126; Dührssen, *Ein Jahrhundert Psychoanalytische Bewegung*, pp. 211–16.
41. Lockot, *Die Reinigung der Psychoanalyse*, p. 282; Domay, *Handbuch*, p. 542.
42. Walter Seitz, "Die Lage der Psychotherapie in Deutschland," p. 400.
43. Marlies von Hattingberg, "Über Psychotherapie," *Medizinische Monatsschrift* 3 (1949): 385–8; Johannes Heinrich Schultz, *Psychotherapie*, pp. 173–9; and idem, *Lebensbilderbuch*, p. 160.
44. Dozentenführer der Universität Tübingen Dr. Usadel to Rektor Stickl, January 6,

1944, BDC: Parteikorrespondenz; and Stickl to Kultusministerium, Stuttgart, January 10, 1945, BDC: Parteikorrespondenz.

45. Johannes Hirschmann, "Psychotherapie," in Kretschmer, *Psychiatry,* pp. 203–14; Baumeyer, "Zur Geschichte der Psychoanalyse in Deutschland," pp. 219–20; Pongratz, *Psychotherapie,* pp. 308–9; and Ernst Kretschmer, *Medizinische Psychologie,* 9th ed. (Stuttgart, 1947).
46. Pongratz, *Psychotherapie,* pp. 51–6; Jung, *Letters,* pp. 542–4.
47. Seitz, "Die Lage der Psychotherapie in Deutschland."
48. Klaus D. Hoppe, "The Emotional Reactions of Psychiatrists when Confronting Survivors of Persecution," *Psychoanalytic Forum* 1 (1966): 187–96.
49. Lockot, *Die Reinigung der Psychoanalyse,* pp. 167–76.
50. Ernst Kretschmer, "Organisationsfragen der deutschen Psychotherapie," pp. 378–9.
51. Pongratz, *Psychotherapie,* p. 61.
52. "Vereinbarung über die Ausübung von tiefenpsychologisch fundierter und analytischer Psychotherapie in der kassenärztlichen Versorgung," *Deutsche Ärzteblatt-Ärztliche Mitteilungen* 73 (1976): 1769; Höck, "Das abgestufte System der Diagnostik," p. 91.
53. Bundesministerium der Verteidigung, personal communication, May 15, 1981; see also Ulfried Geuter and Bernhard Kroner, "Militärpsychologie," in Gunter Rexilius and Siegfried Grübitsch, eds., *Handbuch psychologischer Grundbegriffe* (Reinbek bei Hamburg, 1981), pp. 672–89.
54. Pongratz, *Psychiatrie,* p. 67.
55. Walter Theodor Winkler, "The Present Status of Psychotherapy in Germany," p. 288.
56. Ibid., pp. 301–5.
57. Dührssen, *Ein Jahrhundert Psychoanalytische Bewegung,* p. 231; Richter, *Die Chance des Gewissens,* pp. 156–7.
58. Dührssen, *Ein Jahrhundert Psychoanalytische Bewegung,* pp. 228–9, 248.
59. Walter Theodor Winkler, "50 Jahre AÄGP—Ein Rückblick," pp. 80–2.
60. Pongratz, *Psychotherapie,* p. 54.
61. Winkler, "50 Jahre AÄGP," p. 82.
62. Annemarie Dührssen, "Zu den neuen Psychotherapie-Richtlinien," *Die Ortskrankenkasse* 23/24 (1976): 836.
63. See the "open letters" published in *Report Psychologie Sonderheft der Landesgruppe Berlin* (1980): 9–11.
64. Cf. Michael Hockel, "Der Beruf des Diplom-Psychologen," *Report Psychologie* 4 (1979): 19–73; and Carl Nedelmann and Klaus Horn, "Gesellschaftliche Aufgaben der Psychotherapie," *Psyche* 30 (1976): 827–53.
65. V. Köllner, "Die Ausbildung im Fach Psychosomatische Medizin und Psychotherapie in der Bundesrepublik Deutschland," p. 120.
66. Seitz, "Die Lage der Psychotherapie," p. 401; "Erläuterungen zum Konzept des 'Klinischen Psychologen'," *Report Psychologie Sonderheft,* pp. 15–18; and Nedelmann and Horn, "Gesellschaftliche Aufgaben," p. 840.
67. Manfred M. Fichter and Hans-Ulrich Wittchen, *"Nicht-ärztliche" Psychotherapie im In- und Ausland: Zur psychotherapeutischen Versorgung durch nicht-ärztliche Berufsgruppen* (Weinheim, 1980), pp. 144–255.
68. Paul L. Janssen and Sven Olaf Hoffmann, "Profil des Facharztes für Psychotherapeutische Medizin," p. 195; on supplementary certification and specialization, see also above, chapters 2 and 5.
69. Janssen and Hoffmann, "Profil des Facharztes," p. 199; see also Paul L. Janssen,

"Von der Zusatzbezeichnung 'Psychotherapie' zur Gebietsbezeichnung 'Psychotherapeutische Medizin'," *Zeitschrift für psychosomatische Medizin und Psychoanalyse* 39 (1993): 95–117.

70. Janssen and Hoffmann, "Profil des Facharztes," p. 200.
71. Ibid.; Schultz-Venrath, "Der Missbrauch von Geschichte," pp. 398, 401.
72. Köllner, "Die Ausbildung im Fach Psychosomatische Medizin," pp. 120, 121.
73. Janssen and Hoffmann, "Profil des Facharztes," p. 196.
74. Dührssen, *Ein Jahrhundert Psychoanalytische Bewegung*, pp. 9, 232–3, 237–49; Kurt Höck, personal communication, September 21, 1979.
75. Kurt Höck, "Das abgestufte System," p. 90.
76. See Dietfried Müller-Hegemann, *Die Berliner Mauerkrankheit: Zur Soziogenese psychischer Störungen* (Herford, 1973); Nomi Morris, "East Germans Suffering 'Psychic Shock'," *Detroit News*, February 24, 1991, p. 12. Gerhard Scheunert returned to Erfurt after the war, but left East Germany in 1949 after he allegedly was asked by the Soviet secret police to spy on his patients: see Scheunert to Nedelmann, March 14, 1993, p. 3.
77. Kurt Höck, personal communication, September 21, 1979.
78. Höck, "Entwicklung und Aufgaben der Psychotherapie in der DDR," pp. 8–23; Adolf Kossakowski, "Psychology in the German Democratic Republic," *American Psychologist* 35 (1980): 450–60.
79. Ludger M. Hermanns, "Bedingungen und Grenzen wissenschaftlicher Produktivität bei Psychoanalytikern in Deutschland 1933 bis 1945—mit einem exemplarischen Versuch über Alexander Mette und sein Novalis-Projekt," *Jahrbuch der Psychoanalyse* 25 (1990): 28–54.
80. Geoffrey Campbell Cocks, "Psyche and Swastika: Neue deutsche Seelenheilkunde, 1933–1945," Ph.D. dissertation, University of California, Los Angeles, 1975.

15

Rebellion and Remembrance

For the first three decades after the war, as we have seen, the professional legacy of the Göring Institute had been ignored by psychotherapists and psychoanalysts in both East and West Germany, who concentrated instead on reconstructing their professional present and repressing their recent professional past. To the extent they thought about their own and their discipline's experience in the Third Reich, it was in terms of oppression, wartime suffering, and an implicit or even explicit assertion of inner resistance to the Nazi regime. As we have seen, the social and professional realities of the Third Reich were much more complicated than these manufactured memories would admit. Most Germans, in one way or another, supported and collaborated with the Nazi regime. For most individuals and groups, however, collaboration was not a straightforward matter, especially over time, of seamless support. Private and public human behavior under Nazism was characterized by various points along a scale ranging from degrees of support through instances of nonconformist behavior, refusal, protest, and even genuine resistance.[1] These attitudinal and behavioral degrees and instances, moreover, could be intentional or unintentional and direct or indirect in terms of both motive and effect. For example, at the end of 1942 the rate of sick leaves went up sharply in German industry to over 5 percent of all workers. This was due to people deciding to use accumulated earnings to buy rationed commodities and take a break from work.[2] Such mass absenteeism was achieved with the help of local doctors and had led to increasing Nazi employment of doctors in the factories who would be more loyal to the firm and the regime.[3] In 1944 Conti announced an order by slave labor boss Fritz Sauckel on behalf of Goebbels, dated July 28, that outlined punishments for physicians who allowed patients to duck work.[4] But the 1942 action, taken in the face of Nazi warnings about absenteeism equaling defeatism and defeatism equaling treason, was based in part on the correct assumption that both labor and life would be getting harder in the near future. Therefore, while this "friction" of individual preference constituted a temporary drag on the system, it also—besides being selfish and not idealistic—represented a longer-term commitment to work, however willingly or unwillingly, for the regime. Such short-term "friction" in fact constituted "letting off steam" in order to survive in the context of long-term functional utility to the Nazi system. The regime itself exploited such dynamics on an organized, collective basis by means of such events as orchestral concerts in the factories.

Even at the rare extremes of heroic principled opposition to Nazism, as we have seen in the case of John Rittmeister, there was the necessity of—and even desire for—some functional role in society. More typical, in any case, was a nonheroic tradition of degrees of quotidian dissidence mixed with compromise and even collaboration. As David Large points out, heroism almost by definition describes actions that are too late while concentrating on heroism devalues "low-level" civil disobedience that if not preempting evil can mitigate it.[5] This is not to celebrate those many who went along at the expense of those few who did not. There is great importance in the example of an individual resister (*Einzelkämpfer*) like Rittmeister.[6] But even Rittmeister's life contains instructive ambiguities in terms of his profession: Alongside resistance was, as Rittmeister noted in his prison diary, enthusiasm for much of his work as director of the outpatient clinic at the Göring Institute.[7] Moreover, a post hoc fixation on resistance heroes can substitute a wish-fulfilling "ego-ideal" for historical inquiry, obscuring lines of continuity between past and present, as we will see below in the descriptions of "usable pasts" generated by John Rittmeister's brutally terminated professional career in the Third Reich.

As aspiring professionals, the situation was even more complicated and morally problematic for psychotherapists than it was for people in general. As a result of their ambitions and skills, the psychotherapists were on the functional side of the social balance rather than on the side of resistance. As we have seen, disciplines like psychology and psychotherapy exploited specific conditions created by the Nazi seizure of power to achieve for the first time a significant degree of professionalization. Psychiatrists, psychotherapists, and psychoanalysts all to one degree or another sought professional advantage in competition with one another during the Third Reich, an instance of what in connection with the Holocaust has been called "the nature of modern sin, the withdrawal of moral concerns from public roles in our lives."[8] There are specific reasons why most members of the German elites did not resist Hitler, as much of it having to do with greed, ambition, and power as with obedience, fear, and cowardice. Professional experts in particular were needed by the regime and the psychotherapists in particular confronted an unprecedented opportunity for individual and collective advancement. This of course further undermined any tendency to bite the hand that fed, although the generally protective presence and nature of Matthias Heinrich Göring made a few good moral choices possible. Ironically, however, the very means by which "nonheroic" psychotherapists could most directly and effectively mitigate the inhumane effects of the regime, that is, by the treatment of patients, were most often also the means by which the regime benefited from their expertise, that is, in maintaining the productivity of the populace. Who then supported the regime more effectively, the incompetent psychotherapist who joined the Nazi party or the psychotherapist who opposed the Nazis but did his or her therapeutic work well?

In West Germany such issues were not confronted until the 1960s. During that decade young Germans began to confront elders who during the "economic miracle" of the 1950s had lied or remained silent about their actions and inactions under Nazism. While these challenges, particularly in their angrier forms, often prompted unenlightening defensive reactions, there was also gradually an opening up of the past to investigation and self-reflection. Among others, psychotherapists and psychoanalysts in particular were confronted with their recent professional past. Along with resistance and denial, there emerged—spoken and unspoken—onto the psychological and political landscape some regret over and empathy with the conditions that rendered resistance problematic, regret over the moral derelictions of their own professional ancestors, and longing for a legacy of resistance as redemption of the past and for moral commitment in the present. In these initial confrontations, which were usually characterized by the generational hostility and political rebelliousness typical of the 1960s, little insight into the specific historical dynamics of the Nazi era was achieved. Issues of party membership and alleged continuities between wartime and postwar "fascism" dominated the debate. With the growth of historical research into the social history of Nazi Germany and the emergence of critiques of professions by their younger members, however, came greater critical insight into the social dynamics of professional collaboration in the Third Reich.

Psychiatrists, psychotherapists, and psychoanalysts have therefore shared in the gradual recapturing of memory after 1945. This process went through three distinct stages in West Germany. First, there was the repression characteristic of the 1950s; second, the angry generational confrontations of the 1960s; and, third, the more complicated and thoroughgoing recollections of the 1970s and 1980s. To be sure, all three styles have overlapped to some degree and both the criticism and the excesses that arose from the social crises and youth rebellions of the late 1960s and early 1970s laid the basis for subsequent professional critiques and self-examinations. But even more important was the fact that avoidance of and confrontation with the past took different forms for each discipline. This was so for two reasons. First, the three disciplines grew increasingly distinct during the twentieth century, especially since 1933; and second, the experience of each in the Third Reich differed in crucial respects.

Psychiatrists displayed an almost seamless repression of the field's activities under Hitler, so much so that instances of genuine resistance as well as collaboration were ignored in the silent assertion of general innocence. The two most prominent attempts by psychiatrists active during the Nazi period to rationalize their own or others' behavior raised more ethical questions than they answered. Karl Bonhoeffer, in an essay published posthumously in 1949, condemned medical killing but at the same time offered a rather tortured justification for sterilization.[9] Viktor von Weizsäcker tried unsuccessfully—in the minds of some even dangerously—to differentiate "between justified and unjustified destruction"[10] as part of an overall therapeutic vision. More critically, in the years immediately following the war only a very few psychiatrists were prosecuted for their roles in this program of involuntary sterilization and murder. Some were even absolved of guilt because German courts ruled that they had acted in the belief that the program was legally constituted.[11] Moreover, there was great demand for medical expertise in rebuilding a devastated society and therefore a distinct carryover of medical personnel from the Third Reich into both German postwar republics.[12] So even though the reputation of traditional university psychiatry suffered in Germany both during and after the war because of its involvement with the destructive racial policy of the Nazis, many of its representatives as well as their students remained in positions of authority after 1945. The continuities were not only personal but conceptual. The psychiatric preoccupation with the hereditary determinants of mental illness had been easily exploited by the Nazis. And apart from the authoritarian social and political views commonly held in the German professorate often linked with this hereditarianism, psychiatrists, like physicians in general, had long been heavily influenced by the eugenic thought, social Darwinism, and racism endemic to Germany during the late nineteenth and early twentieth centuries.[13]

A systematic confrontation with psychiatry's past did not occur until the 1980s. At first, this critique was part of a larger critical "history of the everyday" directed "from below" by students and citizens against the silent bastions of academic and political authority. These campaigns took the form of conferences and the collection, exhibition, and publication of documents, recollections, and studies concerning the activities of individuals, communities, and groups under National Socialism. Some of these concentrated on the medical profession, including psychiatry, and constituted criticism primarily from outside the profession from sociologists, pedagogues, historians, theologians, and the like, but also issued from inside the profession as well.[14] Much of this critical work was neo-Marxist or structuralist in orientation and saw Nazi medicine as a culmination of a Western bourgeois trend toward "social control" and eugenic engineering. Especially since the fall of communism in the Soviet Union and Eastern Europe, however, there has also been a greater need and willingness to confront the abuse of psychiatry by totalitarian socialist regimes. While some inside and outside of the profession adopted a radical "antipsychiatry" stance, others pressed for a "humanistic" reform of psychiatry.[15]

Only recently, therefore, did members of the psychiatric community begin to question their collective past. And instead of seeking distance between themselves and their compromised predecessors, as was characteristic of the radical confrontation of the late 1960s with "fascism" at home and abroad, these inquiries focused with some humility on those processes and structures for dealing with the mentally ill that contribute *now as then* to inhumanity. This did not constitute a facile equation of contemporary society with Nazi Germany but, rather, an attempt to deal with those tendencies toward categorization and evaluation within psychiatry that can stigmatize mental patients as especially disruptive of society and the economy. Klaus Dörner, one of the very few psychiatrists to address the subject relatively early on,[16] later expressed concern that he had only intellectualized the subject rather than confront it emotionally and that such an emotional confrontation involved for him an effort to work with relatives of mental patients killed by the Nazis who were denied compensation under the Federal Compensation Law. This effort, Dörner said, brought him face to face with a continuity of attitude and issue between the Nazi period and the present.[17] Such emotional confrontation, however, allowed Dörner to buttress his original continuity thesis. Moreover, according to Dörner, such continuity extends back into the late eighteenth century. He characterized modern European psychiatry as an exercise in "therapeutic idealism" by which "industrial-capitalist bourgeois society" could "deal with those who, by its gauge of rationality, it deems irrational."[18] The coercive social effects of this tyranny of reason ushered in by the Enlightenment and the Industrial Revolution were aggravated in Germany by Prussian authoritarianism. According to Dörner, the Nazi period represented the extremity of both of these traditions.[19] In line with this thinking, more recently Dörner's was a strong voice raised in protest against Peter Singer's argument for euthanasia of severely handicapped newborns.[20] Of course, one can support Singer's arguments without espousing a Nazi point of view, just as one can distinguish between Nazism and "bourgeois society."

A similar ethic pervaded the documentation by a group of young mental health care workers of the operations of the asylum at Wittenau in Berlin between 1933 and 1945. The authors asked why they had failed during the 1960s to take their teachers to task for their collaboration with the Nazis. The answer, they felt, lay with their own desire to divorce themselves from the horrors of the Nazi era by broadening and thus diluting their criticism into a radical condemnation of society in general and fascism in particular. What they found in scouring the archives at Wittenau was that the procedures and judgments involved in the sterilization and murder of mental patients under Nazi direction blended in rather smoothly with the workings of what up until 1933 had been an institution renowned for its progressive treatment of the mentally ill. This continuity of operation was the reason why documents detailing these measures were found in the archives while documents dealing with Jewish patients had long since disappeared.[21] While one must question whether such "progressive" attitudes lead ineluctably to Nazism and thus constitute a critique of modernity per se (see chapter 16), these investigations and attitudes displayed a healthy regret for failure in the past and an equally healthy call for commitment in the present.

This is not to say, however, that there are no professional, political, or ideological agendas involved in these efforts at confronting psychiatry's past. Most of the criticism came from various left-of-center segments of the West German polity who, with considerable justification, saw distinct continuities in professional attitudes among psychiatrists before and after 1945. These critiques most often were part of a general rejection of the conservative West German establishment embodied principally by the Christian Democratic Union which dominated political life after 1945. Moreover, while this confrontation was to a great extent one across generations, with the postwar young challenging the wartime old, the more recent concern with the moral ambiguities inherent in the social place of the mentally ill carried with it an implicit critique of professionalization that could be applied to all practitioners, particularly those of the postwar generations who were advancing professionally in a prosperous Germany. At the same time, the unification of Germany injected a great deal of Marxist-inspired research into the relationships between fascism and capitalism in the Third Reich.[22] Two basic moral positions evolved out of this combination of Western and Eastern scholarship which posed questions relevant to the debate over the role of psychiatry in Nazi Germany. The first maintained that moral choice is obviated by membership in historically determined collectivities; the second emphasized individual choices between good and evil that can and must be made: Which is it more important to change, structures or people? Which are more susceptible to change?

While psychotherapists and psychoanalysts did not have to confront direct participation in Nazi atrocities, their history, as we have amply demonstrated, displayed some disturbing lines of professional continuity extending through the Nazi years. Psychotherapists largely ignored their professional past, in part because they were busy first surviving the difficult years after the war and then exploiting their newly professionalized position to meet a growing demand for psychological services in both the Federal and the Democratic Republic. It is also true that time is necessary for historical perspective and that psychotherapists, like psychiatrists and psychoanalysts, are not professional historians, but a distinct unwillingness to deal with the legacy of the Nazi years also marked their treatments of the past. The accepted—and incorrect—professional view among psychotherapists in West Germany was that the "political events following 1933 pushed German psychotherapy . . . into the background for a long time."[23] In 1977, on the occasion of the fiftieth anniversary of the founding of the General Medical Society for Psychotherapy, its president, Kretschmer's student and successor Walter Theodor Winkler, was forced by recent inquiries and revelations to acknowledge the existence of the Göring Institute. But even this acknowledgment took the form of the inaccurate and protective observation that the only significance of the psychotherapeutic institute in Nazi Germany was the degree of protection and enforced cooperation it provided for those psychotherapists who had not emigrated.[24]

In East Germany an even greater distance was put between postwar psychotherapy and its precedents under German fascism, even though in the socialist republic there was a similar emphasis placed on expert service to the state and a reliance on the short-term methods pioneered in Germany by, among others, Johannes Heinrich Schultz, deputy director of the Göring Institute.[25] Former East German psychotherapists and psychiatrists now face the task of confronting a likewise compromised association with the late communist regime. The difficulty of this task is compounded by the fact that former East Germans in general never had to confront questions of collaboration with the Nazis since by official German Democratic Republic definition all former Nazis lived in the Federal Republic. On the other hand, the infamy and incompetence that prompted the collapse of the communist regimes may combine with the relatively advanced state in the West of confrontation with the Nazi past to produce an easier and quicker coming to terms with this even more recent compromised past. And whatever the psychiatric and psychotherapeutic injustices perpetrated by the East German government in aping its big Soviet brother, they of course pale in comparison to collaboration with the much more evil Nazi regime.

Challenges to the assertion of professional innocence among psychotherapists first came across disciplinary boundaries in West Germany from psychologists as a result of the professional competition sharpened and even created under National Socialism. Psychologists, too, were repressing their professional past as part of a process of defending their newly won professional turf. The findings of young psychologist Ulfried Geuter in the 1980s on the technical contributions made by psychologists in the Third Reich (see chapter 10) would demonstrate that charges of party membership or rhetorical support for the Nazis were not the only—or even chief—measure of collaboration with the Nazis.[26] The postwar attacks from psychologists on psychotherapists, however, raised defenses and not curiosity or consciousness. As a result, the first study of the history of psychotherapy in Nazi Germany came from abroad in the 1970s. By the 1980s some additional work was being done by historians of medicine at the University of Leipzig, but its thematic comprehensiveness was limited by a Marxist-Leninist approach emphasizing a top-down Nazification of psychotherapy.[27] By this time as well research in the West had integrated the history of psychotherapy in the Third Reich into the study of professions and professionalization in Germany.[28] This work had little discernible effect on psychotherapists in Germany, at least partly because the course of their profession's development scattered them throughout several disciplines and the nature of their practice oriented them toward issues of application rather than of introspection.

It was the good fortune of this author to have been the first historian to have stumbled onto the subject of psychotherapy in the Third Reich. My major field as a graduate student at the University of California in Los Angeles was German history and one of my minor fields was in psychohistory, which is the application of psychoanalytic methods to history. As a result, I became interested in the history of psychoanalysis in Germany. In searching for a topic for my dissertation I quite by accident came across some bound volumes of the *Zentralblatt für Psychotherapie*. Upon noticing that the volumes covered the years from 1928 to 1939, I immediately assumed that the journal was Austrian or Swiss, because I already knew that psychoanalysis had been banned in Germany in 1933 and that therefore anything like psychotherapy certainly could not have survived there. I was wrong. A year in West Germany conducting interviews with former members of the institute and scouring archives and libraries produced the first history of the Göring Institute. Early in my research abroad I found myself disliking the people whom I was interviewing and about whom I was reading. At the time I had not found evidence that any of the members of the Göring Institute had been involved in atrocities, but I was bothered by an understandable desire on the part of the people I was interviewing to justify and defend their activities in Nazi Germany, including their acquiescence, or worse, in the purging of Jewish colleagues. But I decided that I should take advantage of the fact that I was a foreigner who had no other purpose than to describe accurately and dispassionately the history of this group of aspiring professionals. The wrestling with the moral consequences could be and has been more successfully carried out by professional descendants in Germany. This did not mean that I would not evaluate the moral consequences of the professionalization of psychotherapy in Germany between 1933 and 1945. Rather, it meant that I would strive to relate all the relevant information I could about psychotherapy in the Third Reich so that as many historical connections as possible could be made by me and by subsequent researchers. It was just about that time that historians of the period were beginning to shift the focus away from the agencies and personalities of Nazi aggression and oppression toward the broader topic of German society under Nazism in order to understand more fully the ways in which everyday "normal" life was part of the environment that allowed Auschwitz to happen. For all of these scholarly reasons, therefore, it simply would not do to label the psychotherapists at the Göring Institute as nothing but just another bunch of Nazis.

Unlike the psychotherapists, psychoanalysts in West Germany (psychoanalysis was officially discouraged in East Germany) finally confronted their past. This had to do with the distinct history as well as the distinct nature of psychoanalysis. Two versions of the history of psychoanalysis in Nazi Germany had literally been institutionalized in the immediate postwar period. The "official" position of the DPG with regard to psychoanalysis in the Third Reich was that it had been "saved" by the Freudian members of the Göring Institute.[29] The DPV, newly aligned with the International Psycho-Analytic Association, argued that psychoanalysis had simply been suppressed by the Nazis.[30] These positions were taken out of both professional rivalry and a common desire to avoid confronting the more uncomfortable truths about the use and abuse of psychoanalysis in the Third Reich. Both the DPG and the DPV in the same spirit attempted to capitalize on the figure of John Rittmeister. There was in this memorialization a distinct sense of "our Rittmeister." For former colleagues at the Göring Institute it was a matter of innocence by association.[31] In East Germany, the figure of John Rittmeister served as the only officially recognized—and highly politicized cold war—link between psychotherapy in East Germany and the Göring Institute. As a communist victim of the fascism that for the East German regime still reigned in the West, Rittmeister was more a tool of foreign policy than he was—especially as a "bourgeois" psychoanalyst—a source of theoretical or practical guidance in the field of psychotherapy. In 1979 the East German Society for Medical Psychotherapy created the John F. Rittmeister Medal for Psychotherapy. Its first recipient was Rittmeister's widow, Eva Hildebrand-Rittmeister.[32] While Rittmeister is certainly worthy of admiration, concentration on him to the exclusion of the other particulars of the history of psychoanalysis and psychotherapy in the Third Reich was part of the process of denial and repression characteristic of both West and East German groups' perceptions of their collective past.

These orthodoxies of memory remained unaltered and unchallenged until the 1970s when psychoanalytic candidates, prominent among them a significant number of young women, began questioning them. Chief among these critics was Regine Lockot (Dipl. Psych) who in 1984 produced with her dissertation a comprehensive critical study of the Göring Institute.[33] By relying on extensive documentary evidence Lockot demonstrated that psychoanalysis was neither merely suppressed nor simply saved during the Third Reich; rather it was used, compromised, abused, and perverted. On the one hand, Lockot sought to follow what she labelled the *realpolitisch* perspective of the earlier historical work I had done and, on the other, to utilize a psychoanalytic point of view to begin the process of what Freud in 1914 called "working through" (*Durcharbeiten*). Freud had argued that what "distinguishes analytic treatment from any kind of treatment by suggestion"[34] is the process by which the patient *works through* resistances to an understanding of the repressed content behind neurotic symptoms. This didactic aim is furthered by transference, whereby the patient reexperiences feelings toward parents in the relationship with the analyst, and by countertransference, whereby the analyst through his or her own emotions created in the analytic situation with the patient comes to understand the patient's unconscious. Lockot argued that psychoanalysts in particular had to work through the repression of their own past and by means of countertransference come to understand not only their history but themselves as well.[35] The alternative was neurotic repetition of actions in place of self-understanding. Lockot argued that this neurotic pattern of behavior had been displayed immediately after the war by leading members of the DPG as they struggled with the emotional consequences of a psychoanalytic identity damaged by compromise and collaboration under National Socialism.[36]

It was this psychoanalytic emphasis on repression that in particular characterized the challenge that young psychoanalysts raised against their professional elders. This challenge mobilized confrontation, regret/empathy, and the tendency to overlook resistance for Resistance. It manifested itself first at a conference in Bamberg in 1980 and was developed by analysts and nonanalysts in the pages of *Psyche* between 1982 and 1986. In 1985 Lockot's book, *Erinnern und Durcharbeiten,* was published in West Germany, the same year as my book on the Göring Institute, appeared in the United States.[37] The appearance of these two monographs further accelerated discussion of this suddenly unrepressed history. The debate within the DPV by and large overshadowed the more timid discussions within the DPG, such as those held at DPG conferences in West Berlin in 1985[38] and in Bad Soden in 1989. Young DPV critics saw their organization's prior treatment of its past as especially objectionable for two reasons: first, because the notion of the complete suppression of psychoanalysis by the Nazis constituted silence on the subject; and, second, because such silence meant forsaking not only the many Jewish colleagues victimized by the Nazi campaign against "Jewish science" but also the ideals embodied in psychoanalytic thought.[39] The DPG, originally displaying the eclecticism in theory and practice promoted by the Göring Institute, had been willing to discuss the saving of psychoanalysis but had been less willing to examine critically the negative aspects of such salvation. Such critical consciousness developed as a result of the growing debate within the DPV and the increasing awareness of the historical research on the subject of psychotherapy in the Third Reich. This change was also helped along by the fact that the DPG began moving away from the "neo-analytic" position established chiefly by the Göring Institute's Harald Schultz-Hencke toward the Freudian tradition represented by the DPV and IPA. This movement was encouraged by increasing contacts among newer members of both groups not divided by traditional rivalries as well as by the growing influence of the DPV both at home and abroad.

Perhaps predictably for a discipline concerned so much with individual cases and characterized organizationally and emotionally by issues of authority between teacher and student, much of the heat (if less of the light) was generated in a controversy between younger and older members of the DPV over the role of Carl Müller-Braunschweig in presiding over the Nazi "coordination" of psychoanalysis.[40] A similar controversy inside and outside of the DPG blew up over the like role of Felix Boehm that involved not only generational dispute but also professional hostility between the two psychoanalytic societies.[41] A more recent dispute about the alleged hushing up of the Nazi party membership of DPV psychoanalyst Gerhard Scheunert was another example of both generational and organizational conflict.[42] While such disputes served the larger task of historical documentation, the ensuing critical scholasticism could also be diversionary. The same was true of the fetishization of the figure of John Rittmeister that affected professional critics as well as apologists. For younger members of the DPV he became the counter-example they held up to their professional elders and from whom they drew inspiration.[43] Surely it is a relevant irony that some who lived ethically compromised lives as members of the Göring Institute could at the time and later rationalize their behavior because of small acts of courage and compassion while later critics could *do* anything either against the Nazis or for their victims except remember for the sake of memory, their contemporaries, and the future. Under such circumstances the figure of a hero provided a certain degree of vicarious satisfaction and emotional nourishment for these critics.

By the early 1970s, wartime psychotherapists and psychoanalysts were at the age of reflection and their recollections were also encouraged by the stirrings of historical interest in the subject of psychotherapy in the Third Reich. The first to publish autobiographical accounts were former members of the Göring Institute, such as Baumeyer and Dräger in 1971 and Kemper, Bitter, Seelmann, and Riemann in 1973. These were followed by the reminiscences of former students of the institute, such as those by Walter Bräutigam in *Psyche* in 1984. These varnished accounts were succeeded and accompanied by critical studies from younger psychoanalysts based on interviews and documents. The original documents upon which Lockot based much of her research for her two books were stolen—or "liberated"—by someone from the "back room" of the DPG and given up to safekeeping at the

Federal Archives in Coblenz.[44] Both published memoirs and the papers left in estates, of course, are usually selective. This is most likely to be true in the case of the history of the Third Reich. But their availability, combined with other primary materials gathered by historians, still constitutes a valuable resource. This is all the more true when one considers that almost any document may reveal more about its author and his or her history than may be intended in the selection and omission of material. Such unintentional revelations can be further clarified by the range of material available to the historian.

Lockot's second book (1994) in particular, on the "purging of psychoanalysis" between 1933 and 1951, sought to use this documentation to destroy the "myth" propagated by the DPG of the "saving" of psychoanalysis under National Socialism. By contrast, the same year Annemarie Dührssen, former director of the Institute for Psychogenic Illnesses in Berlin and honorary member of the DPG, published a history of psychoanalysis in Germany during the twentieth century that tried to justify the deviations from orthodox psychoanalysis undertaken by, among others, Dührssen's teacher Schultz-Hencke. Her characterization of the Göring Institute was as a place where "rational" Enlightenment Freudians opposed "mystical" Nazi Jungians. This polarization of good and evil is of course a distortion of the history of psychotherapy in Third Reich. Such distortion serves Dührssen's view of the history of psychoanalysis in Germany as an ongoing campaign toward the ultimate integration of primarily short-term modes of psychoanalysis and psychotherapy into medicine that culminated in the specialization of 1992.[45] Aside from taking strident issue with Lockot and other critics, moreover, Dührssen's highly contentious and problematic treatment of the question of the relationship between Judaism and psychoanalysis elicited a particularly strong burst of criticism.[46] This divergence of views demonstrates that the lifting of repression among German psychoanalysts with regard to their discipline's history in the Third Reich has not only produced insight but also contention and distortion along the old divide between the refounded DPG and the secessionist DPV. Dührssen's book in particular suffers from partisan distortions of history. Such distortions stem not only from the vagaries of personal subjectivity but also from defense of a current professional position and ongoing denial of the ethical ambiguities and outrages associated with psychotherapy's profitable collaboration in the Third Reich. Dührssen, who argues that psychoanalysis in Germany benefited as a result of its escape during the Third Reich from the elitist Jewish environment of Freud's international movement, at the same time makes no mention of her own training at the Göring Institute.

Central to all these conflicts and debates was the discovery and evaluation of new historical evidence. The Archive for the History of Psychoanalysis has in just the past few years made efforts to deposit materials pertaining to the history of psychoanalysis in Germany at the archives in Coblenz. Just as my earliest work had encouraged and contributed to the first attempts by psychoanalysts in West Germany to explore their professional past, the ensuing achievements of the critical history in Germany based on further documentation during the 1970s and 1980s benefited my own ongoing work on the subject. The purloined Göring Institute papers from the DPG, combined with my own subsequent documentary discoveries at the Library of Congress, the Wiener Library in London, and in the East German archives allowed me to think and write more extensively and effectively on the subject. During the 1980s, moreover, there had been an explosion of research by historians in Germany, England, and the United States into the social history of Nazi Germany and on the professions in modern Germany, the fruits of which have greatly enriched the reach and depth of this second edition of *Psychotherapy in the Third Reich*.

The scholarly implications of the German psychoanalysts' confrontation with their history have therefore been quite significant. Perhaps such a confrontation was inevitable. Psychoanalysis, unlike psychiatry or psychotherapy, is based on detailed excavation of the past. In Germany especially, patients in psychoanalysis included those whose lives were directly or indirectly affected by the horrors of the Third Reich, even if for a long time the topic was largely taboo in analytic sessions.[47] Moreover, the DPV in particular was the inheritor of an intellectual tradition that was largely Jewish in origin and many of whose practitioners were persecuted by the Nazis. German psychoanalysts were reminded of this in 1977 when at the Jerusalem meeting of the IPA a proposal to meet in Berlin was turned down. Yet in 1985 the IPA did meet in Hamburg and devoted a day to discussion of "identification and its vicissitudes in relation to the Nazi phenomenon."[48] In conjunction with the congress a group of young German analysts set up their exhibition on the history of psychoanalysis in Germany highlighting the activities of psychoanalysts at the Göring Institute, a history that they saw as being repressed and not worked through by the international as well as the West German psychoanalytic leadership. But although the DPV was quite willing to benefit from the international success of the Hamburg exhibition, the IPA did not encourage confrontation with the discipline's German past, preferring at Hamburg as before to concentrate on technical issues of psychoanalytic theory and practice. Such a neutral "scientific" posture constituted the original response of the IPA to the depredations of Nazism in the 1930s.[49]

Even before reunification, the Germans made up the second largest national contingent of psychoanalysts in the IPA, behind only the Americans. But the popularity of psychoanalysis in West Germany has also been due to its being "a Jewish heritage in the German language" uncontaminated by the Nazi past that long served, in the eyes of some, to blind the DPV in particular to its compromised past.[50] Moreover, it can be argued that the introspection inherent in psychoanalysis carries a particular appeal for the German Romantic cultural tradition and that such self-absorption can be a means of avoiding rational confrontation with unpleasant truths. Left-wing psychoanalysts such as the Siegfried Bernfeld Group, who wish to effect what they see as the radical social and political implications of psychoanalysis, perceive contemporary German conservatism in social, political, environmental, and military affairs being reflected in the authoritarian practices of psychoanalytic institutes and in the ongoing failure to work through the Nazi past.[51] From this standpoint, the integration of psychoanalysis into the state health care system only aggravated inherent tendencies toward political and social quiescence.[52] More generally, it is anything but clear that Germans as a people have laid to rest the legacy of anti-Semitism, particularly with regard to feelings about health and illness. As we have seen, psychoanalysts, like psychiatrists and psychotherapists, have tended to concentrate on the actions of individuals independent of the broader context of institutional and professional history. But within the dynamics of regret/empathy, for whose exercise the analytic emphasis on intra- and interpersonal psychodynamics is peculiarly suited, German psychoanalysts also had to deal with the structural continuities in the history of their discipline to, through, and beyond the Third Reich. Such continuities raise the disturbing question of the ethical problems inherent in a professionalizing society. For all three disciplines, therefore, there exists the task of working through the present as well as the past.[53]

Notes

1. Peukert, *Inside Nazi Germany,* p. 83.
2. United States Strategic Bombing Survey, Morale Division, Medical Branch Report, *The Effect of Bombing on Health and Medical Care in Germany* (Washington, D.C., October 30, 1945), p. 113.
3. See, for example, Sudetenländische Treibstoffwerke A.G., Brüx, Bericht des Vorstandes, July 24, 1941, microcopy T-83, Hermann-Göring-Werke, roll 76, frames 6983–4, National Archives.
4. *Deutsches Ärzteblatt* 74 (1944): 147.
5. David Clay Large, "The Legacy of Resistance in West German Politics," paper presented at the University of Chicago, March 4, 1990.
6. Klemens von Klemperer, "'What is the Law that Lies Behind these Words?' Antigone's Question and the German Resistance," in Michael Geyer and John W. Boyer, eds., *Resistance Against the Third Reich, 1933–1990* (Chicago, 1994), p. 145.
7. Rittmeister, Tagebuchblätter, pp. 3, 4, 15, 19, 23.
8. Rainer C. Baum, *The Holocaust and the German Elite* (Lanham, Md., 1981), p. 266.
9. Karl Bonhoeffer, "Ein Rückblick auf die Auswirkung und die Handhabung des nationalsozialistischen Sterilisationsgesetzes," *Der Nervenarzt* 20 (1949): 1–5.
10. Kater, *Doctors Under Hitler,* p. 229; Viktor von Weizsäcker, "'Euthanasie' und Menschenversuche," *Psyche* 1 (1947–48): 68–102; Walter Wuttke-Groneberg, "Von Heidelberg nach Dachau," in Gerhard Baader and Ulrich Schultz, eds., *Medizin und Nationalsozialismus: Tabuisierte Vergangenheit—Ungebrochene Tradition?* (Berlin, 1980), pp. 113–44.
11. Ernst Klee, *"Euthanasie" im NS-Staat. Die "Vernichtung lebensunwerten Lebens"* (Frankfurt am Main, 1985), pp. 384–6.
12. Kater, *Doctors Under Hitler,* pp. 223–4.
13. Sheila Faith Weiss, *Race Hygiene and National Efficiency: The Eugenics of Wilhelm Schallmayer* (Berkeley, 1987).
14. See, for example, Baader and Schultz, *Medizin und Nationalsozialismus;* and Dirk Blasius, *"Einfache Seelenstörung": Geschichte der deutschen Psychiatrie 1800–1945* (Frankfurt am Main, 1994).
15. Richter, *Die Chance des Gewissens,* pp. 183–92; see also Mark S. Micale and Roy Porter, eds., *Discovering the History of Psychiatry* (Oxford, 1994), pp. 311–444.
16. Klaus Dörner, "Nationalsozialismus und Lebensvernichtung," *Vierteljahreshefte für Zeitgeschichte* 15 (1967): 121–52.
17. Gerhard Baader et al., "Podiumsdiskussion" in Baader and Schultz, *Medizin und Nationalsozialismus,* pp. 23–4.
18. Klaus Dörner, *Madmen and the Bourgeoisie: A Social History of Insanity and Psychiatry* (1969), trans. Joachim Neugroschel and Jean Steinberg (Oxford, 1981), pp. 218, 291. Cf. Robert Brown, "The Institutions of Insanity," *Times Literary Supplement,* January 8, 1982, p. 24. Brown criticizes Dörner's thesis as lacking in evidence.
19. Dörner, *Madmen and the Bourgeosie,* pp. 216–217, 329, n. 157.
20. Johann S. Ach and Andreas Gaidt, "Kein Diskurs über Abtreibung und 'Euthanasie'?" Zur Rechtfertigung der Singer-Debatte," *Das Argument* 32 (1990): 769–76. Dörner argues that Singer's view represents a mentality concerning ex-

pendable life, which replaces or disguises earlier eugenic arguments based on social cost with arguments based on sympathy for severely handicapped newborns. Any discussion of such ideas, Dörner says, provides them with a valuation they do not deserve.

21. Arbeitsgruppe zur Erforschung der Geschichte der Karl-Bonhoeffer-Nervenklinik, eds., *Totgeschwiegen 1933–1945. Die Geschichte der Karl-Bonhoeffer-Nervenklinik* (Berlin, 1988).
22. V.R. Berghahn, "Big Business in the Third Reich," *European History Quarterly* 21 (1991): 97–108.
23. Winkler, "The Present Status of Psychotherapy in Germany," p. 288.
24. Winkler, "50 Jahre AAeGP—ein Rückblick," p. 79.
25. Kurt Höck, *Psychotherapie in der DDR* (n.p., 1979), pp. 7, 14; Dietfried Müller-Hegemann, "Psychotherapy in the German Democratic Republic" in Ari Kiev, ed., *Psychiatry in the Communist World* (New York, 1968), pp. 51–70.
26. Ulfried Geuter, "Die Professionalisierung der deutschen Psychologie im Nationalsozialismus," inaugural dissertation, Free University of Berlin, 1982.
27. C. Schröder, "Programm und Wirksamkeit der 'Neuen deutschen Seelenheilkunde'," in Achim Thom and Ivanovič Caregorodcev, eds., *Medizin unterm Hakenkreuz* (Berlin, 1989), pp. 283–306.
28. Geoffrey C. Cocks, "Psychoanalyse, Psychotherapie und Nationalsozialismus," *Psyche* 37 (1983): 1057–1106; idem, "The Professionalization of Psychotherapy in Germany."
29. Baumeyer, "Zur Geschichte der Psychoanalyse in Deutschland"; Rose Spiegel, Gerard Chrzanowski, Arthur Feiner, "On Psychoanalysis in the Third Reich," *Contemporary Psychoanalysis* 11 (1975): 477–510.
30. Gerhard Maetze, "Psychoanalyse in Deutschland" in Dieter Eicke, ed., *Die Psychologie des 20. Jahrhunderts. Freud und die Folgen (I),* (Zurich, 1976), pp. 1145–79; Zapp, "Psychoanalyse und Nationalsozialismus."
31. Kemper, "John F. Rittmeister zum Gedächtnis"; Walter Bräutigam, *John Rittmeister—Leben und Sterben* (Ebenhausen bei Munich, 1987).
32. Höck, "Psychotherapie in der DDR," p. 7; and Höck, personal communication, September 21, 1979.
33. Regine Lockot, "Erinnern und Durcharbeiten: Zur Geschichte der Psychoanalyse und Psychotherapie im Nationalsozialismus," inaugural dissertation, Free University of Berlin, 1984.
34. Sigmund Freud, "Remembering, Repeating and Working Through (Further Recommendations on the Technique of Psycho-Analysis II)," in James Strachey, ed. and trans., *The Standard Edition of the Complete Psychological Works of Sigmund Freud* (London, 1958), 12:155–6.
35. Lockot, *Erinnern und Durcharbeiten,* pp. 17–38.
36. Regine Lockot, "Wiederholen oder Neubeginn."
37. Geoffrey Cocks, *Psychotherapy in the Third Reich: The Göring Institute* (New York, 1985).
38. Friedrich Beese, "Psychoanalyse in Deutschland. Rückblick und Perspektiven," in Gerd Rudolf et al., eds., *Psychoanalyse der Gegenwart: Eine kritische Bestandsaufnahme 75 Jahre nach der Gründung der Deutschen Psychoanalytischen Gesellschaft* (Göttingen, 1987), pp. 15–29; Geoffrey Cocks, "Psychoanalyse und Psychotherapie im Dritten Reich" in Rudolf et al., *Psychoanalyse der Gegenwart,* pp. 30–43.
39. Volker Friedrich, "Psychoanalyse im Nationalsozialismus."
40. "Dokumentation des DPV-Vorstands zum Briefwechsel Ehebald/Dahmer" (DPV,

September, 1984, typescript); Hans Müller-Braunschweig, "Fünfzig Jahre danach. Stellungnahme zu den in PSYCHE 11/1982 zitierten Aeusserungen von Carl-Müller-Braunschweig," in Lohmann, *Psychoanalyse und Nationalsozialismus,* pp. 113–19; and Ernst Federn, "Weitere Bemerkungen zum Problemkreis 'Psychoanalyse und Politik'," *Psyche* 34 (1985): 367–74.

41. Dührssen, *Ein Jahrhundert Psychoanalytische Bewegung,* p. 192.
42. Ibid., pp. 210–11; Lockot, *Die Reinigung der Psychoanalyse,* pp. 227–8 n. 59. Scheunert's "denazification" had designated him "a fellow traveler without sanctions." This allowed him to join the DPG and the DPV after the war. He did not reveal his former Nazi party membership to his training candidates on the grounds of the then reigning psychoanalytic principle of abstinence from sharing personal information with analysands. He also claimed to have undergone another psychoanalysis in order to understand why he had joined the party. The revelation of his political past led in 1992 to plans for a demonstration against him at a DPV meeting: see Scheunert to Nedelmann, March 14, 1993, pp. 1–2, 3–4. The BDC, which holds over 90 percent of the NSDAP membership cards, has no record of Scheunert's party membership: Berlin Document Center, Ermittlung von Unterlagen, November 5, 1973; and Daniel P. Simon, personal communication, September 4, 1985.
43. Ludger M. Hermanns, "John F. Rittmeister und C.G. Jung," *Psyche* 36 (1982): 1022–31.
44. Lockot, *Die Reinigung der Psychoanalyse,* p. 15.
45. Dührssen, *Ein Jahrhundert Psychoanalytische Bewegung,* p. 183; see also idem, "Zur Frühgeschichte des Facharztes für psychotherapeutische Medizin," *Zeitschrift für Psychosomatische Medizin und Psychoanalyse* 38 (1992): 299–309; and Geoffrey Cocks, "The Politics of Psychoanalytic Memory in Germany," *Psychohistory Review* 24 (1996): 207–15.
46. Schultz-Venrath, "Der Missbrauch von Geschichte," p. 394.
47. Lutz Rosenkötter, "Schatten der Zeitgeschichte auf psychoanalytischen Behandlungen."
48. Edith Kurzweil, "The Freudians Meet in Germany," *Partisan Review* 52 (1985): 337–47; see also idem, "The (Freudian) Congress of Vienna," *Commentary* 52 (1971): 80–83; and idem, *The Freudians: A Comparative Perspective* (New Haven, 1989), pp. 231–6, 294–8, 313–15.
49. Edward Glover, "Report of the Thirteenth International Psycho-Analytical Congress," *International Journal of Psycho-Analysis* 15 (1934): 485–88; Richard F. Sterba, *Reminiscences of a Viennese Psychoanalyst* (Detroit, 1982), p. 163.
50. Hermann Beland et al., "Podiumsdiskussion: Psychoanalyse unter Hitler—Psychoanalyse heute," *Psyche* 40 (1986): 425; Hans Keilson, "Psychoanalyse und Nationalsozialismus," *Jahrbuch der Psychoanalyse* 24 (1989): 23; and Robert S. Wallerstein, "Psychoanalysis in Nazi Germany: Historical and Psychoanalytic Lessons," *Psychoanalysis and Contemporary Thought* 11 (1988): 360.
51. Janice Haaken, "The Siegfried Bernfeld Conference."
52. Paul Parin, "Warum die Psychoanalytiker so ungern zu brennenden Zeitproblemen Stellung nehmen," *Psyche* 32 (1978): 385–99.
53. Franzíska Henningsen, "Von Dialog zur Institution? Reflexionen über DPV-Kontakte in den Neuen Bundesländern," *Luzifer-Amor* 9 (1996): 156–76; Klaus Behnke and Jürgen Fuchs, eds., Zersetzung der Seele: Psychologie und Psychiatrie im Dienste der Stasi (Hamburg, 1995).

16

Psychotherapy, the Third Reich, and the Course of Modern German History

Class, occupational identity, and interest alone do not suffice to explain the motives of individuals. The complex political motives of human beings within specific cultural and historical contexts[1] combine, as we have demonstrated in this study, with structural and institutional entities and dynamics to shape human actions over time. As much as psychotherapists were motivated by professional aims, each was also a member of social environment that was filled with the less tangible but no less significant percolations of culture, tradition, and personal experience. Such individual combinations of traits are even more historically significant the higher one goes in the social and political hierarchy, especially in the Third Reich, the black core of which can only be grasped through an understanding of the brutal fantasies of individuals with the power to act on their fantasies.[2] But to explain how such people came to power, to comprehend the historical ramifications of their rule under the various and complex conditions set by their time and place, and to locate the aspects of their regime in the contexts of German, Western, and human history is the task of an approach that takes into serious account what Max Weber in 1903 saw being constructed, namely, an "iron cage" of institutions. Still, such an explanation also requires some exploration of the less tangible influences of individual experience and attitude within the established culture.

In this dual sense, then, what is the general significance of the history of psychotherapy in Germany in the twentieth century? First, this history contributes to a growing body of knowledge about professional life in modern Germany, and about the social, political, and economic dynamics of the educated middle class (*Bildungsbürgertum*). It does this by revealing the institutional structures and processes that were responding to—as well as creating—the demand for technical expertise by the complex industrial society that Germany had become by the twentieth century, often (as was most evident under the Nazis) at the expense of the interests of clients and of higher morality. More specifically, the incomplete professionalizing project of psychotherapists in Nazi Germany typified the importance of the state in German professional life. But in this case, as in others, the state had—and has—been an entity whose recognition was an indispensable part of the goal for a professional group organizing from below and, in this case, in conflict with a part of the medical establishment within the university system, the state bureaucracy, and the military. The result in the postwar era was a mix of practitioner dominance that is typical of free-market Western systems and, particularly in the German Democratic Republic, a German tradition of socialized medicine.

Second, this history reveals not only much about modern German society in general but the structure of government and society under the Nazis in particular. This is a phenomenon that has often and necessarily been ignored in the historical literature out of concern for the broad, characteristic extremes comprised of Nazi victimizers and their victims. The Nazis presided over a generally anti-Semitic social environment in which "the overwhelming majority of . . . citizens . . . were ready to complain but willing to comply . . . , maintaining a clear sense of their own interests and a profound indifference to the suffering of others."[3] Nazi policy toward this great mass of *Volksgenossen* (racial comrades) was driven by anxiety as well as by arrogance, however. The Nazis recognized that "carrots were needed as well as sticks" to ensure at least the "passive loyalty" required for the privations occasioned by rearmament and war.[4] As a result, Nazi social policy displayed not only the ideological fanaticism applied most gruesomely against "racial enemies" and in service to a fantasized "racial community" they wished to create. It also exercised a pragmatism, however muddled by organizational chaos and individual incompetence, arising from their mastery of a modern industrial society that they desperately as well as callously wished to exploit. The Nazi emphasis on productivity so professionally beneficial to the ambitious and opportunistic psychotherapists created an environment of competitive individualism that was at odds with reactionary Nazi rhetoric about the comradely *Volksgemeinschaft*. This not only gave an advantage to technically educated elites, but had the effect of subverting opposition throughout society, leaving workers, for example, with vague feelings of cultivated nationalism, self-interest, and a certain resentment over sacrifices, shortages, and, finally, the sufferings brought on by the war.[5]

Third, the history of psychotherapy in the Third Reich contributes to a rethinking of the issues of continuity and discontinuity in German history. This in turn allows us to see anew the nature of modern German history and its place in the modern history of the West as a whole. Nazi Germany did not represent a clean break with either the past or the future. The Nazi system itself was much more riven with discontinuities than earlier studies of the aims and actions of its leaders had led us to believe. These discontinuities in the structure of National Socialism in power, however, allowed for social and economic continuities with developments before 1933 and after 1945, thus lodging the Nazi years more firmly into the course of modern German history. There was in general after 1933 a distinct carryover of social and economic conditions and trends along a scale of oppression, opportunity, collaboration, and contribution. These continuities were not merely a function of structure or process, but reflected dynamic and dialectical conditions that resulted in displacements one way or another in the constellation of forces involved. An excellent relevant example is the success of doctors in achieving recognition from the state as a profession in 1935, an occurrence that marked not only the assertion of Nazi control over the medical profession but also a victory—though a hollow one—for politically conservative doctors as a result of the Nazi destruction of socialist and working-class control over the state health insurance system. The resultantly strengthened professional hegemony of doctors over their patients continued, though not without challenge, particularly in the Federal Republic, after the war.[6] In the realm of psychotherapy, whereas some prominent older practitioners with Nazi ties were kept from the professional mainstream after 1945, the developments in psychotherapy in both the Federal and Democratic Republics coursed primarily from domestic continuities consistent with, rather than caused by, foreign influences revived in Germany after the war.

Such lines of continuity seem unlike those "peculiar" to the traditional liberal view of a Germany dominated by preindustrial elites. A more recent functional view of modern German history as well as some critical explorations in "the history of the everyday" have uncovered the degrees of influence of modern professional elites in an increasingly industrial and technological social environment. Old elites, as Michael Geyer has shown in the case of the officer corps, were reforming their practices along modern professional lines in response to the institutional and technical demands of the modern era.[7] By the twentieth century Germany had largely been transformed into a modern industrial society, although one still bearing some marked traces of specifically German preindustrial ideals, institutions, and influences. In recent times the German's head has often been crowned by a spiked helmet, although, like the crippled German officer von Rauffenstein played by Erich von Stroheim in Jean Renoir's film *Grand Illusion* (1937), his body was held erect not only by Prussian rigor but also by braces of steel. But German spike and German steel did not represent a dichotomy either within Germany or between Germany and the West, but rather, over the course of the modern era, a synergy. Fourth, therefore, the foregoing history provides, as we shall see in this chapter, the opportunity for a challenge through reconciliation of old and new views of German history.

These new views of German history rest upon a critique of "modernization" as a force for political and economic progress. The history of modern Germany, it has been argued, is a particularly good example of the "illiberal," inegalitarian, and inhumane aspects of modern Western political and economic development. An early postwar application of modernization theory, for example, argued that the Third Reich was an entity that swept away a "pre-modern" state and society, thereby in ironic fashion paving the way for democracy.[8] More recently, the "modern" features and ambitions of Nazi programs and plans have been viewed as the culmination of the modern trend toward the political and economic machinery of control.[9] Alternatively, the modern features of Nazi Germany have been argued to reveal a barbarous face of modernity as only a possible "pathological" outcome of modern trends.[10] Even the racism of the Nazis was, in great measure, a late nineteenth- and early twentieth-century pseudo-biological tradition. The hierarchical thinking embedded in such a racist view approved of the upward mobility not only of vulgar Nazi party hacks but also of technical elites. At the same time, in the grab bag of Nazi thought and action, the rhetoric of *Volksgemeinschaft* and the shared privations of the war created some manipulated degrees of the social levelling and solidarity advanced by modern socialism.[11]

Applications and critiques of modernization theory, however, do not constitute adequate models for the understanding of the course of modern German history. First of all, when applied to the Third Reich, such approaches run the risk of relativizing and trivializing Nazi genocide and other crimes against humanity. Second, the rubric of modernization too easily folds German history into Western history without taking adequate account of particular features of the course of modern German history itself. This does not mean that a concentration on the "modern" feature of modern German history has not contributed significantly to our understanding of Germany in general and the Third Reich in particular. Most of the work along these lines has avoided the very real danger of "'relativizing' Nazi genocide, of trivializing the significance of the Third Reich, or of relieving German historians of the responsibility for providing explanations of Nazism."[12] More generally, the study of German society under Nazism should contribute to greater understanding of the contexts for the Final Solution by drawing the *differentiated* circles of contribution and responsibility more widely, not, as has been implied or asserted, more narrowly. But the great amount of new research and thought on the social history of Germany and of the Third Reich still also has to be worked into a comprehensive whole that takes account of both the unique and general features of modern German history. Psychotherapists, more than other technical experts serving the Nazi regime, exemplify the mix because of their social and professional place between more or less specific German cultural and academic traditions and attitudes and the more general characteristics of the growing "technocracy" in Germany and the West.[13]

There are significant problems standing in the way of this task but these problems—like the difficult outcroppings on a sheer rock face that at the same time offer footholds—also represent significant opportunities. The difficulties stem primarily from the nature of the history of Nazi Germany. The Third Reich is a black hole in German history. Like hypothetical black holes in space, it draws everything towards itself. At the edges of black holes massive gravitational forces slow time to a stop. Anything falling toward a black hole, therefore, would appear to an observer to fall forever. Similarly, since 1945 historians of Germany have found themselves gripped by the gravity of teleology. The pull exerted by the Third Reich has often led, in the words of Richard Evans, to a teleological view of modern German history "from Hitler to Bismarck."[14] Such a pull is a necessary and useful one, since the crimes of Hitler's Germany are without parallel in human history, particularly when it comes to the hellish alliance of modern industrial means and ends with virulent racism.[15] But it is also useful and necessary to pull the history of the Third Reich back into the history of Germany, Europe, and the West, rendering it less of a black entity unto itself than a part of other, broader constellations characterized as much by differentiation as by the historiographical problem of teleology. This very task and result, of course, only underscores the reach and press on German history of the dark gravity of the Third Reich. But the heavy presence of Hitler's Germany constitutes a vital opportunity for historians—and humanity—to confront the lessons of the German past for the sake of the human present. The weight of moral gravity thus takes over from that of teleology.

Parallel to the problem of teleology in German history lies the historical problem of continuity and discontinuity between the history of the Third Reich and the history of modern Germany as a whole. The problem of continuity, as we have already mentioned, is particularly important for assessing fully the importance of the history of psychotherapy in Third Reich. How does Nazi Germany fit into the history of the Germans and of the German nation? Before, during, and even after the Second World War, this question elicited some rather crude answers. Some charged that Nazism was the inevitable outcome of German society, culture, character, and history. Others contented themselves with the striking but most often shallowly conceived conundrum of the land of Goethe, Beethoven—and Hitler. Still others in the West, deeply influenced by the cold war, equated German National Socialism with Soviet Marxism as manifestations of the uniquely modern form of rule of totalitarianism. Conservative and apologist Germans seized upon this interpretation, among others, to argue that Nazism was an imported accident in German history occasioned by modern secular revolutionary impulses in Europe. On the other hand, various Marxist models saw European fascism in general as symptomatic of the mortal crisis of late monopoly capitalism.

The predominant postwar paradigm among historians in the West, however, was the liberal idea of the German *Sonderweg* ("special path"). This was the thesis that, unlike Britain and France, Germany during the nineteenth century had not undergone a socially, politically, and economically modernizing bourgeois revolution; this failure allowed pre-industrial feudal elites to lead the country down a uniquely German authoritarian path to Hitler.[16] The issue of the power of the Prussian-German state in particular, therefore, has an important dual quality: not only the matter of government intervention unique in degree and kind to Germany but the *type* of government and the interests of its masters. Since the 1960s, however, historians have generated new varieties of sophisticated questions and answers about the nature of the Third Reich, its place in the history of Germany, and the course of modern German history as a whole. Many of these findings have come about as a result of work in other periods and aspects of the history of modern Germany. In particular, the study of the various stations and conditions of the modern industrial society Germany had become by the onset of the twentieth century has provided great insight into significant developments to and through the Third Reich. Arguments over the impact of modernization have therefore been especially important in evaluating the course and consequences of German history in the era of the two world wars. The "Bielefeld School" used social science methods to refine the *Sonderweg* model of the uniquely German authoritarian divergence from the evolution of modern democracy in the West.[17] Neo-Marxist approaches have been most persistent in posing the questions of the degree to which Germany had in fact undergone a transformation into a bourgeois state and society, the degree to which as a result "feudal" elites were in fact in control, and thus the extent to which it was in fact political and economic liberalism itself that was responsible for the conditions that led to the rise and rule of the Nazis.[18]

Ongoing research into the social, economic, and political complexities of modern German history has significantly qualified both the *Sonderweg* approach and that of its critics. In the history of psychotherapy as of medicine in general, issues such as the professionalization of doctors, the "medicalization" of society, the role of the state in medical professionalization, health, and public hygiene, the political battles over health insurance, the relationships between medicine and Nazism before and after 1945, the rise of eugenic thinking, and the places of women and patients all engage the question of the respective roles of a unique German past and of a general Western pattern of development. The various complex functions within the "polycracy" of a somewhat chaotic Nazi party and state, it has been argued, created a continuity of such established systems. Moreover, distinctly modern technical capacities in medicine—as elsewhere—were required by Nazi policy as well as preserved by Nazi political disorder. As we have seen in the case of psychotherapy in modern Germany, medicine and public health have been the subject of critical study for their role in furthering economic, political, and military demands for social productivity (*Leistung*) through the "practical utility" of various prophylactic policies and therapeutic methods.[19] Closer to the black core of Nazi ideology and policy—the singularity, to extend our astrophysical metaphor, of its biological racism and the resultant Holocaust—discontinuity takes on greater, though not exclusive, importance. In all of this, as in other specialized fields of German history, historians of medicine have had to consider the relative importance, particularly with regard to the rise of Nazism, of various traditional junctures: To what extent have longstanding German political, social, and cultural characteristics antedating the nineteenth century played a role? What is the relevance of the founding of a Germany dominated by Prussia in 1871? Was industrialization and its impact on the German economy, polity, and society the most crucial determinant? Or was it the series of disastrous events after 1914 and 1918 that constituted the more decisive elements?

Recent achievements in social history have greatly expanded our understanding of the place and power of intellectual and professional elites. The reigning bourgeois ethos of the nineteenth century highlighted heroic men of science clearing away ignorance and helping impose the rational order of freedom upon a chaotic and superstitious society. In the twentieth century, Marxist thought, similarly preoccupied with progress, gradually turned some historians to the history of the proletariat. Marxist historiography was no less a bourgeois heir of the Enlightenment in its preoccupation with progress. The only difference was that while liberals saw the bourgeoisie as a means to the future through its ongoing success, Marxists saw the bourgeoisie as a means to the future through its ultimate failure. This tendency, ghettoized politically—and then also geographically during the cold war—eventually contributed to a growing historical interest in social history in reaction to the traditional emphasis upon the ideas and activities of political leaders and cultural elites. Much of the initial interest of these historians centered on the working class, the most numerous class of modern urban industrial society.[20] During the 1950s this historical school was dogmatized in East Germany and ignored in West Germany; it grew in the Federal Republic during the 1960s and was partially suppressed there in the 1970s; increasing academic exchange on the subject across the intra-German border characterized the 1980s; and unification brought even fuller collaboration but also some evaluation and weeding out of Marxist-Leninist historians in the former Democratic Republic.

By this time, however, increased interest in the history of the middle classes[21] spawned studies of the process of its professionalization during the late nineteenth and early twentieth centuries. The subject of professionalization had been pioneered by sociologists in the 1930s and 1940s. This early work tended merely to validate "the normative claims of professionals and . . . [to link them] to the advancement of modernization."[22] Beginning in the 1960s, more critical studies concentrated on the powerful organized self-interest manifested among the professions.[23] For their part, historians of the German professions have highlighted the differences—in particular the greater role of the state in professionalization—as well as the similarities to the Anglo-American model. Historians of Germany have also had to examine the whys and ways of the involvement of professionals with Nazism and the Third Reich, an issue particularly acute in the case of medicine.[24]

In this regard, the history of psychotherapy in Germany also allows us to see the old *Sonderweg* controversy in a new way. The key lies in a tradition of corporatism evident, among other things, in the development of professions in Germany. This tradition as it persisted in Germany into the modern era anticipated certain corporatist features of Western postliberal industrial statism, just as the holism peculiarly strong in German psychotherapeutic thought also informs modern and postmodern critiques of mechanistic science. This process requires us to qualify not only the *Sonderweg* thesis but also modern critiques of it. Corporatist thought, particularly common in nineteenth-century Germany, was first a reaction against the French Revolution that finally envisioned "in some kind of non-Marxian, non-liberal social ideal the promise of class harmony, national solidarity and economic stability."[25] Such solidarity can produce benefits for the whole and protect the members of the group against the depredations of individuals, as was the case with the German health care system. But it can also lead to organized violation of the rights of individuals and of groups inside and outside the larger group in the name of solidarity. Corporatism cultivates a sense of duty, degrees of conformity, and even fanaticism. Moreover, the range of German corporatist thought more often than not displayed a "feudal" hierarchical political and social tradition preserved in and through nationally dominant Prussian authoritarianism. This tradition was strengthened by statist nationalism after 1870 and further radicalized against individualism, egalitarianism, pluralism, populism, and socialism by disastrous military, economic, and political events between 1914 and 1933. And, finally, corporatist thought in Germany of course only reflected broader social habits, attitudes, and convictions in both public and private life.

In Germany corporatism was thus part of a similarly generalized historical tradition of illiberalism, a tradition that significantly affected the professions. This illiberal corporatist tradition was advanced by capitalist trends toward hierarchical public/private control of organized interests. Especially during the early twentieth century, the corporate organization of the interests of experts and their employers was accelerated by the growth of the state as a source of money to be granted and regulation to be influenced. These trends in turn were magnified by the two world wars and institutionalized in the resultant "military-industrial complex." The world wars, which came about chiefly as a result of German difficulties, miscalculations, and ambitions, accelerated the "economic militarization" of modern societies throughout the West, a process also advanced by governmental responses to the Great Depression. The growth in scale and influence of what Michael Geyer has called the "organization of violence" by the modern state helped further the trend toward corporate professional and technical service to the state.[26] The growing influence of corporate bodies attempting to monopolize knowledge and technology and to advance economic interests marginalized the power of political parties and the general public. Professionals therefore were only one—albeit increasingly influential—element of a postliberal state of large interlocking public and private institutions and organized interests.

Germany, therefore, did not follow a *Sonderweg* in the sense of a departure from a liberal political standard achieved in the West. The false dichotomy between the "peculiar" and the "modern" that twentieth-century liberal historians imposed upon German history was a function of the American and Western European struggle with their own political and social ambiguities as projected onto "the other" in the form, first, of Germany, particularly as a result of the two world wars, and then Russia, particularly during the cold war. For example, the "domino effect" used by cold war policymakers in the United States to describe the spread of communism was in part a carryover from Second World War descriptions of the inexorable spread of German and Japanese military expansionism. There was no "special path" in German history because there was no "path" that led to an ideal liberal democracy in the West. Instead, in the West and in Germany there were elements of various political and social realities, including liberal democracy. But Germany, like any nation, has its own history and culture. And it was precisely some of that which was peculiar in kind and degree to Germany—here the military and professional corporatism preserved chiefly by Bismarck's *kleindeutsch* answer to the German question—that evolved under other conditions in Western nations during the twentieth century. Michael Geyer has argued that the traditional portrayal of two Germanies, the one rational and industrial, the other militaristic and backward, was a function of "a corporate *pax Americana* and of 'America' as the imaginary fulfillment of the Western course of (liberal capitalist) development."[27] To the extent that a nation is a meaningful entity for a historian, there was of course only one Germany, even if made up of various constituencies and conceptions from both inside and outside.[28] The question is how to evaluate the specific conditions of German history without reducing that history to a function of Western ideological concerns. Germany was not the antipode of political developments in the West. Germany also was not simply a somewhat more illiberal version of the Western bourgeois state.[29] Part of the problem is that the primary subject matter of each of these approaches to German history—"pre-modern" elites and modern bourgeoisie, respectively—determines the nature and scope of the findings. If one studies the feudal one finds the feudal. If one studies the bourgeois one finds the bourgeois. Understanding Germany on its own unitary terms, however, permits us to avoid a static dichotomy posed around the standard of a liberal model and scale of modern historical development.

In Germany strong traditions of corporatism in society and state had been preserved and strengthened by the unique manner of German state-building through the unification of Germany by Prussia.[30] As in the West, powerful new commercial and industrial interests in the

Reich too displayed inherent corporate instincts. Bismarck, like Napoleon III in France and Benjamin Disraeli in England only with more success—for the short term—harnessed the new political forces of liberalism and democracy in service to old standards and structures of paternalistic governance. With little success, Bismarck also attempted to woo the working class to the paternalistic state by means of a state health insurance system. Even Wilhelm II, that bumbling avatar of Prussianism, maintained a significant degree of royal influence among the German people through a striking and effective mix of old and new methods of rule.[31] The early Prussian political repression of Catholics and socialists had "touched off the political mobilization of the masses much earlier in Germany than elsewhere in Europe."[32] Yet the imperial government, the bureaucracy, and the military remained impervious to parliamentary control, further aggravating the trend among the parties toward the protection and advance of corporate interests. Such "soft" and "hard" paternalism of thought and deed in Germany contrasts with the liberalism of England during the same period, where the institutionalization of greater economic and political individualism helped create the greater effectiveness of political parties and Parliament and also greater disparities between rich and poor.[33] In France, too, the situation was different. The cumulative effect of the revolutions of 1789, 1830, 1848, and 1871 had left royalty on the outside trying to get back in. Such attempts at the reassertion of royal control, abetted by frequent royalist majorities in the legislature after 1871, ultimately withered away in the political fallout from the Dreyfus Affair just before and after the turn of the century. In the newly united Germany of 1871, however, the Prussian house of Hohenzollern experienced continuity of formal and actual—if hardly uncompromised—power until 1918.

The process of professionalization in Germany was problematic along these same corporatist lines. The growing power of professions in Germany was advanced by a traditional German respect for learning, rapid industrialization, a growing technical sophistication in disciplines like medicine, and, in the end, the Nazi demand for organized technical expertise for purposes of racial selection, social control, and military expansion. Professions in the West, however, have traditionally been associated with liberal ideals such as individual liberty, a free market, meritocracy, and representative government. Had, therefore, German professionals represented a challenge to corporate traditions in Germany? This was most certainly not the case with doctors in Germany after 1869, when liberal Berlin physicians had led a successful effort to establish medicine legally as a free trade rather than as a profession. From the founding of the Reich in 1871 onward, doctors (and, to one degree or another, most other professions) confronted and courted a powerful state bureaucracy in search of collective professional status and advantage. In the case of medicine, Bismarck's construction of a state health insurance system and the subsequent growth of socialist influence within it prompted aggressive collective action among doctors in defense of their interests. This included the threat of strikes to improve the position of doctors in the state health insurance system, a campaign to gain recognition from the state as a profession (achieved with ambiguous political and professional effects in 1935), and ongoing attempts to regulate the market for physicians' services. Moreover, during the twentieth century—and especially with the national and economic disasters following the First World War—many doctors were radicalized toward the political right. The German experience of professionalization has alerted historians not only to what the "liberal" professions in Germany confronted (and courted), that is, a powerful bureaucratic state, but also to what "liberal" professions are, or at least have become. Thus has the recent study of the German experience of professionalization contributed to an established critique of the Western ideal type of the liberal professional.

Charles McClelland has argued that "the German experience of professionalization, with its complicated tangle of private sphere and bureaucratically controlled dimensions, may prove more typical of professionalization throughout the twentieth-century world than the Anglo-American 'model'."[34] The trend toward "professional neocorporatism" began in late imperial Germany, according to Konrad Jarausch, when "professionals participated in the bourgeois shift from liberal to national attitudes," assuming a "postliberal" position based on a "rising tide of 'academic illiberalism.'"[35] This shift away from liberalism aggravated the tendency among professionals everywhere in the twentieth century toward using "the state to secure income and social position" and "rejecting its control over practice and organization."[36] It can also be argued that no such turn from "liberal" to "national" was necessary to produce the type of corporate behavior Jarausch describes. Such an argument views liberalism as inherently corporate rather than as a more or less Western "ideal type" corrupted by special German conditions. Whatever was precisely the case in Germany, professionalization there drew upon an especially strong tradition of institutionalized corporatist thought, practice, and feeling at all levels of polity and society. This tradition encouraged both obedience to state authority in pursuit of professional recognition and defense of the profession's own corporate interests against the state and against competitors and clients. And particularly in medicine, even the enlightened liberal scientific ethic of individual and social improvement through technical and therapeutic intervention and prevention could itself help advance inhumane state imperatives.[37]

Within this "iron cage" of professional institutions, the particular accidents of German society and culture as well as the events of history thus worked a significant influence. The psychotherapists who forged their discipline's professional way in Germany between 1918 and 1945 had been born, raised, educated, and in some cases had established themselves professionally before the Nazis came to power. Each one of them, had, as child, youth, and young adult, internalized values, habits, and attitudes of an Imperial Germany at the height of its powers and in the depths of its final crisis. During the twentieth century, moreover, the *Bildungsbürgertum* as a whole was characterized by a growing fear and resentment of both the urban masses and the moneyed elite of what they viewed as a dangerously democratizing and materialistic society: "Doctors were part of the educated middle class, and their social and political attitudes were shaped as much by this fact as their own specialist training and concerns."[38] Many doctors, especially after 1918, displayed conservative and nationalist prejudices easily exploited by the Nazis. World War I had an especially significant effect on doctors and psychiatrists, who were drafted in unprecedented numbers to deal with the staggering physical and mental casualties of industrial warfare. Military service itself only aggravated the authoritarianism common among doctors as increasingly effective and sought-after experts in matters of life and death. The same was even truer in the Second World War, especially on the embattled home front. By that time doctors had become even more therapeutically effective, largely through the medical and surgical advances of the First World War as well as the introduction of a wide range of effective and aggressively marketed drugs in the 1930s. The increasing initiative of patients only heightened doctors' defense of their prerogatives and authority, now backed up by ruthless Nazi wartime sanctions. In such an environment, the relative corporatist disregard for the individual could manifest potential and actual consequences for patients. To a significant degree, all of these dynamics of course affected psychotherapists, most of whom in any case were also physicians by background, training, and practice.

The effects of all these experiences and attitudes were intensified by the Nazi environment right from the beginning in 1933. In power were men violently acting out bloody racist and misogynist fantasies.[39] In a very real sense, the Nazis were at war already from 1933 onward. While the Nazis may have atomized German society by dissolving traditional social groupings, a competitive "hierarchical continuum of achievement"[40] also allowed groups such as psychotherapists to advance their ongoing culturally shaped and encouraged corporate interests in both service and sacrifice to the state. The Nazi system was one that, as we have seen, cultivated the self-serving aspirations of both individuals and groups in the name of national and racial solidarity. The war cut both ways, creating an environment both of individual "survivalism" and of shared purpose and misery.[41] While the Göring Institute itself would not survive Hitler's Reich and Hitler's war, it had, as a result of all these historical circumstances, served as a vital component of the continuous professional development of psychotherapy in modern Germany before 1933 and after 1945. Moreover, as we have seen, there is no clear distinction between "German" and "Western," but rather vital linkages between modern German conditions and Western outcomes in the twentieth century. The history of the Göring Institute, as we have amply demonstrated, therefore provides insight not only into the social history of the Third Reich but also into at least some of the decisive and instructive vectors of German society and history as a whole in the modern era.

Notes

1. James J. Sheehan, "National Socialism and German Society: Reflections on Recent Research," *Theory and Society* 13 (1984): 858, 860.
2. Peter Loewenberg, "The Kristallnacht as a Public Degradation Ritual," *Leo Baeck Institute Yearbook* 32 (1987): 319.
3. Sheehan, "National Socialism and German Society," pp. 865, 867; Daniel Jonah Goldhagen, *Hitler's Willing Executioners: Ordinary Germans and the Holocaust* (New York, 1996). While helpful in reminding us of the pervasiveness of anti-Semitism in Germany, Goldhagen's thesis that Germans "almost universally"

during the Nazi period held to an "elminationist" prejudice against Jews is, by Goldhagen's own admission, not "definitive . . . [because] the proper data simply do not exist" (p. 47). Goldhagen's observation, however, that "Germans conceived of Jews in corporate terms" (p. 65) seems to constitute evidence for the argument in this chapter for a tradition of corporatist thinking in modern German society.

4. Peukert, *Inside Nazi Germany,* pp. 31, 188.
5. Ibid., pp. 108, 113, 117.
6. Stephan Liebfried and Florian Tennstedt, "Health-Insurance Policy and Berufsverbote in the Nazi Takeover," in Donald W. Light and Alexander Sculler, eds., *Political Values and Health Care: The German Experience* (Cambridge, Mass., 1986), pp. 127–84. This hegemony confronted institutional and popular challenge in all professions: Geoffrey Cocks, "Psychiatry, Society, and the State in Nazi Germany," paper presented at Miami (Ohio) University, February 24, 1989.
7. Michael Geyer, "The Past as Future: The German Officer Corps as Profession," in Cocks and Jarausch, *German Professions, 1800–1950,* pp. 188, 198–9.
8. Ralf Dahrendorf, *Society and Democracy in Germany* (Garden City, NY, 1967).
9. Michael Prinz, "Die soziale Funktion moderner Elemente in der Gesellschaftspolitik des Nationalsozialismus," in Michael Prinz and Rainer Zitelmann, eds., *Nationalsozialismus und Modernisierung* (Darmstadt, 1994), pp. 297–327.
10. Frank Bajohr et al., eds., *Die Widerspruchlichen Potentiale der Moderne: Detlev Peukert zum Gedenken* (Hamburg, 1991).
11. Michael Prinz, "Nachwort: Einige Bermerkungen zur neueren Debatte über Modernisierung und Nationalsozialismus," in Prinz and Zitelmann, *Nationalsozialismus und Modernisierung,* pp. 337–8, 340, 342.
12. Crew, "General Introduction," in idem, *Nazism and German Society,* p. 26; on this danger, see also Saul Friedländer, "Some Reflections on the Historization of National Socialism," *Tel Aviver Jahrbuch für deutsche Geschichte* 16 (1987): 310–24.
13. Monika Renneberg and Mark Walker, eds., *Science, Technology and National Socialism* (Cambridge, 1994).
14. Richard J. Evans, "From Hitler to Bismarck: 'Third Reich' and Kaiserreich in Recent Historiography," *Historical Journal* 26 (1983): 485–97, 999–1020.
15. See, for example, Alexander Mitscherlich and Fred Mielke, *Wissenschaft ohne Menschlichkeit: Medizinische und Eugenische Irrwege unter Diktatur, Burokratie und Krieg* (Heidelberg, 1949); Alice Platen-Hallermund, *Die Tötung Geisteskranker in Deutschland* (Frankfurt am Main, 1948); Robert Jay Lifton, *The Nazi Doctors: Medicalized Killing and the Psychology of Genocide* (New York, 1986); and Henry Friedlander, *The Origins of Nazi Genocide: From Euthanasia to the Final Solution* (Chapel Hill, 1995).
16. Dahrendorf, *Society and Democracy in Germany*; Jürgen Kocka, "Ursachen des Nationalsozialismus," *Aus Politik und Zeitgeschichte,* June 21, 1980, pp. 9–13.
17. Hans-Ulrich Wehler, *Das deutsche Kaiserreich 1871–1918* (Göttingen, 1973).
18. Geoff Eley, "What Produces Fascism: Pre-Industrial Traditions or A Crisis of the Capitalist State?" in idem, *From Unification to Nazism: Reinterpreting the German Past* (Boston, 1986), pp. 254–82; David Blackbourn and Geoff Eley, *The Peculiarities of Germany History: Bourgeois Society and Politics in Nineteenth-Century Germany* (New York, 1984).
19. Michael Hubenstorf, "'Aber es kommt mir doch so vor, als ob Sie dabei nichts

verloren hätten.' Zum Exodus von Wissenschaftlern aus den staatlichen Forschungsinstituten Berlins im Bereich des öffentlichen Gesundheitswesens," in Wolfram Fischer et al., eds., *Exodus von Wissenschaften aus Berlin: Fragestellungen—Ergebnisse—Desiderate; Entwicklungen vor und nach 1933*, Akademie der Wissenschaften zu Berlin Forschungsbericht 7 (Berlin, 1994), pp. 368–9, 448; Alfons Labisch, *Homo Hygienicus: Gesundheit und Medizin in der Neuzeit* (Frankfurt, 1992), p. 133.

20. For an early classic example of the genre, see E. P. Thompson, *The Making of the English Working Class* (New York, 1964).
21. See, for example, Peter Gay, *The Bourgeois Experience: Victoria to Freud*, 4 vols. (New York, 1984–95).
22. Konrad Jarausch, "The German Professions in History and Theory," in Cocks and Jarausch, *German Professions, 1800–1950*, pp. 9–10.
23. See, for example, Margaret S. Larson, *The Rise of Professionalism* (Berkeley, 1977); and Paul Starr, *The Social Transformation of American Medicine* (New York, 1982).
24. Claudia Huerkamp, "The Making of the Modern Medical Profession, 1800–1914: Prussian Doctors in the Nineteenth Century," in Cocks and Jarausch, *German Professions*, pp. 66–84.
25. Ralph H. Bowen, *German Theories of the Corporative State with Special Reference to the Period 1870–1919* (New York, 1947), p. 6.
26. Geyer, "The Past as Future," pp. 191, 197, 205; see also Alan Cawson, *Corporatism and Political Theory* (Oxford, 1896), p. 26; and Bowen, *German Theories*, pp. 16–17, 217–18. For an analysis restricted to economic corporatism, see Werner Abelshauser, "The First Post-Liberal Nation: Stages in the Development of Modern Corporatism in Germany," *European History Quarterly* 14 (1985): 285–318. By concentrating on "corporatist interest mediation" (p. 287), Abelshauser posits a dichotomy between authoritarian "state" corporatism and "democratic welfare" corporatism that understates the historical confluence in modern German society and culture of "preliberal" and "postliberal" corporatist institutions and attitudes. On postwar economic militarization, see Michael S. Sherry, *In the Shadow of War: The United States Since the 1930s* (New Haven, 1995).
27 Michael Geyer, "Looking Back at the International Style: Some Reflections on the Current State of German History," *German Studies Review* 13 (1990): 113.
28. Michael Geyer, "The Stigma of Violence, Nationalism, and War in Twentieth-Century Germany," *German Studies Review* 15 (Special Issue, Winter 1992): 86.
29. On the distinctiveness of German liberalism, see Dieter Langewiesche, *Liberalismus im 19. Jahrhundert. Deutschland im europäischen Vergleich* (Göttingen, 1988). See also Hermann Beck, *The Origins of the Authoritarian Welfare State in Prussia: Conservatives, Bureaucracy, and the Social Question, 1815–70* (Ann Arbor, 1995); and Shelley Baranowski, *The Sanctity of Rural Life: Nobility, Protestantism, and Nazism in Weimar Prussia* (New York, 1995).
30. John Breuilly, "State-Building, Modernization and Liberalism from the Late Eighteenth Century to Unification: German Peculiarities; Liberalism and Modernization in Wilhelmine Germany," *European History Quarterly* 22 (1992): 257–84, 431–8; Shelley Baranowski, "East Elbian Landed Elites and Germany's Turn to Fascism: The *Sonderweg* Controversy Revisited," *European History Quarterly* 26 (1996): 209–40.
31. Thomas A. Kohut, *Wilhelm II and the Germans: A Study in Leadership* (New York, 1991).

32. Chris Lorenz, "Beyond Good and Evil? The German Empire of 1871 and Modern German Historiography," *Journal of Contemporary History* 30 (1995): 745.
33. Kenneth Barkin, "Germany and England: Economic Inequality," *Tel Aviver Jahrbuch für deutsche Geschichte* 16 (1987): 200–11.
34. Charles E. McClelland, *The German Experience of Professionalization: Modern Learned Professions and Their Organizations from the Early Nineteenth Century to the Hitler Era* (Cambridge, 1991), p. 10.
35. Konrad H. Jarausch, *The Unfree Professions: German Lawyers, Teachers, and Engineers, 1900–1950* (New York, 1990), p. 24. "This characterization employs a historical Central European meaning of 'corporatism' as calling for a sociopolitical order based on *Berufsstände*. The prefix 'neo' indicates the postliberal thrust of the attempt to reintroduce premodern elements into high industrial society" (p. 269 n. 97).
36. Ibid., p. 24.
37. Hubenstorf, "'Aber es kommt mir doch so vor, als ob Sie dabei nichts verloren hätten'," pp. 444–55; Labisch, *Homo Hygienicus,* p. 133.
38. Richard J. Evans, "In Search of Social Darwinism: The History and Historiography of a Concept," in Berg and Cocks, *Medicine and Modernity,* p. 78; Jeremy Noakes, "Nazism and Eugenics: The Background to the Nazi Sterilization Law of 14 July 1933," in R. J. Bullen et al., eds., *Ideas into Politics: Aspects of European History 1880–1950* (London, 1984), pp. 75–94.
39. Klaus Theweleit, *Male Fantasies,* 2 vols., trans. Erica Carter et al. (Minneapolis, 1987, 1989); Michael Burleigh and Wolfgang Wippermann, *The Racial State: Germany, 1933–1945* (Cambridge, 1991).
40. Peukert, *Inside Nazi Germany,* p. 95; on resistance to the destruction of traditional social groupings, see Jill Stephenson, "Widerstand gegen Soziale Modernisierung am Beispiel Württembergs 1939–1945," in Prinz and Zitelmann, *Nationalsozialismus und Modernisierung,* pp. 93–116.
41. Cf. Tilla Siegel, "Wage Policy in Nazi Germany," *Politics and Society* 14 (1985): 37; Christa Wolf, *Patterns of Childhood,* trans. Ursule Molinaro and Hedwig Rappolt (New York, 1980), p. 200.

Appendix 1

Göring Institute Instructors and Courses[1]

(I, III = Summer Semester; II, IV = Winter Semester, 1937–45; arabic numeral = no. hrs.)

Achelis, Waldtraut
Biological-Medical Course for Nonmedical Training Candidates (IV 40–41, I 41, II 41–42, III 42, II 43–44: 9)

Achelis, Werner
Psychotherapy and Politics (36–37: 2)
The Significance of Fundamental Ideological Judgment for the Theory and Practice of Psychotherapy (IV 40–41: 2)
Ideas as Forces in Mental Occurrences (I 41, IV 41–42: 2)
Good and Evil in Psychology (IV 41–42: 3)

Aichhorn, August
Introduction to Educational Counseling (I 42, II 42–43, I 43: 4)
Introduction to the Treatment of Delinquents (I 42, II 42–43, I 43: 4)

Bilz, Josephine
Physical and Mental Development of the Child from Depth Psychological Points of View (II 42–43: 4)
Parental Problems (II 42–43: 2)
Origin, Development and Structure of Neuroses of Children and Youth (II 43–44: 5)

1. Excluding technical seminars and some minor courses.

Bilz, Rudolf
- Psychology as Psychophysics (IV 41–42: 2)
- On the Biology and Psychology of the Father Role (II 42–43, IV 43–44, II 44–45: 3)
- Paleopsychology (III 44: 2)
- Early Medieval Superstition According to a Depth Psychological View (IV 43–44: 3)

Boehm, Felix
- (w/Müller-Braunschweig) Theory and Practice of Psychoanalysis (36–37: 12)
- Strindberg in Light of Psychoanalysis (36–37: 7)
- Seminar on the Literature of Medical Histories: (37: 12)
- On Difficulties in Therapeutic Practice (II 39, IV 39–40, III 40: 4)
- Technical Difficulties and Their Elimination in the Treatment of Core Neuroses (IV 40–41, III 41, IV 41–42: 3)
- Introduction to the Formulation of Medical Histories and Expert Opinions (III 42, III 44, IV 44–45: 8)
- (w/Göring) Seminar on Criminal and Civil Expert Opinion (IV 42–43: 6)
- Colloquium on an Introduction to Psychotherapeutic Diagnostic Disposition (IV 42–43, III 43, IV 43–44: 5)

Clauss, Ferdinand
- Racial Psychology (II 38–39, II, IV 40–41: 3)

Curtius, Friedrich
- Racial Biology (II 37–38, II 38–39, II 39–40, II 40–41: 4)

Dürck, Johanna (III 43: Herzog-Dürck)
- Disturbances of We-Relationships (II 38–39: 4)
- The We-Cultivation in the Healing Process (III 39: 4)
- Concerning Dream and Symbol (II 39–40: 4)
- Exercises in Therapy (IV 39–40, IV 42–43: 5)
- The Healing Process (II 40–41, III 43, III 44: 4)
- Aspects of the Neurotic Personality (III 40, III 41: 5)
- The Nature of Neurosis (II 40–41, II 43–44: 5)
- Depth Psychological Therapy (IV 43–44: 4)
- Basic Questions of an Existential Psychology (II 44–45: 4)
- The Religious Problem and Psychotherapy (IV 44–45 4)

Eyferth, E. (Gauamt Berlin der NSV)
Forms of Medical Pedagogy (IV 42–43: 2)
Youth Assistance in War (I 43: 3)

Gebsattel, Viktor von
Symptomatology and Differential Diagnosis in Psychic Disturbances (II 39–40, I 40, II 40–41: 4)
Characteristics of a Biopsychological Anthropology (III 41–42, I 42, IV 42–43, III 43, IV 43–44: 4)

Göring, Matthias Heinrich
Psychotherapy in its Importance for National Health and Character Development (36–37: 2)
The Psychology of the Process of Mental Elucidation (36–37: 4)
Symptomatology and Differential Diagnosis in Psychic Disturbances (II 37–38, II 38–39: 4)
Legal Regulations (IV 38–39, IV 41–42, IV 43–44, IV 44–45: 4)
(w/Boehm) Seminar on Criminal and Civil Expert Opinion (IV 42–43: 6)
Introduction to Psychiatry (II 43–44, II 44–45: 8, 4)

Hattingberg, Hans von
Common Fundamentals in Depth Psychology (II 37–38, II 38–39: 6)
Fundamentals of the Theory of Neuroses (II 39–40, II 40–41, II 41–42, II 42–43, II 43–44: 6)
History of Psychotherapy (I 39, I 40, I 41, I 42, I 43, I 44: 4)
Science of Expression (I 39: 3)
Marital Problems in Psychotherapeutic Practice (IV 40–41: 4)

Hau, E.
Introduction to Psychiatry (II 41–42: 9)

Herzog, Edgar
Synthetic Forces in the Construction of Character (36–37: 5)
Education and Punishment (36–37: 10)
Training in Psychotherapeutic Literature (IV 39–40, III 40: 5)
The Development of the Living Personality and Its Endangerment (I 40: 4)

Dream and Symbol (II 40–41: 3)
Exposition of Medical Histories (II 40–41: 3)
Seminar in Literature: Carus (IV 40–41: 5)

Heyer, Gustav Richard
The Problem of Body and Mind (II 39–40: 6)
Training in Dream Interpretation (III 40, IV 43–44, III 44, IV 44–45: 6)
Training in Breathing Therapy (III 40, II, IV 40: 5, 10)
Symbolism with Special Regard to Dreams (Psychobiology) (II 40–41: 13)
Consideration of Unconscious Images (III 41: 6)
On Unconscious Mental Life (IV 41–42, I 42, III 43: 9)

Kalau vom Hofe, Marie
Depth Psychology and the Administration of Justice (IV 41–42: 4)

Kemper, Werner
Biology and Psychology of the Sexual Processes (36–37: 7)
Systematic Description of Psychoanalysis (36–37: 14)
Development, Structure and Function of the Sexual Apparatus (II 37–38: 6)
Seminar on Technique of Analytic Therapy (37: 12)
Endocrinology (II 37–38, II 38–39)
Developmental History, Anatomy and Function of the Sexual Processes (II 38–39, II 39–40: 5, 6)
The General Conditions of the Generation of Neurosis (Constitution, Defense, Fixation, a.o.), Narcissism, Anxiety (II 38–39, II 39–40, II 42–43, I 44: 4)
General Theory of Neuroses (II 40–41: 5)
Special Theory of Neuroses I: (Transference and Actual Neuroses) (II 38–39, II 40–41: 5)
Special Theory of Neuroses II (Character Neuroses, Psychoses, Mania) (III 39, III 40, III 41, III 42, III 43: 6, 4)
Special Theory of Neuroses III (Character Neuroses) (IV 40–41, IV 41–42: 5)
Normal Psychology I/II (Self, Child, Drives, Family) (I 39, II 39–40, I 40: 4)
Biology and Psychology of Sexual and Love Life (I 41, I 42, I 43, I 44: 7, 8)

Colloquium on Particular Questions of Practical Therapy (IV 40–41, IV 41–42, IV 42–43: 10, 5, 8)
Hormonal Neurovegetative Psychotherapy (II 41–42: 3)
On Relations with Patients, Colleagues and Agencies (III 44: 5)

König-Fachsenfeld, Olga von
From the Practice of Complex Psychology (II 38–39: 4)

Kranefeldt, Wolfgang
Basic Concepts of C.G. Jung's Psychology (36–37: 8)
Jungian Psychology: The Neurosis as Shadow Problem (II 37–38: 6)
Archetypology (II 38–39, I 39, IV 39–40, III 40, IV 40–41, III 41: 4)

Künkel, Elisabeth
Applied Characterology (36–37: 8)
Normal Development and its Endangerment (II 38–39: 4)

Künkel, Fritz
Applied Characterology (36–37: 8)
Theory of Neuroses (II 37–38: 12)
Method of Therapy (IV 38–39: 5)
Disturbances of We-Relationships (III 39: 4)

Linden, Herbert
Hereditary and Racial Improvement (II 39–40: 3)

Luxenburger, Hans
Introduction to Psychiatric Racial Biology (II 41–42: 3)
Fundamentals of Racial Biology (II 42–43, II 43–44: 2)
Psychiatric Racial Biology (II 42–43, II 43–44: 3)

Mohr, Fritz
The Problem of Body and Mind (II 37–38: 2)

Moritz, Eva
The Psychology of Pregnancy (II 37–38: 4)
Psychological Typology (III 41, IV 41–42, III 42: 5, 6)

Müller-Braunschweig, Ada
Seminar on Analytic Understanding, Education and Treatment of the Neurotic Child (IV 39–40, III 40: 5)

Müller-Braunschweig, Carl
Systematic Description of Psychoanalysis (36–37, 37: 12, 9)
(w/Boehm) Theory and Practice of Psychoanalysis (36–37: 12)

Neumann, Johannes
Introduction to General Psychology (I 43: 5)
Childhood Conflicts in the Character Structure of Adults (II 43–44: 4)
The Psychological Discoveries of Schiller (I 44: 3)

Pasche, Karl
Introduction to Depth Psychology of the Community (II 41–42, II 43–44: 2)

Prosch, Mila von
Child Psychology (I 39: 4)
Depth Psychology and Social Insights (I, III 44: 6)

Rittmeister, John
Casuistry on the Theme: Mythology and Schizophrenia (III 42: 4)
Psychiatry and Depth Psychology (II 42–43: 3)
Fundamental Questions of Method (II 41–42: 3)

Roellenbleck, Ewald
Seminar on Theoretical Literature (37: 12)
Introduction to the Theory and Analysis of the Dream (II 37–38: 9)

Scherke, Felix
Practicum in Industrial Psychology (II 41–42, III 42: 5)
Mental Health Care in the Factory (III 42: 6)
Colloquium on Industrial Psychology (IV 42–43, III 44: 4, 5)

Schirren, Julius
A Series of Dreams as Education of Character (36–37: 5)
The Mutual Effect of Dream and Fate (36–37: 14)
Dream Interpretation (II 37–38: 9)

Training in Dream Analysis and the Art of Interpretation (IV 38–39, IV 39–40, III 40, IV 40–41, III 41,III 42, IV 42–43, III 43, IV 43–44, IV 44–45: 5)
Normal Psychology I (Individual, Community, Powers of the Soul) (I 39: 4)
Theory of Healing (III 40, IV 41: 4)
German Fairy Tales as Portrayals of the Maturational Processes of the Human Soul (I 39: 4)
On Normal Development and its Endangerment (II 39–40, II 40–41, IV 41–42, II 42–43, I 43, II 43–44, II 44–45: 5, 9)
Exegesis of Fairy Tales (I 40: 2)
Introduction to the Nature of the Symbol (II 42–43: 2)
The Fight with the Demon in Dream and Fairy Tales (IV 40–41: 4)
The Argument of the Ego Within the Authority of the Collective (IV 41–42: 4)
Four German Fairy Tales as Allegories of Mental Development and Self-Discovery (III 42, IV 42–43, III 43, IV 43–44, III 44, II 44–45: 4)

Schmaltz, Gustav
Images from the Unconscious in the Individuation Process with a View to the Early Art of Peoples (I 42: 4)

Schultz, Johannes Heinrich
Overview of the History of Psychotherapy (36–37: 2)
Symptomatology and Differential Diagnosis of Organic Disturbances (II 37–38, II 38–39, II 39–40, II 40–41: 6)
The Problem of Body and Mind (II 38–39: 2)
Theory of Hypnosis and Autogenic Training (II 38–39, II 39–40, II 40–41, II 41–42, II 42–43, II 43–44: 3)
Practicum in Hypnosis (IV 38–39, IV 41–42: 4)
Psychology (I 39: 4)
Psychotherapeutic Propadeutic: Nature and Boundaries of Psychotherapy (I 42, I 43: 4)
Sleep and Its Disturbances (III 43: 2)
Bionomic Psychotherapy (II 43–44: 3)
Seminar on Forms and Means of Short-Term Therapy (IV 43–44, III 44: 5)
History of Psychotherapy (II 44–45: 8)

Schultz-Hencke, Harald
Fate and Neurosis (36–37: 2)
The Basic Rule of Psychoanalysis as Psychological Problem (36–37: 7)
Seminar on Dream Interpretation (37: 12)
The Essential Structure of Neurosis (II 37–38: 6)
The Dream as the Inhibited Expression of Instinctual Demands (II 38–39: 4)
Therapeutic Method (IV 38–39, IV 39–40: 4)
Training Seminar in Dream Analysis (IV 38–39: 5)
On the Psychological Analysis of the Healing Process (III 39, III 40, III 41: 5, 6)
Practicum on the Taking Up of an Anamnesis (II 39–40, II 40–41: 4, 3)
Training in Dream Analysis and the Art of Interpretation (IV 39–40, IV 40–41, III 41, IV 41–42, III 42, IV 42–43, III 43, II 43–44, III 44, II 44–45: 5)
Anxiety, Dream Theory and Dream Analysis (II 40–41, II 41–42, II 42–43: 4)
The Structure of Neurosis (I 42: 3)
Casuistic Seminar (IV 40–41: 10)
Depth Psychological Therapy (IV 43–44, IV 44–45: 3)

Seiff, Margarete
Points of Departure for Neurosis (II 44–45: 5)

Selbach, Heinz
Introduction to Psychiatry (III 42: 6)

Staabs, Gerdhild von
Demonstrations from Child Psychiatry (III 44, IV 44–45: 3)
Technique of Child Psychiatry (IV 44–45: 3)

Vetter, August
Science of Expression (II 39–40, I 40, III 41, II 41–42, I 43, I 44: 6)
Introduction to Characterology (II 40–41, I 41, I 42, IV 42–43, IV 44–45: 6)
Primary Questions of Philosophical Anthropology (III 40–41: 6)

Zippert, Erwin
Introduction to Mythology (IV 43–44: 9)

Sources: Deutsches Institut für Psychologische Forschung und Psychotherapie, Veranstaltungen (Berlin: 1936–41); Deutsches Institut für Psychologische Forschung und Psychotherapie, Ankündigung der Veranstaltungen (Berlin: 1941–44); and Reichsinstitut für Psychologische Forschung und Psychotherapie im Reichsforschungsrat, Ankündigung der Veranstaltungen (Berlin: 1944–45).

Appendix 2

Four-Semester Course of Theoretical Study

Summer Semester

I. Introductory Lectures on:
  1. Psychotherapeutic Propadeutic: Nature and Limits of Psychotherapy, a.o.
  2. History of Psychotherapy
  3. Science of Expression, Part I
  4. Biological-Medical Course for Nonmedical Training Candidates, Part I
  5. Psychotherapy as Profession

II. Lectures on:
  1. Psychotherapeutic Psychology (Depth Psychological Anthropology), Part I (Psychology of Human Development from Child to Adult, Psychology of their Crises and Phases; Psychology of the Child's Instinctual Relationships to the Environment and the Familial Constellation; Psychology of Youth; Psychology of Aging, a.o.)
  2. Biology and Psychology of Sexual and Love Life
  3. General Theory of Neuroses

III. Clinical Demonstrations from the Outpatient Clinic and Educational Assistance

IV. Auxiliary Methods (Breathing Exercises, Movement, Music)

V. Courses on Psychology, Psychotherapy and Education of Children and Youth

Winter Semester

I. Lectures on:
   1. Science of Expression, Part I
   2. The Problem of Body and Mind
   3. Hereditary and Racial Biology
   4. Biology, Endocrinology
   5. Psychic and Organic Disturbances
   6. Introduction to Psychiatry (mandatory for nonmedical training candidates)
   7. Biological-Medical Course for Non-Medical Training Candidates, Part II

II. Lectures on:
   1. Psychotherapeutic Psychology (Depth Psychological Anthropology), Part II (the Unconscious, the Dream, the Symbol, the Structure of the Mental Organism, Psychological Types, a.o.)
   2. Depth Psychological Theory of the Dream and the Understanding of the Dream
   3. Photographic Demonstrations of Dream and Fantasy Pictures
   4. Special Theory of Neuroses, Part I (Hysteria, Compulsion Neurosis, a.o.)
   5. Depth Psychological History of the Origin, Rise and Structure of the Neuroses of Childhood and Youth
   6. Depth Psychological Pathology of Sexual and Love Life
   7. Theory of Hypnosis and Autogenic Training

III. Seminars on:
   1. Medical Histories from the Literature or the Experience of the Instructor, Part I
   2. Training in Depth Psychological Understanding of Dreams and the Science of Symbols, Part I

IV. Clinical Demonstrations from the Outpatient Clinic and Educational Assistance

V. Auxiliary Methods (Breathing, Exercises, Movement, Music)

VI. Courses on Psychology, Psychotherapy and Education of Children and Youth

Summer Semester

I. Lectures on:
   1. Depth of Psychological Content of Myths, Legends and Fairy Tales
   2. Depth Psychological Peoples and Religions
   3. Depth Psychological Content of Creations of Philosophy, Literature and Art

II. Lectures on:
   1. Characterology, Part I
   2. Archetypology
   3. Special Theory of Neuroses, Part II (Perversions, Psychoses, Mania, a.o.)
   4. Therapy, Part I: The Theory of the Healing Process

III. Seminars on:
   1. Medical Histories from the Literature or the Experience of the Instructor, Part II
   2. Training in Depth Psychological Understanding of Dreams and the Science of Symbols, Part II
   3. Theoretical Literature (Systematic-Substantive and Historical-Critical Discussion of Theoretical Works of the Psychotherapeutic Literature), Part I

IV. Characterological Examination of Methods (Testing Methods)

V. Seminar for Assistants (so-called "Triseminar") (Description of Cases by Assistants and Discussion under the Direction of Three Instructors)

VI. Casuistic-Technical Seminar (Discussion of Depth Psychological Healing Processes and Their Applied Procedures on the Basis of Completed Treatments under the Direction of an Instructor)

VII. Introduction to Training in Psychotherapeutic Diagnosis

VIII. Proseminar in Preparation for Practical Work (Preliminary Interview and Relationship with Patients, Questions concerning Honoraria, Relations with Agencies, a.o.)

IX. Practicum in Autogenic Training

X. Clinical Demonstrations from the Outpatient Clinic and Educational Assistance

XI. Auxiliary Methods (Breathing, Exercises, Movement, Music)

XII. Courses on Psychology, Psychotherapy, and Education of Children and Youth

Winter Semester

I. Lectures on:
   1. Legal Regulations
   2. The Place of Psychotherapeutic Psychology (Depth Psychological Anthropology) within Science and Culture
   3. Importance of Fundamental Ideological Judgment
   4. Philosophy of Psychotherapeutic Theory
   5. Philosophical Anthropology

II. Lectures on:
   1. Characterology, Part II
   2. Archetypology
   3. Depth Psychological Exegesis
   4. Special Theory of Neuroses, Part III (Character Disturbances)
   5. Therapy, Part II (Forms and Means of Procedure in Therapy)
   6. Prophylaxis

III. Seminars on:
   1. Training in Depth Psychological Understanding of Dreams and Science of Symbols, Part III
   2. Literature of Therapy (Systematic-Critical Discussion of Works on Therapeutic-Practical Questions from the Psychotherapeutic Literature of Past and Present)
   3. Theoretical Literature, Part II

IV. Characterological Examination Methods (Testing Methods)

V. Seminar for Assistants

VI. Casuistic-Technical Seminars

VII. Introduction to Training in Psychotherapeutic Diagnosis

VIII. Introduction to Formulation of Medical Histories and Expert Opinions

IX. Practicum on Hypnosis

X. Clinical Demonstrations from the Outpatient Clinic and Educational Assistance

XI. Auxiliary Methods

XII. Courses on Psychology, Psychotherapy and Education of Children and Youth

Source: Reichsinstitut für Psychologische Forschung und Psychotherapie im Reichsforschungsrat, Ankündigung der Veranstaltungen des Winter-Semesters 1944/45, pp. 14–15.

Appendix 3

Clinical Diagnostic Schema

A. Unsuited for Causal Psychotherapy
   1. Psychoses (e.g.)
      a. Schizophrenia
      b. Manic-Depressive Insanity
      c. Result of Chronic Alcoholism
   2. Suspicion of Psychosis
   3. Idiocy
   4. Hereditary Degenerative Psychopathies (e.g.)
      a. Schizoid
      b. Paranoid
      c. Cyclothymic
      d. Epileptoid
      e. Hysterical
      f. Drive-Disrupted
   5. Constitutional Nervousness
   6. Infantilism (on an organic basis)
   7. Organic Neurological Ailments
      a. Brain Diseases (e.g.)
         Cerebral Sclerosis
         Paralysis Agitans
         Postencephalitis
         Brain Damage
         Progressive Paralysis
      b. Diseases of the Spinal Cord (e.g.)
         with Pernicious Anemia
      c. Hybrid Forms from a. and b. (e.g.)

Multiple Sclerosis
   d. Diseases of the Peripheral Nerves (e.g.) Trigemal Neuralgia
8. Epilepsy
9. Primary Inner Secretionary Disturbances (e.g.)
   a. Basedow's Disease (Hyperthyroidism)
   b. Diabetes
   c. Eunuchoidism
   d. Thyroid Insufficiency
10. Neurasthenia (e.g.)
   a. through Poisoning or Infection
   b. through Exhaustion
11. Mental Disturbances on account of General Organic Diseases (e.g.)
   a. Uremia
   b. Blood Diseases
   c. Arteriosclerosis
12. Genuine Allergic Diseases (e.g.)
   a. Bronchial Asthma
   b. Urticaria
   c. Eczema
   d. Hay Fever
13. Other

B. Assignment of Causal Psychotherapy
   1. Neurotic Personalities ("Character Neuroses," "Core Neuroses") (e.g.)
      a. Compulsive Personalities
      b. Infantile Personalities
      c. Depressed Personalities
      d. Schizoid Personalities
      e. Pseudological Personalities
      f. Hysterical Personalities
      g. Generally Neurotic Personalities
      h. Manifestly Sexually Disturbed Personalities
         1. Male Homosexuality
         2. Female Homosexuality
         3. Exhibitionism
         4. Sado-Masochism
         5. Transvestism

2. Manias (e.g.)
   a. Drug Addiction (Alcohol, Morphine, a.o.)
   b. Compulsive Onanism
3. Impulsive Acts (e.g.)
   a. Pathological Restlessness
   b. Pathological Incendiarism
   c. Pathological Stealing
4. Compulsion Neuroses
5. Hysterical Neuroses
6. Phobias (e.g.)
   a. Agoraphobia (Space)
   b. Aphephobia (Touching)
   c. Molysmophobia (Contagion)
   d. Ereuthophobia (Blushing)
7. General Anxiety Neuroses (e.g.)
   a. Consequence of Sexual Abuse
   b. Conditioned Reflexes, Signal Fixation
8. "Organ Neuroses" (e.g.)
   a. Disturbances of Circulation
   b. Disturbances of Digestive Process
   c. Disturbances of Sexual Organs (Impotence, Frigidity, Disruption of Orgasm, a.o.)
   d. Disturbances of Breathing
   e. Stuttering
   f. Writer's Cramp
   g. Tic
   h. Bed-Wetting
9. Neurotic Reactions (e.g.)
   a. Compulsive
   b. Hysterical
   c. Phobic
   d. Abnormal Affectual Reaction (Reactive Depression, Affective Blocks)
10. Conflict Neuroses, Life Crises, Developmental Inhibitions
11. Traumatic Neuroses
12. Childlike Pathological Habits (e.g.)
    a. Lying and Stealing
    b. Pathological Onanism
    c. Nail-Chewing

13. Neurotic Inhibitions (Shyness, Inability to Concentrate)
14. Professional Difficulties
15. Developmental and Educational Difficulties, Delinquency
16. Without Exact Diagnosis
17. Other

C. No Pathological Finding

Source: Reichsinstitut für Psychologische Forschung und Psychotherapie im Reichsforschungsrat, Richtlinien der Poliklinik (Berlin, April 1, 1944), pp. 11–14.

Bibliography

Interviews

Franz Baumeyer, West Berlin, November 1, 1973
Käthe Dräger, West Berlin, October 25, 1973
Ernst Göring, Waibstadt/Baden, November 21, 22, and 23, 1979
Gustav Graber, Berne, February 12, 1974
Erika Hantel, Altstädten/Allgäu, March 16, 1974
Lucy Heyer-Grote, Schlangenbad, January 21, 1974
Eva Hildebrand, Reckenberg/Schwarzwald, February 10, 1974
Franz Jung, Küsnacht/Zurich, June 7, 1974
Marie Kalau vom Hofe, Neuhaus am Schliersee, January 11, 1974
Werner Kemper, West Berlin, November 28 and December 3, 1973
Olga von König-Fachsenfeld, Aalen Fachsenfeld, May 25, 1974
Wolfgang Kranefeldt, West Berlin, October 23, 1973
John Kunkel, Ann Arbor, April 23, 1983
Gerhard Maetze, West Berlin, November 11, 1973
Dietfried Müller-Hegemann, Essen, January 30, 1974
Fritz Riemann, Munich, January 8, 1974
Gerhard Scheunert, Hamburg, July 10, 1974
Kurt Seelmann, Munich, January 7, 1974
August Vetter, Ammerland am Stanberger See, January 10, 1974
Kurt Zierold, Bad Godesberg, January 27, 1974

Unpublished Sources

Archives

Berlin Document Center (now Bundesarchiv, Aussenstelle Berlin/Zehlendorf)
Korrespondenz Wi
Kulturkammer
NS-Lehrerbund
NSDAP-Zentralkartei

Oberstes Parteigericht
Parteikorrespondenz
Parteistatistische Erhebung 1939 (Berlin)
Reichsärztekammer
Reichskartei-Warnkartei
SA
SS-Ahnenerbe
SS-Führer

Bundesarchiv Coblenz
B 339 Nachlass Julius Georg Schirren
B 339/9 Nachlass Gerhard Scheunert
Kl. Erw. 762 Deutsches Institut für Psychologische Forschung und Psychotherapie
NS 5 Deutsche Arbeitsfront
NS 19 Persönlicher Stab des Reichsführer-SS
NS 21 Das Ahnenerbe
R 18 Reichsministerium des Innern
R 21 Reichsministerium für Wissenschaft, Erziehung und Volksbildung
R 22 Reichsjustizministerium
R 36 Deutscher Gemeindetag
R 43 Reichskanzlei
R 86 Reichsgesundheitsamt
R 89 Reichsversicherungsamt
R 96 Öffentliche Einrichtungen der Gesundheits- und Wohlfahrtspflege

Bundesarchiv-Militärarchiv, Freiburg
H 1 Generalstab des Heeres
H 20 Heeres-Sanitätsinspekteur
H 34 OKW
RL 4 Reichsluftfahrtministerium
RW 2 OKW, Chef des Wehrmachtsanitätswesens

Geheimes Staatsarchiv Preussischer Kulturbesitz, Berlin/Dahlem
Berlin, Psychiatrische/Nervenklinik Charité

Hoover Institution, Stanford University
Collection Himmler

Imperial War Museum, London
FD 545/46 Speer Collection

Institut für Zeitgeschichte, Munich
MA 116 HA Wissenschaft

Library of Congress, Washington, D.C.
RFR 107/12850 German Captured Documents/Reichsforschungsrat

National Archives, Washington, D.C.
M-887 Records of the United States Nuernberg War Crimes Trials: U. S. v.Karl Brandt et al.
T-77 Records of the Headquarters of the German Armed Forces High Command
T-78 Records of the Headquarters of the German Army High Command
T-83 Private Enterprises
T-84 Miscellaneous German Records Collection
T-175 Records of the Reich Leader of the SS and Chief of the German Police
T-321 Records of the Headquarters of the German Air Force High Command

T-1021 German Documents Among the War Crimes Records of the Judge Advocate Division, Headquarters, United States Army, Europe
Nordrhein-Westfälisches Hauptstaatsarchiv, Düsseldorf
RW 53 Deutscher Gemeindetag
Reg. Aachen
Reg. Düsseldorf
Staatsarchiv Potsdam (now Brandenburgisches Staatsarchiv)
Pr. Br. Rep. 3 B Regierung Frankfurt (Oder) Abteilung I, Präsidialabteilung Medizinalwesen
University of Michigan Graduate Research Library, Ann Arbor
Rowland M. Myers Collection
Wiener Library, London
Press Archives
Zentrales Staatsarchiv, Potsdam (now Bundesarchiv, Abteilung Potsdam)
Reichserziehungsministerium, Amt Wissenchaft
2954 Kongresse der Internationalen allgemeinen ärztlichen Gesellschaft für Psychotherapie, 1934–41
2797 Eranos-Tagung, Ascona, 1935–41

Dissertations and Documents

Blanck, Gertrude S. "The Development of Psychotherapy as a Profession: A Study of the Process of Professionalization." Ph.D. dissertation, New York University, 1963.

Boehm, Felix, "Bericht über die Ereignisse von 1933 bis zum Amsterdamer Kongress: Im August 1951." In Deutsche Psychoanalytische Gesellschaft e.V. "Dokumente zur Geschichte der Psychoanalyse in Deutschland 1933–1951."

Cimbal, Walter. "Familienchronik." Hamburg-Eppendorf, c. 1958.

———. "Gründungsgeschichte der 'Allgemeinen ärztlichen Gesellschaften für Psychotherapie'." Hamburg-Eppendorf, 1950.

Deutsches Institut für Psychologische Forschung und Psychotherapie e.V. in Berlin. Ankundigung der Veranstaltungen. Berlin, Summer 1941 to Winter 1943–44.

———. Richtlinien für die Ausbildung. Berlin, n.d.

———. Thesen zur Neurosenlehre. Berlin, n.d.

———. Veranstaltungen. Berlin, Winter 1936–37 to Winter 1940–41.

Hermanns, Lüdger, and Schultz, Ulrich, "Interview mit Marianne Stark-Henning," videotape, March, 1984, Archiv zur Geschichte der Psychoanalyse e. V., Berlin.

Hippke, Erich. Anweisung für die Truppenärzte über gesundheitliche Betreuung der jugendlichen Lw.-Helfer und Lw.Helferinnen. Sanitätsinspekteur der Luftwaffe, December 21, 1942. H 20/122 (Heeres-Sanitätsinspekteur, Beratender Psychiater). BA-MA. T-78, roll 92, National Archives.

Höck, Kurt. "Psychotherapie in der DDR: Eine Dokumentation zum 30. Jahrestag der Republik, Teil I." Berlin, 1979.

Hummel, Konrad. "Vergleichende Untersuchungen der psychogenen Störungen bei Kriegsteilnehmern des 1. und 2. Weltkrieges unter besonderer Berücksichtigung der Sympotomatologie." Medical dissertation, Tübingen, 1946.

Müller-Braunschweig, Carl, "Skizze der Geschichte der 'Deutschen Psychoanalytischen Gesellschaft' von 1936 bis 1947." In Deutsche Psychoanalytische Gesellschaft e.V. "Dokumente zur Geschichte der Psychoanalyse in Deutschland 1933–1951."

Reichsinstitut für Psychologische Forschung und Psychotherapie im Reichsforschungsrat, Ankündigung der Veranstaltungen. Berlin, Summer 1944 to Winter 1945.

———. Richtlinien der Poliklinik. Berlin, April 1, 1944.

[Rittmeister, John F.] Tagebuchblätter aus dem Gefängnis von Dr. med. John Rittmeister geb. 22.8.1898 hingerichtet 13.5.43. Akten der Staatsanwaltschaft am Landgericht Lüneburg Strafsache gegen Dr. Manfred Roeder. Nds 721 Acc. 69/76 Lüneburg, vol. 10, pp. 126–57. Niedersächsisches Hauptstaatsarchiv, Hanover.

Rutschky, Michael, "'Wir wollen da wieder anfangen, wo wir '33 hatten aufhören müssen.' Das Berliner psychoanalytische Institut," videotape, NDR, Hamburg, 1984, Archiv zur Geschichte der Psychoanalyse e. V., Berlin.

[Schneider, Carl.] Schlussbemerkungen: Wissenschaftliche, wirtschaftliche und soziale Bedeutung und Zukunft der psychiatrischen Therapien. Berlin, 1941. R 96 I 9 Reicharabeitsgemeinschaft Heil- und Pflegeanstalten: Denkschriften und wissenschaftliche Veröffentlichungen. BA.

Schultz, Johannes Heinrich. Anweisung für Truppenärzte über Erkennung und Behandlung von abnormen seelischen Reaktionen (Neurosen). Berlin, n.d.. RW 2, vol. 251. BA-MA. Microcopy T-77, roll 857. National Archives.

Schultz-Hencke, Harald. *Psychoanalyse und Psychotherapie: Gesammelte Aufsätze*. n.p., n.d.

Wuth, Otto. Psychopathen in der Wehrmacht nebst Bepreschung einiger einschlägigen Fragen. Berlin: Reichsluftfahrtministerium, March 9–10, 1939. H20/128. BA- MA. Microcopy T-78, roll 192. National Archives.

Zapp, Gudrun. "Psychoanalyse und Nationalsozialismus. Untersuchungen zum Verhältnis Medizin/Psychoanalyse während des Nationalsozialismus." Medical dissertation, Kiel, 1980.

Published Sources

Achelis, Werner. "Psychologische Hygiene." In Pintschovious and Zeiss, *Zivilisationsschäden am Menschen*, pp. 247–67.

———. "Psychologische Zivilisationsbilanz." In Pintschovious and Zeiss, *Zivilisationsschäden am Menschen*, pp. 53–81.

———. "Zivilisation und Gesundheit." *Die Gesundheitsführung "Ziel und Weg"* 3 (1941): 381–6.

Arnhold, Karl. "Arbeitspsychologie." *Deutsches Ärzteblatt* 64 (1934): 155–7.

———. *Der Deutsche Betrieb: Aufgaben und Ziele Nationalsozialistischer Betriebsführung*, 2nd ed. Leipzig, 1942.

———. *Leistungsertüchtigung*. Berlin, 1942.

Ash, Mitchell G. *Gestalt Psychology in German Culture, 1860–1967: Holism and the Quest for Objectivity*. Cambridge, 1995.

Bally, Gustav. "Deutschstämmige Psychotherapie." *Neue Zürcher Zeitung*, February 27, 1934, p. 2.

Bartels, Fritz. "Die Gesundheitsführung des deutschen Volkes." *Deutsches Ärzteblatt* 66 (1936): 334–7.

Baumeyer, Franz. "Zur Geschichte der Psychoanalyse in Deutschland. 60 Jahre Deutsche Psychoanalytische Gesellschaft." *Zeitschrift für Psychosomatische Medizin und Psychoanalyse* 17 (1971): 203–40.

Becker, Hellmut, and Nedelmann, Carl, eds. *Psychoanalyse und Politik*. Frankfurt am Main, 1983.

Becker, Werner. "Psychotherapie bei Geisteskranken." *Psychiatrisch-Neurologische Wochenschrift* 45 (1943): 275–7.
Bellak, Leopold, ed., *Contemporary European Psychiatry*. New York, 1961.
Berg, Manfred, and Geoffrey Cocks, eds. *Medicine and Modernity: Public Health and Medical Care in Nineteenth- and Twentieth-Century Germany*. Cambridge, 1996.
Bilz, Rudolf. *Lebensgesetze der Liebe: Eine anthropologische Studie über Gefühlselemente, Bewegungen und Metaphern menschlicher Liebe*. *ZfP* supplement no. 4, Leipzig, 1942.
———, ed. *Psyche und Leistung: Bericht über die 3. Tagung der Deutschen allgemeinen ärztlichen Gesellschaft für Psychotherapie in Wien am 6. und 7. September 1940*. Stuttgart, 1941.
Bleuel, Hans Peter. *Sex and Society in Nazi Germany*. Translated by J. Maxwell Brownjohn. Philadelphia, 1973.
Bockhacker, Werner. "Die betriebliche Gesundheitsführung," *Monatshefte für Nationalsozialistische Sozialpolitik* 10 (1943): 28–9.
Boehm, Felix. "Bericht über die Ereignisse von 1933 bis zum Amsterdamer Kongress im August 1951." In Boehm, *Schriften zur Psychoanalyse*, pp. 301–10.
———. "Erhebung und Bearbeitung von Katamnesen." *ZfP* 14 (1942): 17–25.
———. "Poliklinische Erfahrungen." *ZfP* 12 (1940): 65–87.
———. *Schriften zur Psychoanalyse*. Edited by Deutschen Psychoanalytische Gesellschaft. Munich, 1978.
Brainin, Elisabeth, and Kaminer, Isidor J. "Psychoanalyse und Nationalsozialismus." In Lohmann, *Psychoanalyse und Nationalsozialismus*, pp. 86–105.
Brauchle, Alfred. "Seelische Beeinflussung in der Gemeinschaft." *Münchener medizinische Wochenschrift* 87 (1940): 317–20.
Bräutigam, Walter. "Rückblick auf das Jahr 1942: Betrachtungen eines psychoanalytischen Ausbildungskandidaten des Berliner Instituts der Kriegsjahre." *Psyche* 38 (1984): 905–14.
Brecht, Karen et al., eds. *"Hier geht das Leben auf eine sehr merkwürdige Weise weiter...": Zur Geschichte der Psychoanalyse in Deutschland*. Hamburg, 1985.
Brendgen, Franz. "Vegetative Stigmatisation und Neurose." *ZfP* 11 (1939): 84–11.
Bresler, Johannes. "Geisteskrankheit als Kampf." *Psychiatrisch-Neurologische Wochenschrift* 42 (1940): 12–14.
———. "Unfallneurose und Reichsgericht." *Psychiatrisch-Neurologische Wochenschrift* 41 (1939): 453–5.
Broszat, Martin. *The Hitler State: The Foundation and Development of the Internal Structure of the Third Reich*. Translated by John W. Hiden. London, 1981.
Bumke, Oswald. *Erinnerungen und Betrachtungen: Der Weg eines deutschen Psychiaters*. Munich, 1952.
———. *Die Psychoanalyse und ihre Kinder: Eine Auseinandersetzung mit Freud, Adler und Jung*, 2nd ed. Berlin, 1938.
Christian, Paul. "Rechtswissenschaft, Ursachenbegriff und Neurosenfrage: Zum gleichnamigen Heft der sozialmedizinischen Schriftenreihe aus dem Gebiete des Reichsarbeitsministeriums." *Der Nervenarzt* 14 (1941): 315–20.
Chrzanowski, Gerard. "Psychoanalysis: Ideology and Practitioners." *Contemporary Psychoanalysis* 11 (1975): 492–500.
Cimbal, Walter. "Aufgaben und Wege einer deutschen Seelenheilkunde." In Göring, *Deutsche Seelenheilkunde*, pp. 108–12.
———, ed. *Bericht über den IV. Allgemeinen ärztlichen Kongress für Psychotherapie in Bad Nauheim 11. bis 14. April 1929*. Leipzig, 1929.

———. "Erinnerungen eines alten Arztes an die Frühzeit der Psychotherapie in Deutschland." *Praxis der Psychotherapie* 8:1 (January 1963): 36–42.

———. "Gedanken zu einer vergleichenden Psychotherapie." *ZfP* 7 (1934): 304–12.

———. *Naturgemässe Wege zum seelischen Gleichgewicht, eine natürliche Seelenkunde.* Berlin, 1941.

———. "Volksgemässe und wissenschaftliche Heilkunst nicht als Gegensatz, sondern als notwendige Ergänzung." *Hippokrates* 4 (1933): 277–87.

Cocks, Geoffrey. "C. G. Jung and German Psychotherapy, 1933–1940: A Research Note." *Spring* 10 (1979): 221–7.

———. "Continuités et developpement de la psychanalyse et de la psychothérapie en Allemagne depuis 1939." *Revue Internationale d'Histoire de la Psychanalyse* 1 (1988): 51–70.

———. "German Psychiatry, Psychotherapy, and Psychoanalysis During the Nazi Period: Historiographical Reflections." In *Discovering the History of Psychiatry.* Edited by Mark S. Micale and Roy Porter, pp. 282–96. New York, 1994.

———. "The Nazis and C. G. Jung." In *Lingering Shadows: Jung, Freud, and Anti-Semitism.* Edited by Aryeh Maidenbaum and Stephen Martin, pp. 157–65. Boston, 1991.

———. "The Professionalization of Psychotherapy in Germany, 1928–1949." In Cocks and Jarausch, *German Professions, 1800–1950*, pp. 308–38. New York, 1990.

———. "Psicanalise, Psicoterapia e Nacional-Socialismo." In *Psicanalise e Nazismo.* Edited by Chaim Samuel Katz, pp. 79–124. Rio, 1985.

———. "La psicoterapia nel Terzo Reich." *Kos* 2:19 (1985): 67–90.

———. "Psychoanalyse, Psychotherapie und Nationalsozialismus." *Psyche* 37 (1983): 1057–1106.

———. "Psychotherapie und Psychoanalyse im Dritten Reich." *In Psychoanalyse der Gegenwart.* Edited by Gerd Rudolf et al., pp. 30–42. Göttingen, 1987.

———. "Psychotherapy in the Third Reich: A Research Note." *Journal of the History of the Behavioral Sciences* 14 (1978): 33–6.

———. "Repressing, Remembering, Working Through: German Psychiatry, Psychotherapy, Psychoanalysis and the 'Missed Resistance' in the Third Reich." *Journal of Modern History* 64 (1992): S204–26. And in *Resistance Against the Third Reich, 1933–1990.* Edited by Michael Geyer and John W. Boyer, pp. 312–24. Chicago, 1994.

Cocks, Geoffrey, and Konrad Jarausch, eds. *German Professions, 1800–1950.* New York, 1990.

Conti, Leonardo, ed. *Reden und Aufrufe Gerhard Wagners.* Berlin, c. 1944.

Crew, David F., ed. *Nazism and German Society, 1933–1945.* New York, 1994.

Curtius, Otto. "Das Kollektiv Unbewusste C. G. Jungs, seine Beziehung zur Persönlichkeit und Gruppenseele." *ZfP* 8 (1935): 265–79.

———. "Kongress der deutschen allgemeinen ärztlichen Gesellschaft für Psychotherapie 3. bis 6. Oktober 1935 in Breslau." *Zeitschrift für angewandte Psychologie* 9 (1935): 358–65.

———, ed. *Psychotherapie in der Praxis: Ein Gesamtüberblick über die 2. Tagung der deutschen Allgemeinen ärztlichen Gesellschaft für Psychotherapie zu Düsseldorf September 1938.* Düsseldorf, 1939.

de Crinis, Max, and Veit, Gertrud. "Stand der heutigen Psychiatrie in Deutschland." *Forschungen und Fortschritte* 19 (1943): 347–50.

Decker, Hannah S. *Freud in Germany: Revolution and Reaction in Science, 1893–1907.* Psychological Issues Monograph 41. New York, 1977.

Detmar, Bernhard. *Die natürliche Behandlung und Heilung der Nervenkrankheiten.* Stuttgart, 1939.
Döhl, Ilse, Gustav Graber, and Fritz Mohr. *Leibniz, Carus und Nietzsche als Vorläufer unserer Tiefenpsychologie. ZfP* Supplement no. 3. Leipzig, 1940.
Dräger, Käthe. "Psychoanalysis in Hitler Germany: 1933–1949." Translated by Jeanette Friedeberg. *American Imago* 29 (1972): 199–214.
Driest, Wolfgang. *Richtlinien über Menschenführung in der Truppe: Seelische Wehrbetreuung,* 2nd ed. Berlin, 1944.
Dührssen, Annemarie. *Ein Jahrhundert Psychoanalytische Bewegung in Deutschland: Die Psychotherapie unter dem Einfluss Freuds.* Göttingen, 1994.
Eggert, Gerhard. "Nietzsche und die Individualpsychologie." *ZfP* 11 (1939): 358–65.
Eghigian, Greg. "Die Bürokratie und das Entstehen von Krankheit: Die Politik und die 'Rentenneurosen' 1890–1926. In *Stadt und Gesundheit: Zum Wandel von "Volksgesundheit" und Kommunaler Gesundheitspolitik im 19.und 20. Jahrhundert.* Edited by Jürgen Reulecke and Adelheid Gräfin zu Castell-Rudenhausen, pp. 203–23. Stuttgart, 1991.
Eliasberg, Wladimir. "Allgemeine ärztliche Gesellschaft für Psychotherapie, 1926–31: History of the Six Congresses." *American Journal of Psychology* 112 (1956): 738–40.
———, ed. *Bericht über den II. Allgemeinen ärztlichen Kongress für Psychotherapie in Bad Nauheim 27. bis 30. April 1927.* Leipzig, 1927.
Eliasberg, Wladimir, and Walter Cimbal, eds. *Bericht über den III. Allgemeinen ärztlichen Kongress für Psychotherapie in Baden-Baden 20. bis 22. April 1928.* Leipzig, 1929.
Ellenberger, Henri. *The Discovery of the Unconscious: The History and Evolution of Dynamic Psychiatry.* New York, 1970.
Fabricius, Helmut. "Gemeinschaftspsychologie—Adler-Seif-Künkel (1889–1956)." *Schwestern Revue* 11 (1975): 11–14.
Farago, Ladislas, ed. *German Psychological Warfare.* New York, 1942.
Feiner, Arthur. "The Dilemma of Integrity." *Contemporary Psychoanalysis* 11 (1975): 500–9.
Fest, Joachim. *The Face of the Third Reich: Portraits of the Nazi Leadership.* Translated by Michael Bullock. New York, 1970.
Friedrich, Volker. "Psychoanalyse im Nationalsozialismus: Vom Widerspruch zur Gleichschaltung." *Jahrbuch der Psychoanalyse* 20 (1987): 207–33.
Gauger, Kurt. *Politische Medizin: Grundriss einer deutschen Psychotherapie.* Hamburg, 1934.
———. "Psychotherapie und politisches Weltbild." *ZfP* 7 (1934): 158–68.
Geuter, Ulfried. *The Professionalisation of Psychology in Nazi Germany.* Translated by Richard J. Holmes. Cambridge, 1992.
———. *Die Professionalisierung der deutschen Psychologie im Nationalsozialimus.* Frankfurt am Main, 1984.
Goitsch, Heinrich. "Heilwege für die erkrankte Seele." *Das Reich,* August 20, 1944, p. 8.
Gold, Herbert. "Auch die ersten Kindheitseinflüsse bestimmen die Lebensgestaltung." *Völkischer Beobachter,* May 14, 1939, p. 5.
Göring, Matthias Heinrich. "Abfassen von Zeugnissen und Gutachten." *ZfP* 14 (1942): 34–7.
———. "Deutsche Seelenheilkunde." *Völkischer Beobachter,* December 3, 1938, p. 5.

———, ed. *Deutsche Seelenheilkunde: Zehn Aufsätze zu den seelenärztlichen Aufgaben unserer Zeit.* Leipzig, 1934.
———. "Die Bedeutung der Neurose in der Sozialversicherung." *ZfP* 11 (1939): 36–50.
———. "Bericht über das Deutsche Institut für Psychologische Forschung und Psychotherapie vom 1. Oktober 1938 bis 30. September 1939." In Göring, *1.Sonderheft*, pp. 1–5.
———. "Erfolgsmöglichkeiten der Psychotherapie," *ZfP* 8 (1935): 219–27.
———, ed. *Erziehungshilfe: 2. Sonderheft des Deutschen Instituts für Psychologische Forschung und Psychotherapie.* Leipzig, 1940.
———. "Grundlagen der Psychotherapie." *Deutsche medizinische Wochenschrift* 63 (1937): 1442–6.
———. *Die Individualpsychologie als Werkzeug der Bibelbetrachtung.* Wuppertal-Elberfeld, 1933.
———. "Individuum und Gemeinschaft im Reich der Psychologie." *Suddeutsche Monatshefte* 33 (1938): 286–8.
———. "Der Internationale und Deutsche Kongress für Psychotherapie." *Deutsches Ärzteblatt* 68 (1938): 868–9.
———. "Körperliche Erkrankungen als Auswirkungen seelischer Störungen." *Hippokrates* 5 (1934): 484–90.
———. "Die Kraft der Seele." *Hippokrates* 10 (1939): 1074–6.
———. "Die nationalsozialistische Idee in der Psychotherapie." In Göring, *Deutsche Seelenheilkunde,* pp. 11–16.
———, ed. *1. Sonderheft des Deutschen Instituts für Psychologische Forschung und Psychotherapie, ZfP.* Leipzig, 1940.
———. *Über seelisch bedingte echte Organerkrankungen.* Stuttgart, 1938.
———. "Weltanschauung und Psychotherapie." *ZfP* 9 (1936): 291–6; and *Hippokrates* 9 (1938): 1097–1103.
———. "Zur Neurosenlehre." *Deutsches Ärzteblatt* 66 (1936): 562–3.
Grunberger, Richard. *The 12–Year Reich: A Social History of Nazi Germany.* New York, 1971.
Grunert, Johannes, "Zur Geschichte der Psychoanalyse in München." *Psyche* 38 (1984): 865–904.
Grunwaldt, Heinrich. "Über die psychischen Bedingungen des Luftschutzes." *Wissen und Wehr* 6 (1937): 39–49.
Gumpert, Martin. *Heil Hunger! Health Under Hitler.* Translated by Maurice Samuel. New York, 1940.
Haag, Friedrich Erhard. *Die geistige Gesundheit des Volkes und ihre Pflege,* 2nd ed. Munich, 1935.
Haaken, Janice. "The Siegfried Bernfeld Conference: Uncovering the Psychoanalytic Political Unconscious," *American Journal of Psychoanalysis* 50 (1990): 289–304.
Haeberlin, Carl. "Die Bedeutung von Ludwig Klages und Hans Prinzhorn für die deutsche Psychotherapie." *ZfP* 7 (1934): 38–51.
———. "Lebensrhythmus und Lebensführung." *Hippokrates* 9 (1938): 826.
———. "Über das vital Unbewusste, Bewusstsein und Charakter mit Bemerkungen über die deutsche Seelenkunde von Goethe und Carus." *ZfP* 8 (1935): 279–95.
Hannah, Barbara. *Jung: His Life and Work: A Biographical Memoir.* New York, 1976.
Hannemann, Karl. "Seelenheilkunde und politische Führung." *Völkischer Beobachter,* South German ed., October 2, 1938, p. 12.
Hanse, August. "Ärztliche Seelenführung." *Ziel und Weg* 6 (1936): 440–3.

———. "Konstitution, Biozentrische Gesundheitsführung und Volksbezogenheit." *Hippokrates* 6 (1936): 701–11.

———. *Persönlichkeitsgefüge und Krankheit.* Stuttgart, 1938.

———. "Zur volksbiologischen und wertphilosophischen Begründung einer deutschen Psychotherapie." *Medizinische Klinik* 30 (1934): 286–8.

Hantel, Erika. "Beginenwesen—ohne Romantik." *Frankfurter Zeitung,* October 24, 1942, p. 4.

———. *Brücken von Mensch zu Mensch: Erfahrungen einer Betriebspsychologin.* Stuttgart, 1953.

———. *Verborgenes Kräftespiel: Die Pflege des Menschlichen als Aufgabe für Industrie und Wirtschaft,* 2nd ed. Stuttgart, 1947.

Hattingberg, Hans von. "Ehekrisen, ärztlich gesehen." *Deutsche medizinische Wochenschrift* 66 (1940): 909–12.

———. "Die Eheproblematik unserer Zeit und der Entwicklungsgedanke." *Europäischer Wissenschaftsdienst* 3 (1943): 11–13.

———. "Neue Richtung, Neue Bindung." *ZfP* 7 (1934): 98–107.

———. *Neue Seelenheilkunde.* Berlin, 1943.

———. *Über die Liebe: Eine ärztliche Wegweisung.* Munich, 1936.

———. "Weltfrömmigkeit: Ein Vortrag von Eduard Spranger." *ZfP* 13 (1942): 278–82.

———. "Die Willensstörung in der Neurose." In Curtius, *Psychotherapie in der Praxis,* pp. 42–59.

———. "Zur Entwicklung der analytischen Bewegung (Freud, Adler, Jung)." *Deutsche medizinische Wochenschrift* 59 (1933): 328– 33.

———. "Zur Problematik des Führertums." *Zeitschrift für Menschenkunde* 7 (1932): 142–56.

———. "Zur Psychologie des Glaubens: Ein Vortrag von Eduard Spranger." *ZfP* 15 (1943): 130–6.

Hattingberg, Immo von. "Medical Care for Flying Personnel." In *German Aviation Medicine: World War II,* 2:1059–68. Washington, D.C., 1950. Reprint. Pelham Manor, New York, 1971.

Hermanns, Ludger. "John F. Rittmeister und C. G. Jung." In Lohmann, *Psychoanalyse und Nationalsozialismus,* pp. 137–45.

Herzog, Edgar. "Psychotherapie und Erziehungshilfe." In Göring, *Erziehungshilfe,* pp. 5–7.

Heyer, Gustav Richard. "Aus der psychotherapeutischen Praxis: Eine Reihe von Briefen." *Hippokrates* 11–14 (1940–43).

———. "Leben und Erkennen: Gedanken zu einer deutschen Seelenkunde," *Suddeutsche Monatshefte* 33 (1935): 279–85.

———. *Menschen in Not.* Stuttgart, 1943.

———. *Der Organismus der Seele: Eine Einführung in die analytsiche Seelenheilkunde,* 2nd ed. Munich, 1937.

———. "Die Polarität, ein Grundproblem in Werden und Wesen der deutschen Psychotherapie." *ZfP* 7 (1934): 17–23.

———. *Praktische Seelenheilkunde.* Munich, 1935.

———. "Prognose in der Psychotherapie." In Curtius, *Psychotherapie in der Praxis,* pp. 110–25.

———. "Sigmund Freud." *Münchener medizinische Wochenschrift* 77 (1930): 1551–2.

Heyer, Gustav Richard, and Friedrich Seifert, eds. *Reich der Seele: Arbeiten aus dem Münchener Psychologischen Arbeitskreis,* 2 volumes. Munich, 1937.

Höck, Kurt. "Das abgestufte System der Diagnostik und Therapie neurotische Störungen," In *Psychotherapie in sozialistischen Ländern: Bericht über die 1. Symposium Sozialistischer Länder über Psychotherapie in Prag von 13.3.-15.3.1973.* Edited by Milan Hausner et al., pp. 89–92. Leipzig, 1975.
———. "Entwicklung und Aufgaben der Psychotherapie in der DDR." In *Psychotherapie in sozialistischen Ländern: Bericht über die 1. Symposium Sozialistischer Länder über Psychotherapie in Prag von 13.3.-15.3.1973.* Edited by Milan Hausner et al., pp. 89–92. Leipzig, 1975, pp. 51–5.
Hoske, Hans. *Die menschliche Leistung als Grundlage des totalen Staates.* Leipzig, 1936.
Huber, Wolfgang. *Psychoanalyse in Österreich seit 1933.* Veröffentlichungen des Ludwig Boltzmann-Instituts für Geschichte der Gesellschaftswissenschaften, edited by Erika Weinzierli and Wolfgang Huber, vol. 2. Vienna, 1977.
"Jahresbericht 1941 des Deutschen Instituts für Psychologische Forschung und Psychotherapie und Hinweise für die Weiterarbeit anlässlich der Mitgliederversammlung am 28. März 1942." *ZfP* 14 (1942): 62–77.
"Jahresbericht 1940 des Deutschen Instituts für Psychologische Forschung und Psychotherapie." *ZfP* 14 (1942): 1–62.
Janssen, Paul L., and Sven Olaf Hoffmann. "Profil des Facharztes für Psychotherapeutische Medizin." *Psychotherapeut* 39 (1994): 195–201.
Jones, Ernest. *Sigmund Freud: Life and Work,* 3 volumes. London, 1957.
Jung, Carl Gustav. *C. G. Jung Speaking: Interviews and Encounters.* Edited by William McGuire and translated by R. F. C. Hull. Princeton, 1977.
———. *Collected Works.* Edited by Herbert Read et al. Translated by R. F. C. Hull. Vol. 10, *Civilization in Transition,* 2nd ed. Bollingen Series XX. Princeton, 1970.
———. "Grundsätzliches zur praktischen Psychotherapie." *ZfP* 8 (1935): 66–82.
———. *Letters.* Edited by Gerhard Adler and Aniela Jaffe and translated by R. F. C. Hull. Vol. 1, *1906–1950.* Bollingen Series XCV: 1. Princeton, 1973.
———. "Zur gegenwärtigen Lage der Psychotherapie." *ZfP* 7 (1934): 1–16.
Jung, Carl Gustav, et al. "Prof. Dr. jur. et med. M. H. Göring zum 60.Geburtstag." *ZfP* 11 (1939): 193–4.
Kalau vom Hofe, Marie. "Kriminalpsychologie." *ZfP* 14 (1942): 37–41.
Kater, Michael H. *Doctors Under Hitler.* Chapel Hill, 1989.
Kellner, Hans. "Betriebsarzt und Psychotherapie?" *ZfP* 11 (1939): 220–8.
Kemper, Werner. "Die Bedeutung des Seelischen für die Fruchtbarkeit beim Menschen." *Die medizinische Welt* 17 (1943): 21–3.
———. "Die Indikation zur Psychotherapie bei Neurosen." In Curtius, *Psychotherapie in der Praxis,* pp. 9–26.
———. *Die Seelenheilkunde in unserer Zeit: Ihre Entwicklung, Ihr Stand, Ihr Anspruch, Ihre Aufgaben.* Stuttgart, 1947.
———. "Der seelische Anteil an der Sterilität." *Deutsches Ärzteblatt* 72 (1942): 397–9.
———. *Die Störungen der Liebesfähigkeit beim Weibe: Klinik, Biologie und Psychologie der Geschlechtsfunktion und des Orgasmus.* Leipzig, 1942.
———. "Weniger bekannte Aufgaben ärztlicher Eheberatung." *Deutsches Ärzteblatt* 74 (1944): 166–9.
Köllner, V. "Die Ausbildung im Fach Psychosomatische Medizin und Psychotherapie in der Bundesrepublik Deutschland." *Therapeutische Umschau* 52 (1995): 199–22.
König-Fachsenfeld, Olga von. "Erziehungshilfe." *ZfP* 14 (1942): 25–34.
"Kongress für Psychotherapie in Breslau." *Deutsches Ärzteblatt* 65 (1935): 1064–6.

Kötschau, Karl. *Zum nationalsozialistischen Umbruch in der Medizin*. Stuttgart, 1936.
Kranefeldt, Wolfgang. "Freud und Jung." *ZfP* 7 (1934): 24–38.
Krauskopf, Alfred A. "Tiefenpsychologische Beiträge zur Rassenseelenforschung." *Rasse* 5 (1939): 362–8.
Kretschmer, Ernst, ed. *Bericht über den VI. Allgemeinen ärztlichen Kongress für Psychotherapie in Dresden 14. bis 17. Mai 1931*. Leipzig, 1931.
———. *Gestalten und Gedanken: Erlebnisse*. Stuttgart, 1963.
———. "Organisationsfragen der deutschen Psychotherapie." *Deutsche medizinische Wochenschrift* 75 (1950): 377–9.
———, sr. auth. *Psychiatry*. Field Information Agencies Technical Review of German Science 1939–1946, no. 83. Wiesbaden, 1948.
Kretschmer, Ernst, and Walter Cimbal, eds. *Bericht über den V. Allgemeinen ärztlichen Kongress für Psychotherapie in Baden-Baden 26. bis 29. April 1930*. Leipzig, 1930.
Krisch, Hans. "Die Lehrbarkeit der psychotherapeutischen Wissenschaft." *ZfP* 8 (1935): 227–34.
Künkel, Fritz. *Charakter, Einzelmensch und Gruppe*. Leipzig, 1933.
———. "Die dialektische Charakterkunde als Ergebnis der kulturellen Krise." *ZfP* 7 (1934): 69–84.
———. *Grundzüge der politischen Charakterkunde*, 2nd ed. Berlin, 1936.
———. "Das Hausarzt und Psychotherapie." *Deutsche medizinische Wochenschrift* 64 (1938): 1730–3.
———. "Die Lehrbarkeit der tiefenpsychologischen Denkweisen." *ZfP* 8 (1935): 235–48.
———. "Psychotherapie: Eine Übersicht über die Neuerscheinungen der letzten Jahre." *Hippokrates* 10 (1939): 1361–9.
———. "Seelenheilkunde." *Suddeutsche Monatshefte* 33 (1936): 294–300.
———. "Vorbeugung der Neurose." In Curtius, *Psychotherapie in der Praxis*, pp. 190–4.
———. *Das Wir: Die Grundbegriffe der Wir-Psychologie*, 3rd ed. Schwerin, 1939.
Künkel, Fritz, and Elisabeth Künkel. *Die Erziehung deiner Kinder*. Berlin, 1936.
Lockot, Regine. *Erinnern und Durcharbeiten: Zur Geschichte der Psychoanalyse und Psychotherapie im Nationalsozialismus*. Frankfurt am Main, 1985.
———. *Die Reinigung der Psychoanalyse: Die Deutsche Psychoanalytische Gesellschaft im Spiegel von Dokumenten und Zeitzeugen (1933–1951)*. Tübingen, 1994.
———. "Wiederholen oder Neubeginn: Skizzen zur Geschichte der 'Deutschen Psychoanalytischen Gesellschaft' von 1945–1950." *Jahrbuch der Psychoanalyse* 22 (1988): 218–35.
Lohmann, Hans Martin, ed. *Psychoanalyse und Nationalsozialismus*. Frankfurt am Main, 1984.
———, ed. *Das Unbehagen in der Psychoanalyse: Eine Streitschrift*. Frankfurt am Main, 1985.
———, and Rosenkötter, Lutz. "Psychoanalyse in Hitlerdeutschland: Wie war es wirklich?" In Lohmann, *Psychoanalyse und Nationalsozialismus*, pp. 54–71.
———. "Nachtrag zu unserem Beitrag 'Psychoanalyse in Hitlerdeutschland'." In Lohmann, *Psychoanalyse und Nationalsozialismus*, pp. 86–105.
Löhr, Hanns. *Über die Stellung und Bedeutung der Heilkunde im nationalsozialistischen Staate*. Berlin, 1935.
Luchsinger, C. "Psychotherapie." *Volksgesundheitswacht* 3 (1936): 3–6.

Luxenburger, Hans. "Die Indikation zur Psychotherapie der Neurosen vom Standpunkt der Erbbiologie aus." In Curtius, *Psychotherapie in der Praxis,* pp. 20–32.
Maetze, Gerhard, ed. *Psychoanalyse in Berlin: Beiträge zur Geschichte, Theorie und Praxis.* Meisenheim, 1971.
Meinertz, Josef. *Psychotherapie—eine Wissenschaft! Untersuchungen über die Wissenschaftsstruktur der Grundlagen seelischer Krankenbehandlung.* Berlin, 1939.
Meyer-Mark, Hans H. "Neurotiker der Wirtschaft." *ZfP* 11 (1939): 228–46.
Mohr, Fritz. "Die Behandlung der Neurosen durch Psychotherapie." In Curtius, *Psychotherapie in der Praxis,* pp. 60–82.
———. "Brief an eine durch Fliegerangriff stillunfähig gewordene Mutter." *Hippokrates* 11 (1940): 1016.
———. "Einige Betrachtungen über Wesen, Entstehung und Behandlung der Homosexualität." *ZfP* 15 (1943): 1–20.
———. "Das Leib-Seele Problem (vom Standpunkt der Psychotherapie aus)." *Münchener medizinische Wochenschrift* 86 (1939): 61–4.
Mosse, George. *Nazi Culture: Intellectual, Cultural and Social Life in the Third Reich.* Translated by Salvator Attanasio et al. New York, 1966.
Müller-Braunschweig, Carl. "Psychoanalyse und Weltanschauung." *Almanach der Psychoanalyse* 6 (1931): 102–16; *Reichswart,* October 22, 1933, p. 22; and in Lohmann, *Psychoanalyse und Nationalsozialismus,* pp. 109–12.
Neumann, Johannes. *Leben ohne Angst: Psychologische Seelenheilkunde.* Stuttgart, 1941.
Nitzsche, Otto. "Kriegswichtiges in der ärztlichen Praxis." *Deutsches Ärzteblatt* 74 (1944): 169–71.
Orlow, Dietrich. *The History of the Nazi Party 1933–1945.* Pittsburgh, 1973.
Peterson, Edward N. *The Limits of Hitler's Power.* Princeton, 1969.
Peukert, Detlev J. K. *Inside Nazi Germany: Conformity, Opposition, and Racism in Everyday Life.* Translated by Richard Deveson. New Haven, 1987.
Pintschovious, Karl. *Die seelsiche Widerstandskraft im modernen Krieg.* Berlin, 1936.
Pintschovious, Karl, and Heinrich Zeiss, eds. *Zivilisationsschäden am Menschen,* 2nd ed. Munich, 1944.
Pongratz, Ludwig J., ed. *Psychotherapie in Selbstdarstellungen.* Berne, 1973.
Prinzhorn, Hans, *Psychotherapie: Voraussetzungen, Wesen, Grenzen.* Leipzig, 1929.
Proctor, Robert N. *Racial Hygiene: Medicine Under the Nazis.* Cambridge, Mass., 1988.
Psychotherapie: Bericht über den 1. Allgemeinen ärztlichen Kongress für Psychotherapie in Baden-Baden 17. bis 19. April 1926. Halle, 1926.
Ramm, Rudolf. *Ärztliche Rechts- und Standeskunde: Der Arzt als Gesundheitserzieher,* 2nd ed. Berlin, 1943.
Reichsmininsterium des Innern. *Der öffentliche Gesundheitsdienst im 3. Reich.* Berlin, 1939.
Reiter, Hans. *Ziele und Wege des Reichsgesundheitsamtes im 3. Reich.* Leipzig, 1936.
Richter, Horst-Eberhard. *Die Chance des Gewissens: Erinnerungen und Assoziationen.* Hamburg, 1986.
Ringer, Fritz K. *The Decline of the German Mandarins: The German Academic Community, 1890–1933.* Cambridge, Mass., 1969.
Rittmeister, John. "Der augenblickliche Stand der Poliklinik und ihre künftigen Aufgaben." *ZfP* 12 (1940): 88–96.
———. "Die mystische Krise des jungen Descartes." *Zeitschrift für Psychosomatische Medizin* 15 (1969): 204–44.

———. "Voraussetzungen und Konsequenzen der Jungschen Archetypenlehre." In Lohmann, *Psychoanalyse und Nationalsozialismus,* pp. 146–55.
Rosenkötter, Lutz. "Schatten der Zeitgeschichte auf psychoanalytischen Behandlungen." In Lohmann, *Psychoanalyse und Nationalsozialismus,* pp. 236–49.
Scheunert, Gerhard. "Über Psychotherapie Kurzbehandlungen." *ZfP* 11 (1939): 206–20.
Schoenbaum, David. *Hitler's Social Revolution: Class and Status in Nazi Germany, 1933–1939.* Garden CIty, N.Y., 1966.
Schoppmann, Claudia. *Nationalsozialistische Sexualpolitik und weibliche Homosexualität.* Pfaffenweiler, 1991.
Schultz, Johannes Heinrich. *Geschlecht, Liebe, Ehe: Die Grundtatsachen des Liebes- und Geschlechtslebens in ihrer Bedeutung für Einzel- und Volksdasein,* 2nd ed. Munich, 1941.
———. "Ist Psychotherapie lehr- und lernbar?" *ZfP* 7 (1934): 146– 58.
———. *Lebensbilderbuch eines Nervenarztes: Jahrzehnte in Dankbarkeit.* Stuttgart, 1964.
———. "Das Leib-Seele Problem in der Heilkunde." *Suddeutsche Monatshefte* 33 (1936): 289–94.
———. "Leistung und Psyche." *Das Reich,* February 14, 1943, pp. 5–6.
———. "Der nervöse Zustand." In Pintschovious and Zeiss, *Zivilisationsschäden am Menschen,* pp. 82–102.
———. *Neurose, Lebensnot und ärztliche Pflicht: klinische Vorlesungen über Psychotherapie für Ärzte und Studiernde.* Leipzig, 1936.
———. "Neurosenbekämpfung als Mittel der Leistungssteigerung: Grundsätzliches über Neurosenformen." *Die Gesundheitsführung "Ziel und Weg"* 7 (1945): 19–21.
———. "Poliklinische Aufgaben und Pflichten." *ZfP* 14 (1942): 12– 17.
———. "Praktischer Arzt und Hypnose." *Deutsche medizinische Wochenschrift* 67 (1941): 1032–4.
———. "Psychopathie und Neurose." *Forschungen und Fortschritte* 17 (1941): 1032–4.
———. *Psychotherapie: Leben und Werk grosser Ärzte.* Stuttgart, 1952.
———. "Rundschau: Psychotherapie 1935/36." *Jahreskurse für ärztliche Fortbildung* 5 (1936): 37–44.
———. *Die seelische Gesunderhaltung unter besonderer Berücksichtigung der Kriegesverhältnisse.* Berlin, 1942.
———. "Seelische Gründe der Unfruchtbarkeit." *Europäischer Wissenschaftsdienst* 2 (1942): 22–4.
———. "Seelische Reaktionen auf die Verdunkelung." *Deutsche medizinische Wochenschrift* 66 (1940): 564–7.
———. "Seelische Schulung, Körperfunktion und Unbewusstes." *ZfP* 8 (1935): 304–18.
———. "Der seelische Schutz des Gesunden in den verschiedenen Lebensaltern." *Medizinische Klinik* 36 (1940): 213–16.
———. "Über kleine Psychotherapie in der allgemeinen Praxis und Kurzverfahren in der Psychotherapie." *ZfP* 11 (1939): 69– 84.
———. "Über den Schutz seelisch Gefährdeter." *Medizinische Klinik* 36 (1940): 699–703.
———. "Über tiefenpsychologische Kurzbehandlungen." *Europäischer Wissenschaftsdienst* 4 (1944): 28–9.

———. "Vom Seelenleben der Jugend." *Die Gesundheitsführung "Ziel und Weg"* 5 (1943): 88–92.
———. "Vorschlag eines Diagnosen-Schemas." *ZfP* 12 (1940): 97–161.
———. "Der Yoga und die deutsche Seele." *ZfP* 7 (1934): 61–9.
———. "Zur Psychologie der Perversionen." *Die Deutsche Polizei* 12:4 (1944): 71–3.
Schultz-Hencke, Harald. *Der gehemmte Mensch: Grundlagen einer Desmologie als Beitrag zur Tiefenpsychologie*. Leipzig, 1940.
———. "Die Tüchtigkeit als psychotherapeutisches Ziel." *ZfP* 7 (1934): 62–97.
Schultz-Venrath, Ulrich. "Der Missbrauch von Geschichte als transgenerationelles Traumatisierungsphänomen." *Psyche* 49 (1995): 392–403.
Schulze-Maier, Friedrich. "Gesundheitspflege der Seele." *Der Hoheitsträger* 5 (1941): 26–7.
Seelmann, Kurt, "Die Erziehung des Schulkindes in Hinblick auf seine Lebensaufgaben." In Bilz, *Psyche und Leistung*, pp. 29–56.
———. *Kind, Sexualität und Erziehung*. Munich, 1942.
Seif, Leonhard. "Prophylaxe gegen Neurose." In Curtius, *Psychotherapie in der Praxis*, pp. 165–74.
———. "Volksgemeinschaft und Neurose." *ZfP* 7 (1934): 52–61.
———, ed. *Wege der Erziehungshilfe: Ergebnisse und praktische Hinweise aus der Tätigkeit des Münchener Arbeitskreises für Erziehung*. Munich, 1940.
Seitz, Walter. "Die Lage der Psychotherapie in Deutschland." *Medizinische Klinik* 46 (1951): 399–402.
Smelser, Ronald. *Robert Ley: Hitler's Labor Front Leader*. Oxford, 1988.
Smith, Harvey L. "Psychiatry in Medicine: Intra- or Inter-Professional Relationships?" *American Journal of Sociology* 63 (1957): 285–9.
Speer, Ernst. "Ergebnisse aus der psychotherapeutischen Praxis zum Typenproblem." *ZfP* 7 (1934): 24–54.
———. *Die Liebesfähigkeit (Kontaktpsychologie)*. Munich, 1937.
Spiegel, Rose. "Survival of Psychoanalysis in Nazi Germany." *Contemporary Psychoanalysis* 11 (1975): 479–92.
Störring, Gustav. "Die Verschiedenheiten der psycho-pathologischen Erfahrungen im Weltkriege und im jetzigen Krieg und ihre Ursachen." *Münchener medizinische Wochenschrift* 89 (1942): 25–30.
Stransky, Erwin. "Rasse und Psychotherapie." *ZfP* 10 (1937): 9–29.
"Tätigskeitbericht 1935/36." *ZfP* 10 (1937): 4–6.
"Tätigkeitsbericht 1937." *ZfP* 10 (1938): 200–9.
"Tätigkeitsbericht 1938." *ZfP* 12 (1940): 2–9.
"Tätigkeitsbericht 1939." *ZfP* 13 (1941): 2.
"Tätigkeitsbericht 1940." *ZfP* 13 (1941): 2–4.
Thomä, Helmut. "Some Remarks on Psychoanalysis in Germany, Past and Present." *International Journal of Psycho-Analysis* 50 (1969): 683–92.
Toren, Nina. "Semi-Professionalism and Social Work." In *The Semi-Professions and Their Organization*. Edited by Amitai Etzioni, pp. 142–62. New York, 1963.
Vollmer, Howard M., and Donald L. Mills, eds. *Professionalization*. Englewood Cliffs, N.J., 1966.
Wagner, Gerhard. "Neue deutsche Heilkunde." *Deutsches Ärzteblatt* 66 (1936): 419–20.
———. *Reden und Aufrufe*. Edited by Leonardo Conti. Berlin, 1943.
———. "Der Weg zu einer neuen deutschen Heilkunde." *Völkischer Beobachter*, April 17, 1936, p. 5.
Wegscheider, Klaus. "Psychotherapie bei Kassenpatienten." *ZfP* 11 (1939): 56–69.

Weizsäcker, Adolf von. "Heim-erziehung (Beobachtungen und Gedanken über den Austausch zwischen Psychotherapie und Heilerziehung)." In Bilz, *Psyche und Leistung*, pp. 88–104.

———. "Die tiefenpsychologische Behandlung von Kinderneurosen und ihr Verhältnis zur Heilerziehung." *Zeitschrift für Kinderforschung* 49 (1942): 255–83.

Weizsäcker, Viktor von. "Ärztliche Aufgaben." *Volk im Werden* 2 (1934): 80–90.

———. "Soziologische Bedeutung der nervösen Krankheiten und der Psychotherapie." *ZfP* 8 (1935): 295–304.

Winkler, Walter Theodor. "50 Jahre AÄGP—ein Rückblick." *Zeitschrift für Psychotherapie und medizinische Psychologie* 27 (1977): 74–84.

———. "The Present Status of Psychotherapy in Germany." In *Progress in Psychotherapy 1956*. Edited by Frieda Fromm-Reichmann and J. L. Moreno, pp. 288–305. New York, 1956.

Wuttke-Groneberg, Walter. "Leistung, Vernichtung, Verwertung, Überlegungen zur Struktur der Nationalsozialistischen Medizin." In *Volk und Gesundheit: Heilen und Vernichten im Nationalsozialismus*. Edited by Projektgruppe "Volk und Gesundheit," pp. 9–59. Tübingen, 1982.

Wyatt, Frederick, and Hans L. Teuber. "German Psychology Under the Nazi System 1933–1940." *Psychological Review* 31 (1944): 229–229–47.

Zabel, Werner. *Grenzerweiterung der Schulmedizin*. Stuttgart, 1934.

Zilboorg, Gregory. *A History of Medical Psychology*. New York, 1941.

Index